STRATEGY AND ORGANIZATION
Text and cases in
general management

Strategy and organization

TEXT AND CASES IN
GENERAL MANAGEMENT

HUGO E. R. UYTERHOEVEN,
Dr. Jur., Dr. en Droit, M.B.A., D.B.A.
Timken Professor of Business Administration
Graduate School of Business Administration
Harvard University

ROBERT W. ACKERMAN,
S.B., M.B.A., D.B.A.
Vice President and Director
Preco Corporation
Former Lecturer, Graduate School
of Business Administration, Harvard University

JOHN W. ROSENBLUM,
A.B., M.B.A., D.B.A.
Associate Professor of Business Administration
Graduate School of Business Administration
Harvard University

1977

Revised edition

RICHARD D. IRWIN, INC. Homewood, Illinois 60430
Irwin-Dorsey Limited Georgetown, Ontario L7G 4B3

Revised Edition

8 9 0 MP 5 4 3 2 1 0

Case material of the Harvard Graduate School of
Business Administration is made possible by the
cooperation of business firms who may wish to remain
anonymous by having names, quantities, and other
identifying details disguised while basic relationships
are maintained. Cases are prepared as the basis for
class discussion rather than to illustrate either effective
or ineffective handling of administrative situations.

ISBN 0-256-01923-1
Library of Congress Catalog Card No. 76–57331

Printed in the United States of America

Preface

THIS BOOK is about business policy. It deals with the general management tasks of strategy formulation and organizational implementation. Its focus is not limited to those who are or want to be company presidents, because general management is not the exclusive province of the chief executive. The modern divisionalized corporation has several intermediate levels of general managers. In addition, executives at functional operating levels or in advisory staff positions need general management skills. The general management viewpoint is also important to professions dealing with business firms from the outside, such as management consultants, financial analysts, commercial or investment bankers, and lawyers.

The text is oriented to the practitioner, describing a conceptual framework for strategic and organizational action. It is not intended to be a theory of the firm. Rather, as an operational guide, its purpose is to help in application—for the businessman in the real situation and for the student in the classroom through the study of real-life case situations. The text, in content and purpose, remains the same as in the first edition. It presents a concise framework for the policy course, which can be supplemented as desired by outside readings. The text, while benefiting from contributions of his coauthors, was written by Hugo Uyterhoeven, who for the past 16 years has taught at the Graduate School of Business Administration of Harvard University, where he has been head of the MBA Business Policy course and chairman of both the Advanced Management Program and the General Management Area.

The cases focus on the management of transition and change. They portray companies in dynamic situations involving opportunities for growth or competitive and other environmental threats. While both large and small companies are described, smaller firms predominate. This choice is deliberate: The total company is easier to comprehend when small, thus permitting a more thorough and meaningful analysis. The cases describe both domestic and international business situations, with the latter covering both the developing and industrial world.

A great variety of industries is covered. In manufacturing, they range from textiles, firearms, cigarettes, pickles, paints, wine, and tableware, to watches, video cassettes, electronic components, recreational vehicles, and mobile homes. Other industries included are shipping, fishing, wholesaling, bottling, and construction. The growing service sector is represented by ski resort management, investment banking, income tax services, movie theaters, and broadcasting. Some of these industries are aiming for the same consumer time and dollar: for example, movie theaters, broadcasting, and video cassettes.

The cases reflect current environmental and other strategic as well as organizational issues. About one third are new in this Second Edition and will strengthen the book substantially. They not only are more recent than the ones they replace but cover dynamic industries and relevant issues. For example, two of the new cases portray the organizational implications of external pressures in connection with affirmative action and OSHA. Cases in the section on General Management in the Divisionalized Organization have been significantly improved and focus on the middle-level general manager. They are action oriented and encourage the student to play the role that many will soon have an opportunity to assume or observe firsthand. Although the preponderance of case situations continues to be in smaller companies that the student can easily identify with, several of the new cases add necessary balance by permitting insights to be gained in the performance of larger organizations. Some of the cases that appeared in the First Edition have been revised: The Tax Man, Marlin Firearms, and Philip Morris have been shortened to facilitate in-depth preparation. The final section of the Note on the Watch Industries in Switzerland, Japan, and the United States has been revised to include recent developments, while the General Cinema case has been completely rewritten and updated.

These cases have been taught in a variety of programs at the Harvard Business School, including the Business Policy course in the MBA Program, the Advanced Management Program, the Program for Management Development, the International Teachers Program, and Executive Education seminars. Several of the cases also have been used in other universities, in-house company programs, and industry association seminars. They have been tested in class with both graduate students and experienced executives.

All cases, with five exceptions, were either written or coauthored by one of us. The remaining five were written by colleagues, but in these too we participated in preparing the revised versions which appear in this book. In developing several of the cases, we were assisted by Robert J. Berman, Robert J. Boehlke, Charles E. Fienning, Michael L. Lovdal, W. Edward Massey, William J. Michaelcheck, Edwin A. Murray, Jr., Ralph Z. Sorenson, Audrey T. Sproat, and Charles R. Weigle. We are particularly grateful for the major contributions made by Howard H. Stevenson in developing the Anglo-Norness cases, by Frederick T. Knickerbocker in the watch note, by Charles E. Summer in the BCI case, by John Archer and the late Ralph M. Hower in the United Latex case, and by Ram Charan in the Bancil case.

This book would not have been possible without the support and stimulus of the General Management Area at the Harvard Business School. Its conceptual framework was developed over many years through joint efforts. It represents the collective product of the members of the Business Policy teaching group, which through the 1960s was guided by its senior members: Robert W. Austin, Kenneth R. Andrews, and C. Roland Christensen. We equally owe much to our many other colleagues, past and present, who have helped shape the Business Policy course through many years of teaching and research.

We owe special notes of thanks to Helen Ford for her superb efforts in editing the cases and supervising the final assembly of the material. Her help and dedication contributed greatly to making this book possible.

We are grateful to the Director and the Trustees of IMEDE for letting us use a number of cases copyrighted by them and to the Dean of the Graduate School of Management of Northwestern University for permitting the inclusion of the Bancil case. Also, some of the cases in this book were prepared with the support of the Young Presidents' Organization, for which we are most indebted. Our thanks also go to Dean Lawrence E. Fouraker and Senior Associate Dean George F. F. Lombard for their leadership at the Harvard Business School, which in the last analysis provided the impetus for this book.

March 1977 · HUGO E. R. UYTERHOEVEN
ROBERT W. ACKERMAN
JOHN W. ROSENBLUM

Contents

Part II
THE GENERAL MANAGER AS ORGANIZATION BUILDER

Corporate staff activities. Role of top management. Implications of the
divisional transition: *Advantages of the divisional organization. Disadvantages of divisionalization. A different "way of life."*

Part I
The general manager as strategist

1

General management is everybody's business

THE GENERAL MANAGER AS STRATEGIST AND ORGANIZATION BUILDER

GENERAL MANAGEMENT, or business policy, focuses on a company in its totality: its external posture (corporate strategy) as well as its internal structure (corporate organization). The general manager, therefore, provides leadership both as strategist and as organization builder. The two major tasks are closely interwoven. A strategic response depends on the organizational ability to implement it. More importantly, the process of strategic decision making occurs within an organizational context. While in theory strategy determines organization, in practice strategy depends heavily on organizational inputs.

As strategist, the general manager defines the corporate purpose. The first part of this text portrays a dynamic framework for formulating strategy, relating the company's internal situation to its evolving external conditions. It involves several steps as well as a number of skills which are discussed in Chapters 2 through 9.

As organization builder, the general manager provides leadership by managing his people as a cohesive unit to accomplish the corporate strategic mission. Again, the challenge is a dynamic one: Today's action must be taken in view of tomorrow's needs. In many ways, the organizational aspects of the general manager's job are the most difficult, especially where they involve the management of transition. While strategy formulation, to a large extent, is an intellectual activity involving abstract plans and physical or financial resources, organizational leadership, in contrast, is an administrative activity involving people, their tasks and their relationships. The general manager is concerned with both organizational diagnosis and action. Chapters 10 through 15 cover the organizational aspects of the general management task. Chapter 16 concludes this text by focusing on the most critical transition in a manager's career, that from specialist to general management.

THE GENERAL MANAGEMENT POINT OF VIEW

To a manager of people, the respect for human dignity comes first and foremost. The general manager greatly influences the quality of the professional life of many people. Obviously, the quality of one's professional environment has a major impact on the quality of one's personal and family life and on the fabric of society. One key element in striving for respect for human dignity is the point of view, stressed in this text, of seeing oneself both as a superior and subordinate. By simultaneously viewing human relationships from both sides, it is possible to provide professional leadership. In a democratic society, one can govern only with the consent of those being governed.

The human element confronting the general manager makes his task a political one. He must deal with the personal and organizational realities: with ambitions, desires, and goals of individuals. These realities will influence motivation and cooperation, particularly when power is sought and contested and when rivalries and conflicts emerge. In fact, politics are a phenomenon of all human interaction, whether in the church, in government, in universities, or in business. The general manager must have a sense—and a stomach—for the political dimension of his organization.

A diagnostic ability is also required. General managers must be able to discover, select, and use the facts. This challenge is more demanding for the generalist because he is confronted by a multiplicity of dimensions. Furthermore, strategic and organizational facts do not manifest themselves as neatly and overtly as do technical or financial facts.

The ability and willingness to make decisions, however, is the most critical aspect of the general manager's job. He must integrate and balance the many elements of the total situation. His actions usually involve long time spans, necessitating a sense of timing. Frequently, he confronts major risks, making the decision process a dangerous and lonely task. Also, he must communicate his decisions to his organization and enlist support for their implementation.

General management is not an exact science. Clarity, purity, and certainty often conflict with a general management point of view. General management is fuzzy, complicated, and imprecise. Balancing the many elements of the total company equation requires tradeoffs, compromises, and accommodations. Timing means predicting and anticipating future events, sequencing one's moves accordingly, and proceeding on a path which involves a continuous back and forth of action and response. General management skills, therefore, are not just analytical. They are judgmental and political as well. It is more important for a general manager to be wise than to be smart.

GENERAL MANAGEMENT IS EVERYBODY'S BUSINESS

Traditionally, the job of the general manager has been equated with that of a company's chief executive. Yet, increasingly, corporate organizations are providing for general management positions at levels below the chief executive, and as a result the number of general management positions is rising.

General management positions at the intermediate level of the corporate hierarchy are a direct outgrowth of the movement toward the divisional organization. While the functional organization requires only one general manager, the divisional organization provides for a variety of business units, each requiring a general manager. Often the process of divisionalization extends several levels down into the organization (that is, group, division, department), further increasing the need for general managers at lower levels. As a result of divisionalization, the number of general managers has increased greatly during the last few decades. Today, in all likelihood, the majority of general managers are not chief executives.

General management, however, is of importance not just to the chief executive and the general managers of operating divisions but also to the functional managers who frequently provide input for the strategic process. Such information can be gathered more effectively if subordinates are able to assume the viewpoints of their superiors. This is particularly important where data gathering involves, as it often does, discretion in what to look for and selectivity in what to present.

More importantly, every functional manager continually makes operating decisions which have policy implications. In theory, a company's strategic and organizational posture results from definitive statements issued by top management. In practice, however, no statement can give categorical guidance when dealing with an uncertain future and highly complex situations. Policy statements, while superficially clear and often confining, typically require clarification and interpretation. Just as no legislature can write crystal-clear laws, so is it impossible for top management to issue unambiguous directives. Implementation requires interpretation. This inevitable need for clarification and amplification gives the manager a great deal of discretion which puts him, whether he wants it or not, in a general management position. In implementing guidance from above, the manager greatly influences it. Policies evolve and become clarified through a manager's daily activities. Every manager, therefore, is a policy maker, even though he may not have the formal authority. His role typically is broader than codified in his job description. If he wants to assume this broader role, however, he must be aware of it, because he cannot discharge a responsibility he does not recognize.

Strategic and organizational action involves all managers; it is part of their daily activities; and it is a continuous process. Because all managers make frequent operating decisions of a policy nature, it is important that everybody in the organization make general management his business. The general management approach in these situations serves as a frame of mind, an awareness, a point of view which guides the manager in recognizing and anticipating the policy implications of his daily activities.

The general management point of view is relevant to managers not only in the conduct of company affairs but also in approaching their own jobs and careers. Just as it is possible to formulate a corporate strategy, so is it feasible to develop a job strategy. The same framework can be used. In fact, the quality of corporate management depends heavily on how each individual manages his own professional life. The general management process and viewpoint help the manager in meeting this critical challenge.

2

The general manager
as strategist

THE PURPOSE OF CORPORATE STRATEGY

CORPORATE STRATEGY can best be defined by looking at the purposes
it serves: to provide both direction and cohesion to the enterprise. Providing direction is the traditional objective assigned to corporate[1] strategy: to give the company a sense of purpose and mission. Providing
cohesion, on the other hand, is an objective of corporate strategy which
is often ignored. Yet it is not only important but also more essential
than providing direction.

Rhetorically, advocates of corporate strategy often pose the alternatives for a company of either having or not having a corporate strategy.
In the latter case, they will cite the famous statement that "if you don't
know where you are going, any road will take you there." However,
lack of a corporate strategy does not necessarily entail a lack of direction.
Rather, in the absence of a corporate strategy, other goals and objectives
will fill the vacuum. Every company consists of various units—for example, marketing, manufacturing, research and development, and administration in a functional organization. Each unit will have its own functional strategy. Manufacturing may wish to mechanize its facilities to

---

[1] In describing the general manager as strategist, the organizational unit is the
company. Hence, the term corporate strategy is used. However, this description is
equally applicable to strategists at lower corporate levels, such as business groups,
divisions, departments, or other profit centers. In these divisionalized organizations,
the strategist is not a single general manager. Rather, the strategic process here
involves muliple levels of general managers.

the utmost in order to reduce the labor component in its cost structure; research and development may wish to explore the frontiers of knowledge; and marketing may aim for a broad and constantly changing product line. The strategy of each unit, furthermore, will be influenced also by the goals and ambitions of the executive in charge. Functional and personal strategies of the various units will fill the vacuum which may exist in the absence of a corporate strategy.

Unit strategies may prevail even where a corporate strategy has been formulated because members of the organization identify more readily with their units, which are both smaller and closer, than with the corporation, which appears to many managers as remote and unfamiliar.

The choice usually is not between either having or not having a corporate strategy but between the primacy of corporate goals and objectives over those of the units, or vice versa. When the unit strategies take over (notwithstanding the lip service middle managers may continue to pay to company-wide objectives), corporate responses to external opportunities and threats become an arbitrary outgrowth of these multiple unit strategies. Sometimes a single function tends to dominate the others, thereby resulting in a one-function strategy. In other instances, unit strategies pull toward their own and often different directions, which may create conflicts and thereby prevent the corporation from responding consistently as an entity. The one-function as well as the conflicting and haphazard unit responses are particularly dangerous when resources are limited or when the external threats are severe. Only by establishing the primacy of the corporate strategy over that of the units is it possible to achieve the internal cohesion which permits effective utilization of corporate resources and quick responses to external opportunities and threats.

In providing cohesion, corporate strategy influences the unit strategies rather than permitting the latter to shape the corporate response. This poses no problem where both corporation and unit pursue similar goals. Where the corporate strategy runs counter to that of the unit, however, strategic leadership requires convincing members of the unit to pursue policies which are not their "first" choice. Corporate strategy may require responses which run counter to the conventional functional wisdom. For example, a company with limited resources operating in a highly cyclical industry may emphasize the need for a low break-even point by minimizing fixed expenses. As a result, it will have to rely heavily on outside suppliers, minimizing its investment in manufacturing plant and equipment even at the penalty of foregoing cost-reducing automation. Such an approach clearly runs counter to conventional manufacturing wisdom. However, the purpose of functional strategies is not to seek self-centered perfection but to implement the corporate strategy.

In establishing cohesion, furthermore, corporate strategy must establish priorities among the units. Rarely can all their shopping lists be satisfied; choices must be made. As a result, some units will be treated as more equal than others. For instance, a company with a weak market share may give preference to bolstering its distribution setup before devoting funds to manufacturing or engineering. Likewise, where the industry is cyclical, debt may be repaid (avoiding future fixed interest and repayment charges) before money is invested in plant and equipment (which would increase fixed expenses).

Finally, cohesion requires that the activities of the various units be interrelated. For example, are product and distribution policy mutually supportive and do they reinforce each other? Do the total actions of marketing, manufacturing, engineering, and finance result in a coordinated response? This integration aspect not only provides a common sense of direction to the units but also permits the total organizational response to be more effective than that of the sum of its parts. This is the final test of a cohesive organization.

THE PROCESS OF CORPORATE STRATEGY

The process of corporate strategy involves several steps. It is useful to begin with a thorough understanding of a company's *strategic profile*. A company may have made its strategy explicit or its strategy can be derived implicitly from the company's actual behavior. The two are not always identical, in which case the strategist judges a company by what it does, not by what it says. The strategic profile concerns itself with how a company has defined (1) its business, (2) its competitive posture, and (3) its concept of itself.

The next step is to arrive at a *strategic forecast*. A first phase sets the framework by identifying the various environmental dimensions, while a second phase involves predicting their future developments. Analysis focuses on the (1) political, social, and economic; (2) market; (3) product and technological; and (4) competitive dimensions. The strategic forecast thus encompasses the company's total external environment. Furthermore, it is a dynamic process: the existing environmental dimensions are not only identified but their future scope is predicted as well. The strategist explores both current as well as future opportunities and threats.

The third step of the strategic process involves the *resource audit*. Here the focus is on the internal dimensions: operational, financial, and managerial. Corporate resources are both identified and evaluated. The strategist defines a company's strengths as well as its weaknesses.

The subsequent step builds upon the preceding two: within the external and internal framework a variety of *strategic alternatives* are explored. What is the range of strategic responses, given the environmental opportunities and threats and the corporate strengths and weaknesses? The purpose of this step is to provide the strategist with a range of choice broader than the company's existing strategic profile and to prevent a myopic focus on either company traditions or on prevailing industry fashions. Given the earlier dynamic appraisal of environment and resources, the development of strategic alternatives aims particularly at the pursuit of future opportunities and the avoidance of emerging threats and risks.

The fifth step of the strategic process entails the *test of consistency*. The existing strategic profile and various strategic alternatives are evaluated by testing their consistency with the external and internal dimensions, both in their identified current and in their predicted future scope. The strategist relates what a company is *able* to do with respect to its resources to what is *possible* in its external environment.

Following the evaluation of a company's strategic options, the strategist moves to the final step: He makes his *strategic choice*. Either the existing corporate strategy is reaffirmed or a new strategic profile is developed. Commitment to a specific strategic plan usually will require not only definition of the elements of the strategic profile but also basic choices in terms of degree of risk and timing.

The steps of the strategic process thus move from the strategic profile to the strategic forecast and the resource audit, followed by the development of strategic alternatives. These, in turn, are put to the test of consistency which leads to the necessity for strategic choice. Three comments are in order. First, the framework of strategy formulation is simple in concept. It is easily described and understood. It is basic rather than esoteric. It represents common sense and will not strike anyone as a profound revelation. Yet this apparent simplicity should not fool its user. While simple in concept, the framework of corporate strategy is difficult to apply. The gap between understanding and application is extraordinarily wide. The test of a successful strategist is based on the latter, not the former.

Second, the framework of corporate strategy is a dynamic one. It deals with today's answers to tomorrow's issues. This requires not only an analytical approach to today's facts but also predictive judgments of tomorrow's conditions. By necessity, therefore, corporate strategy formulation is an inexact science. Those seeking certainty should not aspire to become strategists.

Third, the framework of corporate strategy operates in two ways. It can be used to appraise an existing strategy by relating it to the external environment and the internal resources. Alternatively, one can begin with an analysis of environment and resources to arrive at a number of strategic alternatives from which a desirable strategy is chosen.

THE SKILLS OF THE STRATEGIST

In its application, the conceptually simple process of strategy formulation places high demands on the strategist. It requires a variety of skills. The first one, identification, is easily overlooked. Every manager will claim that he knows his own business. Yet it is surprising how many elements are discovered or seen in clearer perspective by embarking on a systematic and explicit process of identifying the company's strategic profile as well as its external and internal conditions.

While many executives carry the data on their strategy and their environment in their heads, it is extremely difficult to assess objectively the completeness and relevance of these data without making them explicit. It is a common experience that thoughts which appear perfect when they flash through one's head pale considerably once they are put down on paper and assessed with detachment. Likewise, being explicit about strategy, environment, and resources is an essential prerequisite if a complete and objective analysis is to take place.

Identification is primarily an analytic process. As such, it has to be thorough to ensure that all factors have been considered; it must be precise in order to give focus to the analysis; and it should be as concise as possible to avoid overburdening the decision process. More importantly, the process of identification establishes the parameters within which the strategic analysis must proceed. Given the multiplicity of dimensions involved as well as their changes over time, it is highly desirable to give structure and analytical discipline to the strategic process. Identification greatly influences the quality of the final outcome.

Analytical skills do not suffice. The predictive elements of the strategic process, especially strategic forecasting, require judgmental skills. The future cannot be identified; it must be predicted. Predictions cannot be based solely on an objective analysis but also require subjective judgments. Where no major environmental changes are anticipated, the role of the strategist is minimal. He earns his way by responding to changes or by bringing them about. Given the usually long lead times needed for strategic decisions, such responsiveness requires anticipation of these changes. This anticipation requires difficult predictive judgments.

The skills of identification and prediction, of analysis and judgment, have to be complemented by a third skill: that of innovation. In developing strategic alternatives the strategist has to apply creative skills, to be an innovator. Within the context of environment and resources a broad range of strategic options has to be explored. As evidenced by several cases in this book, the rewards of a unique and imaginative strategy can be great.

After identification, prediction, and innovation comes evaluation as a fourth skill. While the test of consistency at first glance appears to be an instrument of logic, in reality it requires both analysis and judgment. In the dynamic framework of strategy formulation the test of consistency matches not only current environment and resources but also predictions of the future external and internal conditions. Because the latter are products of judgment, so also is the process of evaluation. Furthermore, the test of consistency does not always result in neat and precise outcomes, again forcing the strategist to rely on his judgment.

The final step of the process confronts the strategist with the necessity of choice, requiring decisiveness. Because strategic decisions usually involve major commitments which have to be made in anticipation of future events and years may pass before the results are known, decisiveness is no easy task. Faced with an uncertain future, several options, and the need to embark on a specific course of action requiring the irrevocable commitment of major resources, decisiveness involves risk taking. It demands not only a clear head but also a strong stomach. The strategist must exhibit both nerve and courage.

The task of strategist, therefore, is not easy. It requires skills of identification, prediction, innovation, evaluation, and decisiveness. These skills require qualities which go beyond those of logical analysis. They demand sound judgments, imagination, and creativity, and a great deal of nerve and courage.

In summary, the strategic process consists of:

Skills Elements	Identification	Prediction	Innovation	Evaluation	Decision
Strategic profile	Step 1				
Environmental dimensions	Step 2				
Strategic forecast		Step 3			
Company resources	Step 4			Step 4	
Strategic alternatives			Step 5		
Test of consistency				Step 6	
Strategic choice					Step 7

3

The strategic profile

EVERY COMPANY, whether it has an explicit strategy or not, has a *strategic profile*. This profile is based on the actions of a company, not on the plans or statements of its executives. Hence, strategic profiles are not secrets available only to those familiar with the inner workings of a corporation. They can be deduced from a company's actual behavior by insiders and outsiders alike. Thus, identification of the strategic profile is a feasible and useful exercise both for one's own company and for its competitors.

Every company in the conduct of its business faces some critical choices which shape its strategic profile. These choices are not entirely free; they are constrained both by the company's internal resources and by its external environment. Within these constraints, however, some basic choices are typically made. Such choices are not always the result of explicit decisions. They may have been inadvertent or may have gradually evolved over time.

The strategic profile consists of three major elements:

How a company defines its business.

How a company defines its competitive posture.

How a company defines its concept of itself.

HOW A COMPANY DEFINES ITS BUSINESS

Typically, a company faces some basic choices in terms of its scope of operations: horizontally, vertically, and geographically.

13

Product scope: The horizontal choices

Every company defines, by one means or another, the business(es) it participates in. A first choice relates to the horizontal range of products: from specializing in a single product or a narrow segment of an industry, on one extreme, to broad diversification into a wide variety of unrelated products on the other. From a strategic and organizational point of view, the choice between participation in a single business versus that of engaging in multiple businesses is a critical one, the organizational implications of which will be discussed in later chapters. At this point, suffice it to say that in a diversified company the strategic process must be undertaken not only at headquarters for the corporation as a whole but also for each separate business unit before the total strategic plan can be formulated. Usually the former focuses on financial goals and the composition of the portfolio of businesses, while the latter deals with specific product-market relationships. Thus, the strategic process takes place on a corporate basis for the single product company and on a divisional (or even lower) as well as on the corporate level for the diversified enterprise.

Within the single business entity, a number of options are typically available. Most businesses are characterized by a range of products that can be grouped along several dimensions, among them price (and quality), product features, and product utility. For instance, in the light aircraft industry planes are sold in various price categories having numerous configurations (single engine, twin engine, turboprop, etc.) for use in several markets (recreational, business, and commercial). The companies in the industry differ in the extent to which they attempt to blanket the market. Some opt for a relatively narrow segment; others seek a full product line.

Within the diversification choice, different approaches are possible depending on the degree of "relatedness" of the various activities. The business units, each catering to a different product and market, may share commonalities in technology, production processes, distribution, and customer base. For example, Litton Industries, in its early years, although represented in numerous fields, including computer and control systems, radar systems, and navigational devices, maintained a relatively homogeneous technical and customer base. Or the relatedness between the units may be virtually nonexistent, as happened later when the company branched out into calculators, cash registers, geophysical research and exploration, shipbuilding, paper, restaurants, and other activities. The common thread became increasingly difficult to find.

Degree of vertical integration

The flow of a product, from its basic raw materials until it reaches the ultimate user, usually involves several stages. For example, crude oil or natural gas are the feedstock for some chemical building blocks which 'are transformed into chemical intermediates which, in turn, are converted into chemical end products used to manufacture a great variety of products such as plastic toys, pipes, or packaging. In some instances, companies have integrated vertically along the product flow to protect or provide markets for intermediate products and to capture a greater share of the value added. In other cases, they have confined their activities to certain aspects of the product flow. The large oil companies, for example, are fully integrated from the well to the gasoline station but also sell by-products of their refineries on a merchant basis, providing feedstock for the chemical companies.

A company situated along the vertical product flow faces both an opportunity and a threat. It can decide to integrate either forward or backward. Concurrently, it is exposed to the threat of either its suppliers or its customers doing likewise. The strategic profile will indicate what choices a company as well as its competitors, customers, and suppliers have made in terms of their involvement along the vertical product flow. These strategic postures raise questions not only in terms of opportunities and threats but also in terms of the competitive conditions of an industry as reflected, for example, in costs, prices, or purchasing patterns.

The tire industry is a well-known example. Fearful of backward integration by the automobile companies, the tire companies have sold to the original equipment market at near cost, relying for their profitability largely on the replacement market. Within the framework of such a strategy, the introduction of longer lasting tires such as radials which delay the replacement cycle has significant strategic implications.

Geographic coverage

The strategic profile also registers a company's geographic involvement. *The New York Times* has achieved leadership only in one section óf the country; its western and European editions were failures, and in spite of its international reputation, its sales are geographically confined. *The Wall Street Journal*, in contrast, has successfully achieved national distribution. Geographic coverage, moreover, confronts a company with the choice of extending its operations to other countries, an option which *The Wall Street Journal* decided to pursue in 1976 when it launched *The Asian Wall Street Journal*. The degree, or absence, of its international commitment may have important strategic implications, for example, in terms of growth opportunities, manufacturing strength, competitive or economic vulnerability. Within the same industry, international coverage may vary significantly among the various companies.

The geographic choices complete the profile of how a company has defined its business. The strategic profiles resulting from these various choices can differ markedly, even for companies in the same industry. The example below has been taken from the farm equipment industry and represents the percentage of total sales in 1965 that each of three major companies derived from North American, international, and non-farm equipment sales.

	Percentage of 1965 sales derived from—		
	North American farm equipment sales	*Overseas farm equipment sales*	*Nonfarm equipment sales*
Deere.	70	14	16
Massey Ferguson	28	49	23
White Motor.	30	1	69

HOW A COMPANY DEFINES ITS COMPETITIVE POSTURE

The choice of competitive weapons

An industrial company typically competes on the basis of its marketing, manufacturing, engineering, research and development, and financial capabilities. In other business sectors, such as shipping, publishing, construction, mutual fund management, or broadcasting, competition is based on different, though often analogous, activities. Because resources and capabilities are limited, companies often place different emphases on these various operational aspects. In effect, they choose the competitive weapons to be used in securing an advantage in the marketplace. For some it may be the posture of the low-cost producer. For others it may be rapid delivery and extensive customer service. For still others it may be product innovation or creative marketing. John Deere, in the example referred to above, achieved leadership in the farm equipment industry through emphasis first on distribution, then on the extension of credit, and finally on product development. Clearly, not every company places special emphasis on one or more aspects of its operations. However, most successful enterprises have a concept of how they wish to compete.

A company's relative position

Beyond a concern for the company's choice of competitive weapons, the strategist identifies its rank relative to its competitors. What is the company's role in the industry? Does it exhibit leadership along some dimensions or does it follow industry convention? Is its leadership based on a unique strategic design or simply on overpowering muscle? Size, of course, does not necessarily connote leadership, nor is the company with the largest market share necessarily the most profitable or the most likely to secure growth in the future. Indeed, being the biggest in an industry often creates penalties and constraints as well as rewards and opportunities.

HOW A COMPANY DEFINES ITS CONCEPT OF ITSELF

Mentality and culture

A company has a mentality and a mode of behavior of its own. In some instances, the company may be a reflection of the drive and leadership style of its chief executive. It was difficult in the mid-70s to separate Polaroid from Dr. Land, or ITT from Mr. Geneen, for example. In other instances, there is a pervasive atmosphere, which may range from aggressiveness, quick responses, and a hard-nosed orientation, as was the case for some of the newer conglomerates, to complacency, slow responses, and paternalism, a not uncommon characteristic of some of the older, long-established firms. These conditions influence not only a company's strategic posture but also its range of potential responses to competitive challenges and environmental changes.

A company's performance goals

A final but important element of a company's strategic profile is the performance goals which management has decided to pursue and which, for the benefit of financial analysts or for internal guidance, have often been made explicit. These goals may be expressed in terms of earnings growth (often expressed as a rate of growth in earnings per share), sales growth, industry position, or in other ways (for example, in terms of sales breakdown, such as between government and civilian sales). Of increasing importance is the intended relationship between the company and various constituencies, such as employees, customers, and the community, which extends beyond the traditional financial and stewardship obligations to ownership interests. In some instances, performance in these areas is also included among the company's goals.

It is important to note that this identification deals with what a company hopes to achieve, not what it has achieved. In order to place these future goals in perspective it is useful to relate them to the actual performance to date. Where goals significantly exceed previous achievements, they provide an indication of the stress that will be placed on future strategy. Thus, performance goals serve as a point of departure for the subsequent steps in the strategic process.

4

The environmental dimensions

IDENTIFICATION OF THE
ENVIRONMENTAL DIMENSIONS

IN IDENTIFYING the conditions prevailing in the external environment, four major dimensions typically have to be considered:

—political, social, and economic dimension;
—market dimension;
—product and technological dimension;
—competitive dimension.

Identification of the external dimensions does not imply that they should be solely considered as "givens." Obviously, they influence a company's strategic flexibility. On the other hand, a company's strategic response may influence or change many of the environmental dimensions. Thus, the interaction between strategy and environment goes both ways: they influence each other. In this chapter, however, the focus will be exclusively on environmental analysis. The strategic response will be discussed later.

The process of identifying the external dimensions begins with the broad political, social, and economic environment within which business operates. In a sense, these are the atmospheric conditions with which corporations have to contend. From there, the more specific market dimension is considered. It describes the terrain on which the competitive battle will be waged. Then the product and technological dimensions must be identified, revealing the weapons with which the competitive battle will be fought. Finally, the competitive dimension itself must be analyzed. Who are the opponents to be faced on the battlefield?

POLITICAL, SOCIAL, AND ECONOMIC DIMENSION

Political factors have become vastly more important to businessmen in recent years. Rare nowadays are the general managers who can ignore the political consequences of their decisions or the impact of public policy on future decisions. Some of the elements which influence the strategic equation have been with us for years, such as tariffs and other trade restrictions or antitrust legislation. Others have surfaced lately, either through private actions in the courts and at stockholder meetings, or through congressional and other government activities. The public concern today over such issues as ecology, equal opportunity, and consumer protection may, in retrospect, appear to have been the inevitable consequences of clearly visible social change. However, few companies devoted time and resources a decade ago to diagnosing or preparing for this more complicated political and social environment.

The economic dimension is also an important input to the strategic equation. In part, the concerns are those traditionally having an influence on supply and demand: economic growth and cyclicality. How does a company's strategy relate to the business cycle? How is it affected by rising affluence and changing spending patterns? For instance, among the case studies in this book, the fortunes of Winnebago and Fleetwood, leaders in the recreational vehicle industry, are intimately related to the performance of the economy. However, given the expanding scope of governmental intervention in the private sector, the relationship between market opportunities and threats and public policy becomes even closer. Thus, Winnebago and Fleetwood must also assess the economic impact of likely government-sponsored regulations concerning safety or of a possible national energy policy.

The political, social, and economic dimension is one over which the strategist clearly has the least control. As a result, many general managers view those factors rather fatalistically as inevitable constraints. However, in many instances they may constitute opportunities. For example, antitrust actions may provide opportunities to the small newcomer. A major event permitting the growth of General Cinema was the breakup after World War II of the integrated companies which had dominated the production, distribution, and exhibition of movies. While the remnants of these giant companies, as they tried to diversify, floundered through an industry depression created in part by television, General Cinema capitalized on an array of social and economic trends to emerge by the early 1970s as the leading theater exhibition company.

Four elements of the political, social, and economic dimension will be discussed in more detail:

—international and national economic policies,
—traditional government regulation of business,
—recent political and social developments,
—economic developments.

International and national economic policies

A relatively recent but highly important phenomenon is economic integration. Spearheaded by the European Common Market, attempts at economic integration have been undertaken by countries in a number of other trading areas as well. The reduction of tariff barriers and the harmonization of other economic policies broaden the market. Not only does economic integration stimulate economic growth but it also permits business strategies hitherto impossible because of the limitations of small fragmented national markets. However, opportunities for some constitute threats to others. The opening of national markets results in the entry of foreign competitors. Historic market positions may be attacked and competitive behavior may be upset by newcomers. More is at stake for participants in the enlarged competitive battle than market shares and prices. Changes in industry structure with the elimination of marginal firms may also result. Patterns of direct investment, manufacturing rationalization, and distribution may be altered as well.

Tariffs and other trade restrictions, such as import quotas or currency regulations, constitute other important elements influencing business strategy. The Swiss watch industry for decades and even centuries pursued an export strategy, supplying world markets from its local production sources. The post–World War II import restrictions, particularly in the developing world, upset this pattern.

Economic policies at the national level also influence corporate strategy. For instance, government attempts to tighten credit may affect the manufacturer of consumer durables which typically sells a large percentage of its products on an installment basis. Price controls may reduce marketing flexibility and, coupled with increasing costs, place pressure on margins. Tax policies, such as investment credits, may have a bearing on capital investment decisions.

Traditional government regulation of business

While the above government actions influence businesses indirectly, other government activities have a direct impact on corporate strategy. Antitrust has already been mentioned. Regulatory agencies, such as the

Federal Communications Commission (FCC) or the Food and Drug Administration (FDA), shape the strategic options available to the industries they regulate. It can be argued that stricter testing by the FDA, while protecting the consumer, also benefits the established pharmaceutical companies and constitutes an additional entry barrier for newcomers. Policies established or interpreted by the FCC are critical inputs to the strategic process for radio and television firms such as the Arkana Broadcasting Company, which is described in a subsequent case.

Recent political and social developments

In recent years, new developments having significant potential consequences have occurred. Consumerism or consumer protection is one of them. It manifests itself in a concern for reasonable prices, as happened in the pharmaceutical industry; for safety, which has become a major issue in the automotive and tire industries; and for truth in packaging, which has affected many consumer goods companies. It is impossible for the Marlin Firearms Company to avoid a concern for product safety and indeed the more pervasive issue of gun controls.

The issue posed by discrimination and equal employment has become another major environmental factor of strategic importance. For example, industries heretofore relying on low-cost minority or female labor, whether in agriculture, manufacturing, or services, are directly confronted by a different and rising cost structure. The more difficult task of integrating women and minorities into the ranks of top and middle management is only now being tackled. The physical and psychic energy consumed in racial disputes is enormous; the risks lie in the company's ability to attract competent managers as well as the diversion of attention from the competitive aspects of the business.

Another set of issues arises from the evolving public policy aimed at the protection of our physical environment. Emissions from manufacturing processes into the air and water are now being widely regulated. The businessman is confronted with rapidly changing laws at federal, state, and local levels which are sometimes at variance with one another. Moreover, the standards are often such that the best available technology is insufficient to ensure compliance. Under these uncertain conditions, the potential cost in the next decade to clean up certain industries including steel, paper, and copper is staggering. Decisions involving marginal facilities and businesses, product policy, and new plant locations will increasingly have to incorporate the direct and indirect (for example, higher fuel rates) costs of environmental protection.

These newer forces in many instances constrain existing strategies. Sometimes they call for revisions, and often they entail higher costs. While threatening or costly to some industries, they present opportunities to others and competitive advantages to more fortunate or farsighted companies in a single industry. As the quality of life increasingly takes precedence over the quantity of output, these environmental trends pose challenges that call for imaginative and novel strategies. However, by virtue of their new and evolving character, coupled with the great uncertainties clouding the formulation of public policy, the strategist often receives unclear and—worse—conflicting signals.

Economic developments

The broad economic development of a country or market obviously is an important input into the strategic equation. The emerging economies of the Central American countries, on the verge of an era of industrialization, create different opportunities and problems than does the large and diverse industrial economy of the United States. In contrast to the relatively unsaturated markets of the developing world, the industrialized nations present the strategist with the problems of maturity and the opportunities associated with affluence. It is difficult to extend the capacity of a full stomach or to find products for the "person who has everything." In fact, deepening concern for ecology has given rise to proposals for a zero growth policy as the only way to halt mankind's predatory use of its limited global resources. Needless to say, a zero growth economy, or one in which energy or raw materials are rationed, has far-reaching implications for many corporate strategies.

Even if growth is to continue, its mix is certain to change. After food and shelter needs have been satisfied, economic activities are directed toward consumer durables, resulting in the vast mechanization of our daily activities, from transportation to household chores. But here, too, saturation becomes evident; with the second automobile and the electric carving knife, consumption tapers off. Expenditures for leisure activities, often of a service nature, then begin to grow. People travel more, increasingly eat in restaurants, and seek a wider variety of entertainment. Function alone ceases to suffice. Convenience and beauty are additional requirements. As such products or services gain acceptance, they move from a class to a mass market, permitting new strategies and industries.

While the structure of the economy changes, the strategist will also have to cope with the persistent presence of inflation as well as the traditional and yet continually important phenomenon of the business cycle. The recessions which occurred in the seventies have reminded many companies, often painfully, of the importance of this element. Admittedly, the business cycle affects various industries differently. Yet the phenomenon of declining margins coupled with rising working capital and fixed asset requirements has adversely affected many companies. The pattern is a common one. As the economy stagnates, companies fight more fiercely for a stagnant market, almost inevitably narrowing the spread between competitive prices and inflationary costs. In an attempt to keep costs under control, more mechanization is called for, resulting in higher fixed asset expenditures which—if debt financed—result in increased charges as well. At the same time, the use of customer service as a compensatory competitive weapon frequently results in larger inventories and receivables. Unable to finance these asset requirements internally with a shrinking cash flow, companies have to resort to more debt, thereby raising their fixed charges and vulnerability still further. The remedy, severe cost cutting, is then instituted, which may choke off those programs in product development and marketing which have been designed to fuel future growth.

Strategies have to be geared to a variety of economic conditions. A strategy which is viable only under good economic conditions is a highly risky proposition. Yet, obvious as this statement sounds, it is surprising how many strategies are in violation of it. Psychologically, it is difficult to plan for disaster under euphoric conditions. Indeed, it is usually during the periods of economic boom that the seeds of disaster are planted, through errors both of commission and omission. Regarding the former, shortages during boom periods pressure a company into plant expansion. Failure to respond to these pressures would result in a loss in market share and would leave the company behind in terms of modern and efficient manufacturing facilities. Thus, it is a matter of economic and competitive necessity for a company to ride with the economic boom. Such behavior, however, aggravates the condition as the business cycle turns downward. The larger manufacturing facilities create a severe excess capacity problem, compounded by a cost structure which, especially for modern, highly efficient plants, includes a high ratio of fixed costs. Where fixed costs are high and incremental variable costs low, the normal reaction is to attempt to maintain volume, even if it entails reducing price. Where everyone has the same idea in a period of declining demand, the obvious result is a vicious circle, with prices being pushed down severely as all manufacturers attempt to avoid a loss in volume. Thus, the logical behavior during economic boom creates conditions which are likely to lead to behavior which aggravates the damage of a subsequent economic downturn.

Errors of omission occur because boom conditions cover up weaknesses which may prove critical during a subsequent recession. Product characteristics and distribution strengths are not truly tested while shortages prevail. Yet they may prove critical in the subsequent fight for a share of a declining market. Because it is easy to gain a false impression of a company's competitive posture during good years, management fails to strengthen its products and distribution. When an economic downturn brutally uncovers competitive weaknesses, it is often too late and too costly.

Strategists in companies subject to changing economic conditions must be cognizant of these dangers. As a result, the strategic demands during an economic boom are twofold: to develop responses for benefiting from the prevailing favorable conditions, while simultaneously to prepare the company's competitive and financial posture for coping with a subsequent economic downturn.

MARKET DIMENSION

The market dimension focuses on the terrain on which the competitive battle is being fought: the customers which are being served; the channels of distribution which are being used; and, importantly, the size and segmentation of market demand. This section will discuss the assessment of:

—market demand,
—market requirements,
—distribution requirements.

Market demand

Determination of market size is an obvious step in identifying a company's environment. Every strategy has to be geared to available opportunities. In doing so, a shortsighted view of the limits of the market is a common error. The dangers are twofold. First, market opportunities may be artificially constrained by too narrow a product-market focus. And, second, competitive interdependencies among alternative means of satisfying demand may be overlooked or minimized. Thus, manufacturers of glass bottles, serving the packaging market, should at least be alert to trends affecting metal, paper, and plastic containers as well as glass.

Paradoxically, too general a view of market size may also mask opportunities and threats. Possible segmentations of market demand also have to be explored. HMH Publishing Company with its flagship, *Playboy*, is a famous (or infamous) example of a fantastic success story in a depressed publishing industry which counts the well-known *Saturday Evening Post, Life,* and *Look Magazine* among the victims of its declining competitive position among entertainment, news, and advertising media. Arthur Keller's company, the introductory case in this book, faces both major growth opportunities and severe market declines in the mature textile industry. General Cinema built its success in a depressed industry, first with drive-in theaters which were least affected by television and subsequently with shopping-center movie houses. As a result, a corporate strategist has to focus not only on the size and growth of his company's total market but also on existing and potential segments within this market. The outlook for these segments is often markedly different from that for the industry as a whole. In fact, even in a stagnating or declining business it may be possible to discover segments providing a company with major growth opportunities.

At the same time, a prediction as to market growth is equally essential. Estimates of growth have to be based on predictions, not solely on projections. Determination of the future size of the market requires strategic judgments. Often other environmental dimensions will influence the outcome. For example, an estimate of Philip Morris' future market will have to include an assessment of the potential impact of government regulation and public response to the alleged dangers of cigarette smoking. Likewise, Marlin Firearms' market potential may be greatly influenced by gun legislation. Consequently, the past cannot always be taken as an accurate guide for the future. Yet the strategist must be cognizant of the impact of the political, social, and economic dimension on historic demand. He must be able to interpret the record of the past with a sensitivity that will enlighten his judgments of the future.

Market requirements

A major input in the determination of market potential is the analysis of market requirements. Customer needs may not be satisfied by existing products and strategies. Needs may be changing, providing opportunities to those who are willing to adapt. Or new needs may emerge.

New needs provide the impetus for an entrepreneurial strategic design. Cartridge Television is a classic example; its strategy is based on the premise of a rapid and significant emergence of a consumer video cassette market. Success, of course, is by no means assured. For instance, General Cinema is betting that movie theaters in suburban locations will continue to draw large audiences. Since these two companies will compete for the same consumer time and dollar with very different products, their assessments of consumer needs are evidently different. The validity of their analysis, involving such factors as price, convenience, and product variety, will be critical for their relative success.

Changing needs are equally important. In some instances, they may result from changes in consumer desires. In other situations, consumers will shift their purchasing patterns because alternate products compete for their time or money. Sometimes these products are directly competitive; for example, cheaper ball-point pens and pin-lever watches damaged the market for more expensive fountain pens and jewel-lever watches, respectively. Or these alternate products may be only indirectly competitive. These instances are equally damaging yet harder to recognize. Frozen foods and other forms of food preservation have an indirect but important impact on the market for tin cans. Television, by competing for leisure-time activities, has been a major competitive threat to both the publishing and the movie exhibition industries.

An assessment of market requirements is one of the critical but difficult steps in identifying and predicting a company's environment. This question looms large for several of the companies portrayed in this book. Taylor Wine faces an uncertain future in the wine industry, Philip Morris in cigarettes, and Marlin Firearms for guns.

Distribution requirements

Most businesses have to operate within a distributive infrastructure. The strategist asks: What impact does the distribution structure have on the formulation of a growth strategy? Are new or rapidly growing products able to find sufficient and qualified outlets? Sometimes a company faces a crucial dilemma: the use of existing channels may permit rapid product introduction but may entail longer run disadvantages, while a restructuring of distribution may be preferable for long-term growth but may create an initial start-up handicap.

Changes in the distribution infrastructure also have a strategic impact. For example, the decline of the jewelry trade greatly influences the strategies of the established watch companies. On the other hand, companies may actively attempt to bring about changes in the distribution infrastructure. For example, in the recreational vehicle industry, Winnebago is pursuing a distribution strategy aimed at reliance on a small number of exclusive dealers, while its competitor Fleetwood continues the traditional approach of supplying a much larger number of non-exclusive outlets.

Two major trends in distribution are frequently encountered. One is the shift from the use of independent channels to that of captive branches. As technological changes place greater emphasis on sophisticated sales effort and skilled service operations, many companies have integrated forward into these activities. Given the costs of operating one's captive and exclusive branches, this trend frequently favors the larger, wider line companies. Economies of scale sometimes are more critical in distribution than in manufacturing. If the tradeoff between benefits and costs for the company with the largest market share favors a direct sales force, the same conclusion may not be appropriate for competing firms. They may have to absorb a higher cost burden per unit sold if they create their own captive distribution network. Their alternative, however, may leave them with a competitively inferior distribution setup as they continue to rely on independent channels which may not have the required skills and resources and may divide their attention among a large number of unrelated products.

Another major trend is the so-called "retail revolution," characterized by the growth of large-scale department stores and supermarkets, on the one hand, and specialty chain stores on the other. In either case, the net effect is greater leverage for the retail outlet in terms of securing price and service concessions from manufacturers, more aggressive merchandising, and, on balance, lower retail prices. The shifting patterns of influence in the distribution system are manifested by the emergence of private brands and, in some instances, moves by the retail company to own or control its sources of supply. Thus, the emergence of the department store as a major outlet for ladies' dresses has an important impact on Arthur Keller's company. Marlin Firearms is faced with the increasing penetration by discount stores into the merchandising of guns.

These trends favor not only size but innovation. The continuous flux in retailing and particularly the large number of recent successes in discount retailing or convenience eating places, such as McDonald's, are vivid testimony to the opportunities open to innovators. In some industries, the many small outlets attempt to stem the tide, as, for example, the neighborhood drugstores and local stockbrokers. Yet even in these industries revolutionary changes in distribution are slowly breaking through. The degree and pace of change has far-reaching implications for the strategies of pharmaceutical and mutual fund companies. Finally, there is the inevitable problem of the middleman. A. G. Brown, a food broker, is affected by the establishment of captive sales forces by food manufacturers, on one end, and by the growing strength of supermarkets and their private brands on the other.

PRODUCT AND TECHNOLOGICAL DIMENSION

The product and technological dimension deals with the weapons with which the competitive battle is being fought: the products or services which are being offered and the processes which are being used to get the goods out the door. In assessing this dimension it is useful to focus on three characteristics:

—the products and services themselves,
—the process required to produce the products,
—the ingredients or materials used in the manufacture of the products.

Products

A critical element in the strategic profile is a company's product-market relationship. The identification of market size and competitive requirements deals with one aspect of this equation; the product and technological dimension focuses on the other. In the second instance, the product policies pursued by the various participants in the industry are highlighted. How broad are the product lines being offered? Do companies pursue "specialist" strategies or do they follow a full-line approach? Also, what choices have been made in terms of price and quality? In the light aircraft industry, for example, Piper has pursued a low-price, basic-quality strategy while Beech has been the leader in the high-price, high-quality segment, producing, as stated by company executives, the Cadillac of the industry. The largest company in the industry, Cessna, markets a line which, with only minor gaps, blankets the field. Tying price, quality, and product policy to the previously discussed market segmentation permits the identification of markedly different strategies even within the same industry.

Products are subject to continuous change as participants in the competitive arena attempt to secure marketing advantages. New products may be seen as competitive weapons to differentiate one's own strategy from that of competitors or as responses to new market needs or even as efforts to create markets. Often competitive and market elements will be intertwined. General Motors' product proliferation strategy that evolved under Alfred Sloan may have been primarily a competitive response, albeit haphazard at first, to differentiate the company from Henry Ford's then highly successful single-product strategy. Yet this strategy turned out to be in line with the changing market needs as the U.S. automobile market matured.

Product innovation may provide major competitive advantages and growth opportunities. For example, in the farm equipment industry the development of highly specialized, sophisticated, laborsaving machinery, geared to the large and increasingly specialized farms, has injected new life into an otherwise relatively stable and mature industry. More dramatically, product innovation has permitted the emergence of entirely new industries and companies. Snowmobiles are a recent example. Industry sales had grown from a few thousand dollars in the early sixties to around $600 million by the end of the decade, creating an estimated employment of around 100,000 people. Interestingly, this new industry is dominated by two newcomers, Bombardier and Arctic, while subsidiaries of large established companies are left with small market shares and often unprofitable operations. It is important to keep in mind, however, the limitations imposed by market size and competitive reaction. Products have life cycles which imply the existence of different strategies as the product passes from an untried innovation in a wary but untouched market to a standard item in a replacement market. During the early seventies, replacement sales began to exceed original purchases of snowmobiles, and the issue of market saturation became critical.

Product innovation may also change the rules of the game in an industry. The advent of supertankers, as described in the Anglo Norness cases, had a major impact on the competitive requirements of bulk shipping. While providing substantial operating economies to shipowners which could be shared with clients, the supertankers require a heavy initial investment, are expensive to have idle, and are relatively inflexible as to cargo. Predictably, the nature of the relationship between owners and shippers has begun to focus on longer term contracts which promise greater price stability. The strategic implications of new products can be far-reaching and have to be fully analyzed.

Product innovation is not without risks. The mortality rate of new products is high. But even where success has been achieved, it may prove to be ephemeral. The rate of technological change may be so rapid that it reduces the time span during which a company can reap the benefits of its product developments and hence requires a continuing commitment of development funds to stay in the vanguard of progress. Among marketing companies, brand proliferation may have an analogous effect. The cigarette industry, dominated in the 1920s by three brands, now boasts nearly a hundred, the most popular having less than 20% of the market. Launching a successful brand, defined as one having at least 1% of the market, is an expensive and risky affair.

More critically, a company with an initial winner does not always find success possible to replicate. In many industries technological change has raised important strategic implications for the participants. Calculators are an example. For years, the industry worked peacefully on improvements and cost reductions for mechanical calculators. Then electromechanical calculators came along, and the technological pace quickened somewhat. It permitted Olivetti to emerge from its position as a small Italian company to that of a major worldwide factor in the office equipment industry. The shift toward electronics shifted the competitive constellation, providing Japanese companies with sizable growth opportunities. The pace of electronic innovation, however, has quickened even more, providing U.S. semiconductor manufacturers with technological and cost advantages that permit them to enter the end-use market for hand calculators. As wave upon wave of new products reached the market, prices eroded, threatening marginal producers who had hoped to ride along on the crest of a growing market.

Product and technological innovation does not always reward its supporters. Sometimes, those who are left behind may turn out to be the beneficiaries. The desire for product differentiation and the flow of ideas from the laboratories may overshoot market requirements. Not all innovation is either needed or accepted. A famous example is George Romney's American Motors which by staying with its old product in the late 1950s became unique, while the "Big Three" introduced larger and larger cars. The traditional American Motors car, later dubbed "the compact," better satisfied the needs of many consumers during those years than the so-called (by Romney) "dinosaurs" of the Big Three. In the packaging industry during the last decade there was a major push toward new and revolutionary packaging materials and techniques, leading some observers to write the obituary of the tin can. As it turned out, the performance of metal container companies was far better than that of many of the companies marketing new materials. Thus, product and technological innovation should not be endorsed automatically but should rather be submitted to a thorough strategic evaluation.

Process innovation

Innovation takes place not only for products and services but for processes and ingredients as well. Innovation in these areas may also have far-reaching strategic implications, and many of the comments made above apply equally to them.

Process innovation has been particularly important in capital intensive commodity industries, such as steel or chemicals, where low manufacturing costs are critical. Innovation in such instances is often combined with increased facility size in an effort to attain greater economies of scale. The benefits, however, do not always accrue to the industry, though the implications of not innovating may be still less attractive because of foreign or interindustry competition. A cost or productivity breakthrough by one firm often triggers a competitive reaction. The result may be an expansion of industry capacity beyond current market needs which, of course, leads to price cutting and a lower-than-expected return on investment. This sequence of events has characterized the experience in recent years of many basic industries.

Process innovation is also important in those industries facing labor shortages and rising wage rates. The typical response in manufacturing areas under these circumstances is to seek ways of substituting capital equipment for manpower. Thus, Marlin Firearms, while continuing to manufacture and assemble in the United States, is attempting to remain competitive with European and Japanese imports through increased mechanization, requiring highly automated equipment. Process innovation in service industries has often been overlooked, though here, too, it may be significant. For instance, by locating multiple auditoriums in the same theater, General Cinema was able to reduce both construction and operating costs per dollar of revenue. In general, where costs are an essential input into the strategic equation, process innovation is a frequent companion.

Cost reduction is, of course, not the only goal of process innovation. It also may provide product-quality improvements and better customer service. New processes may also be linked to new ingredients. Thus, the strategist should bear in mind a number of questions: Have process technologies changed frequently or dramatically? Have plant sizes or machine speeds escalated? Has labor productivity increased and, if so, have capital expenditures followed suit?

New ingredients or raw materials

Finally, new ingredients often permit both cost reductions and product innovations. Frequently, innovations in ingredients originate outside the user industry. Moreover, users do not always possess the technology required to apply these innovations and are sometimes inclined to ignore them. Their impact has to be broadly identified and carefully assessed, since potential opportunities and threats are easily overlooked. Classic examples of this phenomenon are the substitutions of aluminum for steel in beer cans, synthetic fibers for cotton and wool in textiles, and plastic for wood in furniture. In some instances, the innovator has sought or been forced to bypass the manufacturers who would normally be its customers and enter the market for end-use products.

COMPETITIVE DIMENSION

The competitive dimension spotlights a company's opponents: the number and characteristics of one's competitors. The first question here is to ask: "Who are our competition?" The general manager is likely to greet the question with laughter. He knows who his competitors are. He already has the answer. However, a visit to a pathology lab of the corporate hospital reveals as a common cause of death: killed by a competitor one did not know or did not take seriously. IBM, which did not make manual typewriters, destroyed Underwood's leadership position in the typewriter business with its electric typewriter. Yet for many years Underwood paid more attention to its traditional rivals, Smith-Corona and Royal-McBee. IBM was seen as a remote outsider with a special luxury product, not as a serious and dangerous challenger. In some ways newcomers are more dangerous than established competitors. In identifying the competitive dimension, the strategist should not limit himself to familiar faces. He should also view the lesser known and, more importantly, potential competitors.

A second question in dealing with the competitive dimension is: "How do we compare?" Often this analysis focuses on a comparison of resources. Clearly, a count of the number of troops which can be sent into battle is important. It will provide clues as to relative strength and probable results. Of greater importance, however, is an assessment of the quality of the strategies. The larger company is not necessarily the one most likely to succeed. One must compare not only the size of available resources but also the characteristics of the respective strategies. John Deere is smaller than the Ford Motor Company yet more successful in farm equipment. Vlasic Foods has achieved leadership in the U.S. pickle market even though it is smaller than its major competitor, Heinz.

In some instances, the single-business company is able to outperform its competitors who accommodate a wide range of products. This is particularly true where new products damage the position of established ones. The electric typewriter, for example, was a threat to the market for manual machines. IBM, unburdened by a position in manuals, could focus all its efforts and attention on promoting and selling the electrics. Underwood, Smith-Corona, and Royal-McBee, on the other hand, were reluctant to endanger the position of their manuals, which accounted for the bulk of their output, and consequently sold the electric typewriter defensively at best. Unless properly trained and compensated, a salesman is not going to endanger his established bread-and-butter line by an uncertain, although potentially desirable, product.

A third question in identifying the competitive dimension is: "How do we compete?" Competitive behavior varies from industry to industry. It is in part a function of how participating companies have chosen to compete, a result of their strategic profiles. It is also influenced by the structure of the industry, its operational requirements, and the number and strength of the companies involved. The metal container industry is dominated by Continental and American Can. Their huge market shares and financial resources impose major restrictions on their smaller competitors, such as Crown Cork and Seal and National Can. At the same time, such a structure creates opportunities because can purchasers are often anxious to have one of the smaller companies as a second supplier. The combination of industry structure, operational requirements, and strategic profiles permits the strategist to identify the degree and type of competition which may be encountered.

Competitive weapons vary from industry to industry. In farm equipment, competition occurred on several fronts: price, product development, dealers, and credit. In the duplicating industry it involved product development, systems development, price, service, and advertising. An analysis of competitive behavior must precede the resource audit, which will be discussed in a later chapter. The adequacy of a company's resources can be judged only in light of the competitive requirements of its industry.

A fourth and final question in terms of this dimension is a determination of the impact of competition. Does competition permit the entry of new companies into the industry? Are the industry leaders increasing their market share at the expense of the smaller participants, as has happened in the beer industry? Of great importance is an identification of price levels and cost-price relationships. In certain industries, competition results in a deterioration of price levels, while in others prices remain at reasonable or even high levels in spite of competition. Cost-price relationships are equally important. It is not unusual for industries to have their margins squeezed between low prices and uncontrollable costs. As the IBM electric typewriter began to take an increasing share of the office typewriter market, the traditional Big Three in manuals competed so fiercely for the declining manual typewriter market that their margins almost completely disappeared. Rising costs resulting from inflationary pressures approached the highly competitive price levels. Trapped by such low margins, the Big Three were unable to generate the resources for either a competitive counterattack or for effective and durable diversification.

Several cases in this book permit an exploration of the competitive dimension, especially those dealing with the watch and recreational vehicle industries. The Philip Morris case permits the exploration of competitive behavior in an oligopolistic industry, while Anglo Norness in the shipping industry illustrates close to pure competition as the forces of supply and demand interact relatively freely.

5

Strategic forecasting

PREDICTIVE JUDGMENTS

THE DESCRIPTION of the environmental dimensions has made clear that they have to be looked at in terms of both the present and the future. The strategist is interested not only in today's market size but also in tomorrow's market growth. Competitive conditions have to be assessed both in current and future terms. In sum, the environmental framework, if it is to be useful to the strategist, must be a dynamic rather than a static description of prevailing conditions. As a result, the focus is not solely on the environment "as is" but also on the environmental trends. While the former requires the analytical skill of identification, the latter involves a predictive skill which is predominantly judgmental in character. Forecasting the environmental trends necessitates primarily strategic judgments and will be referred to here as strategic forecasting.

Strategic forecasting, therefore, is the judgmental process through which the strategist attempts to predict the future shape of the environmental dimensions. It involves the totality of the dimensions and therefore is more than just a market forecast. It includes a forecast of the economic, political, market, technological, and competitive dimensions. Once the forecasts of the various dimensions have been made, the total picture must be viewed.

Given the broad scope of the forecast and the difficulty in predicting many of the dimensions, strategic forecasting by necessity is a highly uncertain process. It is one where judgments by reasonable people may

34

vary significantly. As a result, critics contend that the general manager may as well throw a pair of dice. Yet uncertain and conflicting strategic judgments made explicitly are preferable to jumping haphazardly with one's eyes closed. The process of strategic forecasting makes the areas of judgment explicit. These areas can be fully analyzed, benefiting from a variety of inputs. And even though the forecast is a judgmental one, if made explicitly it can be monitored subsequently, so that changes can be made quickly if later events disprove the basis on which the judgment was made.

Anyone who is called on to forecast, in this day and age, almost feels a moral obligation to predict change. Change is glamorous, it gets the publicity, and it provides the justification for modifying one's strategic posture. Also, the grim stories of those companies which failed to respond to changing conditions make the headlines and are fresh in everybody's mind. Yet strategic forecasting should be done with an open mind. There are many situations which are not subject to appreciable change. In fact, many a strategic forecast will come to the conclusion that conditions will remain the same. No one should be ashamed of such a conclusion. However, it must be based on a thorough predictive analysis rather than on traditional thinking, which satisfies itself that tomorrow will be a carbon copy of yesterday because "that is the way it has been over the last several decades."

Strategic change is often characterized by its suddenness. Conditions which have been stable for years change abruptly, often without warning. It frequently happens in those industries where change is least expected: the older, mature ones. The challenge for the strategic forecaster is to call these sudden major changes in industries which have been stable for years. It is, in many respects, more difficult than predicting changes in industries which are in constant turmoil.

PREDICTIONS, NOT PROJECTIONS

Strategic forecasting involves primarily predictions, not projections. Yet the strategic forecaster will constantly seek refuge in the latter. Projections have their roots in the past. They are essential in making operational forecasts. However, even if dressed up with the most elegant, esoteric, and modern analytical techniques, a projection still has its roots in the past. While the general manager can learn from history, history should not be the sole basis for his prediction of the future, especially when strategic change involves major structural change as well.

Major change cannot be predicted by relying on past experience. New products may either dislodge existing ones or they may satisfy hitherto unfulfilled needs. Projecting history into the future would not have predicted Heublein's phenomenal success with vodka during the fifties and sixties. During the early fifties the liquor industry was faced with a stagnating market; vodka accounted for only a minimal share of alcoholic beverages consumption. Yet vodka sales, and especially those of Heublein's Smirnoff brand, rose rapidly in the next decade, increasing vodka's share of the liquor market from about 2% to roughly 10%. This success was based on structural changes in liquor consumption; on the increased involvement of women and young people who preferred to dilute alcohol with the familiar taste of tomato juice, orange juice, or soft drinks rather than swallow straight rye or bourbon. The trend toward long drinks also helped, as did the trend toward lightness. Furthermore, the growth of the vodka market was greatly enhanced by Heublein's aggressive and imaginative marketing policies, coupled with the absence of immediate competitive retaliation. Heublein's larger competitors were busy diversifying outside the liquor industry and were also reluctant to endanger their other well-established products by aggressively marketing vodka.

This vodka example indicates some of the variables entering into the strategic forecast. As has already been stated, they cover all or several of the environmental dimensions. The anticipated competitive response was one variable. Would Heublein have been able to make Smirnoff the leading vodka brand if competition had retaliated immediately and vigorously? The strategic forecaster has to judge whether such a response is likely or whether a preoccupation with established lines and diversification will give the new entrant several years of grace. The market dimension as it relates to changing consumer needs was another key variable in the Smirnoff success. So was the product dimension, in that Smirnoff was not just another alcoholic beverage; Heublein's marketing approach made it much more than that. In fact, to achieve product differentiation and premium prices with a product that is tasteless, colorless, and odorless must rank among the major marketing achievements. .

During the sixties, Heublein attempted to repeat its Smirnoff success with bottled cocktails. Here again, history was a most inadequate guide to the future. The strategic forecast required judgments in terms of competitive response, the uniqueness of the product, and the needs and desires of the market.

Another strategic forecast relates to the future of the metal container. Will users continue to rely on it as the staple package, or will the need for food processing techniques or beverage characteristics permit or even force a switch to other forms of packaging? Will new raw materials be developed with characteristics superior to those of the metal container? Will the established can companies have access to these new technologies or will they be developed by material companies who may supply the users directly? Will new technologies be developed by a single can company, giving it a major competitive advantage over its rivals? Or will new technologies encourage backward integration through increased self-manufacture by users? Alternatively, will rapid technological change discourage backward integration as users avoid freezing their commitment to a single technology, retaining their freedom of choice of where they want to obtain their packaging materials?

Uncomfortable as it may be, the strategist must predict the answers to such questions as these and, further, be prepared to allocate resources to strategic action programs based on his environmental assessments. In making these judgments, he should be guided by an analysis that encompasses the multiplicity of dimensions described earlier and the interdependencies among them.

CYCLICAL OR STRUCTURAL CHANGE

A critical dilemma frequently faced by the strategic forecaster is whether the industry is suffering from a common cyclical decline or is confronted with major structural change. The farm equipment industry during the early fifties suffered a sales decline. Some executives in the industry interpreted it as a cyclical slump which they saw as inevitable after the postwar boom had satisfied the prevailing shortages. Others saw a concurrent structural change resulting from fewer but larger farms with different and more sophisticated product needs. The former group simply set out to weather the storm, whereas the latter concluded that changes in strategy were called for. During the 1970s, many a company, faced with a sales decline, had difficulty interpreting whether the cause was the recession or a declining competitive position in terms of product development and marketing.

The same dilemma may be posed during times of economic prosperity. IBM's electric typewriter counted its first successes during the immediate post–World War II period. Was this an indication of forthcoming structural change, a major shift from manual to electric typewriters? With the benefit of hindsight we now know that such a strategic forecast would have been correct. Yet at that time one could have argued persuasively that IBM's success with electrics was the result of the then prevailing shortages and that once the pent-up war demand was satisfied industry would return to purchasing low-cost and lower maintenance manual typewriters for all but a very specialized market segment. Who would have dared to predict in 1948 that electric typewriters would conquer virtually the entire office typewriter market rather than remaining the Cadillac of the industry with its use limited to the presidential secretary?

The strategic forecast dilemma, whether we are confronted with the impact of the business cycle or with basic structural change, does not solely confront the businessman. The London *Economist*, in its November 6, 1971, issue, posed the same dilemma for the United States:

. . . the chances of the United States recovering its confidence in the reasonably near future are either even worse than they seem at the moment, or rather better than most people think; and it cannot be ruled out that the trouble in America goes so deep that the Americans may be incapable of running a coherent foreign policy for years to come. The United States may be experiencing something that no other country has yet had to go through. It may be experiencing the first full flowering of the Protestant revolution. What happened in the sixteenth century was the rebirth of an idea that had long lain dormant: the idea that the responsibility of the individual is the ultimate criterion of both politics and religion. The rebirth of that idea changed the face of Europe; among other things, it made democracy possible on a scale larger than that of the Greek city-state. But its full impact was never felt by the majority of people. It remained largely a concept of the educated. It is possible that the United States, which has been the first country to do so many things, and was the first to bring material plenty to most of its people, is now the first country to face the consequences of the fact that widespread prosperity universalises the revolution of individualism. If that is the explanation of what is happening to America, the place could be almost ungovernable for a very long time: it could be living through the first onset of the war of all against all. The rest of us had better wave the Americans goodbye while we wait for the same cataclysm to hit us in our turn.

The chances of recovery

That is one interpretation of the American crisis. But there is an alternative which does not depend on believing that something unique is taking place there. The more hopeful explanation merely assumes that the United States is suffering from a particularly vicious downturn in the normal cycle of expansionist self-confidence and inward-looking masochism that every country rides up and down on; and that sooner or later the normal corrective mechanism will send it back on the upswing.

If that is how it turns out—if history has not intervened this time with one of its secular twists of pattern—there is reason to hope that better times could be coming fairly soon. Three different things have contributed to the American disaffection of the past few years: the Vietnam war, the racial crisis and America's share of the pseudo-revolution of the young that exploded all over the western world in 1968. The American part in the Vietnam war will be almost over next year, and although the enemies of the war will continue to attack the residual American connection they may find the rest of the country increasingly reluctant to feel very strongly about it. By most of the measurable tests, the condition of the majority of America's blacks has improved markedly over the past decade. The gap in living standards that separates them from the whites has narrowed; the number of middle-class jobs open to them has increased; their children have a better chance of going to mixed schools. None of this will end racial antagonism, in America or anywhere else, but it may keep it off the streets. And the most telling fact of all is the failure of the would-be revolutionaries of 1968 to produce an ideology to justify their appeal to violence. That is why 1968 does not look like being another 1848. The upheaval of 1848 in Europe was followed by the formulation of marxism. The new left today has been able to produce very little more than warmed-over Marx.

Given the uncertainty involved in strategic forecasting it may be useful to develop alternative scenarios. Thus, the subsequent evaluative and creative processes may be based on different assessments of the future outlook. The final choice then awaits the last phase in the process when the strategic commitment has to be made.

6

The resource audit

RESOURCES ARE RELATIVE

THE TEMPTATION is great to begin the resource audit with an identification of a company's resources. Such an approach easily yields a long list of attributes. However, in terms of the strategic process this is putting the cart before the horse. Resources are relative. A company's strengths and weaknesses can only be appraised by relating them to its external environment and its strategic profile.

The environmental dimensions prevailing in its industry, and especially the competitive conditions, determine whether resources can be rated as strengths or weaknesses. In early 1967, American Motors ran a full-page advertisement containing an interview with its new president, Mr. Chapin. In it, the following conversation took place:

MR. CHAPIN: Our engines are the most modern on the road. They're one important result of the more than one-quarter billion dollars we've invested in recent years in plant and equipment and tooling.

INTERVIEWER: Over a quarter billion? That's more than most major companies are worth in total.

MR. CHAPIN: You're right. But when you talk about American Motors, you're talking about a company that outsells such major companies as National Cash Register and Campbell Soup, and has greater assets than General Mills and Armstrong Cork.

American Motors' size in sales and assets would be magnificent if the company were competing in either the soup or the cereal business. They are of little comfort, however, in its existing business: automobiles. In 1967 Chrysler's assets were 10 times, Ford's 21 times, and General Motors' 35 times as large as those of American Motors. In spite of the large dollar figure of American Motors' sales and assets, it was—relative to its competitors—a dwarf in its particular business.

The management of a capital goods company saw its resources as perfectly adequate. New plants had been constructed to permit the firm to supply a growing market; a highly liquid financial situation was viewed as allowing great future flexibility. Profit margins were most satisfactory. However, major structural changes and a cyclical downtrend hit the industry. Severe excess capacity conditions made the expanded plant useless, creating heavy fixed expense burdens. Credit competition lengthened the average period outstanding for receivables from three to nine months, thereby absorbing the company's liquidity and forcing additional debt charges upon it. Price competition eroded profit margins, reducing the company's flexibility to incur marketing as well as research and development expenses to bolster its deteriorating market position.

Resources have to be related not only to the company's *current* but also to its *future* external conditions. It is essential to view them as relative not just in a static but also in a dynamic sense. A certificate of health in today's situation may turn into a fight for life under tomorrow's changed conditions. Henry Ford's single-model, single-color car was an outstanding product in an immature market; it was a liability in a more mature market which had shifted from utility and function to features and style. The same happened to Howard Head's metal ski.

Resources must be related to a company's strategic profile as well. Fashion skills are more critical to a company specializing in women's shoes than for one concentrating in ski boots. Broad distribution is more important to Piper selling low-priced aircraft than for Beech with its luxury planes. However, by changing its strategic profile to include a low-priced plane, Beech's selective distribution setup becomes a weakness. American Motors' limited resources may suffice if it concentrates on some narrow segments of the automobile market, but they may be disastrously weak if it tries to meet the Big Three on many fronts.

THE RESOURCE DIMENSIONS

The resource audit encompasses a company's:

—operational dimension,
—financial dimension,
—management dimension.

The operational dimension will vary with the company's field of endeavor. In an industrial company it will typically consist of marketing, manufacturing, engineering, and research and development. In a publishing company the operational requirements will be editorial, circulation, and advertising, while in a mutual fund management company distribution, portfolio execution, and money management are involved. The financial dimension focuses on money as a strategic variable, while the management dimension analyzes a company's human resources.

The operational dimension

In viewing the operational dimension, it is useful to begin by asking what it takes to succeed in a particular business. What are the key requirements for success? The strategist begins with the portrayal of the ingredients of both a successful and an unsuccessful company. What does it take to become a hero or a bum in a particular business? Another look at *Playboy* magazine exemplifies the successful strategy. Its content shielded the magazine against "me too" competition on one side and against television and regular entertainment on the other. The protection against "me too" competition came from a balanced content, which included several literary pieces by well-known and highly respected authors, with only a relatively small percentage of the pages allocated to pictorial sex. No printing expense was spared to give the magazine a high-class appearance. *Playboy* also was able to differentiate itself from other entertainment magazines, and especially from television, through those few pages on which it revealed its distinctive competence. Operationally, filling the content of the magazine according to this formula was a simple proposition. Professional authors submitted their material in the early sixties at the rate of about 100 manuscripts per week. Cartoons also largely originated on the outside, while photographers from all over the country were invited to submit film strips of prospective playmates. Printing, too, was subcontracted. The operational task of putting the magazine together was further facilitated by the fact that (*a*) the magazine appeared infrequently, that is, monthly, (*b*) its content was largely timeless, (*c*) it appealed to a large audience, and (*d*) its focus was extremely broad.

In terms of distribution, the formula was equally simple. Given its unique position, the magazine was sold at a high price, thereby avoiding the cost-price squeeze common to the industry. The high price furthermore gave the magazine great discretion in terms of its advertising policy: it did not have to rely on advertisers to make ends meet. Also, by relying primarily on newsstand sales, the company avoided the high circulation costs of obtaining and servicing subscribers. Mr. Hefner had simplified the operational requirements by adopting a strategy of relying to a large extent on outside help.

Yet, the same Mr. Hefner went through another lesser known and disastrous magazine experience when he launched *Show Business Illustrated* in 1961. In terms of content, *SBI* was much more demanding than *Playboy:* (a) it appeared more frequently, (b) its content was highly current, (c) it appealed to a specialized audience, and (d) its focus was predominantly local, depending on the entertainment offered in particular cities. Nor were outside contributors beating on the door with manuscripts and photographs. Competitively, the magazine was at a disadvantage in terms of timing vis-à-vis the daily newspapers or the weekly magazines. Nor did it have a distinctive competence to set it apart from other media. In terms of distribution, it was impractical to rely mainly on newsstand sales, and therefore it incurred heavy expenses in obtaining subscriptions. In addition, its high price, making it the most expensive semimonthly on the newsstand, proved to be a liability.

Within the context of the current and future environmental dimensions, the company's existing strategic profile, and the established success requirements, the strategist identifies and evaluates the firm's operational condition. By way of illustration, the Marlin Firearms Company is used here. Its research and development capabilities must be assessed. Do they permit the necessary product development? Does the company have the required skills to stay abreast of technological developments? Manufacturing also has to be analyzed. Is it capable of meeting the company's growth objectives? What happens to its cost structure if demand fluctuates, either upward or downward? Are its costs competitive, especially with imports from Europe and Japan? What future manufacturing investments are anticipated to meet the market and competitive requirements? Marketing is another function which must be scrutinized. Does Marlin have an appropriate distribution setup? Does its consumer franchise, and especially its brand name, provide protection against domestic and foreign competitors? Are its prices competitive? Does its product policy aim at the appropriate market segments?

Not only do the various operational elements have to be related to the external conditions, to the strategic profile, and to the success requirements of the particular business; these operational elements also have to be interrelated. The strategist thus has to build on his functional knowledge, in marketing, manufacturing, and research and development. A vast literature is available, particularly on the first two of these functional elements. The task of the strategist is to take the available expertise in all functional areas and integrate them with each other and with the above-mentioned aspects of the strategic equation. Furthermore, the operational dimension has to be related to the financial dimension.

The financial dimension

Money often is an important strategic variable. A company's financial resources have to be related to its strategic requirements. In this connection, the strategist must have a clear notion of several aspects of the financial dimension, as will be illustrated by using Philip Morris, another of the companies included in this book. In simplified form, its balance sheet in 1969, a year in which several important investments were made, looked as follows (in millions):

Receivables	$ 83	Current and other liabilities	
Inventory	447	(excluding debt)	$130
Net fixed assets	147	Current and long-term debt	490
Investments in subsidiaries	228	Equity	356
Other assets	29		
Cash	42		
	$976		$976

The first three categories of assets, totaling $677 million, were required in operations for both working capital and plant and equipment. Netted against the $130 million in liabilities, this figure is reduced to $547 million, which was used to support $1,142 million in sales. In addition to the operational assets, Philip Morris carried $228 million in investments and $71 million in cash and other assets. To finance all these assets it relied on $490 million of debt and $356 million in equity. Its earnings before taxes in 1969 were $115 million; after taxes, $58 million. Its price-earnings ratio was approximately 12 times. One other item of interest was that $364 million of its inventory consisted of leaf tobacco.

The strategist is particularly interested in the following elements:

1. What are the asset requirements per dollar of sales? A quick analysis reveals the following:

> 7 cents for receivables
> 39 cents for inventory, of which 32 cents was in leaf tobacco
> 13 cents for net fixed assets
> 59 cents for total operating assets
> 11 cents for liabilities
> 48 cents for net operating assets

In other words, for each dollar of sales the company invests approximately one-half dollar in net operating assets.

2. What does the company earn? The figure is roughly 5 cents per dollar of sales, hence its return on its net operating assets is about 10%. Debt leverage increases this return on the basis of equity.

3. How much cash is generated internally? Philip Morris, in addition to its $58 million profit after taxes, benefited from a $13.5 million depreciation cash flow but paid out about $23 million in dividends, leaving a net cash flow of a little under $50 million.

4. How has the company committed its resources and where has the money come from? A 1968–69 funds flow shows (in millions):

Uses		Sources	
Working capital	$ 8	Liabilities	$ 14
Fixed assets	9	Debt	135
Investments	160	Equity	41
Other assets	13		
	$190		$190

During this period sales increased by $122 million. Thus, Philip Morris was keeping its existing assets nearly constant (in spite of substantial growth) in order to use its retained earnings as well as substantial amounts of debt to diversify into other fields. In part, the company could keep its existing operating assets constant by virtue of the flexibility given to it by its large inventory in leaf tobacco and the alternative of relying on government tobacco stockpiles.

With the above elements in mind, a company's current performance can be appraised and its ability to grow as well as its ability to diversify can be analyzed. By having a feel for the asset requirements per dollar of sales (in terms of working capital and plant and equipment) the financial requirements of growth can be assessed. (Of course, average and incremental asset requirements per dollar of sales may differ and have to be analyzed in detail in the specific situation.) The ability to generate funds has to be related to these requirements: How much growth can be financed internally? Where borrowing is required, the company's debt capacity must be analyzed, as well as its vulnerability to debt. The company's flexibility to influence its asset requirements has to be explored, such as keeping its inventory constant, reducing inventory, or utilizing excess capacity. In this case, the strategist has to determine how long such an approach is feasible. The company's performance permits one to compare it with alternate opportunities. Will diversification improve or reduce profitability? Is it desirable to reduce operations in some segments of the business and use its currently committed resources elsewhere?

The financial dimension also has to be viewed dynamically. What is the impact of credit competition on working capital needs? What happens if service competition increases inventory requirements? What are the fixed asset requirements resulting from mechanization forced upon a company to keep its costs competitive? What happens to a firm's cash flow if competitive conditions force a reduction of its margins either through lower prices or through higher marketing and research and development expenses? What is the impact of rising interest costs? In other words, in relating a company's financial dimension to the future it may be necessary to construct different financial profiles based on growth or stagnation (if not decline) as well as on more or less severe competitive conditions.

Management dimension

The management dimension is probably the most critical. To many a company the depth of its management resources constitutes its greatest strategic constraint. In many ways, and in contrast to the financial aspects, this dimension is the most difficult to assess. Some of the later chapters on corporate organization will focus more closely on this dimension. The following poem from an unknown author describes it nicely:

> Though your balance sheet is a model
> of what balance sheets should be
> Typed and ruled with great precision
> in a type that all can see.
> Though the grouping of the assets
> is commendable and clear
> And the details which are given
> more than usually appear.
> Though investments have been valued
> at the sale price of the day
> And the auditor's certificate shows
> everything O.K. . . . . .
> One asset is omitted—and its
> worth I want to know:
> That asset is the value
> of the men who run the show.

The capabilities of management, like the other resource dimensions, have to be related to the environmental requirements and the company's strategic profile. A watch company may have the world's best mechanical engineers, but they may prove of little help in developing an electronic watch. An insurance company may have salesmen who are outstanding in selling life insurance policies but ill-equipped and little motivated to sell mutual funds. A company's labor force may be highly skilled but unable to compete costwise with imports from the Far East. Management may be highly skilled in establishing and running movie houses, but can these skills be transferred to managing bottling plants?

Not only the abilities of management have to be assessed but also its depth. Some companies, particularly the smaller and rapidly growing ones, have barely enough talent to fill the necessary positions. Departure by one of the members of management, and especially the president, may leave a critical gap. In contrast, other companies may have several competent candidates available for each position. The organizational machinery, under these circumstances, continues to run smoothly even when key managers depart. In some instances, the capable specialist is critical. In others, however, specialists can be relatively easily replaced, and it is the generalist, the coordinator and integrator, who is a most vital and nearly irreplaceable member of management. In some cases, managers control the business they have helped to create: if they leave, as in the case of investment bankers, they frequently take their accounts with them.

One aspect of the managerial dimension which may have a critical impact on a company's strategic behavior is the nature and application of its control system. Lack of an efficient and clear control system can hinder strategic decision making. It is difficult to analyze and evaluate a situation if it is impossible to find out exactly what is going on. On the other extreme, too efficient a control system can be equally damaging. If results are measured frequently over short time spans, managerial responses will be geared to the system. When the paycheck is at stake, it is difficult to be a strategic statesman and favor the long run. Yet, responses which are keyed to a quarterly or annual profit and loss statement inevitably favor improvisation over long-haul strategy and foster a reluctance to commit investments and expenses which are reflected in the current statement but which are expected to yield results only in a future period. Short-term measurement may easily destroy the dynamic aspect of the strategic framework. Management plays it safe and aims for early results, which inevitably leads to a static approach. General Electric in the early 1970s instituted a major effort in "strategic business planning." According to *Business Week*, GE's new president "thinks GE's new planning approach . . . reduces a manager's temptation to go for short-term results, sacrificing long-term gains—a criticism leveled at GE's decentralized structure. Performance of managers is now rated on adherence to their strategic plans rather than on short-term profits."[1]

---

[1] *Business Week*, July 8, 1972, p. 58.

7

Strategic alternatives

THE CREATIVE PROCESS

DEVELOPING strategic alternatives is a creative process. This creativity, however, takes place within the now well-defined framework of the external and internal dimensions, both in their current and future configurations. The strategist asks: Given the prevailing environmental conditions and given the resources at a company's disposal, what strategic options are available? Does the strategic forecast suggest the opportunity for innovative strategies? Can existing or future resources be put to new or more desirable uses?

Combining the discipline of the strategy framework with the innovative strategic creativity has some important advantages. In established organizations, especially large ones, there is a tendency to hold back unconventional ideas. The reasons are simple: the mortality rate of such ideas is high, and no one wants to harm his track record. Also, unconventional ideas, creative as they may be, easily get labeled as crazy because the borderline between creative and crazy ideas is often very thin. A solid company man with balanced judgment, therefore, is likely to play it safe. The penalty of such an atmosphere is that sound but unconventional approaches never see the light of day. This need not be so, however. Within the strategic process unconventional or even crazy ideas are welcome. As long as they are cycled through the evaluative framework, there is a good chance that the bad ones will be weeded out and the occasional good ones retained for future exploration. Within

48

the discipline of the strategic framework, it is possible to extend an open invitation to creativity.

Analysis of successful entrepreneurial strategies shows that they were frequently aided by two conditions: (1) the entrepreneur did not know that it could not be done and (2) he had nothing to lose and everything to gain. In developing strategic alternatives, the strategist should approach the creative process from the vantage point of these entrepreneurial conditions.

. Product or strategy innovations, when they are introduced by entrepreneurs, are often laughed at by the established companies. The industry leaders, after all, are the experts, and their expertise tells them that what the entrepreneur is attempting cannot be done. Underwood, Royal, and Smith were the experts in the typewriter business, and they knew that the electric typewriter was neither feasible from a technical nor desirable from a marketing point of view. The Big Four in the liquor industry were attempting to build brand loyalty around drinks with a distinctive taste. Heublein's attempt to develop a brand franchise in vodka, both tasteless and odorless, appeared to them as destined for defeat. Howard Head, when he carried his early samples of metal skis into the snow country, was told by the professional skiers that wood was the only suitable material for a quality ski.

This phenomenon is not confined to business. As stated by C. W. Ceram: "No matter how far back we go in the history of science, it seems that an extraordinary number of great discoveries were made by dilettantes, amateurs, outsiders—the self-taught who were driven by an obsessive idea, unequipped with the brakes of professional training and the blinkers worn by the specialists, so that they were able to leap over the hurdles set up by academic tradition."[1] Ceram then proceeds to give a long list of examples.

Expertise, indeed, can be a severe handicap in creatively developing strategic alternatives. Expertise, in fact, is often a result of an existing strategic profile. If the strategy is one of manufacturing a quality product with highly skilled labor and selling it through selective distribution channels by granting high retail margins and relying on dealer push, such a company is unlikely to consider mass-producing a lower quality product with unskilled labor and selling it through intensive distribution backed up by mass advertising to create customer pull. Likewise, to a Henry Ford who produced a low-cost utility vehicle for basic transportation, the General Motors strategy of model proliferation may have appeared as nonsensical.

The brake which expertise places on creativity is compounded by the opposite of the second entrepreneurial condition. While the entre-

---

[1] C. W. Ceram, *Gods, Graves, and Scholars,* 2d ed. (New York: Bantam Books, 1972), p. 58.

preneur or the challenger often has nothing to lose and everything to gain, the established company, in contrast, may have everything to lose and little to gain. To them a most painful aspect of the creative process is when certain appealing strategic options are developed which constitute threats to the existing strategy, sometimes to the point of making it obsolete. The natural reaction is to quickly close this Pandora's box. Yet any strategist who does so and closes his eyes to such options must be very sure that no one else thinks of them. In strategy formulation there is no monopoly on ideas. Regularly, companies which ignore options detrimental to their own strategy find that others, who may have nothing to lose, are less reluctant. When faced with the inevitable obsolescence of one's strategy, one may be better off in grasping that opportunity oneself rather than leaving it exclusively to others.

Developing a strategic alternative which calls into question the existing strategy is difficult not only because of the emotional and human reluctance to upset the traditional and often successful prevailing strategy but also because a novel strategic approach requires a shift in a company's resources. It may require building on weaknesses rather than on strengths. A company's existing commitment to selective distribution may make a shift to mass distribution difficult. Its reservoir of skilled manpower may make it reluctant to shift to mass production.

To advocate the creative process does not imply that the existing strategic profile will inevitably be superseded by an imaginative new strategy. The subsequent evaluative process will frequently result in the conclusion that the existing strategic posture is most appropriate. The purpose of developing strategic alternatives is to ensure that the strategist considers his existing strategy at this point only as one amongst many. There is a latent danger that the process of developing strategic alternatives becomes no more than the writing of variations on an established theme: that of the traditional strategy. Thus, the strategist should be cautioned not to consider his existing strategic profile as too much of a given.

The creative process, furthermore, is a powerful guarantee against a company blindly following industry or functional conventions. Just as a company may become a prisoner of its own strategy, it may also become a victim of industry practices or traditional approaches in terms of manufacturing, marketing, or finance.

Finally, the strategist should be cautioned that the exploration of strategic alternatives does not always lead to "either-or" choices. The issue is not necessarily between either the retention or the rejection of the existing strategy. The creative process which searches for options frequently leads to minor modifications and improvements in the existing strategy, which on balance emerges as the most desirable choice. However, retention and modification of the current strategic profile constitutes a more meaningful decision if it is made in full view of the various alternatives.

TYPICAL STRATEGIC ALTERNATIVES

In developing strategic alternatives, the strategist typically faces a number of basic options which can be explored in somewhat more detail.

The "do nothing" alternative

This one is the all-time favorite. Why not continue the existing strategy? While the recipe is simple, the reasons leading to it must be explored. Is retention of the status quo suggested on the basis of a thorough investigation? Or is it simply a matter of convenience or laziness? Is it a convenient way of sticking one's head into the sand?

There is a great temptation to put forth this strategic alternative. There may also be a great deal of justification for it. Innovation is risky, sometimes esoteric and possibly unwise. Thus, there is an opportunity to benefit from the mistakes of others. George Romney became a hero as champion of the compact car by sticking to his existing product line and by benefiting from the errors of the Big Three as they misread the trends in their industry. To draw on a football analogy, the fundamentals of strong blocking and tackling may be more crucial than the fancy pass patterns.

The do-nothing alternative, however, may also be a convenient escape from the uncomfortable pressures for change. Where the strategic forecast calls for a shift in strategy, action may be delayed by questioning the predictive judgment. Or a "wait and see" attitude may be adopted to await further evidence as to whether the predicted trends will indeed occur. Such reactions are especially convenient where the strategic response to new developments is either very risky or very costly. For example, major marketing or research and development investments may be required. Since most of these would have to be expensed in the current profit and loss statement, thereby reducing earnings per share or even resulting in losses, management may be reluctant to take such necessary strategic action. Instead, it may adopt the "do nothing" attitude by keeping these expenses within what it considers an acceptable level. The focus on the security analyst may overrule the strategic forecast.

The liquidation alternative

While "do nothing" is the favorite, "liquidation" is the black sheep among the strategic alternatives. Yet, there are circumstances where this alternative may be best for all parties concerned. Too often, management holds on to an obsolete strategy or fights a constantly escalating war with inadequate and diminishing resources. Such a strategy may destroy managerial careers as well as the shareholders' equity and, in many instances, is also detrimental to the employees. Unfortunately, it is both difficult and painful to reach the verdict of liquidation. Management is unlikely to put itself out of work.

Liquidation is particularly difficult in the single-product company, where it entails terminating the corporate existence. In the diversified company, on the other hand, liquidation is a more common occurrence. Some of the newer conglomerates are particularly known not only for their acquisitions but also for their disinvestments. The older diversified enterprises, however, also follow this route. General Electric's new president in 1972 rose to fame through the successful sale of the computer business. During the week of his appointment, the company also sold off its television broadcasting equipment business. *Business Week* commented that the new president, Reginald Jones, "was vaulted into GE's top spot largely because of his intimate identification with 'strategic business planning'—a technique that treats the company's vast array of ventures as an investment portfolio, sorting out the winners and losers through systematic analysis. The aim is to decide which ventures deserve the most investment capital and which should be dumped. TV broadcasting equipment turned out to be the loser."[2]

The alternative of specialization

During the boom years of the conglomerate it was not fashionable to stress the merits of a specialist strategy. Yet many companies owe their success to specialization. Of the subsequent cases, both Timex and Vlasic are eloquent examples. Indeed, the power of a single purpose can be substantial, particularly where competitors spread their energies and resources over a variety of activities. Thus, specialization may provide a competitive edge.

If one asks managers of the operating divisions of diversified companies who their most dangerous and difficult competitors are, they rarely cite other conglomerates. Instead, they usually mention much smaller specialized companies, which excell in a single product or service and which are able to react quickly and decisively.

In addition to providing a competitive edge, specialization also permits companies with limited resources to use them most effectively. Under George Romney, American Motors, with its limited resources vis-à-vis its giant competitors, aimed at one market segment: the compact car. Under Romney's successor, the company broadened its product scope with disastrous results. Vlasic, as a privately held company starting at a sales level of a few million dollars, has been able to compete successfully with the giant food processing companies.

---

[2] *Business Week,* July 8, 1972, p. 52.

A strategy of specialization permits a company to exploit particular market segments, sometimes resulting in spectacular performances even where the general industry conditions are stagnant. *Playboy's* success in the otherwise difficult magazine industry has already been mentioned. A large and well-known British shoe company more than quadrupled its sales during the fifties while the industry was virtually stagnant. It increased its market share in women's shoes from about 3% to over 8% and in children's shoes from 4% to nearly 12%, largely specializing in shoes for young children and older women. As such, it was able to compete and excell on the basis of comfort and reputation, thereby avoiding the vicissitudes of the fashion game.

Specialization also entails major risks. A company's fortunes are tied to a particular industry. If the industry declines, the company may be trapped. Changing market needs or major technological innovation may even put it out of business. Also, where a firm specializes in a cyclical industry, its fortunes may be subject to major swings. While management may accept such swings as a fact of life and prepare the company financially for it, the stock market may penalize it through a lower valuation of its shares. Another negative aspect is that specialization often creates a high level of expertise in a narrow area. This kind of expertise, as was pointed out earlier in this chapter, may be a hurdle to creatively developing strategic alternatives.

The vertical integration alternative

A common strategic alternative, as was pointed out in Chapter 3, is to integrate backward in terms of one's supplies or to integrate forward into one's outlets. Vertical integration is a constant temptation because it permits a company to expand the scope of its activities and yet remain on relatively familiar ground. There are also powerful strategic reasons for integrating either backward or forward.

Backward integration may aim for a steady source of supplies, thus minimizing the risk of shortages in the merchant market. Backward integration may also seek to ensure a low-cost position, if not a cost advantage relative to one's competitors. Oil companies seek ample and low-cost crude oil sources to supply their refineries and market outlets. Steel companies want to be assured of sufficient supplies of iron ore at constant quality and reasonable cost.

Backward integration does not necessarily entail advantages. Given the usually high capital requirements it may place a heavy strain on a company's financial resources. Also, a company with its own sources of supply becomes more vulnerable to technological change. It is tied to a particular technology requiring existing plant and equipment. Where new products or processes are developed, the vertically integrated company either has to write off its supply investments and invest in the new innovations or be placed at a competitive disadvantage. Its competitors who have not integrated backward are flexible enough to switch to merchant suppliers who deliver the new products or utilize the new processes. In the early 1970s, the leader in the snowmobile industry, Bombardier, had integrated backward by acquiring its engine supplier, while its main challenger, Arctic, in contrast, purchased engines on a merchant basis, permitting it to feature a model with the Wankel engine.

Forward integration may be undertaken to secure outlets, thereby guaranteeing a steady volume. Such a move may make the company less vulnerable to pressures from its customers. Particularly, the guaranteed volume, even if it is sold internally at market prices, becomes most important during periods of excess capacity in highly capital intensive industries. The few extra percentages in plant utilization may make a substantial difference in profitability. Even if prices are depressed, the margins on incremental volume may be substantial where fixed costs are high and variable costs are low.

Forward integration also often helps a company to achieve greater product differentiation, thereby reducing the price sensitivity of its products. In the early phases of the vertical product flow, products usually are of a commodity nature: within the framework of technical specifications they are identical and hence extremely sensitive to price. At the end of the vertical product flow when they reach the ultimate consumer, products are often differentiated: marketing activities become more critical, price may prove to be less important, while brand loyalty provides the differentiated product with a secure market position. For example, the chemical intermediates used to make detergents are commodities highly sensitive to price, while the branded detergents are differentiated products, enjoying a more stable price and market position.

In addition to seeking a guaranteed volume and more stable prices, forward integration may also be pursued to achieve better margins. For commodities fixed assets are usually high and market expenses low, while for differentiated products the opposite is true. Greater price stability combined with lower asset requirements may become a tempting proposition. However, many a company integrating forward does not have the marketing know-how to succeed with differentiated products. To stay with the detergent example, Monsanto as a supplier was able to make a good detergent, but its efforts several years ago to market its own brand were a fiasco.

One common problem encountered in terms of both backward and forward integration is that of balance. The minimum efficient size at one part of the product flow may be substantially different from that at the other end. The iron ore mine may be too large an investment even for a good-sized steel company. The problem is sometimes compounded, especially in the chemical industry, by the necessity to dispose of various by-products.

While vertical integration may be tempting to some companies, others refrain from it as a matter of policy. Dansk Designs prefers to rely for the manufacture of its products on subcontractors. Vlasic is relying increasingly on outsiders to harvest the cucumbers needed for its pickles. Along the lines of the specialization alternative, these companies want to concentrate on their strengths. Other firms, however, may not have the freedom of choice. Of the companies described in this book, Hedblom and A. G. Brown are confronted with vertical integration developments in their competitive environments which require a strategic response from them.

The diversification alternative

Of all the strategic alternatives, diversification is undoubtedly the most glamorous. Admittedly this glamour has paled somewhat as several well-known conglomerates have come upon hard times. Yet, whenever a company faces a strategic dilemma, diversification is immediately put forth as a quick and easy remedy. This is precisely what diversification should not be. It does not solve old problems. Nor is running away from one's problems through diversification the way to solve them. In fact, under these circumstances, diversification can be harmful by draining resources away from the problems which need to be solved. Opening a second front is not the way to solve a delicate situation on one's first front. Thus, diversification is not a solution to the problems encountered in one's existing business. These problems have to be faced separately and directly.

Diversification is an alternate way of committing one's resources. The strategist may decide that his existing business does not hold sufficient potential. He may wish to cut back or even liquidate it and commit his resources elsewhere. Alternatively, he may keep his existing activities at current levels or exploit their growth to their full potential but seek additional growth elsewhere. Thus growth through diversification may not always be a better utilization of existing resources but may aim at a better spreading of business risks or at achieving a growth rate which cannot be accomplished within a company's original given field of endeavor.

Diversification by moving into a more profitable and rapidly growing business and at the same time reducing one's commitment in a less profitable and stagnant business makes a great deal of sense. Unfortunately, many a strategist aims to do the former without the latter. Under these circumstances, the original business continues to deteriorate and drain company resources while also diverting management's attention from the more attractive diversification opportunities. These get short-changed in terms of management and money and therefore may fail to reach their full potential.

Diversification to achieve a more ambitious growth rate than is possible with the existing business creates other problems. This approach is frequently taken by companies which have achieved fame with a brilliant entrepreneurial strategy and which are eagerly looking for an "encore" to maintain their successful performance as well as the value of their shares. Unfortunately, success does not easily repeat itself, and a rapidly growing and highly profitable company finds it equally difficult to discover a counterpart which is for sale at a reasonable price. Faced by such a dilemma, many companies either reject one diversification proposal after another or acquire companies with lower growth and profitability rates, and often more problems, than their own.

When choosing between growth through the expansion of existing businesses and diversification, the strategist makes an intriguing tradeoff. With existing businesses he faces the uncertainty of future sales and profits but the certainty of knowing the industry. Diversification brings him the opposite: he may be able to add a certain amount in sales and profits but faces the uncertainty of a new and different business. Moving into an unknown business is the key variable in diversification. If company A which is in X business wants to acquire company B which is engaged in Y business, we know how A has performed in X and B in Y. The unknown and critical element of the equation, though, is how A will perform through B in Y. The same holds true where

a company develops by starting from scratch except that it does not have the experience, good or bad, in the new business that is secured with the acquired firm.

In assessing how a company may perform in a new industry, it is helpful to compare and contrast the success and competitive requirements in its own industry with those of the industry into which it plans to diversify. For example, when Heublein was contemplating diversifying into beer through the acquisition of Hamm, it would have been useful to compare and contrast the liquor and beer industries.

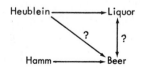

Such an analysis may save the diversifying company from a common error: that of applying its original and successful strategic recipe to the acquired company in a different industry. Diversification into another business often requires drastically different strategies. Yet it may be difficult for a company to follow one strategic approach in one industry and a totally different one in another industry. This danger applies especially to companies taking their first diversification steps. The highly diversified conglomerate, on the other hand, is forced, given the vast diversity of its units, to treat them separately and is, therefore, less tempted to transfer strategic responses.

This chapter describes diversification only as one of several strategic alternatives. It is not a guide for diversification decisions. In this respect, a vast literature is available detailing criteria and all the financial and negotiating elements. Obviously, the industry and company to be chosen as well as financial terms are important elements. Before these questions can be answered satisfactorily, however, it is necessary to place the diversification choice within a company's overall strategic context. The basic strategy has to be decided first before the details can be worked out. This is particularly important because diversification is not without risk. Errors here do not only affect the diversification move but they may backfire on the original strategic posture. A failure in diversification may entail the downfall of the entire company.

The international alternative

Instead of product diversification a company may embark on a strategy of area diversification. In the former, the products are different but the country is the same, while in the latter the products are the same but the countries are different. The prospect of repeating a successful strategic formula elsewhere around the world is a tempting one. Of the companies discussed in this book, Timex and Philip Morris have done so successfully. The firms in the Capital International case see a major opportunity in such an alternative.

A critical question is whether foreign markets will be as receptive as the company's home market to both the products and the strategic formula. Will the strategy have to be adapted to different foreign conditions? Furthermore, what kind of competitive constellation will the strategist encounter overseas as he seeks to repeat his domestic success?

During the fifties international expansion was seen as a luxury, during the sixties as an opportunity, but during the seventies it may well become a necessity. Some industries have been international for years. Often this was the result of nature in that sources of supply, such as crude oil, were in different parts of the world from the major consuming areas. Companies in other industries, such as Nestlé, Unilever, Singer, and

Colgate-Palmolive, have also been on the international scene for a long time. These companies essentially introduced successful products or applied effective strategies around the globe. Often, in spite of the international scope of these firms, the various national markets were largely separate entities harboring subsidiaries which were engaged in all facets of operations. The international connections were primarily in terms of ownership, dividends, or royalties rather than in terms of operations. Increasingly, however, competition is shifting from a national to an international scale. Worldwide• sourcing supplants national sourcing. Companies borrow money all over the world. Research and development is geared to the needs of products and facilities sold and located in widely different contexts. Marketing confrontations occur in several markets simultaneously. Internationalization, where it provides major competitive strengths through worldwide rationalization, may become not just a matter of choice but one of necessity.

In viewing international alternatives it is useful to separate the developing from the industrialized countries. The former used to be supplied from central sources located in the latter. During the last several years, however, the developing nations have made great strides in terms of import substitution, a topic raised by the Central American paint case in this book. Using the "infant industry" argument, these countries have typically closed their borders to imports. As a result, the developing world has increasingly been fragmented in separate and often small markets. The industrial world, on the other hand, after about a half a century of compartmentalization and protectionism is slowly moving to a freer interchange, sparked by developments such as the European Common Market. Also the predominance of the United States has dwindled, and in the early seventies at least three major industrial areas confront each other: Europe, Japan, and the United States. The Note on the Watch Industry portrays this phenomenon and permits an exploration of its implications.

8

The test of consistency

THE TEST of consistency is the process by which a given strategy or strategic alternatives are evaluated. Strategies are tested for consistency with a company's external and internal dimensions, both in their identified current and in their predicted future scope. In simple terms, the strategist relates what a company is *able* to do with respect to its resources to what is *possible* in its external environment. The test of consistency seeks the most appropriate response by relating corporate strengths and weaknesses to environmental opportunities and threats.

Like most other aspects of the strategic process, this is more easily said than done. Conceptually, the test of consistency appears to be a logical and exact approach. Practically, however, it is a difficult and judgmental process. Three factors, especially, complicate the application of the test of consistency. First, the test involves the multiplicity of external and internal dimensions, resulting in a highly intricate network. Second, the multiplicity of these dimensions and hence the complexity of this network are further compounded by the dynamic nature of the test, in that both current conditions and future predictions are taken into account. Third, the various current and future dimensions which enter into the equation often lead to conflicting conclusions. As a result, the test of consistency does not always produce clear-cut answers. Instead, the general manager is often forced to make tradeoffs.

The need to consider a multiplicity of dimensions is evident from the earlier discussion of the environmental conditions and the company resources. The key challenge here is to give full consideration to all the elements involved. For example, companies in the watch industry have to contend with the full scope of environmental dimensions. Politically and economically they are affected by tariff policies, import restrictions, and variations in the foreign exchange rates of several currencies. In terms of the market dimension, they are confronted with changing distribution patterns and a role of lesser importance for the watch among consumer durables. Technological developments in the manufacture of better quality throwaway watches and highly advanced electronic watches are of great importance. With respect to competition, the success of Timex and the Japanese companies as major competitors as well as the recent emergence of the electronics firms are of vital importance to the established companies. In terms of resources, the competitive battle demands a full display of the operational dimensions. Marketing is critical in conquering a share of the hotly disputed market. Production is essential in maintaining competitive costs. Research and development has risen in importance as the pace of product development quickens. The financial dimension is also highly relevant as the stakes increase and larger and larger companies begin to dominate the industry. Needless to say, with the above challenges, the managerial dimension is also a critical variable.

In practice, it is easy to overlook several of the important dimensions. This results not only from the natural human tendency to simplify problems but also from the fact that some elements may overshadow others. A given resource may represent such an obvious weakness that it calls for urgent repair; or it may be such a tempting asset that its full utilization is irresistible. The same may be true for an environmental opportunity or threat. Yet, where a particularly squeaky wheel asks for oil, the other wheels are easily overlooked. In Marlin Firearms, the lack of productive capacity represented such a crying need. However, was the corporate response to this need consistent with the other environmental and internal dimensions? The test of consistency requires that all external and internal conditions be taken into account. As will be discussed subsequently, however, this does not mean that all dimensions are equally important.

The multiplicity of dimensions is further compounded by the need to consider both the identified current and the predicted future conditions. A strategic response must be tested under both today's and tomorrow's situations. Strategic decisions take time, and their impact is felt over a long time span. Therefore, the test of consistency must be a dynamic and not just a static one. Furthermore, since the predictive dimensions are necessarily judgmental in character, the test of consistency becomes judgmental as well. Under these circumstances, the strategist easily seeks refuge in the more certain current dimensions. Yet such an approach casts doubt on the validity of the test, especially where a number of dimensions are changing. As a result, if the test of consistency is to be dynamic, it must be judgmental. If the strategist demands certainty, he will only be able to perform a static test.

Where the strategic forecast predicts major change, the test of consistency may well expose the obsolescence of the established and hitherto proven strategic recipe. There is no need to repeat here the conditions described in earlier chapters which lead to such strategic obsolescence: changes in the political, social, and economic constellations; in the marketplace; in technology; or in competitive conditions. The critical challenge here is to anticipate this obsolescence, because when it actually occurs, it may be too late for meaningful corrective action. Unfortunately, anticipation means (1) abandonment of a still successful strategy and (2) doing so on the basis of uncertain judgmental predictions. Obviously, the tendency under these circumstances is to rely more heavily on today's consistent test than on tomorrow's prediction of inconsistency. In other words, it is a perfectly human reaction to refuse to apply the predictive level of consistency precisely in those situations where it is most needed.

Frequently, a given strategic response is consistent with certain of the internal and external conditions but inconsistent with others. When a multiplicity of dimensions enters into the equation, it is difficult to satisfy all of them. Inconsistencies may occur between a strategy and certain current dimensions, or different results may emerge when relating a strategy to both current and future conditions. Under these circumstances, the strategist has to make tradeoffs. As was pointed out earlier, it is important to take all dimensions into account. An intelligent choice can only be made if one knows what one is choosing from. However, postulating a complete analysis does not mean that all elements are of equal importance. (Here again, as earlier, urgency should not necessarily be equated with importance.) Where a strategy relates positively to some dimensions but negatively to others, it is not simply a question of offsetting pluses and minuses. Some inconsistencies may be critical, while others may prove to be minor. As a result, in making these inevitable tradeoffs the strategist again has to rely on his judgment.

The test of consistency in practice is both complex and judgmental. Yet not only is it often erroneously portrayed as a product of simple logic but also as a device permitting the strategist to obtain the best of all worlds. Through the test of consistency a strategy should attempt to maximize external opportunities and internal strengths and to minimize external threats and internal weaknesses. And, indeed, many a strategic plan postulates the vigorous pursuit of unexploited opportunities with the support of established and proven resources. Unfortunately, while it is common to aspire to a strategic equation which incorporates the best of all worlds, this is not always possible. Maximizing both opportunities and strengths and minimizing both risks and weaknesses may be inconsistent.

For example, in the farm equipment industry Deere sought to maximize its opportunities by entering the European markets, while Massey Ferguson attempted to increase its penetration in the United States. Each company thus confronted the other where it was weak and its competitor was strong. Not surprisingly, neither Deere nor Massey Ferguson's efforts were successful. By chasing what they considered unexploited opportunities, they were forced to attack from a position of weakness on a terrain where competition was firmly established. Instead of maximizing opportunities, both companies ended up by maximizing their weaknesses, with an adverse impact on the earnings of both companies. Luckily for each other, they both made the same mistake. A similar situation prevailed in the light aircraft industry, where Piper attempted to trade up and Beech to trade down.

Thus, maximization of opportunities often involves maximizing rather than minimizing one's weaknesses. It also may entail maximization of risks. Reliance on company strengths may involve closing one's eyes to new opportunities; and as a result, maximization of internal strengths may result in minimizing external opportunities. Thus, the test of consistency may confront the general manager with some basic strategic choices rather than with perfect answers. The resolution of these choices will be discussed in the next chapter.

9

Strategic choice

NECESSITY FOR STRATEGIC CHOICE

STRATEGIC decision making, in the final analysis, is a matter of choice. As stated by Zaleznik, "the essence of leadership is choice, a singularly individualistic act in which a man assumes responsibility for a commitment to direct an organization along a particular path."[1] Strategic choice thus becomes the capstone of the strategic process. It involves a number of key choices which periodically confront the general manager:

1. A tradeoff between maximizing opportunities and minimizing risks.
2. The timing of strategic moves based on anticipated changes.
3. An assessment of the potential competitive confrontation which may result from strategic action.

Not surprisingly, strategic choice is the most difficult step in the strategic process. Having established the framework and facts, having made predictive judgments, having scanned strategic alternatives, having applied the test of consistency, the general manager now must decide. This decision cannot be based solely on facts and analysis. It is also influenced by uncertain predictive judgments and qualitative tradeoffs among a multiplicity of dimensions. The strategist will need the nerve and courage to make major and often irrevocable commitments in the face of uncertainty and imperfect analysis. Under these circumstances,

---
[1] Abraham Zaleznik, "Management of Disappointment," *Harvard Business Review*, November–December 1967, p. 68.

strategic choice becomes a highly personal decision. As such, it will be shaped by the personality of the strategist, particularly by what he sees as (1) his individual goals and ambitions and (2) his obligations to society.

KEY CHOICES

The opportunity-risk tradeoff

As was pointed out in the previous chapter, it is not always possible to obtain the best of all worlds. Maximization of opportunities may involve simultaneously maximizing threats. Specialization and diversification involve a similar tradeoff. As was discussed in Chapter 7, specialization permits a company to fight its battle on familiar territory but also makes it totally dependent on the economic fortunes of its industry. Diversification makes a company less vulnerable to the business cycle and the ups and downs of a particular industry, but requires it to compete simultaneously in several businesses, in some of which management may not be entirely expert, possibly causing a dissipation of its resources and efforts.

These tradeoffs cannot be made on the basis of logic. The decision depends, in the final analysis, on the willingness of the strategist to shoulder risk. For example, if he is reluctant to do so, he is likely to elect a strategy which minimizes the external threats to which his company is exposed. At the same time, such a strategy will probably result in minimizing the company's opportunities. On the other hand, if the strategist is an eager risk taker, he will be ready to maximize opportunities even if it involves exposing the company to a great many external threats. Thus, before committing the company to a specific strategic plan, the strategist has to determine how much of a risk taker he really is. Where the decision process is a collective one, the board of directors or management committee has to make clear how much risk it is willing to shoulder.

Too often, these risk assessments are not made. They are avoided because the necessity for choice is not made explicit. Management saves itself from this painful confrontation by assuming that it can indeed obtain the best of two worlds: that opportunities can be maximized and threats minimized. This ostrich-like approach can simplify strategic decisions but it certainly does not enhance their quality.

The timing dilemma

Where judgment accounts for a high proportion of the strategic process and where uncertainty is great, the tendency is to go slow and adopt a wait-and-see attitude. This is not always possible. Not all strategic decisions can be made in increments. At times it is necessary to make a commitment one way or another.

Even where a wait-and-see approach is feasible, it may not be desirable. Timing is a critical element. While the risk of early action is usually highest, so is the payoff. Furthermore, early action typically entails lower costs. Delays in action usually will be accompanied by risk reduction, payoff reduction, and cost increases. As opportunities become more certain and widely recognized, costs frequently become very high, accompanied by minimal payoffs.

Thus, timing entails a necessity to choose between a high-risk, high-reward strategy of moving early and the low-risk, low-reward attitude of wait and see. Sometimes, there is not even a choice because the wait-and-see approach may prove to be—in terms of results—a high-risk strategy. If a company does not move early, it may subsequently find itself totally outclassed by those who had the courage to do so. Early action, therefore, requires not only foresight but also a willingness to take risks.

Assessing competitive confrontation

Strategic action usually is either a challenge or a response to existing strategies of competitors. The familiar questions asked in deciding on a strategy are whether (1) it is superior or at least equal to those strategies which it confronts, (2) it is innovative or imitative, and (3) it attacks competition squarely or attempts to avoid competitive confrontation. This analysis, however, has to be carried one step further. What will be the possible counterresponse to a new strategy? What counterattack may be expected? Thus, two interrelationships must be explored:

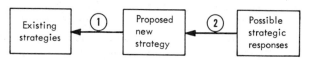

This way of viewing the competitive interplay focuses on an additional strategic choice. The strategist through his proposed new strategy is able to influence the possible strategic counterresponses by competitors. The nature of the attack greatly determines the likelihood and extent of a counterattack. Certain innovative strategies make it difficult and costly for the established companies to respond. Also, where the opposition feels that a new strategy is likely to fail, which is not uncommon with an unconventional new strategy, a quick and major response is less likely. In other instances, a competitive reaction follows immediately.

For example, technological innovation in steel processing gave newcomers a significant advantage over established companies. The oldtimers, in turn, responded by building new facilities themselves, creating a great deal of excess capacity which left the entire industry worse off. Ideal are those situations, in contrast, where a preemptive strategy is possible, giving the early entrant a strong and durable hold over the market.

THE STRATEGIST'S PERSONAL CHOICE

Individual goals and ambitions

Strategic choice, as exemplified above, is tough and risky. How does the strategist resolve these choices? In the absence of a logical and compelling answer, strategic choices for the corporation often will be influenced by the chief executive's personal strategy. Strategic decision making inherently is a matter of personal choice. How bold does the strategist want to be? Is he willing to suffer the consequences of wrong judgments, both in terms of the company's strategic posture *and* in terms of his own career? As stated by Harry B. Henshel, President and Chief Executive Officer of Bulova Watch Company, Inc.:

The president's decision, if it is to have maximum effect, is bound to reflect his own attitudes, philosophy, and capabilities to a considerable extent. As a result, he may very well find himself standing alone behind his personal analysis of a situation and his response to it. He may also find himself putting his job on the line as collateral for his judgment.[2]

The heavy dose of judgments and tradeoffs involved in the strategic process makes it inevitable that the personal attitudes of the strategist influence the final commitment. Yet it is a common practice to hide personal inputs under a cloak of rational decision making. Nevertheless, it is important that the strategist be explicit about these personal influences. Often when we hide something from others, we end up fooling ourselves. Many an executive becomes the victim of his own rationalizations.

The strategist's attitude toward alternate courses of action, first of all, may be influenced by his ambitions. He may want to be known as the person who shaped the character of his company. Second, his attitude may be determined by the situation he has inherited. He may succeed a strong and well-known personality and be anxious to differentiate his regime from that of his predecessor by exploring totally new paths. Third, it may be a result of his background. For example, in

[2] Harry B. Henshel, "The President Stands Alone," *Harvard Business Review,* September–October 1971, p. 38.

making tradeoffs under the test of consistency a chief executive having risen through the sales route may place major, if not exclusive, emphasis on the environmental market dimension. Fourth, the strategist's attitude toward risk may be shaped by external pressures, for example, from the financial community. Fifth, it may be influenced by organizational pressures. This is particularly the case in divisionalized organizations, where the general managers of the operating divisions have to make strategic decisions but are also subject to a measurement and compensation system which may focus excessively on the short run. Also, where collective decisions have to be made, the strategist may avoid risks because by doing so it will be easier to arrive at a common denominator encompassing everybody's opinion and thereby facilitating consensus.

It is important to be explicit about the personal inputs which influence the strategist's attitude toward alternate actions because these elements, too, have to be submitted to the test of consistency. Is what the chief executive *wants* consistent with what *is possible* in the external environment and with what the company *is able* to do in terms of its internal resources? Management may not want to acquiesce in the union demands, but its limited resources and its weak competitive position may make it essential to avoid a strike. The division manager in a diversified company may not wish to incur marketing or research and development expenses which reduce his immediate profitability, but his division's position may make such expenditures imperative. Where, under these circumstances, a strategist follows his wishes, he may be courting disaster.

Social responsiveness

The strategist is influenced in his choice not only by his own individual goals and ambitions but also by his attitude toward society and by what he sees as his own and his corporation's obligations.[3] Strategic choice is not solely an economic equation. It is also influenced by noneconomic considerations, which are often encapsulated in an overworked phrase "corporate responsibility." Society has an impact on the strategic process in two ways. First, as described in Chapter 4, the political and social dimension is an important element of the environmental framework. It influences the strategic equation as an external force in much the same way as technology or competition. Second, perceived obligations to society cause managers to make strategic choices which obligate the corporation to social goals of a noneconomic nature, which, in some

---

[3] For a comprehensive discussion of a company's social responsibilities, see Kenneth R. Andrews, *The Concept of Corporate Strategy* (Homewood, Ill.: Dow Jones–Irwin, Inc., 1971), chap. 5, and Robert W. Ackerman, *The Social Challenge to Business* (Cambridge, Mass.: Harvard University Press, 1975).

instances, may reduce economic performance. It is the latter which has a direct bearing on the strategist's personal choice and thereby on the strategic posture of his corporation. In responding to these societal obligations, how are they to be incorporated into his strategic choice?

First, the corporate posture on these issues involves tradeoffs between performance as it has been traditionally measured and social benefits. Moreover, the penalties in terms of increased costs or lower revenues are generally more easily determined than the benefits, which are often intangible, long-term, or indirectly obtained. Second, the difficulty of the calculation does not absolve the strategist from the need to apply the same degree of rigor that he applies elsewhere to defining strategy in this area. To neglect analysis of both environmental and resource dimensions because such analysis is difficult or because the results may conflict with a philosophical conviction is to risk frivolity and ineffectiveness. Third, the strategy, if it is to be effective, requires a level of commitment to subsequent achievement at least as great as that for competitive responses. Before making statements about the intended performance of his company in equal employment, for instance, the chief executive should be sure of his willingness and ability to secure compliance from his organization. He must be ready to incur the costs and exert the leadership necessary to attain results or he may be justly criticized for merely reflecting a professional corporate piety.

FROM STRATEGIST TO ORGANIZATION BUILDER

The strategic process described up to this point is largely intellectual in character. It is a process which the strategist can accomplish by himself, possibly using some staff or professional inputs. The many judgments and the ultimate strategic choice must be made by him and often by him alone. The job of the general manager does not end here, however. The strategy has to be implemented, requiring support and commitment from other people in the organization. The task of implementation involves not only ideas and facts but people as well. Therefore, it is not just intellectual but also administrative in character. The general manager must not only be a strategist but also an organization builder. Part II of this text focuses on that aspect of the general manager's job.

Part II

The general manager as organization builder

10

Organizational diagnosis

INTERRELATIONSHIP BETWEEN STRATEGY AND ORGANIZATION

In MANY instances, business policy or general management courses, having covered the concept of corporate strategy and its application, will come to an end. Yet, from the general manager's point of view, it is like a baseball manager who posts his lineup and then calls the game. A general manager is not solely a paper strategist. It is his task to convert the intellectually formulated strategy through his organization into an operationally effective one.

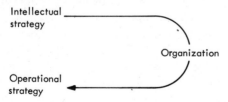

This task is compounded in the growing enterprise by the dynamics of change. First of all, growth entails a larger size, resulting in more people, more facilities, and, for everybody, more work. Is it possible to manage increasing size without losing the organizational and human strengths that made this growth possible? Second, growth often involves

71

a broader geographic dispersion, whether nationally or internationally, placing additional and sometimes different demands on the organization and its people. Third, growth may be based on diversification into different products, posing new challenges as dissimilar activities must be managed simultaneously. In sum, in a growing enterprise the general manager's job of converting an intellectual into an operational strategy is compounded by the fact that both tasks and people change significantly. The organizational challenge is similar to building a house on constantly shifting grounds.

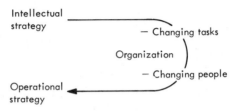

The general manager cannot evade this challenge. Continued growth requires a strong but frequently changing organization. Thus, if growth is to be more than ephemeral, the general manager must be not solely a successful strategist but a capable organization builder as well. Organizational change in support of a successful strategy will be a regular facet of the general manager's job in a dynamic enterprise.

Corporate organization and its people are not only the means through which strategy is implemented; they are also the major constraint. In fact, a significant hurdle to the successful execution of a strategy is the inability of the organization to carry it out. In these circumstances, it is convenient to, place the blame on the organization. Yet how many strategic plans specifically take into account the fact that organizationally they entail changing tasks and people? The general manager as architect has to relate his plans to the organizational and human dimension.

Organization is not only a constraint in shaping strategy; it also greatly influences the strategic process. Suggestions, demands, and ambitions of organizational units or their members shape the strategic direction of the company. These influences may not always surface boldly or be recognized explicitly, but they prevail nevertheless. In several of the cases which follow, it is possible to recognize the organizational inputs which influence strategy.

The general manager, in summary, faces the task of (1) building and constantly adapting his organization to the demands of his strategy, (2) ensuring that his strategy takes into account organizational constraints, and (3) recognizing the organizational inputs which influence the strategic process.

This chapter deals with organizational diagnosis. It focuses (1) on the concept of organization by asking "what" the general manager manages and (2) on the test of organizational adequacy to determine whether the organization is sound. Both these questions are easier to pose than to answer. In fact, organizational diagnosis is one of the most difficult tasks confronting the general manager. The next chapter is devoted to organizational action. It describes (1) the tools of the general manager, that is, "how" he manages; (2) stages of corporate development identifying varying characteristics of different forms of organization; (3) the need to manage reality, which may involve compromises in terms of both decisiveness and clarity; (4) the need to manage time by giving specific attention to the timing and speed of organizational action; and (5) the risks confronting the general manager as he copes with his organizational challenges. Chapters 12 and 13 describe the management of organizational transition by highlighting two major and frequently occurring organizational shifts which are caused by growth: the process of institutionalization, when a company shifts from entrepreneurial to professional management, and the process of divisionalization, when a company moves away from a functional setup to one organized around business units. The shift to a divisional organization structure creates multiple levels of general management. Chapter 14 describes the divisional and Chapter 15 the corporate general management job. Chapter 16 concludes this text by focusing on the most important transition of a manager's career: the shift from specialist to generalist.

CONCEPT OF ORGANIZATION

Organizational diagnosis requires definition. The general manager asks, "What am I managing?" and the student asks, "What am I analyzing?" This section proposes a way to view an organization. For this analysis the organization is seen as consisting of (1) a set of functional or divisional strategies, (2) a set of personal strategies, (3) a set of personal abilities, and (4) a set of relationships.

Organizational diagnosis begins with an identification of the various key activities which the general manager has to manage. In a specialized industrial company these will be functions such as manufacturing, marketing, engineering, research and development, finance, and control. A diversified industrial company, as will be discussed later, usually is divided into business units, each encompassing functional departments. Service companies will be organized around the activities peculiar to their businesses.

These activities should be viewed not as static stereotypes (that is, production, marketing) but in strategic terms (that is, the company's production strategy or its marketing strategy). Usually, each function, by virtue of its assigned responsibilities in the organization, has its own goals, ambitions, and plans. These various functional strategies should be identified. In the divisionalized company, identification focuses on the strategies of the various business units. For example, in the functionally organized Dansk Designs, marketing and design pursue different strategies, as do the project management and superintendent functions in Vappi.

The next step in organizational diagnosis is to identify the people. This task should not be confined to listing their names, titles, and job histories. Just as each function has its own goals, ambitions, and plans, so does each individual. Thus, an organization not only represents a group of people, it consists of a set of personal strategies. In Dansk Designs it is possible to attempt to identify the personal strategies of several of the key executives. In United Latex the five line and staff executives interviewed pursue quite different personal strategies.

Corporate, functional, and personal strategies, in the final analysis, are confined by the abilities of the people who carry them out. Hence, in identifying the people in the organization, it is necessary to look not only at their strategies but also at their abilities. Abilities, like corporate resources, must be viewed as relative to the demands placed upon them by the nature of the tasks to be performed. In National Franchise Management, Mr. Fisher has to assess the abilities of the manager of the Flowers-By-Phone organization. The managing director of United Latex has to take into account the abilities of his managers in dealing with the issue of corporate-division relationships.

People as well as functions interrelate. As a result, each organization consists of a network of relationships. Beyond the formal links suggested by the organization chart or the flow of goods and services, there is inevitably an array of informal ties based on friendships, alliances, and background. Animosities or rivalries may also exist. In identifying the interconnections between the functions and between the people, it is important to do so again in strategic terms.

In a small packaged and branded foods company the marketing and manufacturing vice presidents were continuously locking horns. Yet, with a commonly accepted corporate strategy aimed at rapid and maximum market penetration, resulting in the allocation of every discretionary dollar to marketing, it was a foregone conclusion that marketing always won and manufacturing always lost. This pattern had been institutionalized and was accepted by both vice presidents. The marketing man saw his primary goal as sales growth, while the manufacturing man made a virtue of necessity, taking great pride in his ability to keep the plant running with an absolutely minimum budget. As a result, the interfunctional conflicts were largely mirror fights, conducted in a sense of good fun and fellowship. This pattern of relationships produced a cohesive organization and permitted rapid growth, albeit without significant profits since all discretionary money was channeled into marketing expenditures. The president then decided to focus more on profits; to implement this goal, he hired—at a salary significantly above that of the other two vice presidents—an administrative vice president. Conflicts immediately followed. The strategy of the marketing department which aimed at growth clashed with the strategy of the administrative department which focused on profits and hence on reduced marketing expenses. (Manufacturing expenses were already at minimal levels.) This clash between the strategies of the two departments was aggravated by a simultaneous conflict between the personal strategies of the marketing and administrative vice presidents. The former had always been the company's crown prince, but his position was now challenged by the new vice president who had a strong personal need for power and a desire to be next in line to the president. While the two old-timers questioned the new control system, the president had a blind faith in the ability and expertise of his new vice president. Relationships became marked by rivalry and hostility, and the company's performance declined. Instead of the hoped-for profits, losses occurred.

The functional and personal strategies and the resulting relationships create a multidimensional framework which the general manager must manage. These multiple dimensions must be identified since one cannot manage what one does not know. Furthermore, these strategies and relationships may involve conflicts, as the above description clearly demonstrates. Conflicts also are found in several of the subsequent cases, such as Vappi, Dansk Designs, or United Latex. In the latter some division managers want to run their operations independently, while others are eagerly looking for help. The corporate staff managers, in turn, see their roles in divisional affairs differently. These conflicting divisional and personal strategies greatly influence the relationships in United Latex between the corporate staff and the operating units.

The framework of functional and personal strategies, abilities, and relationships is a dynamic one. People change, as do their attitudes, ambitions, and abilities. Functional opportunities and risks change. So do relationships. Organization is thus a dynamic concept. As a result, the general manager must constantly update the identification of his multidimensional organizational framework. Also, as organizational modifications are contemplated, their impact on this framework can be assessed. Thus, organizational diagnosis provides the general manager not only with the parameters within which he has to work but also with a framework to predict the implications of organizational change. The Vlasic Foods and Dansk Designs cases portray such dynamic situations, involving changes in several elements of the framework.

TEST OF ORGANIZATIONAL ADEQUACY

Diagnostically, the general manager must not only identify his organizational framework but he must also evaluate its adequacy. The test of organizational adequacy determines whether a company's organization as defined in the previous section is able (1) to support its corporate strategy, (2) to meet the environmental threats, and (3) to discharge its key operational requirements. The test of organizational adequacy, therefore, relates the *internal* dimensions of functional or divisional strategies, personal strategies, personal abilities and relationships to *external* dimensions resulting from a company's strategy, the environmental threats confronting it, and its key operating requirements.

The first question to be tested is whether the organization is able to support the corporate strategy. Given the many possible strategic postures, it is impossible to generalize by developing an all-encompassing prescription. Some examples must suffice. Vlasic Foods is engaged in a strategy of continued and rapid growth through geographic expansion. Will its organization be able to support this growth strategy? Dansk Designs is contemplating entry into a different product line. Will its organization be able to satisfy the new and possibly more demanding requirements of this line?

The second question focuses on the environmental threats, such as a business recession, which a company must face regardless of its strategic posture. The Vappi company must cope with increased external pressures. Is its organization, hitherto geared to rapid expansion, able to meet these new challenges?

The third question tests the organizational adequacy in terms of the industry's key operational requirements. Given the operating characteristics of the construction industry, how is Vappi's organization to be evaluated? How well is the Vlasic Foods organization able to cope with the critical coordination of farm and field, manufacturing and marketing, or the Dansk Designs organization with the balancing of the differing requirements of design, sourcing, and marketing?

In applying the test of consistency the general manager frequently meets three difficulties. First, as he attempts to relate organization to strategy, he may find the strategy unclear, emerging, or changing. How does the general manager test the adequacy of his organization? Can National Franchise Management decide on an organizational response with respect to Flowers-By-Phone until it has formulated a strategy for this new acquisition? Yet, it may have to make organizational decisions before the strategic choices can be sorted out.

A second difficulty results from the fact that symptoms of organizational malfunction are not always explicit. It is a common human tendency to cover up unpleasant things, and organizational situations are no exception. A malfunctioning machine will squeak or leak oil and alert the engineer; organizations do not so readily exhibit their malfunctions to the general manager. Hence, he has to be part detective to assess his organizational situation. Alternatively, members of the organization may exaggerate the symptoms. Are the complaints in Vappi serious or simply a manifestation of normal human discontent?

A third hurdle in applying the test of organizational adequacy is that symptoms often have multiple causes. If profits are down or new business is lost, is it because of uncontrollable external forces, because of an inadequate strategy, or because of a weak organization? Is a business recession to blame? Is the strategy at fault? Or is the organization the cause for unsatisfactory performance? This dilemma is faced by Vappi. If there are multiple possible causes, where does the blame lie? Given an uncertain diagnosis of the causes, how can the general manager evaluate the adequacy of his organization?

The test of organizational adequacy must be applied dynamically. How will the organization look some years hence? Will the functional and personal strategies change? Which people will contribute to the organization and what will be their abilities? What will happen to their relationships? Will a struggle be waged for the succession of the retiring chief executive? Will key people retire? Will it be possible to find enough new people with the same skills and commitment as the old-timers? How does one evaluate Dansk Designs without its chief designer? Will Vlasic Foods be able to find enough skilled people to support its rapid growth? What is the impact on Vappi of the departure of several project managers? Once the future scope and strength of the organization have been predicted, they have to be appraised as to how they will satisfy the requirements of the future. The general manager must constantly pose the question whether his strategy, emerging environmental threats, or changing operational requirements will outgrow his organization. Today's organization has to be related to tomorrow's strategy, risks, and tasks. As a result, future conditions have to be predicted. The test of organizational adequacy must be built on the strategic forecast. Thus, this chapter which began by stressing the interrelationships between strategy and organization ends on the same note, leading to a conclusion and a question. The conclusion is that the test of organizational adequacy, being dependent on the strategic forecast, is by necessity judgmental. The question is whether general managers give the same time to organizational prognosis that they give to environmental prognosis.

11

Organizational action

TOOLS OF THE GENERAL MANAGER

ORGANIZATIONAL diagnosis concerns itself with *what* the general manager manages; organizational action focuses on *how* he manages. Typically, the general manager uses three tools: (1) he acts as architect through the use of organizational structure; (2) he manages the various systems which have been designed, such as the budgeting or compensation system; and (3) he manages through his direct dealings with people. The general manager uses these three tools simultaneously. Thus, even though they will be described sequentially, they are in actual life closely and continuously interrelated. The choices which he makes in terms of these three tools greatly influence the organizational climate. They determine in large part the "way of life" of a particular company.

The design of the organizational structure is the general manager's most visible tool. The basic choice between a functional and a divisional organization will be discussed later. The latter is frequently a response to diversification, dictating a structure which (1) places the divisional manager in the best position to direct the business, (2) permits his success to be measured by observing the profits he produces, and (3) prevents the corporation, bent on further diversification, from burdening the divisional manager with the problems of new businesses. In addition, the divisional structure is often chosen as a deliberate tool to change management behavior. The United Latex case is one such example. Another example is a 120-year-old company producing a broad and varied line of paper products. After years of stagnation, this company had changed from a "paternalistic, sleepy firm" to a "growth" company. Yet, its strategy had remained relatively constant. Management felt that its "new look" had resulted from changes in the organizational structure and in the bonus system. Its chairman of the board commented: "I am convinced that the biggest single factor in our recent success was the assignment of profit responsibility for the product line to a well-trained group of managers in a single operating unit. The second biggest factor was that we began paying management based on results."

Within the basic alternatives of a functional or divisional organization are a number of subordinate choices. The choices for the divisionalized company will be discussed in more detail in Chapter 13. In the functional firm, the general manager faces such questions as whether to assign the credit function to the financial staff or to the marketing manager, or the technical customer service activities to manufacturing or to sales. In a greeting card company, the president was wondering whether sales, merchandising, and product design, each under a separate vice president, should be combined into a single marketing department or whether sales and merchandising at least should be placed under a single vice president.

The design of the organization structure involves both task definition and allocation. In assigning responsibility to subordinates, the general manager must ensure that his structural design (1) relates effectively to the elements determining organizational adequacy, that is, corporate strategy, environmental threats, and key operating requirements; (2) relates the various tasks effectively to each other, permitting a cohesive and coordinated functioning of specialized activities; and (3) permits meaningful motivation and commitment, both of a monetary and nonmonetary nature.

The general manager should not apply structural design mechanistically. It encompasses more than mere job descriptions and organization charts. In the consumer goods company example cited in the previous chapter, the president had used structural change, that is, the hiring of a new administrative vice president, to implement his goal of changing the corporate strategy from maximizing sales to enhancing profitability. Yet this change alone was not enough. The new strategy and structure had to be managed within the dynamic organizational context of functional and personal strategies, abilities, and relationships. A fancy title will not overcome a lack of ability, nor will a large corner office guarantee effective relationships. Organizational design must take place in a dynamic and strategic setting. In the earlier example, it resulted in a clash of both functional and personal strategies and destroyed hitherto effective relationships. The general manager as architect designs his organization structure not only around tasks but also around people and their relationships. As a result, he must take into account the operational as well as the political requirements. He must not only determine the most effective way of getting the goods out the door but also how to deal with power, influence, and personalities.

These comments raise the perennial dilemma of whether the organizational structure should be built around people or around tasks without regard to the existing members of the organization. In reality, however, this dilemma is a nonissue. The general manager must calibrate both requirements and must take into account and manage both tasks and people. Organizational design does not involve a choice between one or the other but the degree of balance and emphasis between the two. Even those who cling to structural purity feel the impact of the people dimension, particularly when one of the key executives departs.

The general manager must be more than an architect who uses structural design as his only tool. He must also design and manage the many systems which focus on *planning, resource allocation, budgeting, control, information, coordination and arbitration, compensation,* as well as *executive selection and development.* These systems provide the general manager with tools through which he influences organizational behavior indirectly. Like structural design, they must (1) relate effectively to the elements determining organizational adequacy, (2) relate effectively to each other, and (3) permit meaningful motivation and commitment. In addition, the various systems must be congruent with the organizational structure, on one hand, and with the way in which the general manager utilizes them on the other. If a general manager evaluates his subordinates through a close and constant use of the control system and relates this system directly to the compensation system by basing the distribution of rewards (or sanctions), in the form of pay and promotions, on performance, then subordinates are likely to pay close attention to this control system. Where, in contrast, compensation and the control system are not interrelated, the latter is likely to be taken less seriously. Also, if performance measurement is determined by relating the control to the budgeting system, requiring managers to submit their own target estimates against which they are subsequently measured, and if the general manager does not permit his subordinates to reestimate their targets when results fall short, both systems will be taken very seriously. As a result, subordinates will submit their estimates carefully, possibly even conservatively, and where results are below target they will resort to early and vigorous action.

The Cases for Part II of this book permit analysis of several systems and their use by the general manager. Compensation systems are described in Vlasic Foods, where the chief executive places a heavy reliance on a performance bonus versus a fixed salary, and in Vappi, where one group of managers is compensated on the basis of total company performance while another group, which has to coordinate closely with the former, receives a bonus based on the execution of a specific job. Both these companies have an intriguing system of achieving coordination through reliance on the team concept. In Dansk Designs a coordination system between the European and U.S. offices is being developed.

A third tool of the general manager is direct intervention. The leadership styles of the chief executives of Dansk Designs and Vlasic Foods, respectively, provide an interesting contrast between the relative influence of direct action and reliance on systems. The former manages largely through personal contact, providing critical inputs for new products as well as day-to-day coordination for existing ones. The latter, on the other hand, uses more formal planning, budgeting, control, and compensation systems in guiding his organization and stays away from daily operating activities. However, certain activities, such as the selection of key executives, require the personal input of the general manager. The chief executive of Dansk Designs wishes to retire but must first select his successor, while the Vlasic Foods chief executive must hire a new manufacturing vice president.

A critical question for the general manager is not just the extent to which he wishes to manage through direct intervention but also the consistency of his behavior. If he has chosen to rely largely on systems but on occasion chooses to intervene directly, he may well arrive at quick and decisive solutions for the specific problem at hand, but he may also be undercutting his subordinates, thereby making the resolution of future problems more difficult.

STAGES OF CORPORATE DEVELOPMENT

The relative emphasis placed on the three tools varies depending on the stage of a company's development, which, in turn, is influenced by its strategic posture. In smaller organizations the importance of direct contact is usually greatest, whereas in larger companies the general manager relies more on structure and systems. Thus, the general management task is significantly different in each type of organization. These differences have led to the formulation of a model of stages of corporate development. Pioneered by Scott, inspired by Chandler's historical work,[1] and supported by Christensen, Salter, and others, it has resulted in a fruitful research effort.

The first stage of corporate development is a "small company with one or a few functions performed largely by one manager."[2] Its strategic

---

[1] Alfred D. Chandler, *Strategy and Structure* (Cambridge, Mass.: The M.I.T. Press, 1962).

[2] This and the following quotations are taken from Bruce R. Scott, "Stages of Corporate Development." (Copyright © 1971 by the President and Fellows of Harvard College.)

posture involves a single product sold through a uniform set of distribution channels. Through growth in volume, geographic expansion, or vertical integration a company moves to the second stage, which—even though the strategic single-product posture remains the same—involves a "multidepartmental enterprise, with specialized managerial departments based upon function." Diversification, leading to multiple product lines and multiple channels of distribution, leads to the third stage of the "multidivisional enterprise, with divisions based largely on product-market relationships." Scott singles out a number of characteristics for each stage in terms of research and development, performance measurement, rewards, control system, and strategic choices.

Research and development is essentially the province of the owner manager in stage 1; it becomes institutionalized in the second stage as a systematic search for product and process improvements; in stage 3 the search broadens to one for totally new and different products. Performance measurement in the stage 1 organization is by "personal contact and subjective criteria," becoming in stage 2 "increasingly impersonal using technical and/or cost criteria," and evolving in stage 3 into the impersonal use of such "market criteria" as return on investment. Rewards similarly move from being "unsystematic and often paternalistic" to "increasingly systematic with emphasis on stability and service" to "increasingly systematic with variability related to performance." Scott describes the control system of stage 1 as "personal control of both strategic and operating decisions," of stage 2 as "personal control of strategic decisions, with increasing delegation of operating decisions based on control by decision rules (policies)," and of stage 3 as "delegation of product-market decisions within existing businesses, with indirect control based on analysis of 'results.'" Strategic choices, finally, pit the needs of the owner against the needs of the firm in stage 1, while stage 2 involves choices in terms of degree of vertical integration, market share objectives, and breadth of product line. Stage 3 strategic choices concern "entry and exit from industries, allocation of resources by industry and rate of growth."

Scott concludes that this "cluster of characteristics suggests not just a form of organization but a 'way of managing' and to a considerable extent a 'way of life' within the enterprise. It is these clusters, their stability by stage, the problems of transition from one stage to another, the relative importance of each type of firm, and the historical trends by industry and by country which are of particular interest."

The cases on organization in this book are broken down into two sections, the first dealing with general management in the functional or stage 2 organization, and the second focusing on the divisional or stage 3 company. Several of the cases as well as Chapters 12 and 13 describe the management of transition from one stage to the next. Before discussing the process of transition, however, three aspects of organizational action must be emphasized: the need to manage within the realm of reality, the importance of timing, and the necessity to shoulder risks.

THE CHALLENGE OF ORGANIZATIONAL ACTION

Managing reality

Organizational action must be rooted in reality, sometimes requiring the general manager to abandon conventional organizational principles. Reality may force him to opt for conflict or confusion, even though theory may prescribe the pursuit of harmony or clarity. It is a common error to assume that all conflicts can be avoided through proper organizational design. Often, they are unavoidable elements of the organizational fabric. The challenge for the general manager is not to avoid them but to manage them properly. Lack of clarity is not necessarily undesirable, either. As organizational relationships emerge or as people prove themselves, it may be appropriate to let them earn their own way without making the assignment or authority explicit.

General managers may centralize activities and provide detailed operating guidance. Within such a setting, however, they may not always enforce the rules but rather permit selective violations of them. The general manager may consider these rules essential as guidance and support for his weaker or newer managers. The stronger and more experienced managers, on the other hand, may be unnecessarily confined by them and may be expected and even encouraged to take more independent action. While theoretically such an approach may appear inconsistent, it permits the general manager to set his rules on the basis of the lowest common denominator without constraining the scope of action of his stronger and more talented subordinates.

Another example of deliberate confusion is the so-called "psychological" decentralization. Here a subordinate is given more authority on paper than he exercises in reality. It happens where corporate staff managers are in a position to influence the scope of activities of operating line managers. Again, such a situation is not necessarily bad. First of all, staff executives may interfere only selectively. Second, the illusionary power may nevertheless be an important ceremonial attribute, providing some motivational benefits and establishing the authority of the operating manager among his own subordinates.

In terms of organizational action, conflicts and lack of clarity should not be summarily rejected and condemned without proper analysis. The key question is whether conflicts and confusion will lead to malfunction which may obstruct the strategy, expose the company to environmental threats, and prevent the proper execution of the key operational require-ments. In a number of situations, conflicts and confusion may not lead to malfunction but will better satisfy the requirements of organizational adequacy than harmony and clarity.

Organizational action deliberately involving conflicts or lack of clarity may encounter resistance or misunderstanding. Under such circum-stances members of the organization will typically blame the general manager for his inability to develop a structure without conflicts and for his indecisiveness in eliminating confusion. They will view harmony and clarity as desirable per se and will view their absence as evidence of the general manager's poor decision-making ability. Organizational action, like strategic choice, is often a lonely task, and the general man-ager may not always be able to achieve popularity and effectiveness simultaneously.

Managing time

Time is even more critical in contemplating organizational action than in formulating strategy. It is easier to change plans than to change people. It is easier to expand a product line or a manufacturing plant than to train people. It is easier to predict rapid growth than to achieve it through organizational action. A strategist must be aware of the digestive capacity of his organization: how much can be done how fast?

Managing time also involves anticipating future needs and taking preventive organizational action. The decision to take preventive action, however, is not an easy one, and the action itself is often resisted by members of the organization. Rather, given the risk, pain, and cost in-volved, organizational change is often contemplated and accepted only when the symptoms of malfunction are so severe that the need is obvious. If delayed, organizational change frequently takes place in an at-mosphere of crisis, adding a major handicap to an already difficult process. The alternative to taking preventive action, however, is not easy. Who wants to undergo preventive surgery when there is still hope that matters will not turn out so badly after all? Where there is hope, there is wishful thinking. As a result, it is much harder, when the existing organization is still reasonably successful, to convince its members that change is in order. Modifying behavior today in anticipation of future needs is a major challenge facing the general manager.

Managing risks

The general manager as organization builder manages risks. It is com-mon to associate risk taking exclusively with strategic responses to ex-ternal forces such as products, technology, or competition. Yet the general manager faces great internal risks as well. Organizational change is often more difficult and riskier than strategic change. It involves shifts in people and relationships as well as in tasks. People and their behavior are not as easily changed as the organization chart or the strategic plan.

In deciding on organizational action the general manager must base his prescription on his organizational diagnosis. This diagnosis, however, may be uncertain, making it both difficult and dangerous for the general manager to be decisive. Unfortunately, the general manager frequently finds himself in this situation. In discussing the cases in the second part of this book, some observers may give a particular company a clean bill of health, others may diagnose a minor disease requiring a modest dose of medicine, while still others may call for major and immediate surgery. Situations eliciting such vastly different and conflicting diagnoses are not uncommon when several experts are consulted. If one wishes peace of mind by arriving at a clear-cut diagnosis, the only safe solution is to call in just one expert. Once faced with diverging diagnoses, however, what does the general manager do? He can wait and see. Or he can be decisive. But what if he sends a healthy patient to surgery? The risk of decisive action can be substantial. On the other hand, the wait-and-see attitude can be equally risky if the severely ill patient is sent home without treatment. Thus, where organizational diagnosis is uncertain, as it often is, organizational action is risky, and the organization builder inevitably has to manage risks.

Another risk results from the inevitable consequence of changing tasks and people: the breakup of old and hitherto successful patterns. In the process of instituting change, the general manager may be forced to destroy his home base. Once he has destroyed his base, he has no place to which to return in case of failure. Thus, organizational change is generally a one-way street. If it fails, the general manager faces an entirely new and usually more difficult beginning, requiring him to rebuild his organization anew.

Organizational change often involves total risk, not just incremental risk. Incremental risks in case of failure affect only the incremental decision. If a person buys a high-risk stock whose value subsequently declines to zero, the loss remains confined to the amount of the stock purchase and does not affect the person's entire net worth. Total risks, on the other hand, have ramifications far beyond the incremental decision. Failure, in such event, endangers the total situation. For example, some observers may argue that failure of Vlasic Foods to grow successfully by another $20 million or of Dansk Designs to launch the Gourmet line may jeopardize the existence of the entire company. Since the success of these strategic steps hinges to a large extent on the organizational underpinnings, the failure of the organizational changes contemplated in those companies might result in the downfall of the entire firm.

12

Process of institutionalization

SYMPTOMS OF MALFUNCTION

IT IS SUCCESS itself which necessitates the transition from entrepreneurship to professional management. Growth strains the existing organizational setup. The only way to relieve these strains is not to grow. If an entrepreneurship wants to retain its existing organization, the sole remedy is to avoid growth by not being successful.

Those entrepreneurships which succeed and which accept the consequences of growth will sooner or later outgrow their organizational setup. Usually this change occurs sooner because in an entrepreneurship all key activities and decisions are typically handled by a few key people, often primarily the president. The process is characterized by several symptoms:

—An overworked chief executive is involved in too many decisions and he has too many people reporting to him.
—The textbook remedy, delegation, is not working.
—The combination of the overworked executive and the failure of delegation inevitably slows down the decision-making process.

There are several reasons why delegation is not effective. First, the chief executive bemoans the fact that his people are not capable of handling the additional responsibilities. His subordinates may have been hired during the earlier stages of the company's existence as operational

86

aides and not as managers. Thus, the size of the company may have outgrown their capabilities.

Second, in an entrepreneurship delegation is simply not a way of life. Normally, decisions are made in the process of daily and constant contact during which everyone checks with the boss. Letting someone run his own show independently is a rare exception. In this atmosphere, even when the chief executive assigns some of his tasks to others, it turns out to be in reality only pseudodelegation. The old habits continue to prevail in spite of written edicts to the contrary. Parenthetically, it is often the chief executive himself who is the prime offender.

Third, there is a simple pragmatic reason why delegation is difficult. In an entrepreneurship, the managers are usually jacks of all trades. Assignments are scattered and haphazard, largely influenced by the most urgent needs prevailing at each particular moment. In such a setting, it is difficult to assign specifically and consistently both authority and responsibility. In fact, most of the delegation may be of one-shot activities rather than defining and assigning a set of recurring tasks.

Fourth, in an entrepreneurship the chief executive may use "eyeballing" rather than formalized control in measuring performance. Where there is no scorecard, it is not unusual to receive no credit for the wins but nevertheless to get blamed for the losses. If assuming responsibility does not generate benefits on the upside but does involve penalties on the downside, one is more than likely to play it safe. When the boss bemoans the fact that his subordinates are unwilling to shoulder responsibility, he should first ask himself whether scorecards are being kept and whether on this basis he distributes the rewards as well as the penalties.

In the absence of delegation, decisions have to wait for the boss. Yet, as the company's size increases, the boss becomes less well informed. As a result, he must obtain more and more information from others. However, this information reaches him haphazardly and not in a standard or systematic fashion. Thus, more and more people are needed for the boss to make his decisions, and soon he will resort to committee management. This, in turn, will aggravate the phenomenon of being overworked as people sit around the table rather than doing their jobs. Also, it gets harder and harder to find times when everybody is available; hence, meetings are delayed, causing further decision slowdowns.

As the waiting time for decisions lengthens, people in the organization inevitably resort to self-help. Everybody begins to improvise in his own fashion. Rarely does this produce harmonious action. Rather, it frequently involves duplication, as people who do not get together do identical things. As everyone tries to do his best on his own, organizational cohesion suffers.

The above symptoms inevitably translate into a decline in performance and a rise in costs. The overworked chief executive then resorts to a typical cure of hiring an assistant or deputy to relieve him of some of his excessive workload. Unfortunately, this action often aggravates rather than remedies the symptoms. Instead of one overworked person there are now two. Both get involved in everything. Subordinates seek guidance from two bosses, and the bosses, in turn, have to coordinate among themselves. Thus, the available time for productive activity declines even further. The malfunction goes from bad to worse.

THE GENERAL MANAGER'S RESPONSE

The organizational engine finally reaches the point where a few drops of oil are not enough to restore it to a smooth-running condition. Instead of the oilcan it needs a major overhaul. In medical terms, what is needed is surgery, not just medicine. Organizational surgery, however, like medical surgery, involves three elements: it is painful, it is risky, and it is costly.

Given the pain, risk, and cost, the general manager often delays organizational surgery. Moreover, the chief executive in this instance shares the privilege of being both the surgeon and the patient. As a patient, he has reason to ask for his own record as a surgeon, only to find that he has none. The successful entrepreneur is a proven obstetrician, but not necessarily a skillful surgeon.

In summary, the management of transition frequently takes place late; it is a painful, risky, and costly activity; and it is managed by someone with no prior experience. Fortunately, many manuals and textbooks stand ready to guide the general manager in this major challenge. The common operation prescribed for the above symptoms is specialization. Sometimes, expansion may take a company into vastly different product lines, in which event the transition may be directly to a divisional form of organization described in the next chapter.

DESIGNING THE FUNCTIONAL ORGANIZATION

Specialization leading to a functional organization involves several elements:

1. It attempts to combine related effort and to segregate unrelated effort. Thus, instead of having everybody do a little of everything, like activities are grouped together. People are able to do what they are best at, hence efficiency is expected to increase.

2. Organizational tasks are defined and formalized, usually by function (such as manufacturing, marketing, engineering). Through this explicit codification, the general manager makes sure that all activities are properly covered.

3. Authority required to discharge each task is delegated to the incumbent in each job. Thus, the general manager explicitly surrenders some of his decision-making power.

4. With delegation goes control. A system of performance measurement is designed to evaluate the delegated activities. An explicit scorecard permits the general manager to determine how well the various tasks are being discharged. Likewise, these reports assist the managers in the conduct of their activities.

5. Reporting relationships are established. Delegation is not always complete; and in certain instances, approval or guidance may be required. Generally, an attempt is made to minimize the number of reporting relationships for superiors and to have a subordinate report only to one boss.

6. Coordination also has to be provided for, particularly horizontally among functions. In a number of instances, the specialized functions have to interrelate in terms of daily decision making or advance planning.

7. Communication and information are essential for both the vertical reporting relationships and the horizontal coordination.

8. Centralization, while the exception, may be necessary for certain activities. In some instances, specialization may be economically undesirable, or it may be necessary to use scarce management talent in a variety of activities.

9. People have to be assigned to the various tasks in accordance with both their desires and abilities.

10. As new people take on new assignments, their selection, training, and development have to be provided for. Often, this cannot be confined to the technical aspects of the job. As a plant superintendent moves to manufacturing vice president, the sales manager to marketing vice president, and the bookkeeper to controller, they shift more from operational to managerial activities. Thus, management development becomes increasingly important as the company grows and the organization becomes more complicated.

IMPLICATIONS OF THE FUNCTIONAL ORGANIZATION

A different general management job

The shift from the entrepreneurial "one-man show" to the specialized functional structure changes both the way of life of the organization and the job of the general manager. Under the previous structure, he was involved in day-to-day management, making specific decisions on current matters, resolving issues through direct intervention while dealing with individuals. This style of management typically is applied to both small and major decisions. Under the new structure, this style has to change.

Instead of dealing directly with specific issues on an "ad hoc" basis, the general manager will have to formulate broad policies encompassing sets of similar issues. Instead of poking his nose into everything, he has to categorize problems and develop guidelines for similar situations. Thus, compensation policies replace specific salary or bonus decisions for each individual. Such policies are necessary to maintain fairness in an increasingly larger organization and to permit meaningful delegation. The general manager's job shifts from direct intervention to delegation within a framework of policies and guidelines.

Instead of dealing with individuals, the chief executive now also manages functions. Again, the style of management shifts from direct action to indirect influence. By managing through guidelines and functional department heads, the chief executive's time horizon changes from a day-to-day orientation more towards the future. He must not only preside over the resolution of today's problems but also anticipate tomorrow's.

The general manager's job, as he withdraws from daily operations, becomes one of leadership through coordination and conflict resolution. Having functional managers reporting to him, he must manage specialists. His task is to mold these specialized functions into a cohesive corporate unit. The cases portraying functional organizations show that general managers use a number of different approaches in meeting this challenge.

Need for adaptation

As a growing enterprise embarks upon the transition from entrepreneurial to functional management, two questions have to be answered affirmatively: first, is the organization able to change; and second, is the general manager able to change? The second question is often ignored. Corporate histories are full of examples of successful entrepreneurs who turned out to be unsuccessful organization builders. Chandler in his historical studies[1] of Du Pont and General Motors describes how both companies were created as large enterprises by entrepreneurs and empire builders, Coleman du Pont and William Durant, but that they were strengthened if not built organizationally by Pierre du Pont and Alfred Sloan. Thus a chief executive contemplating such a transition may wish to pause and reflect whether he has the qualifications to manage it by changing his leadership style. Alternatively, the

---

[1] Alfred D. Chandler, *Strategy and Structure* (Cambridge, Mass.: The M.I.T. Press, 1962).

entrepreneur may decide to withdraw, leaving the management of transition to a successor, who, even though he may not possess the same entrepreneurial drive, may be better equipped in terms of organizational talents.

The ability of the general manager to adapt is crucial. Yet, equally critical is the ability of the organization to move to a different way of life. Even if successfully implemented, however, a more formal and systematic organization may stifle the entrepreneurial spirit on which previous growth was based. This tradeoff must be recognized and managed.

The ability of an entrepreneurially based company to evolve toward a more formal functional organization should not be taken for granted. Organizational transition involves changes in tasks, in people, and in their interrelationships. Such change in established patterns of behavior is upsetting and frequently resisted. Its implementation requires patience, guidance, and a great deal of teaching. An organization builder is in large part an educator.

Risks of transition

Education is difficult. First of all, the organization builder must assess the digestive capacity of his people. Are they able to change to the new patterns of behavior required by increased formalization and are they able to discharge independently the tasks delegated to them? Just as a parent has to assess his child's driving ability before giving him the car keys, so must the general manager evaluate the ability of his organization. How much training and coaching are required to accomplish effective delegation?

Education is even more difficult where it is resisted. Such may be the case for organizational transition. It may take place against a background of success. Thus, the architect of organizational change in a growing company does not come to correct failure but to ensure continued success. Yet people resisting such a change may not see it this way. To them the argument of ensuring the future health of the organization is dwarfed by the argument that the existing setup has brought the company its proven success. Organizational surgery in this setting is like breaking up a winning team. To destroy the basis of previous success in order to ensure continued success in the future is often perceived as risky and perhaps unwarranted.

Thus, while the need and benefits of organizational transition are obvious to the general manager, they may be perceived differently by his people. The "new" life may seem less desirable than the "old" way of doing things. As Scott points out: "a company tends to lose some of its 'family like' nature as it grows, not just through the introduction of formal task specialization, but through the increased social 'distance' which separates people in a hierarchy."[2] Furthermore, newcomers have to be brought into the company. They may be seen as threats by the old-timers, who may resist their entry. Sometimes, newcomers bring expertise gathered through education, as in the case of Dansk Designs, or they contribute experience acquired through many years of work, as in the case of Vlasic Foods. Transition may require the hiring of new people with different skills and expertise. In these situations, the general manager must not confuse the organizational need for such people with the organizational acceptance of them by the old-timers in his company.

In managing organizational transition, the general manager must not only cope with the above difficulties and risks. Simultaneously, he has to continue his company's rapid growth pattern. To return to the surgery analogy, the patient has to return to work immediately after the operation and is given no time for rest and recuperation. While tasks, people, and relationships change, existing problems have to be solved, products have to be shipped, and capacity has to be expanded. The general manager cannot stop the world while he changes his organization.

---

[2] Bruce R. Scott, "Stages of Corporate Development," p. 29. (Copyright © 1971 by the President and Fellows of Harvard College.)

13

Process of divisionalization

SYMPTOMS OF MALFUNCTION

WHILE GROWTH forces an entrepreneurially organized company onto the path of institutionalization, growth through geographic expansion and product diversification necessitates the process of divisionalization. Both forms of expansion are a frequent phenomenon. Not only have companies achieved national coverage for their products or services, but many of them have expanded internationally as well. As they seek to adapt to special local conditions and to the many pitfalls of currency, trade, and tax regulations, the organization, hitherto geared exclusively to domestic operations, begins to show the strains. Likewise, diversification into different products has been a popular strategic response. Here, too, the organization with its activities originally aimed at a single product may find it difficult to cope simultaneously with a variety of dissimilar products. Demands imposed by internationalization and diversification are not limited to the giant companies. The process of divisionalization affects smaller companies as well.

As in the case of institutionalization, the need for organizational transition resulting from internationalization and diversification manifests itself through certain symptoms of malfunction:

1. Interfunctional coordination and conflict resolution by necessity must be handled by top management, because beneath this level all managers are specialized by function. As top management gets further

and further removed from increasingly varying activities, its intimate operational knowledge declines to the point where it can no longer discharge this task effectively. The result under these circumstances is described as follows by the president of a large, functionally organized company engaged in several different product lines:

> It soon became apparent that for almost every decision, even the smallest, three to four people were needed, depending on how many functions were involved. Each man would enter the meeting having been briefed by his subordinates. However, in many cases, this information would not be the same. Yet, the top functional men usually were not sufficiently familiar with the details of the issue to resolve these discrepancies during the meeting. Hence it was often necessary to delay the decision and request further information and assistance from the lower echelons.

The breakdown of multifunctional coordination leads to organizational malfunction. In one company lack of direction by top management resulted in marketing, production, and engineering personnel not working together effectively, causing poor exploitation of opportunities for developing new products based on existing skills and markets. Also, managers in this company cited continual squabbles concerning improvements in manufacturing methods between process engineers and line production supervisors. Often, decisions by top management on these conflicts were postponed and the issues were never resolved. Under these circumstances, personal influence of certain managers rather than leadership from the top guided decisions on manufacturing improvements, production control, scheduling priorities, and research time allocations.

2. Even where decisions are reached by top management, it becomes increasingly difficult to have them understood and accepted by the company's lower echelons. A president contemplating divisionalization commented on this difficulty:

> The three or four people involved in a particular decision, agreement, or conflict could not bring their subordinates to the meeting, since this would have made the executive committee too cumbersome a body. Yet decisions made this way, in an exclusive circle, were not always understood by the people below, with a resulting decline in their commitment. We also felt this lack of participation by middle management to be a waste of our human resources.

3. Where functional managers at headquarters are far removed from operations but have to ensure coordination and conflict resolution—for example, in terms of resource allocation or transfer pricing—they are less likely to approach these matters pragmatically. Instead, these issues often become a matter of principle and prestige, leading to political maneuvering and power plays in which saving face becomes more important than reaching quick and reasonable decisions in the best interest

of the company. Thus, a dispute involving a few pennies in the internal transfer price of a product may delay production schedules or result in poor pricing decisions. Even though in theory the transfer price should have no impact on the total profits of the corporation, unresolved disputes may lead to behavior clearly detrimental to the corporation.

4. Compromise, rather than vigorous leadership, becomes a way of life in the company. In one large international company the president explained: "the members of the board are all specialists in their own sectors. It was only natural that in the final analysis each of them would defend his own sector and his own point of view during discussions." In addition, according to an observer outside this company, "the board members were too involved in day-to-day operational problems to devote the necessary time to planning or establishing an overall corporate mission. The result was that the president was not able to truly manage the company. He could only compromise among the managers at meetings."

5. Where overall corporate leadership is not forthcoming, the units will go their own and separate ways, resulting in *de facto* independence. Under these circumstances, it becomes difficult to formulate and implement an overall business policy for the corporation. Overlapping activities or even competition between the functional units may result.

6. Secrecy is another common symptom. Managers are familiar only with their own specialized activities. In the political atmosphere of a corporate environment they may be unwilling to share their data with other functions in the organization. Consequently, sales executives may have to make marketing decisions without having the cost structure of a product or the facts on plant capacity utilization.

7. The span of control of the chief executive frequently becomes unmanageable. As the corporation diversifies, new operating units are added, often resulting in new subordinates reporting to him. As this occurs, it becomes harder and harder for him to exercise effective leadership, especially where these reporting relationships involve him in a mass of minute details.

8. Finally and importantly, within the context of the above malfunctions it becomes very difficult to focus on profitability. Lines of accountability and responsibility become less clear, and with all the confusion and detail it may be virtually impossible to establish and maintain standards for measurement, evaluation, and reward. As in the process of institutionalization, where the scoreboard is out of order, the incentive to strive for exceptional performance diminishes. Managers are unable to obtain clear feedback on their achievements. Even where profit information is available, it may not relate to critical decisions or controllable items. In a functionally organized company it is usually only possible to measure profitability for the total organization. For each of the func-

tions, the measurement is normally on the basis of costs or quotas. Given the fact that all functions influence the total cost structure and that they are closely interrelated, it is always possible to pass the buck, blaming deficiencies in performance on lack of cooperation from another functional counterpart. This problem is compounded when operations involve different products or take place all over the world.

THE GENERAL MANAGER'S RESPONSE

The general manager confronted with the above symptoms will be tempted to prefer prescribing medicine over performing surgery. Yet attempts to improve operating efficiency rarely resolve the fundamental structural problems resulting from internationalization and diversification. The impact of diverse product lines and of geography, especially as it extends across borders, requires a different organization structure. Such organizational surgery, however, has far-reaching implications in terms of tasks to be performed, relationships, and behavior of people. Such a break with established patterns involves risks similar to those described in the process of institutionalization. Surgery to reorganize the company along divisional lines is also painful, costly, and risky.

Nevertheless, divisionalization has become fashionable. Starting with Chandler,[1] the trend toward divisionalization has been documented in a number of studies. The vast majority of large U.S. companies have adopted a divisional structure during the last two decades, and a similar development is currently taking place in Europe. Interestingly, the first experimentation with such a structure took place in the early twenties at Du Pont. Chandler[2] renders a fascinating account of this transition which had its origins in Du Pont's World War I diversification into chemicals, paints and varnishes, celluloid, artificial leather, dyestuffs, and rayon. The organizational move, though, was triggered by losses in some of the new businesses, such as paints. The diagnosis of the organizational roots of these profit problems was facilitated by the fact that while Du Pont incurred losses, other smaller companies were making money in paints. A committee of junior executives analyzed the situation, concluding in March of 1920 that given the different sales requirements of the various businesses, the problem was not one of strategy but of organization. They proposed the realignment of management responsibilities around products rather than functions. Top management, however, rejected these recommendations, feeling—according to Chandler— that "the answer was not reorganization but better information and knowledge." Unofficial efforts toward *de facto* diversification, however,

---

[1] Alfred D. Chandler, *Strategy and Structure* (Cambridge, Mass.: The M.I.T. Press, 1962).

[2] Ibid., chap. 2.

continued to be made. They were disguised in reports dealing with profit improvements and statistical controls. A loss of close to $2.5 million during the first half of 1921 provided the final impetus, convincing top management to adopt in August of 1921 the organizational recommendations which had been made by the junior managers one-and-a-half years earlier.

Although in the years following the Du Pont experience a number of other organizations adopted a divisional structure, it took another three decades before this form of organization really took hold. In the fifties the best-known case of divisionalization was probably that of General Electric under Ralph Cordiner. So fashionable became the divisional organization that even companies which were not widely diversified adopted it. Divisionalization became prestige surgery, recommended as the instant answer for any company in trouble.

Indeed, divisionalization has certain temptations for general managers. The symptoms described earlier in this chapter may make him feel helpless. He recognizes that his company is not performing as it should—a declining profit picture may add a touch of urgency to his concern—but he does not quite know what to do about it. The problems have become too many and too vast, making it impossible to pinpoint and correct all the causes. Furthermore, as the company's scope expands geographically or productwise, the general manager becomes less and less expert on operating affairs. Where he lacks the necessary intimate knowledge, he is less capable of exerting a direct influence. As a result, he feels even more helpless. The divisional organization gives him a convenient way out of this dilemma because it permits him to delegate some of his general management tasks and, thereby, some of his problems.

DESIGNING THE DIVISIONAL ORGANIZATION

The divisional structure

The divisional organization is built around business units. Each unit has its own general manager who is responsible for the basic functions, such as manufacturing, engineering, and marketing. The performance of the unit is measured on the basis of its own profit and loss statement. In many ways a divisional organization consists of a number of relatively independent companies, with staff services provided either at the corporate or the divisional level or both (Exhibit 1). In large companies, divisionalization covers several levels (Exhibit 2). Staff services in such an organization may be located at either the corporate, group, divisional, or departmental level.

EXHIBIT 1

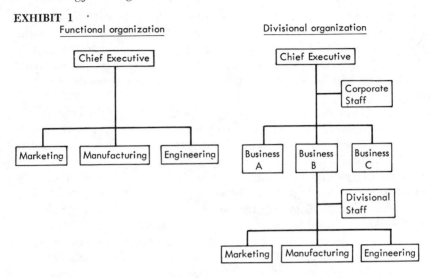

Functional organization   Divisional organization

EXHIBIT 2

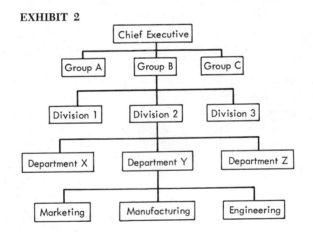

In designing a divisional organization a variety of alternatives is available. Some of the important and regularly occurring issues in terms of design are discussed below.

Number of divisions

A first choice confronting the organization builder who contemplates divisionalization is how many divisions to create. On what basis are business units to be set up? Should the company be divided into a few large or several small divisions? The perennial problem here is the degree of overlap and the extent of interdependence which will be created between divisions. Minimizing overlap and interdependence means that only a few divisions can be created. The benefits of divisionalization, therefore, will be smaller than if a larger number of divisions is set up. A large number of divisions, on the other hand, makes overlap and interdependence unavoidable.

In one company a potential division sold raw materials both to outsiders and to another potential division. Should they be combined into one? If separately constituted, should the latter be permitted to have its own raw material facilities and, if not, should it be required to purchase its raw materials from the other division? If it is to rely on the other division for its sourcing, a complex problem of transfer pricing will be created. Also, do supplying divisions owe their counterparts any scheduling favors during periods of shortages? The decision on the number of divisions thus forces the organization builder to make tradeoffs. While costs and benefits of different organizational approaches can be analyzed, a general manager nevertheless has to rely to a large extent on his judgment because not all critical costs and benefits are objectively measurable.

The issue of the number of divisions arises in two ways. First, how many divisions immediately below the corporate level should be created? Second, should these divisions, in turn, be broken down into separate business units, thus carrying the principle of divisionalization deeper into the organization? Where this is done, several layers of general managers are created, and the organization builder must ponder what role the in-between general manager is to play.

Proponents of multilayer divisionalization cite several reasons for such an approach. In one company they stressed that it would (1) permit profit centers below the divisional manager level, (2) require the development of general management skills at lower organizational levels rather than retaining a specialized functional orientation up to the top of the division, (3) allow coordination of product or customer-centered plans below the division manager level, (4) give each business unit the flexibility of a small company and yet also provide the support and strength which goes with being part of a larger firm, and (5) result in an improved product and/or customer orientation, such as more appropriate technical services or more rapid introductions of new products.

Single-layer divisionalization with functionally organized divisions, on the other hand, avoids intensifying the problems of overlap and interdependence. For example, under a further breakdown into business units, different salesmen may call on the same customer, whereas a functional setup avoids such overlap as well as the problem of plant interdependencies. Use and allocation of joint services within the division may also prove simpler under a functional structure. In research and development, for example, activities can be centralized (1) to achieve the most efficient and balanced use of funds and (2) to avoid splitting the research effort into too many small teams.

Corporate staff activities

Regardless of the degree of divisionalization, certain activities are likely to be centralized as part of a corporate staff. One company used the following criteria in deciding what to centralize:

1. To achieve economy in the use of specialized staffs: for example, personnel.
2. To consolidate tasks affecting the entire company: for example, legal work and insurance activities.
3. To achieve optimal use of scarce resources: for example, research and development and data processing.

Companies have taken vastly different approaches to the role of corporate staff activities. Berg in his research has documented that companies which have diversified by recent and often unrelated acquisitions generally have lean corporate staffs, while companies which have been diversified for a longer period of time and have entered into different product lines through internal expansion have opted for large corporate staffs. He refers to the former as "conglomerates," companies like Textron, Litton, or Gulf & Western, and to the latter as "diversified majors," like Bendix, Ingersoll-Rand, Westinghouse, or General Electric. Exhibit 3 gives intriguing data on some of the companies covered by the research, with sales in the $500 million to $2 billion range.

Centralization of certain activities into a corporate staff inevitably complicates reporting relationships. If there is a centralized controller's office or research and development staff, does the controller or R & D manager in the division report to the central staff directly (thereby reducing the authority of the divisional general manager), or through a so-called "dotted line" relationship, or not at all? The second or third alternatives are frequently followed, thereby giving the central staff merely an advisory role. The implications of such a situation for the central staff will be discussed in more detail in Chapter 15.

Role of top management

When Du Pont pioneered the transition to the divisional organization in the early twenties, it faced the issue of whether top management should have operating responsibilities. In the old organization, the top-management committee consisted of the functional managers who were in charge of day-to-day operations. The architects of the new Du Pont

EXHIBIT 3
Organizational data on companies

Functions	Diversified majors						Conglomerates						
	Company				Four companies		Company					Five companies	
	A	B	C	X	Total	Avg.	F	G	H	I	J	Total	Avg.
General executives	5	5	4	2	16	4	4	1	4	3	14	26	5
Finance	28	61	101	144	334	84	8	22	29	91	106	256	51
(of which control)	(10)	(36)	(78)	(107)	(231)	(58)	(6)	(12)	(8)	(38)	(49)	(113)	(23)
Legal-secretarial	4	10	22	42	78	20	1	7	5	6	66	85	17
Personnel administration	11	6	20	25	62	16	1	2	3	10	20	36	7
Research and development	54	130	139	232	555	139	0	0	0	0	0	0	0
Marketing	5	0	34	0	39	10	0	0	0	0	0	0	0
Manufacturing	5	1	0	5	11	3						0	0
Public relations	1	6	9	16	32	8	5	3	5	6	9	28	6
Purchasing and traffic	10	1	33	4	48	12	0	0	0	2	0	2	0
Corporate planning	3	3	2	6	14	5	5	4	1	7	9	26	5
Totals	126	223	364	476	1,189	297	24	39	47	125	224	459	92

Note: Numbers shown indicate professional personnel in corporate functions as determined from field research.
Source: Norman Berg, "Corporate Role in Diversified Companies" (Harvard Business School, Division of Research, Working Paper, 1971).

organization, however, felt that operating management could not be objectively critical and analytical and decided that the members of the executive committee should have no direct operating duties. Instead, they were—according to Chandler[3]—"to concentrate on overall planning, appraisal, and coordination." Also, "each was to help oversee one set of functional activities in all five of the new product divisions," but only "in an advisory way." The counter argument to this approach rests primarily on the fact that it adds additional overhead and that sufficient management resources may not be available to staff both nonoperating and operating tasks. The ideal solution may have to be watered down for practical reasons. A collective top-management group without direct operating responsibilities has grown in importance in recent years through the creation of the so-called "president's office."

Another important element of the top-management role is the degree of autonomy granted to the divisions. On one extreme, a strong top management may be constantly involved in divisional affairs, while on the other hand divisions may be allowed to operate independently, only being monitored through the control system. In the former, the job of divisional management will be narrow and the degree of decentralization reduced, while in the latter the organization takes on the characteristics of a holding company. The relationship between corporate and divisional management is a constantly evolving one, as illustrated by the United Latex case in this book. The resolution of this dilemma depends not so much on organizational theory as it does on the respective corporate and divisional strategies as well as on the abilities and ambitions of the corporate and divisional general managers.

IMPLICATIONS OF THE DIVISIONAL TRANSITION

Advantages of the divisional organization

Proponents of the divisional organization cite several advantages. First, by breaking the organization into smaller units, each with its own functions, the divisional organization is able to combine the advantages of a small company with the benefits of belonging to a large corporation. The small, relatively autonomous divisions under the command of a single general manager with coordination closer to the action permit better and quicker responses to market needs than the large centralized functional organization. Thus, the symptoms of malfunction arising in the overextended functional corporation are corrected. Yet in their strategic responses divisions can rely on the total resources of the corporation. Critical managerial talent can be transferred, money can be made

---

[3] Ibid., p. 106.

available, a strong research and development group can be of assistance, and so on.

Second, as will be discussed in more detail later, the availability of more general management positions facilitates management development and enhances career opportunities. Thus, the divisional organization may provide a better climate for attracting and motivating younger managers.

Third, divisionalization permits profit measurement at various organizational levels, enabling collection of control information on all the factors critically affecting profits of each business, with the result that unit and individual performance can be measured against goals and plans. Thus, divisionalization facilitates an action-oriented, future-centered management style. The functional organization, in contrast, prevents profit measurement below the top-management, total-company level; and consequently efforts at instituting administrative procedures and information systems must necessarily be limited to one function only. This forces control reports to focus on volume or costs. It is argued that cost-based management frequently becomes a breeding ground for comparisons against the past rather than against goals and plans and that such measurement results in a focus on cost minimization rather than on profit maximization. Also, stressing sales volume does not necessarily enhance profitability.

Fourth, divisionalization combined with profit-center reporting permits the assignment of authority and responsibility to a single person who can be given clear performance guidelines. In a functional organization, on the other hand, operating responsibilities are often shared among the functions, making it difficult to hold a particular person responsible for overall financial performance.

Disadvantages of divisionalization

The divisional organization is not without drawbacks. First and foremost, it frequently entails higher costs. The additional levels of general managers add overhead. Especially when each division has full control over its line and staff activities, it is virtually impossible to avoid duplication. Different divisions may have similar but independent manufacturing facilities, which—if shared—could be run more efficiently. Market research staff and control departments have to be constituted for each division, thereby probably requiring more people and other costs than if they were handled by a functional corporatewide department. Thus, an organization contemplating divisionalization should carefully assess its ability to support such a costly structure.

Secondly, the divisional organization surrenders some of the functional expertise. Each division going its separate way may not generate the power and cohesion of a single, centrally coordinated effort. In the latter, responsiveness to changes within the functional area is increased and a broader base is provided for the collection and application of special know-how and other such intangibles.

Third, the corporation embracing divisionalization often faces an embarrassing lack of manpower. In the functional organization there was only one general manager. Suddenly a large number of general managers is required. From where in the organization will they come? How are potential candidates to be evaluated and trained? Also, the shift to divisionalization may be seen by some managers as involving a demotion. For example, plant managers report to a vice president of manufacturing. After divisionalization they report to a general manager who may be one or more layers away from the president. Hence, the plant manager may see his new boss as being of lesser stature (and also closer by) and thus view change as a personal demotion.

Fourth, divisionalization, while it permits clear-cut assignments of responsibility through the profit-center setup, also may produce an excessive focus on the short run by virtue of the stress placed on the current year's profit objective. This danger has already been alluded to in Chapter 6.

A different "way of life"

In the functional organization, the general manager relates to specialists. In the divisional organization, in contrast, he manages general managers (Exhibit 4). As a result, the divisional organization has at least

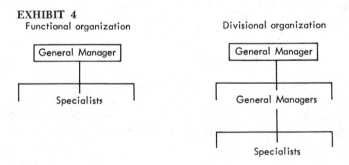

EXHIBIT 4

Functional organization   Divisional organization

two levels of general managers, that is, at both the corporate and divisional level. Also, as a generalist the corporate general manager no longer relates to specialist managers but to other general managers. Thus, the divisional organization creates a larger number of general management slots than the functional organization. Having general managers as his subordinates permits the chief executive to delegate some of his troubles.

It changes his job significantly. In the functional organization, he must coordinate the functions through specific operating decisions, requiring detailed expertise on the issues at hand. In the divisional organization, he delegates this task to the divisional general manager who must provide the coordination and specific guidance. The chief executive is able to treat his divisions conceptually like independent companies, guiding them through abstract business plans and financial performance goals. Subsequent performance can be measured neatly and precisely on the basis of the division's profit and loss statement, permitting the chief executive to reward the winners and punish the losers.

Where interdependencies among divisions are minimal, it is possible to embrace the "every tub on its own bottom" theory. In allocating corporate resources, the chief executive can expand certain divisions while starving others. In the functional organization, in contrast, he is forced to balance functional demands given their interdependence.[4] Also, by treating divisions separately, it is possible to compartmentalize risks not just in terms of business risks but also in terms of the success or failure of the divisional general managers. Furthermore, within the divisional organization new divisions can be added or existing ones dropped with a minimum of disturbance to the other parts of the organization, providing the chief executive with an organizational vehicle which gives him great strategic flexibility.

Interdependencies and tradeoffs frequently prevent the creation of a "pure" divisional organization. Certain activities, such as research and development, sales offices, or manufacturing plants may have to be shared or centralized at the corporate level. It may be too costly or impractical to move all the way toward pure divisionalization. In one company, this dilemma was described as follows:

> One significant question here is how to organize the sales force. These men are highly skilled and quite expensive to employ—each salesman should enter commitments of at least $1 million yearly in order to justify his expenses. Since our customers are spread all over the country, it would appear economical to assign field salesmen by geographical areas each to sell all, or at least a number of, our products. Unfortunately, this system might take a good measure of the responsibility for the sales effort from the product group and place it at the level of centralized sales supervision. Our problem here is to leave sales responsibility at the product group level without having an undue duplication of field sales personnel.

Where compromises between divisionalization and centralization must be made, the chief executive and his managers face the issue of the degree of involvement and authority of the corporate vis-à-vis the divi-

---

[4] For a more detailed discussion, see John H. McArthur and Bruce R. Scott, *Industrial Planning in France* (Boston, Harvard Business School, Division of Research, 1969), p. 125.

sional level. This issue has become a perennial bone of contention in many divisional organizations.

In spite of the above impurities, the divisional organization is a much more performance-oriented institution than the functional company. As stated by Scott, "This distinct 'way of life' is due in large measure to the internalization of market pressure for economic results, with upper levels of management typically applying more 'profit pressure' within the enterprise than is characteristic of the external environment. . . . This 'internalization' of the market mechanism is one of the crucial innovations of the divisionalized organization."[5]

This form of organization not only changes life for the chief executive and changes his role but it also shapes the role of the divisional general manager who is subject to precise performance measurement. The scoreboard may compare divisions, leading to a highly competitive constellation among division managers. The market mechanism will have unpleasant career implications for the poor performer but it also will reward the "stars." The next chapter describes the job of the divisional general manager, while Chapter 15 focuses on the jobs of the corporate general manager and his corporate staff.

---

[5] Bruce R. Scott, "Stages of Corporate Development," p. 12. (Copyright © 1971 by the President and Fellows of Harvard College.)

14

General management at the
divisional level*

JOB OF THE MIDDLE-LEVEL GENERAL MANAGER

OF THE SEVERAL levels of general managers in the divisional organization, this chapter focuses on the divisional general manager, the person who is in charge of one of the operating units of the company. Because organizations use different words to describe their business units, such as divisions or departments, the manager in charge will be referred to as middle-level general manager. The job of the middle-level general manager is discussed first because their number probably exceeds that of corporate general managers by a wide margin. Also, it is a job which is available to younger as well as older managers. General management in the divisional organization does not necessarily require many years of service. Therefore, a discussion of the middle-level general manager's job is of both actual and potential value to a large number of managers. Furthermore, and most importantly, while this job is of greater relevance to a larger number of people earlier in their careers than is the job of the corporate-level general manager, the literature has focused largely on the latter. One approach would be to refer to what is known about the top-level general manager. However, this knowledge is not necessarily applicable. The middle-level general management job is signifi-

---

* This chapter, in slightly revised form, appeared in the March–April 1972 issue of the *Harvard Business Review,* pp. 75–85, under the title "General Managers in the Middle."

cantly different. Furthermore, it is, in a number of respects, more difficult. It involves:

—managing multiple relationships,
—acting as "playing coach,"
—translating goals into action,
—translating action into measurement,
—assuming full responsibility while having limited authority,
—managing in a "political" environment.

Managing multiple relationships

The middle-level general manager, like most managers, accomplishes his goals largely by managing relationships. There are few things which a manager can do alone; he must usually rely on the support, cooperation, or approval of a large number of people. As the textbooks say, "he gets things done through others."

Managing relationships at his level in the organization, however, is a threefold task requiring the middle-level general manager to act, at the same time, as subordinate, equal, and superior. Upward he relates to his boss as a subordinate; he takes orders. Downward he relates to his team as a superior; he gives orders. Laterally, he often relates to peers in the organization as an equal; for example, he may have to secure cooperation from a pooled sales force or solicit assistance from corporate staff services. Thus, the middle-level general manager wears three hats at the same time. In contrast, the top-level general manager acts primarily as a superior.

Managing this triple set of relationships is most demanding. It is difficult for any one person to excel in all three simultaneously. To be at once a decisive superior, a cooperative colleague, and a loyal subordinate is quite a challenge, similar to a baseball player having to excel simultaneously in hitting, fielding, and pitching. Not only does the middle-level general manager have to be good at all three; he also has to be able to shift quickly and frequently from one role to another.

In view of these conflicting and changing demands, it is often difficult for the middle-level general manager to arrive at a consistent pattern of behavior. Moreover, in the process of satisfying the requirements of one set of relationships, he may reduce his effectiveness in managing another. For instance, a middle manager who follows orders from headquarters to the letter may thereby, in the eyes of his subordinates, either weaken his authority or appear unreasonable and unresponsive. For one division, headquarters restricted its freedom to purchase from the outside; this order threatened to undermine the authority of the general manager. He was torn between the dilemma of asserting his authority with his subordinates by ignoring or fighting headquarters' orders, or weakening his image as a superior by following headquarters' directives. Being a good subordinate would have weakened him as a superior; yet, by being a strong superior, he would have been a disloyal subordinate. Also, prolonged negotiations with a peer in the pooled sales force to arrive at a mutually satisfactory solution made the general manager appear inconclusive and indecisive to his subordinates.

To successfully manage these multiple relationships with their often conflicting and changing demands, the middle-level general manager may want to—

1. Make his network of relationships explicit. To whom does he have to relate? Which are the key relationships?
2. Identify, in his specific situation, the triple set of requirements: What is expected of him as a good subordinate? What is required to be an effective colleague and equal? What does it take to provide leadership as a superior? This analysis forces the middle-level general manager to focus not only on his own goals and abilities but also on those of his "opposite numbers" at all three levels.
3. Recognize the difficulty of achieving consistent behavior in view of the differing demands of the triple set of relationships and be willing to "wear three hats" simultaneously. To do so successfully involves balancing all three roles. Sometimes it requires tradeoffs. Under these complex circumstances, it helps to proceed explicitly.

Others in the organization who are relating to the middle-level general manager may, in turn, bear in mind that they are but one of the multiple relationships which he has to manage. Their expectations and responses should take this into account.

Acting as "playing coach"

In managing multiple relationships, the middle-level general manager—at his particular level in the organization—may have to act in a dual role. In some respects, he is the leader of his unit who delegates, guides, and plans. In other respects, however, he has specific operating responsibilities and must "roll up his sleeves" to achieve output and to meet his targets. Therefore, he is both a delegator and a doer, both a strategist and an operator, or, to use the sports analogy, both a coach and a player. In contrast, his superiors are usually exclusively coaches and his subordinates are normally players.

This dual role requires a man to excel simultaneously at coaching and at playing. Continuing the analogy, sports experience indicates that it is easier to excel either as a coach or as a player and that the playing coach job is clearly the most difficult. The skills required to succeed as player are different from those of a successful coach, but the playing coach needs to possess the skills of both. Likewise, the dual role of a middle manager combines different skills and actions. On the one hand, he needs a broad overview, detachment, and a long-run perspective. On the other hand, he needs detailed knowledge and experience, the ability to involve himself directly and deeply, and a sense of urgency. The middle-level general manager must attempt to combine all these characteristics simultaneously.

Acting both as player and as coach, the middle-level general manager must constantly balance the two roles and sometimes make tradeoffs. Is he going to be too much of a player, too involved in operating details and in doing things himself? Or is he becoming too much of a coach by staying aloof, by delegating too much, by not getting sufficiently involved? It is easy to misperceive one's role, especially in regard to the latter. For example, top management of a large divisionalized corporation assigned a promising manager to a recent acquisition. Charged with enthusiasm for his new position, he saw himself as primarily a delegator, an organizational builder whose job was to oversee the installation of parent company procedures and guide the acquisition's integration with staff services of the parent. He had not considered becoming directly involved in operating details or concentrating attention on increasing sales, both of which his immediate superior, the former owner/manager, saw as primary responsibilities of the middle-management position.

This question of balance—of asking oneself, "To what extent do I get involved in actual operations and to what extent do I delegate?"—is most delicate. "To what extent do I try to be coach and to make the decisions, and to what extent do I try to be a player and wait for the coach upstairs to call the plays?" The balancing of the two roles is, of course, also influenced by the demands, expectations, and abilities of the middle-level general manager's superior and subordinates. The choice is not entirely free.

Translating goals into action

The middle-level general manager usually receives abstract guidance from his superiors in the form of goals that he must translate into concrete action. If, for example, a company's chief executive sets the goal of a certain percentage increase in earnings per share (and mentions it to financial analysts, thereby making it an even stronger commitment), how does he go about achieving this goal? He will communicate it to his group vice president, who will salute and pass it on to his divisional general manager, who, in turn, will salute and pass it on to the middle-level general manager. The latter will salute, turn around, . . .

and find nobody to pass the goal on to. To use Harry Truman's famous dictum, this is where the buck stops.

The buck stops at the middle-level general manager, who must translate the abstract guidance of more earnings per share or meeting the budget into the concrete action required to achieve these goals. He has to translate the budgetary, financial, strategic language into operational language. He has to talk the general-manager language with his superiors and translate it into the functional-specialist language for his subordinates. His superiors, by contrast, are all general managers and are able to communicate in the same general management language. His subordinates, however, communicate in their common functional-specialist language. It is the middle-level general manager who must be bilingual and who must assume the job of translator: from abstract guidance handed down from above into concrete action to be followed below.

Often these abstract goals or financial budgets carry the label "difficult but achievable." While such labels may have a motivating purpose, they are basically a euphemism for the following proposition: Top management knows the results it wants to see, has no idea how to achieve them, and assigns to the middle-level general manager the twofold duty of figuring out how to perform the task and then getting it done. Orders from above are usually result-oriented and do not specify the means to be used to achieve these results. The boss tells what he wants, not how he wants it accomplished.

There are several reasons for the foregoing results-oriented procedure. One explanation is that the middle-level general manager is closest to the action; therefore, he has most of the data, and hence is in the best position to make the decisions relevant to translating goals into action. A second explanation states that it is a superior's privilege to push decision making down and let his subordinates sweat it out. Why should the boss stick his neck out when he has a subordinate to do it for him?

The implications of top management's approach, however, are more important than the explanations. First of all, the middle-level general manager is provided with a much broader *de facto* responsibility than is usually codified in job descriptions or organization charts. Consequently, he must often be more of a strategist than he realizes. It is important, therefore, that he go beyond the formalistic definition of his job, functioning broadly enough so that he deals explicitly with the full scope of his real responsibilities. A narrow definition of his job, by contrast, may cause him to ignore some critical tasks. He cannot assume a responsibility he does not recognize.

But, with responsibility goes risk, particularly where the goals are abstract and the charter is unclear. This risk is further compounded by the many constraints, external as well as organizational, within which the middle-level general manager operates. However, along with risk also goes opportunity. As Harry Truman put it, "If you can't stand the heat, get out of the kitchen." To be a strategist rather than just an order taker is exciting, even without the job's ceremonial attributes.

The opportunity to translate abstract goals into concrete action is in large part a strategic one. It requires the ability to develop plans. In doing so, the middle-level general manager must take into account external factors of an economic, political, marketing, technological, or competitive nature. Moreover, in line with his dual role, he must achieve congruence between the goals of subordinates (whose commitment is essential) and the goals imposed by superiors (whose approval he seeks).

This strategic task is both intellectual and administrative in nature. Furthermore, not only the development but also the communication of his plans is critical. Often, communication is most effectively accomplished not through proclamation but, rather, through "teaching" the general management point of view during day-to-day activities.

To translate goals into action the middle-level general manager must—

1. Define his job realistically and broadly.
2. Assume full responsibility for translating the abstract goals into concrete action through strategic decision making and planning, taking into account both external and organizational factors.
3. Effectively communicate his decisions and plans to both his superiors and subordinates.

Translating action into measurement

Translation is required in both directions: not only from abstract guidance into concrete action but also from concrete action into abstract measurement. The boss measures success in terms of results; he is less interested in how it has been accomplished. Consequently, the middle-level general manager's performance is more often appraised by matching the abstract results of his actions with the abstract guidance that he has been given than by evaluating the quality of the specific action taken.

This fact of organizational life sometimes leads to misunderstanding. In one company, for instance, a middle-level general manager was unable to meet his goals and invoked his actions to show why. Top management, however, perceived the explanations as excuses. Concrete action was not part of its measurement system.

In terms of the total equation, there can be real problems when the signals from abstract measurement contradict those from abstract guidance. Where this occurs, the translation process frequently gets reversed. Instead of starting with the abstract guidance (goals) to develop specific action, the middle-level general manager starts with the abstract measurement (required results) and translates backward to his plan of action. For example, in one company, top management emphasized the need for its divisions to have ample productive capacity. In the measurement of performance, however, excess capacity was looked on unfavorably. As a result, division managers added capacity very cautiously, achieving high plant-utilization ratios at the expense of lost sales (which did not show up in the measurement system).

Translating action into measurement involves the same skills as translating goals into action. One language is operational and involves a variety of dimensions, whereas the other is abstract and is often in terms of a single dimension. The required ability is to relate these two different languages. And when measurement and goals are contradictory, the middle-level general manager must be able to tread a thin line between the two, sometimes making tradeoffs.

Furthermore, he must cope with an additional problem: the language of corporate measurement is sometimes inadequate for measuring and guiding the activities of his subordinates. While top management typically measures him on the basis of profit and loss, the middle-level general manager has to evaluate his subordinates in terms of different quantitative measures (such as costs, production and sales volume, number of rejects, and so on) as well as qualitative judgments (such as adequacy of the plant layout, effectiveness of the R & D effort, comprehensiveness of the marketing activities). These measures not only are different in kind and more numerous but also require greater expertise and more intimate knowledge of specifics.

Assuming full responsibility and limited authority

The middle-level general manager typically assumes full responsibility for his unit and is evaluated on the results of his total operation. There is no way to shift the blame as might be done in a functionally organized setup, where marketing could claim that production did not deliver on time or where production could point the finger at marketing for not bringing in enough orders.

Like the chief executive, the middle-level general manager has to account for the performance of others. It is up to him to see that they work harmoniously and effectively toward the accomplishment of the required results. Unlike the chief executive, however, he has only limited authority in the pursuit of his goals. He often needs cooperation from equals, such as a pooled sales force or a centralized R & D department, and he receives solicited, or unsolicited, guidance from superiors. Thus, responsibility and authority do not overlap. The former exceeds the latter.

Textbooks state categorically that such an imbalance is wrong and that responsibility should be backed up with the necessary authority. Yet, this responsibility/authority discrepancy is an inevitable fact of life where divisionalization is carried far down into the organization. The choice is between few divisions with general managers who control almost everything and several divisions where the general manager has to rely on joint activities, such as a pooled sales force. Where the second alternative has been chosen, the middle-level general manager may become frustrated by the discrepancy between responsibility and authority. However, without this discrepancy his division would not exist and he would not have a general management job. From a career point of view, an imperfect general management job at age 32 may be preferable to a perfect one at age 57.

To function effectively in this imperfect world, the middle-level general manager must meet two requirements. First, in spite of the limited authority, he must be willing to accept full responsibility and take his action accordingly. At the same time, he should recognize that he cannot do everything himself, that he must cooperate and coordinate with others. The ability to manage multiple relationships is critical here.

Second, the middle-level general manager always has the opportunity to "go to court," to appeal to his superiors when cooperation from equals is not forthcoming. However, he should pick his fights wisely, carefully, and infrequently. By going to court, he asks somebody higher up to stick his neck out. The fact that this "somebody" has attained this higher position probably means that he is good at not sticking his neck out. A middle-level general manager often finds that taking a case to court does not necessarily resolve it and that the issue may be pushed down by his superior. As a result, this route should be relied on only as a last resort or where the issue is clear-cut. Otherwise, preventive settlements, even if they involve compromises, may be preferable.

Managing in a "political" environment

The setup involving multiple relationships, playing-coach elements, translation from goals to action and back to results, and discrepancies between responsibility and authority necessarily results in a structure which requires coexistence among managers in an atmosphere inevitably political. There are different interests and interest groups, conflicting goals and ambitions, and positions of power and weakness. Organizationally, they are all tied together: the situation is one of coexistence.

This coexistence, moreover, is not always peaceful. The parties involved are not always neutral. Career objectives are at stake. Positions of power are created or reduced. Prestige may be an important factor. Tempers, feelings, and ambition may overrule analysis. In this environment the middle-level general manager is an easy, accessible, and often permissible target. The malcontent soldiers do not pick on the general directly; they go for his officers.

The general manager in the middle, furthermore, is in a vulnerable position. He needs cooperation and assistance and is therefore exposed to sabotage. Particularly, with a measurement system requiring immediate and frequent responses, his position is delicate. In a political sense, he is up for reelection continuously.

Thus, the middle-level general manager must possess political sensitivity as well as the constitution to stomach pressures and conflicts. He has to be aware of the configuration of the power structure and the direction of political winds. Unfortunately, in this potentially volatile atmosphere, managers often fail to ask an obvious but key question: "Who are my friends, and who are my enemies?"

IMPLICATIONS OF THE MIDDLE-LEVEL GENERAL MANAGEMENT JOB

Some important implications can be drawn from the characteristics of the middle-level general management job. They affect not only the manager himself but his superiors as well.

One common pitfall is that superiors tend to judge middle-level managers in terms of their own jobs. They believe that middle-level general managers have the same opportunities, prerogatives, and power that they do and therefore should shoulder similar responsibility. The same belief is frequently shared by the middle-level general managers themselves. However, the above characteristics of the middle-level general management job make it quite different from that of the top-level general manager. These differences, as well as the resulting difficulties, should be recognized. The job itself is demanding enough. It should not be made more difficult by an incorrect understanding of its scope and characteristics.

Top management often fails to recognize that imperfection is a fact of life in the middle-level general management job. Furthermore, formal job descriptions frequently reflect sacred dogmas like overlapping authority and responsibility. Such ostrich-like attitudes create unrealistic expectations among all parties involved. Unrealistic expectations inevitably produce disenchantments and failures. Reality, even though it may not correspond to the demands of theoretical elegance, must be faced. If reality imposes imperfection, as it does, then imperfection must be recognized and accepted. Only by acknowledging imperfection rather than sweeping it under the rug will it be possible to manage its challenges.

ADVANTAGES OF THE MIDDLE-LEVEL GENERAL MANAGEMENT JOB

The preceding description of the characteristics of the middle-level general management job portrays it as a major challenge, as indeed it is. Why would anyone want to accept such an ill-defined, open-ended, risky assignment? Yet, with risk goes opportunity and with open-endedness goes a job of considerably broader scope than what is stated on the formal job description. Why is it not possible, then, to design this job by including all the positive elements and eliminating all the drawbacks? The answer is that the drawbacks are inherent in the divisional organizational structure. They can be eliminated only by eliminating the structure itself.

A divisional structure is essential to the conduct of operations for a diverse range of products in a variety of countries. From the individual's point of view, it permits a large number of managers to assume general management responsibilities early in their careers, sometimes in their early or middle thirties after less than 10 years of business experience. In contrast, the functional organization usually offers an individual manager his first attempt at general management only during his middle fifties, after some 25 to 30 years of business experience. The choice, as indicated under the full responsibility/limited authority heading, is between having a broad opportunity to assume an imperfect general management job at an early age or having a very limited opportunity to hold a "perfect" general management job late in one's career. To put it in the context of Churchill's famous statement: early in a manager's career, the middle-level general management job is the worst assignment except for all the others.

The advantages of the middle-level general management job and the resulting opportunity of becoming a general manager early in one's career are many, both for the company and for its managers.

First, it is a major motivational factor. The opportunity to run one's "own show" at a young age, rather than having to wait for a quarter of a century, should make a business career more exciting. Also, by having a large number of general management slots in an organization, it is possible to attract and retain many capable managers rather than having an elimination contest for the company's single general management position.

Second, the shift of a manager from specialist to generalist early in his career is less perilous, and failure is less painful. If a manager has spent some 25 years as a specialist, he is apt to be firmly set in his ways and will find it difficult to make a major change. A younger manager, on the other hand, should still be flexible and able to adapt more easily to a different set of job requirements. Failure is easier to take—and to overcome—early in one's career than it is later on. Putting a 25-year track record on the line is a major risk and one that might well destroy an entire career.

Third, the early shift from specialist to generalist is also less risky from the company's viewpoint. When a manager who has been a specialist for a quarter of a century is selected for the president's job, the total conduct of the company is entrusted to someone with no record in general management. It is not at all certain that a successful engineering, marketing, manufacturing, or finance vice president will turn into a first-rate general manager. Yet, the entire fate of the corporation will have been placed in his hands. In the divisional organization, in contrast, the middle-level general manager typically manages one of several profit centers. Thus risk is greatly reduced by entrusting to an unproven general manager only a small segment of the total enterprise.

Fourth, a corporation with many middle-level general management jobs will develop a reservoir of general managers. They can be transferred and promoted as new opportunities arise. Since the scarcest resource of a company is usually competent management, a reservoir of middle-level general managers helps corporations overcome this hurdle and constitutes a major competitive advantage.

Fifth, the middle-level general management phenomenon is conducive to management development and training. A manager can start in a small profit center, establish a track record there, transfer to a larger unit, and so on. Thus, both the breadth and challenge of the general management job can be increased as a manager moves up in the ranks. His confidence and versatility will be increasingly enhanced, fostering personal career development as well as strengthening corporate competence.

Sixth, middle-level general managers are close to the action. Leadership and coordination, therefore, take place on the battlefield rather than from distant headquarters. Decisions can be made more quickly by better informed people who can more closely monitor an action's impact and ensure its proper implementation.

15

General management at the corporate level

THE CREATION of middle-level general management positions in the divisionalized company forces a redefinition of the tasks and responsibilities retained at the corporate level. The implications for both the corporate staff and the top executives are significant. This chapter focuses first on the job of the staff manager and second on the critical functions of the chief executive. The point which has already been made for the chief executive, that is, that in the divisional organization he relates to general managers instead of to specialists, also applies to the corporate staff manager.

THE JOB OF THE CORPORATE STAFF MANAGER

The job of the corporate staff manager will be explored through focus on the corporate planner.[1] While this job has much in common with other frequently encountered corporate staff activities such as personnel, control, and central engineering, it has been selected for emphasis here for two reasons. First, in many companies the job is a relatively new one that has been specifically created to help manage the diversified, divisionalized organization. Second, the planner is concerned with the formulation of corporate and divisional strategies which permits putting

[1] This section on the corporate staff manager is based on a paper, "The Role of the Corporate Planning Executive," prepared by Robert W. Ackerman for the Fifth Annual Conference for Planning Executives in 1972 held at the Harvard Business School.

the earlier chapters on the process of strategy in the context of the organizational structure.

The illusionary power of the system

The most obvious, though perhaps the least useful, way of describing the planner's role is in terms of the tasks demanded of him by the system he manages. Executing the procedures required by the system defines the need for certain communications, relationships, and activities.

To those who take a professional's view of planning, these aspects of the job are of commanding importance. This view hinges on the assumption, however, that a well-designed system, professionally administered, will result in effective planning. Such, unfortunately, is not always the case. The system itself cannot dictate (1) either the contents of the plans or (2) the level of organizational commitment to using them as a basis for setting corporate strategy. Securing relevance for planning in the decision-making process may relate more to the planner's interpersonal competence than to his skills as a planner.

On the other hand, the corporate planner should be aware of the implications of the system for his job, especially when he is given the responsibility for initiating planning. In the start-up situation he frequently has the choice between installing a prepackaged system or developing one of his own. Ironically, interpersonal skills may be considerably more demanding in the former situation than in the latter. With the basic design questions decided beforehand (and without wide participation), the prepackaged system can be activated more rapidly. Relationships, which might otherwise evolve over time, must be managed under the strained conditions of a new but fully elaborated system.

The illusion of neutrality

Corporate staff managers, as implementors of the system which they manage, may see themselves in a neutral role. They view their job as the scientific implementation of their discipline. They like to relate their role to that of the doctor, the psychologist, or the lawyer. However, the corporate staff manager frequently encounters situations where he is not considered neutral by others or where a neutral position is impossible. This may occur when the flow of resources is to be diverted from normal channels. For instance, in times of corporate crisis (or a national crisis, for that matter) chief executives frequently seek to reassert their authority over the affairs of operating units. If divisions are to be liquidated or divested, the chief executive may find it foolhardy to expect those involved to adopt corporatewide views. Similarly, planning for entry into a major new field and implementing that decision by accumulating the necessary resources from existing businesses may also be a task that cannot be delegated to middle-level general managers. Instead, the chief executive turns to his staff for support and guidance. In short, a neutral role for the corporate planner may rest on the assumption that the firm is functioning satisfactorily relative to its potential and that the chief executive does not see the need for intervention in the initiation of business plans and resource allocation proposals.

Furthermore, the needs and ambitions of other managers involved in planning constitute a major influence on the corporate planner. The power and attitudes of, for instance, the controller, the manager of the most profitable division, the executive who was passed over for the presidency, the executives who are vying for the top spot next, are all relevant concerns. The corporate planner must be aware of likely allies and likely enemies and the intensity and significance of their feelings. He is, after all, dealing with a process that affects the careers of the managers involved; it is natural that they calibrate its usefulness in personal terms.

Managing relationships

Thus, like the middle-level general manager, the corporate staff manager must structure his relationships. In doing so, it is important to view these relationships from both sides. The corporate planner asks not only how he sees his job but also how others with whom he must interact see it. Likewise, the corporate planner must ask how the others see their own jobs. If the parties involved perceive their respective

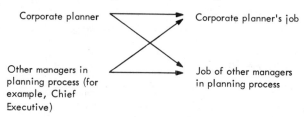

jobs differently, misunderstandings or even conflicts may arise. Because multiple relationships must be managed, this analysis is required along a number of dimensions.

Frequently, the planner's principal client is the chief executive, whose respect and trust must be earned. If there is one basic truth in the lore of planning, it is that the exercise is futile unless it has the continuing, visible support of the chief executive. Without his dedication to the proposition that planning is useful and, more importantly, without his willingness to make commitments to his division managers on the basis of their planning activities, the function loses its effectiveness.

On an interpersonal level, the perceived relationship between the chief executive and the planner will, of course, have a major bearing on how the latter is viewed by the rest of the organization.

In relating to the chief executive, the corporate planner must consider at least two types of inquiry. The first relates to the personal needs of the chief executive and the pressures placed on his job. The new president brought into a crisis situation clearly has different concerns than his long-tenured counterpart in a successful company. The former may view planning as a mechanism for sorting out what is to be kept from what is to be liquidated, while the latter may hold planning to be one means of developing managers and insuring against unforeseen long-term consequences of environmental change. Their time horizons, mandates for change, and power in the organization may be radically different. Moreover, the nature of the relationships they must manage may vary, and this should be of great importance to their advisers. Most presidents have personal needs and goals that help to define what they expect from the planning function.

The second inquiry relates to the chief executive's management style and in particular the means he adopts to solve problems. For example, what is his tolerance for detail and how deeply does he tend to intervene in the decision-making process? Some chief executives place great reliance on delegated responsibilities and indirect methods of guiding decisions through performance appraisal and rewards; others are willing to share responsibility in exchange for the chance to influence the outcome directly. The emphasis has a great deal to do with how much the chief executive needs or wants to know about operating matters and where he looks for guidance.

The planning executive must also manage his relationships with division managers. It is naive for him to think that they will happily grasp the benefits of corporate planning. Their concerns have to do with the course of their careers as well as the chart they have plotted for their division. They are continually monitoring the opportunities for securing resources and are sensitive to the nuances of performance evaluation. The planner and his system represent elements at least partially beyond the operating manager's control and to that extent constitute a disruption and possibly a threat to previously existing decision processes.

Finally, the planning executive must relate to other staff functions, especially those responsible for financial controls. Unless he is to build a sizable analytical and clerical staff, the planner may have to depend on the controller's office for assistance. Without it, his efforts may be either hopelessly mired in detail or so far removed from the detail that his advice is not grounded in fact. There is, of course, a tension between planning and budgeting; to give precedence to one tends to lessen the influence of the other. It is not unusual that the planner and the controller find themselves in competition for the attention of both the chief executive and the operating managers. Given the importance frequently accorded the budget in the evaluation of executive performance and the greater bulk of the controller's task and organization, it is not surprising that the planning executive finds the odds untenable in the event of battle.

Challenge of the corporate staff job

In the context of these relationships, none of them easy to manage, the corporate planner has a difficult task. He is generally expected to secure information from managers down the line regarding the nature of their activities and future plans. This information is to be forthright and truthful. More importantly, it is to be useful in guiding the future activities of the corporation. He is also expected to help the corporation develop objectives and goals and strategies for attaining them. One planner commented, "My job is to be the manager in charge of tomorrow." For him to be successful in measuring up to that responsibility, he will have to secure influence in the process through which strategic decisions are made. Unhappily for him, his office is rarely endowed with the power of position. His portfolio at the outset is thin and his mandate often superficial. In a head-to-head confrontation with divisional management, he will normally lose. With good reason, a strong chief executive will most likely sacrifice his staff advisers rather than disrupt reporting relationships with those responsible for operations.

Thus, even though the corporate staff is often referred to as the eyes and ears of the president, it rarely has his hands. It has to achieve action without power. Furthermore, it is difficult to measure its effectiveness. Its task usually is to assist others, to enhance their effectiveness, or to assess their competence. Where the assistance proves beneficial, it is difficult to separate how much is due to staff assistance. Would the operating manager have achieved identical (or even better) results without staff help? Where operating results are poor, it may be caused by operating management with the staff manager being an innocent bystander. Yet he may get blamed nevertheless. Thus, within the divisional structure, the job of the corporate staff manager is a highly delicate one. Unfortunately, many a staff executive fails to recognize these difficulties, or even aggravates them by relying primarily on the illusionary power of the system which he has been asked to manage.

Success hinges more on an ability to manage multiple relationships than on technical competence. A corporate staff manager in order to be effective must take a general management point of view. Taking into account his own objectives and capabilities, he must determine his role. Three basic options are available. On one extreme, the corporate staff manager may see himself as a neutral middleman, while on the other extreme, he may choose to play an independent and activist role. In between, he may see himself as a presidential emissary. While there may be some overlap, these roles are by and large distinct and will be described in more detail for the corporate planner.

Possible roles of the corporate planner

Planning broker.   In this role, the corporate planner struggles to maintain neutrality and impartiality in his relationships with other managers. He manages the long-range planning system, insures that the plans are comprehensive, and promotes the ideas and techniques of planning. However, he avoids taking positions whenever possible on the strategic issues confronting the corporation or its components. In a sense, he acts as a weather bureau by reflecting the chief executive's concerns to managers down the line and as a broker by giving advance exposure for their plans in corporate circles. He tends to view his career as a planner in professional terms and avoids getting caught in the cross-fire between operating managers on the same or different levels in the organization. He limits his exposure to criticism, keeping, as the current saying goes, a "low profile."

Presidential adviser.   Alternatively, the corporate planner may see the president as his client and the president's needs as his concern. Rather than attempting to maintain neutrality, the planner may take advantage and make use of "the president's ear" to further his client's purposes. He ties his success and influence to the strength and resolve of the chief executive. While this position may seem extreme and dangerous for the planner, it is not necessarily so. It depends heavily on the relationships between the chief executive and his division managers. If the chief executive is a respected leader, the planner benefits from his close association. Moreover, the organization understands his point of view, knows how to approach him, and may in fact deal with him as the chief executive's stand-in.

Strategic evaluator.   Finally, the planner may attempt to define a role which permits him to have his own position on strategic issues. In this case, he seeks independence rather than neutrality or subjugation to the chief executive. His client is the corporation, and his efforts are directed toward defining strategy that will be to its long-run advantage. In fulfilling this role, the planner must have freedom to evaluate plans and the influence to have his assessments taken seriously. To assess, however, is to judge the competence of the managers submitting plans, and to influence is to exert some control over the allocation of resources. In effect, the corporate planner adopts a position akin to that of a line manager. While clearly the most active role, it is also the most exposed. The stakes are higher, and the planner must decide whether the opportunities justify the risks.

A serious consideration of alternative roles forces the planning executive to diagnose his position in the organization. He should think through very carefully such questions as: (1) "Who is my client?" (2) "What distance should I maintain in my relationships with various other executives?" and (3) "What degree of independence do I want or need for my views on the substantive issues confronting the enterprise?" With an identification of his role or the role he would like to have, the planning executive can then begin to develop a strategy that will serve as a guide for future action. If planning is useful in managing the corporation, the planner has the responsibility for insuring that his office is managed in a fashion that insures that the benefit is obtained.

THE JOB OF THE CORPORATE GENERAL MANAGER

Given the preceding description of the middle-level general manager's job and that of corporate staff managers, what job is left for the chief executive, the corporate general manager? An immediate answer usually given to this question is that he handles corporate relations with the outside, especially with the financial community and the government. If being "president in charge of public relations" were his only major task, then public relations would be by far the best-paid position in a firm. With the operating task delegated to middle-level general managers, the corporate general manager's job becomes one of managing managers. While the tools remain the same as those described in Chapter 11, that is, structure, systems, and personal intervention, the emphasis falls more heavily on the first two elements. The emphasis also shifts away from operational aspects to those which shape the scope and performance of the company: planning, resource allocation, performance measurement and compensation, and management selection and development.

Ralph Cordiner, the architect of General Electric's major move toward divisionalization in the early fifties, described the role of corporate general managers as follows: "They have been freed of operating responsibility and administrative details so that they can devote their time to long-range planning, appraisal of current performance, bringing divisional objectives and plans into a working pattern with over-all company needs, and making sure of the needed continuity of competent managerial and other personnel in the decentralized businesses."[2]

Managing the strategic process

Among the tasks of the corporate general manager, planning is most frequently cited. Repeatedly, the statement is made that the chief execu-

---

[2] Ralph T. Cordiner, *New Frontiers for Professional Managers* (New York: McGraw-Hill, 1956), p. 68.

tive officer is now freed from operating details, being able to spend his time on policy. He is seen, by himself and others, as the corporation's chief strategist. His tools are the long-range plan and the resource allocation process. Bower, in his research on the management of the resource allocation process,[3] challenges this notion. In the large divisionalized corporation, given the vast array of different activities, the intimate knowledge of the businesses, their markets and technologies rests inevitably with divisional management. The critical link between strategic planning and action is the process through which resources are allocated. Bower has found that middle-level general managers provide what he calls the "definition" and "impetus" for specific projects. Definition is the process leading to the determination of the "technical and economic" characteristics of a proposal, while impetus is the willingness of the middle-level general manager to put "his reputation for good judgment on the line,"[4] by submitting and sponsoring the proposal to corporate general management. He obtains corporate approval in large part through securing their commitment to his strategic plan for the division and to him as a general manager capable of executing it.

Bower's findings lead him to the conclusion that the critical inputs to the resource allocation process are made at the stages of definition and impetus and that corporate general management acts largely as a ratifier. In fact, corporate general managers seldom have unbiased strategic alternatives presented to them by division executives for decision. Bower states: "That boards and appropriations committees in most companies recognize the extent to which they have delegated their capital appropriating power, is evidenced by the very low rate of project rejections which characterizes their actions."[5]

The role of corporate general management in planning and resource allocation encompasses several other aspects. First of all, financial and strategic goals have to be set. This process is not solely influenced by corporate or personal ambitions or by the demands and expectations of the financial community. It is also organizational in nature. Performance goals often result from a tug of war between corporate expectations and divisional forecasts, which occurs through the various phases of the formal planning and budgeting process. Corporate general management performs the delicate task of balancing its expectations of superior performance with what the divisions forecast as achievable goals. Sometimes, the challenge to forecast and deliver high-performance goals results not from corporate demands but from peer group pressure

---

[3] Joseph L. Bower, *Managing the Research Allocation Process: A Study of Corporate Planning and Investment* (Boston, Mass.: Harvard Business School, Division of Research, 1970).

[4] Ibid., p. 68.

[5] Ibid., p. 15.

as division managers all contend for the first-place spot in the corporate pennant race. In that event, the alleged disadvantage of bottoms-up goal setting, that is, that operating divisions will play it safe by submitting conservative estimates, is thus avoided.

Another aspect of the role of corporate general management is that of acting as catalyst, ensuring that divisional general management conducts its strategic planning. Berg[6] points out, on the basis of his research, that

many conglomerates make a determined effort to force the division manager to do more strategic planning for his division than was done for his company when it was independent. . . . A significant contribution of the conglomerate to the acquired company, therefore, can often be a new structure which *forces* more strategic planning.

The usual approach of conglomerates is to make small groups of line executives—not large committees and staff groups—directly responsible for planning the future of the business. The focus is on economic return and search for opportunity, rather than on commitment to a given product or way of doing business simply because "we have always done it this way."

A further important responsibility of corporate general management is to make decisions to embark on new business ventures, utilizing the financial resources generated by the existing divisions, as well as to divest existing businesses. The divisional organization, as has already been pointed out, provides greater freedom of action in this respect than the functionally organized company. Hence, corporate general management is able to focus explicitly and objectively on the full scope of available strategic alternatives.

Managing structure and systems

If corporate general management, lacking the intimate knowledge of its diverse activities, has delegated not only the operating but also to a large extent the strategic responsibility for its businesses to its middle-level general managers, how does it provide strategic leadership? Bower cites two sources of top-management influence in the planning and resource allocation process. One is called "context," described as "the set of organizational forces that influence the processes of definition and impetus."[7] Some of the forces mentioned are structure as well as information, control, and compensation systems. The other source of

---

[6] Norman A. Berg, "What's Different about Conglomerate Management?" *Harvard Business Review*, November–December 1969, p. 116.

[7] Bower, *Managing the Research Allocation Process*, p. 71.

influence is the use of abstract strategic guidance and measurement typically reflected by return on equity or rate of growth objectives.

The significant role of "context" in permitting corporate general management to influence the strategic process in the large divisionalized corporation underlines the close interconnection between strategy and organization as well as the strategic impact of the latter. The corporate general manager influences the strategic decision-making process indirectly through organizational structure and systems.

Such remote control vastly extends his range of influence, but it also removes him from the action. Use of the abstract strategic, financial, or budgetary language does not permit a portrayal of the richness of the actual operating data. Not every corporate general manager feels comfortable in relying exclusively on the abstract results (as communicated by the profit and loss statement) as evidence that actual divisional behavior is congruent with his intentions. To seek more information, however, is to assume more responsibility. Hence, the chief executive may be reluctant to violate his intentions of delegation.

Where corporate goals are primarily economic in nature, remote guidance through structure and systems can be measured relatively accurately and top management will feel comfortable that actual behavior is consistent with corporate policy. The worry here is largely whether the long term suffers by excessive focus on short-term results. However, where corporate goals are not solely economic, their measurement and hence the assurance of their implementation are much harder to determine. The profit and loss statement does not reveal whether divisional management is following corporate directives on equal opportunity employment or pollution control. In fact, the pressures generated by frequent abstract performance measurement may be critical obstacles to the successful implementation of noneconomic directives. Delegating the pursuit of noneconomic goals to divisional management poses an entirely new set of challenges to the chief executive in managing structure and systems.

Managing relationships

Managing managers involves more than the use of structure and systems. Like the middle-level general manager and the corporate staff manager, the chief executive must manage relationships. One set of relationships involves the board of directors as a source of guidance and advice. Does the chief executive seek objective guidance and evaluation or does he prefer a symbolic body to rubberstamp his decisions? Once the board has been committed to a certain course of action, does it retain its objectivity?

The chief executive furthermore must manage relationships with his division managers. The respective roles of corporate and divisional management must be defined. As witnessed by the BCI case, clashes in this connection are not infrequent. It is useful to ask these questions: (1) how does the corporate general manager see his own role; (2) how does the corporate general manager see the division general manager's role; (3) how does the division general manager see his own role; and (4) how does the division general manager see the corporate general manager's role:

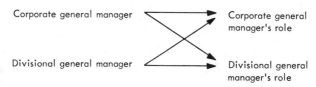

It is not unusual to find drastically different perceptions. Where these differences exist and are not made explicit, they can lead to major conflicts.

Relationships with his corporate staff also have to be managed. Corporate staff managers importantly assist the chief executive. As has already been described, they derive their effectiveness less from the systems and more from the multiple relationships which they manage. The chief executive faces the dilemma that strong support of his corporate staff may harm the latter's relationships with line managers. By putting all his weight behind his corporate staff managers, the chief executive may actually impair their effectiveness. Throwing his power around may be dangerous for his subordinates.

Managing executive selection and development

In managing structure, systems, and relationships the corporate general manager, in the final analysis, must rely on the quality of his managers. Delegation of responsibility requires confidence in subordinates. Furthermore, success in leadership depends not only on the quality of the strategic choices, the organization and its people, but also on the ability of the chief executive to provide for his own succession. Many a prominent leader, whether in business or government, has failed on this score. Executive selection and management development are crucial tasks for the corporate general manager. The corporate and organizational climate are critical elements in attracting managers and helping them to develop. A chief executive must constantly ask: "Why do people want to work for my organization? Why do they want to upgrade their skills?"

16

The transition to general management

Up to now, this text has dealt with both strategic and organizational transition. The general management task was viewed to a large extent within the context of dynamic situations requiring adaptations in terms of corporate strategy and organization. The final chapter focuses on transition from the job point of view: the shift from specialist into general management. It is probably the most critical point in a manager's career. The elements involved in this transition apply primarily to the manager who assumes a new and usually his first general management assignment. However, some of these elements have equal relevance to the experienced general manager.

Major career transition

General managers are usually promoted to this position on the basis of outstanding achievement as functional specialists. Hence, as general managers they operate on a new terrain to which their previous experience is not transferable. This new job represents a major transition. The shift from functional to general management often is considered to be the greatest challenge of a manager's entire career.

Indeed, the skills and activities which led to a functional manager's success—whether in marketing, manufacturing, engineering, R & D, control, or finance—are usually those of specialization, of deep involvement in a narrow area. The specialist knows more and more

129

about less and less. In the medical and legal professions specialization is the usual route to excellence and eminence. The famous doctors and lawyers normally are authorities in special and narrow fields. The manager, too, during the early phases of his career, follows this pattern; he establishes his track record by excelling in a particular specialty. But, unlike the doctor and the lawyer, his career progression pattern is brutally shifted. Having earned his spurs as a specialist, the manager is given a new and drastically different challenge, that of excelling as a generalist. Instead of knowing more and more about less and less, he now shifts to knowing less and less about more and more. Different skills are required and different activities have to be undertaken. His job is not only new in terms of title but also in terms of substance. It represents a major career transition.

This transition, in turn, represents a major risk. The recently promoted general manager puts his track record in jeopardy on new and unfamiliar ground. Previously, each step up the functional specialization ladder led to familiar challenges which required proven skills. Now, the challenges are new and the skills unproven. Not all managers will be able to make this transition; not all will possess the required general management skills. In spite of earlier success, not all will successfully meet the new challenge.

Resentment

In making this major and risky transition, the general manager does not always face a friendly working environment. Rather, his promotion to his new job may cause resentment. Not everybody will see his promotion positively. Some may ask themselves why they did not get the job. They may consider themselves better qualified, because of age or seniority, and they may view the general manager's promotion as undeserved and his capabilities and background as insufficient for the job. Others may resent the promoted individual because he represents an "educated elite."

Yet the general manager needs the cooperation and support of those very people who may resent his appointment. Their cooperation is essential, and he will face constant obstacles until he has it. In overcoming this possible handicap of resentment, administrative skills and experience are of utmost importance. Unfortunately, however, these skills are typically the new general manager's short suit; he is more often long on technical abilities and experience, which are obviously less relevant in coping with resentment. Thus, the skills most needed are often lacking.

Newcomer

Sometimes a new general manager is brought in from the outside, or in the divisional organization he comes from another segment of the organization. As a newcomer, he will probably be unfamiliar with his unit's history, opportunities, and problems. Also, he will have no established relationships and will be dealing with a new set of people.

Obtaining facts or information to diagnose the situation in his new unit will not be easy for the newcomer. First, while the board of directors or corporate management may have assessed the unit's performance in terms of its abstract results, the general manager has to evaluate it in terms of concrete action. The latter is much harder to determine than the former. Second, the new general manager will have to acquaint himself not only with the "formal" organization of his unit but with its "informal" structure as well. While the formal structure can be found in the manuals and organization charts, the informal one has to be discovered through daily activities and interpersonal relationships. Third, "politics" may color the facts. Certain information may be deliberately withheld, while other aspects may be overemphasized. In summary, the newcomer's fact-finding mission is difficult and hazardous and he will be required to sift through information that is often contradictory, tough to evaluate, and not always obvious.

Establishing relationships is no easy task, either. It is a particularly difficult challenge to the manager who is not only undertaking his first general management job but is also possibly resented as a newcomer. Since relationships cannot be ordered from above, the new general manager will have to earn his own way. He will have to gain the confidence and respect of his counterparts not by virtue of the uniform he wears but instead by the quality of his daily activities.

Without essential facts and established relationships it is difficult for a newly appointed general manager to get off to a fast start. Yet, he often walks into a situation which requires quick and decisive action. In such an event, he will have to walk a tightrope between (1) an early commitment based on inadequate facts and nonexisting relationships or (2) indecision while he establishes his facts and relationships. The first course of action is often preferred since it establishes a manager's authority and image. He may also be responding to pressures which are pushing him in this direction. The risks, however, are great. Before he proceeds on such a path, it is worthwhile for him to pause and consider the long-run implications of action that precedes the establishment of facts and relationships. What, for example, are the chances of making major mistakes? While it is often argued that the wrong action is preferable to no action at all, it is important for the new general manager to get off to a good start, not just a fast one. Things that start badly usually get worse.

Experimental leadership

A new general manager often functions as an agent of change. He may have received his assignment in order to bring about changes, or his own ambition may push him to develop new approaches. However, such change may have to be experimental. Obvious solutions may not be available. It may be necessary for him to learn through trial and error. In a divisional organization, the manager's unit may have been chosen as the experimental laboratory for the entire organization.

Experimentation, however, means vulnerability. Since an experiment is easier to defeat than a long-established policy, the forces of resistance may be encouraged to mount opposition, or even sabotage. Where the agent of change is an inexperienced newcomer, it is particularly easy to shift the blame to his shoulders.

Experimental leadership, furthermore, has an inherent weakness, especially for the inexperienced newcomer. It involves using trial and error as well as constant adjusting and testing, rarely permitting one to move ahead at great speed in a single direction. The slow testing and the occasional backtracking, however, may be viewed by subordinates as indecision and defeat. They may interpret experimental leadership as lack of leadership, withholding their respect and support and blaming their leader for inexperience and ignorance. Thus, experimental leadership may be perceived wrongly, especially where the general manager is unknown, inexperienced, and new to the job. Under this handicap it may be difficult for him to generate the necessary support, to obtain the required feedback, and to perform the inevitable education for a new course of action.

In the divisional organization, top management, under these circumstances, may not always come to the rescue. They may be watching rather than supporting the experiment. This is their privilege. From their vantage point, why should they stake their reputations, possibly their careers, on the uncertain outcome of an experiment? Thus, it is often unrealistic to expect rescue from above. More importantly, it is often wise for top management to remain neutral. Experiments are not always sound. Change is not a priori desirable. To judge the soundness and desirability of the experimental change, objective and neutral top management is needed. A neutral superior can act as a mutually acceptable arbiter where conflicts arise, as in situations of limited authority. The middle-level general manager may be better served in the long run by having such a neutral arbiter above him rather than a prejudiced ally. In the latter instance, resistance by others will go "underground," which obviously makes the task of obtaining cooperation and support more difficult. In the former instance, cooperation and support can be obtained through candid and open negotiation. The availability of an objective judge encourages reasonable attitudes by all parties concerned.

Ratification

One important characteristic of the general manager's job is the need to obtain ratification for his actions. He can govern effectively only with the consent of those being governed. If this consent is withheld, it is exceedingly difficult to succeed. While the general manager formally is promoted or demoted by his board of directors or by his superior in the divisionalized organization, the jury usually consists of his subordinates and his peers. By giving or withholding their support, they greatly influence the general manager's career.

This need for ratification is easily overlooked or underestimated by the general manager. He may approach his job with supreme confidence in his own abilities, viewing his new appointment as evidence of his importance and talents. Where change is required, he may see himself as the new leader destined to bring order out of chaos and turn failure into success. At the same time, he may see his subordinates as old-timers who have failed in the past to meet the challenge. Hence, he may doubt their abilities and downgrade their importance. A general manager who approaches his job by overestimating his own importance and underestimating that of his subordinates is erecting a self-imposed barrier to ratification. He is creating the conditions for a self-fulfilling prophecy—with himself as the ultimate victim.

Accommodation and compromise

Another important implication for the general manager is the necessity of finding his way in a maze of accommodation and compromise. He cannot always make quick decisions, take a straightforward course of action, or follow completely rational and logical solutions. The network is too complex, the parties involved are too many, and the interests affected too delicate. There is a constant need for accommodation and compromise to bring what he judges as necessary within the realm of what is possible.

Often, it is difficult to adjust to such a complex challenge. While he may have made his mark as a technical expert whose previous successes were based on purely rational solutions to technical problems, optimization may not be the most successful approach for the new general manager. He may have been the company's efficiency expert: logical, rational, decisive, hardnosed, constantly searching for the "best" answer.

Yet, the French saying, "le mieux est l'ennemi du bien" (the best is the enemy of the good) can be applied to him. Rarely do perfect solutions exist for the general manager. There are viable solutions, however, and they require constant accommodation and compromise.

Job strategy

Given the difficulty and challenge of general management, the job should be approached as explicitly as possible. The general manager must identify the difficulties, challenges, opportunities, and risks. He must be explicit about the organizational structure of which he is part, about the relationships which he has to manage, and about the people to whom he has to relate. In terms of his job, he can identify his total organizational environment. He can match this with his own strengths and weaknesses as well as with his own personal goals and ambitions. Just as companies formulate their corporate strategy by matching their resources to their environment, so can the general manager formulate his own job strategy.

Looking at his job in strategic terms should help the general manager face his varied daily challenges, overcome frustrations, and develop a consistent pattern of behavior. Obviously, a job strategy should be not a ceremonial proclamation but, instead, a plan of action which the general manager "carries in his back pocket" to guide him in his daily actions. A managerial record, like a judicial one, is established through the cumulative impact of a series of decisions, many of which set precedents. If these decisions can be related not only to the specific demands of each separate issue but also to an overall philosophy and master plan, their internal consistency and cumulative impact will establish a strong and cohesive organizational fabric. This is the landmark of an effective and successful manager.

CASES FOR PART I

The general manager as strategist

THE PROCESS OF
CORPORATE STRATEGY

*Arthur Keller**

On MONDAY, March 13, 1967, Mr. Arthur Keller,[1] age 31, MBA 1965, entered the offices of Hedblom in Boxholm, Sweden, for the second time, having just been appointed its new managing director. Mr. Keller had first visited Hedblom, a company making ladies' dresses, in December 1966. As assistant to the president of Wientex A. G. from Vienna, Austria, a textile yarn producer and 50% shareholder in Hedblom, he had been sent to investigate Hedblom's deteriorating sales and profit performance. This investigation had led to bitter negotiations between Wientex and Hedblom's owner manager, who held the other 50% of the stock. As a result, Wientex had assumed full ownership on Friday, March 10. While Mr. Keller had been closely involved in the negotiations, he had not been able to participate in the final stages. He was informed of the acquisition on Sunday, March 12, and was asked to take the first possible plane for Sweden. It was during this trip that Mr. Keller, much to his surprise, was asked by Wientex's president to become Hedblom's managing director, this assignment being his first at the general management level.

Mr. Keller took control of a company which had suffered a severe decline in sales accompanied by mounting losses. (See Exhibits 1 and 2a and 2b for Hedblom's balance sheet since 1965 and its income statement since 1962.)

---

[1] Names and figures have been disguised.

	1964-65	1965-66	1966-67 (6 months)
Sales (Skr million)*	16.2	11.5	4.0
Profit (Skr million)†	(0.06)	(2.3)	(1.7)

*Skr = 19.3 U.S. cents; $1 = Skr 5.17.
†Before depreciation on fixed assets.

The company had been continuously short of cash during the previous 12 to 18 months and on the verge of bankruptcy since the fall of 1966. From the middle of January 1967, its owner manager had given almost exclusive attention to his negotiations with Wientex, thereby neglecting operating decisions, which had been all the more serious given his highly centralized and authoritative leadership style. As a result, morale of the Hedblom managers had suffered greatly, while operations were often near a standstill and important decisions were left unmade. The general feeling of work force and town alike was that Hedblom would soon join the long list of defunct textile firms, a common occurrence in European textile towns like Boxholm during the middle 1960s.

EXHIBIT 1

HEDBLOM
Balance Sheets,* June 1965–March 1967
(in thousands of Swedish kronor)

	6/30/65	6/30/66	3/31/67
Assets			
Cash	236	915	19
Receivables	2,651	3,300	3,757
Inventories.	6,562	4,074	4,302
Net fixed assets	1,834	2,244	3,433
Miscellaneous assets	218	94	99
Total assets	11,501	10,627	11,610
Liabilities			
Payables	5,276	5,187	7,881
Loans	2,926	4,391	5,271
Capital	3,299	1,049	(1,542)
Total liabilities	11,501	10,627	11,610

*These balance sheets represent a consolidation and simplification of the original unaudited balance sheets given to Mr. Keller. Like the original statements from which these figures were derived, the inventory and capital accounts may not reconcile with the corresponding income statements.

On becoming managing director, Mr. Keller knew very little about Hedblom and its managers. While holding its 50% share, Wientex had exercised only a loose financial control, leaving operating decisions entirely to the owner manager. As a result, very little information on Hed-

EXHIBIT 2a

HEDBLOM
Income Statements, 1962–March 1967
(in thousands of Swedish kronor)

	1962	1/1/63 to 6/30/64	7/1/64 to 6/30/65	7/1/65 to 6/30/66	7/1/66 to 3/31/67
Gross sales	10,196	23,739	16,196	11,529	7,723
Sales taxes	8	24	20	26	8
Rebates	301	665	414	321	146
Net sales	9,887	23,050	15,762	11,182	7,569
Cost of sales	6,549	15,251	12,269	9,358	6,061
Materials	3,461	8,203	7,397	5,109	3,028
Wages	1,979	4,435	3,683	3,455	1,882
Payments to subcontractors	902	2,148	912	563	954
Utilities and maintenance	207	465	277	231	197
Gross margin	3,338	7,799	3,493	1,824	1,508
General and administrative costs	383	970	1,063	1,249	1,065
Administrative salaries	611	1,019	732	796	631
Sales commissions	553	1,267	826	853	476
Sales salaries	279	490	340	387	264
Shipping	212	509	318	401	227
Income from operations	1,300	3,544	214	(1,862)	(1,155)
Interest	69	186	285	378	479
Other expenses (income)	(2)	(9)	(6)	11	(14)
Net income	1,233	3,367	(65)	(2,251)	(1,620)
Insurance and pensions	105	127	143	143	107
Depreciation	270	952	288	. . .	588
Bad debts	21	40	31	41	19
Inventory writedowns	208	460	739	202	246
Increase (decrease) in general reserves	335	1,679	(1,281)	(1,844)	. . .
Increase (decrease) in reserve for cyclical fluctuations	135	. . .	. . .	. . .	. . .
Increase (decrease) in pension reserve	. . .	79	5	. . .	. . .
Taxes other than income and sales	140	9	7	1	4
Loss (gain) on sale of property	(1)	(16)	(1)	(1)	(15)
Total income	20	37	4	(791)	(2,569)

Source: Company records.

blom was available at Wientex's headquarters. On Mr. Keller's first trip in December 1966, the owner manager had made only himself and his tight-lipped controller available for discussions. These, plus a quick plant tour, took up the whole four hours of the visit. During the subsequent negotiations, Hedblom's owner manager had formally forbidden his subordinates to maintain any contacts with Wientex, going so far as to stop all yarn purchases. The various managers at Hedblom, furthermore, were left in the dark regarding the negotiations. It was left to Mr. Keller to inform them of Wientex's complete takeover.

EXHIBIT 2b

HEDBLOM
Income Statements as a Percentage of Net Sales

	1962	1/1/63 to 6/30/64	7/1/64 to 6/30/65	7/1/65 to 6/30/66	7/1/66 to 3/31/67
Net sales	100.0	100.0	100.0	100.0	100.0
Cost of sales	66.2	66.2	77.8	83.7	80.1
Materials	35.0	35.6	47.0	45.7	40.0
Wages	20.0	19.3	23.3	30.9	24.9
Payments to subcontractors	9.1	9.3	5.8	5.0	12.6
Utilities and maintenance	2.1	2.0	1.7	2.1	2.6
Gross margin	33.8	33.8	22.2	16.3	19.9
General and administrative costs . . .	3.9	4.2	6.7	11.2	14.1
Administrative salaries	6.2	4.4	4.7	7.1	8.3
Sales commissions	5.6	5.5	5.2	7.6	6.3
Sales salaries	2.8	2.1	2.2	3.5	3.5
Shipping	2.1	2.2	2.0	3.6	3.0
Income from operations	13.2	15.4	1.4	(16.7)	(15.3)
Interest	0.7	0.8	1.8	3.3	6.3
Other expenses (income)	*	*	*	0.1	(0.2)
Net income	12.5	14.6	(0.4)	(20.1)	(21.4)
Insurance and pensions	1.1	0.6	0.9	1.3	1.3
Depreciation	2.7	4.1	1.9	. . .	7.8
Bad debts	0.2	0.2	0.2	0.4	0.2
Inventory writedowns	2.1	2.0	4.7	1.8	3.2
Increase (decrease) in general reserves	3.4	7.3	(8.1)	(16.5)	. . .
Increase (decrease) in cyclical fluctuations	1.4	. . .	. . .	. . .	. . .
Increase (decrease) in pension reserve	. . .	0.3	*	. . .	. . .
Taxes other than income and sales	1.4	*	*	*	0.1
Loss (gain) on sale of property	*	(0.1)	*	*	(0.2)
Total income	0.2	0.2	*	(7.1)	(33.9)

*Less than .05%.

While Mr. Keller knew little about Hedblom, he knew even less about Sweden, which he had first visited during his December trip. He spoke hardly a word of Swedish and had to communicate with Hedblom's managers in English or German. Since the lower echelons and some of the managers were not fluent in these two languages, direct communication was impossible. Also, Mr. Keller was uncertain whether all the managers would be willing to stay. The previous owner manager, who was to withdraw immediately and completely, had asked his entire commercial staff to leave with him. During their first meeting, the commercial manager told Mr. Keller that he would stay for two to three months, since he felt that his immediate departure would be disastrous to the company, but that he was uncertain of his willingness to cooperate in the long run. Finally, Mr. Keller was able to devote only half his time to Hedblom, since he retained his earlier duties in Vienna as assistant to the Wientex president. These had involved him primarily in planning and implementing Wientex's forward integration from spinning and texturizing into knitting, weaving, dyeing, finishing, and, eventually, dressmaking.

In spite of the fact that he did not have any experience or know-how in either knitting or dressmaking, Mr. Keller, immediately after his arrival at Hedblom, was faced with some urgent operating decisions. The most critical was the introduction of the autumn line, which was already three weeks late and which had to be ready within 10 days if the company expected to write any sales for delivery during August and September. Also, before the middle of May, fabric selections were to be made and basic design issues settled for the 1968 spring collection, which would be introduced in early September 1967. The departure a few months earlier of one of the two directresses of design had left Hedblom short in design skills and required the immediate hiring of a new directress. Furthermore, during Mr. Keller's early days at Hedblom a delegation of workers came to him to complain that they lacked sufficient work; that production runs in sewing were too short; that too much sewing work, especially longer runs, was being subcontracted; and that certain working conditions left much to be desired.

It was against this background that Mr. Keller took charge of Hedblom and began to formulate his strategy. This case describes his activities through the end of April 1967, as he was learning about the company and its employees, making the necessary operating decisions, and beginning to develop plans which he hoped would restore Hedblom to profitability. Some basic background is provided on the textile industry, Wientex A.G., and Mr. Keller himself.

TEXTILE INDUSTRY

"If you had told me when I was an MBA student that two years after graduation I would be working in the textile industry, I would have said you were crazy," stated Mr. Keller. "In fact, today when I meet classmates they think I am out of my mind in working for so old-fashioned and traditional an industry as textiles, especially in my field, the dressmaking business, which is called the ragtrade." He continued:

In fact, while the stereotypes of small family-owned companies, no innovation for over 100 years, poor profits, declining sales, fierce competition, and weak management apply to large sectors of this industry and to many companies, there are at the same time plenty of opportunities, a great deal of innovation, and an urgent need to apply modern management techniques. These opportunities and challenges have career implications. Since textile companies are short on management, young and relatively inexperienced people like myself are able to assume major responsibilities early in their careers, witness my job at Hedblom. On the other hand, both tradition and lack of management skills can make for fierce resistance to change, particularly to young newcomers like myself. Thus, we are continuously involved in arguments, and it is not always easy to keep a cool, analytical head amidst the politicking. At Harvard, we fight our battles in the classroom with guys who basically think alike, are the same age, and share similar ambitions. In the textile business, on the other hand, you are pretty much a lone wolf. However, I wouldn't want it any other way. I love the fights, the challenges, and particularly the responsibility. Less than two years after graduation I am sure that, among all my classmates, I have one of the most interesting jobs, permitting the maximum of personal growth. Where would I be two years out of school if I had joined an automobile or chemical company? Also, in my job I have true operating responsibility and I have to live with my decisions. I consider this quite a bit more exciting and challenging than if I had joined a management consulting outfit, going from job to job, certainly seeing and learning plenty of interesting things, but never having to stick my neck out and implement and live with my decisions.

The changes and innovations stressed by Mr. Keller affected all phases of the textile industry, from raw materials to cutting and sewing.

Changes in *raw materials* came through the increasing use and new developments of synthetics, especially acetates, nylon, and polyesters. In contrast to the natural fibers which were sold unbranded by many different producers, synthetic fibers were produced by only a few large chemical companies. These commonly branded their fibers and advertised them heavily. (For example, Dacron was Du Pont's and Terrylene and Crimplene were ICI's brand names for identical polyester fibers.) As a result, producers of synthetic fibers were in a much more powerful position vis-à-vis their customers than the suppliers of natural fiber. In fact, they were so powerful as to pose a threat of forward integration. Also, in terms of management, synthetic fiber producers were both sophisticated and powerful.

The traditional process in *yarn manufacturing* was spinning, whereby the fibers were given both the necessary length and thickness. In this complicated seven-stage process, both natural and synthetic fibers could be used. Synthetic fibers, however, permitted a new process called texturizing, which allowed yarn manufacturing to be done on faster machines and in one single operation, hence resulting in lower costs. During the early and middle 1960s, the entire growth of yarn manufacturing capacity was in texturizing. This expansion, in turn, resulted in severe competitive pressures for traditional spinners. Shortages in texturizing capacity had prevailed until the late 1960s, by which time continuous entry was creating a threat of excess capacity. The heavy capital requirements for texturizing and the rapid growth of this segment made manufacturers particularly vulnerable to forward integration by the large synthetic fiber producers. This threat led the yarn manufacturers to contemplate forward integration into fabric manufacturing as a step for reducing their vulnerability.

The traditional dominant process for *fabric manufacture* was weaving, a complicated and costly process which required four or five steps. Recently, the development of stronger and more standardized synthetic fibers had vastly broadened the application of the knitting process. Subsequent improvements in circular knitting machines (called Jacquards) by a handful of leading German machine manufacturers permitted the production of knitted goods which looked to the consumer identical to woven fabrics. These new machines allowed enormous flexibility in creating patterns. Knitting, a one-step operation, was also more economical than weaving. Hence, expansion of knitting capacity was rapid, being largely a function of the ability of the knitting machine manufacturers to deliver.

Traditionally, *finished clothes* were manufactured by large numbers of small companies (usually consisting of the family and few employees), by tailors, or by people at home. With the increased popularity of printed media and the changes in retail and mail-order distribution, larger and larger units began to supply finished clothes. These were often sold under a brand name which, in turn, was supported through advertising and promotion. Thus, the structure of the clothing manufacturing industries was changing from many small companies selling unbranded goods to fewer but larger companies selling branded goods. This development opened the opportunity for fabric manufacturers to integrate forward into finished clothes.

The combination of all these changes had revolutionary implications. The greater simplicity of the texturizing and knitting processes more than offset the higher cost of the raw materials. At the same time, improved styling possibilities plus, most importantly, new wash-and-wear characteristics endowed clothing made in the new way with greater consumer appeal, even without the benefit of a favorable price differential.

Besides changes in materials and processes, the textile industry was undergoing changes in its structure. On these Mr. Keller commented as follows:

One of the most interesting aspects of the textile business is that at the beginning of the vertical product flow we have the large, sophisticated, and professionally managed synthetic fiber producers like Du Pont or ICI, while at the end we have equally powerful and sophisticated large retailers like Sears and Macy's in the United States or Domus, Åhléns (Tempo), and Turitz (Epa) in Sweden. The Swedish retail chains are growing rapidly, accounting yearly for increasing segments of retail textile sales, having increased their market share from below 10% in the late 1950s to about 45% in 1967. In between, however, we have much smaller, and often poorly managed, companies.

Different phases of the textile industry had quite different characteristics. At the beginning of the vertical product flow, long life cycles for products and especially for capital equipment were required, while fashion imposed a very short life span on the end product. Synthetic fiber manufacture was highly capital-intensive, but also fabric manufacture required costly knitting machines. Moreover, it took production personnel about one year to familiarize themselves with these machines. In contrast, fabrics themselves had an 18-month life cycle (even shorter if subject to fashion), and dress fashions changed every six months.

The vertical product flow also made for long lead times, especially during the earlier steps. To be bought in the store in April–May, a spring dress had to be shipped during February–March, produced during October–January, and introduced to the trade during early September. Fabrics had to have been designed by early May of the previous year, or 12 months before the final purchase. Yarns used for the fabrics, if dyed, had to be presented six months earlier still. These lead times, combined with the inherent fashion risks, made timing critical: early production could result in gambling on the wrong yarns, fabrics, or dresses with the risk of severe inventory losses, while delays in manufacturing commitments could result in the producer's inability to deliver on time, usually resulting in cancellations given the short fashion life of the product.

As already indicated, forward and backward integration were constant possibilities in the textile industry. In the United States, large firms such as Burlington or Stevens had combined yarn and fabric manufacture but had not integrated forward into end products, such as dresses and suits. The situation in the United Kingdom was similar to that in the United States. On the Continent the industry had not integrated vertically, and separate companies usually limited their activities to one single step in the product flow. Industry observers, however, wondered whether increased vertical integration, especially among the larger and more dynamic firms, would not just be a matter of time.

WIENTEX A. G.

Wientex A. G. was one of the leading yarn producers in Europe with manufacturing facilities in two countries belonging to the European Common Market[2] and two belonging to the European Free Trade Asso-

---

[2] European Economic Community (EEC), commonly referred to as European Common Market, comprised France, West Germany, Italy, and the three Benelux countries.

ciation.[3] Traditionally, Wientex had produced yarn by spinning, but with the advent of synthetic fibers it had started to use the texturizing process as well. While its spinning activities had been subject to fierce competition during the 1960s, its texturizing sales had grown rapidly and profitably, benefiting from the prevailing shortages of texturized yarn.

During December 1964, Wientex had purchased 50% of Hedblom, a Swedish knitter and dressmaker as well as the pioneer in Scandinavia of dresses made from the new synthetic fabrics. The reasons for the interest in Hedblom were (1) to acquire fabric and dress manufacture expertise which might pioneer new uses of Wientex's texturized yarns and thereby assist its sales efforts to other yarn customers, and (2) to secure a stable outlet for its yarns. Wientex management decided to leave most operating decisions with Hedblom's owner manager on the premise that (1) Wientex knew nothing about dressmaking and little about knitting, and (2) Hedblom's owner manager had proven highly competent and successful.

ARTHUR KELLER

Arthur Keller had been graduated in 1959 as Diplom Ingenieur (Master of Engineering) from Vienna University, where he had specialized in civil engineering. Upon graduation he joined the production division of Chrysler International in Geneva, and had worked largely on setting up new assembly plants in developing countries. Mr. Keller commented on his Chrysler experience as follows:

After one and one-half years as a trainee, doing everything and nothing and meeting a lot of people, I was one day put on a plane to Pakistan and had to assist our truck distributor in setting up a very small, very inexpensive assembly plant for trucks. I was in a foreign culture, with different values, away from home, and alone with no staff, no tools, no connections, and only 18th century materials and techniques to set up a 20th century plant. These factors quickly made me rely on common sense, gave me experience in adaptability, and taught me to take risks and responsibility. Similar assignments in the Philippines and Turkey contributed greatly to my personal growth before my business school training.

Married in 1962, Mr. Keller left Chrysler in 1963 to enter the MBA program at the Harvard Business School. After his MBA graduation, he joined a leading U.S. textile firm as assistant to the executive vice president. Here he worked on various short-run projects: investment policies and guidelines for the international division in Europe; market investigations for European textiles in the United States; and negotia-

---

[3] European Free Trade Association (EFTA) comprised the United Kingdom, the Scandinavian countries, Austria, Switzerland, and Portugal.

tions and investigations for plant sites in Europe. It was planned that after one to two years Mr. Keller would join this company's Austrian operation. For a variety of reasons this did not materialize, and in the fall of 1966 Mr. Keller was offered higher pay but a less exciting job. At the same time he met the president of Wientex. A job offer resulted, and Mr. Keller decided to accept. Looking back on his 17 months at the U.S. textile company, Mr. Keller reflected:

It was a very frustrating but useful experience. In one way, I didn't have responsibility and couldn't push anything myself. On the other hand, I gained tremendous experience and insight into the working relationships of top management and division management in a large corporation and what each one could and was supposed to do.

At Wientex in Vienna Mr. Keller assumed his duties on November 15, 1966, as assistant to the president. While initially assisting on regular daily activities, Mr. Keller's main responsibility soon crystallized around the issue of vertical integration: Should Wientex, as a yarn producer, integrate forward, and, if so, how should this policy be implemented? This responsibility resulted in his first visit to Hedblom in December 1966. Early that month Hedblom's balance sheet for June 30, 1966, had arrived, along with its income statement for the 1965–66 fiscal year. These statements indicated severe losses and a serious sales decline. Mr. Keller reviewed the previous financial statements and learned that control by Vienna had largely taken the form of social visits, given Wientex's policy of operating freedom for Hedblom. Once a young man from the controller's department had asked some highly pertinent questions, but this had resulted in a stormy protest to the Wientex board by the Hedblom owner manager, who forbade the young man ever to set foot in the Boxholm office again. After this high-level protest, younger staff members and even upper management from Vienna refrained from further investigation.

Mr. Keller described his own initiation into Hedblom, which occurred on his December 1966 visit. Arriving at the Stockholm airport at 8:00 A.M., he was met by the Hedblom chauffeur and driven the 150 miles to Boxholm in the company Rolls-Royce. On arrival, he was ushered into the owner manager's office where the following exchange took place:

KELLER: Good morning. Are you Mr. Hedblom?
OWNER MANAGER: Who the hell else would you expect to see here!

Afterwards, Mr. Keller commented on this incident as follows:

The owner manager's initial reaction was an outburst against management in Vienna, which, in his words, had really affronted him by hiring me for the verticalization strategy of the company. Afterwards, I did not see or learn anything. My plant tour lasted one-half hour without any figures, details, or questions answered.

Mr. Keller left with the suspicion that the situation at Hedblom had further and seriously deteriorated. On requesting the quarterly financial statements for September 30, he was told that they were not yet completed.

On his return to Vienna, Mr. Keller resumed his analysis of the available financial statements. Making projections, he predicted to the Wientex president that, on top of the already generous supplier credit given by Wientex, Hedblom would require Skr 1.5 million in fresh funds by January of 1967, or else face bankruptcy. His analysis met with disbelief in Vienna and was shrugged off with the comment that "things couldn't be that bad." However, on January 23, 1967, the December 31 quarterly financial statements arrived, together with a request for Skr 1.5 million in new funds. At that point, Wientex top management decided to move. Mr. Keller suggested that a Swedish lawyer be hired to assist in negotiations to assume complete ownership of Hedblom. His suggestion was accepted, and he went to Sweden. Several weeks of tough high-level negotiations ensued, resulting in the changes described at the beginning of this case.

HEDBLOM

During his early weeks at Hedblom, Mr. Keller tried to learn about the company's history as well as the reasons for its successes and its recent failures. The following picture emerged: Hedblom had been founded in the 1880s as a wholesaling firm and had entered the knitting industry in 1919, when control passed to the second generation of owner managers. For the next 30 years, Hedblom specialized largely in warm knitted underwear, becoming one of the leading brands in Sweden. Large military orders during the war years led to very substantial profits. The line was expanded to include some knitted dresses and sweaters. These, too, were made from Hedblom's own fabrics, none of which were sold on a merchant basis.

In 1948 the next generation took over, and Hedblom's new owner manager was more interested in running a ladies' dress company than in spending his efforts on underwear. Thus he somewhat changed the company's emphasis, while retaining the same product line. This personal inclination was justified by subsequent changes in competition and customer requirements. The underwear market collapsed during the early 1950s as a result of (1) cheap foreign imports, (2) domestic excess capacity, and (3) fewer and different customer demands as houses were better heated and military orders disappeared. Hedblom responded by dropping its underwear line and by concentrating on ladies' dresses and sweaters. Its knitting capacity was used first for wool dresses and subsequently for mixed fabrics (such as 60% wool and 40% rayon). Hedblom dresses and two-piece suits were largely made of jersey. Jersey was the standard word in Europe for knitted fabrics with simple stitch, which could be used during three to four seasons. This heavy use of jersey reduced manufacturing and inventory problems.

The company's dresses derived their distinctive features from special trimmings, made on its flat knitting machines which had originally been purchased for its sweater line. With most competitors making dresses only and buying their fabrics, and with fabric suppliers not having these special machines and therefore not supplying trimmings, Hedblom acquired a unique position on the market. Competitors found it impossible to copy its models. Also, jersey materials were in short supply at that time. Thus, Hedblom during the late 1950s and early 1960s was able to base its strategy on (1) the advantage of having its dresses largely consist of standard jersey, which was not subject to fashion changes, and for which it had ample capacity while merchant supplies were insufficient; and (2) the advantage of giving its dresses distinctive features through trimmings which could not be copied by most competitors (only a few of whom had their own flat knitting machines). During these years, Hedblom began to support its brand name with modest press advertising.

The next major change started with the arrival of the Wientex salesman who attempted to interest the company in the brand-new texturized polyester yarns sold under the Crimplene brand. His major selling tool was a generous advertising allowance, the traditional approach of the synthetic fiber companies. Hedblom was willing to experiment and became the first company in Scandinavia to knit Crimplene yarn. Later, the commercial manager commented:

> Our technical expert was curious and interested, but the owner manager did not believe in it. Without the advertising allowance he probably would never have tried. We made some 2,000 Crimplene dresses in late 1962 and sold them as a specialty at the Göteborg dress fair. Our spring collection for 1963 was still entirely based on the traditional fabrics. During the early months of 1963, I got lots of calls from customers for those dresses they had bought at Göteborg with a name starting with "C." This is unheard of in the dress business. It happens once in your lifetime that customers spontaneously ask for things. As a result, when we were planning an interim collection between the spring 1963 and autumn 1963 collections, I suggested that it consist of Crimplene dresses. We sold 20,000 of them, which at that time was unbelievably high for an interim collection. We had struck gold. We were the first and only ones with a new product which had unique features in that it could be put in the washing machine and required no ironing.

As a result, Hedblom's sales increased rapidly, based on jersey and Crimplene dresses and also on sweaters. The company had become one of the largest dressmakers in Scandinavia. The commercial manager stated:

Hedblom alone was able to advertise Crimplene on a big scale and for several seasons. As introducer of Crimplene we got priority on the yarn quantities. Fabric manufacturers could not always execute the orders for Crimplene because of lack of yarn. The typical comment of the trade during these 1963 and 1964 years was, "Better a late delivery from Hedblom than no delivery at all." However, by 1965 times had changed. First of all, Hedblom was forced to drop the sweater line because of Italian and especially Far Eastern competition. Secondly, switches in fashion finally caught up with the jersey-trimmings combination, aggravated by the fact that Crimplene materials had replaced the wool or half-wool jerseys. Thirdly, Crimplene-based fabrics caught up with demand, and more and more Swedish dressmakers included Crimplene dresses in their collections. Both fabrics and dresses were predominantly of the cheaper variety. Also, cheap U.K. Crimplene dresses began to be sold aggressively in Scandinavia. These three changes reduced Hedblom's product line to Crimplene dresses only, which, in turn, were subject to increasing competition. It was just before these changes occurred that Wientex acquired its 50% share in Hedblom.

In spite of increased competition and a smaller product line, Hedblom remained late with its deliveries. But, whereas before we got away with it, the tolerance of our customers weakened as other supplies became available. Thus' orders dropped, or were canceled when deliveries were late, or goods delivered late were returned. While our customers do not have a return privilege for goods which they can't sell, they are able to return merchandise which arrives after the promised date. Faced with stiffer competition, Hedblom increased its advertising expenditures and the number of models in its line. Of course, the latter move further aggravated our delivery problem. Our problem in not getting the goods out of the door on time also made for higher shipping costs: single dress shipments increased at the expense of bulk shipments because orders for a single customer could not be accumulated.

As to the reasons for the late deliveries, Mr. Keller learned that (1) the owner manager had the final say in all design decisions and often procrastinated, thus making Hedblom collections late; (2) fabric and dress manufacturing commitments were usually delayed until orders on the already late collection had been placed, resulting in production bottlenecks; and (3) manufacturing was the Cinderella in terms of top-executive attention, which went almost exclusively to merchandising. As a result, manufacturing considerations were ignored in style decisions; production scheduling was given low priority, resulting in hand-to-mouth operations; and expenditure and investment requests by manufacturing were often acted on only after considerable delays, if at all.

Losses started in 1965. They were aggravated in 1966 when the owner manager rented a brand new factory in Boxholm at the beginning of the year, into which he moved manufacturing during July. This building was located about a five-minute walk from the office building where the managing director, commercial manager, and controller were located, along with their respective departments. Until July 1966, production operations had been conducted in Sandvik, a small village about eight miles from Boxholm, where Hedblom had been one of the two employers. The move from Sandvik resulted from a disagreement between the owner manager and the town fathers concerning the extent of town support for the planned plant expansion.

After July 1966, the Sandvik plant stood idle, housing some obsolete machinery and inventory. Mr. Keller learned that this plant, while not modern, was still in decent shape and could possibly command a sales price of Skr 500,000. The Boxholm plant, in turn, had a maximum capacity of about 1.0 to 1.2 million meters of fabrics and between 500,000 and 600,000 dresses. At the average sales price of Skr 80 per dress, the plant could support a sales volume of over Skr 40 million. Yet several production executives, who had never been consulted concerning the move, commented that the plant was not ideal for fabric manufacturing. After the move, the owner manager threw out all the old piece rates and hired a consulting engineer to establish a new set. By March 1967, however, little progress had been made in this direction. The consulting engineer, hired at an annual expense of Skr 400,000, had also been charged with the installation of an IBM punch-card system for production scheduling and with the development of automatic materials handling systems.

Of great interest to Mr. Keller was the leadership style of his predecessor, whom he had only been able to observe across the bargaining table as a brilliant negotiator. The former owner manager was described as extremely authoritarian. Even the smallest detail required his approval. As the company grew in size and complexity, difficulties and delays resulted, according to several managers. Said one of them, "He wanted to hold everything in his hand, but his hand was getting too small." Delays were also caused by the owner manager's reluctance to make quick decisions; most issues were tossed back and forth before being decided. The implications of these delays in bringing out the collections (often as much as two months late) and for production have already been mentioned, as well as the owner manager's almost exclusive focus on merchandising and his neglect of manufacturing. Another factor mentioned was his great reliance on outside help: for example, the use of the consulting engineer in manufacturing and the use of an expensive Paris designer. Expense was never a hurdle, from the use of outside help to the company Rolls-Royce. In fact, the owner manager was described as quite a showman who had an impulsive tendency to be Number One wherever he went and to dominate his environment. Also, his working hours were unconventional, and he often kept his managers in the office far into the night, regardless of their prior social commitments. One manager commented:

Time had no meaning for him; life seemed a continuous improvisation, sometimes brilliant, sometimes less so, but never did we get the feeling that he went by a specific timetable. I think he considered himself to be an artist; aesthetics came first, and in fact his primary devotion went not to the business but to his private art collection.

Some incidents during the early weeks of Mr. Keller's management provided further indications on how Hedblom had been managed. Around the middle of April, Mr. Keller saw one of his top managers near the time clock. The following discussion followed:

KELLER: Are you checking the time-clock cards?
MANAGER: No, I am punching my own card.
KELLER: What do you mean, punching your own card?
MANAGER: Didn't you know that all of us here from the top down use the time clock?

During his first day, Mr. Keller found all the company's mail on his desk. Asking one of his managers why it had not been distributed, he was told, "But sir, the previous owner manager used to open and distribute the mail himself." Later that day Mr. Keller received the company checkbook with several checks made out but not signed. Again, he was told that the top executive himself signed all the checks. Likewise, all incoming orders passed Mr. Keller's desk before going to the sales department. Every day, he received a tabulation of orders from his secretary with the explanation that this, too, was company tradition. At the end of the month, Mr. Keller added these daily sheets and was shocked to find the figure so low. Immediately he called in the commercial manager and was told that his tabulation was incomplete since many orders came in by telephone and that these had never been included in the daily tabulation. If he wanted to know total orders for the month, he would have to ask the sales department.

Manufacturing operations

One of the first tasks Mr. Keller set himself was to learn in detail about the company's manufacturing operations. These can be described by following the product flow through the factory.

The basement of the plant housed storage facilities for yarn. About 70% of this was white 150-denier Crimplene polyester supplied by Wientex for which Hedblom paid the same price as other Wientex customers. The remaining yarns covered a wide variety: they might be made of different materials (such as wool, Dacron-wool, or rayon-wool mixtures), or they might be colored. Dyed yarn was about 30% more expensive than white and was subject to fashion obsolescence. Obsolete dyed yarn commanded only about one third of the original price because the only way to use it was to knit it into fabrics which would be dyed darker.

The yarn moved by elevator to the first-floor knitting department. Producing entirely for in-house use, this department employed 20 men, all of them highly skilled in setting up machines and supervising operations. In spite of the sophisticated technology of the equipment, running the machines was still very much a craft. Up to 48 yarns were knitted simultaneously, and if only òne broke the entire machine would stop. Errors or unevenness in the fabrics were not uncommon and would sometimes show up only after dyeing. As a result, constant and careful supervision was essential to ensure that faults be caught before too much yarn had been wasted. Because of the skill required, knitting machine operators were in short supply, even in a textile town like Boxholm which otherwise had a large labor surplus. As a result Hedblom had retained the skilled knitting operators and other scarce skilled workers from its Sandvik plant, and a special company bus shuttled the men back and forth between their homes in Sandvik and the plant in Boxholm.

In March 1967, the knitting department contained 59 machines: 36 flat knitting, 21 interlock, and 2 old Jacquard. Machines differed in terms of width of cloth produced, gauge of yarn handled, speed (with the Jacquards able to produce the widest variety of patterns). Annual capacity[4] on a three-shift basis amounted to 1.1 tons (or 3,300 meters) for a flat knitting and to 14 tons (or 42,000 meters) for an interlock or old Jacquard machine. Originally, the flat knits had been used for sweaters. Being obsolete for this purpose in 1967, they were used for knitted trimmings which could not be made on the circular interlock and Jacquard machines. To meet demand at 1967 levels, Hedblom needed on a one-shift basis only 8 to 12 flat knitting machines and 14 to 16 interlocks and old Jacquards.

Besides the existing machines, 10 new 24 "systems" (or sets of needles) Jacquards had been ordered by the previous management for delivery in June 1967 at a cost of Skr 100,000 each. Mr. Keller learned that these new machines were anxiously awaited and were expected to provide a significant competitive advantage through ability to knit special fabric designs that could not be handled on interlock machines.

---

[4] If continuously operated, machine capacity would be higher. The above figures take into account estimated downtime for setups and maintenance or because of breakdowns and also include use of machines in trying out new fabric designs.

Their annual three-shift capacity amounted to 10 tons of fabric per year, or 30,000 meters.

After knitting, fabrics not made of colored yarn were sent out for dyeing unless they were intended to remain white. Although dyeing accounted for a large share of production costs and although it could create a competitive advantage, it was subcontracted on the grounds that Hedblom did not produce enough fabrics to justify the large investment in dye facilities. Two weeks were typically required for fabrics to be dyed, to which one week of transit time had to be added.

The dyed fabrics were returned to Hedblom's third-floor cutting department, which comprised 10 men and 15 women. On a large table, 10 meters long by 2 meters wide, about 40 layers of fabric were laid out by a special machine. The pattern girl would then arrange the dress patterns, trying to cover as much cloth as possible. Subsequently, a net would be placed over the patterns and the whole would be sprayed with light red paint. The cloth covered with the patterns would be shielded, while the cloth painted red would have to be discarded. Arranging the patterns was a highly skilled and most crucial operation, since up to 20%–25% of the fabric could be lost in the cutting process. Also, defects in the fabric, about which the pattern girls complained frequently, made it even more difficult to achieve an efficient arrangement. With the red paint indicating how the cloth was to be cut, the actual cutting was done in two steps: rough cutting on the table, and finer cutting on special machines. The cut pieces were then assembled in batches to be sent to sewing.

Sewing employed 70 people, all women, and was located on the second floor. Operations were conducted pretty much the same way as around the turn of the century. There were two lines of 62 machines, with a conveyor line supplying and taking away boxes of dress parts. A lady dispatched these boxes, attempting to maximize long production runs.

On the same floor, 10 people in the pressing department prepared the dresses for shipping. Employing eight people, shipping was located on the ground floor. According to industry practice Hedblom assumed all freight costs to the customer. Hence it was important to accumulate all dresses ordered by a single account to permit cost-saving bulk shipments. Since shipping was viewed as part of customer relations, it reported to the commercial manager. Also reporting to this department was a third-floor unit where 15 people under a directress prepared dress patterns and produced sample dresses on a hand-cut, machine-sewn basis.

The top floor of the building stood empty. On seeing this floor, Mr. Keller inquired about converting part of it to offices and using the rest for storage. Estimates indicated that this would cost Skr 300,000 for fixed installations and Skr 100,000 for furniture. Mr. Keller also learned that Hedblom held a long-term lease on the office building which could not be canceled until 1972. Thus a possible move would not save any rent, since renegotiation of the lease appeared highly unlikely given the fact that several office buildings in Boxholm stood empty.

Marketing operations

By March 1967 Hedblom specialized in ladies' dresses and two-piece suits, mostly but not entirely using Crimplene-based fabrics. Typically, a spring and autumn collection was presented, with a limited number of models. Hedblom catered largely to the 25- to 30-year age group, its price range being too high for younger customers. Dresses were sold on the basis of an image of atmosphere and quality. The line always included some high-fashion models, which were emphasized in Hedblom advertising, even though the bulk of sales occurred in the traditional models. Hedblom had also acquired a reputation for certain patterns, especially those using trimmings which it had been able to emphasize because of its flat knitting machines. All dresses were sold under the Hedblom brand except for end-of-season closeouts, which were sold unbranded.

Factory prices of Hedblom dresses averaged Skr 80 and ranged from Skr 50 to Skr 204. With retail markups amounting to 90% to 100% (sometimes 100% to 110% in Stockholm), retail prices averaged Skr 150 with a range of Skr 98 to Skr 395. Hedblom stamped its price on the label but did not enforce retail price maintenance. Because of its reputation, Hedblom commanded a 10% to 15% price premium for its dresses which were the only well-known branded ones in its price range. Most dresses in Sweden retailed for under Skr 100, although one other well-known brand retailed between Skr 300 and Skr 400. Competition came primarily from unbranded dresses made by small producers who purchased their fabrics. Entry of these firms into the industry was easy and high, as was their mortality rate. These companies always found it possible to pick up sales, especially with their low prices. Low-price imports, especially from the United Kingdom, also posed a competitive threat. Hedblom did not have data on the size of the Swedish dress market nor a breakdown in terms of prices and channels.

Hedblom followed a selective distribution policy, attempting to sell through the best dress retailer in town. Especially in the larger towns this exclusive policy was not pursued rigidly; however, Hedblom did not sell to the large department store chains or other mass merchandising outlets such as mail-order houses. The reasoning was that Hedblom's high price required a great deal of sales push, on which the company could not count in mass distribution channels. In department stores, also, a Skr 100 retail price was a limit which store buyers were reluctant to exceed. Hedblom had about 250 accounts in Sweden, of which 30 were in Stockholm. Five salesmen, of whom one took care of Stockholm alone, covered these accounts. They were paid a base salary and a 1% commission on sales. They placed their main sales emphasis on the introduction of the spring and autumn collections which they showed with mannequins to their customers in local hotels. They averaged about two to three customers a day when showing the collection.

Advertising was largely placed in local newspapers, often on a co-operative basis with Hedblom's better customers. Hedblom did not devote a fixed percentage of sales to advertising, the amount rather being a function of the advertising support received from the synthetic fiber companies. Expenditures in 1966 had amounted to Skr 400,000. In addition to its press advertising, Hedblom participated in fashion shows such as the Scandinavian Fashion Week in Copenhagen. Furthermore, the company employed a public relations adviser, a Mrs. Westman from Stockholm, who had been most successful in providing free publicity for Hedblom in newspaper accounts on fashions. In April 1967 Mr. Keller was faced with the decision on whether to spend Skr 40,000 as Hedblom's share of expenses for a trip by Mrs. Westman to South America, during which she would get the Hedblom collection photographed and write travel accounts which would provide the company with free publicity in the Swedish press as well as photographs of its collection in a unique setting.

Exports accounted for 20% of Hedblom's sales, with the bulk going to Denmark and Norway where the line was sold through independent agents who took a 10% commission. Advertising in export markets was paid for by Hedblom and amounted to Skr 50,000 in 1966. Hedblom also had sales offices in Germany and Switzerland. In Germany, which was not a member of EFTA, dresses paid an import duty of 30%. In Denmark, Norway, and Switzerland, which were members of EFTA, no import duties were levied. Freight costs to foreign markets were 30% to 40% higher than for domestic sales, but still only about 1% to 1½% of the cost of dresses.

Design was done in-house under a directress. The company also used the services of a Paris dress designer. Dress design involved travel by the directresses to gather inspiration for the models. Hedblom pretty much followed prevailing trends, and hence fashion risks were not very high. Timing in introducing dresses was critical, and it was just as dangerous—according to the commercial manager—to come out with some model too early, before the trend would catch on, as too late. Also, he indicated the need to synchronize design and selling to permit continuous feedback from the marketplace and quick responses to new market trends.

Control and planning system

It was the absence rather than the existence of a control and planning system which struck Mr. Keller during his early investigations. The company lacked budgets, a standard cost system, and inventory control. Mr. Keller found no records to measure the efficiency and output of knitting, cutting, sewing, pressing, and shipments. He found only what he considered to be a complicated, unusable production report. Mr. Keller received two daily reports: the one on incoming orders has already been described; the other was a daily report on bank balances. A balance sheet and income statement was prepared yearly, but was ready only several weeks, if not months, after the closing date. At Wientex's request, some quarterly statements had been prepared in the past. Mr. Keller also noticed that all communications were centralized via the top executive. Managers did not have an information system to keep one another posted on important current events. Also, no system of copies of important letters or memos existed. In fact, the company had no memo forms.

Departments and their managers

During his first weeks on the job, Mr. Keller tried to learn as much as possible about the company managers, operations, and problems. Talks on these aspects started the very first day, and from these and subsequent discussions he was able to construct the following picture.

The organization structure under the previous owner manager had five managers (in charge of control, purchasing, production, fabric design, and commercial) reporting to him as well as two directresses (in charge of dress designs). Mr. Jansson, age 44, had been controller since 1956. He had joined the company in 1950 and had previously held positions in the bookkeeping department. Mr. Keller recognized that for him the adjustment might be the most difficult. He had assisted the former owner manager during the negotiations with Wientex and hence had faced his new boss across the negotiating table. He had been the owner manager's confidant (his salary had been raised by 50% after Wientex took its 50% interest) and was the only manager who knew about the serious sales decline and disastrous losses. (The commercial manager, of course, knew the former and suspected the latter, but the other managers had no idea that the company situation was so grave.) Mr. Jansson's duties under the previous management had been confined to bookkeeping and his department had not been asked to provide the top executive with management control and planning reports. Hence Mr. Jansson had no expertise in these areas.

Purchasing was managed by Mr. Nilsson, age 40, who had joined Hedblom in 1948 as clerk and was promoted to his present position in 1952. Mr. Keller learned that Hedblom bought practically all its yarn from Wientex, particularly in recent months when supplier credit had become increasingly important. Mr. Nilsson's main problem was that, because of the late presentation of the Hedblom collections, he was forced to purchase on a hand-to-mouth basis. Also, he indicated that the company had a large excess inventory of fabrics and dresses, part of it three to four years old. This was not currently used and probably only worth one third of its book value of Skr 4.0 to Skr 4.5 million. Not counting the excess supplies, Mr. Nilsson estimated that Hedblom had supplies for about 10 to 12 weeks in storage. These supplies tied up about Skr 2.0 million at current output levels.

Production was managed by Mr. Lanner, age 40, who had joined the company as a time-study man in 1955. He took on his present job during the move in 1966. His main problem in the past had been the lack of attention to production and its subordination to the company's commercial activities. For example, the owner manager had only once set foot in the plant during the previous two months. Mr. Lanner also indicated that manufacturing was forced to operate in high gear when the collections were to be delivered, while operations were nearing a standstill during the intermediate periods. Also, special orders by sales frequently made long runs difficult. He stated that in terms of authority he had been subordinated to the consulting engineer. Also, because the lack of piece rates had resulted in maintaining people's previous Sandvik salaries, the decline in volume meant they were being overpaid. Furthermore, without piece-rate schedules, lower costs could not be realized by making layout or procedure more efficient. Mr. Lanner also stated that, much to his chagrin, the previous owner manager had unilaterally discarded the previous piece-rate schedule.

Production scheduling was managed by Mr. Carlsson, age 46, who had joined the company in 1956. On arrival at Hedblom, Mr. Keller did not know about Mr. Carlsson since he was not listed among the top managers. Toward the end of his first day, Mr. Keller was told by one of the managers that he might want to talk to Mr. Carlsson, who reported to both the manufacturing and commercial managers but who was described as one of the key men in plant operations. Mr. Carlsson mentioned the same problems as his purchasing and production colleagues. He had found it exceedingly difficult to do any forward planning, instead having to operate on a day-to-day basis. Particularly since the previous owner manager was unwilling to make advance fabric commitments (that is, to knit fabrics for certain dresses before orders had come in), production bottlenecks were inevitable. He also stressed the difficulties resulting from a complete lack of standardization, which made it necessary to juggle an excessive number of fabrics, dress models, and dress sizes. Finally, he questioned the appropriateness of the punch-card system which was being installed by the consulting engineer, stating that it was a standard system which the same man had installed for fabric companies but that it was inappropriate for a company making dresses. Also, he indicated that the system was overly complicated and that prior to its installation, planning and record keeping were done by hand.

The consulting engineer, age 60, was highly respected and well known in Boxholm. He was a specialist in the textile industry with wide connections. During their first meeting, the consulting engineer called Mr. Keller by his first name, and added:

> I am an engineer like you, and surely you will appreciate my services and help. Mr. Hedblom previously gave me a free hand to make this the most automated, most modern textile company. I would like to continue this way, particularly having the production manager remaining my subordinate.

Mr. Sundman, age 58, who had joined Hedblom in 1931, was in charge of fabric design. He was recognized as an authority on knitting, and his expertise had in large part been responsible for Hedblom's strong fabric position. He also made the comments already described concerning the company's manufacturing problems. Mr. Sundman had one assistant and shared the knitting foreman with manufacturing in order to experiment with fabric designs. He also cooperated closely with the directresses in developing new fabric designs in tune with dress fashions.

Mr. Filipsson, age 42, had been commercial manager since 1963, having joined the company in 1955. He reiterated the great influence which the previous owner manager exercised over style decisions. He also voiced the opinion that with its two basic collections and its current product, price, and distribution policies, Hedblom would be able to sell at most 125,000 dresses a year, allowing sales of about Skr 10 million. He indicated that the desire of the manufacturing department for fewer models within the present assortment was impossible. Rather, Hedblom should have a wider range of models, especially if the bulk of sales were to be made in Scandinavia with only marginal sales elsewhere. His customers preferred to buy less in primary orders at collection time and more articles with short delivery times during the season. This pressure gave a competitive advantage to the flexible manufacturer. He explained that this trend stemmed from the reluctance of the dress stores to make large, firm commitments at the time collections were presented, or six months ahead of actual sales. The commercial manager finally expressed his disappointment on a recent experience with the most fashionable Swedish department store chain; it had placed a modest order for Hedblom dresses but had not reordered. He commented:

> They simply used our dresses for the prestige and in their show windows and advertising, but they continued selling the cheaper dresses. It proves

that department stores are only interested in the below Skr 100 range and are unable to sell the more expensive merchandise like ours. Also, this experience was with our high-class department store chain. I wouldn't even dare to sell Hedblom dresses to the other, lower price, department store chains or mail-order houses because of a real risk of losing sales to our regular clients as a result of such a move. Particularly, the mail-order houses are very unpopular with our customers.

The Tax Man, Inc.

THE TAX MAN, INC., provided assistance to individuals and other clients in the preparation of tax returns through 25 owned offices in eastern Massachusetts and 6 franchised offices. In June 1970, Robert Murray, president, and Roger Servison, chairman, indicated that they believed The Tax Man was on the threshold of an exciting era of growth; they intended to make the company one of the leaders in its industry while at the same time seeking profitable fields for diversification. As results for the 1970 tax season were tallied, however, an unexpected loss of $89,000 on revenues of $183,000 appeared, creating the prospect of a severe near-term working capital problem. Securing additional financing, in management's judgment, depended in large part on their ability to define and articulate a means of developing the growth and profit potential in the business.

THE TAX PREPARATION "INDUSTRY"

In 1913 the shortest amendment to the Constitution was passed, bringing into law 31 words which have since affected nearly every resident of the United States. Amendment XVI reads: "The Congress shall have the power to lay and collect taxes on income, from whatever source derived, without apportionment among the several states, and without regard to any census or enumeration."

In the years following the passage of this law, individuals wrestled annually with the preparation of their income tax returns. Assistance

160

was available initially from lawyers, auditors, bookkeepers, and even IRS agents who viewed tax preparation as a source of additional compensation. In the mid-1950s businesses devoted specifically to assisting large numbers of taxpayers were formed, most notably H&R Block, Inc. Nonetheless, the vast majority of federal tax returns continued to be computed either by the taxpayers themselves or by local part-time preparers such as real estate brokers, insurance agents, and assorted friends and relatives.

Tax preparation—1970*

	Returns (millions)	Percent
Self-prepared returns	34.6	45
Local part-time preparers	25.4	33
Lawyers and accountants	9.3	12
Income tax service business	7.7	10
Total.	77.0	100

* For a distribution of tax returns by adjusted gross income, see Exhibit 1.

EXHIBIT 1
Number of federal tax returns by adjusted gross income categories—1968

Adjusted gross income	Returns (in thousands)	Percent
Less than $5,000	31,921	43.3
$ 5,000–$ 10,000	23,367	31.7
10,000– 15,000	11,987	16.3
15,000– 20,000	3,666	5.0
20,000– 25,000	1,180	1.6
25,000– 30,000	519	0.7
30,000– 50,000	716	1.0
50,000– 100,000	301	0.4
100,000– 200,000	62	0.1
200,000– 500,000	16	. . .
500,000– 1,000,000	3	. . .
Over $1,000,000	1	. . .
Total.	73,739	100.0

Source: Internal Revenue Service, preliminary 1969 statistics on individual income tax returns.

By 1974 the number of tax returns was estimated to reach 87 million, an annual growth rate of roughly 3%. Furthermore, several recent developments suggested a substantial increase in the proportion of people seeking outside tax assistance. First, the federal income tax Form 1040 underwent a major revision in 1970 and the 1040A (short form) was eliminated altogether. The added complexities, real or imagined, of these changes received wide publicity. Moreover, during the next few years further modifications would be necessary to accommodate changes in the tax laws resulting from the federal tax legislation of 1969.

Second, the tax law revisions themselves involved important changes in the treatment accorded a wide variety of income and expense items, including both the standard deduction and the personal exemption. Virtually all taxpayers would be affected to some degree, further complicating the task of filing the typical return. As Henry Block, president of H&R Block, the leading tax service company, noted in a recent speech, "We have a saying in our business that if Congress simplifies taxes once more, even we won't understand it." He later added, "Another thing that has contributed to our success is what is referred to as the 'Martinsburg Monster' and that is the computer that checks every tax return. For it is the fear of the IRS that drives a lot of people to our door."[1]

Third, the aggregate number of returns has grown more rapidly than the number of taxpayers because states and cities have instituted income taxes in an effort to meet the enormously inflated costs of government at these levels. By 1969, 38 states and many cities had tax returns, each different from the other and each different to some degree from the federal return. Industry observers expected this trend to continue. The implications were further intensified in a society in which approximately 15% of the people moved every year.

Fourth, rising income levels in the United States created both an increased opportunity for tax savings and a demand for a greater variety of personal financial services. Indeed, some observers claimed that taxpayers with moderate incomes had, in percentage terms, the most to gain from the professional handling of their tax affairs, since many of the special deductions or exclusions were directed toward their needs.[2]

Competitors

The independent operator. A wide variety of individuals were engaged in part-time tax preparation, including real estate brokers, insurance agents, pawnshop operators, bookkeepers, and people who simply had gained a working knowledge of the tax laws. In some instances, the independents prepared only as many returns as they could personally handle during the tax season. They solicited clients by word of mouth or

---

[1] Speech to the Omaha-Lincoln Society of Financial Analysts, March 5, 1969.

[2] For instance, the dividend exclusion, the retirement credit, sick pay, child care, educational expenses, employment fees, and so forth.

through customer contact established in the normal course of their business, perhaps supplemented by a sign in their offices or storefronts.

In other instances, the independents hired assistants and rented an office for the tax season. They often advertised on local radio, in the local newspapers and telephone book, and in general sought to establish a tax preparation business. While undoubtedly numerous, no estimates were available to suggest the number or average size of such establishments. They were characterized by industry sources as offering vastly differing degrees of technical competence and preparation quality as well as widely differing terms of performance guarantee, if any, and fee structures.

The professional. Frequently reluctant competitors for the individual tax return were the lawyers and the CPAs. In particular, the larger law and CPA firms tended to view such work as a goodwill gesture for their legal, trust, or audit clients and they exhibited little desire to expand these services beyond the levels required to satisfy client requests. In general, the professionals dealt with individuals in relatively high income tax brackets who filed complex returns and who frequently relied on their professional guidance and services in other matters as well.

H&R Block. H&R Block was reputed to have retained over 85% of the market accounted for by income tax service businesses. In 1969, 3,286 H&R Block offices were spread throughout the United States and Canada; 5,300,000 individual returns were calculated, and tax preparation revenue for owned and franchised offices amounted to $56 million and net profits after taxes to $3.3 million. Moreover, growth continued at a rapid pace: total offices in 1969 increased 37%, tax preparation volume 46%, and net income 60% from 1968. Summary financial data for H&R Block are provided in Exhibit 2.

The company had consistently followed five policies over the years. The first was to expand the number of offices as rapidly as capable managers and financing permitted.[3] Recently, H&R Block management had begun to reserve large city locations for company-owned offices and had even repurchased some franchises. Second, the company was prepared to locate offices in towns with as few as 500 people through the use of satellites; in essence, these were individuals franchised to prepare returns under the H&R Block name. Third, the fee structure, which was based on the complexity of the client's return, had remained unchanged since 1955, although the average charge per client had increased steadily. H&R Block management attributed this phenomenon to the growing size and diversity of clients' sources and uses of funds.

Fourth, H&R Block stressed a high-quality, high-volume, low-cost

---

[3] Mr. Block claimed, in his speech to the Omaha-Lincoln Society of Financial Analysts on March 5, 1969, that the number of offices opened during 1969 could have been 1,600 had the company wished to maximize growth.

EXHIBIT 2

H&R BLOCK, INC.
Profit and Loss Statements
(highlights)

	Year ended July 31					Nine months ended April 30, 1966	Year ended April 30		
	1961	1962	1963	1964	1965		1967	1968	1969
Volume									
Owned offices	$715,034	$1,114,226	$1,834,586	$2,876,707	$5,010,412	$7,702,447	$12,907,125	$19,785,785	$29,543,635
Franchised offices	589,151	985,469	1,805,479	3,321,187	6,553,700	9,406,333	13,172,662	18,539,913	26,600,164
Total volume	$1,304,185	$2,099,695	$3,640,065	$6,197,894	$11,564,112	$17,108,780	$26,079,787	$38,325,698	$56,143,799
Revenues*									
Owned office volume	$715,034	$1,114,226	$1,834,586	$2,876,707	$5,010,412	$7,702,447	$12,907,125	$19,785,785	$29,543,635
Franchise fees and other	116,543	154,471	191,580	258,628	690,356	1,054,660	1,807,285	3,018,529	4,821,855
Total revenues	$831,577	$1,268,697	$2,026,166	$3,135,335	$5,700,768	$8,757,107	$14,714,410	$22,804,314	$34,365,490
Earnings									
Total revenues	$831,577	$1,268,697	$2,026,166	$3,135,335	$5,700,768	$8,757,107	$14,714,410	$22,804,314	$34,365,490
Operating expenses	658,639	995,618	1,667,226	2,528,204	4,487,431	6,785,583	11,701,891	18,248,645	26,722,916
Earnings before taxes	$172,938	$273,079	$358,940	$607,131	$1,213,337	$1,971,524	$3,012,519	$4,555,669	$7,642,574
Taxes on income	82,694	124,076	170,564	296,506	559,775	910,330	1,421,500	2,509,320	4,363,000
Net earnings	$90,244	$149,003	$188,376	$310,625	$653,562	$1,061,194†	$1,591,019	$2,046,349	$3,279,574
Earnings per share‡	$.02	$.03	$.04	$.06	$.12	$.20	$.30	$.39	$.62
Tax returns prepared (not including state tax returns)	150,000	250,000	400,000	650,000	1,150,000	1,700,000	2,600,000	3,650,000	5,300,000
Number of offices§	140	206	353	495	806	1,190	1,712	2,406	3,286

* For 1969, franchise fees and other revenues includes $586,771 of resident school tuition fees which were included in owned office volume for prior periods.

† The earnings for the nine-month period are not representative of those for a full fiscal year. Net earnings for the 12 months ended April 30, 1966 (unaudited) were $962,947 or $.18 a share on total revenues of $8,839,349.

‡ Based on shares outstanding at the end of each period retroactively adjusted for the five-for-four stock split in the form of a stock dividend declared May 2, 1969, for stock dividends in prior years, and for shares issued in connection with poolings of interest and the acquisition. As so adjusted there were at April 30, 1969, and 1968, 5,305,001 shares outstanding, and at the end of each prior period 5,277,512 shares outstanding.

§ H&R Block had 162 offices, or about 5% of the total offices in the six New England states for the 1969 season: Connecticut, 46; Maine, 12; Massachusetts, 95; New Hampshire, 6; Rhode Island, 1; and Vermont, 2. The population of New England was roughly 11.5 million, or 5.8% of the national figure.

Source: H&R Block 1969 Annual Report.

operation directed primarily at the taxpayer with income in the $5,000 to $15,000 range. Quality was fostered by a tax preparation school, attended by 30,000–40,000 people annually at a fee of $60 per person. In addition to providing income for Block, the school was an excellent recruiting ground for office managers. Increased volume was the objective of an extensive nationwide television advertising campaign each year during the tax season in addition to ads placed in local print media. Low costs were achieved through a minimum of overhead and office frills, centralized purchasing of supplies and office services, and, in 1970, experimentation with computer-assisted tax return preparation.

A fifth element in the H&R Block success formula was diversification. Partly the thrust was geographical; by 1969, 166 offices had been located in Canada and others in Puerto Rico and New Zealand. The company had also enlarged the scope of its activities; for instance, in the education field a home-study course had been initiated. More important, prior to the 1970 tax season, a joint venture with the Pennsylvania Life Insurance Company was formed, called H&R Block Financial Services, to sell mutual funds and life insurance nationally. It was too early for industry observers to determine the success of this last activity, however.

Other tax service companies. A number of smaller tax specialist companies were in operation during the 1970 tax season in addition to The Tax Man. Typical of the older, established companies was Weiss Tax Service, Inc., a family business with 16 owned offices in the greater Chicago area. Despite a spinoff in 1968 to accommodate certain members of the Weiss family, the company had attempted to expand by enlarging existing offices and opening new ones in nearby communities. At various times in the past, Weiss had been involved in merger negotiations with other tax companies, including H&R Block, but in each case it had been unable to reach an agreement. Summary operating data are noted below:

WEISS TAX SERVICE, INC.*

Year ending December 31	Revenues	Net profits	Offices
1966	$141,620	$ (1,912)	19
1967	197,216	(1,863)	15
1968	162,497	13,116	10
1969 (five months)	247,381	16,743	16

* Disguised name.
Source: Weiss Tax Service annual reports.

A second company, located in New York City, was Witt Tax Centers, Inc., which had begun as a proprietorship in 1962. After raising nearly $500,000 in public and private equity placements in 1968, the company launched an acquisition and franchising program for the 1969 tax season, increasing the number of owned offices from 5 to 21 and the number of franchised offices from none to 20, including 10 which, immediately prior to the transaction, had been company owned. These policies were abruptly changed later in 1969. Witt management decided to own rather than franchise offices and "establish a national network of financial service centers initially offering income tax preparation, mutual funds and life insurance."[4] Sixty-two tax centers were open for the 1970 season, 59 company owned. Financial results of late, however, were unfavorable:

WITT TAX CENTERS, INC.

Year ending Sept. 30	Revenues	Net profit
1967	$ 56,790	$13,404
1968	88,383	26,986
1969	259,898	(271,536)

Source: Witt Tax Centers annual reports.

A third tax specialist organization was the Ben Franklin Income Tax Service Company, formed in 1969, financed by a private placement estimated by industry sources to be $2 to $2.5 million, and managed by a group of experienced executives formerly with Litton Industries and IBM. The company pursued a policy of rapid growth in both owned and franchised offices. By the beginning of the 1970 tax season, Ben Franklin reportedly owned as many as 100 offices in California and had embarked on an aggressive franchising program. The franchisee, under Ben Franklin terms, would pay $2,500 per office initially plus a fee of 20% of gross revenues; in addition, the company would have the option of repurchasing the franchise for cash or stock according to a formula based in part on historical earnings.

Personal finance companies. Several of the major personal finance companies offered tax services for the first time in 1970. Most significant among them was the Beneficial Finance Company which, through its newly formed Benevest subsidiary, opened 80 offices in California for the 1970 season and intended later to expand nationally. The Benevest offices were separate from the Beneficial Finance outlets,[5] the latter being subject to strict regulation under California small-loan statutes.

Benevest offered its clients an instant refund without interest[6] for tax overpayments, securing in return a pledge that the client would repay Benevest when he received his government check. Beneficial's motives were interpreted in *Business Week* as follows:

---

[4] 1969 Annual Report, Witt Tax Centers, Inc., February 18, 1970.

[5] Beneficial Finance had approximately 800 offices nationwide.

[6] The IRS has reported that 72.5% of returns filed claimed a refund.

The refund ploy is, of course, expected to generate a large chunk of tax preparation business, but it is really a "kicker" to entice people to come in and sign up for a wide range of "family financial services"—especially mutual funds and life insurance—that Benevest's salesmen will peddle after the tax season closes. . . . For Beneficial, the nation's largest personal loan company, profit margins on sales of funds and insurance are likely to be higher than those on lending activities now being squeezed by rising interest rates. . . . Thus, the company will avoid the problem some fund-insurance sales organizations face of having to pay advances to salesmen until they can generate enough commission income to support themselves.[7]

Benevest was reported to expect revenues of $3 million to $5 million the first year, requiring an estimated $50 million in cash to support anticipated refunds. The average tax preparation charge per client of $25, however, was considerably above the industry average. A Benevest advertisement noted, however, that "not every taxpayer qualifies for an 'instant refund,' of course, but if you're a homeowner with an income of $12,000 or more, you probably qualify easily."

Insurance companies. At least one insurance group, the St. Paul Companies, Inc., had entered the tax preparation business directly. Through its subsidiary, Form 1040, Inc., St. Paul planned to open 46 offices in the Minneapolis–St. Paul area for the 1970 tax season. The 1968 annual report stated that, while insurance was still the primary business, competition for the public's investment funds and a cost-premium squeeze were forcing the company to diversify its services and products and to find more aggressive ways to market insurance.

Retail chains. J. C. Penney, Sears, Roebuck, and Montgomery Ward offered tax preparation services during the 1970 tax season by placing booths in selected stores. In each case pricing and service were patterned after H&R Block. For Penney and Sears, the service was new and experimental; for Montgomery Ward, 1970 was the eleventh year. The size of these companies and some measure of their potential strength in the tax preparation industry are provided in the following statistics:

Operating data for retail chains

	Sales (millions)	Stores	Estimated tax preparation centers in 1970	Projected 1970 growth in stores
J. C. Penney	$3,756	1,646*	24	35
Sears, Roebuck	8,863	826	88	28
Montgomery Ward†	2,715	468	135	22

*Includes 1,438 "soft line" stores.
†Now Marcor following a merger with Container Corporation.
Source: Annual reports and estimates by industry executives.

---

[7] "Luring Clients with On-the-Spot Tax Refunds," *Business Week,* December 20, 1969, p. 80.

Computer service companies. A less easily defined, though potentially significant, factor in the industry was the computer service company which provided tax assistance either on a time-share basis or through a processing center. Such companies were of two types: those offering wholesale computer services to "professional" tax preparers and those offering assistance directly to the taxpayer. Typical of the former were Tax Computer Systems, Computax Systems, and Programmed Proprietary Systems. Skeptics noted several drawbacks in the use of such services, most notably the possibility of breakdown or overloading on and just prior to April 15 and the problem of accuracy. Other industry observers, however, pointed out that much of the time-consuming detail work in filling out a return could be eliminated. The ultimate effect might then be more competition for tax return preparation from (1) lawyers and CPAs who might then view the business as less time consuming and more profitable; (2) part-time preparers who would enjoy a substantially increased capacity; and (3) others such as banks, which might perceive tax work as a means of enlarging customer services. For instance, the National Bank of North America, Chase Manhattan, and The First National City Bank already provided tax services for their customers in 1970 on a limited basis.

Fiscal Systems, Inc., typical of computer service companies offering assistance directly to the taxpayer, distributed Tax-Pak through banks and department stores. For $2.50 the customer could buy a package of instructions and forms which included questions about personal income and expenses. About seven days after returning the forms to the company, the individual received a completed return ready to be signed. Sales of Tax-Pak were cut off on April 3 due to the processing and mailing time required prior to the April 15 filing deadline.

Operating characteristics

The operations of tax preparation companies were influenced considerably by the seasonal nature of the demand for tax services. Typically, over 90% of a company's total income from this and related sources was received in the January-to-April period. An estimate by one industry spokesman of the level of activity during this period is provided below:

Month	Percent of Revenues
January	6
February	34
March	25
April (through the 15th)*	35
	100

* April 15th alone = 5%.

One impact of this operating pattern was financial. A tax preparation company which maintained a year-round central staff had administrative overhead costs to absorb in the "off season" as well as rent for individual offices. Moreover, funds were necessary for supplies and possibly for advertising and promotion prior to the next tax season. Securing long-term financing was complicated by the fact that the business and most of its tangible assets virtually disappeared for eight months of the year, to return only if management was successful in launching another tax-season effort.

A second, perhaps more fundamental, impact of seasonality on employees who were reasonably highly skilled was described by Roger Servison:

One of the major problems confronting the income tax industry concerns the seasonal employment needs of the business. The heavy reliance on part-time, seasonal help makes it difficult to motivate and instill a sense of company pride and job responsibility in these employees. In addition, people who are readily available on a part-time basis are frequently people who for various reasons are not capable of holding a full-time job. Yet it is these people who must represent the company to the public. The impression created by a tax preparer is the only impression the customer receives, since none of the other employees have any personal contacts with the customers.

This large demand for seasonal help during the tax season results in a high rate of turnover among employees and makes recruitment of personnel a major problem for tax companies.

The high rate of employee turnover also has an adverse effect on the repeat business of a tax office. An office that is staffed by the same people year after year is able to develop a personal rapport with its clients that is more meaningful to the customer than the name of the company he is dealing with. Many people hesitate to divulge confidential information about their personal income to a new person each year.

The personnel requirements for a multioffice income tax business of the H&R Block type fell naturally into five categories, none of them, according to industry practice, requiring a college education. As one industry spokesman put it, "Any person with a high school education and an ability to work with numbers can be taught to compute income taxes with only eight to ten weeks of formal tax training." These positions are noted below in order of increasing skill and including the typical means of compensation:

1. *Tax return processors* made copies of completed income tax returns, compiled the various sheets in the proper order, and mailed the returns to the customer. This job was frequently performed on a part-time basis by high school students who were paid by the hour.

2. *Tax return checkers* reviewed all completed returns, a task which entailed verifying the appropriateness of tax law application, the mathe-

matical accuracy of computations, and the completeness of the return. Normally checkers were also paid on an hourly basis. One checker was typically required for five preparers.

3.   *Tax preparers* interviewed clients and prepared their tax returns. Tax preparers were normally paid a commission of 20% to 25% of the gross amount of revenues derived from the returns they prepared. An experienced preparer could prepare about four returns of average complexity per hour.

4.   *Office managers*, in addition to preparing returns themselves, were responsible for scheduling work, insuring that all cash was deposited promptly, submitting weekly reports on office performance, maintaining a proper inventory of supplies, and overseeing general office appearance. Office managers generally received a commission based on the total revenues of an office and were usually expected to work 55 hours a week during the tax season.

5.   *Area managers* were responsible for recruiting and training personnel, equipping offices, checking on office performance, scheduling local advertising and promotions, and resolving operating problems. Area managers were typically responsible for approximately five offices and were paid a salary plus a percentage of the net profit of their operation. These people were frequently employed year-round to operate the tax schools and handle customer complaints during the period from May to January.

Financial characteristics of an income tax office

Income tax offices were potentially high-margin operations. The variable costs associated with preparing a return were estimated by industry sources to be about $1.33, excluding the preparer's commission. With an average client charge of $11.50 per return, the contribution to overhead after commissions was about 61% of revenues, and the break-even volume for an office was roughly $6,200 (Exhibit 3). While The Tax Man management felt that the H&R Block break even might, if anything, be somewhat lower, the above figure was thought to be representative of the other tax specialist companies. Under these assumptions, the contribution from a large office was impressive.[8]

Marketing characteristics

A variety of competitive devices had historically been employed in marketing tax services. Location was one important factor in the success

---

[8] H&R Block was reported to have some locations whose revenues exceeded $120,000.

EXHIBIT 3

THE TAX MAN, INC.
Typical* Income Tax Office Break-Even Calculations

Average revenue per return		$11.50	100.0%
Variable costs (excluding preparer commission)			
Coffee	$ .05		
Tax forms	.09		
Copy paper (10 copies/return)	.08		
Copy developer	.03		
Checking and processing labor	.65		
Postage (optional)	.24		
Large envelopes	.05		
Client folders	.05		
Government envelopes (2/return)	.018		
Customer receipt	.015		
Tax saver envelope	.047		
Check list	.005		
Total variable costs		1.33	11.5
Average contribution per return before commission		$10.17	88.5%
Preparer commission	$ 2.88		
FICA tax	.29	3.17	27.5
		$ 7.00	61.0%
Fixed costs			
Payroll	$2,700†		
Rent (five months)	800		
Advertising and promotion	1,370		
Repairs and maintenance	200		
Utilities	200		
Insurance	25		
Miscellaneous	125		
Total fixed costs	$5,420		

Break-even
Volume: $5,420 ÷ .885 = $6,200
Returns: $6,200 ÷ 11.50 =   540

*Typical of operations patterned after H&R Block.
†The first $2,700 in commissions and FICA taxes is considered fixed since preparers are generally given advances approximating this amount in anticipation of commissions.
Source: Casewriter's notes based on Tax Man calculations.

of an office. Since most tax companies relied heavily on walk-in business, the ideal location was a street-level storefront in a high-traffic shopping center. An office appealing to this clientele was thought to have an effective drawing radius of two to four miles and required a population of 15,000 to 20,000 households. Consequently, the tax company had to consider office density as well as location. Once a company had established itself in an area, however, it appeared that the number of offices per thousand households could be profitably increased.

Pricing was a second important element in marketing policy. Although the majority of tax companies advertised their prices as "$5 and up," the average charge per client in the industry was about $11.50. The average charge for small single-office companies was somewhat lower than the industry norm, while for companies offering instant refunds or computerized services it was considerably higher. Most companies based their prices on the complexity of the return. Thus, the basic fee for a nonitemized federal return was $5; additional schedules typically cost about $2.50 each. A few companies set fees by the amount they "saved" their clients. This practice had been criticized in the industry by those who contended that it encouraged the preparer to deduct questionable items on the client's return.

Providing guaranteed year-round service was a third method of attracting clients. The importance of continuing service and guaranteed accuracy was partially a result of the emphasis given to these factors by the IRS and the Better Business Bureau. Such organizations attempted to discourage the public from having their taxes computed by individuals who would not cosign the return or be available after the tax season to deal with client problems.

Finally, tax companies depended on client loyalty to generate a repeat business frequently as high as 75% to 80%. Thus, in January, tax companies generally sent a reminder to each of their former clients encouraging them to return. To this was often added an advertising program in newspapers and on local television.

THE TAX MAN

The Tax Man, Inc., was organized by Mr. Joseph Rossi, a man in his mid-50s, on September 29, 1967, to purchase a single-office tax preparation proprietorship. The stated purpose of the corporation was "to assist individuals and others in the preparation and filing of tax returns of whatever nature and to license or franchise others to use the name of The Tax Man." During the 1968 tax season, eight offices were opened and approximately 4,600 returns were prepared, yielding $40,527 in gross revenue.

On November 18, 1968, the corporation filed a prospectus for a public offering in accordance with Regulation A of the Securities and Exchange Act for 39,500 shares at $2.50 per share. Approximately $60,000 of the proceeds was to be used in the establishment of 30 new offices. The prospectus stated that Mr. Rossi owned 12,000 shares and had options to purchase another 45,000 shares at $1 per share until July 31, 1971, and thereafter until July 31, 1975, at $5 per share, at which time the options would expire. Other members of management were stated to own 3,300 shares and to have options to purchase an additional 6,000 shares under similar terms. On November 13, 1968, the offering was made and a month later was fully subscribed.

On March 6, 1969, the U.S. District Court in Boston, on the basis of an affidavit filed by the SEC, temporarily enjoined The Tax Man from further sale of common stock under Regulation A. The injunction was made permanent on April 17, 1969. The principal complaints brought by the SEC against the corporation and the principal investors were inadequate or false disclosure of material facts in the registration statement and the prior and subsequent sale of unregistered shares to the public. The market price of The Tax Man stock fell from a high of $15 per share on March 6 to $2 in June of the same year.

During May and June of 1969 Messrs. Robert Murray and Roger Servison, both stockholders in the company and both in the process of obtaining a master's degree in business administration, began consulting for Mr. Rossi regarding plans for the 1970 tax season. During their study, they discovered that the company would report a large operating loss for the year ended July 31 and that additional financing would be required to reopen existing tax offices, then numbering 27, for the 1970 season.

A special meeting of the board of directors was held on July 12, at which time, among other actions, Messrs. Murray and Servison were elected to an expanded board, giving them, with one outside investor, a three-to-two majority. Subsequent events, including a still larger estimate of the operating loss and an absence of planning or progress in securing funds, prompted a second special meeting of the board on August 2. At that time Mr. Rossi was asked to resign as president and chairman of the board and, among other requests, to cancel approximately two thirds of his existing options.

The new managers

Robert Murray and Roger Servison rationalized the risks involved in assuming the direction of The Tax Man by citing the fact that they were young (24), single, and able to start over again should the venture fail. Both men had a great deal of confidence, however, in their ability to turn the company into a successful growth business. They saw it as a means of gaining wide experience in general management and of ultimately obtaining some measure of financial independence, though in the beginning they were willing to work for very modest salaries. In terms of long-range career goals, they indicated a willingness to devote 8 to 10 years to operating the business, but then hoped to become more heavily involved in forward planning and administration.

Management tasks were divided as follows: Mr. Murray was to handle the legal and accounting functions while Mr. Servison was to concentrate on marketing and franchising. Responsibility for finance and personnel would be shared, and operations would be handled by dividing the offices geographically between the two men.

New management's actions

The most immediate problem confronting the new management team was a financial crisis: as indicated by the balance sheet (Exhibit 4), current liabilities of $16,000 exceeded current assets by slightly more than $2,000 on July 31, 1969. Servison and Murray responded, on October 6, with a private placement of 200,000 shares at $.50 per share,[9] of which they each subscribed to 30,000 shares,[10] while the remainder was divided among a group of 10 investor friends. Mr. Servison indicated that the placement not only provided funds to sustain and expand the business but insured that voting control would be retained in friendly hands.

While the financial situation was being clarified, management also turned its attention to preparing for the 1970 tax season. During the next four months, action was taken along three dimensions. First, a tax school was opened in an effort to attract and train competent tax preparers and office managers. About 18 students were enrolled in the course at a fee of $50, of whom about half continued with The Tax Man as preparers or office managers.

Second, Mr. Frank Kelley, a former manager of H&R Block, was hired as operations manager with the hope that he would provide the day-to-day management expertise and training skills necessary for a multioffice operation. He had discussed the possibility of joining The Tax Man with the new principals prior to their assumption of control. Mr. Kelley subsequently hired two former associates as area managers.

Third, the new management sought to expand the number of offices through the sale of franchises and the acquisition of established tax practices. The former goal was implemented through the sale of one franchise in Massachusetts and another for Illinois, excluding Cook County, with the expectation that five offices would be opened in that state for the 1970 season. These transactions produced gross revenues of $22,150. The latter goal was implemented through five acquisitions encompassing eight offices in Massachusetts. The terms of the acquisitions are noted in the table on p. 176.

With these steps taken and with sufficient funds remaining for supplies and working capital, management in the late fall of 1969 had looked forward to a tax season that would enable The Tax Man to break even financially in fiscal 1970 while also providing a solid base for future expansion and for securing bank loans to finance the 1971 tax season.

---

[9] The market price of the common stock fluctuated between $1 and $2 per share during this period.

[10] In addition, Mr. Servison and Mr. Murray each agreed to purchase an additional 30,000 shares over a five-year period at $1 per share.

EXHIBIT 4

THE TAX MAN, INC.
Balance Sheet

Assets	July 31 1968	July 31 1969	April 30 1970
Current assets			
Cash	$ 3,239	$ 6,722	$ 7,660
Note receivable	. . .	5,423	23,579*
Employee advances	. . .	400	300
Prepaid expenses	. . .	782	3,110
Total current assets	$ 3,239	$13,327	$ 34,649
Fixed assets—at cost			
Land	. . .	$30,835	$ 30,835
Buildings and improvements	. . .	$16,480	15,714†
Office equipment.	$ 4,660	16,391	44,070†‡
Automobiles	. . .	2,000	2,000
Total.	$ 4,660	$65,706	$ 92,619
Less: Accumulated depreciation	583	2,697	. . .
Total fixed assets.	$ 4,077	$63,009	$ 92,619
Intangible assets§	$11,592	. . .	$ 50,050
Total assets	$18,908	$76,336	$177,318
Liabilities and Stockholders' Equity			
Current liabilities			
Mortgage payable—current portion.	. . .	$ 1,400	. . .
Note payable	. . .	655	$ 16,350
Accounts payable.	$ 257	4,061	51,958
Accrued and withheld taxes.	. . .	9,227	21,866
Accrued payroll and commissions	. . .	200	6,396
Total current liabilities	$ 257	$15,543	$ 96,570
Long-term liabilities			
Mortgage payable—less current portion shown above	. . .	$30,297	$ 30,961
Notes payable.	. . .	. . .	6,250
Total long-term liabilities	. . .	$30,297	$ 37,211
Stockholders' equity			
Common stock, $1			
Authorized 500,000 shares; issued and outstanding, 68,500 shares at 7/31/69, 339,286 at 4/30/70	$15,000	$68,500	$169,643
Capital surplus	. . .	57,375	58,228
Retained earnings (deficit)	3,651	(95,379)	(184,334)
Total stockholders' equity	$18,651	$30,496	$ 43,537
Total liabilities and stockholders' equity.	$18,908	$76,336	$177,318

*Includes $14,000 in franchise initiation fees, $7,000 due in July 1970 and the remainder in July 1971.
†Net of depreciation.
‡Major items include copy machines and office signs.
§Reflects difference between purchase and book value of acquisitions.
Source: Company records.

Acquisition terms

Acqui- sition	Number of offices	Revenues 1969 season	Method of acquisition		
			Cash	Stock (shares)	Terms
A	4	$26,700	$35,000	2,000	$20,000 cash and 2,000 shares down, remainder over two years
B	1	16,500	15,000	...	50% down, 50% over a year
C	1	6,700	2,150+	286	$2,150 cash and 286 shares down, plus 125% of revenues from returning clients
D	1	3,850	2,450+	...	Book value of office equipment plus $5 per returning client
E	1	4,000	2,000	...	25% down, remainder over two years
	8	$57,750	$56,600	2,286	

The 1970 tax season

The 1970 tax season fell far short of expectations, and as of April 30 a loss of $89,000 had already been incurred for the current fiscal year (see Exhibit 5). Mr. Servison reviewed the shortcomings of the past five months as follows:

Our biggest problem, in retrospect, was our own lack of experience in the tax business. We made several costly mistakes, which hopefully can be avoided in the future.

Back in August 1969 we had no organization in the company. This, combined with our age and inexperience, created two kinds of problems. First, we had difficulty establishing our ideas. The operations manager and those men he brought with him had a concept for running the business that was different from ours. They wanted the kind of high-volume, low-cost operation that has made H&R Block successful. We, on the other hand, wanted to introduce new marketing techniques, upgrade the offices, and build a base for diversified services. Communications broke down. To keep these managers from resigning before the tax season began, we divided up the offices—one third using their methods and the others ours. Curiously, our offices turned out to yield better financial results, in part at least because we encouraged aggressive marketing. Anyway, that won't happen again since, as of April 15, we parted ways with Frank Kelley and the two area managers who came with him.

Second, we were critically short of good office managers. As a result, several of the offices had severe problems and one was not even able to open until March 21.

Cost control was another problem area. We didn't handle purchasing of

EXHIBIT 5

THE TAX MAN, INC.
Comparative Income Statements
Years Ending July 31

	1967	Percent	1968	Percent	1969	Percent	1970 (9 months)	Percent
Gross revenues								
Tax preparation	$3,360.00	100.0	$40,527.00	100.0	$ 83,786.50	95.5	$153,665.54	83.7
Franchise initiation fees and royalties	...	...	...	...	...	...	22,145.50	12.1
Miscellaneous	...	...	...	...	3,960.00	4.5	7,567.07	4.2
Total revenues	$3,360.00	100.0	$40,527.00	100.0	$ 87,746.50	100.0	$183,378.11	100.0
Operating expenses								
Preparers' salaries	$2,300.00	68.5	$15,640.26	38.5	$ 69,237.34	78.8	$102,216.26	55.7
Office supplies and services	220.60	6.7	3,546.17	8.7	20,393.08	23.3	40,835.53	22.3
Advertising	624.70	18.5	8,181.25	20.2	22,874.39	26.0	32,853.13	17.9
Rent	450.00	13.4	4,650.00	11.5	10,882.50	12.4	16,985.90	9.2
Other operating costs	272.02	8.1	4,275.08	10.5	24,448.79	27.9	28,602.04	15.6
Total operating expenses	$3,867.32	115.2	$36,292.76	89.4	$147,836.10	168.4	$221,492.86	120.7
Operating profit (loss)	(507.32)	(15.2)	$ 4,234.24	10.6	$ (60,089.60)	(68.4)	$ (38,114.75)	(20.7)
Administrative costs								
Salaries	...	...	...	...	$ 22,455.35*	25.6	$ 25,281.53	13.8
Rent	...	...	...	...	...	...	2,070.00	1.1
Other administrative costs	...	...	$ 583.00	1.4	3,383.41	3.9	23,588.92	12.8
Total administrative costs	...	...	$ 583.00	1.4	$ 25,838.76	29.5	$ 50,940.45	27.7
Net profit (loss)	$ (507.32)	(15.2)	$ 3,651.24	9.2	$ (85,928.36)	(97.9)	$ (89,055.20)	(48.4)

*Reflects the opening of a corporate office.
Note: Number of returns processed in 1970 was roughly 17,000, including 1,000 by the franchised offices.
Source: Company records.

supplies very well and costs in that area were excessive. With a better understanding of competitive bidding practices and better planning, I believe we
could double volume next year and reduce supply costs $5,000 (about 12%).
In addition, our bookkeeping department was not adequately staffed, with
the result that we didn't have close control over labor costs. Many of our
offices were overstaffed, and this, probably more than anything else, contributed to the operating loss.

Finally, we had some conditions left over from the prior year that turned
out to have more serious implications than we expected. First, we had to
relocate all but one of the original offices because leases for the 1969 season
covered only a four-month period. The problems involved in finding suitable
locations and getting supplies delivered caused the opening dates for most
offices to be delayed until February 1, and unfortunately we were unable
to relocate in Waltham and Salem at all. This probably meant at least $25,000
in lost revenues. More importantly, however, we discovered that less than
50% of last year's Tax Man customers returned this year, well below the
normal industry average. This can be partially attributed to changed office
locations, but we suspect that the service given in 1969 was inferior in many
instances as well. Also, in three locations former employees went into competition with us, using our customer lists from the prior year.

The spring of 1970 was not, however, without its bright spots. Mr.
Servison continued in this vein:

In other respects, 1970 was an encouraging year. We had about four
offices that together accounted for over half of the operating loss. The better
offices, on the other hand, showed very substantial volume increases which
lifted several of them from break even to a solid profit. Here are the historical
figures for our best managed office that shows this trend. [See table on page
179.] The acquired offices in particular were strong performers. The return
before taxes on gross investment was nearly 16%, which isn't bad for the first
season, and it should improve considerably next year.

Management also felt that valuable experience had been gained in
the conduct of the business. More specifically, progress was cited in
the areas of procedures and control, marketing, and organization; however, particularly in the last instance, significant work remained to be
done.

Procedures and controls.   By the end of the tax season, data had
been gathered for a comprehensive manual on policy and procedures
which was to be made available for a management training session
in January 1971. Mr. Murray hoped that the manual and the thought
behind it would assist in consolidating the varied experiences of the
office managers into a booklet of helpful advice on the efficient operation
of a tax office.

Similarly, a cost control system comparable to that thought to be
used by H&R Block was introduced during the tax season. With con-

"Best managed" office

	1967	1968	1969	1970	1970
Revenues.	$3,360	$9,850	$16,500	$22,600	100.0%
Operating costs					
Payroll.	$2,500	$4,825	$ 6,940	$ 8,668	38.4%
Rent	800	800	2,400	2,400	10.6
Advertising	650	800	1,000	1,000	4.6
Supplies	370	1,080	1,815	2,750	12.1
Utilities	100	100	300	300	1.3
Insurance	10	10	10	10	. . .
Telephone	100	100	600	600	2.6
Total costs	$4,530	$7,715	$13,065	$15,728	69.6%
Net profit (loss).	$(1,170)	$2,135	$ 3,435	$ 6,872	30.4

tinuing refinements, Mr. Murray believed that it would be instrumental in achieving reductions in operating cost ratios on the order of 10% during the next tax season.

Marketing. Mr. Servison indicated that the results obtained from some of the marketing techniques introduced during the tax season had been very encouraging. For instance, an employee discount plan was marketed in some areas to companies employing 50 or more people as a special fringe benefit. Under this arrangement, the employer simply included a coupon with the wage and tax statement (W-2 form) mailed to employees each January which entitled them to a 10% discount on returns prepared by The Tax Man. In large part due to this effort, one new office opened with a volume well above the break-even point. Mr. Servison also felt that some companies might be willing to underwrite some or all of the service in future years, providing The Tax Man with temporary offices and in-plant promotion in exchange for reduced rates.

Organization. Progress in building an organization was viewed as mixed. Vacancies existed in three of the five area-manager positions, and although the remaining incumbents were seen as competent in this role, none was thought to be immediately able to assume the position formerly held by Mr. Kelley.

Messrs. Murray and Servison were, however, quite optimistic about the progress they had made in recruiting and training office managers. About half of the 25 company-owned offices were headed by what management considered to be capable managers who were likely to return to The Tax Man in 1971. These men promoted their offices aggressively and derived considerable satisfaction from directing an efficient operation.

Management also indicated that efforts to recruit competent part-time tax preparers had been very successful. Over 140 preparers had worked for the company in the course of the 1970 season, about 100 of whom were considered capable of performing this function at a satisfactory level. It was hoped that the existence of such a large number of experienced preparers would reduce the time and effort needed to recruit personnel in 1971. In addition, there was a possibility that some of them would be offered the position of office managers for the next season.

Financial condition

One immediate problem confronting The Tax Man management was a shortage of working capital. The proceeds from the 1969 private stock placement had been expended and operations for the 1970 tax season had drained rather than replenished funds. Mr. Murray estimated that a minimum of $150,000 would be needed to support overhead (currently running at about $3,000 per month), to reduce accounts payable, and to finance start-up expenses for the 1971 tax season. An additional $150,000 would be necessary to undertake the acquisition, franchising, and diversification programs that management felt were important for the company's long-term growth.

Obtaining equity was complicated by the court injunction prohibiting the further sale of stock under Regulation A. To sell shares registered with the SEC, Mr. Murray felt that a full registration under the Securities and Exchange Act would be necessary. In view of The Tax Man's history, the legal expenses of such a registration would be high, requiring, in management's judgment, an issue of at least a million dollars to be economical. Alternatively, additional unregistered or "letter" stock could be sold privately to individuals. Mr. Murray thought the purchasers of the 1969 placement would be unwilling to invest sufficient additional funds, however, and he was concerned about the terms that would be demanded by a new investor group.

Messrs. Murray and Servison had initially approached several banks in an effort to secure a combination of term and seasonal financing. While the banks were sympathetic to the latter during the early months of the tax season, they were negatively disposed to the former, citing the absence of a profitable operating history, a weak balance sheet, and the relative inexperience of management.

More recently, management had contacted a number of venture capital organizations. The preliminary response in several instances had been favorable, although discussions had not progressed to the point of formulating a specific financing arrangement.

Included in the presentation to potential investors or lenders was a forecast of projected revenues for the 25 existing offices for the following three tax seasons. Taken together, the profit pattern was estimated as follows:

	1971 (000)	1972 (000)	1973 (000)
Revenues.	$278	$372	$492
Break-even revenue @ $6,200 each	155	155	155
Revenues above break even	$123	$217	$337
Contribution @ 61%	75	132	206
Less: Area manager bonus @ 40%.	30	53	82
Contribution to general overhead.	$ 45	$ 79	$124
Less: General overhead.	65	65	65
Profit before taxes	$ (20)	$ 14	$ 59

Mr. Servison indicated that 1973 revenues could easily be doubled by acquisitions and new offices.

Alternatives for growth in income tax services

Management regarded growth in income tax services as both necessary and desirable. Mr. Servison reflected these views:

We have developed what we think to be a sound method of operation and are enthusiastic about opening new tax offices. Growth in this business is going to be exciting over the next few years as tax law changes drive some of the untapped market to professional tax preparers. In addition, we need greater volume to generate the contribution to support overhead in the off season and provide working capital for the next season.

Unfortunately, opening new offices ourselves presents some problems. One is money. A relatively modest office requires about $1,500 in furniture and equipment and another $2,000 in working capital to get started. Then we have to find a qualified manager. He and the preparers he has working for him are essential for the success of the office. Upgrading staff in existing offices has been a big job for us that isn't over yet. I doubt that we'll have people to spare for some time. Lastly, a new office typically doesn't show a profit for two to three years. With our financial status as it is, we are very much aware of the need for establishing a track record for our stockholders and potential sources of financing.

While not discounting entirely the possibility of opening company-owned offices, management was more inclined to pursue new office possibilities through franchising. The franchise arrangement included three important provisions. First, the franchisee would pay Tax Man $5,000 for exclusive rights to service a population center of 15,000 households. The fee would increase $500 for each additional 5,000 households. In return, The Tax Man would provide training and administrative services which, added to the expenses associated with selling the franchise, Mr.

EXHIBIT 6

THE TAX MAN, INC.
Projections for Franchisees*

	1st year	2nd year	3rd year	4th year	5th year	5th year summary
Revenues						
1st office	$5,000	$10,000	$17,500	$22,000	$25,000	$ 79,500
2nd office	...	...	5,000	7,500	10,000	22,500
Total revenues	$5,000	$10,000	$22,500	$29,500	$35,000	$102,000
Operating costs						
Payroll	$2,500	$ 3,000	$ 5,750	$ 8,650	$10,500	$ 30,400
Rent	1,000	2,400	3,400	4,800	4,800	16,400
Advertising and promotion	800	800	1,000	1,000	1,000	4,600
Supplies	550	1,100	2,475	3,025	3,850	11,000
Repair and maintenance	200	200	300	200	200	1,100
Sign rental	200	200	400	400	400	1,600
Utilities	200	400	600	800	800	2,800
Insurance	100	100	200	200	200	800
Contingency fund	...	100	225	295	350	970
Miscellaneous	50	50	100	100	100	400
Total costs	$5,600	$ 8,350	$14,450	$19,470	$22,200	$ 70,070
Operating profit (loss)	$ (600)	$ 1,650	$ 8,050	$10,030	$12,800	$ 31,930
Royalty fees	...	1,000	2,250	2,950	3,500	9,700
Net profit (loss)	$ (600)	$ 650	$ 5,800	$ 7,080	$ 9,300	$ 22,230
Owner's draw	1,750	2,000	2,500	2,500	2,500	11,250
Total owner proceeds	$1,150	$ 2,650	$ 8,300	$ 9,580	$11,800	$ 33,480

*The figures are based on a market area of 12 square miles or less and a minimum of 15,000 households.
Source: Company records.

Murray estimated to cost about $2,500. Supplies and equipment were billed separately at cost (about $1,500). Second, the franchisee would pay The Tax Man 10% of gross revenues after the first tax season. While the initiation fee was thought to be among the highest in the industry, management felt the percentage of revenue was less than average.[11] Third, The Tax Man agreed to repurchase the franchise after five years at the option of the franchisee for 10 times the average profit after taxes, The Tax Man fee, and normal "owner's" salary for the previous two years payable in cash or marketable securities. The financial estimates provided with the franchise were predicated on opening a second office in the same population center in the third year, as shown in Exhibit 6.

Despite the opportunity for short-term gain, Mr. Servison had two reservations about mounting a major franchising program. He was concerned, first, by the initial expenses involved in assembling sales materials and procedure manuals, office design, travel, and so forth, which he estimated at about $20,000. Second, he was uncertain about the effect of possible legislation directed toward regulating franchise activities. Should future law require a registration of some kind for each franchise,[12] the added time and legal expenses involved would seriously diminish the attractiveness of franchising.

A final possibility for expanding geographically in tax services was the acquisition of established practices. Management was of the opinion that a sizable number of profitable practices could be purchased from owner managers who would be willing to continue as office managers. In fact, nine proprietors in eastern Massachusetts had already contacted The Tax Man offering to sell their practices. The number of returns and approximate revenues are shown in Exhibit 7.

Typically, the purchase price approximated the prior year's revenues, often with roughly half the amount payable immediately and the remainder after the tax season, the second payment sometimes based on a factor related to the percentage of returning clients. The Tax Man's financial condition posed a serious limitation to an acquisition program, however, since in management's view acquisitions would have to be made for cash rather than for stock.

Diversification

Management was also actively considering a number of alternatives for using The Tax Man capabilities to provide other services. Three

---

[11] For instance, H&R Block received 15% of gross revenues from franchisees but required no initiation fee.

[12] "A Law Shapes Up on Franchising," *Business Week*, January 31, 1970. According to *Business Week*, the Senate Small Business subcommittee was considering full disclosure of franchise agreements, possibly through a registration statement and control over advertising statements by franchisers.

EXHIBIT 7

THE TAX MAN, INC.
Immediate Single-Office Acquisition Candidates

City	Returns	Approximate revenues*
A	372	$ 4,300
B	1,000	11,500
C	750	8,700
D	500	5,800
E	1,500	17,300
F†	1,000	11,500
G	225	2,600
H†	1,000	11,500
I†	1,000	11,500
	7,347	$84,700

*At $11.50 per return.
†Could be consolidated with existing Tax Man office.
Source: Company records.

types of businesses with widely differing characteristics were currently being evaluated: bookkeeping services, miscellaneous simple businesses, and personal financial services.

Bookkeeping services. Individuals with multiple income sources, proprietors, and small businessmen frequently needed part-time accounting services on a continuing basis. Tax Man bookkeepers could be assigned to several clients, providing the client with services and flexibility and the bookkeeper with full-time employment.

For The Tax Man there were several advantages to be gained from entering such a business. Overhead charges would be low, since personnel would work in client offices, and billings would not have dramatic seasonal fluctuations. At the same time, management felt that this type of service would be entirely consistent with the company's image and would probably result in new tax customers. Moreover, people qualified as bookkeepers could probably be trained to prepare tax returns with little difficulty.

The business also had certain drawbacks, identified by Mr. Murray as follows:

Not all of The Tax Man's present employees would be qualified to provide bookkeeping services. We would be confronted with another recruiting problem and possibly a training effort as well. In addition, bookkeeping services aren't seasonal, so we couldn't use them to offset tax work. It's possible that an entirely different staff would be needed, which might just aggravate our personnel problems.

Also, we, as management, don't have any particular expertise with this service, especially how to market it. We might find it necessary to hire an aggressive man to get it moving.

Simple businesses. With 25 office locations and a pool of reliable part-time employees, The Tax Man provided the basis for a variety of relatively uncomplicated businesses. Management had discussed using the offices as duplication centers or as driving schools during the off-season months. Alternatively, offices could be converted to the sale of real estate and casualty insurance. Sufficient data had not been gathered, however, to assess in detail the advantages and disadvantages of such ventures.

Personal financial services. Finally, personal financial services were being considered, including the sale of mutual funds and life insurance as part of a family budgeting and financial counseling service. Mr. Servison noted some of the reasons for his interest.

Depending on how The Tax Man is conceived of as a business, selling a broad range of financial services could be a natural extension of our existing business. Tax customers could be screened for sales potential, and the salesmen could capitalize on the rapport established during the tax-return preparation. Conversely, cold calls and continuing client contact would enhance the tax business.

Unlike the bookkeeping service, sales efforts for mutual funds and life insurance may be made seasonal so that some of the same people can prepare tax returns as well. Also, if the salesman begins work as a preparer or office manager during the tax season, he will build up a cash reserve as well as a customer list, which will reduce the need for us to provide him with working capital.

Mr. Servison felt that falling stock market prices and the financial difficulties experienced by numerous brokerage firms in the spring of 1970 would assist in recruiting securities salesmen. He was less sanguine, however, about finding individuals with this background who would also be interested in tax work.

At present, The Tax Man was exploring the possibility of selling the insurance and mutual fund product line of an established agent, thus avoiding the difficulties involved in registering a new program. With this arrangement, management believed that only its salesmen, as individuals, would need to be registered. The Tax Man would receive a share of the commissions and would provide certain administrative and accounting services. No investment would be required, however.

RECENT EVENTS

In the first two weeks of June, The Tax Man management had begun to receive some indications of the performance of competing tax service companies during the 1970 season. The results were mixed. H&R Block had experienced another record-breaking year: revenues increased 43% and profits 83%, and approximately 1,100 new offices were opened.[13] On the other hand, many of the newer companies appeared to have had dismal results.

During this time The Tax Man received three tentative invitations to consider acquiring or merging with competing companies. While figures were not available, Mr. Servison had the impression that as of June 15 these companies could be characterized in the manner below:

Company	Number of offices	Losses	Age of company (years)	Approximate unobligated cash*
1	About 80	About $500,000	1	$400,000
2	About 25	Small	6	nil
3	8 mobile units	About $100,000	1	$ 50,000

*Remaining after payment of 1970 tax season expenses.

Mr. Servison was uncertain whether such opportunities should be pursued. Placing a value on The Tax Man was one difficulty,[14] accommodating his and Mr. Murray's personal desires another, and identifying the business benefits of a merger, acquisition, or sellout a third.

---

[13] H&R Block stock, traded on the NYSE, closed at 46 on June 15, 1970 (the range in 1970 was 37 to 68). At this price the stock commanded a P/E ratio of about 40 based on 1970 earnings per share.

[14] As of June 15, Tax Man stock traded at $1 per share, indicating a market value of about $340,000, although the market for the stock was very thin.

Prelude Corporation

In June 1972, Prelude Corporation could look back on 12 years of pioneering in the newly developed offshore segment of the northern lobster fishing industry. (See Appendix.) Having accounted for 16% of the offshore poundage landed in 1971, this Massachusetts company ranked as the largest single lobster producer in North America. Mr. Joseph S. Gaziano, president since 1969, looked forward to a still more dominant position and, in the long run, to further vertical integration beyond what he had already introduced:

Basically, we're trying to revolutionize the lobster industry by applying management and technology to what has been an 18th century cottage industry heretofore. Other companies have become giants by restructuring such commodity businesses as crab, tuna, avocados, celery and chicken; we want to become the Procter & Gamble of the lobster business. Until we opened up the offshore resource there was no way to bring about this revolution, but now the chance is there. Furthermore, the technology and money required to fish offshore are so great that the little guy can't make out; the risks are too great. The fishing industry now is just like the automobile industry was 60 years ago; 100 companies are going to come and go, but we'll be the General Motors.

We have toyed with the idea of establishing a restaurant chain featuring the Prelude lobster, similar to Black Angus or Red Coach [local chains which offer only a small selection of beef as their fare], but have never really gotten serious about it. We find we have enough to manage now. The Deep Deep and Wickford distribution systems, which we purchased in the past fiscal year, have given us some vertical integration.

187

EXHIBIT 1

PRELUDE CORPORATION
Average Monthly Company Landings per Trip
(as percentage of fiscal 1971 average)

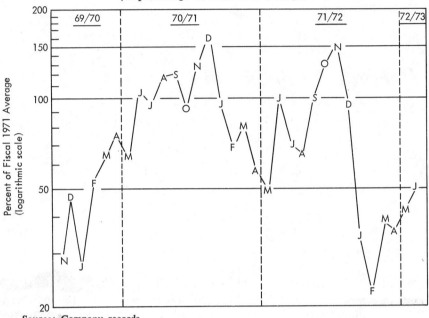

Source: Company records.

As Mr. Gaziano voiced these expectations, Prelude hopefully saw it-self as starting to recover from a recent precipitous and unexplained decline in its per trip catch (Exhibit 1). This decline had plunged the company back into the red for the fiscal year ending in April (Exhibit 2) and had raised the specter of depletion of the offshore lobster popula-tion by pollution or overfishing. Mr. Gaziano viewed these possibilities as bleak, but discounted them:

The vessels we have are especially designed and constructed for our lobster gear and couldn't be used for any other purpose without costly re-fitting. I suppose we could go south into the Caribbean for crawfish or go after finfish that are amenable to the long line techniques. We could even use the vessels for research, laying cables, or as oil-survey ships. Practically speaking, if someone said tomorrow that we couldn't sell lobsters due to mercury con-tent or some other reason, I guess we would be forced to close the doors. However, I foresee this risk as minimal. Certainly it is possible, but there are no studies or indications that this is at all a likely occurrence.[1]

---

[1] In support of his belief that depletion of the resource was unlikely, Mr. Gaziano employed a widely used argument—namely, that the average weight of offshore lobsters caught was holding steady at about 2½ pounds (with a range of 1–11 pounds or more), a fact taken to indicate that the more mature lobsters were not being fished at a rate higher than their natural replacement.

EXHIBIT 2

PRELUDE CORPORATION
Statement of Operations and Accumulated Deficit, 1967–1972
(in thousands of dollars)

Year Ended April 30

	1967	1968	1969	1970	1971	1972 (consolidated)*
Net sales	$ 128	$ 176	$ 152	$ 371	$1,511	$ 3,064
Costs and expenses:						
Cost of vessel operations	$ 108	$ 161	$ 225	$ 445	$ 832	$ 1,175
Cost of purchased seafood	...	...	...	...	...	1,062
Depreciation	22	23	21	68	135	253
Selling, general and administrative†	53	90	193	249	271	565
	$ 183	$ 274	$ 439	$ 762	$1,238	$ 3,055
Income (loss) from operations	$(55)	$(98)	$(287)	$(391)	$ 273	$ 9
Other income (expense)	...	(1)	(69)	(21)	(107)	(157)
Income (loss) before income taxes and extraordinary items	$(55)	$(99)	$(356)	$(412)	$ 166	$(148)
Provision for income taxes	...	...	...	...	84	...
Income (loss) before extraordinary items	$(55)	$(99)	$(356)	$(412)	$ 82	$(148)
Extraordinary items:						
Write-down of vessels	...	...	...	(133)	...	...
Credit arising from carryforward of operating losses	...	...	...	...	72	...
Net income (loss)	$(55)	$(99)	$(356)	$(545)	$ 154	$(148)
Accumulated deficit at beginning of year	...	(55)	(154)	(510)	(1,055)	(901)
Accumulated deficit at end of year	$(55)	$(154)	$(510)	$(1,055)	$ (901)	$(1,049)
Income (loss) per share of common stock assuming full dilution	$(.23)	$(.41)	$(1.25)	$(1.15)	$ .28	$ .27
Shares assumed outstanding	240	240	285	474	550	550

* Includes the results of subsidiary operations from November 1, 1971, on.
† Includes all operating costs incurred after landing, such as vehicle operations, salaries of delivery and restaurant personnel, and tank maintenance as well as executive salaries and general overhead.
Source: Company records.

HISTORY

Prelude's predecessor company had been organized in 1960 to develop techniques for deep-sea lobster fishing. Its founder was an ordained minister, the Reverend William D. Whipple, and its name reflected Mrs. Whipple's profession—music. In the course of raising money for a company that was never in the black until 1971, Rev. Whipple had incorporated in 1966 and had arranged a private placement of 140,000 shares (58% of the total). This brought in $350,000, which was supplemented by debt. Late in 1968, when Rev. Whipple felt ready to start commercial operations, prospects for growth plus creditor pressure led to additional financing (Exhibit 3), some of it completed before the ending of the go-go market in 1969:

Date	Financing	Amount
February 1969	250,000 common shares @ $8.50	$2,125,000 gross
September 1969*	10% senior notes (John Hancock Insurance Co.)	500,000
September 1969	40,000 rights @ $6.75 (John Hancock)	270,000
June 1970	50,000 common shares @ $3.00 (private placement)	150,000

* This financing became necessary when an expected government subsidy for fishing fleets failed to materialize.

Also during 1969, Mr. Whipple agreed to bring in Mr. Gaziano as president and to have him put together a professional management team. The purchase of two 101-foot trawlers for $1,585,000 completed Prelude's makeready, and the year ending April 30, 1971, brought operating earnings of $273,000 from a lobster catch of 1.1 million pounds.

Spurred by this success, Prelude purchased two more ships of 96 feet and 125 feet for $1,118,000 and acquired two nearby subsidiaries in the lobster distribution business. The latter were the Wickford Shellfish Company and the distribution segment of Deep Deep Ocean Products; these would, it was hoped, reduce price fluctuations and raise margins by reducing Prelude's dependence on independent wholesalers. In the three fiscal years prior to their purchase, Wickford had had two nominal profits and one nominal loss. Deep Deep had suffered significant losses, but these were laid by management chiefly to Deep Deep's operation of three ships[2] which Prelude did not buy, although it agreed to market their catch. Prelude saw both firms as competently managed but beset

---

[2] By June 1972 one of these ships had been sold.

by inability to raise enough capital to finance their rapidly expanding sales:

	1969	1970	1971	1972
Dollars in Thousands				
Wickford (years ending February 28).......	...	$ 870	$1,000	$1,600
Deep Deep (years ending December 31)	$950	1,623	1,414	...

EXHIBIT 3

PRELUDE CORPORATION
Balance Sheet
(in thousands of dollars)

		April 30	
Assets		*1971*	*1972 (consolidated)*
Current assets:			
Cash and marketable securities.........................		$ 460	$ 253
Accounts receivable		22	243
Lobster and seafood inventories		13	62
Trapping supplies....................................		158	323
Prepaid expenses		55	108
Total current assets		$ 708	$ 989
Fixed assets...		$2,743	$3,471
Less—accumulated depreciation......................		189	420
		$2,554	$3,051
Goodwill		...	315
Total assets		$3,262	$4,355
Liabilities and Stockholders' Equity			
Current liabilities:			
Notes payable.......................................		$ ...	$ 350
Current portion of long-term debt......................		79	270
Accounts payable....................................		107	257
Accrued taxes and expenses		46	75
Total current liabilities		$ 232	$ 952
Long-term debt......................................		$1,616	$1,857
Stockholders' equity:			
Common stock			
Authorized—1,100,000 shares			
Issued and outstanding—569,985 shares in 1972,			
530,000 shares in 1971...........................		$ 265	$ 285
Additional paid-in capital		2,065	2,325
Accumulated deficit................................		(901)	(1,049)
		$1,429	$1,561
Less—6,200 treasury shares		15	15
		$1,414	$1,546
Total liabilities		$3,262	$4,355

Source: Company records.

Both Prelude's new ships (which began fishing in July 1971 and January 1972) and its acquisitions (effected in December and January) led to additional financing:

Date	Financing	Amount
April 1971	Two ships' mortgages consolidated @ 1% above prime	$1,200,000
December 1971	Paid 17,500 common shares, valued @ $6.50* for Wickford, plus cash	122,000
January 1972	Paid 22,845 common shares valued @ $7.00 for Deep Deep distribution, plus assumption of certain liabilities	170,000

* According to the terms of sale, if the former owner should sell his stock at less than $6.50 a share, the company would pay the difference.

Still another episode in Prelude's history deserves mention because of the worldwide attention it received. In the spring of 1971, Prelude became the focus of a well-publicized international incident involving the United States and Russia. Early in the year, ships of the Russian commercial fishing fleet had caused the loss of more than $70,000 of Prelude's gear by dragging fishing nets over the bottom on which Prelude's traps were resting, clearly marked by buoys and radar reflectors. Such fixed gear had legal right-of-way, so Mr. Gaziano not only sued the Russian government for $177,000 in actual damages plus $266,000 in punitive damages, but also caused a Soviet merchant ship to be attached in San Francisco. The actual out-of-court settlement was for only $89,000, but it was hailed as a precedent in commercial relations between the two countries.

PRELUDE IN 1972

In mid-1972, Prelude was organized primarily along functional lines, with departments for operations, engineering, research, and finance and administration. Distribution functions were divided among the Deep Deep and Wickford subsidiaries (Exhibits 4, 5).

Operations

Fishing. Fishing operations and the logistics involved in landing and distributing the lobster catch were under the direction of Robert E. (Gene) White, age 33, vice president, operations. Prelude's four ships operated year-round on a two-week cycle, ten days fishing and four days in port for unloading and resupply. Each ship carried a crew of ten: captain, mate, engineer, cook, and six deckhands. After a 12-hour steam to the offshore lobster grounds, the crew would begin "hauling pots" 12

EXHIBIT 4

PRELUDE CORPORATION
Organization Chart

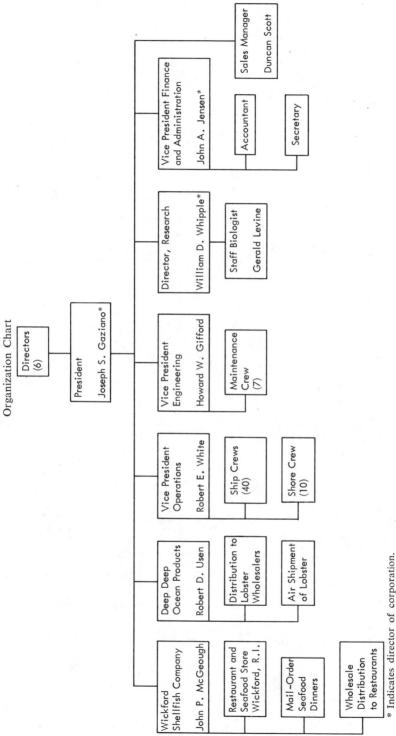

* Indicates director of corporation.
(☐) Indicates number of personnel involved.
Source: Company records.

EXHIBIT 5

PRELUDE CORPORATION
Personal Data on Officers and Management Personnel

	Joseph S. Gaziano	John A. Jensen	W. D. Whipple	Howard W. Gifford	Robert E. White	John P. McGeough	Robert D. Usen
Title(s)	Director, President, CEO	Director, VP Finance and Administration	Director, Director of Research	Vice President Engineering	Vice President Operations	President, Wickford Shellfish Co., Inc.	President, Deep Deep Ocean Products, Inc.
Age	36	33	41	37	33	31	42
Education........	MIT, B.S.E.E., 1956 AMP programs: Harbridge House Sloan School	Babson Institute BS/BA, 1962 MBA, 1963	Princeton, BA 1953; Boston Univ. School of Theology, STB *cum laude*, 1958	New Bedford Institute of Technology. B.S.	U.S. Navy Nuclear Sub School.	Providence College BS. 1962	Tufts University, BA
Previous experience	Raytheon Co., 1962–67, rising to manager, Major Space Systems Allied Research Associates, Engineering and Systems Div., 1967–69, VP and GM.	U.S. Army, Sept. 1963–Feb. 1964 Price, Waterhouse, & Co., 1964–June 1968.	Owner of a charter yacht business, 1954–1958 Inventor and innovator in the area of fishing equipment, especially for deepwater lobster fishing, 1958–59. Founded predecessor company, 1960. President 1960–1969	Electric Boat Division of General Dynamics, rising to supervisor in the Mechanical Engineering Dept.	U.S. Navy, 1960–69, rising to I/C Engineman. Held technical assignments, including mechanical inspection, systems and machinery testing.	Former professional football player. Increased sales of Wickford almost tenfold in the five years prior to its acquisition.	Over 15 years experience in several family-owned seafood businesses, including the Tabby Cat Food Company. As president, Mr. Usen had expanded this to $25 million sales volume prior to its sale. Founded Deep Deep in 1968.
Date of entry	January 1969 Exec. VP	June 1968		May 1969	March 1969	December 1971	January 1972
Officer(s) held	President	VP, June 1970 Director. Sept. 1971	VP, Sept. 1971	VP, Sept. 1971	Vice President	President of subsidiary	President of subsidiary

Note: The three outside directors were: Chester A. Barrett, Chairman, Merchants National Bank of New Bedford; Joshua M. Berman, Partner, Goodwin, Procter and Hoar; Robert F. Goldhamer, Vice President and Vice Chairman of the Executive Committee, Kidder, Peabody and Co.
Source: Company data.

hours a day. (See Appendix.) When the lobsters were brought up and removed from the pots, their claws would be pegged with a red plastic peg which displayed the Prelude brand, and then they would be stored in the hold. The empty trap would be rebaited and stacked until the line was ready to be payed out again for another three days of fishing.

Whether the trawl was relaid where it had been or in another location was a decision made by the captain, depending very much on how the catch was running. In any event, the captain was charged with bringing in as many pounds of lobster as possible on each trip, an amount which could vary tremendously. Although Prelude's ships averaged about 20,000 pounds per trip, the results of a single trip could range from 4,000 to 40,000 pounds. (An indication of the variation in the size of the catch can be obtained from Exhibit 1.) In Mr. Gaziano's words:

The biggest problem in the production process is the variability in the size of the catch. It is not like a manufacturing business. The size of the catch is uncertain. There is no proven way of forecasting where the lobsters will be on a given day. Mating habits, weather, etc., are some of the many variables which determine the size of the catch. Black magic is used by the captains to find lobsters. Presently, it is an art, not a science. Actually it is on a trial and error basis. If one canyon is not producing, the skipper moves to another location.

Workforce. Along with dispatching and supplying the vessels, Mr. White was responsible for staffing both the ships and Prelude's truck fleet and storage facility. These operations used 50 people who were engaged in manning the ships or moving lobster. Because Prelude was located in Westport Point, these workers were nonunion. In nearby New Bedford, where the larger portion of the fishing industry was located, unions were a predominant force. Unlike most others in the fishing industry, who were required by the union to pay their crews a staright percentage of the catch, Prelude paid a base salary plus a sum of 20 cents a pound on everything over 25,000 pounds, to be divided among the crew on a pro rata basis. Mr. White commented on some of the problems with people:

The fisherman is an independent worker. He is always in demand and has a job waiting at his beck and call. His reputation stays with him, although references are not easy to evaluate. Since there is "always a ship leaving," he does not hesitate to tell his boss to "get screwed" if he is unhappy about something. How do you get a reference on somebody who has told his last three bosses to "get screwed"? So we end up hiring them and taking a chance based on their informal reputation which I get from my sources in the industry. We spin our wheels on quite a few. We attempt to hire experienced fishermen, but 20% of our crews are bank tellers and "potato farmers" who want to try something more exciting and more financially rewarding. We start the experienced fisherman at $225 per week and the layman at $150. If the latter pans out after two or three trips, he goes to $225 also.

The cook is one of the most important men on the ship. If I get a bad cook, morale goes to hell. Most ship cooks are drunks—it is just a question of whether they are good drunks or bad drunks. I try to have at least one crewman on each ship to have welding expertise. This avoids having to return to shore to make minor repairs. Engineers are hard to get—their education allows them to earn good money on shore and avoid the hard sea duty. Lobstering is a hard and demanding job. Guys over 40 break up after several trips.

Logistics.   Since the inlet leading to Prelude's headquarters in Westport Point was not deep enough for the draft of the four ships, the company rented 225 feet of pier space at the State Pier in Fall River, about 15 miles away. Here the vessels tied up for unloading, maintenance, and resupply. The company owned and maintained a fleet of refrigerated trucks with which to transport the catch. After a returning ship had docked, the mesh baskets of pegged lobsters were lifted out of the hold and into these trucks. If the catch had already been sold, the truck, driven by a member of the shore crew, began its delivery rounds immediately.

If there was an excess, however, or if it was desired to hold the catch for better prices, then the truck would make the 20-minute run to Westport Point, where the lobsters would be transferred to the Prelude holding tank. This tank, built during 1968 and 1969 at a cost of $250,000, was capable of holding 125,000 pounds of lobster in seawater cooled to 42°F. The tank was designed around an experimental system aimed at reducing handling costs by keeping the lobster in mesh baskets aboard ship and stacking these baskets in the storage tank. The system had not worked out well in practice, however, since one dead lobster could cause the loss of 10% to 15% of its tankmates within a 24-hour period. As a result, the baskets had to be hauled out and culled regularly. Prelude management felt that if they did expand their holding capacity it would be with conventional three-tier tanks which, even though they required more space and lobster handling, could be culled more efficiently and could be built for only $1 per pound of storage capacity. Security measures, both at the holding tank and on the trucks, were important since lobster was a readily marketable commodity at any roadside stand.

Engineering

Engineering activities at Prelude were under the direction of Howard W. Gifford, age 37, vice president, engineering. These activities included the maintenance and procurement of vessels and equipment as well as the development of gear, and so forth.

Maintenance. With each ship representing an investment of over $500,000 and subject to continual stress at sea, maintenance was an important and continual activity. This work was carried out by a seven-person maintenance department located at the pier in Fall River. Available there were complete facilities for the welding and machining necessary to overhaul and repair a ship's engines, life-support equipment, and trap-handling gear. Additionally this crew performed periodic preventive maintenance on the holding tank at Westport Point. This life-support system was particularly important since its failure, if full, would result in the loss of 125,000 pounds of lobster. Mr. Gifford was responsible for the hiring and firing of the maintenance personnel. Also, even though the ship's engineers were under the operational command of Mr. White, Mr. Gifford was responsible for their technical direction.

Purchase of ships and gear. Mr. Gifford was responsible for evaluating potential vessels for use as fishing platforms; writing the specifications for their conversion; and initiating, supervising, and approving their fitting out. In all these activities Mr. Gifford worked closely with Rev. Whipple in improving designs. Mr. Gifford also spent considerable time working with manufacturers' representatives on developing improved refrigeration technology for the life-support systems. The corrosive nature of the seawater coupled with the lobster's sensitivity to trace amounts of certain metals which were traditionally used for refrigeration systems made this a difficult area.

Research

Rev. Whipple, age 41, held the title of director of research. Since 1958 he had devoted a major portion of his time to commercial fishing and to developing a number of improvements and innovations in its equipment. Among these were an hydraulic power block and various rigging and hauling devices related to high-speed handling of deep-water lobster trapping systems.[3] Rev. Whipple was constantly evaluating the operational design of the ship's fishing gear and experimenting with ways to improve it. A qualified captain himself, Rev. Whipple would often take a ship out when for some reason a captain was sick or missing. In any case, he was generally at sea whenever there was a new idea to be tried out, a frequent occurrence.

In an effort to enhance their knowledge about the habits of the lobster,

---

[3] Although the company held design patents on certain of these mechanisms, management stated that the patents were no protection against competitors' using similar but not identical equipment.

Prelude's management had recently hired a marine biologist. Mr. Gaziano remarked regarding research on the "product":

> We knew a lot about management and lobster fishing when we started, but we didn't know a damn thing about the lobster. We hired Jerry [a marine biologist] to give us some expertise in this area. He started with the task of accumulating all the data he could find on the lobster. It turned out nobody really knows a heck of a lot about them. He has three current projects. One is to set up a lobster rearing facility downstairs [corporate headquarters] and see what we can learn from that. The second project is to help us figure out what to do with the crabs we catch in our traps along with the lobsters. They are highly perishable and only bring 25 cents per pound. There is not much market for them, but, since we haul them in from the sea in quantities equal to or greater than the lobsters, we would like to exploit the resource. And lastly, we've chartered a little research sub. Jerry's going to spend five days on the bottom seeing what really goes on down there. It's going to cost us $25,000, but we will have information that no one else has.

Marketing

Prior to the acquisition of Wickford and Deep Deep late in fiscal 1971, Prelude sold most of its catch directly to wholesale lobster dealers in large lots, usually an entire shipload. As a result, the number of transactions was limited, and Mr. Gaziano was able to handle the telephone negotiations himself. He commented on the bargaining process as follows:

> The distributor knows when you have a large catch. He may say, "You have 30,000 pounds—well, we don't really want any today," and thereby drive down the price. Even with our large holding capacity we have been caught in this situation. There are no long-term, fixed-price contracts. It is cutthroat haggling to a great degree. We are really in the commodity trading business—buy and then sell at a profit; there is very little value added.

With the acquisition of Wickford and Deep Deep, each of which owned a variety of trucks and sorting tanks of 50,000 pounds capacity, marketing arrangements had changed. The original plan was for the two acquisitions combined to handle some three-fourths of Prelude's catch, although, in line with the intent to treat all three entities as profit centers, each could sell or buy where it got the best price. In any event, the Wickford and Deep Deep acquisitions happened to coincide with the precipitous drop in lobster catches, so all of Prelude's lobsters were sold "inside" during the first half of 1972.

Wickford, located in North Kingston, Rhode Island, had brought Prelude a business in live lobsters (about 70% of sales) and in other types of seafood, including other shellfish and frozen-fish products. It distributed in various ways. Thus, it had a combined retail seafood store and restaurant located in its home town, which accounted for 30% of its sales; it had a mail-order business in prepackaged clam and lobster dinners; and it operated a wholesale business in a market area that extended along the eastern seaboard south to Pennsylvania. Customers were restaurants and small dealers, whom it reached by making four delivery runs a week, locally, and to Pennsylvania, Connecticut, New York, and New Jersey.

Deep Deep, located in Boston, Massachusetts, brought Prelude a business that consisted of distributing lobsters to dealers and restaurants in New England, New York, the Midwest, West, and South, the latter three markets being served by air shipments. Deep Deep's major accounts, however, were wholesalers serving restaurants in New York City. Shipments to these accounts had to be made by common carrier, since Prelude's nonunion drivers could not gain safe access to the city's highly organized Fulton Fish market.

Critical to selling all accounts of both companies was knowing who wanted to buy what, where, when, and at what offered price. "Contacts" were a marketer's paramount asset in the lobster trade. Prelude's management believed that Mr. John P. McGeough, former owner of Wickford, and Mr. Robert D. Usen, founder and ex-president of Deep Deep, were highly qualified in this regard, basing this opinion partly on a three-week cross-country trip that the financial vice president had made with Mr. Usen prior to the Deep Deep acquisition.

Both Messrs. Usen and McGeough had agreed to follow their companies into Prelude, where they continued to serve as presidents of the two subsidiaries. Here the compensation of each would be based primarily on the total profit of his unit. Although the decline in the lobster catch had prevented a full-scale testing of the two companies' performance, Prelude management indicated that their expectations had been largely fulfilled to date.

Besides bringing in Mr. Usen and Mr. McGeough, Mr. Gaziano had in November 1971 hired a new sales manager, Mr. Duncan Scott. The new manager had been on the road since his arrival, "cold calling" potential new distributor and restaurant accounts and visiting old ones. Any business Mr. Scott turned up was referred to either Wickford or Deep Deep.

In still another marketing move in the spring of 1971, $15,000 had been invested in advertising on two Boston radio stations, WBZ and WHDH. This advertising was aimed at raising the ultimate consumer's awareness of Prelude's offshore lobster. Mr. Gaziano outlined the rationale behind this program:

> We are trying to establish brand identification for the Prelude lobster. We want people to ask for Prelude lobster—not just lobster—similar to the

Chiquita Banana strategy. Towards this end we have used radio advertising and promotional devices in the form of handouts and red plastic lobster pegs with the Prelude name etched on them. The handouts are put in our lobster shipping boxes, and Scott leaves them wherever he goes. We plan to start direct mailings. But our radio advertising was ill-timed in that we didn't follow up soon enough with sales calls, and our catches were not large enough to satisfy the demand we created.

Finance and administration

Mr. John A. Jensen, age 33, was in charge of the financial affairs of the company. In the past he had been responsible for shepherding the financial transactions required to raise needed capital. Mr. Jensen kept close tabs on the day-to-day state of affairs, maintaining an eight-week cash flow projection which he revised weekly, monitoring the daily transactions of the subsidiaries, and monitoring accounts receivable. (Restaurants and their suppliers were notoriously slow payers.)

His most current concern was centered around providing the funds needed to finance the two new ships which were planned for 1973. Exhibit 6 shows the projected income statement assuming the two new ships were added. The cost of the two vessels was estimated at $1.3 million, of which all but $300,000 could be mortgaged. Additionally, Mr. Jensen and Mr. Gaziano were concerned about the impact of interest charges on net income, interest being the main component of the fairly substantial figure carried in the operating statement as "other" income and expense (Exhibits 2 and 6). They felt that they needed a reduction in short-term debt of between $200,000 and $450,000 to "clean up" their balance sheet and reduce interest charges.

The company's underwriter had prepared a prospectus proposing a private placement of 100,000 to 150,000 shares of stock at $5 per share in order to secure the needed funds. Unfortunately, the release of the prospectus in March 1972 coincided with the drop in the catch, and the issue had had to be withdrawn.

THE OUTLOOK FOR THE FUTURE

By the summer of 1972, Prelude had weathered the downturn of fishing catches which had so far occurred that year. The company's boats had been able to bring in enough lobster to meet its $190,000 per-month cash flow breakeven (including the subsidiaries). Breakeven costs were divided as follows:

Vessel operations	$120,000	SGA	$23,000
Selling	42,000	Taxes, interest	13,000

EXHIBIT 6

PRELUDE CORPORATION
Projected Statement of Operations
(in thousands of dollars)

	Actual 1972	Pro- jected 1973	Pro- jected 1974
		For years ending April 30	
Sales*			
Prelude	$ n.a.	$2,656	$3,990
Wickford†	n.a.	1,250	1,360
Deep Deep†	n.a.	850	840
Total	$3,064	$4,756	$6,190
Costs and expenses			
Vessel operations	$1,175	$1,464	$2,246
Purchases	1,062	1,420	1,416
Depreciation	253	312	362
S, G&A	565	780	1,084
Total	$3,055	$3,976	$5,108
Operating income (loss)	9	780	1,082
Other income (expense)‡	(157)	(123)	(180)
Income (loss) before taxes	$ (148)	$ 657	$ 902
Provision for income taxes	...	338	464
Income (loss) before extraordinary credit	$ (148)	$ 319	$ 438
Extraordinary credit from operating loss carryforward	...	272	347
Net income	$ (148)	$ 591	$ 785

* Assumes that fishing conditions parallel those of May 1970–January 1972; that two new ships for a total of six begin fishing in fiscal 1974; that sales of the subsidiaries continue at mid-1972 levels; and that Prelude receives a price per pound of $1.33, with 25% of its sales to outsiders.
† Assumes that the subsidiaries will handle 75% of sales reported by the parent.
‡ Primarily interest expense.

Sources and Uses of Funds
(in thousands of dollars)

	1973	1974
	For years ending April 30	
Uses of funds:		
Increase in fixed assets (new vessels)	$ 300	$ ...
Increase in current assets (32% of sales)	531	460
Reduction in note payable	350	...
Reduction in long-term debt	370	270
Total uses of funds	$1,551	$ 730
Sources of funds:		
Increase in accounts payable (11% of sales)	$ 191	$ 157
Net operating income	319	438
Anticipated operating loss carryforward	272	347
Depreciation	312	362
Total sources of funds	$1,094	$1,304
Funds needed (surplus)	$ 457	$ (574)

Source: Company records.

In terms of breakeven per trip, this monthly $190,000 (which excluded depreciation of about $25,000) worked out to about $22,000. The breakeven catch in pounds varied, of course, with the price attainable in the market. In the spring of 1972 it ran about 8,000 pounds a trip, since the wholesale price of "select" lobster had risen to more than $3 per pound during some of this period.

Although the lobster catch had recently risen (Exhibit 1), no one knew when or whether it would return to normal. On the one hand, industry optimists argued that the scarce condition was only a transient event and that there were still "plenty of lobsters out there for everybody." On the other hand, industry pessimists, championed by federal fishery officials, raised doubts about the long-term viability of the resource and were calling for some form of management to sustain the yields.

Competition

Even under "managed" conditions, Prelude's leaders expected the company to survive if not to prosper—barring total disappearance of the offshore lobster. They felt that they had the staying power to outlast the one-boat competitors who had come in on a shoestring and, further, that they had an edge of experience and success which would enable them to outdistance the newer and better capitalized multiboat competitors. Chief among these had been Deep Deep; Mr. Usen had had three new boats fishing out of Boston since 1968 but had not been able to make them pay. He was presently operating two of these boats under a separate company but selling his catch at market price to Prelude and attempting to dispose of the fleet. A second established competitor, MATCO, which fished five boats off the Virginia coast, was also reported to be in financial trouble, having been dragged under by its allegedly overextended parent, Marine International Corporation. Although three other firms were putting three to five boats each out to sea, Mr. Gaziano was not particularly worried about the threat they presented. He summed up his feelings as follows:

> This is going to be one hell of an interesting summer [1972]. We're going to have some new boats out there, each backed by some rich Johnny who is fascinated by the sex appeal of lobstering. They're going to find out the hard way how much it really costs to pot fish offshore. We've got a real shakeout coming.

In management's eyes a more real threat was that Prelude itself would be "taken over" by a larger company. Although there were no blocks of stock large enough to make for an easy takeover, the depressed state of

Prelude's stock made a tender bid not unlikely.[4] For example, Mr. Jensen had heard a speech in which a spokesman for a West Coast seafood firm with 1971 sales of $25 million had stated:

We are, then, a seafood company. And we want to remain a seafood company. The potential in utilizing the rich harvest of the sea is enough to keep any company of our size busy for as long into the future as we care to look.

Already we are expanding from a solid base in the Pacific salmon industry into a much broader segment of the total spectrum of Alaskan and Northwestern fisheries. But we do not see ourselves as confined to Alaska and the Pacific Northwest. Rather we are interested in fisheries virtually anywhere on the globe if we can find a way to enter them in a sound and profitable manner. And, yes, we are constantly looking for acquisitions which could expand and complement our activities in the seafood industry.[5]

Expansion and diversification

With the acquisition of Wickford and Deep Deep, Prelude had achieved integration all the way through to the consumer, and management was considering expanding this chain in several ways. One way would be to develop more restaurant/lobster stores similar to the one in Wickford, Rhode Island. Another way would be to enlarge on the branding program already underway. One California firm, Foster Farms, Inc., had been very successful in branding its fresh chickens and placing them in supermarkets.

A third alternative entailed broadening the product base by marketing other types of seafood that could be purchased outside and then resold through the company's distribution system. Flounder, trout, clams, oysters were among the types of gourmet seafood products bought by restaurants in much the same way as lobster was.

Processing and marketing crab meat was another possibility, but somewhat remote. Canning crab meat required a multimillion dollar investment in centrifuging equipment and a continuous supply of crab meat. Although Prelude did catch a lot of crabs, they could not be stored together with lobsters; furthermore, the catch was sporadic. There was, however, a minority small business company in New Bedford which was using government funds to develop a crab processing plant, and Prelude was watching this development with interest.

---

[4] In June 1972, the bid price of Prelude's stock was in the range of $2¼–$3. Five brokers made an over-the-counter market in the 530,000 shares outstanding. Of these, Rev. Whipple held 92,400; a prominent Boston family, 70,000; Mr. Usen, 22,845; and Mr. McGeough, 17,500. The balance of the holdings were widely fragmented, with no individual or institution owning more than 15,000 shares. No other officer or employee held more than a few thousand shares, although this group as a whole held qualified options granted at prices of $6.50 to $9 on 53,500 shares.

[5] Larry M. Kaner, Vice President, Whitney-Fidalgo Seafoods, Inc. Speech to Boston Security Analysts, February 9, 1971.

Nor were Mr. Gaziano's interests entirely confined to seafood. Previously the company had looked at the possibility of acquiring a manufacturer of small boats but had been beaten out by the CML Group, Inc. In any event, Mr. Gaziano did feel that any future expansion or acquisition efforts should be seaward-oriented, once the present difficulties were resolved.

APPENDIX ON THE LOBSTER INDUSTRY

Having graced the Pilgrims' first Thanksgiving, the northern lobster remained a U.S. gourmet delicacy, demand for which was growing abroad. Supply had not kept pace, however, even though the U.S. market drew 80%–90% of the Canada-landed catch, thereby roughly doubling poundage available for domestic consumption and export.

From a 1960 peak of 73.2 million pounds live weight, supply had dropped to 56.5 million pounds in 1967, but rose again thereafter, partly owing to the success of new techniques of offshore fishing:

Total U.S. supplies of northern lobster (live weight in millions of pounds)

	1968	1969	1970	1971
U.S. landed	32.6	33.8	34.2	33.3
Imports*	31.3	31.6	30.2	34.5
Total†	63.9	65.4	64.3	67.9

* Converted to live weight equivalent.
† Includes exports (about 1% in 1968, and growing).
Source: National Marine Fisheries Service.

Shortage had sent prices rising even faster than general inflation, and in 1971 the 33.3 million-pound, U.S. landed catch brought fishermen $35.1 million in sales, making lobsters the second most valuable single species (after Gulf shrimp) in the $643 million fishing industry.

The resource

The northern lobster inhabited the chilly waters of the North Atlantic from Newfoundland to North Carolina. Two populations had been observed, one in the shallow water from Canada's Maritimes south to New Jersey, the other further out, usually in the deep, cold canyons of the continental shelf from Massachusetts to the Carolinas. During the spring and fall the latter population migrated and could thus sometimes be found crawling across the flats of the shelf. Estimated weights and numbers for "legal sized" (legally fishable) lobsters in the two populations were as follows:

Popu- lation	Total weight (millions of lbs.)	Annual replenishment (millions of lbs.)	Number (millions)	Average weight (lbs.)
Inshore	25–31	15–20 est.	20–25	1¼
Offshore	100–120	25 est.	25–30	4

Besides fluctuating from year to year, lobster catch rates were seasonal, being lowest in the winter when lobsters and fishermen were least active and highest in October and May. Since demand was highest in mid-summer (shore-dinner time), prices rose then, giving dealers a motive to buy and hold lobsters in enclosed tidal pools until values increased.

Harvesting the resource

Inshore fishing. Inshore and offshore lobster fishing differed in technique, the inshore method being much the same in the 1970s as in the 1840s. A 30-foot boat, manned by its owner and a relative, could manage 300–800 lathe traps or "pots," sinking each at depths of less than 30 fathoms and hauling it up with a power winch to empty, bait, and toss overboard again.

By 1971 some 8,000 individuals were engaged in inshore lobster fishing, and a million pots were being used. Fishing was so intensive that government sources estimated that 90% of the legal-sized inshore lobster population was caught every year. Of this total, some 70% was delivered to ports in Maine. Optimum investment for entering this trade was estimated at $8,000–$10,000, but anyone could enter who had a few used traps, an outboard motorboat, and a license.

Offshore fishing. Only after World War II were feasible methods devised for fishing the offshore lobster population, and only in the late 1950s did the industry start significant growth. By 1968, two techniques were being used: trawling and potting on long lines.

Trawling involved scooping up migrating lobsters from the offshore flats by dragging weighted nets along the bottom. With the government pointing the way on methods, catches rose quickly, fluctuating around 5.5 million pounds a year in 1965–71 but ranging between 3.9 million in 1966 and 7.1 million in 1970.

Attractive features of offshore trawling included the absence of competition from Canada and Maine (where it was illegal to land the catch), relatively modest manning requirements compared with other types of fishing, and the low investment needed to equip a boat for switching back and forth from ground fish to lobsters. Increasingly unattractive features included overcrowding, loss of expensive gear when nets were dragged across the rising number of offshore pots, and injuries to the catch which might render 50%–70% of it unsalable. Thus, government sources believed that this industry segment would level off at 100–130 boats.

Offshore lobster potting started with experiments to develop gear for trapping lobsters in the deep canyons of the continental shelf, where government researchers reported a year-round abundance. Prominent among the first experimenters was Prelude's Rev. Whipple, who finally settled on a method that entailed a mile-long line, buoyed and anchored at each end, to which 50–75 weighted traps were attached by four-foot wires. Keys to his system were gear strong enough to haul the heavy line and a special clip to permit the automatic attachment and detachment of the traps as the ship steamed along.

In 1970 this technique proved its worth when Prelude landed nearly all of the 1.5 million pounds attributed to offshore potting in the first statistics to segregate this figure. In 1971 the offshore potting catch rose to 2.3 million pounds, but this was shared by a growing number of competitors, lured in part by Prelude's success. By mid-1972, 92 vessels were fishing 50,000 offshore pots, nearly half of which had come into service during the previous six months.

Such an influx brought technical problems. These included loss of gear when one's boat line was laid across another's or when the lines were cut by boats pursuing fin fish. Crowding, too, was a problem in the canyons, with the result that some pot lines had been set upon the flats, where they ruined the offshore trawlers' nets and motivated trawlers to retaliate.

Costs varied widely for putting a vessel into offshore lobster potting, some vessels having been converted from dragging to potting for as little as $50,000, whereas Prelude's fourth ship came to almost $600,000, including both cost of the hull and conversion.

Regulation

Lobstering was a regulated trade, the regulations being set by the states, the Federal Government, and international conventions. Thus, to protect the resource, all states except North Carolina and Virginia set a minimum size for a landable lobster, and most states forbade the harvesting of egg-bearing females. To protect the consumer, the Federal Government required all lobsters to be alive when sold and forbade U.S. ships to process them at sea. To govern fishing rights, nations had agreed not to fish within 12 miles of one another's coasts, and most had signed an international convention establishing a court-enforced code of conduct for vessels.

One clause in this code, of special interest to lobstermen, gave right of way to "fixed" equipment such as pot lines. This requirement tended, however, to be ignored by ships in "hot pursuit" of fin fish, particularly, lobstermen believed, by foreign ships. In any event, losses were frequent and significant: one incident alone could damage or destroy several trap lines costing about $7,000 each and thereby put a one-boat operation out of business. Lobstermen vociferously complained, but the U.S. Coast Guard lacked enough patrol boats for adequate policing. New England congressmen, however, had been persuaded to sponsor a bill to reimburse fishermen for cumulative gear losses of about $500,000.

In other future plans, the Federal Government was pressing the states to enact uniform and more stringent laws for resource protection within the three-mile limit, which was the area of state jurisdiction. To protect the resource further out, the Federal Government might take several steps, from imposing a federal license requirement to extending the 12-mile limit to a highly controversial 200 miles. What fishermen favored was bringing foreign as well as domestic deep-sea lobstermen under federal control, an objective that could be accomplished by officially declaring lobsters to be "creatures of the shelf" as opposed to "free-swimming" fish.

How urgent it might be to take protective action on the offshore resource was not clear. Reported removal of 14 million pounds[6] by all takers was well below the 25 million pounds a year that government biologists estimated could be removed without depleting the resource, but no one knew how many pounds were being taken out unreported or how many were maimed and killed through fishing operations. One highly placed official admitted, "It would not be at all unreasonable to speculate that as much as 25 million pounds might be being removed."

Handling and transport

Unlike inshore lobstermen, offshore lobstermen making 10-day runs required refrigerated tanks to hold their catch, not just barrels and some seaweed for moisture. Once delivered to the dock, most lobsters again went into holding: perhaps for a few days in a dockside "car" or floating tank, then for a few months in a "pound" or tidal pool, and then for a few more days in a dealer's sorting and culling tank. In total, cars, pounds, and dealers' tanks in the Northeast could accommodate an estimated 7 million pounds.

With the advent of refrigeration and lightweight packing containers, shipments by rail or truck posed no problem, and shipment by air could carry northern lobsters to far-distant points.

Over the years, consumers had come to expect their lobsters live. Weak and dying lobsters could be culled and cooked, then canned and frozen, but despite high prices these operations barely recovered their costs, so dealers pressed suppliers for a high-quality catch.

---

[6] In 1972, U.S. offshore trawling and potting reported 5.7 million and 2.3 million pounds; foreign lobstermen about 5 million, and U.S. groundfish fishermen about 1 million.

Aquaculture

Although worked on for some time, techniques to supplement lobster fishing by "farming" remained undeveloped in 1972. Progress had been made, however, especially on the biological side: lobsters had been developed to breed in captivity, and experiments had been started to breed selectively for fast growth, bright color, two crusher claws, and high meat content. Already, lobsters had been grown to one-pound size in two years compared with six years in the wild. And lobsters had been grown to half-pound size in six to seven months, with tails bigger than any commercially available shrimp.

The big problem lay with engineering the life-support system. Depending on investment in development and plant, the start of commercial operations was put at two to five years away by the best known authority in lobster hatchery.

Marketing the resource

Channels. As indicated by solid lines on the diagram, lobsters typically moved from the fishermen's barrel or tank to a local buyer with a lobster car or so, who then sold to a large dealer operating a lobster pound. From thence, the lobsters passed to a primary wholesaler, who sold to a retail outlet—most likely to a restaurant, since about 80% of all lobsters reached the consumer that way. Lobsters could pass to the retailer in several alternate ways, however, as indicated by dotted lines. These could either add or eliminate a step.

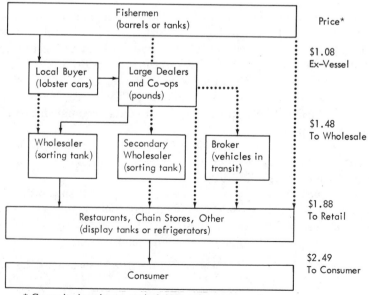

* Casewriter's estimate, typical 1971 price per pound.

Price. As indicated by the price data on the diagram, prices more than doubled between the fisherman and the consumer, with retailers (largely restaurants) accounting for the biggest rise. The estimated price figures shown conceal wide seasonal variations, as well as variations for different weights of lobsters, and a steep, year-to-year uptrend:

Liveweight wholesale prices per pound,
Fulton Fish Market, New York City

	"Chix" *1⅛ lbs.*	*"Quarters"* *1¼ lbs.*	*"Duces"* *2 lbs.*
1970			
High	$1.85	$1.88	$1.89
Low	1.24	1.34	1.36
1971			
High	2.06	2.14	2.66
Low	1.45	1.46	1.47

Source: National Marine Fisheries Service, *Shellfish Situation and Outlook, Annual Review, 1971.*

Weighted average annual price per pound paid to Maine fishermen

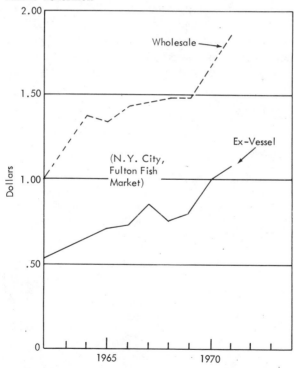

Two major market segments combined to yield these aggregate statistics. Restaurants and fancy seafood stores, which favored "select" (1½–2½ pound lobsters) had a relatively constant demand, so that prices sometimes reached astronomical levels. Supermarkets and volume restaurants had a price-sensitive demand and tended to drop out of the picture when prices went above a certain level. When prices were low, however, chains tended to buy for promotions, thus helping to stabilize the market.

Competition among distributors. Companies of varying types and sizes were engaged in lobster distribution, and they competed fiercely to handle the limited supply on a price basis favorable to themselves.

Two of the largest entities in the business were J. Hook and Bay State, both of Boston, who together handled an estimated 30 million pounds a year. Despite their size, they might find themselves outbid by "small lotters," who were able to sell crate lots in Europe for twice what their large competitors were getting from a high-volume restaurant account.

Hook and Bay State operated quite differently, thus illustrating the wide variety of ways that entities in lobster distribution could be linked together or combined. Bay State specialized in furnishing the restaurant trade with sorted lobster at a stable year-round price, which might be above or below the current market. While it had preferred to confine itself to a wholesale function, it had recently been forced to enter the dealer function of running a pound in order to secure its sources of supply. In contrast, Hook maintained only a skeleton staff year-round, but geared up when the market was good to provide tremendous quantities of case lots of unsorted lobsters to secondary wholesalers. Hook also brokered a large volume to chains.

A. G. Brown and Son, Ltd.

A. G. BROWN AND SON of Halifax, Nova Scotia, was the largest food broker in the Canadian Maritimes, which included the provinces of New Brunswick, Prince Edward Island, Nova Scotia, and Newfoundland. Mr. Garnet Brown, president and majority owner,[1] maintained that the brokerage business was ideal for an entrepreneur since it required no inventory and little capital, and provided a continuing, valuable service to its clients. However, despite his considerable success in expanding revenues by over 125% from 1965 to 1969, Mr. Brown was disturbed by the steady decline in profits during this period, culminating in a small loss in 1969. At one point he mused:

Dad and I alone once sold $1,000,000 from our homes. Now it takes 14 salesmen and an office staff of five to sell $7,000,000. Of course, we wouldn't have the accounts if we didn't give the service. But one would think some of those added revenue dollars would reach the bottom line. I've been giving some thought to a couple of possibilities which might help, though—some having to do with the way we run the business and others having to do with how we might expand it.

HISTORY

After graduating from high school in 1946, Mr. Brown left Halifax to play baseball for two years in the Brooklyn Dodgers farm system.

---

[1] Garnet Brown owned 89%, Donald Brown, a brother, 9%, and other members of the family 2%.

211

In 1948 he returned to Halifax and played ball with a local team for two more years. His athletic reputation then helped him obtain a job as an apprentice draftsman in a local shipyard.

In 1953 Mr. Brown's father, who had quit his job as a candy salesman to start a brokerage business in 1946, was offered the account of an expanding biscuit maker. Feeling that he had reached his capacity to provide service to the retailer, he arranged for his son to take the account. In 1970 it was the largest annual revenue producer for the company.

A. G. Brown and Son was formed as a partnership in 1956 and handled a retail sales volume of $500,000 that first year. Earle Hilchey, formerly a biscuit salesman for a national company, became the first nonfamily employee four years later; and in 1965, the year Mr. Brown's father passed away, responsibility for the New Brunswick territory was given to Donald Carlton. Then in 1968 the firm moved from a cramped, dimly lit two-room office of 800 square feet into a new 4,200-square-foot building constructed for the company and owned personally by Mr. Brown.

Financial statements are provided in Exhibits 1 and 2, and the growth in employees, revenues, and principals since 1962 is reflected in Exhibit 3.

THE MARITIMES

The economy of the Maritimes had historically been dependent on farming, fishing, and commerce rather than industry, due in large part to the distance from major markets, their small population, rough topography, and a relative absence of industrially useful resources. The Canadian government, however, had recently begun a series of projects designed to speed economic development and increase the level of disposable income in the Maritimes, then among the lowest in the country. Unlike neighboring Quebec, the predominant language and ethnic background in these provinces was English rather than French. The population tended to be split evenly between towns and the countryside, with a few large cities such as metropolitan Halifax (population 200,000) containing most of those classified as urban in Exhibit 4. Many small food stores, listed as "others" in Exhibit 5, and a few chains served the people of the Maritimes and were at least partially dependent upon the information and services supplied by food brokers.

FOOD BROKERS

In the United States and Canada, the food broker was an agent of one or more principals and was paid a commission of 3%–8% of sales to sell the principals' products and provide detail services to accounts and retailers. In Canada brokers did not normally obtain custody, pos-

EXHIBIT 1

A. G. BROWN AND SON, LTD.
Income Statements

	1965	100.0%	1966	100.0%	1967	100.0%	1968	100.0%	1969	100.0%
Approximate yearly sales*	$2,782,720		$3,561,980		$4,813,420		$5,740,260		$6,267,600	
Commission revenue	$ 139,136	100.0%	$ 178,099	100.0%	$ 240,671	100.0%	$ 287,013	100.0%	$ 313,380	100.0%
Expenses										
Advertising and promotion	$ 5,223	3.8%	$ 6,826	3.8%	$ 6,938	2.9%	$ 10,136	3.5%	$ 7,795	2.5%
Association and club dues	1,046	0.7	1,535	0.9	1,444	0.6	1,658	0.6	3,074	1.0
Audit and legal fees	1,088	0.8	2,817	1.6	4,404	1.8	4,880	1.7	8,304	2.7
Interest	2,183	1.6	2,554	1.4	4,943	2.0	6,573	2.3	7,171	2.3
Car expense	17,366	12.5	22,974	12.9	31,176	12.9	33,487	11.7	39,285	12.5
Depreciation	298	0.2	405	0.2	580	0.2	2,259	0.8	2,100	0.7
Donations	95	0.1	195	0.1	946	0.4	1,128	0.4	400	0.1
Group insurance	1,604	1.2	1,853	1.2	1,213	0.5	2,662	0.9	2,834	0.9
Property expense	1,531	1.1	2,450	1.1	1,491	0.6	1,126	0.4	1,710	0.6
Insurance	134	0.1	146	0.1	220	0.1	418	0.1	165	0.0
Office supplies	1,570	1.1	3,517	1.1	3,068	1.3	3,937	1.4	5,010	1.6
Pension	1,036	0.7	1,353	0.7	1,909	0.8	2,018	0.7	2,243	0.7
Rent and storage	480	0.3	620	0.3	1,839	0.8	11,265	3.9	13,709	4.4
Salaries and bonuses	55,179	39.7	68,526	39.7	114,441	47.6	153,457	53.5	162,131	51.7
Sundry	1,712	1.2	2,179	1.2	2,243	0.9	4,449	1.5	7,961	2.5
Taxes	30	0.0	48	0.0	104	0.0		0.0	1,486	0.5
Telephone	2,968	2.1	3,759	2.1	4,819	2.0	6,429	2.2	7,563	2.4
Travel	18,047	13.0	24,900	13.0	34,115	14.2	38,312	13.4	40,428	12.9
Unemployment insurance	201	0.1	335	0.1	531	0.2	349	0.1	1,359	0.4
Heat, light, water		0.0		0.0		0.0		0.0	2,593	0.8
Total expenses	$ 111,791	80.3%	$ 146,992	81.5%	$ 216,424	89.8%	$ 284,543	99.1%	$ 317,321	101.2%
Net profit from operations before taxes	27,345	19.7	31,107	18.5	24,247	10.2	2,470	0.9	(3,941)	(1.2)

* Based on an average commission rate of 5%.
Source: Company records.

EXHIBIT 2

A. G. BROWN AND SON, LTD.
Balance Sheets
As of December 31

	1967	1968	1969
Assets			
Cash	$ 2,003	$ 11,791	$ 5
Accounts receivable	35,072	50,900	39,555
Stock subscriptions receivable.	4,996	3,888	3,888
Loans to directors	17,604	50,672	59,247
Travel advances	650	875	. 975
Prepaid rent	. . .	13,500	. . .
Tax overpayment	. . .	1,157	585
Fixed assets, net of depreciation	7,738	14,149	13,181
Cash value of life insurance	7,163	13,154	21,885
Investments at cost	207,652	149,082	114,080
Land	12,995	. . .	. . .
Total assets	$295,873	$309,168	$253,401
Liabilities			
Bank loan	$ 61,961	$ 86,028	$ 69,011
Accounts payable	16,744	32,480	29,591
Accounts payable to securities dealers	47,679	36,811	. . .
Employees' tax deductions	877	6,870	3,498
Taxes payable	4,853	. . .	7,560
Loans from directors	2,032	. . .	. . .
Capital stock	10,000	10,000	10,000
Surplus*	151,727	136,979	133,741
Total liabilities	$295,873	$309,168	$253,401

* Surplus account will not balance with income statement because corporate income taxes and losses on sales of investments are not reflected in the profit or loss figures in Exhibit 1.
Source: Company records.

session, or control of the actual product and did not have an interest in the buyer or the seller of the product.[2] The National Food Brokers Association[3] maintained as a policy that brokers should act as sales agents only and not speculate or purchase for their own accounts, reasoning that such actions would jeopardize the fundamental relationships of broker service to both principals and accounts.

Principals were generally manufacturers of a processed consumer food product, such as canned peas, although some dealt in fresh produce which was also sold to canners. *Accounts* were either wholesalers who distributed to independent retail grocers, affiliated retail groups such as IGA (Independent Grocers Association) which joined together to

[2] These activities were prohibited in the United States by the Robinson Patman Act which made the collection of brokerage fees on one's own purchases illegal. The purpose of this provision was to prevent large buyers from owning their own brokerage operation and thereby receiving an unfair price advantage over small buyers who could not support their own brokerage operation.

[3] The association represented brokers from Canada and the United States.

EXHIBIT 3

A. G. BROWN AND SON, LTD.
Business Statistics

	1962	1963	1964	1965	1966	1967	1968	1969
Growth in revenue over previous year		34%	15%	14%	35%	35%	19%	9%
Profit/revenue				+19.6%	+17.5%	+10.1%	+0.9%	-1.3%
Trial accounts or accounts with commissions of less than $1,000								
Number added		4	7	4	6	5	8	9
Number lost*		1	2	1	3	2	3	3
Total accounts	7	10	15	18	21	24	29	35
Accounts with commissions of over $1,000								
Number added		4	4	2	4	2	5	6
Number lost*		0	1	0	0	0	2	2
Total accounts	4	8	11	13	17	19	22	26
Revenue added†		$ 13,900	$ 23,700	$ 5,500	$ 25,800	$ 9,100	$ 12,800	$ 27,600
Revenue lost‡		300	1,100	100	800	900	3,100	13,700
Revenue for year		99,188	114,094	139,136	178,099	240,671	287,013	313,380
Total net change§		+25,242	+14,906	+25,042	+38,963	+62,572	+46,342	+26,367
Number of employees:								
Salesmen	6	6	8	9	9	14	13	12
Office staff	2	3	3	3	3	4	4	4

* Accounts voluntarily lost or withdrawn by seller.
† Commissions in first full year with A. G. Brown.
‡ Commissions in last year with A. G. Brown.
§ Over previous year, including growth of old accounts.
Source: All figures based on casewriter's interpretation of company-supplied data.

EXHIBIT 4
The Atlantic provinces: Demographic data

	New Brunswick	Nova Scotia	Prince Edward Island	New-foundland
Population (in thousands)*				
Urban†	312	439	40	267
Rural	304	317	69	227
Total	616	756	109	494
Ethnic background				
British	55%	71%	80%	94%
French	39	12	17	4
German	1	6	1	. . .
Dutch	1	3	1	. . .
Other	4	8	1	2
	100%	100%	100%	100%

* 1966 census.
† Living in a town or city.
Source: *Market Data,* Survey of Markets 1969.

pool their buying and merchandising power, or chain supermarkets which owned many stores. *Retailers* were the individual consumer outlets for merchandise supplied by their buying organization.

The food broker acted as a sales representative for his principals at both account and retail levels. At the account level the broker dealt with buyers or buying committees. As new principals and products were added to his line, the broker sought to have his accounts accept the products · by providing samples and market data. If a product was "listed," the broker's salesmen carried samples to the retail stores to introduce it to the owners or managers and solicit orders.

If the retailer was an independent, orders taken by the salesmen were usually relayed to .the wholesaler who delivered the merchandise from his inventory. Orders could also be "drop shipped" directly from inventory maintained by the principal in a public warehouse, in which case the principal billed the wholesaler who in turn billed the retailer. Wholesalers also had salesmen, but they usually took orders for only those items which a retailer needed immediately or called specifically to obtain.

If the retailer was an affiliate or part of a chain, the headquarters staff determined which products were mandatory and which were optional for a store and stocked most of them in its own warehouse. Store managers then ordered their requirements from this warehouse, and headquarters reordered through the broker when their supply ran low.

In addition to order taking and inventory checking, the broker's salesmen communicated information on special allowances, planned promo-

EXHIBIT 5
Grocery market statistics

	B.C.	Alta.	Sask.	Man.	Ont.	P.Q.	Maritime provinces				
							Total	N.B.	N.S.	P.E.I.	Nfld.
Sales (millions)											
1961	$365	$242	$129	$164	$1,399	$1,078	$325	$101	$147	$15	$63
1968	613	363	176	257	2,100	1,707	455	151	190	20	93
1969 (est.)	650	398	180	273	2,317	1,794	471	154	202	21	94
Increase, 1969/1968	6.1%	9.6%	2.7%	5.9%	10.3%	5.1%	3.6%	1.9%	6.2%	2.2%	1.5%
Chains' share of sales											
1961	48.3%	50.4%	35.6%	40.1%	60.2%	33.8%	29.1%	28.8%	30.4%	15.7%	15.7%
1968	59.1	47.9	47.9	40.4	62.0	34.4	31.2	31.7	36.2	22.0	22.0
1969	55.7	47.5	47.5	42.5	64.6	35.6	33.9	32.2	36.4	31.6	31.6
Sales as a percent of total Canadian market	10.7%	6.5%	3.0%	4.5%	38.1%	29.5%	7.7%	2.5%	3.3%	0.3%	1.5%
Food stores											
Chains	252	108	82	105	1,306	486	103	...	...	...	...
Groups	744	805	454	609	2,125	2,860	412	...	...	...	...
Others	928	466	697	611	2,761	6,083	4,219	...	...	...	...
No. of chains	6	8	8	8	19	10	4	...	...	...	...
No. of groups	10	22	22	22	18	63	13	...	...	...	...
No. of wholesalers	4	10	10	10	8	26	8	...	...	...	...
Population increase, 1969/1966	10.3%	6.7%	0.4%	1.7%	7.1%	3.5%	n.a.	1.3%	0.9%	1.3%	4.3%
Per capita PDI*											
1963	$1,805	$1,617	$1,742	$1,541	$1,824	$1,382	n.a.	$1,081	$1,221	$1,047	$ 958
1968	2,370	2,260	2,060	2,290	2,520	2,050	n.a.	1,640	1,780	1,490	1,280
1969	2,460	2,365	2,160	2,395	2,625	2,150	n.a.	1,735	1,870	1,570	1,350
Per capita FSS†											
1963	$235	$190	$145	$193	$238	$223	n.a.	$183	$210	$168	$141
1968	305	238	183	265	287	288	n.a.	242	251	187	183
1969	308	255	188	278	311	300	n.a.	246	265	191	183

*Personal disposable income.
†Food store sales.
n.a. = not available.
Source: *Canadian Grocer*, February 1970.

tions, and new merchandising techniques. They also constructed displays to promote their principal's products and paid close attention to perish-able or easily damaged items, calling attention to unsalable ones or removing them from the shelves. Since food stores typically stocked from 4,000 to 7,000 items, the broker traditionally assisted the retailer in merchandising his store and maintaining a balanced inventory.

Some of the functions of the food broker are summarized in Exhibit 6; major product groups, special services, and potential accounts other than wholesalers and chains are listed in Exhibit 7.

EXHIBIT 6

Major functions of a food broker

Order and control—taking orders from a retailer and transmitting them to the account serving the retailer; taking orders from the account and transmitting them to the manufacturer; following the progress of orders in the supply pipeline.

Creative selling—using marketing techniques to encourage the purchase and acceptance of products.

Product introduction—the process of first getting an account to stock a new item and then making certain that retailers know of its existence, purpose, and availability, encouraging an initial order, and checking to be certain that it reaches the shelf.

Promotional follow-through—informing accounts and retailers of coming promotions, encouraging participation and cooperation, and checking at the retail level to insure adequate preparation and stocks.

Retail display—advising retailers on the best means to display products and encouraging them to use special fixtures, end-of-aisle, or promotional displays.

Local-level supervision—educating retailers and accounts to new methods of selling, promoting, pricing, and displaying; checking to ascertain that adequate inventories are on hand, that damaged or overage products are removed from the shelves.

Establish prestige—helping create brand images for their principals' products with accounts and retailers.

Clerical—assembling information as required by the accounts and principals on cost, volumes, prices, etc.

Field reporting—apprising principals of competitive activity directed against their products and suggesting countermeasures.

Source: National Food Brokers Association *Handbook.*

Competitive aspects

Since one broker's products often competed with those of another broker, it might be assumed that they viewed one another as competitors. However, because a broker was seldom permitted by the principals involved to represent competing products, and because most grocery stores stocked multiple brands of an item anyway, brokers felt that their main competition came from direct sales forces, on the one hand, and private brands, on the other. The threats were very different in nature.

EXHIBIT 7
Product groups, special services, and nongrocer accounts

Product Groups

1. Alcoholic beverages
2. Baby foods
*3. Candy and chewing gum
*4. Cereals
*5. Coffee and tea
*6. Condiments, olives, pickles, sauces, vinegar
*7. Crackers, biscuits, cookies
*8. Dairy products, cheese, margarine
*9. Dietetic (low calorie) and health-food specialties
10. Feed, hay, grain
*11. Fish, canned
*12. Fish, other than canned or frozen
*13. Flour—barreled, sacked, packaged
*14. Food products, miscellaneous
15. Frozen foods, consumer sizes
16. Frozen foods, food service (institutional) and industrial
*17. Fruits, vegetables, juices—canned
18. Fruit, dried
19. Gourmet foods
*20. Health and beauty aids, drug products
*21. Household supplies and equipment, such as cleaning supplies, insecticides, home canning supplies, wraps
22. Industrial equipment and supplies, such as cans, cartons, and caps
23. Ingredients for industrial users
*24. Jams, jellies, honey, spreads
*25. Laundry supplies, such as soaps, detergents, bleaches, starch, softeners
*26. Meat and poultry, canned ·
27. Meat and poultry products; other than canned or frozen
*28. Nonfood products, miscellaneous
29. Nuts
30. Paper products
*31. Pet foods and supplies
32. Prepared foods—canned, packaged
33. Produce, fresh fruits and vegetables
*34. Salad dressings, mayonnaise
35. Salt, seasonings, spices
*36. Shortenings—solid, liquid
37. Snack foods
38. Soft drinks
39. Soft goods, such as towels, hosiery, clothing
40. Store supplies, such as bags, trays, wraps
41. Sugar
42. Vegetables, dried, such as beans, rice, peas

Special Services

1. Exclusive sales agent—the broker acts for one or more sellers through other brokers
2. Exporting services
*3. Importing services
4. Industrial users—broker maintains special department for sale of products to industrial users
5. Food service (institutional)—broker maintains special department for sale of products for distribution to food-service users
6. Food service (institutional): end-user service—broker maintains sales personnel available for end-user merchandising, sales service, and detail work
*7. Merchandising service—broker maintains a force of salesmen available for retail merchandising, sales service, and detail work
*8. Private-label products

Nongrocer Accounts

*1. Bakery and dairy supply wholesalers
*2. Candy and tobacco wholesalers
*3. Drug trade
*4. Hardware trade
5. Industrial users (bakeries, dairies, meatpackers, bottlers, other manufacturers and processors)
6. Food-service (institutional) wholesalers
7. Janitor-supply wholesalers
8. Military installations
*9. Rack merchandisers
*10. Variety and/or department store trade

*Handled by, performed by, or sold to by A. G. Brown and Son, Ltd.
Source: National Food Brokers Association *Handbook.*

Manufacturers used brokers in large part to avoid the cost of a sales force and to gain distribution rapidly through established sales organizations. In the case of a small manufacturer with one or two products, the economics were perhaps obvious, since broad distribution could be accomplished internally only with many salesmen, whose time traveling between accounts and retailers would represent a sizable expense. However, for a large multiproduct manufacturer or a manufacturer who required significant amounts of service at the retail level, the economic advantage and perhaps the effectiveness of brokers were less apparent. Some manufacturers used both direct sales forces and brokers, although not in the same region.

Conversely, a grocery chain which had its own private brand usually established direct connections with a manufacturer, supervised all activities related to selling the products, and in doing so was able to offer the line at a lower price than comparable products. Further, it was not uncommon for a chain to restrict the number of competing brands or sizes in its retail stores to give the private brand an advantage.

Thus, both seller and buyer were evaluating the cost and effectiveness of the broker's services in the context of their own marketing and distribution strategies. Complicating the broker's task were a number of trends that appeared to be gathering force in food manufacturing and retailing in the United States and Canada.

First, the product lines of many manufacturers were expanding through the introduction of new products or the acquisition of other manufacturers. This tended to increase the frequency with which a broker experienced conflicts among the products of the companies he represented. To resolve the conflict, the broker frequently had to part with some or all of one principal's business, retaining the principal which provided the greater revenues. In addition to increasing the importance to the broker of a few conglomerate manufacturers, proliferating product lines hastened the point at which direct selling became economically feasible.

Second, as competition among manufacturers for market share intensified, promotions and deals to consumers, retailers, and wholesalers multiplied dramatically. This, coupled with the proliferation of processed foods, greatly increased the complexity of the salesman's job. Proper timing and accurate communication became increasingly important since buyers were limited in the number of promotions they could execute.

Third, grocery trade publications such as *Grocery Manufacturer* reported that supermarket growth appeared to have slowed as specialty stores[4] and fast-food operations captured more of the retail food market.

---

[4] Chains of small, neighborhood stores which carried only high-turnover items such as bread and milk usually charged lower prices than supermarkets and usually remained open when supermarkets closed.

Moreover, traditional segments of the supermarket business such as canned goods were decreasing in importance as frozen and precooked food and nonfood items gained acceptance. These trends not only slowed the growth of the traditional lines but also created a need for new distribution and selling techniques to cope with new and often more complex transportation, storage, and display requirements.

Fourth, many supermarket operators, caught in a web of rising costs, increasing retail competition, and consumer resistance to high prices, were experiencing increasing pressure on profit margins. One response was to reduce salary expenses at the store level. The broker's salesmen frequently attempted to fill the gap by performing the duties of stock clerks, such as shelf arrangement, stock taking, and display building. In some cases, union sentiment developed against this, forcing some chains to issue "hands-off" policies to brokers. A second response was to reduce inventory levels. In 1970, several chains in the United States were reportedly testing programs and equipment which would allocate shelf space by product profitability and volume and make reordering as simple as passing a hand-held reading device over a precoded card placed on the front of the shelf. This innovation could reduce inventories, making reorders more frequent and smaller in quantity, and hasten the delisting of less profitable products.

Confronted by these and other trends, the National Food Brokers Association underscored three areas of concern to its members. The first was inadequate compensation for services. Brokers felt that sales and commissions were rising but net income was declining as principals, accounts, and retailers demanded more service. Principals resisted brokerage rate increases, telling brokers to sell more if they needed more revenue. The second was a need for better field relations and closer ties with manufacturers to aid communications. An increasing turnover in the manufacturers' field supervisors sometimes resulted in misunderstandings and broker switching when a new supervisor was unfamiliar with a broker's market situation. Thirdly, increased broker switching and more dependence on large accounts caused brokers to desire more security in the form of longer term contracts with principals.

COMPANY OPERATIONS

A. G. Brown and Son received commissions for brokering the products of approximately 35 principals. This figure is somewhat misleading, however, because a number of the principals had very limited product lines and sales in the Maritimes. More representative was the fact that the largest seven principals accounted for about 62% of the company's revenues. While most of the principals were food manufacturers, six were in nonfood businesses ranging from hockey sticks to beauty aids and

EXHIBIT 8

A. G. BROWN AND SON, LTD.
Products and Sales Rankings of Principals

Product	No. of items	1969 revenues	Percent of total*	Share of market rank†	Principal advertising expenditures: rank†
Cookies, cakes, hard candy	74	$ 61,569	19.6	1	None‡
Jams and marmalade	15	30,626	9.8	1	§
Chinese foods, sauces, pickles, olives, fruit drinks, frozen cocktail snacks	167	29,080	9.3	4	None
Canned fruits and vegetables	75	20,184	6.4	3	3
Cheeses	42	19,578	6.2	2	None‡
Powdered milk	12	17,249	5.5	2	3
Margarines, shortenings, and oils	18	16,310	5.2	§	§
Pet foods	30	13,310	4.2	1	3
Tea	2	10,000	3.2	5	5
Liquid detergents	4	9,045	2.9	2	None‡
Molasses	18	9,027	2.9	2	None‡
Flour	6	8,881	2.8	3	3
Batteries	27	7,778	2.5	2	1
Candy bars, cocoa	22	7,286	2.3	3–10	None‡
Canned tuna	6	6,309	2.0	1	1
Beauty aids	61	5,766	1.8	5	None‡
Australian fruits	10	4,639	1.5	§	§
Canned clams	4	4,021	1.3	3	None‡
Cereals, snacks, cake mixes, frostings	55	3,832	1.2	3	3
Canned meats and fruit juices	29	3,328	1.1	§	1
Honey	14	3,275	1.0	1	None
Canned chicken and turkey	20	3,158	1.0	§	§
Household cleansers	10	3,036	1.0	§	§
Coffeecake	25	2,207	0.7	1	1
Skin creams	2	1,735	0.6	§	§
Mothballs, aerosol insect sprays	60	1,055	0.3	§	§
Nine others, including spaghetti and macaroni products, baby foods, soup mixes, kosher meats and fish, and salt cod	70	11,096	3.5		
Total	878	$313,380	100		

* Rounded.
† Relative ranking in terms of sales volume and advertising expenditures according to Garnet Brown. The share of market for multiproduct principals may vary by product.
‡ Competing products were advertised.
§ No estimate given.
Source: Company records.

together accounted for roughly 10% of revenues. The largest nonfood account, a line of detergents, ranked tenth in commissions with $9,045 in 1969. A description of the principals is provided in Exhibit 8. By U.S. standards, A. G. Brown could be classified as a medium-size broker in terms of retail volume, as shown in Exhibit 9, although it was thought

EXHIBIT 9
Comparisons of broker size

	Small	Medium	Large	A. G. Brown
Sales volume.	Under $3,000,000	$3-7,000,000	Over $7,000,000	$6,300,000
Average number of principals represented	21.1	23.4	26.0	35.0
Average number of items sold.	513	532	738	880
Average number of items per principal.	24	23	28	25
Average number of accounts				
Chain headquarters*	5.2	6.8	11.8	17
Wholesale grocers.	17.9	19.7	25.3	8
Institutional accounts	9.5	14.1	26.6	0
Industrial accounts	7.6	16.9	24.5	0
Average staffing				
Managers.	1.1	1.3	2.5	2.5
Salesmen	5.0	7.0	21.3	12.5
Clerical.	1.5	2.3	5.9	4.0
Other.	0.1	0.1	0.3	0.0
Total.	7.7	10.7	30.0	19.0

*Includes affiliated groups.
Source: *Grocery Manufacturer*, December 1969.

to be as large as the next two companies in the Maritimes combined in terms of number of salesmen.

Brokerage commission rates averaged 5% but varied from 3% to 8%, depending in part on the service required and the expected volume. In practice they were negotiated, since very few brokers or principals really knew the costs of service per dollar of sales for specific products. Mr. Brown commented:

> If I can determine the sales volume expected and the number of men needed as a direct sales force, I can apply some pressure. For instance, if a manufacturer who has $120,000 in sales with one salesman wants to use a broker, I know that his current selling expense is about $12,000 or 10%, so I'll shoot for 7%.

In some cases pressure was exerted by manufacturers for reduced commissions. For instance, large principals who converted part of their production to private brands for chain stores often requested reduced brokerage rates. The company might agree to accept one half to one third of the normal commission as a means of remaining involved at a reduced level of service. Small principals who private branded, however, were requested to pay the full commission or take all of their business elsewhere. On the other hand, rarely was it possible for

A. G. Brown to secure an increase in commission rates once they had been established.

The company serviced virtually all accounts and retail outlets in the Maritime Provinces which, as shown in Exhibit 5, numbered as follows:

Accounts	Number	Retail outlets
Chains	4	103
Affiliated groups	13	412
Wholesalers	8	4,219

Two chains and one affiliated group were estimated to account for 60% of the sales volume of the A. G. Brown line, and one wholesaler, representing roughly 1,000 independent retailers, another 20%.

The accounts were visited regularly by Don Brown and Don Carlton, both vice presidents. Their duties were to present new products for listing, take orders from accounts, and inform the buyers of deals and secure their participation in promotions and cooperative advertising. These men also called on certain large stores in Halifax and New Brunswick. The remainder of the detail work at the retail level was performed by 10 salesmen and 2 directors.

Since about 80% of the stores were small and geographically separated, the salesmen were assigned territories as shown in Exhibit 10. Salesmen were to visit all the stores in their territory on a regular basis, take orders, inform the retailer of promotions and deals being offered by principals, and encourage the use of available merchandising materials. In practice, larger stores required more time because they stocked more items and had a higher merchandise turnover than small stores. The salesmen might visit small retailers once every six weeks but would rarely let two weeks pass without a visit to a large chain or group account store.

In the independent stores the salesman wrote a separate order for each principal. These orders were mailed to Halifax daily, where clerks typed them onto the order form of the wholesaler who handled the pricing, billing, and delivery of the merchandise. Only orders for drop shipments were taken from the chain and group retail stores and sent to the Halifax office for processing. Principals calculated the commissions due the company on the basis of retail sales. While A. G. Brown did not maintain sales records to verify the accuracy of these calculations, spot-checks in the past had revealed only minor errors.

Salesmen received a fixed salary of from $5,000 to $10,000, a car, and expenses. Mr. Brown thought that most brokers paid their salesmen

EXHIBIT 10
Territories of A. G. Brown salesmen

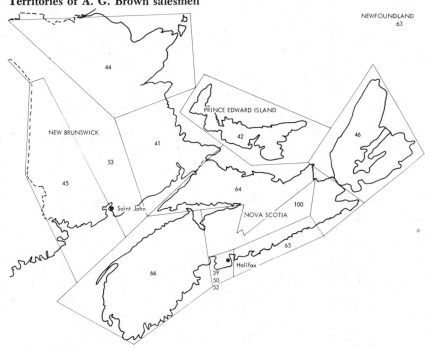

Note: Numbers refer to salesmen identified in Exhibit 13.
Source: Company records.

on commission but felt that this was an incentive to sell only the easiest lines or stores. Each salesman lived in or near his territory, visiting the Halifax office for special meetings involving large-scale promotions or the introduction of a new principal with a broad line of products.

Sales quotas, expense budgets, and revenue forecasts were not used because Mr. Brown felt that the vast differences in culture, geography, population, income, and size of stores among the territories, as well as the fact that most accounts purchased centrally but distributed widely, would make the data expensive to prepare and complicated to use. Instead, Mr. Brown used sales statistics on individual products which compared current year cumulative sales with the prior year as a means of control. The data were supplied monthly or quarterly by principals and were usually broken down by account as shown in Exhibit 11. If sales were lower than the previous year for the same period, the salesmen were asked to explain the difference and to augment their efforts. Salesmen also used these reports to encourage accounts to buy if they were lagging behind last year, or to congratulate them if they were ahead. Independent market share rating services were also used as a performance indicator.

EXHIBIT 11

A. G. BROWN AND SON, LTD.
Sales Summary from Principal*
Customer Sales Summary, Nine Fiscal Months to June 1970

Wholesaler 611† product	Fiscal year to date					Current month				
	Cases			Dollars		Cases			Dollars	
	1970	1969	Percent change	1970	1969	1970	1969	Percent change	1970	1969
Apricot halves	1		100	5		1		100	5	
Fruit cocktail	98	83	18	587	492	9	8	13	72	67
Peaches	20	15	33	316	224					
Orange juice	39	25	56	238	161	10		100	77	
Pineapples—sliced	200	195	3	2,835	2,845	30	53	-43	393	861
Prune nectar	14	2	600	98	9					
Peas—assorted	150	135	11	981	796	30	25	30	201	163
Zucchini	5	5	- 29	40	31					
Spinach	5	7	100	35	45	1	2	-50	7	13
Corn	1		100	4		1		100	4	
Stewed tomatoes		5	-100		26					
Customer Total	533	472	13	5,139	4,629	82	88	-8	759	1,104

*This report is typical of sales summaries received by A. G. Brown from its principals.
†Wholesaler refers to an account serviced by A. G. Brown. A. G. Brown received a similar report from the principal for each wholesaler.
Source: Company records.

ORGANIZATION

Garnet Brown provided general supervision of all selling and administrative activities and regularly sampled the orders sent in by the salesmen. Routine supervision and training, however, were handled by the vice presidents or directors in the field. The four-man office staff reported to George Lauder. An organization chart is shown in Exhibit 12, and certain personal data on the company's employees are given in Exhibit 13.

Prior to 1965, Mr. Brown had traveled extensively in the provinces supervising salesmen and selling to accounts. That year Don Carlton and Earle Hilchey were promoted and assumed these functions for New Brunswick and Nova Scotia, respectively, and in 1966 Leo Deveaux was given the same responsibilities for Cape Breton and Newfoundland. Don Brown was promoted to vice president in 1967 and assumed the remainder of the account work in the Halifax area. Garnet Brown said:

Since 1965 my selling and travel activities have fallen off a lot, and my appearances at our accounts are mostly for public relations. Now I work most of the time with the problems of our principals and negotiate with prospective principals as they come along. Actually, I sometimes don't have enough of this work to keep me busy.

Accounts were divided among the vice presidents and directors, as Mr. Hilchey explained:

We used to communicate independently with all of the accounts. In several instances this caused mix-ups since no one knew what everyone else was doing. Now we meet regularly in the conference room to discuss new developments and keep everyone informed. In addition, our largest accounts have been put under the direct supervision of one of us.

In 1968, after several months of discussion among the management group, the decision was made to seek a general manager from outside to aid the organization in controlling its growth. His duties were to include the direct supervision of the salesmen and office staff. Caleb Benson, formerly the regional sales manager of a large U.S. food firm on the West Coast, was hired. He stayed with A. G. Brown 18 months and then left to form his own brokerage firm in Halifax. Garnet Brown described the relationship in these terms:

1967 was a very good year for our accounts, and 1968 looked as though it would be even better. We all felt that someone with experience in controlling a large sales force was needed. Everyone talked to Caleb when he was interviewed and agreed that he was the man, but somehow things got off on the wrong foot immediately after he was hired. He was a good salesman and should have been out in the territories assisting the men, but he put

EXHIBIT 12

A. G. BROWN AND SON, LTD.
Organization Chart

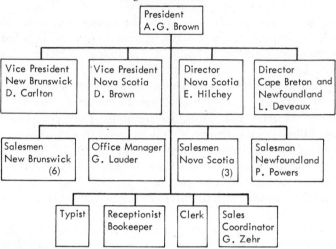

Note: Figures in parentheses refer to number of salesmen.
Source: Casewriter's notes.

his effort into building an empire here at the office. He did improve our office routines, but he wanted more responsibility, and his aggressive behavior seemed to be a source of irritation and conflict with the others.

Caleb seemed to feel superior and never really set a selling example. I backed him in what he was doing because I had brought him a long way and felt he deserved a chance. After several threats to leave, he finally quit. I think he might have been the right guy if we were in Toronto, but he was the wrong guy here.

Mr. Brown continued to feel that better field supervision was needed and was considering a new position of field supervisor to train new salesmen, monitor their performance, and insure good communications with the office. These tasks were now handled by the vice presidents and directors, but their selling activities consumed most of their time and their supervising functions tended to be a secondary concern. Mr. Carlton added:

A new salesman takes almost two years to train, with very close supervision the first six months to determine if the man can handle the job. A supervisor could increase sales by helping the salesmen learn the finer points of selling and by providing the additional knowledge which comes with experience.

Mr. Brown also agreed that a field supervisor could do much to improve sales, but he was unwilling to make an investment in the position until one or two more accounts with revenues sufficient to cover the added costs had been obtained.

EXHIBIT 13

A. G. BROWN AND SON, LTD.
Personnel Data

Name	Age	Year joined	Position	Years in present job	Previous job	Education	Salesman number*
A. Garnet Brown	39	1956	President	5	Salesman	High school	(39)
Donald Brown.	26	1964	Vice president	3	Salesman	1 yr. college	(52)
Earle Hilchey	53	1960	Director	4	Salesman, AGB	High school	(50)
Donald Carlton	47	1961	Vice president	4	Salesman, AGB	High school	(41)
Leo Deveaux	40	1966	Director	4	Salesman, AGB	High school	(46)
George Lauder.	50	1963	Office manager	5	Salesman, AGB	Jr. high school	
					Royal Canadian Navy		
Lorne Milburn.	29	1965	Salesman	5	Tea salesman	High school	(45)
Austin Vye.	45	1966	Salesman	4	Food salesman	High school	(42)
Al Reardon	51	1967	Salesman	3	Food sales supervisor	High school	(65)
Pat Powers.	44	1967	Salesman	3	Shipyard storesman	High school	(63)
Wayne Devine	30	1967	Salesman	3	Canned milk salesman	High school	(66)
Bob Banks	25	1969	Salesman	1	Biscuit salesman	High school	(64)
Al Thomson	42	1970	Salesman	½	Biscuit salesman	High school	(44)
Chuck Craig	26	1970	Salesman	½	Floor salesman	High school	(100)
Keith Johnson.	59	1970	Salesman	½	Floor salesman	High school	(53)
George Zehr.	40	1970	Office staff	½	Office manager	High school	

*To identify salesmen's territories as shown in Exhibit 10.
Source: Company records.

GROWTH

Mr. Brown attributed the growth of the firm to several decisions he and his father had made in 1958.

Food brokerage used to be a telephone operation that ended when the owner retired or died. We also noticed that more and more large, chain-type markets which required increased service were opening. We decided to provide that service better than a manufacturer's sales force could. Since then we have put our profits into more men to upgrade our services. Our cheaper distribution is winning the battle against direct sales forces. Although advertising is being relied upon more and more to sell products to the consumer, nothing can replace a service which insures the manufacturer that his product is on the shelf.

We also decided to stay away from specialty items since the real money is in volume selling. Imports weren't attractive to us, either, since we couldn't be certain of continuing supplies. How could we tell what's going to happen to the mushroom crop in Taiwan next year or to tariff and import regulations?

As new principals were added or old principals acquired new products, salesmen had to spend more time servicing each store, thus reducing the number of stores they could cover without reducing the number of visits to each. In addition, new and larger stores were opening in many areas. Consequently, Mr. Brown continued to add new salesmen and reduce the territories of the old salesmen. He admitted, however, that measuring a salesman's capacity was difficult because of the diversity of stores and the number of products. He concluded:

Don and I try to visit the territories to sense what a man's load is and how he is performing, but we don't give this nearly enough attention. Salesmen are always complaining about something. When the complaints get loud enough, we reduce the size of the man's territory.

Mr. Brown indicated that growth beyond that of aggregate food sales meant taking principals from other brokers, displacing direct sales forces, or attracting new principals to the Maritimes. Considering the first alternative unethical, he relied on the company's reputation for performance to attract new principals. In part, Mr. Brown related the success of this policy and the ability of the company to retain principals to the business climate in the Maritimes.

We try to handle product duplications by giving the item of conflict to another broker while retaining the rest of the account. If the other broker then tries to steal the whole account from us, the manufacturer would think him a pig and probably remove the portion given to him. Business in the Maritimes isn't as cutthroat as it is in Toronto or the United States. If a manufacturer doesn't want his account split, then we have to choose who leaves.

We did lose one account because a new field manager convinced his company that he could double their current sales of $400,000 in the Maritimes by using a direct sales force. I tried to show them it would take more men than they expected, but they persisted. A year later their costs had doubled, their sales were still $400,000, and they had fired the field manager and the salesmen. They asked me to take them back, but I refused.

We also lost a big cheese manufacturer a while back because it merged with a company which had a direct sales force, but soon afterward another cheese company switched brokers to come to us.

On this last point, an A. G. Brown salesman commented that it was a little awkward to promote a new cheese as the best on the market when last month he had promoted a competitor's brand, but he felt that the stores were very appreciative of the service received from A. G. Brown. In fact, one chain delisted the principal which A. G. Brown had lost and listed the new one.

A. G. Brown stood willing to accept principals and service retail outlets without regard to size. Mr. Brown said:

We really haven't any average-type principals. Each has its own service needs. Biscuit code dates are very important, but canned goods are relatively trouble free. Our low-volume lines pay for our postage and bookkeeping. It's the overall picture that counts; we can sell all our lines at small stores and spread the cost.

On this point there was not total agreement in the company, however. Mr. Hilchey offered a rebuttal:

But small-volume lines take almost as much thought and trouble as big ones, in the sense that we are expected to do them justice. This is a distraction of a salesman's time. The same goes for stores that don't do a certain volume of business with our lines. You can go broke trying to service everybody. The mom and pop stores don't buy all of our lines anymore, and they only purchase a case at a time of what they do buy.

RECENT OPERATING PROBLEMS

The decline in profitability had prompted Mr. Brown to seek ways of controlling expenses and holding back on expanding manpower until new principals had been secured. His efforts had been complicated in recent months by the loss of a large principal through merger and the addition of a comparably sized principal which wanted to switch from a direct sales force to a broker. To obtain the latter, however, A. G.

Brown agreed to hire three of the principal's salesmen. Garnet Brown summarized the problem as follows:

I don't know a lot about accounting, but I do know that our expenses are continually rising. Take car expense. I've tried leasing and owning, but both seem about as expensive to me. Our population has remained fixed while our principals want more service. We can't raise our brokerage percentage because of contracts, so we have to add new principals to keep up.

Another aspect of the problem was the increasing paperwork requested by manufacturers and accounts. For instance, Mr. Hilchey had recently been asked by an account to prepare a summary report on scheduled promotions and deals, including their timing and duration, costs, discounts, and cooperative allowances. The report took several hours to prepare and was supposedly a one-time affair, but Mr. Hilchey indicated that the account might now expect it routinely.

OPPORTUNITIES

In addition to considering means of controlling costs, Mr. Brown was evaluating several opportunities for increasing revenues. The first involved the addition of a principal new to the Maritimes, whose only product, canned shrimp, was expected to reach $250,000 in volume. The commission was expected to be about 5%. Since the product did not conflict with any of the items currently represented by the company, accepting it appeared to present few difficulties.

The second opportunity was of greater significance. Mr. Brown had explored in a very preliminary way the possibility of representing a large, narrow-line manufacturer currently selling about $1,000,000 in the Maritimes through a direct sales force. He elaborated on this prospect:

From the number of men this company has in the field, I know they must be spending at least $100,000 distributing their line. And they aren't doing as well as they might, either. If they came with us, I think we could increase their sales by 20% because we have twice as many men in the field. What's more, our lines don't conflict. If they came with us, I would hire three new men and could then have two sales supervisors and another salesman.

Third, additional revenues could be sought from institutional or non-food lines. Mr. Brown was skeptical of the frozen foods and institutional areas because they involved troublesome aspects, such as refrigeration and time wasted chasing dietitians, but he was working to establish a split-representation system with a manufacturer of ethical and non-ethical drugs. The manufacturer had approached him with the proposition that A. G. Brown's salesmen service grocery stores with the nonethicals, such as cold syrups and cough drops, while the manufacturer's salesmen detailed the ethical drugs to doctors and pharmacies. A volume of about $100,000 with a 5% fee for brokerage was expected. Although he had not previously considered selling such items, Mr. Brown commented, "Until Berec approached me last year, I never considered selling batteries, either."

Manufacturing was a fourth area under consideration. Mr. Brown knew of a prominent local food manufacturer with a large market share in the Maritimes and sales and profits of roughly $2 million and $20,000, respectively. He felt that the company was overburdened with expenses and that, were he able to buy it, the salaries of the owner and three of the managers estimated to total about $60,000 could be saved. In addition, by disbanding the direct sales force in favor of A. G. Brown, he maintained that substantial reductions could also be achieved in selling costs, thought to be currently on the order of $125,000 a year. Mr. Brown had one important reservation in this case, however. A. G. Brown had begun representing a competing imported product recently introduced in the Maritimes. Sales had grown to nearly $200,000 which Mr. Brown attributed to a retail price about 4% lower and a package 20% larger in content than competing brands. He was uncertain whether the favorable response traditionally accorded local products could withstand this differential.

A final opportunity was private labeling. Although he did not like to be dependent on imports, Mr. Brown was negotiating with an English producer of jams and jellies from whom he could purchase a quality product at a price substantially below that of existing brands. He felt that the manufacturer would finance his inventory and that, perhaps through a separate corporation, he could net 5% on sales after all expenses. Should imports be cut off for some reason, he was confident that a source of preserves could be located in Canada. With the A. G. Brown reputation and access to the food markets, Mr. Brown estimated that $200,000 could be sold the first year.

A PERSONAL ADDENDUM

The Brown family had been natives of Halifax for several generations. Having been a local sports personality and a successful businessman, Garnet Brown felt an obligation to the community and expressed a desire to devote some of his energy to civic affairs. Within the last five years he had become active in politics and had been elected in July 1969 to the Legislative Assembly of Nova Scotia as a Liberal member. He recounted his involvement:

I had always been in the organizational end of politics until last year. Elections were approaching then, and we didn't have a candidate. I ran because there wasn't anyone else. It takes some time, but I don't curl or belong to a home or school association, so I have no other outlets aside from the business. Being an opposition member makes it that much easier since we don't have executive or administrative responsibilities. We could very possibly win a majority in the next election, though: a change of only 4% in voting patterns could give us a landslide. Since I'm one of five opposition members in the legislature now, I suppose I would be considered for the cabinet in a Liberal government.

The Marlin Firearms Company

THE MARLIN FIREARMS COMPANY, founded by New Haven gunsmith John Marlin in 1870, was nearly defunct when Frank Kenna purchased it at auction for $100 and the assumption of a $100,000 mortgage in 1924. From those precarious beginnings, the Kenna family had succeeded in revitalizing the company.

Sales for 1969 were $13.6 million, equal to nearly three times the 1959 sales volume. Since 1959, net income had increased by as much as 650% to $748,000 in 1967, but in 1969 a net income of only $269,000 was recorded, partially as a result of Marlin's recent move into a new plant in North Haven, Connecticut. The new facilities were designed to increase significantly Marlin's manufacturing capacity and thereby its sales and earnings potential. As evidence of this, sales for the first six months of 1970 were $8.8 million and profits after taxes of $340,000 were posted. (For financial data, see Exhibits 1, 2, and 3.)

Despite a new factory and the hope of continued growth, Marlin's corporate horizon was not cloudless. Imports which threatened Marlin's competitive position in the marketplace were one source of concern. Marlin had recently spent more than five years developing a centerfire, bolt-action, high-powered rifle designed to compete in the high-price end of the market. It was considered by management to be an excellent rifle, but in 1967 Mauser rifles from Spain, Argentina, Finland, and Sweden flooded U.S. markets. As a consequence, Marlin had postponed plans to sell the rifle until after July 1971 when a new pump-action shotgun was scheduled for introduction.

EXHIBIT 1

THE MARLIN FIREARMS COMPANY
Condensed Comparative Statements of Income
For the Years Ended December 31

	1966	1967	1968	1969	6 mos. 1970*
Net sales	$11,334,318	$12,558,056	$14,563,346	$13,578,915	$8,758,839
Less: Cost of goods sold	7,523,710	8,295,897	9,808,448	9,354,900	6,007,005
Gross profit	$ 3,810,608	$ 4,262,159	$ 4,754,898	$ 4,224,015	$2,751,834
Less: Selling expenses	$ 1,625,318	$ 1,762,560	$ 1,925,401	$ 1,904,775	$1,135,480
General and administrative expenses	393,551	463,241	573,628	648,107	237,147
Operating profit	$ 1,791,739	$ 2,036,358	$ 2,255,869	$ 1,671,133	$1,379,207
Other income					
Miscellaneous	$ 28,122	$ 11,431	$ 20,106	$ 8,694	$ 15,286
Gain on sale of equipment	...	260	...	...	500
Total other income	$ 28,122	$ 11,691	$ 20,106	$ 8,694	$ 15,786
Other expenses					
Contributions	$ 14,436	$ 12,140	$ 9,975	$ 21,693	$ 1,548
Sale of equipment—loss	$ 1,127	60			
Employees pension plan	142,057	144,732	146,373	74,832	75,000
Interest	88,494	148,432	173,432	428,426	300,883
Total other expenses	$ 246,114	$ 305,304	$ 329,840	$ 524,951	$ 377,431
Profit before depreciation	$ 1,573,747	$ 1,742,745	$ 1,946,135	$1,154,876	$1,017,562
Depreciation	186,053	246,223	324,049	489,824	271,920
Profit before prior years' expenses	$ 1,387,694	$ 1,496,522	$ 1,622,086	$ 665,052	$ 745,642
Less: Prior years' sales commissions	...	...	49,813	...	...
Profit before taxes	$ 1,387,694	$ 1,496,522	$ 1,572,273	$ 665,052	$ 745,642
Less: State and federal taxes	670,736	748,144	850,254	151,505	405,735
Income before extraordinary items	$ 716,958	$ 748,378	$ 722,019	$ 513,547	$ 339,907
Extraordinary item—cost of relocation of plant facilities, net of federal income tax benefit of $273,851				244,807	...
Net profit	$ 716,958	$ 748,378	$ 722,019	$ 268,740	339,907

* Comparable figures not available for June 30, 1969.
Source: Company records.

EXHIBIT 2

THE MARLIN FIREARMS COMPANY
Condensed Comparative Balance Sheets

Assets	For the years ended December 31				For six months ended June 30	
	1966	1967	1968	1969	1969	1970
Current assets						
Cash and equivalent	$1,612,778	$1,226,981	$ 775,426	$ 330,099	$ 1,087,331	$ 274,889
Accounts receivable (net)	2,088,012	2,597,507	2,922,695	3,339,440	6,218,669	7,416,214
Accounts receivable (U.S. government)	....	....	....	482,587*	....	....
Inventories	2,143,644	2,180,528	2,470,469	4,286,918	3,166,213	3,999,358
Prepaid expenses	25,333	28,366	93,835	136,421	108,033	114,332
Total current assets	$5,869,767	$6,033,382	$ 6,262,425	$ 8,575,465	$10,580,246	$11,804,793
Fixed assets	$1,924,239	$2,374,021	$ 5,029,317	$ 8,223,567	$ 6,888,424	$ 8,241,528
Less: Reserve for depreciation	817,252	1,017,335	1,110,833	1,271,703	1,366,872	1,347,289
Net fixed assets	$1,106,987	$1,356,686	$ 3,918,484	$ 6,951,864	$ 5,521,552	$ 6,894,239
Other assets						
Cash surrender value—life insurance	$ 65,727	$ 97,300	$ 132,091	$ 145,084	$ 131,227	$ 163,770
Accounts receivable—long term	369,978	401,173	493,727	338,470	529,435	997,790
Miscellaneous assets	12,521	24,607	24,180	23,360	5,118	108,896
Trademarks	355	355	355	355	355	355
Total other assets	$ 448,581	$ 523,435	$ 650,353	$ 507,269	$ 666,135	$ 1,270,811
Total assets	$7,425,335	$7,913,503	$10,831,262	$16,034,598	$16,767,933	$19,969,843

EXHIBIT 2 (*continued*)

| | For the years ended December 31 | | | | For six months ended June 30 | |
	1966	1967	1968	1969	1969	1970
Capital and Liabilities						
Current liabilities						
Notes payable—bank	$	$	$	$ 1,980,000	$ 4,300,000	$ 4,880,000
Notes payable—stockholders	74,714	48,607	48,607	70,500	48,607	48,607
Accounts payable	686,993	656,646	1,642,609	1,693,129	934,207	1,915,755
Accrued liabilities	270,662	264,900	393,333	688,405	452,945	1,079,113
Accrued taxes	498,966	373,277	400,921	52,126	401,834	405,735
Dividends payable	5,985	5,977	5,919	.....	.....	.....
Total current liabilities	$1,537,320	$1,349,407	$ 2,491,389	$ 4,484,160	$ 6,137,593	$ 8,329,210
Other liabilities						
Mortgage payable	$	$	$ 850,000	$ 3,120,000	$ 2,324,000	$ 3,120,000
Deferred income—contracts (net)†	1,808,402	1,853,886	2,247,922	2,173,700	2,533,590	2,249,748
Notes payable—stockholders	231,460	208,960	110,957	37,048	83,244	27,808
Loans—affiliated companies	21,556	.....	.....	.....	.....	.....
Deferred income taxes	.....	.....	.....	590,909	.....	271,324
Total other liabilities	$2,061,418	$2,062,846	$ 3,208,879	$ 5,921,657	$ 4,940,834	$ 5,668,880
Capital and surplus						
Preferred stock, 4%, $25 par	$ 172,375	$ 172,375	$ 172,375	$ 172,375	$ 172,375	$ 172,375
Common stock, 120,000 shares issued‡	300,000	2,907,500	2,907,500	2,907,500	2,907,500	2,907,500
Surplus	3,415,865	1,690,143	2,320,512	2,592,749	2,653,474	2,937,520
Less: Treasury stock, 4,000 shares	61,643	268,768	269,393	43,843	43,843	45,642
Net worth	$3,826,597	$4,501,250	$ 5,130,994	$ 5,628,781	$ 5,689,506	$ 5,971,753
Total capital and liabilities	$7,425,335	$7,913,503	$10,831,262	$16,034,598	$16,767,933	$19,969,843

* Investment credit and tax refunds.

† Marlin Industrial Division two-year contracts to be fulfilled.

‡ Of the 116,000 shares of common stock outstanding, the Kenna family as a group owned 39,550 shares directly and 75,440 additional shares were held by the Marlin Voting Trust, a 10-year trust expiring on December 31, 1971. Beneficiaries of the voting trust were various members of the Kenna family. The remaining 1,010 outstanding shares were owned by nonfamily members.

Source: Company records.

EXHIBIT 3

THE MARLIN FIREARMS COMPANY
Other Financial Data

	Year ended				First 6 months	
	1966	*1967*	*1968*	*1969*	*1969*	*1970*
I. *Financial ratios*						
A. Measures of profitability						
1. Gross profit/sales	.336	.340	.327	.311	n.a.	.314
2. Operating profit/sales	.158	.160	.155	.124	n.a.	.157
3. Income before extraordinary items/sales	.063	.060	.050	.038	n.a.	.039
4. Return on net worth	.187	.166	.141	.048	n.a.	.057
B. Measures of current position						
1. Current assets/current liabilities	3.800	4.500	2.500	1.800	1.700	1.400
2. Accounts receivable/sales	.180	.210	.200	.250	n.a.	.840
3. Inventories/sales	.190	.170	.170	.320	n.a.	.460

II. *Funds flow: 1966–69 (millions)*

Sources		Uses	
Cash	$0.8	Accounts receivable	$1.2
Accounts payable	1.0	Inventories	2.1
Bank notes payable	1.9	Other	0.1
Long-term debt	3.1	Fixed assets	5.9
Contracts	0.3	Notes payable	0.2
Deferred taxes	0.6		$9.5
Retained earnings	1.8		
	$9.5		

n.a. = not available.
Source: Exhibits 1 and 2.

Recently Marlin had been confronted by a new threat from one of its old competitors, The Browning Arms Company. In 1967 Browning, long an importer of firearms sold under its own name, had introduced a .22-caliber, lever-action rifle made in Japan that competed directly with one of Marlin's best-selling rifles, the Model 39. By capitalizing on low manufacturing labor costs and marketing directly to retail gun dealers, Browning had been able to price the rifle at $75, compared to a list price of $94.95 for the Model 39. Marlin management was particularly concerned because they considered the Browning gun to be a high-quality product.

The issue of gun-control legislation had aroused additional concern. It was clear to Marlin management that the Federal Gun Control Act of 1968 had not completely settled the issue of gun control. (See Appendix for a brief summary of the Act.) State and local gun-control legislation was anticipated across the country in a variety of forms. However, as only the fourth ranking manufacturer of long arms (rifles and shotguns) in the United States, Marlin did not feel it had the resources to lead any movement against gun-control legislation at either the federal, state, or local level.

Despite these problems, Marlin's president, Frank Kenna, Jr.,[1] was optimistic in July of 1970:

As far as the issue of gun-control legislation goes, I think it is just about over except in the pistol field. As a manufacturer of shoulder arms, Marlin has not been severely affected by gun-control legislation.

With regard to foreign competition, I think it is good for us. As yet, we don't really know how seriously the Japanese-made .22 rifle will affect our sales, but we have prepared a defensive move.

One thing the recessions of 1958, 1960, and now 1968–70 have shown me is that Marlin is nearly recession-proof. In 1966, when I saw we were nearly at capacity in our old plant, I decided to build a new one. We moved in June 1969 and now have the room to expand our production. Before, our sales were limited by capacity, but now sales should increase again. My objective is at least 10% growth in sales per year. You need at least that to keep even with inflation.

Actually, for the growth I foresee in the firearms industry, Marlin is probably undercapitalized; therefore we need to go public, and I would like to do it soon. This would be in the form of a primary rather than a secondary offering with the purpose being heavy acquisition of numerically controlled machines. Even though equity market conditions are currently poor, we've had our 1969 financial statements audited by one of the very best national auditing firms. This is all in preparation for going public.

THE INDUSTRY

The firearms industry was one of the nation's oldest, dating back to 1798 when Eli Whitney first demonstrated the feasibility of mass production by developing interchangeable musket parts. The industry was characterized by a few major segments: handguns, long arms, ammunition, and accessories.

The Sporting Arms and Ammunition Manufacturers' Institute (SAAMI) reported that domestic wholesale shipments of nonmilitary arms and ammunition totaled $253 million in 1967 and $158 million in the first six months of 1968. Handgun sales accounted for about 8%; long arms, 45% (rifles, 25%, shotguns, 20%); and ammunition, 47% of these totals.

Approximate figures for gun sales for 1967 are reflected below (value and units in millions):

---

[1] In 1947 Frank Kenna, Sr., died; his son Roger succeeded him. When Roger died in 1959, his brother Frank, Jr., stepped into the presidency. Frank, 47 in 1970, had attended Yale University, had served three years with the Marines during World War II, and had completed his education at Clarkson College of Technology. He had started his career with Marlin in 1949 as an apprentice toolmaker.

	Domestic shipments*		Imports	Total
	Value	*Units*	*(units)*	*(units)*
Handguns	$ 19.5	.45	1.20	1.65
Rifles.	63.2	1.52	.26	1.78
Shotguns.	49.6	.97	.28	1.25
	$132.3	2.94	1.74	4.68

* Excludes shipments to government agencies. Industry observers felt this to be significant only in the case of handguns sold to law enforcement agencies.

The fastest growing segment of the long-arms market had been center-fire rifles. Total unit production had increased 180% from 1960 to 1967, while rimfire production had increased 93% and shotgun production had risen only 90% (see Exhibit 4). It was suggested by one executive that conservation funds and road-building programs were responsible for opening up and making accessible new hunting areas across the country. This, he pointed out, would cause an increased demand for both center-fire and rimfire rifles.

The National Commission on the Causes and Prevention of Violence estimated the number of firearms in civilian hands in the United States to be 90 million: 35 million rifles, 31 million shotguns, and 24 million handguns. Most firearms owners were thought to own more than a single gun. According to Attorney Mark Benenson:

> Spot checks suggest that NRA club members may own an average of 12 rifles and shotguns, and that nonclub members may own an average of 6 rifles and shotguns. Hunters generally own at least three guns—a .22 rifle, a high-power rifle, and a shotgun. Other citizens also frequently have more than one firearm.[2]

In the long-arms segment, four manufacturers, three of them owned or controlled by larger companies, were thought by industry observers to account for roughly 80% of domestic sales.

Manufacturer	*Parent company*	Approximate market share
Winchester-Western	Olin Corporation	24%
Remington Arms	DuPont (owning 60%)	24
Savage Arms	Emhart Corporation	17
Marlin Firearms	. . .	15

(Additional information on these and other long-arms manufacturers is provided in Exhibits 5 and 6.) In the handgun segment, the Colt Fire-

[2] Mark K. Benenson, "Statement Representing the New York Sporting Arms Association, Inc., before the Subcommittee on Firearms Control of the City Affairs Committee, New York City Council," August 25, 1967.

EXHIBIT 4
Marlin's share of shoulder-arms market (January 1, 1960–June 30, 1968)

	Rimfire			Centerfire			Shotguns		
	Total (units)	Marlin (units)	Marlin (percentage)	Total (units)	Marlin (units)	Marlin (percentage)	Total (units)	Marlin (units)	Marlin (percentage)
1960	461,000	112,000	24	224,000	29,000	13	517,000	23,000	4
1961	472,000	141,000	30	213,000	30,000	14	534,000	29,000	5
1962	517,000	138,000	27	270,000	39,000	14	552,000	31,000	6
1963	566,000	150,000	27	271,000	44,000	16	595,000	31,000	5
1964	695,000	168,000	24	342,000	55,000	16	687,000	27,000	4
1965	768,000	190,000	25	392,000	53,000	14	834,000	19,000	2
1966	826,000	201,000	24	562,000	76,000	14	913,000	13,000	1
1967	892,000	216,000	24	633,000	84,000	13	970,000	13,000	1
1968 (6 mos.)	539,000	151,000	28	420,000	45,000	11	547,000	7,000	1
7-yr. % increase (decrease)	93%	93%	..	183%	190%	..	88%	(43%)	..
Average retail price	$60			$150			$200		

Source: Company records.

EXHIBIT 5

Marlin's principal competitors in long-arms sales (in thousands)

Manufacturer	1968-69 sales	1968-69 Net income	1968-69 Total assets	Rimfire rifles	Centerfire rifles	Shotguns	Handguns	Telescopic sights, traps, accessories	Ammunition	Hunting clothing	Leisure time equipment	Tools, hardware	Other
Browning Arms Company	$ 42,621	$ 1,262	$ 34,712	x	x		x			x	a		
Emhart Corporation	239,550	13,876	183,322										
Savage Arms Division	n.a.	n.a.	n.a.	x	x	x		x					
Leisure Group, Inc.	39,694	1,678	52,967										
High Standard Division	n.a.	n.a.	n.a.	x		x	x						
Marlin Firearms Company	14,563	722	10,831	x	x	x		x					
O. F. Mossberg & Sons	n.a.	n.a.	n.a.	x	x	x							
Olin Mathieson	1,156,896	50,342	1,078,108										b
Winchester-Western Division	238,200	11,400	n.a.	x	x	x		x	x	x	c	d	
Remington Arms Company	129,499	12,834	11,281	x	x	x	x	x	x			f	e
Sturm-Ruger	9,068	1,401	8,803	x	x		x					g	

a Archery equipment and boats.
b Employee Communication-Motivational Service.
c Camping equipment, skis.
d Cartridge-activated fastening tools.
e Hunting and fishing, travel agency services, safari lodges in East Africa, and high-quality books, art, films about outdoors.
f Chain saws, abrasive cutting tools, and powder-metal parts.
g Castings and winches.
n.a. = not available.
Source: Moody's Industrial Listings.

EXHIBIT 6
1970–71 Gun models by manufacturer

Manufacturer	Rifles — Rimfire $0–$59.99	$60–$149.99	$150–$299.99	$300+	Centerfire $0–$59.99	$60–$149.99	$150–$299.99	$300+	Shotguns $0–$59.99	$60–$149.99	$150–$299.99	$300+	Handguns $0–$59.99	$60–$149.99	$150–$299.99	$300+	Total long arms	Total all guns
Browning	6	1					8	2			12	10		5	1	1	39	46
Colt	2													22	7		2	31
High Standard	2									9	8	1	3	14			20	37
Marlin*	8	1				4	1		1								15	15
Mossberg	7					4	7		8	5	10	1					42	42
Remington	9	10†	1	1		6	9	4	4	6	4			1			54	55
Ruger	2					3	7	2					2	10			14	26
Savage	9	6	4	1		8				2	1						31	31
Savage/Anschutz		7	5	1													13	13
Savage-Fox										13	4						17	17
Smith & Wesson							5						1	34	4		5	44
Winchester	4					10	8	14	1	4	13	7					61	61
Other manufacturers	14	13		1	1	5	23	2	13	10	29	36	17	27		–	147	191
Total	63	38	10	4	1	40	68	24	27	49	81	55	23	113	12	1	460	609

* Glenfield models excluded.
† Includes two 5-millimeter models; otherwise, all rimfire rifles use .22-caliber ammunition.
Source: 1971 Shooter's Bible, published by Stoeger Arms.

arms Division of Colt Industries; Smith and Wesson, a division of Bangor Punta; and Sturm-Ruger were the acknowledged leaders in sales. Winchester-Western and Remington were thought to account for about 75% of ammunition sales.[3] At present, none of the large firearms manufacturers dealt heavily in government contracts for shoulder arms.

Despite recent efforts to introduce new models and manufacturing innovations, gun making remained steeped in tradition. Patent infringement suits were almost nonexistent because gun mechanisms had remained virtually unchanged for many years. Those patents that were issued were generally very restricted. For example, Marlin's "time-honored" Model 39 was first designed in 1893. It had been modified only slightly since then and was advertised as a "direct descendent of the Model 1891," Marlin's first .22 rifle made in 1891.

Remington was generally regarded as the leader in production engineering and product development. For example, nylon parts which were both durable and self-lubricating had been developed first by Remington. In 1956, they introduced a .22-caliber semiautomatic rifle with a nylon butt stock. After considerable consumer and dealer advertising, the rifle had become the best-selling .22 automatic on the market, according to industry sources. Remington also attempted to introduce plastic butt stocks on their bolt-action rifles, but poor market acceptance prompted a return to wooden stocks. Other companies had been less successful with new product innovations. Winchester, for instance, had attempted to popularize rifles with plastic sights and cast-metal actions instead of traditional machined actions. Although the economics of such construction were significant, the rifles never sold well and eventually were removed from Winchester's product line.

Product innovation, however, was being forced on the industry by rising labor and material costs and the diminishing number of skilled gunsmiths in the country. Manufacturers were turning more and more to automated assembly lines and numerically controlled milling machines, routers, and wood carving machines.

THE MARLIN FIREARMS COMPANY

In 1970 Marlin consisted of two operating divisions: the Marlin Industrial Division (MID) and the Marlin Firearms Division (see Exhibit 7 for the organization chart). The industrial division, owned 90% by the company and 10% by the Kenna family, accounted for about 20% of 1969 sales. Profit margins for the industrial division were described by one executive as "substantially higher than the firearms division—up to 50% higher." Motivational employee communication programs were

---

[3] Federal Cartridge Co. was in third place, specializing in private label ammunition for K-Mart, Montgomery Ward, Western Auto, and Sears, Roebuck.

EXHIBIT 7

THE MARLIN FIREARMS COMPANY
Organization Chart

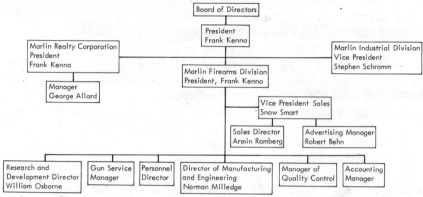

Source: Company records.

supplied to industrial firms, hospitals, and transportation companies. The service consisted of a high-quality bulletin board, or "News Center," on which topical events and messages to employees were displayed. MID selected and produced the display literature and illustrated news and sports stories which were mailed out at least once a week to 8,000 clients.

The service was sold nationwide through a 30-man sales force. Typically the client signed a two-year contract, and division experience indicated about a 75% renewal rate. Clients included many of the nation's largest industrial firms, such as General Motors, Ford, Olin, and North American Rockwell.

The firearms division accounted for approximately 80% of total sales and employed the bulk of Marlin's 700 employees. It produced over 300,000 units per year, with prices ranging from $25 to several hundred dollars per gun.

Product policy for firearms

Marlin sold rimfire rifles, centerfire rifles, and shotguns under the Marlin name. The company also marketed a lower price Glenfield line, the chief difference being that a less expensive birch stock was substituted for the traditional walnut stock. Some private-label selling was also done for national chain stores, such as Sears, Roebuck, Montgomery Ward, and Western Auto. The company believed its guns were generally of superior quality to comparably priced competing brands. The emphasis on quality was often described in terms of Frank Kenna's "walnut and steel" philosophy. Mr. Kenna noted that companies like Remington had

EXHIBIT 8
Marlin 1970 models

Model	Caliber	Description	Price	Date model introduced	Comment
Rimfire					
Marlin 39CL..........	.22	Lever-action repeater	$125.00	1970	Commemorative—(originally introduced in 1922)
Marlin 49	.22	Automatic	59.95	1968	New model
Marlin 99 C/M.......	.22	Automatic	49.95	1957	New model
Marlin 989..........	.22	Automatic	49.95	1962	New model
Marlin 980..........	.22	Bolt-action repeater	49.95	1962	Minor modifications
Marlin 81	.22	Bolt-action repeater	46.95	1937	New model
Marlin 80	.22	Bolt-action repeater	44.95	1935	New model
Glenfield 60.........	.22	Automatic	43.95	1966	Reproduction
Marlin 101..........	.22	Bolt-action single shot	29.95	1959	New model
Glenfield 10.........	.22	Bolt-action single shot	26.95	1966	Reproduction
Centerfire					
Marlin 444..........	.444	Lever-action repeater	135.00	1964	Minor modification
Marlin 1894.........	.44	Lever-action repeater	105.00	1970	Reproduction
Marlin 336 c/t.......	.30/30	Lever-action repeater	105.00	1947	Minor modification
Glenfield 30.........	.30/30	Lever-action repeater	99.95	1966	Minor modification
Shotgun					
L.C. Smith Sidelock Double....	12 gauge	Sidelock double barrel	300.00	1968	Reproduction
Marlin 55 Goose......	12 gauge	Bolt-action single shot	59.95	1962	Reproduction
Glenfield 50.........	12/20 gauge	Bolt-action single shot	49.95	1966	Reproduction

Source: Company records.

recently tried without success to use plastic stocks and stamped metal parts for critical parts of rifle actions. In contrast to such cost-cutting methods, he felt that he owed customers reliable firearms in the best gun-making tradition.

In Marlin's 1970 centennial catalog, Mr. Kenna wrote:

And while our improved facilities and modern equipment will enable us to achieve increased production volume, I assure you that Marlin will continue to make guns the right way. We know there is no substitute for solid steel forgings, American walnut, hand-fitted stocks and actions, and all the fine touches that make the name Marlin synonymous with traditional gun quality. As we begin a second century of American gun making, we remain dedicated to that goal.

A summary of the 1970 catalog including a description of each gun and its date of introduction is provided in Exhibit 8.

Markets and customer profile

In a mid-1968 study summarized in Exhibit 4, the sales department estimated that Marlin accounted for approximately 13% of domestic long-arms sales: 28% in rimfire rifles, 11% in centerfire rifles, and 1% in shotguns. Marlin executives asserted that the company's inability to obtain a larger share of the centerfire rifle market was due, in part, to insufficient production capacity in the old plant.[4]

In the new facilities, Marlin expected to increase the production of higher priced guns with only a moderate increase in overall volume. For instance, by mid-1970 Marlin's production was within 1,000 units of comparable 1969 production figures, but revenues from gun sales were $800,000, or roughly 10% higher than 1969.

Marlin sold about 1% of its annual production abroad through Dodge and Seymour, a worldwide distributor. Although sporting-arms sales had recently picked up in West Germany, France, and Italy, restrictive gun laws abroad generally limited Marlin's export business. Many nations in Asia and Africa had banned or severely restricted the sale of firearms. In South America, some military governments had made the importation of sporting arms illegal.

On the basis of warranty cards returned on about 15% of unit sales, Snow Smart, vice president of sales, was confident that he had a profile of the average Marlin customer. Characterized as a young male factory worker, the "typical" Marlin customer was highly conscious of technical features and generally purchased a rifle for hunting or target practice.

Traditionally, retail gun sales were highest in July, August, September, and October when new rifles were purchased in preparation for the

---

[4] Maximum production in the old plant had been 300,000 units per year.

hunting season. Recently, however, a strong sales trend was discerned just prior to Christmas, indicating that guns were also a large gift item. As a consequence, more intensive promotion campaigns were slated by Marlin for the Christmas season. Other sales peaks had been identified around Father's Day and graduation time. Shipments to dealers tended to precede retail sales by about three months.

Marketing policies

Marketing was headed by the vice president of sales, Snow Smart, 61, who had come to Marlin in 1951 after extensive hardgoods merchandising experience at Sears, Roebuck, Montgomery Ward, and Spiegel. Mr. Smart lived in Chicago to be near the headquarters of the larger retail chains. His office was equipped with a kitchen, pool table, and a large fireplace. On the walls were approximately 50 game heads he had collected on hunting trips around the world. Mr. Smart had a collection of about 40 sporting arms, many of them Marlins.

Mr. Smart visited the New Haven plant for one week each month to consult with production personnel and his sales director, Armin Romberg. Mr. Romberg, 53, had been with Marlin 34 years, 11 of them as sales director. In addition to supervising in-house marketing activities, he administered Marlin's credit policies.

Marlin firearms were sold by a combination of 20 sales representatives and five company regional salesmen. Salesmen were on commission, which averaged 4% on sales to jobbers. The company had over 300 active accounts, most of them jobbers who, in turn, sold to some 7,000 retail establishments.[5] Marlin had not incurred a bad-debt loss since 1961, which Mr. Smart attributed to the company policy of accepting only those jobber accounts listed as AA or AAA by Dun & Bradstreet. In recent years the company had sold an increasing proportion of sales directly to certain large customers, including Montgomery Ward, Western Auto Supply, J. C. Penney, Spiegel, Aldens, Jewel Companies, K-Mart Sporting Goods, and Sears, Roebuck.

Prior to 1970 Marlin had not devoted a great deal of attention to the retail dealers, concentrating instead on securing financially stronger jobbers and providing them with better promotion aids and service. Recently, however, increased consideration was being given to the retailers. According to Snow Smart:

We have never made love to the dealers until this year. Actually, there are only about 5,000 good dealers in the country. This year for the first time we mailed kits containing catalogs, brochures, and sweepstakes contest in-

---

[5] Jobbers received a markup of 20% on wholesale price and retailers a markup of 25% on retail price. A few manufacturers such as Colt Firearms, Browning, and Ithaca Gun Company did not rely on jobbers but sold direct to retailers. Colt Firearms had about 10,000 outlets and Browning about 4,000.

formation to 10,000 dealers. This was an attempt to generate interest among the dealers and make them more aware of Marlin.

The reason we are approaching the dealers directly is to prepare the way for bringing out a broader line of rifles and shotguns. Right now, we are only selling to about 40% of the sporting long-arms market; by expanding into shotguns, we can move into the other 60% of the market.

Advertising and promotion

Media advertising was placed in sporting magazines such as *Outdoor Life, Sports Afield, Shooting Times, Field and Stream, The American Rifleman* (published by the National Rifle Association), and various trade journals. No cooperative advertising was done. The importance of tradition, craftsmanship, and quality was emphasized by Marlin's advertising and promotional literature.

Mr. Robert Behn, 29, had been director of advertising for seven months. Before coming to Marlin in the spring of 1969, he had worked in Remington's shaver advertising department. Mr. Behn discussed Marlin's advertising.

With 60% of our customers under age 30, we cater to the younger male, but we are not really in the youth market, such as the *Boy's Life* magazine audience. Given our present advertising and promotion budget, which is only about 5% of sales, such advertising still represents a luxury. However, as our budget allows, it will be important to cultivate these kids—particularly in the face of foreign imports. We need to stress the importance of high-quality, traditional American craftsmanship to educate the novice and first-time hunter.

To this Frank Kenna added:

Customers are generally very emotional about guns. There is a very manly feeling of deeply rooted Americana in owning a gun. This feeling actually extends to nearly everyone. A guy might buy one of our Model 39 Century Limited .22s just to put up on the wall of his den for a conversation piece, never intending to shoot it. The Model 39 is our "Cadillac" of the .22s, and its handsome workmanship, including a solid brass butt plate and octagonal barrel, makes it very decorative.

New product development

The research and development department was responsible for working with sales and production to develop new models of rifles and shotguns. It was headed by 34-year-old William Osborne and consisted of four engineer-designers, three model-makers, and a technical and historical adviser. Mr. Osborne had been director of R & D for one year. Before coming to Marlin in 1966, he had worked as a project manager in Winchester's Ramset Tool Division.

Three to five years generally elapsed between the conception of a new rifle or shotgun and the development of an actual working prototype. For the rush design of a simple gun, two years could be expected. Typically, the new product idea was accompanied by performance, appearance, and cost objectives. R & D engineer-designers then made several preliminary sketches to define alternative design approaches to be reviewed by Bill Osborne, Snow Smart, and Frank Kenna.

The production department performed a thorough engineering job that encompassed specifying production methods and estimating costs. Norman Milledge, production manager, commented:

At $500,000 per major model change, such as we experienced on our new pump-action shotgun, we have to be careful in our approach to each new model proposed. Even minor modifications of existing models cost $50,000 to $100,000. Most new model ideas come from salespeople. We make up the prototypes and often make suggestions that help us in producing a more uniformly reproducible gun.

Of particular importance in any new product decision were Frank Kenna and Snow Smart, both of whom hunted extensively and were gun collectors. According to Mr. Osborne:

Market research comes from Snow Smart and Frank Kenna. They talk to their field people and their friends in the firearms industry. There are some internally generated ideas, too, but because firearms are very personal in such matters as a long or short stock, pistol grip or straight grip, etc., it is difficult to keep personal preferences separate from what the customer wants. The final say has to come from marketing.

Mr. Kenna discussed what made a good gun in these terms:

You can't do it by motivational research, as the Edsel fiasco proved. An intuitive feel is necessary, and all of Marlin's salesmen are gun men. One very important feature is quality, and that is stressed above all else.

We also offer new models, like the automobile industry. As with new cars, we don't change the basic "engine" but add new styling features. For example, we might change the shape of the stock, add some etching on the barrel, and so forth.

The new pump-action shotgun was presently in its third design cycle; a working prototype was expected to be available October 1. If the design was accepted for regular production at that time, the gun would probably be ready to market by July 1971. Temporarily shelved were production plans for a new bolt-action centerfire rifle; under the pressure of foreign imports, Marlin had postponed its introduction, although Mr. Osborne described management's attitude as "still positive" about the gun.

Production

The firearms division had a work force of approximately 640 nonunion employees, 80% of whom were compensated on an incentive system related to piecework. Pay was competitive within the community and averaged about $3 per hour for the production workers. Production was conducted in one full eight-hour shift followed by a partial shift of only 60 people. The plant was closed for the first two weeks in August, and production was fairly even throughout the year because guns were produced for inventory during the slack selling seasons. In its new factory, Marlin was set up to produce 350,000 guns per year, but it was estimated that by going to two full shifts over 500,000 units per year could be turned out.

The manufacturing costs for one representative moderately priced gun were estimated by Mr. Milledge to be 18% materials, 25% direct labor, and overhead calculated at a rate of 230% of direct labor. In addition to occupancy costs—utilities, depreciation, etc.—major overhead expenses included the indirect costs associated with testing and engineering as well as indirect labor and fringe benefits.

Foreign competition

Browning's introduction of the Japanese-made .22-caliber lever-action rifle was viewed with concern by Marlin management. In 1970 sales were expected to approach 6,000 units at a "fair-trade" price of $75. Marlin understood that delivery problems had limited volume to date but that these were now under control. Moreover, Browning had indicated to the trade that a higher caliber rifle would be introduced next, parts of which were made in Japan.

Marlin was reasonably sure that the combination of import duties and increased labor costs would force Browning's price on the .22-caliber rifle to $85 in 1971. Using this assumption and certain further assumptions concerning costs and margins, Marlin estimated that the price of the rifle in Japan was $30.16.

Retail price	$85.00
Retailer's margin	28.00
Price to retailer ("wholesale" price)	$57.00
Browning margin (15% of "wholesale")	8.50
Excise tax (11% of import price)	4.80
Import price	$43.70
Per-gun tax	3.50
Import duty (20% of import price less per-gun tax)	8.04
Landed price	$32.16
Transportation from Japan	2.00
Purchase price of gun in Japan	$30.16

For 1971 Marlin was contemplating a defensive move calling for the reintroduction of the Model 39 which had been withdrawn in 1970 in favor of the custom-engraved commemorative model. The gun was to be priced at $99.95 and designed especially for "competitive" selling.

The high quality of the Browning imports had made them competitive with several $100 American models, and in 1969 Marlin's Model 39, then priced at $94.95, had been discounted by many dealers. Armin Romberg explained that although Marlin guns were "fair-traded," the company was not as stringent as Browning in policing retail pricing, and only in the most flagrant cases of price cutting had Marlin requested that the jobber terminate a retail account. Actually, Marlin was counting on aggressive merchandising to maintain its market position. According to Mr. Kenna, K-Mart was one of the best gun merchandisers in the country because of its aggressive marketing techniques and computerized inventory system. By concentrating on the low-price, high-volume sales outlets like K-Mart, Mr. Kenna felt that Marlin could protect its market share in the face of low-price imports.

Gun-control legislation

Snow Smart thought that gun-control legislation had had its biggest impact on the sale of Marlin guns when the over-18 restriction on the sale of ammunition caused a slump in the sale of .22 automatic rifles in 1969. Sales had recovered in 1970, and he concluded:

Sales depend primarily on the economics of the country just like auto sales, and management must come up with new models. With the possible exception of some handgun legislation and some local gun-control laws, the gun-control legislation has pretty much passed. Guns, like automobiles, are so widely held by individuals in American society that it is unlikely they will be more stringently controlled.

PLANS FOR THE FUTURE

Mr. Kenna's chief objective was to expand Marlin's product line to a full line of shoulder arms. By introducing new models of centerfire rifles and shotguns, he indicated that the company could reach additional segments of the firearms market. He stated:

With our new facilities, I plan to go full line in shoulder firearms. Right now we make rimfire and centerfire rifles in a limited number of models, and only two models of shotgun. We have some heady plans for the future which include further expansion into the shotgun field with a new pump-action shotgun we are developing. As we get established in the plant, we will add more shotgun models and also introduce more models of our centerfire rifles.

These new models in production will require new machinery, of course, but we spent about $1,000,000 last year on equipment because of the new plant and expect to spend $500,000 annually in the future for new machinery. We are buying mostly numerically controlled machines, and they range in price from $40,000 to $130,000 per machine.

Unless an opportunity presents itself, I see no need to diversify from the firearms and employee-communications fields we're in right now. We do want to go full line in shoulder arms, but we don't contemplate, for example, going into the ammunition business.

I am open-minded about diversifying into some new field, but someone will have to make a pretty good case for it. Of course, when we go public, it will be a lot easier to diversify if we want to do it later.

APPENDIX
SUMMARY OF THE FEDERAL GUN
CONTROL ACT OF 1968

—Federal firearms business licenses would have to be obtained by all those connected with firearms transactions. This included manufacturers of "destructive devices" (grenades, rockets, etc.), firearms, and ammunition; importers, dealers, collectors, and pawnbrokers.

—A holder of a federal firearms license could not sell any firearms or ammunition to anyone under 18, nor handguns or handgun ammunition to anyone under 21. Records of all firearms and ammunition sales had to be maintained.[6]

—A license holder could not sell any firearms or ammunition to anyone whom they knew to be under indictment or convicted of a crime punishable by more than a year's imprisonment, to be a fugitive from justice, a narcotics user or addict, or to be judged mentally defective or committed to a mental institution.

—A license holder could not, even under a contiguous state's laws, sell handguns to any unlicensed out-of-state resident.

—A license holder could not deliver any firearms over the counter to unlicensed persons from other states unless returning a firearm sent for repair or parts replacement.

---

[6] In November 1969, the Gun Control Act of 1968 was amended, exempting shotgun shells and ammunition suitable for use only in rifles (excluding .22-caliber rifles) from record-keeping requirements.

Cartridge Television Inc.

On July 13, 1971, Cartridge Television Inc. went public with a $22 million offering. The prospectus stated:[1]

The common stock of the Company offered hereby involves a high degree of risk. In evaluating these securities, a prospective investor should carefully consider the following factors:

1. The Company has been in existence only three years and has had no operating revenues since its inception.

2. Numerous firms, both in the United States and abroad, are engaged, or have announced their intention to engage, in the development of home video systems which are or would be competitive with the CARTRIVISION system. Most of these companies are substantially larger and possess greater resources and more extensive operating experience than the Company.

3. . . . . From its inception in 1968 to March 31, 1971, the Company incurred approximately $6,076,000 of research and preoperating costs in developing its CARTRIVISION system, and it estimates that at least an additional $7,509,000 of preoperating costs must be incurred before the first units can be sold. . . . The Company also estimates that approximately $8,640,000 will be spent to acquire additional capital equipment and tooling before the first units can be sold.

4. To date, commercial application of video tape systems manufactured by others has been limited primarily to industrial and business uses. In view of the novelty of the home video tape system developed by the Company, the substantial estimated retail prices of CARTRIVISION units and cartridges,

---

[1] Hornblower & Weeks-Hemphill, Noyes, *Cartridge Television Inc. Prospectus*, July 13, 1971.

and the difficulty of predicting public demand for the programming which will be available for use with the system, no assurance can be given that the CARTRIVISION system will meet with general public acceptance.

5.   As production and sale of the CARTRIVISION system have not yet commenced, the Company has no experience as to whether CARTRIVISION units manufactured in production quantities will operate satisfactorily under conditions of home use or whether they can be sold profitably.

6.   The Company does not have, nor does it presently plan to establish, its own plants to manufacture components of the CARTRIVISION system, other than its cartridge and video head manufacturing plant located in San Jose, California. The Company must depend on making satisfactory contractual arrangements with other manufacturers to assure adequate production and sales of its system.

7.   Failure by the Company to retain the services of its present key technical personnel or to attract additional qualified personnel, as required, could have an adverse effect on its operations.

8.   Published reports indicate that efforts are being made by various firms in the industry to standardize the technical characteristics of the tapes and cartridges used or to be used in home video tape systems. Since no tapes or cartridges other than those being developed by the Company are presently compatible with the CARTRIVISION system, industry standardization on a different type of tape or cartridge could have a seriously detrimental effect on the Company's prospects.

9.   Much of the earnings potential of the Company appears dependent upon its ability to offer customers pre-recorded tapes covering attractive subject matter. Keen competition is developing among the potential participants in this industry to conclude contractual arrangements covering a wide variety of popular programming. Because of its recent organization, small size and lack of demonstrated manufacturing and marketing abilities, the Company may be at a competitive disadvantage in obtaining satisfactory programming for the CARTRIVISION system.

10.   Although the Company has filed a number of patent applications pertaining to various aspects of the CARTRIVISION system, it does not expect to obtain fundamental patent protection for the basic concept or design of its system. No assurance can be given that patent infringement claims will not be asserted which may adversely affect the Company or that any valid patent protection will be obtained by the Company. The Company may be required to obtain patent licenses in order to produce and market the CARTRIVISION system, but no assurance can be given that such licenses can be obtained.

11.   Although the Company believes that the net proceeds of this offering will be sufficient to meet its long-term financing needs, no assurance can be given that unforeseen factors, such as problems in production or marketing, may not result in a need for additional financing. The Company anticipates, furthermore, that after production and sale of the system have commenced, it will require additional bank or commercial financing for its working capital needs. No assurance can be given, however, that any such financing can be obtained or, if obtained, as to the terms thereof.

12. The Company is not in a position to pay any cash dividends on its common stock, nor is it likely to be in such a position in the foreseeable future.

HISTORY

On June 27, 1968, Ernest S. Alson, Victor Elmaleh, and Frank and Arthur Stanton organized Cartridge Television Inc. (CTI). Alson and Frank and Arthur Stanton were senior officers of World-Wide Volkswagen Corporation, the Volkswagen distributor for New York, New Jersey, and Connecticut, which had pioneered the introduction of the VW "beetle" in the late forties and early fifties and was rumored to be the largest VW distributor in the world. Elmaleh was president of Magna-Dolphin Inc., an automobile distributor. Elmaleh and Frank Stanton were also senior officers of Cragstan Industries, Inc., a toy manufacturer. The founders had obtained 218,100 shares of CTI for $7,270 at about $.03 per share, with 15,600 shares going to Alson and 67,500 each to the other three.

CTI acquired all the rights and interests of Playtape, Inc., pertaining to the invention, design, and development of a preliminary prototype home video tape recorder-playback system. Playtape was a wholly owned subsidiary of World-Wide Volkswagen Corporation, of whose stock CTI's four founders owned 92.1%. CTI's agreement with Playtape specified a basic purchase price of $120,000 and provided for annual royalties equal to the lesser of $500,000 or 2% of the income of CTI derived from the Cartrivision system before income taxes for each fiscal year in perpetuity commencing with the fiscal year beginning December 1, 1973. Also, CTI's principal executive offices, including furniture and equipment, were sublet at an annual rental of $42,000 under an agreement with Playtape which expired December 31, 1972.

Recognizing that their recorder-playback prototype required substantial further development before its commercial feasibility could be fully determined, the principal stockholders of CTI approached the large financial services and aerospace conglomerate, Avco. In May 1969 CTI and Avco executed contracts which provided for (1) the issuance and sale to Avco of 50.2% of CTI's outstanding shares for a cash purchase price of $500,000, (2) an agreement by Avco to lend CTI up to an additional $1,000,000 and to assist CTI in securing such further financing as might be required during the developmental stage, and (3) an agreement by Avco's electronics division to provide technical and engineering assistance in further developing the Cartrivision system. The latter agreement provided for future royalty payments by CTI to Avco in the same amounts and on the same terms as provided under the agreement with Playtape. Since May 1969 Avco had advanced CTI $7.5 million. Of this debt, $7.1 million was exchanged shortly before the public offering for 355,000 newly issued shares, increasing Avco's holdings to 670,000 shares, and 10-year stock purchase warrants for 12,500 shares at $20 per share.

The July 1971 public offering involved 1.1 million shares at $20 per share. After deducting underwriting discounts and commissions of $1,980,000 and expenses payable by the company of $170,000, CTI received $19,850,000. CTI planned to use its proceeds, according to the prospectus,

. . . to defray its additional preoperating costs (estimated at $7,509,000 as of March 31, 1971, of which approximately $1,173,000 will be used to reimburse Avco for startup expenses to be incurred in connection with production of CARTRIVISION recorder-playback units), to acquire additional capital equipment and tooling (estimated at $8,640,000 as of March 31, 1971, of which approximately $6,267,000 is expected to cover equipment and tooling to be located in Avco plants), to pay accrued interest and accounts payable (including amounts, $751,000 at March 31, 1971, payable to Avco), to repay $400,000 of short-term notes payable to Avco and any additional short-term borrowings which may be needed prior to the Company's receipt of the proceeds of this offering, and to provide funds to meet other operating needs of the Company. . . .

The underwriting also involved the issuance to the underwriter, Hornblower & Weeks-Hemphill, Noyes, of five-year warrants to purchase an aggregate of 50,000 shares of CTI's common stock at $24 per share. The following table from the prospectus shows the percentage of ownership of CTI's common shares before and after the refinancing of Avco's debt, after the public offering, and after Avco's and the underwriter's common stock purchase warrants of CTI have been fully exercised:

	Before refinancing	After refinancing	After offering	After exercise
Avco Corporation.	50.2%	68.2%	32.2%	31.8%
Other present stockholders	49.8	31.8	15.0	14.6
Public.	. . .	. . .	52.8	51.3
Hornblower & Weeks-Hemphill, Noyes	. . .	. . .	. . .	2.3

Total common stock outstanding after the offering, but before exercise of the warrants, was 2,082,750 shares. Exhibit 1 presents CTI's assets, intangibles, deferrals, and liabilities, while Exhibit 2 provides its statement of cash receipts and disbursements.

EXHIBIT 1

CARTRIDGE TELEVISION INC.
Statement of Assets, Intangibles, Deferrals, and Liabilities
March 31, 1971
(pro forma and unaudited)

Assets, Intangibles, Deferrals

Current assets

Cash	$ 38,522
Advances and prepaid expenses	37,444
Total current assets	$ 75,966
Additional loan commitment from Avco Corporation*	1,050,000
Property, plant, and equipment, at cost	$2,373,782
Less: Accumulated depreciation	(184,186)
Net property, plant, and equipment	$2,189,596

Intangibles and deferrals

Patent applications, at cost	60,521
Research and preoperating costs†	6,075,700
Total assets, intangibles, deferrals	$9,451,783

Liabilities

Current liabilities

Notes payable to Avco Corporation	$ 400,000
Trade accounts payable, including $440,232 payable to Avco Corporation	539,740
Accrued interest payable to Avco Corporation	311,074
Accrued payroll and payroll taxes	58,894
Other accrued liabilities	33,275
Long-term debt due within one year	130,200
Total current liabilities	$1,473,183
8½% note payable	368,100
Commitments and contingencies‡	...
Total liabilities	$1,841,283

* A commitment by Avco Corporation as of March 31, 1971, to lend the Company an additional $1,050,000 (all of which has been received and substantially all of which has been used for research and preoperating costs and to purchase property, plant, and equipment) has been reflected in the above pro forma financial statement, as has the exchange by Avco on July 12, 1971, of $7,100,000 (including $650,000 of the foregoing $1,050,000) of the Company's then outstanding notes payable held by Avco for 355,000 shares of the Company's common stock and 10-year warrants exercisable at any time to purchase 12,500 shares of its common stock.

† The Company intends to continue deferring all costs incurred until sales of its products commence. The Company plans to amortize research and preoperating costs applicable to each product by charges to earnings based on units expected to be sold, subject to increased amortization if sales exceed projections, during the 36 months beginning with the first sales of the respective products.

‡ The Company has entered into agreements with the owners of certain film properties for the purpose of licensing the Company to use such properties with its video tape cartridges. The agreements are for varying periods of time, none of which extends beyond 1976. The agreements call for royalties to be paid by the Company at varying rates, based on sales and rentals of the video tape cartridges. Certain of these agreements call for minimum royalty payments aggregating $275,000.

The Company has entered into an engineering services agreement with Barger Corporation which obligates the Company to pay royalties up to an aggregate maximum of $300,000 based on future sales of certain products.

Source: Cartridge Television Inc. Prospectus, July 13, 1971.

EXHIBIT 2

CARTRIDGE TELEVISION INC.
Statement of Cash Receipts and Disbursements

	June 27, 1968 (date of incorporation) to November 30, 1968	Year ended November 30, 1969	Year ended November 30, 1970	Four months ended March 31, 1971	Total
Cash receipts					
Sales of common stock..........	$ 10,000	$515,000			$ 525,000
Proceeds of loans from Avco Corporation...............		200,000	$4,900,000	$1,350,000	6,450,000
Total cash receipts..........	$ 10,000	$715,000	$4,900,000	$1,350,000	$6,975,000
Disbursements (accrual basis)					
Research and preoperating costs*					
Salaries of officers and directors		$ 15,000	$ 162,369	$ 79,416	$ 256,785
Other salaries and employee benefits		256,556	1,414,233	625,312	2,296,101
Materials and supplies		29,990	573,384	147,471	750,845
Travel		112,712	111,905	34,265	258,882
Advertising, promotion and market surveys		47,316	189,100	18,340	254,756
Taxes		250	47,000	17,575	64,825
Rent and utilities............		23,098	146,433	62,977	232,508
Industrial design		804	102,982	17,765	121,551
Engineering services and consulting fees		54,550	260,816	33,015	348,381
Interest (net of $9,673 interest income)...............		(1,554)	263,487	179,512	441,445
Employment expenses.........			133,521	9,545	143,066
Purchase of invention	$120,000				120,000
Avco's production startup costs				393,779	393,779
Other		24,705	134,915	48,970	208,590
	$120,000	$563,427	$3,540,145	$1,667,942	$5,891,514
Property, plant, and equipment		63,029	2,300,815	9,938	2,373,782
Patent applications...........		31,098	23,604	5,819	60,521
Principal payments on 8½% note				151,700	151,700
Other...................		34,144	17,856	444	52,444
Total disbursements (accrual basis)	$120,000	$691,698	$5,882,420	$1,835,843	$8,529,961
Accrual adjustments.........	115,000	214,734	781,060	482,689	1,593,483
Total cash disbursements	$ 5,000	$476,964	$5,101,360	$1,353,154	$6,936,478
Net increase (decrease) in cash	$ 5,000	$238,036	$ (201,360)	$ (3,154)	$ 38,522
Cash at beginning of period		5,000	243,036	41,676	
Cash at end of period............	$ 5,000	$243,036	$ 41,676	$ 38,522	$ 38,522

* Approximately $1,659,000 of research and preoperating costs (including interest of $385,000) have been charged to the Company by Avco Corporation.
Source: Cartridge Television Inc. Prospectus, July 13, 1971.

THE CARTRIVISION SYSTEM

Cartridge Television Inc.'s system, identified by the registered trademark, "Cartrivision," consisted of a solid-state video recorder-playback unit which was integrated with a color television receiver. The system was designed (1) to play prerecorded cartridges in color or monochrome on the television receiver, (2) to record either color or monochrome television programs off the air for subsequent playback without processing, and (3) to play cartridges on which home movies with sound had been recorded with a special camera (initially available only in monochrome). The unit incorporated a timing device which permitted television programs to be automatically recorded off the air in the absence of the set owner, enabling the programs to be viewed later at the owner's convenience. Normal television viewing was available when the Cartrivision system was not in use or while programs were being recorded. CTI had begun development of an adaptor unit with recording and playback capabilities that could be adapted to a regular television receiver.

The tape used with the Cartrivision system was one-half inch wide iron oxide magnetic video tape which resembled the audio tape currently in general use. The tape came in different lengths and was wound in cartridges which permitted up to 114 minutes of continuous playing time, sufficient to display an average full-length motion picture without interruption. The tape could be erased and had an estimated life of more than 100 playings.

In the recording process, one of the system's three video heads placed on the tape a magnetic imprint which conformed to the electronic impulses derived from the picture. Separate audio heads recorded and reproduced the sound by the same method used by conventional audio stereo tape recorders. For playback, the three video heads scanned the video magnetic imprint sequentially, generating three picture fields from each one recorded. This technique, according to the prospectus, "increases by a factor of three the duration of program which can be recorded on a given length of tape, but produces a slightly less smooth image transition which could be perceptible to the trained eye under certain circumstances."

Prototype Cartrivision units had been exhibited publicly, but CTI did not expect production of the system and the cartridges to be sufficiently advanced to permit sales to consumers before mid-1972.

OPERATING POLICIES

The prospectus stated:

Marketing

Marketing plans for the CARTRIVISION system have not yet been finally determined. Initially, the Company will depend on sales of its system components to television receiver manufacturers who will market, for their own account, the completed CARTRIVISION system to consumers through distributors and retailers. Admiral Corporation[2] has agreed to purchase from the Company 10,000 recorder-playback units (with an option to purchase an additional 10,000 units), integrate the units with its own television receivers and sell the completed CARTRIVISION systems . . . In addition, Warwick Electronics Inc., a corporation associated with Sears, Roebuck and Co., has placed an order with the Company for 3,001 recorder-playback units to be delivered commencing in mid-1972 to cover the introduction of the CARTRIVISION system by Sears. The Company also intends to market, for its own account, CARTRIVISION units to commercial, industrial, and governmental customers.

The Company estimates that the retail price of the CARTRIVISION system, including the color television receiver, will be approximately $900–$1,000, although the Company may have no control over the price of certain elements of the system such as the receiver. The CARTRIVISION cartridges are expected to be offered for retail sale at prices ranging from approximately $10 to approximately $40, depending upon length (in the case of blank cartridges) and length, content, and artist (in the case of prerecorded cartridges). Distribution of cartridges is expected to be made initially through CARTRIVISION system dealers and selected music, record and audio cassette/cartridge distributors. Prerecorded cartridges will also be offered for rent at rentals starting at approximately $3 per use, and are expected to be available through a variety of retail outlets.

Arrangements have been made with United Artists Corporation and Time-Life Video, a division of Time Incorporated, giving each company the right to purchase CARTRIVISION cartridges containing programming supplied by them at specified wholesale prices. The agreement with Time-Life Video. also provides for certain mutual promotional efforts on a nonexclusive basis. No other arrangements have yet been made for distribution of the CARTRIVISION cartridges.

Programming

Although blank cartridges will be offered for use in recording television programs off the air, or for making "home movies" with an auxiliary camera, much of the market appeal of home video systems is expected to revolve around the availability of prerecorded cartridges offering a broad range of subject matter. Accordingly, the Company is actively engaged in negotiating agreements making available to it movies, sporting events, musical and educational programs, "how-to" instruction, travel subjects, documentaries, cartoons, and dance and poetry performances for distribution on CARTRIVISION cartridges.

The Company has acquired nonexclusive license rights to more than 800 film presentations. These include 95 feature films from Avco Embassy Pictures Corp. (a subsidiary of Avco), 50 from United Artists Corporation, 28 from

---

[2] In addition to selling its own branded sets, Admiral produced TV sets for Montgomery Ward.

Lion International Films, and 15 from American International Pictures, Inc. Rights have also been negotiated for the use of National Football League films, a film series of well-known prize fights, instructional films dealing with a variety of participatory sports, and filmed classical music productions.

Substantially all of the Company's initial programming will consist of previously exhibited subject matter. The Company is seeking to obtain rights to original musical programs, including full-length symphonies, rock and pop concerts, country and western music, and opera and ballet productions. In this connection, the Company may participate in some production financing, but most of its programming is expected to be acquired from outside sources without Company participation.

The programming license agreements which are being negotiated give the Company the right to distribute the subject matter on CARTRIVISION cartridges for a specified period (normally at least three years) in return for royalties based upon the receipts derived by the Company from the sale or rental of the cartridges. Renewal rights for varying periods of time are customarily included, and minimum royalty guarantees are sometimes required. . . .

Keen competition is developing for home video programming rights, but since most of the subjects are being made available to potential competitors on a nonexclusive basis, the Company does not anticipate any major problems in securing rights to a broad range of material.

Production

The Company has entered into agreements with two divisions of Avco providing for the production of 25,000 CARTRIVISION recorder-playback units in the presently agreed configuration, and for an option to purchase up to an additional 175,000 units. Using capital equipment and tooling owned and supplied by the Company, Avco's Electronics Division will produce electronic and mechanical components of the system at Huntsville, Alabama, and its Precision Products Division will manufacture and assemble the CARTRIVISION recorder-playback units at Richmond, Indiana. The Company has agreed to reimburse Avco for certain startup expenses aggregating approximately $1,567,000 incurred and to be incurred for the Company's account.

The agreements with Avco specify unit target costs and prices (including an 8% profit) based on delivery of a total of 200,000 units. If the Company does not exercise its option to acquire this entire quantity in accordance with the agreed delivery schedule, additional charges (estimated at a maximum of $2,900,000 if the Company does not exercise any part of its option) may be made by Avco based on its incurred costs, and equitable adjustments will be made in the target costs and prices based on any changes in the presently agreed configuration. On completion of delivery of 200,000 units, Avco's actual costs will be reviewed and cost savings or overruns from the agreed target cost will be shared equally by the Company and Avco, provided that the final price cannot exceed 116% of the adjusted target cost.

The Company does not intend to establish its own facilities for manufacturing the CARTRIVISION system but expects to contract with various domestic and foreign television receiver manufacturers to produce and market for their own account CARTRIVISION units on a nominal royalty or royalty-free basis. The Company has granted Admiral Corporation a five-year nonexclusive royalty-free license (renewable on certain conditions) permitting Admiral to manufacture and sell CARTRIVISION recorder-playback units.

The cartridge producing facility which the Company is equipping at San Jose, California, is expected to have the capability of producing more than 200,000 blank and prerecorded CARTRIVISION cartridges per month when fully operating on a single shift basis. If sufficient demand for its cartridges develops, the Company may establish additional cartridge manufacturing facilities or license other manufacturers to produce cartridges under the CARTRIVISION name on a royalty basis.

The Company recognizes the importance of quality control and continuous supply of video heads for its CARTRIVISION system, and has been conducting video head preoperating work with the intent of creating an internal source of supply. Prototype video heads are currently being produced at the San Jose facility, and the Company plans to install additional equipment at that location to enable it to establish a video head production capability. The Company also plans to purchase video heads from other sources.

Several sources of magnetic video tape are presently available to the Company, and the plastic material used in fabricating cartridges is available from a number of suppliers.

Management

As of May 31, 1971, CTI had 136 full-time employees: 59 in technical operations; 33 in production, programming, and marketing; and 44 in administrative and clerical operations. The board of directors consisted of the four founders and four members of Avco management. Thor W. Kolle, Jr., a general partner of Hornblower & Weeks-Hemphill, Noyes, David L. Coffin, president of The Dexter Corporation, a producer of specialty chemicals and specialized long-fiber products, and George S. Trimble, president of The Bunker-Ramo Corporation, a diversified manufacturer and supplier of electronic components, information systems, and services and other products, were expected to be elected directors of CTI shortly after completion of the public offering. Mr. Frank Stanton, age 51, was president and was assisted by four vice presidents who had joined CTI between December 1969 and June 1970. Charles D. Brown, general manager of West Coast operations, had previously held management positions in the electronics division of Avco and had served as president of an electronics division of Textron. Samuel W. Gelfman, vice president of production and programming, had been vice president of the motion picture department of General Artists Corporation as well as assistant to the president of United Artists Corporation. Donald F. Johnston, vice president of marketing, had been a vice president of Philco-Ford Corporation. Denis B. Trelewicz, treasurer and secretary, had served in various staff positions with Avco and, prior to joining CTI, had been a Sloan Fellow at the Massachusetts Institute of Technology. The prospectus listed executive remuneration as follows:

Name	Capacity in which remuneration is being received	Aggregate annual remuneration
Frank Stanton	President	$ 75,000
Donald F. Johnston	Vice president	65,000
Samuel W. Gelfman	Vice president	50,000
All 12 officers and directors as a group		265,000

The prospectus continued:

The Company has adopted a Stock Option Plan, pursuant to which options to purchase a maximum of 175,000 authorized but unissued or treasury shares of the Company's stock may be granted to officers (including officers who are directors) and other key employees of the Company. . . .

✿   ✿   ✿   ✿   ✿

The Company's Board of Directors has approved the grant of qualified options to acquire an aggregate of 41,500 common shares at the Price to Public, effective as of the date of this Prospectus, including 2,500 shares each to Messrs. Johnston and Gelfman and 10,000 shares to all officers and directors of the company as a group. The directors have also approved the grant to Frank Stanton of an option to acquire 50,000 common shares on similar terms. This option cannot be qualified due to the number of common shares owned by Mr. Stanton.

Competition

The prospectus described CTI's competition as follows:

Various types of video tape recorders, different from the CARTRIVISION system, have been available and used for a number of years by the television industry, and a limited number are also being produced for the industrial and general consumer markets. However, the high price and operating complexities of these devices have prevented them from becoming mass market consumer items. Currently, a number of firms are devoting considerable research efforts to the development of lower cost home video systems.

To date, a number of different varieties of home video systems have been publicized. One is the magnetic tape cartridge system, of which the CARTRIVISION system is an example. Other magnetic tape systems are being developed by Sony Corporation of Japan, Ampex Corporation and Philips of Holland, among others.

A second approach is represented by Columbia Broadcasting System's Electronic Video Recording system which relies on miniaturized film coiled in a cartridge and run through a separate playback unit connected to a television set. Units incorporating this system are presently being produced by Motorola, Inc. Another proposed system is RCA Corporation's SelectaVision process based on holographic photography. Using a laser beam, RCA embosses an encoded picture on vinyl tape which is played through a module connected to a television set. Other approaches include the use of Super 8mm film in conjunction with a television set, and systems utilizing plastic discs on which the video images have been recorded in phonograph fashion.

Each of these home video systems presently being developed is incompatible with the others. In an effort to avoid the expense and consumer confusion inherent in the marketing of incompatible but competitive products, attempts are being made by certain electronics firms to standardize magnetic tape and cartridge configurations.

The foregoing information, which has been summarized from published reports and news articles, indicates that the major potential competitors of the Company and its CARTRIVISION system appear to be Sony, Ampex, Philips, CBS, and RCA. Each of these companies is substantially larger than the Company and has greater financial and other resources and more extensive operating experience in electronics. If general agreement is reached by a significant number of the Company's potential competitors on magnetic tape and cartridge standards incompatible with the CARTRIVISION system, the Company could be at a competitive marketing disadvantage.

The potential competitive clash thus was not only one among rival companies but also among technologies. Two more proven and established recording materials (magnetic tape and super 8mm film) were pitted against two drastically new techniques. CBS had introduced EVR, which used film but exposed it by a fine electron-beam scanner rather than by light, permitting the film to contain considerably more information and thereby reducing costs. Also, the EVR system was the only one which could be built directly into TV sets, avoiding duplication of player circuitry, which allowed further cost reduction. RCA's SelectaVision used a simple vinyl tape, combining a low-cost material with a highly advanced technology. Although the prototypes of both the CBS and RCA systems had not yet reached the quality of reproduction of the more established materials, they offered the prospect of major further advances both in terms of quality improvement and of cost reduction. The latter was a major questionmark for both magnetic tape and regular film. They used costly materials, and mass reproduction was both expensive and slow. The lowest cost product was the video disc. Like EVR and SelectaVision, however, it permitted playing only prerecorded programs. Magnetic tape, on the other hand, allowed its user to self-record

TV programs off the air and also use the system for immediate or delayed replay of home movies. However, the camera initially was limited to black and white, was bulky, and was therefore restricted in terms of mobility. Super 8 did not allow self-recording and handled only delayed (that is, after outside development) viewing of self-made movies. The playing time varied from a maximum of 15 minutes on video discs, to above 30 minutes for EVR, up to a maximum of 60 minutes for the other techniques. Cartrivision, however, by using its special technique had been able to reach 114 minutes of playing time. Also, Cartrivision used one-half inch tape compared with the three-quarter inch tape used by several other companies. As a result, it was expected that Cartrivision tape costs would be lower. Also, in terms of projected equipment prices, which were largely guesswork, Cartrivision was at the lower end of the scale. By and large it seemed that companies using magnetic tape or EVR (especially Motorola) would be among the early entrants. Most of these companies, such as Sony, were concentrating their initial efforts on the industrial market while Cartrivision aimed primarily at the consumer market. According to *Fortune:* "since none of the playbacks use any part of the public airwaves, all being confined to individual TV chassis, the Federal Communications Commission has no power—at least not yet—to regulate or impose standards on them."[3]

MARKET ESTIMATES

Opinions on the outlook for video cassettes ranged from undisguised pessimism to strongly worded optimism. Some observers felt that video cassettes could never dislodge television, which was viewed an average of six to seven hours per day. *Broadcasting* in its April 26, 1971, issue stated:

Companies are spending millions of dollars a year wrestling with their various systems. But timetables for production and marketing keep getting pushed back. . . .

✿　✿　✿　✿　✿

. . . how much time is likely to pass before a significant proportion of the television audience acquires playing machines? The short answer, based on information, opinions and parallels on both sides of the dispute, is: at least five years and probably not in this decade.[4]

The article cited a number of reasons, including the slow initial growth of color television. It concluded:

---

[3] "Stand By for the Cartridge TV Explosion," *Fortune,* June 1971, p. 81. © 1971 Time Inc.

[4] "Cassette Revolution Slow a 'Borning," Special Report by Rufus Crater, *Broadcasting,* April 26, 1971, p. 60. © 1971 by Broadcasting Publications, Inc.

Where the prophecies of wholesale takeover by cassettes break down, in the opinion of many, is in the assumption that John Doe will want to spend the kind of money necessary to make the prophecies come true. In fact, it is pointed out, the average U.S. household's total expenditure for all box-office entertainment currently comes to less than $37 a year—a fraction of the money being talked about for cassette equipment and programs.[5]

On the other side, *Fortune* reported that "Peter Goldmark of CBS Laboratories, a major contributor to the new technology, has been talking about 'the greatest revolution in communications since the book.' "[6] Paul J. Caravatt, Jr., senior vice president of the Interpublic Group of Companies, predicted at a seminar for the American Association of Advertising Agencies that cassettes:

"Will ultimately seriously erode television network audience sizes" and "have revolutionary effects upon education, entertainment, public service, retailing and even religion."

Will provide a "mature market" for program material that at current retail prices could be as high as $11 billion a year.

"Represent a major breakthrough in human freedom," providing the individual for the first time with "a full spectrum of communication" and giving him "complete control over the output of his television set—to see and hear what he wants, when he wants, as long as he wants."[7]

CTI's Samuel Gelfman had also expressed optimism:

If you have ageless product . . . you don't have to make your money back right away. You make it over a period of years. Television and the theater have to be concerned with immediacy. Cartridge TV doesn't. If a program reaches a thousand homes a week, by the end of a year it's reached a good audience. By the end of 10 years, it's reached a hell of an audience.[8]

An Arthur D. Little study in 1971 had estimated the U.S. market as shown in the table at the top of page 269.

The Arthur D. Little study, noting that penetration of 44% of U.S. TV households through 1970 by color sets indicated a willingness to spend more than $300 for entertainment devices, also commented:

. . . The most significant new product of the early 1970s will be videoplayers; we forecast that factory sales of videoplayers, video-cassettes, and software will reach $0.9–1.5 billion worldwide in 1975. Growth in industry sales and profits will depend to a great extent on the willingness of manufacturers to standardize on videoplayers and cassettes and thereby permit full exploitation of this major potential market, while stimulating a substantial by-product demand for color TV sets, at present the industry's most important product. . . .

[5] Ibid., p. 64.

[6] Lessing, *Fortune*, p. 81.

[7] *Broadcasting*, April 26, 1971, p. 64.

[8] Ibid.

Videoplayer market in the United States, 1972–80* (factory sales in 1970 dollars)

	1972	1974	1976	1978	1980
Estimated TV households (million), year-end	64	66	70	75	80
Videoplayer penetration (%), year-end	0.3%	2.6%	5.6%	9.3%	14.0%
Videoplayer households (million), year-end	0.2	1.7	3.9	7.0	11.2
New videoplayer households for year shown (million)	0.2	0.8	1.2	1.7	2.2
		(in millions of dollars)			
Consumer market:					
Hardware sales†	$ 53	$213	$319	$451	$ 584
Software sales‡	11	51	93	152	223
Software rentals§	11	51	93	152	223
	$ 75	$315	$505	$755	$1,030
Institutional and government market‖	90	125	150	175	200
Total	$165	$440	$655	$930	$1,230

*John P. Thompson, "International Outlook for Consumer Electronics," Arthur D. Little, Inc., April 1971.
†Calculated at average factory price of $266 ($400 at retail).
‡Calculated at average factory sales of $50 × new videoplayer households (basic library) and $12.50 × old videoplayer households (additions to library). ($100 and $25 at retail, respectively.)
§Estimated at same volume as sales.
‖Does not include software.

Free world sales of consumer electronics products: 1969–75 (millions of U.S. dollars, at factory prices)

			1975	
Products	1969	1970	Low	High
Videoplayers and prerecorded cassettes	$ 0	$ 0	$ 900	$ 1,500
Television sets				
Black and white	2,265	2,300	2,000	2,600
Color	3,900	4,100	6,200	7,500
Audio tape equipment and software				
Cassettes and cartridges	372	585	1,475	2,235
Players and recorder/players	565	710	1,245	1,610
Phonographs and hi-fi components	1,400	1,475	1,300	1,775
Radio	1,370	1,425	1,555	1,990
Cable television equipment	100	135	435	575
Interactive TV equipment	0	0	55	235
Home facsimile systems	0	0	30	75
Total (rounded)	$9,970	$10,700	$15,200	$20,100

Source: Arthur D. Little, Inc. estimates.

CORPORATE STRATEGY AND
ENVIRONMENTAL CHANGE

Note on the commercial broadcasting industry

THE COMMERCIAL broadcasting industry is composed of two major segments, television and radio, which together generated about $4 billion in revenues in 1970. This note develops the structural characteristics of these industry segments and some of the economic, political, and social forces at work in them.

TELEVISION

Structure and performance

There were 862 television stations in the United States at year-end 1970, an increase of 303 or 54% from the 559 stations on the air in 1960. The highest percentage of increases, as shown in Exhibit 1 and in Table 1, had been in UHF rather than VHF channel allocations[1] and in educational rather than commercial stations.

Both UHF and educational television enjoyed the strong support of the Federal Communications Commission, which was responsible for granting and renewing licenses. Conversely, with the VHF bands already crowded, only two new VHF commercial stations had been authorized from 1967 to 1970. The FCC had demonstrated its interest in UHF by increasing the allowable power of UHF transmission, thus ex-

---

[1] UHF (ultra high frequency), channels 14–83, operate at 470–890 megacycles and VHF (very high frequency), channels 2–13, operate at 174–216 megacycles.

EXHIBIT 1
Television stations on the air (1945–70)

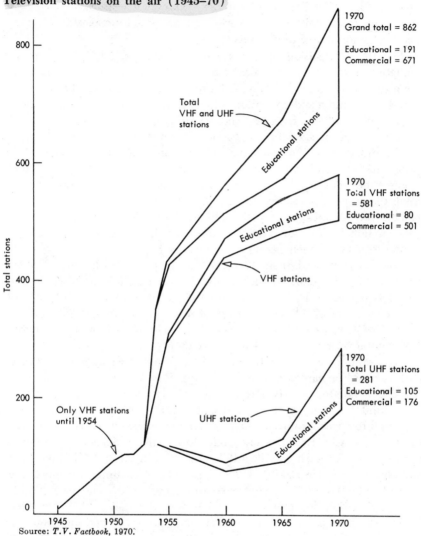

Source: *T.V. Factbook*, 1970.

TABLE 1

	VHF		UHF		
	Commercial	*Educational*	*Commercial*	*Educational*	*Total*
1960	440	34	75	10	559
1970	501	80	176	105	862
Increase	61	46	101	95	303
Percent.	14%	135%	135%	950%	54%

panding the broadcast range to be more competitive with VHF, increasing the UHF license allocations, making some areas all UHF, and requiring, after 1964, that television set manufacturers install UHF receiving capability on all new sets.[2]

The three television networks (ABC, CBS, and NBC) entered into affiliation agreements with local stations, about 530 in total, across the country. Each network originated programs, produced in-house or secured from independent studios, including national and international news, public affairs features, and sporting events. The networks sold advertising on the show or event to national accounts, remitting a portion of the proceeds as "station payments" to affiliates which broadcast the program. While affiliates relied on the networks to cover most of their prime time, they produced or acquired much of the daytime programming themselves, purchased their own movie rights, and, of course, were responsible for local news. Stations also had sales representatives who sold "national spot" advertising (time sold independently of the program) to national accounts on a commission basis.

The networks and their 15 owned and operating stations (O&Os)[3] were dominant factors in the profitability of the industry (see Exhibit 2). Network activities accounted for 41% of 1969 total television broadcast revenues of $2.8 billion and 17% of total pretax profit of $554 million. Their O&Os, representing about 2% of the nation's stations, had another 12% of total revenues and 24% of pretax profits.

Looking beyond ABC, CBS, and NBC, performance among TV broadcasters could be categorized in four ways. First, the largest metropolitan markets generated a very large share of television revenues, as shown in Exhibit 3. Many of the important stations in these markets were part of broadcast groups owned by companies such as Westinghouse, Metromedia, Cox Broadcasting, and RKO General. Second, profitability appeared to increase significantly with size for both VHF and UHF stations, as shown in Exhibit 4. Third, despite FCC support, a substantial majority of UHF stations continued to be both small and unprofitable. One explanation for this phenomenon was the fact that UHFs were frequently latecomers to the market and faced competition from entrenched stations with network affiliations. Finally, affiliates, as one would suspect, were mostly VHFs and were substantially more profitable than nonaffiliates, as reflected in the FCC sample shown in Table 2.

Industry observers pointed to several competitive reasons for the superior performance of network affiliates. For instance, expensive programming and special events which were beyond the financial means of independents were obtained from the networks. Moreover, media

---

[2] According to the FCC, 68% of TV homes were able to receive UHF channels.

[3] Each network had five VHF stations in the top 10 markets, the maximum number of VHFs allowed by the FCC to any single owner.

EXHIBIT 2

1969 broadcasting industry revenues, expenses, and income

	Broadcast revenues		Broadcast expenses		Broadcast income before taxes	
	Dollars (millions)	*Percent of industry*	*Dollars (millions)*	*Percent of industry*	*Dollars (millions)*	*Percent of industry*
Television						
3 networks*.	1,144.1	41	1,051.3	47	92.7	17
15 network stations*.	323.3	12	189.9	8	133.4	24
All other stations						
489 VHF	1,214.9	43	844.2	38	370.7	67
169 UHF	114.0	4	157.2	7	(43.2)	(8)
Total television industry.	2,796.2	100	2,242.6	100	553.6	100
Radio						
3 networks	44.1	4	50.4	5	(6.3)	(6)
20 network stations	48.8	4	43.0	5	5.8	6
4,174 other stations reporting to the FCC	955.8	92	844.1	90	111.7	100
Total radio industry.	1,048.7	100	937.5	100	111.2	100

*The percentage share of the $1,467,400 ($1,144,100 + $323,300) held by each major network was as follows: CBS (38.4); NBC (35.4); ABC (26.2).

Note: To avoid double counting, station payments of $254 million and $10 million have been excluded from network revenues and expenses for television and radio, respectively.

Source: FCC Annual Report, 1970.

buyers found it simpler and safer to allocate advertising budgets to network programming or national spot salesmen who could offer packages on proven stations covering many markets.

As a network, CBS had generally been the leader in prime-time ratings by a narrow margin over NBC, with ABC in third place. The CBS lead in total national advertising revenue had dwindled in recent years and in 1970 stood at CBS, 34.5%; NBC, 34.5%; ABC, 27.3%.[4] It was not unusual, however, for the order of finish to change depending on the success of the prime-time program lineup. For local stations, the specific affiliation was not necessarily a good indication of relative market share. In other words, competition at the local level encompassed many factors relating the station to the community of which network programming was only one.

---

[4] *T.V. Factbook*, 1970.

TABLE 2

	Network affiliated		Independents		Total	
	VHF	UHF	VHF	UHF	VHF	UHF
Number of stations reporting.	422	94	34	48	456	142
Number reporting profits	357	48	21	2	378	50
Percent profitable. . . .	85%	51%	62%	4%	83%	35%

Source: Federal Communications Commission.

EXHIBIT 3
1969 revenues of commercial television and radio stations in metropolitan markets (thousands of dollars)

	Number of stations	Network payments	National spot advertising	Local adver- tising	Total revenues	Percent of total
TV stations in—						
10 largest markets .	68	$ 65,300	$ 555,700	$153,500	$ 773,500	41.0
15 next largest markets	66	39,000	209,350	95,600	353,950	19.8
264 smaller markets	549	149,800	343,050	269,850	753,700	39.2
All metropolitan markets	683	$254,100	$1,108,100	$518,950	$1,881,150*	100.0
Radio stations in—						
10 largest markets	229	$ 2,550	$ 154,950	$151,000	$ 308,500	35.7
15 next largest markets	208	1,900	51,050	86,400	139,350	16.3
333 smaller markets	1,618	4,150	98,250	307,000	409,400	48.0
All metropolitan markets	2,055	$ 8,600	$ 304,250	$544,400	$ 857,250*	100.0

*These figures do not represent total TV and radio industry revenues of $2.8 billion and $1.05 billion, respectively, because networks retained a substantial portion of their advertising revenues and made network payments to stations carrying network advertising.
Source: Compiled from *FCC News*, No. 53051, July 24, 1970, Table 17; and *FCC News*, December 14, 1970.

Television advertising

Broadcast media, particularly television, had increased its share of total advertising expenditures in the 1960s at the expense of print and other media (see Table 3). Significantly, 64 of the top 100 advertisers spent more than 50% of their media dollars on TV. Television's "big

EXHIBIT 4
Profitability of VHF and UHF television stations by total broadcast revenues, 1969

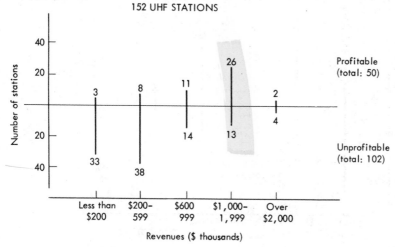

152 UHF STATIONS

Profitable (total: 50)

Unprofitable (total: 102)

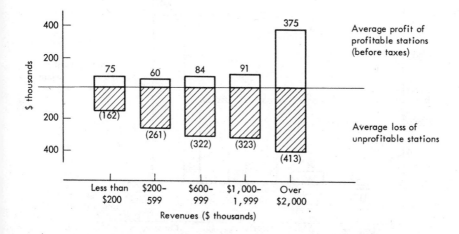

Average profit of profitable stations (before taxes)

Average loss of unprofitable stations

spenders" in 1970 included foods and beverages (20%); toiletries (17%); drugs (12%); transportation (11%); household products, chiefly soap (11%); tobacco products (10%); other consumer goods (14%); utilities and trade associations (5%).

Contributing to revenue growth were a modest rise in the number of commercial minutes per day (from 145 in 1964 to 162 minutes in 1969, according to one survey of the top 75 markets)[5] and increases in advertising rates averaging 6.6% per year for the top 10 markets and

---

[5] *Advertising Age*, November 2, 1970, p. 2. The NAB code permitted 10 minutes per hour.

EXHIBIT 4 (*continued*)

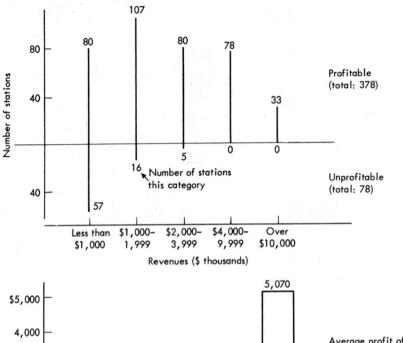

456 VHF STATIONS

EXHIBIT 4 (*continued*)

Profitable
(total: 378)

Number of stations this category

Unprofitable
(total: 78)

Revenues ($ thousands)

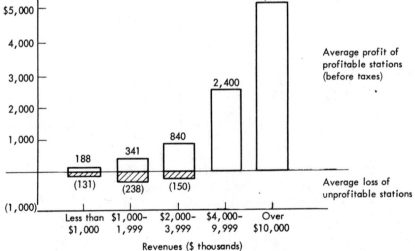

Average profit of
profitable stations
(before taxes)

Average loss of
unprofitable stations

Revenues ($ thousands)

Source: FCC Annual Report, 1970.

3.4% for the next 40 markets during the 1960s.[6] Since expanding the
number of minutes devoted to commercials was subject to public criticism for "cluttering" and advertiser criticism for downgrading message
retention, revenue growth was dependent primarily on how rapidly rates
could be increased.

[6] Ibid.

TABLE 3

	Share of expenditures		Annual growth rate
	1960	*1969*	
Television	13.4%	18.3%	9.3%
Radio.	5.8	6.5	6.9
Newspapers	31.1	29.8	5.2
Magazines	7.9	7.0	4.3
Other.	41.8	38.4	4.1
	100.0%	100.0%	5.7%

Source: *T.V. Factbook*, 1970, p. 58a.

Broadcasters had been successful in raising advertising rates for several reasons. First, although the proportion of households with a television set topped 90% in 1962, the penetration of color into 37% of the households by 1970 and the surge in multiple-set households were thought to increase the attention given television. In fact, the average TV viewing per household had leveled off at about five hours in 1965 but then rose to six hours and nine minutes in 1969.

Second, broadcasters had argued that it was possible for advertisers to target their messages at specific geographic or demographic audience segments, thus increasing the efficiency of the expenditure. For instance, in February 1970, the major networks signed a contract with the National Football League for $184 million to broadcast NFL games for the next four seasons on radio and TV, an increase of $76 million over the previous four-year contract. In February 1971, networks signed a one-year pact with the major baseball leagues for $40 million. Having signed contracts with the leagues, the networks then sought sponsors desiring to reach a highly concentrated male audience. Advertising was sold at prime-time rates (about $60,000 per minute) or higher ($200,000 per minute for the Super Bowl, $100,000 per minute for the World Series).

Revenue-cost relationships and trends

Despite the ability to secure rate increases, the networks were confronted with a number of difficulties in 1971. It should be noted, of course, that with the supply of advertising minutes essentially fixed, the networks had good reason to be concerned about their rate cards. Their concern was heightened by the fact that programming costs accounted for about 80% of total network expenses after station payments in 1969. Such costs were largely fixed in the short run and bore no direct relationship to the program ratings which determined audience size and hence influenced advertising rates. Moreover, network programming costs had been increasing at a rate of 9.7% during the 1960s, somewhat in excess of network revenue growth of 8.5%. The networks had protected their margins by reducing the proportion of revenues remitted to affiliates as station payments.[7]

A major problem for the networks was the drop in ratings for their programs which almost exactly balanced the increase in the number of TV households.[8] This in turn was a reflection of two further adverse factors. First, the market shares of affiliates in many cases were being fragmented by the intrusion of new stations and CATV into their broadcast areas. Second, as local broadcasters assessed the implications of lower station payments, some of them began to substitute local programming for network shows and sold the program time themselves to local advertisers. Consequently, it was becoming more difficult for the networks to deliver the full affiliate lineup to national advertisers, which necessitated rebates in the short run and over the longer term encouraged advertisers to consider buying national spots rather than network program time.

Prime-time access rule

In 1971 the FCC adopted a rule designed to encourage nonnetwork programming in prime time, that is, generally 7:00 P.M. until 11:00 P.M. The rule limited network programming to not more than three hours per day (down from three and one-half hours), which had the effect of increasing program costs to the local station and reducing network revenue. On the other hand, the decrease in network time available seemed to firm up network rates, which had sagged about 10% following the January 1971 ban on cigarette advertising. Cigarettes had accounted for about $210 million in revenue, most of it in prime time.[9]

For television station operators, trends of major significance were shifts in the sources of revenue and increasing programming costs evident in Table 4.

---

[7] Station payments declined from 25% of total network revenues in 1960 to 18% in 1969.

[8] For instance, the Nielsen rating for the top-rated show dropped from 42.4 in 1960 to 31.1 in 1970. As a result, despite the increase in TV hours, the number of homes reached by this program dropped from 18.9 million to 18.2 million. *Advertising Age*, November 2, 1970, p. 66.

[9] CBS estimated this would reduce the network's pretax profits by $5 to $15 million in 1971. *Advertising Age*, November 2, 1970.

TABLE 4

	(In millions)		Five-year growth rate
Revenues	1964	1969	
Network station payments.	$ 214	$ 254	3.5%
National spot	711	1,108	9.3
Local.	276	519	13.5
Total broadcast revenue (net)*	$1,081	$1,652	8.9%
Total broadcast expenses	725	1,191	10.4
Total pretax profit	$ 355	$ 461	5.3%

*Total sales plus miscellaneous revenue less commissions to advertising agencies, representatives, and brokers.
Source: *Broadcasting*, March 22, 1971.

CATV

Community antenna television was regarded by some as the most noteworthy development in broadcasting in the sixties. CATV companies erected towers capable of picking up signals of television stations from 60 to 100 miles away from the communities they served. Microwave relays could be used to bring in programs from even more distant stations. The signals received were then fed to homes of subscribers by means of coaxial cables. Subscribers usually paid about $20 for initial installation of the cable plus a monthly fee ranging from $5 to $7. Originally, CATV companies confined their efforts to small communities having limited TV coverage. Starting in 1964, however, CATV systems were set up in a number of major markets in which the nature of the terrain or the number of tall buildings interfered with reception of the signals of local TV stations.

Growing at a compound annual rate of 20% since 1960, 2,800 CATV systems served 4.5 million subscribers or about 6% of U.S. households in 1970. The seven largest systems accounted for 25% of total subscribers. CATV revenues totaled approximately $400 million in 1970. One source forecast that 28 million homes would be served by 4,400 systems in 1980.[10]

Since a typical system carried 6 to 12 channels, a viewer was offered the potential for increasing by two to four times the number of available channels. Most systems had excess channel capacity, and entrepreneurs in CATV looked to the day when these channels might be used commercially for such services as "TV shopping-at-home," information retrieval, and newspaper facsimile. In 1971 excess channels were often devoted to weather, stock market, and wire-service news reports and limited program origination.

[10] *Advertising Age,* November 2, 1970, p. 98.

In 1969 the FCC ruled that CATV systems would not be permitted to carry distant signals into the top 100 markets. CATV operators were required to delete commercials, with priority going to nonaffiliated UHF stations. However, a directive scheduled to become effective in March 1972 would allow two distant signals to be imported into the top 100 markets.

CATV operators were not permitted to import network programs if they duplicated the broadcast of a local network affiliate. Nevertheless, the impact on ratings, especially for nonaffiliates and those stations which depended heavily on local advertising, could be severe. One survey of three market areas in which 50% of the homes were CATV subscribers revealed that local stations suffered an audience loss ranging from 14% to 25%. Indignant station owners argued that CATV operators got a "free ride" by not paying for programming, on the one hand, and collecting fees from subscribers on the other.

RADIO

Structure and performance

Radio stations on the air in the United States numbered 6,991 in 1970, up 2,673 or 60% from the 4,368 stations in operation in 1960, as shown in Exhibit 5. FM accounted for 1,838, or about 70% of the station additions.[11] Since 1968, the FCC had virtually stopped issuing licenses for AM broadcasting, due primarily to growing congestion in the AM frequency band which was having the effect of reducing the effective range of broadcast signals. Approximately 76% of FM radio stations were part of AM/FM combinations, though the FCC had a long-term goal of separate ownership.

Unlike television, the radio networks and their 20 owned and operated stations were relatively minor factors in this segment of the industry. Network and O&O revenues of $44.1 million and $48.8 million, respectively, were together only 8% of the 1969 radio total of $1,048.7 million, as shown in Exhibit 2. Moreover, network pretax losses of $6.3 million more than offset O&O profits of $5.8 million. Nonnetwork stations, by contrast, had pretax profits of $111.7 million.

Prior to the advent of television, the networks had been powerful forces in radio. However, centralized programming proved less effective in holding diverse audiences than locally produced shows, and gradually the networks' role was reduced to news, public affairs, and an occasional

---

[11] FM had the advantages over AM of higher fidelity characteristics and relative freedom from static, fading, and background overlapping of other stations' programs.

EXHIBIT 5
Radio stations on the air (1945–69)

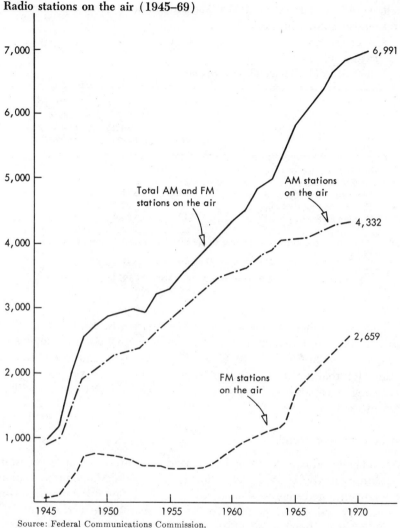

Source: Federal Communications Commission.

holdover such as "The Arthur Godfrey Show."[12] In addition, the number of stations in individual markets steadily increased (for instance, there were 34 stations in New York City) and were supported by independent news services.

Like television, profitability could be categorized in several ways. One indicator was size; the bigger the station, the more likely it was

---

[12] The Arthur Godfrey Show, produced by CBS, was scheduled to go off the air in 1972.

to be profitable (see Exhibit 6). Second, FM stations, at least those which were not part of an AM/FM combination, generally were loss operations, as shown in Table 5.

TABLE 5
1969 FM radio financial performance

	Stations reporting	FM revenues (millions)	FM pretax profits (millions)
AM/FM combinations			
No FM revenues	387	. . .	. . .
FM profits not reported	953	$21.9	n.a.
FM profits reported	179	12.1	$(4.8)*
FM independents	442	33.4	(5.5)†

*45 reported profits averaging $18,929; 134 reported losses averaging $42,114.
†136 reported profits averaging $16,674; 306 reported losses averaging $25,541.
Source: FCC AM/FM Broadcast Financial Data, 1969.

While the number of independent FM stations rose from 218 in 1960 to 442 in 1969 and revenues from $5.8 million to $33.4 million, losses increased from $2.4 million to $5.5 million. Growth had been limited by the fact that until the mid-1960s few radios were produced with FM receiving capability. This situation was rapidly changing, as illustrated in Exhibit 7.

Cost and revenue trends

As indicated above, radio had increased its share of total advertising expenditures in the United States during the 1960s. Many radio station owners maintained that the medium was in a favorable position for continued growth. They pointed to the fact that there were about 303 million radios in the United States in 1969, almost five on the average per household, and the figure had been growing at a rate of 10% to 15% per year. Opportunities for market segmentation through programming policy were thereby enhanced. The peak listening period occurred between 6:00 and 10:00 A.M.; to the extent that this was a result of commuters (75 million of the radios were in automobiles), station owners argued that the quality of the audience during these hours was higher than normally obtainable.

The future growth of radio was, of course, by no means assured. Population migrations to the suburbs and beyond were tending to shrink and reduce the affluence of metropolitan markets. With the limited range

EXHIBIT 6

Profitability of commercial radio stations by total broadcast revenues, 1969*

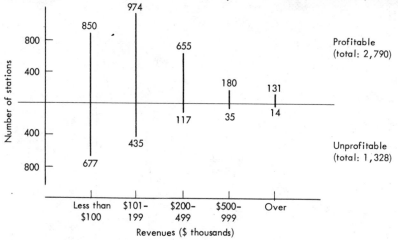

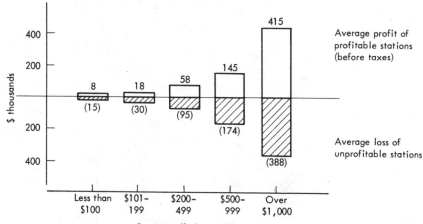

Revenues ($ thousands)

* Includes AM and FM stations.

Source: *FCC News*, December 14, 1970.

of most radio signals, this meant larger potential audiences for outlying stations. The commuter market was also undergoing change as industry moved from the cities and more emphasis was placed on mass transit. Furthermore, the impact of audio cassettes in automobiles or miniature television sets was as yet unknown.

One factor was clear to most radio station operators: local advertising was becoming steadily more dominant among their sources of revenue, as shown in Table 6.

EXHIBIT 7
U.S. sales of radio sets*

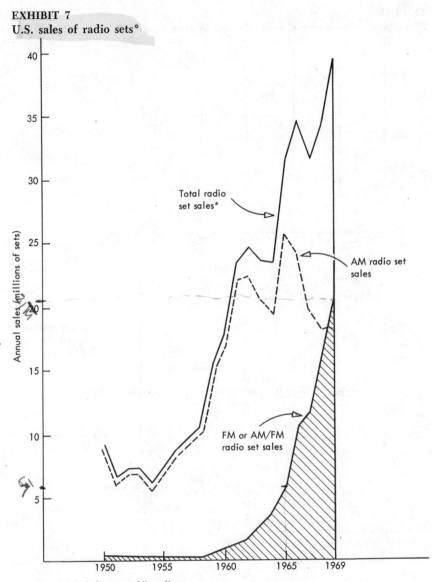

* Does not include automobile radios.
Source: Electronics Industries of America, *Market Data Book* 1970.

THE FEDERAL COMMUNICATIONS COMMISSION

The Federal Communications Commission, created by Congress in 1934, was an independent federal agency charged with regulating interstate and foreign communication (radio, TV, telephone, cable, and satellite). Its seven commissioners, appointed for seven-year terms by the

TABLE 6

	1964 (millions)	1969 (millions)	Five-year growth rate
Revenues			
Network station payments	$ 11	$ 10	(1.9%)
National spot	244	350	7.5
Local	504	800	9.7
Total broadcast revenue (net)*	$732	$1,086	8.2%
Total broadcast expense	661	985	8.3
Total pretax profit	71	$ 101	7.3%

*Total sales plus miscellaneous revenue less commissions to advertising agencies, representatives, and brokers.
Source: *Broadcasting*, March 22, 1971.

President, reported directly to the Congress. The FCC had quasi-legislative and judicial powers and was charged with "providing for the orderly development and operation of communication services." The seven FCC Commissioners in 1971 included four Republicans and three Democrats, four of whom had been appointed by President Nixon since 1969. One Democrat's term expired on June 30, 1973, and one Republican's term expired on June 30, 1974.

The powers of the FCC were far-reaching, as the President and Congress relied heavily on the Commission for advice on communications matters. The FCC allocated broadcasting spectrum frequencies to different types of civilian broadcast services, reviewed radio and TV station licenses every three years, and regulated telephone, telegraph, and civil defense communications. With regard to broadcasting stations, the FCC did not regulate advertising rates, profits, or accounting procedures. However, it did scrutinize editorializing and political broadcasting to insure fairness in the presentation of controversial issues. In addition, the Commission worked in conjunction with other regulatory agencies such as the Federal Trade Commission and Food and Drug Administration to prevent false or misleading advertising from appearing over the air.

Renewing licenses

Until the late sixties, few stations encountered problems in renewing their broadcasting licenses every three years. However, beginning with a pact between black groups in Texarkana, Texas, and KTAL-TV in June 1969, citizens' groups had been bargaining for minority group programming in return for withdrawing (not filing) petitions with the FCC to deny a station's renewal license. Many of these attempts had been successful in getting station owners to present more programming relevant to minority groups and to hire black and Spanish-surnamed Americans.

The FCC had recently proposed that all commercial TV stations be required to file detailed annual reports on their programming. In addition, the same proposal would require stations to make announcements at specified intervals throughout their license period, inviting comments on their service to the community. The president of the NAB complained that "these proposals, if adopted, would produce a jumpy, responsive, subservient broadcasting system . . . stations will become the sounding boards for a cacophony of narrow interests."[13]

Major FCC issues and rulings

Multiple ownership of media. In March 1970, the FCC proposed a rule prohibiting commonly owned broadcasting stations (radio and TV) and newspapers from operating in the same market (as defined by the Commission). In addition, the Commission set a limit on the number of stations a single owner could control of seven AM, seven FM, and seven TV stations.[14] Present licensees were given five years to reduce their holdings.[15] In February 1971, the rule was relaxed somewhat to allow AM/FM combinations and to permit joint ownership of radio and UHF–TV stations in the same city. In June 1971, the Commission was reviewing the comments received on the ruling prior to issuing a final statement.

The "fairness doctrine." In 1967 the FCC enunciated its famous fairness doctrine: "Licensees must give adequate coverage to public issues . . . and coverage must be fair in that it accurately reflects the opposing views."

In 1970 the fairness doctrine was strengthened by a ruling that "licensees must *actively seek* individuals whose opinions differ from those of the station management."

Public complaints. Private interest groups had petitioned the FCC with increasing frequency to enact rules with regard to advertising and public affairs coverage. In 1970 the Commission received petitions from Action for Children's Television (ACT) and Termination of Unfair Broadcasting Excess (TUBE). The ACT group proposed (1) no com-

---

[13] *Broadcasting*, April 5, 1971, p. 55. Statement by Vincent T. Wasilewski.

[14] Of the seven TV stations, no more than five of them could be VHF stations.

[15] *Broadcasting* (April 5, 1971, p. 48) noted 600 broadcast combinations of TV and radio stations in the same market areas. The article also mentioned that 14% of all TV stations were controlled by individuals or companies which also owned a newspaper.

mercials on children's programs and (2) a requirement that each TV station provide daily programming for children (14 hours per week minimum) during specified hours. TUBE asked the Commission to adopt more stringent rules to prevent deceptive advertising. Although the FCC had not made judgments involving these petitions by June 1971, public hearings had been scheduled for September 1971 to determine the real effects of ads directed at children.

BROADCASTING AND OTHER PUBLIC AGENCIES

Congress

Congressional action was necessary to effect regulation of rates and the admissibility of advertising subject matter. Two recent examples of Congressional action were the 1970 ban on cigarette advertising and a 1968 law requiring radio and TV stations to sell time to all candidates for federal, state, and local offices at the lowest rate charged to commercial advertisers with long-term contracts.

Federal Trade Commission

The FTC worked in conjunction with the FCC to identify "false, misleading, and deceptive advertising." Commercials for headache remedies, gasoline additives, and automobiles were among the products which had been questioned by the FTC in recent years. For instance, in 1970, the FTC charged that Standard Oil (Chevron) had misrepresented its product by claiming that its gasoline "reduced air pollution." Chevron was forced to devote 25% of its print advertising (for a specified period of time) to a publication of FTC findings. In a similar vein, the manufacturer of Wonder Bread was told to prove that its product "helps build strong bodies 12 ways" or submit to the 25% "corrective" penalty.

Justice Department and federal courts

In 1971 the Justice Department's antitrust division ordered CBS to divest itself of a CATV subsidiary, Viacom International. The federal court system provided appellate review of FCC decisions. For example, in June 1969, a U.S. Court of Appeals overturned an FCC decision to renew the license of a Jackson, Mississippi, television station. The court ruled that the station had not served the needs, tastes, and interests of the substantial black population in its area and that, in programming on the racial issue, it had presented only a segregationist viewpoint.

CRITICISM OF THE NETWORKS

Comments by Vice President Agnew

On several occasions, Vice President Spiro Agnew had lashed out at news media for what he termed "irresponsibility." In a speech delivered in Des Moines, Iowa, on November 18, 1969, the Vice President said:

. . . According to Harris polls and other studies . . . for millions of Americans the [TV] networks are the sole source of national and world news. . . . Now how is this network news determined? A small group of men . . . settle upon the 20 minutes or so of film and commentary that's to reach the public. This selection is made from the 90 to 120 minutes that may be available. Their powers of choice are wide. They decide what 40 million Americans will learn of the day's events in the nation and in the world. . . . These men can create national issues overnight.

. . . We do know that to a man these commentators and producers live and work in the geographical and intellectual confines of Washington, D.C. or New York. . . . We can deduce that these men read the same newspapers. They draw their political and social views from the same sources. Worse, they talk constantly to one another, thereby providing artificial reinforcement to their shared viewpoints.

. . . Is it not fair and relevant to question the concentration [of power] in the hands of a tiny, enclosed fraternity of privileged men elected by no one and enjoying a monopoly sanctioned and licensed by the government? The views of the majority of this fraternity do not—and I repeat, *not*—represent the views of America.[16]

Dr. Frank Stanton, president of CBS, reflected the sentiments of the networks toward the charges levied by Mr. Agnew:

. . . The public, according to opinion polls, has indicated again and again that it has more confidence in the credibility of television news than in that of any other medium. Our newsmen have many times earned commendations for their enterprise and for their adherence to the highest professional standards. Since human beings are not infallible, there are bound to be occasions when their judgment is questioned.

Whatever their deficiencies, they are minor compared to those of a press which would be subservient to the executive power of government.

"The Selling of the Pentagon"

Immediately following the broadcast of the CBS documentary "The Selling of the Pentagon" in April 1971, the question of broadcaster responsibility and "truthfulness" was aired in the public forum through

---

[16] *New York Times,* November 24, 1969.

a heated exchange of views between the news media, on one hand, and disgruntled congressmen, senators, and Defense Department officials on the other. The latter questioned both the factual accuracy and editorial tone of the documentary. CBS, while refusing to release all of the film used to produce the documentary, claimed that it had acted in the public interest by directing viewers' attention to an important aspect of national defense policy.

As it had done during the Agnew controversy, the FCC elected not to intervene, expressing its collective opinion as follows:

It would be unwise and probably impossible for the Commission to lay down some precise line of factual accuracy—dependent always on journalistic judgment—across which broadcasters must not stray. Any attempt to do so would be inconsistent with the national commitment to wide-open debate of public issues and would involve the FCC deeply and improperly in the journalistic functions of broadcasters.

Arkana Broadcasting Company*

In June 1971, Mr. James E. Pickett, president of Arkana Broadcasting Company, headquartered in Nashville, Tennessee, was evaluating the prospects for his company. Although Arkana had grown steadily since its founding in 1964, several events had increased the uncertainties associated with the broadcasting business.

First, the Federal Communications Commission had proposed a ruling that would have the effect of prohibiting multimedia ownership in the same market of VHF television stations and radio stations or newspapers. Comments on the ruling had been solicited and received by the FCC; should it be put into effect, five years would be granted for compliance. Arkana owned AM/FM radio as well as VHF television stations in both Nashville, Tennessee, and Greensboro, North Carolina. In addition, the organization that owned Arkana also controlled the largest newspaper in Nashville.

Second, the previous two years had been characterized by a lively debate among public interest groups, broadcasters, and government officials over the nature of the public interest to be served by the media, in particular television. Recently, the controversy over the CBS documentary, "The Selling of the Pentagon," followed by the *New York Times*' disclosure of secret government documents on the Vietnam war, had sharpened the focus of the public on the role of news media in the United States. When WLRA–TV sought to renew its license in 1970,

---

* Names, locations, and certain financial information have been disguised.

Arkana had been subjected to criticism from a Nashville resident who filed a complaint with the FCC alleging that the station had failed to program for the entire community and had presented programming favoring its own viewpoint. After considering the matter for several months, the FCC renewed the license.

Third, CATV (community antenna television) had grown rapidly in the past decade and had steadily increased its penetration into Arkana's markets. Mr. Pickett believed that CATV posed a major competitive threat to free "over-the-air" television stations by fragmenting audiences and thereby endangering advertising revenues. Coupled with increasing costs of TV programming, it posed a potential threat to Arkana's profits.

It was in this context that Mr. Pickett had decided to review Arkana's situation in relation to the complex factors which affected operations and future plans. Although a large part of the company's profits were derived from its two TV stations, Mr. Pickett had negotiated the acquisition of several FM radio stations in recent years, including one in Chicago, and was convinced that as the number of radios in use with FM receiving capability increased, the profits and value of these stations would increase as well. He was uncertain, however, whether to seek expansion in radio or television or, in the event Arkana was required to divest one or the other in its major markets, which one to retain.

HISTORY

Arkana Broadcasting was incorporated in 1964 as a subsidiary of the Arkana Investment Company (AIC), which in turn was owned by five long-time friends and associates, several of whom had worked together in state and local political and civic affairs. Through another corporation, AIC operated the *Nashville Post,* the largest paper in the city in terms of circulation and advertising revenues. Revenues were comparable to those for WLRA, although profits were lower. The newspaper, however, had been the initial investment of AIC and several of the directors had helped to build it in earlier years. When AIC had been formed, its initial purpose was to serve and invest in the Nashville community. This remained an important consideration for individual board members, although activities by 1971 extended beyond the confines of Nashville.

Mr. Pickett, 56, a native of Nashville, had been a career officer in the U.S. Army Signal Corps and had attained the rank of Colonel. He had retired in 1962 to join the National Association of Broadcasters in Washington, D.C., remaining there until 1964 when he was recruited to serve as president of the newly formed Arkana Broadcasting Company. Mr. Pickett had been the architect of Arkana's expansion program. He had made recommendations to Arkana's board of directors and had personally taken the lead in consummating subsequent acquisitions and in selecting management for the acquired stations.

Arkana Broadcasting had been formed with the primary objective of becoming an effective instrument for service in communities where its facilities would be located, as well as for returning a reasonable profit. The company immediately assumed ownership of WLRA AM/FM/TV in Nashville, stations long operated by AIC, and subsequently acquired several broadcast facilities, most of them in southeastern cities. In 1971 the company owned two VHF television, three AM radio, and six FM radio stations. Financial data on Arkana are contained in Exhibits 1, 2, and 3.

ARKANA MANAGEMENT AND BOARD OF DIRECTORS

Working with Mr. Pickett at Arkana's headquarters were two staff vice presidents (finance and special affairs), a corporate secretary, and an assistant to the president. The Nashville and Greensboro AM/FM/TV stations were each headed by a vice president and general manager. All other units had general managers. The nine-man board of directors consisted of Mr. Pickett, four vice presidents, the corporate secretary, and three members of the AIC board. The latter three men, none of whom had operating experience in the broadcasting industry, also served on the board of directors of Arkana Investment Corporation. Information on the officers and directors of Arkana Broadcasting is presented in Exhibit 4. An organization chart is contained in Exhibit 5.[1]

Mr. Pickett reviewed some of the major decisions he had made in acquiring new stations:

When I was given the opportunity of managing and developing Arkana, I looked for big-city stations where we could reach the greatest number of people. In the past seven years, we have acquired at least one metropolitan radio or TV station in each of six states. Basically, the stations have been turn-around situations which could be bought for cash. My policy has been to build up a first-rate reputation in each of our areas.

In 1968 we decided to buy an FM radio station in Chicago, even though it was run-down and had little audience. However, the station had great potential and is now a leading good music station in the city. Some of our directors felt we should run very conservative programs and take strong positions on national issues, as they had done at times with the newspaper. I had to convince them that under the Communications Act and FCC regulations we had to serve the whole community and furnish fair and objective programming.

[1] In keeping with the objective of community service, each station had a board of directors comprised of prominent local figures. These directors are not listed in Exhibit 5.

EXHIBIT 1

ARKANA BROADCASTING COMPANY
Income Statement for Year Ended December 31, 1970
(thousands of dollars)

	Television		Radio							Total Arkana
	Nashville	Greens-boro	Nashville (AM/FM)	Tulsa (AM/FM)	Greens-boro (AM/FM)	Houston (FM)	Chicago (FM)	Monroe, La. (FM)		
Sales										
Network payments	$ 665	$ 630	$ 25	$ 8	$ 11	$ 0	$ 0	$ 0		$ 1,339
National spot revenues	1,432	1,320	400	290	289	98	508	24		4,361
Local advertisers	1,390	1,290	425	328	510	188	901	140		5,172
Total sales	$3,487	$3,240	$850	$626	$810	$286	$1,409	$164		$10,872
Expenses										
Technical	$ 198	$ 201	$ 84	$ 64	$ 98	$ 55	$ 106	$ 50		$ 856
Program	1,232	1,148	276	186	225	107	391	62		3,627
Selling	425	340	151	88	162	70	200	38		1,474
General and administrative	955	851	279	172	211	150	348	68		3,034
Total expenses	$2,810	$2,540	$790	$510	$696	$382	$1,045	$218		$ 8,991
Profit before taxes	$ 677	$ 700	$ 60	$116	$114	$ (96)	$ 364	$(54)		$ 1,881

Source: Company records.

EXHIBIT 2

ARKANA BROADCASTING COMPANY
Summary Financial Data 1967–70
(in thousands of dollars)

	Television		Radio							Total
	Nashville	Greensboro	Nashville (AM/FM)	Greensboro (AM/FM)	Tulsa (AM/FM)	Houston (FM)	Chicago (FM)	Monroe, La. (FM)		
Revenues										
1967	$3,081	$2,562	$793	$606	$447	...	...	...		$ 7,489
1968	3,356	3,095	841	687	520	$222	$1,016	...		9,737
1969	3,489	3,121	834	763	540	245	1,321	$137		10,450
1970	3,487	3,240	850	810	626	286	1,409	164		10,872
Pretax profit										
1967	960	503	55	49	23	...	...	...		1,590
1968	1,022	647	73	61	63	(127)	249	...		1,988
1969	916	778	62	86	51	(117)	369	(67)		2,078
1970	677	700	60	114	116	(96)	364	(54)		1,881
Year acquired	1964	1967	1964	1967	1965	1968	1968	1969		

Note: Figures restated to include the full year's results in the year of acquisition.
Source: Company records.

ARKANA BROADCASTING COMPANY
Consolidated Balance Sheet, December 31, 1969 and 1970

Assets

	1969	1970
Current assets		
Cash and cash items	$ 1,647,380	$ 1,064,163
Marketable securities—at cost	278,890	147,397
Trade accounts receivable	$ 1,878,810	$ 2,701,784
Accounts receivable—other	629,888	496,479
Total accounts receivable	$ 2,508,698	$ 3,198,263
Note receivable	$ 707,000	$ 64,770
Broadcasting films—current portion		717,000
Prepaid expenses (TV tubes, insurance, travel, etc.)	$ 129,806	$ 117,157
Total current assets	$ 5,271,774	$ 5,308,750
Real estate contract receivable (interest at 7¼% due monthly; principal balance due on or before May 21, 1973)		$ 100,100
Investments—at cost	$ 320,636	$ 295,698
Property—land, buildings, equipment, leasehold improvements, etc.—at cost (less accumulated depreciation and amortization)	$ 7,345,232	$ 8,572,457
Other assets		
Network contract—at cost	$ 4,535,329	$ 4,535,329
Licenses—at cost	1,968,919	1,968,919
Other intangibles—at cost less amortization	1,414,586	1,412,142
Broadcasting films—less current portion	1,258,703	714,378
Excess of cost over net equity in consolidated subsidiaries	394,742	418,363
Other	88,313	111,895
Total other assets	$ 9,660,592	$ 9,161,026
Total assets	$22,598,234	$23,438,031

Liabilities

	1969	1970
Current liabilities		
Notes payable to banks—current portion	$ 359,370	$ 240,000
Film contracts payable—current portion	1,033,504	533,687
Trade accounts payable	433,445	427,813
Advertising services due	261,487	425,332
Accrued liabilities	479,514	550,610
Income taxes due		41,000
Total current liabilities	$ 2,567,320	$ 2,218,442
Long-term debt		
Notes payable to bank	$ 3,500,000	$ 4,760,000
Mortgage note payable	138,108	
Film contracts payable	403,672	226,171
Total long-term debt	$ 4,041,780	$ 4,986,171
Minority interest in subsidiaries	$ 65,068	$ 57,559
Stockholders' equity		
Common stock—no par value, authorized 500,000 shares; issued and outstanding, 350,000 shares	$11,075,168	$11,075,168
Additional paid-in capital	4,357,043	4,357,043
Retained earnings	491,855	743,648
Stockholders' equity—net	$15,924,066	$16,175,859
Total liabilities	$22,598,234	$23,438,031

Source: Company records.

EXHIBIT 4

ARKANA BROADCASTING COMPANY
Officers and Directors
June 1971

Name	Title	Age	Background
James E. Pickett	President	56	See text of case
Samuel Caruthers	VP finance	44	BA degree 15 years with General Electric finance department 4 years as controller for WLRA VP since 1968
Larry R. Crawford	VP special affairs	50	BA, LLB degrees 10 years in CBS legal department 12 years as Congressional liaison for National Association of Broadcasters VP since 1965
Billy Ray White	VP and general manager	48	BA degree 25 years in radio and TV Sales manager, then VP and general manager of WLRA AM/FM/TV, Nashville VP since 1966
Judd A. Shipley	VP and general manager	47	BA degree 22 years in radio and TV VP and general manager of Greensboro station since 1967
Cyrus Lawton	Secretary	53	BA, LLB degrees Partner in Nashville law firm Secretary and director since 1946
J. Robert Simpson	Director	74	BA degree Banker. Director, Arkana Investment Co.
Robert Lee Jones	Director	72	BA degree Chairman, small manufacturing enterprise. Director, Arkana Investment Company
C. Jefferson Davis	Director	70	BA degree Cotton farmer. Director, Arkana Investment Company

Source: Company records.

Mr. Pickett himself was active in the community. He had served as president of the Rotary Club and of the Chamber of Commerce, had been on several state committees, and had assumed positions of increasing responsibility in his church. He was also a respected spokesman in the broadcasting industry.

COMPETITIVE POSITION

Arkana management had guided the company's television stations, both CBS affiliates, to leadership positions in their markets. In Nashville,

EXHIBIT 5

ARKANA BROADCASTING COMPANY
Organization Chart

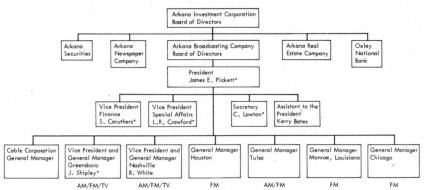

*Officer and director of Arkana Broadcasting Company.
Source: Company records.

ranked 30th nationally in the number of TV homes, Arkana had increased its share of advertising dramatically from 1964 to 1967, particularly advertising from local accounts. More recently, however, the station had lost some ground, which was attributed to several factors in the market. First, competition from the other network affiliates had stiffened in response to Arkana's aggressive community action programming and through new program formats at key hours. They were successful in narrowing the gap in daytime and nonprime-time ratings. Second, in August 1968 a UHF station went on the air. Although the signal from this new competitor reached less than 30% of the homes receiving signals from the major stations, it nonetheless siphoned off some advertising dollars and proved unsettling in the market. A VHF noncommercial education channel had also entered the market in the early 1960s and appeared to be attracting more attention as the quality of child and adult programming improved.

Finally, CATV had come to town attracted by the mountainous terrain in the area surrounding Nashville. Should the FCC permit the importation of distant signals, the effect could be a general dip in ratings for the local broadcasters. Particularly upsetting to Mr. Pickett was the difficulty he had encountered in securing permission from the FCC to build translators, essentially microwave relay towers, which would enable him to improve the clarity of his station's signal. The Commission took the position that the translators would allow Arkana to increase its broadcasting range, thereby infringing on the territory of stations in contiguous markets.

Arkana also owned the leading television station in the Greensboro-Winston-Salem-High Point area, the 49th-ranked market in terms of TV homes. The market was shared by three network affiliates and had not, at least as yet, attracted independent stations or been seriously affected by CATV. Competitive and market data are provided in Exhibits 6 and 7.

In radio Arkana was also the leader in Nashville and Greensboro in terms of advertising revenues. The same was true of the AM/FM combination in Tulsa and the FM station in Monroe, Louisiana. While the Houston station was considerably smaller than several in its 18-station market, it was nonetheless thought to be the Number 2 FM broadcaster and was making steady progress in increasing market share and reducing losses. Finally, Arkana's station was among the largest overall in the Chicago area and was the leading FM station. The Nashville, Greensboro, and Tulsa stations were affiliated with CBS; the remainder were independents.

EXHIBIT 6

ARKANA BROADCASTING COMPANY
Market Statistics

I. *Television competition*

	Advertising rates*		Circulation†		TV† homes (000)
Station	Prime-time prog./hr.	Daytime spot/30 sec.	Daily (000)	Weekly (000)	

Nashville—Number of stations: 3 VHF, 1 UHF, 1 education (VHF)

ABC Affil. (VHF).	$1,000	$ 33	233	408	635
NBC Affil. (VHF).	1,200	.45–90	325	477	680
CBS Affil. (VHF)‡	1,180	70–180	347	474	652
Independent (UHF)§	250	n.a.	5	21	186

Greensboro—Winston-Salem—High Point—Number of stations: 3 VHF

ABC Affil. (VHF).	$1,000	$40	253	444	876
NBC Affil. (VHF).	1,000	41	207	361	616
CBS Affil. (VHF)‡	1,000	65	270	416	798

II. *Market characteristics*

	TV homes (thousands)	National rank		
		TV homes	Consumer spending	TV advertising
Nashville	474	30	38	40
Greensboro.	327	49	52	50
Tulsa	340	52	60	55
Houston	705	14	16	14
Chicago	2,508	3	3	3
Monroe.	138	104	119	n.a.

Exhibit 6 (*continued*)

III. *Consumer buying indices* ‖

	Nashville	Greensboro	Tulsa	Chicago	Monroe
Beer.	37	31	54	131	n.a.
Coffee (instant)	97	128	67	74	n.a.
Coffee (regular)	73	83	108	104	n.a.
Deodorants	99	103	97	94	n.a.
Dog food.	120	123	142	75	n.a.
Gas	106	114	105	95	n.a.
Hair coloring	108	69	124	103	n.a.
Headache remedies	101	102	90	108	n.a.
New cars	94	101	91	105	n.a.
Soft drinks.	114	157	108	106	n.a.
Supermarkets	85	88	87	109	n.a.
Wash loads.	93	89	99	94	n.a.

* Rate charged by the network to advertisers. The station received a share as a station payment.
† Circulation refers to the number of TV homes expected to view the station daily and weekly. TV homes reflects the number of homes reached by the station's signal.
‡ Arkana station.
§ Went on the air August 1968.
‖ Relative to national average of 100.
n.a. = not available.
Source: I and II, *TV Factbook*, 1971; III, American Research Bureau Survey, 1971.

COMPANY POLICIES

Programming

Arkana management felt that success in achieving strong positions in radio as in television was due to programming and marketing policies. In FM, the basic programming format was music suitable for background and for comfortable listening.

Mr. Pickett commented on the programming philosophy he encouraged at Arkana:

The first objective for Arkana is public service, to be an effective instrument for responsible action in the community. Each of our managers is required to select the 10 most pressing problems in his community—pollution, school busing, drugs, transportation, etc.—and design programs which will provide the public with various points of view on these problems. We give free air time to get the issues discussed.

We are also not afraid to say and do what we think is right. For instance, people get excited about Vietnam and LSD, but alcohol kills 28,000 on the highway each year. Thirty-five times that many are injured. In one case we succeeded in getting the highway patrol, the Med Center, and the Bar Association to conduct tests to determine if the permissible alcohol content was safe. We demonstrated that with a much lower alcohol content subjects were drunk, and we produced a film on the disaster caused by drunk driving. We succeeded in getting the legislature to pass a law tightening the criterion for drunk driving.

EXHIBIT 7

ARKANA BROADCASTING COMPANY
Summary Financial Data for Arkana Markets
(dollars in thousands)

	Television		Radio					
	Nashville	Greensboro	Nashville	Greensboro	Tulsa	Houston	Chicago	Monroe
Revenues (total market)								
1968	$7,259	$6,092	$4,381	$2,937	$2,280	$ 8,199	$31,100	$484
1969	8,371	6,571	4,909	3,608	2,730	9,702	36,370	561
1970	9,587	7,328	5,467	3,758	2,912	10,617	35,576	529
Station income (total market)								
1968	1,813	1,311	821	393	114	1,961	6,405	(1)
1969	2,095	1,655	779	592	264	2,168	9,882	49
1970	1,787	1,790	917	594	279	2,075	8,882	63
Percent of 1970 revenues for the total market accounted for by—								
Network	16%	19%	2%	1%	1%	1%	3%	...
National/regional spot	46	46	37	20	34	51	51	24%
Local	38	35	61	79	65	48	46	76
Total	100%	100%	100%	100%	100%	100%	100%	100%
Arkana share of market—1970								
Network	43%	45%	33%	32%	40%	0%	0%	0%
National/regional spot	32	39	19	38	29	2	2	18
Local	36	50	13	17	17	4	5	32
Share of total market	36%	44%	16%	22%	21%	3%	3%	26%
Number of stations	5	3	12	12	9	18	32	4

Source: *Statistical Trends in Broadcasting*, John Blair & Co., 1971.

In another case, one of our managers discovered that millions of dollars of state funds were lying fallow in no-interest bank accounts. We waded in with both feet, criticizing the state for not earning interest on taxpayers' money. We succeeded in persuading the state to put the money in certificates of deposit. The banks retaliated for awhile by switching their advertising to competing stations.

Mr. Pickett was particularly concerned with the development of strong managers able to deal effectively as individuals with the needs of their communities. Station managers reported that the freedom granted them to respond to community needs contributed significantly to the enthusiasm which they brought to their work and to their sense of professional pride. Mr. Kerry Bates, assistant to the president, described Mr. Pickett's management style in the following anecdote:

It's not his style to ride herd on his managers. During the November elections, he was appalled at our news coverage, and he watched other channels. Our manager got cheerleaders from the university to post election returns. The girls wore miniskirts. The station's switchboard was flooded with calls. The station manager, however, let them continue. Mr. Pickett voiced his displeasure but didn't try to discipline the manager.

The newscasters are in "show biz." They're hard to fire because they're stars. Mr. Pickett is almost too humane. He works through the "rub-off method." He wants to develop managers who are independent, and I must say he's succeeding. Those managers effectively set the policy for their stations.

Mr. Larry Crawford, vice president for special affairs, commented further on Arkana's programming:

We believe that good news coverage is a major ingredient for success in broadcasting. That's why we have more of it than most of our competitors and pay attention to what our audience says about our news coverage, right down to comments about the kind of tie the sportscaster wears! Another important thing about news is that advertisers want to identify with *strong, public-minded* stations. It's a fact that most stations which rank first in audience ratings at news time also lead the market overall.

In FM, we're selling music and news all day long. AM radio is more complex because the critical period is "drive time" [7:00 to 9:00 A.M. and 4:00 to 6:00 P.M.]. An AM station must have a good disc jockey for those two time periods. Having a good sportscaster is also a big plus for coverage of local sports which aren't televised. Since our AM stations usually concentrate on the over-25 audience, we're not as concerned with the top 20 rock-and-roll tunes. Two of our AM stations have been successful with a late evening show called "Take a Stand," which features advocates representing opposing views on a significant public issue supplemented with phone calls from the audience.

In television we carry practically all of the network programs. With TV, of course, the opportunities for impact from public affairs broadcasting is greater than with radio, and we have tried to exploit that. Our objective is to serve the whole community. We don't believe in pushing our opinions on others.

Marketing

Mr. Caruthers, vice president of finance, described Arkana's approach to marketing:

The underpinning of our success lies in market analysis. In determining what is needed to build and hold market share, we look at our markets to determine what population segments aren't fully exploited. We utilize a university professor's research team and various rating services to give us a detailed profile of those segments and what they desire in the way of TV and radio programming. Once we think we have the "target audience" analyzed, we tailor programming and advertising to suit its needs. Most of our competitors do only a cursory job of this, which gives us a big advantage.

As shown in Exhibit 6, advertising rates for Arkana's TV stations were more or less the same as those for the other network affiliates for prime-time programs but were substantially higher for daytime spots. The company had also been successful in increasing rates in radio as audience surveys portrayed increasing market shares.

Mr. Bates commented on matters of advertising subject matter:

There is some feeling among our board members that beer and pills should not be advertised on television. However, we have said that, if we eliminated these ads, we would be charged with being "self-serving," imposing our values on the community.

Anticipating the ban on cigarette advertising, Arkana was among the first broadcasters to decline such ads—before the law cleared Congress. Several agency media buyers were reportedly upset by this, and some revenue was lost as a result. On a wider issue, Mr. Bates expressed some concern over the impact of consumerism on television advertising:

The media are going to be in trouble in 10 years because of exaggerated product claims. My seven-year-old son was watching TV the other night, and during a commercial he turned to me and said, "That isn't true, is it, Dad?" The advertisers are building cynicism among viewers. They're prostituting themselves for a buck. Pretty soon viewers won't believe any advertising message.

Public affairs

Mr. Pickett was active in promoting the interests of local broadcasters before legislative and other groups. In particular, he sought more comprehensive regulation of CATV and greater latitude for VHF stations to construct translators.

TV should be a local medium, and CATV threatens local broadcasting with extinction because it fragments the audience. By bringing in distant signals it can make the market more oriented to the large population centers and large national events than to the local markets and occurrences in the locality. But let's face it, CATV is here to stay. Our objective is to have it put under common carrier regulations, since all it does is carry signals. This would prohibit cable operators from substituting advertising and from programming in competition with local stations.

Indirectly, the importance of local stations is being reinforced by attacks on network news coverage. Much of what Vice President Agnew has said is justified. We have a top-flight Washington correspondent. After one speech in which Mr. Agnew attacked the "news establishment," our correspondent sent me a Gallup poll of college students which showed that in every region except the Northeast better than half of those interviewed supported what Mr. Agnew had said. In the Northeast, however, 65% of the students interviewed reacted negatively to the Vice President's remark. It is our correspondent's opinion that the networks are trapped by being located in the liberal Northeast. They tend to look down on the rest of the country. Since these news executives are located in New York, for the most part, they are continually subjected to liberal philosophies.

THE FUTURE

The course to be followed by Arkana in the future was not altogether clear to Mr. Pickett. Originally, it had appeared logical for Arkana to acquire additional broadcast properties in both radio and television up to the limit allowed by the Commission. In total, Arkana could add one radio and five television stations, no more than three of which could be VHF.[2] Moreover, it was possible to "trade up" by selling stations and buying others in larger markets. Such a course would address Mr. Pickett's second and third objectives for the company: increasing revenues and profits.

The recent FCC proposals on multimedia ownership, the turmoil in television broadcasting, and the competitive threats of CATV and market fragmentation had caused Mr. Pickett to reevaluate the company's position. It was possible that a divestment of either the radio or television stations in Nashville and Greensboro would be required. Should the company keep the more profitable television franchises or keep those in radio and embark on a major development of that medium?

Mr. Pickett remained enthusiastic about the pattern of success Arkana had had in serving its communities. However, while there appeared to be no lack of commitment from the board to the broadcasting industry, it was clear that under most circumstances growth would have to be financed internally. Indeed, it was possible that Arkana Investment

---

[2] Broadcasting stations typically sold for 15 to 25 times after-tax earnings.

Corporation would look to Arkana Broadcasting as a source of funds, particularly in the event that cash generated in the business remained unused. Yet he commented:

We have demonstrated that we can take lackluster stations and make them profitable. On the other hand, our problems have never been greater. In this business, you face all the drama of an afternoon soap opera—outside interference, threats, and two-timing. We are caught up in so many problems, I don't know where to begin. Sometimes I think I shouldn't sleep at night.

A note on the recreational vehicle industry

With a growth rate of over 35% annually in the decade after 1962, recreational vehicles (RVs) by 1973 had become a major industry in the United States with retail sales of $2.5 billion. Perhaps more than any other industry, the RV industry had benefited from a changing American life style that emphasized mobility, leisure, and outdoor activity. There were five basic classes of RVs:

Travel trailers were compact housing units on wheels designed to be towed by a passenger vehicle. They averaged 8 feet in width, 10 feet in height, and from 10 feet to 30 feet in length and sold for $700 to $18,000. There were three basic types of travel trailers: a standard rectangular shape, an aluminum rounded-top style, and a newer "fifth wheel" style which extended over the top of a pickup truck bed.

Motor homes[1] were self-propelled vehicles placed on standard truck chassis. Averaging 8 feet wide, 10 feet high, and 10 feet to 35 feet long, motor homes sold for $5,000 to almost $30,000. There were three basic types: the conventional (A body) was constructed directly on a heavy-duty truck chassis which included drive components and engine and was usually the largest motor home; the van-conversion (B body) consisted of the conversion of the interior of a van-type truck by an RV manufacturer; the chopped-van (C body) was a motor home built on the aft

---

[1] It is important to emphasize here that *motor* homes, self-propelled vehicles used for recreational purposes, were different from *mobile* homes which were much larger units used for permanent housing.

frame section of a van-type truck and usually fell between the A and B styles in size and price.

Truck campers were units which either slid onto the bed of a pickup truck or else were permanently affixed to the back end of a truck chassis. Truck campers, which generally had fewer amenities than travel trailers or motor homes, were from 7 feet to 15 feet long and sold for $800 to $6,000 exclusive of the truck.

Camping trailers were designed to be towed behind passenger automobiles. They were constructed with folding walls for fast expansion to form a large living space and for lowering to provide a low profile for easy towing. Camping trailers were usually not self-contained and sold for $300 to $2,500.

Pickup covers were protective enclosures placed over the bed of a pickup truck and designed for easy removal. They ranged in price from $200 for a simple cover to $1,600 for a unit with living facilities.

THE MARKET FOR RECREATIONAL VEHICLES

Growth of the recreational vehicle industry had been most dramatic. From 1961 to 1972 unit shipments from manufacturers to dealers had increased at an annual rate of 23%. During the same period, dollar retail sales had increased at a 35% rate (see Exhibit 1). The industry's growth had been strong in every year except 1970 when unit shipments had declined 8.2% from 1969, a decline attributed to the general recession in the American economy.

The consumer

Because recreational vehicles were often expensive and required ample leisure time, the typical consumer was older and had an above-average income. There were, however, demographic differences among consumers. Buyers of travel trailers, truck campers, and camping trailers tended to be skilled blue-collar or white-collar workers between the ages of 45 and 55; they were usually married with children and earned between $9,000 and $12,000 annually. Buyers of motor homes, on the other hand, tended to have higher incomes and more education; often they had no children. Some changes in the typical profile of an RV consumer had become evident by 1973 as both younger people and senior citizens were increasingly attracted to RVs.

The number of families that already owned or could be expected to purchase RVs was an important consideration for the industry. One measure of current saturation is given in the following table:

	Travel trailers	Motor homes	Truck campers	Camping trailers	Total
RVI estimates of vehicles in use	1,730,000	240,000	801,000	1,055,000	3,826,000
Saturation of total families*	3.2%	0.4%	1.5%	2.0%	7.1%
Saturation of "key" families†	4.6%	0.6%	2.2%	2.9%	10.3%

* Based on Census Bureau estimate of 53.7 million families in March 1973.
† "Key" families are those with head of household over 25 years old and income over $7,000. Estimated at 37 million in March 1973.

Estimates of the maximum saturation level for RVs ranged from 10% to 50% with no strong consensus. Commerce Department projections were for a 2 million increase in "key" families between 1970 and 1975 and a 7.3 million increase from 1975 to 1980, with a total potential market for RVs of about 38 million families in 1975 and 45 million in 1980.

One important factor in buying behavior was a "trade-up" phenomenon that had become evident in 1973. The *RV Dealer* study revealed that 36% of RV consumers were first-time buyers while 60% were purchasing at least their second vehicle. The first-time buyer generally bought a small travel or camping trailer; then, within three years, he would trade up to a larger, more expensive unit of the same type or to a larger product of a different type (see Exhibit 2). Since the RV industry continually developed new models and features, trade-ups resulted more from obsolescence than from physical deterioration of the vehicle. With only limited use generally, RVs had quite long lives, estimated at over 15 years.

One aspect of trading up was the large number of used units generated. For years used RVs had been scarce, and some dealers actually advertised for second-hand units. By 1973, however, many used units were beginning to appear on the market, and some industry observers were predicting that sales of new units could be hurt. "The real question is whether our industry can attract enough new buyers to absorb the high volume of used camping vehicles and yet maintain sales on new models simultaneously."[2]

Geographical markets

Within the United States, recreational vehicle sales varied according to population density, recreational area availability, and weather conditions. Most owners lived in rural areas or in cities with a population of less than 100,000. In general, sales tended to be concentrated in the

---
[2] Lee Oertle, "Used Units Causing Problems," *RV Dealer*, November 1972, p. 54.

EXHIBIT 1
Growth of the recreational vehicle industry
Unit shipments

Year	Total production	Travel trailers	Motor homes	Truck campers	Camping trailers	Pickup covers
1961	62,600	28,800	n.a.	15,800	18,000	n.a.
1962	80,300	40,600	n.a.	16,700	23,000	n.a.
1963	118,600	51,500	n.a.	26,800	40,300	n.a.
1964	151,000	64,200	n.a.	34,800	52,000	n.a.
1965	192,830	76,600	4,710	44,300	67,220	n.a.
1966	219,810	87,300	5,710	54,500	72,300	n.a.
1967	244,430	94,500	9,050	61,600	79,280	n.a.
1968	483,100	115,200	13,200	79,500	125,200	150,000
1969	514,100	144,000	23,100	92,500	141,000	113,500
1970	472,000	138,000	30,300	95,900	116,100	91,700
1971	549,400	190,800	57,200	107,200	95,800	98,400
1972	747,500	250,800	116,800*	105,100	110,200	164,600

Retail sales (in thousands of dollars)

Year	Total production	Travel trailers	Motor homes	Truck campers	Camping trailers	Pickup covers
1961	$ 87,040	$ 52,122	n.a.	$ 26,818	$ 8,100	n.a.
1962	112,033	73,256	n.a.	28,427	10,350	n.a.
1963	156,478	92,753	n.a.	45,590	18,135	n.a.
1964	198,535	116,136	n.a.	58,999	23,400	n.a.
1965	308,236	168,986	$ 33,912	75,089	30,249	n.a.
1966	370,781	201,497	42,825	92,574	33,885	n.a.
1967	446,441	217,350	68,875	104,720	55,496	n.a.
1968	791,790	357,120	113,850	141,100	137,720	$42,000
1969	1,077,067	452,592	251,790	175,750	162,885	34,050
1970	1,149,924	445,326	318,150	183,169	175,311	27,968
1971	1,629,483	650,246	572;458	223,619	150,885	32,275
1972	2,421,861	971,080	1,010,542*	217,767	165,520	56,952

Other data

	All RVs	Travel trailers	Motor homes	Truck campers	Camping trailers	Pickup covers
Average retail price:						
1967..............	$1,826	$2,300	$ 7,610	$1,700	$ 700	...
1970....:........	2,436	3,280	10,500	1,910	1,510	$305
1972..............	3,240	3,872	8,652	2,072	1,502	346
Industry share 1967:						
Unit shipments	100.0%	38.6%	3.7%	25.2%	32.4%	...
Retail sales	100.0	48.7	15.4	23.5	12.4	...
Industry share 1972:						
Unit shipments	100.0%	33.5%	15.6%	14.2%	14.7%	22.0%
Retail sales	100.0	40.1	41.7	9.0	6.7	2.5

n.a. = Data not available.
 * Motor home sales in 1972 for the different classes were 64,600, 23,800, and 28,400 in units and $665,021,000, $127,211,000, and $218,310,000 for Type A, B, and C.
 Source: "Facts & Trends," Recreational Vehicle Institute, and casewriter's analysis.

Travel trailer and A-body motor home pricing comparisons*

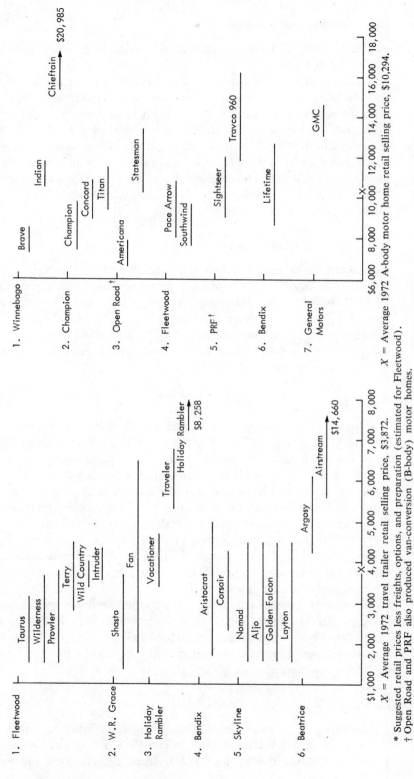

Travel Trailers

1. Fleetwood
Taurus
Wilderness
Prowler
Terry
Wild Country
Intruder

2. W.R. Grace
Shasta
Fan
Vacationer

3. Holiday Rambler
Traveler
Holiday Rambler → $8,258

4. Bendix
Aristocrat
Corsair

5. Skyline
Nomad
Aljo
Golden Falcon
Layton

6. Beatrice
Argosy
Airstream → $14,660

$1,000 2,000 3,000 X 4,000 5,000 6,000 7,000 8,000

X = Average 1972 travel trailer retail selling price, $3,872.

A–Body Motor Homes

1. Winnebago
Brave
Indian
Chieftain → $20,985

2. Champion
Champion
Concord
Titan

3. Open Road †
Americana
Statesman

4. Fleetwood
Pace Arrow
Southwind

5. PRF †
Sightseer
Travco 960

6. Bendix
Lifetime

7. General Motors
GMC

$6,000 8,000 10,000 X 12,000 14,000 16,000 18,000

X = Average 1972 A-body motor home retail selling price, $10,294.

* Suggested retail prices less freights, options, and preparation (estimated for Fleetwood).
† Open Road and PRF also produced van-conversion (B-body) motor homes.
Source: *NADA Recreational Vehicle Appraisal Guide,* May 1973; *Recreational Vehicle Directory;* and casewriter's analysis.

Pacific, eastern, and west north central areas, with most other areas lagging far behind.

Recreational vehicles had been a particularly American phenomenon, and for some time there was little international activity. By 1973, however, the international market was thought to be growing quite rapidly. While no exact data existed, the strongest markets were thought to be Western Europe, South Africa, and Australia. These areas were generally serviced by local manufacturers and sales were concentrated in units such as camping trailers and small travel trailers. A few domestic U.S. manufacturers had made some inroads into markets outside North America, but these were relatively limited.

INDUSTRY COMPONENTS

In addition to the manufacturers, the recreational vehicle industry included a large number of suppliers, dealers, and campgrounds. The RV industry was also closely related to the mobile home industry. Since the first travel trailers had actually been used as mobile homes before evolving into recreational vehicles, almost all the segments of the modern RV industry either grew out of or were still actively involved with mobile homes in 1973.

Suppliers

Component parts accounted for 65% to 75% of the factory price of an RV, and the supplying of components was a $1.2 billion business in 1973. Since few manufacturers produced their own parts, there was a large supplier sector of about 1,000 companies. While most suppliers were small, privately held firms that served local markets, several large companies had also become active in the area. These were of two types: those that made a majority of their sales to the RV industry and those that derived only a small portion of their total revenues from the RV industry. The latter group included primarily appliance manufacturers, such as Coleman and Magic Chef, and the large automobile companies which manufactured motor home chassis.

The most expensive component was the motor home chassis, costing between $2,500 and $3,500. Dodge produced 80% of all chassis, while Chevrolet, Ford, and International Harvester supplied the balance. All four companies, however, competed quite vigorously for this business, as did the suppliers of other RV components.

Dealers

According to a Recreational Vehicle Institute estimate, there were 10,000 recreational vehicle dealers in the United States compared with 25,000 automobile dealers and 22,000 truck dealers. One source estimated that 7,000 of the RV dealers handled only recreational vehicles, 350 were automobile or truck dealers, and the remainder sold farm equipment or mobile homes.[3] There were no wholesale distributors in the industry; all sales were made directly by the manufacturer to the dealer.

In 1972 the average RV dealer had sales of $242,000 or about 75 vehicles. Most were small, one-leased-lot type of operation run by an owner manager with perhaps one or two salesmen, a small service area, and a few rental units. Promotion was generally through local newspaper advertising, and most manufacturers engaged in cooperative advertising with the dealers. Perhaps 10%–15% of the dealers had sales over $1 million, and a few had multiple lot operations. The largest dealer in the country was a Winnebago outlet with annual sales of $9 million.

The manufacturer generally sold the RVs for cash. Sales were almost entirely F.O.B. factory, with the dealer paying freight. The inventories of most dealers were financed on a "floor plan" basis by a lending institution.[4] The average dealer markup was 25%, and most manufacturers published suggested retail prices for their products. A few provided "sticker" prices on the vehicle as was the practice with automobiles.

Dealers occupied an especially important position since they represented the industry to the public. With few exceptions, consumers did not identify with manufacturers or brands. One survey revealed that only about a fourth of the retail customers had decided on a certain make of RV before approaching a dealer, and that 86% of those might be persuaded by the dealer to buy another brand. Thus dealers, who usually carried three or four brands of an equal number of manufacturers, could easily replace the products of a manufacturer with which they were not satisfied.

Parks and campgrounds

By 1973 there were 18,767 camping areas in the United States, Canada, and Mexico that were suitable for RV use. Of these sites, 7,400 were publicly owned and run by a state, local, or federal government, and the other 11,367 were privately owned and operated. The leading company in the industry was Kampgrounds of America which had developed and franchised over 700 campgrounds in the United States, Canada, and Mexico. In total, about 50 firms were building multiple-outlet operations and several large corporations had been attracted to the field, including

---

[3] "The Recreational Vehicle Industry," White Weld and Co., Inc., August 1972, p. 40.

[4] Under this agreement a dealer borrowed substantially all of the purchase price of a unit, usually with the requirement that consumer financing be directed exclusively to the lender. While in many cases the manufacturer had to agree to repurchase its merchandise if the dealers defaulted, few manufacturers had encountered significant losses from repurchase agreements.

Exxon, Gulf Oil, Holiday Inns, Ramada Inns, and Pet. Such activity resulted in both a general upgrading in the quality of parks and an increase in their size. In 1973 the average private U.S. park had 54 sites as compared with 39 in 1968. Another trend was the development of condominium parks where campsites were sold for $5,000 to $8,000.

A major shortage of parks and campgrounds existed, however, especially in popular vacation spots. There were only some 900,000 sites for the estimated 3.8 million RVs, or about one site for each four vehicles. The situation was further aggravated in 1973 when the Federal Government announced that it would not build any additional camping facilities and also began to place restrictions on the use of national parks because of overcrowding.

Manufacturers

The Recreational Vehicle Institute estimated that there were 650 manufacturers of RVs and 704 plants in operation as of January 1, 1973, compared with 800 producers on January 1, 1972. The large number of RV manufacturers could be attributed to the ease of entry into the industry. The basic technology, similar for all producers, was a simple assembly operation performed in a one-floor, inexpensive plant containing little sophisticated equipment. Most suppliers, in tight competition with each other, sold component parts on open credit of at least 30 days. With an independent distribution system, market access presented no problem for the small producer, especially in times of rising sales when large, established manufacturers could not keep up with the demand.

On the other hand, the decline in the number of manufacturers from 1972 to 1973 was viewed by many as evidence of a long-term trend towards concentration as small one- and two-plant firms either failed or were acquired. One executive predicted "tremendous consolidation in the next ten years" with the field narrowing to 25 "solid companies."[5] The RV industry in 1973 was often compared to the U.S. automobile industry in the 1920s which was on the brink of evolving from a highly fragmented industry to one with a much smaller number of large producers.

MAJOR RV MANUFACTURERS

Product strategies

The large RV manufacturers had adopted quite different product strategies. Several had concentrated in a certain product class, such as

---

[5] Alan Robin, president of Open Road, in "Motor-Home Sales Build Up Speed," *Business Week*, April 29, 1972, p. 44.

motor homes for Winnebago, Champion, and PRF, and travel trailers for Beatrice, W.R. Grace, and Holiday. Other manufacturers, such as Open Road, Coachmen, and Skyline, produced full lines of almost all types of recreational vehicles. A few, such as Fleetwood and Bendix, were strong in both motor homes and travel trailers but did not produce other types of RVs.

Differences also existed in product identification. Some companies, believing that brand or manufacturer identity was impossible or of limited value, had a large number of brand names for relatively similar products. Most of these firms were the mobile home manufacturers— Fleetwood, Champion, Skyline, and Bendix—that had diversified into RVs but had retained the brand strategy that was common in the mobile home industry. Other firms had emphasized a corporate identification for their entire product line. Open Road, Winnebago, and Coachmen were the best examples of this practice (see Exhibit 3).

Marketing strategies

Most large manufacturers had national dealer organizations but used substantially different approaches. The mobile home companies followed the practice of building a large dealer organization, with Fleetwood, Skyline, and Champion having the largest number of dealers in the industry—approximately 1,800, 1,500, and 1,200, respectively. At the other extreme was the approach of building a smaller dealer network of larger, often exclusive dealers. Winnebago, with only 328 dealers, and Open Road, with several large company-owned outlets, were the best examples of this approach. Generally, all manufacturers contacted and serviced their dealers with field salesmen operating out of a local plant.

The main promotional device employed by manufacturers was the trade show. While traditionally no manufacturer had engaged in extensive consumer advertising, this situation was changing by 1973. Several large manufacturers advertised heavily in selected consumer magazines such as *Travel Trailer* and *Wheels Afield*. Only Winnebago and Open Road, however, had attempted to use mass media such as *Newsweek* or television for consumer advertising.

Production strategies

Most manufacturers operated several small plants that averaged about 70,000 square feet. Such plants were inexpensive, rapidly built, had low break-even points, and kept transportation charges to a minimum. (Transportation costs averaged 25 cents to 41 cents per mile for different RVs.) Delivery costs, paid for by dealers and passed on to consumers, were especially important for the price-competitive RVs. Location also

EXHIBIT 3
Major recreational vehicle manufacturers

Company	No. of brands*	No. of plants	Sales†			1972 unit shipments		1972 market share	
			RV sales	Total sales (millions)	RV % of total sales	MH	TT	MH	TT
Winnebago	1	1	$212	$ 212	100%	22,000	1,900	18.8%	0.7%
Fleetwood	6 TT, 4 MH	21	147	354	42	5,200	30,000	4.5	12.0
Champion	3 TT, 4 MH	14	86	291	30	8,700	3,500	7.5	1.4
Beatrice Foods (Airstream)	2 TT	3	75	2,787	3	...	10,000	...	4.0
Open Road	1	6	71	71	100	7,200	2,000	6.2	0.8
Bendix	2 TT, 2 MH	11	70	1,777	4	3,500	16,000	3.0	6.4
Holiday Rambler	1	2	70	70	100	...	16,500	...	6.5
W.R. Grace (Shasta, Fan)	2 TT	8	57	2,315	2	nil	17,000	...	6.8
Skyline	4 TT, 3 MH	11	54	357	15	1,100	14,000	0.9	5.6
Coachmen	1	6	45	53	85	1,200	3,500	1.0	1.4
PRF Industries (Travco)	4 MH	4	40	44	91	4,500	...	3.8	...
Total top 11			$927			53,400	114,400	45.7%	45.6%
Other producers						63,400	136,400	54.3	54.4
						116,800	250,800	100.0%	100.0%

* MH = motor home, TT = travel trailer.
† For calendar 1972 or closest fiscal year end.
Source: Casewriter's analysis and estimates. Unit shipment estimates from "Recreational Vehicle Industry," Dataquest, Inc., August 1972, pp. 37 and 39.

helped to keep labor costs down since most RV plants were situated in remote areas where unskilled nonunion labor was plentiful. Location was also important in the supply of component parts as nearby vendors enabled manufacturers, most of whom carried little raw material inventory, to obtain parts as needed.

The main exception to the multiple-plant practice was Winnebago which operated from one location of over 2 million square feet. Winnebago also had integrated into component production and by 1973 could supply an estimated 60% of its raw material needs. Only one other RV manufacturer, Champion, had integrated substantially, supplying 25% of its raw materials from 13 small component supply plants located around the country.

Service strategies

One of the most common complaints of recreational vehicle owners was the lack of convenient and complete service. Few RV dealers could provide service on an entire unit—structure, appliances and heating, electrical and plumbing systems. The problem was especially acute for motor homes with their additional complications of a chassis and engine. Several manufacturers, however, had by 1973 attempted to deal with the service problem. Champion had opened service centers at its manufacturing plants; Winnebago and Open Road emphasized a more critical selection of dealers with an emphasis on large, full-service outlets; and several manufacturers undertook training of dealer service personnel.

Another aspect of the service problem was the manufacturer's warranty. Originally most companies guaranteed their products for only 90 days, but by 1973 all major producers had one-year warranties. Differences still existed, however, over the extent of the warranty. Some manufacturers gave a broad warranty covering almost all parts of an RV. Winnebago, the leader in this approach, had devoted substantial advertising revenues to its "complete warranty" coverage. Other firms required a purchaser to utilize suppliers' warranties for the engine, chassis, appliances, and other features and agreed only to service assembly problems. This type of coverage forced a consumer to seek service from several sources.

CHALLENGES TO RV MANUFACTURERS: 1973

Safety

The most significant problem for the industry was safety, especially for motor homes, as stringent federal safety regulations were an imminent possibility. The RVI had tried to stay ahead of federal regulations by developing in 1971 a standard code for plumbing, heating, and electrical systems in all RVs. These standards were limited to just the three systems, however, and for this reason the National Highway Traffic and Safety Administration (NHTSA), the body that set federal automobile standards, was taking an active interest in RVs. In 1972 an advisory group, the National Transportation Safety Board, published a report in which it concluded that the design and construction of some motor homes "are such that they are incapable of maintaining structural integrity in a crash."[6] The large amount of wood used in the bodies of motor homes was the main focus of criticism. As a result, several large RV manufacturers had added steel frames to their motor homes even though the NHTSA had not announced standards for body construction.

The government's main areas of interest in 1973 were visibility for motor homes, hitches and lighting for trailers, and braking, flame retardancy, and tires and rims for all RVs. Each of these areas was to come under regulation by 1974, after which the NHTSA was expected to move into other areas, the most significant of which would be coach construction. Since the elapsed time from standards proposal to implementation often was four years or more, there was little danger of immediate imposition of harsh standards. To insure up-to-date continued information, the RVI had a Washington legal staff that worked closely with government regulators on matters relating to RV safety.

The relationship, however, was in some danger of being interrupted by outside parties. One of these groups was Ralph Nader's Center for Auto Safety which, together with Consumers' Union, had petitioned the NHTSA to make automobile standards immediately applicable to motor homes. The Nader group was also preparing a major study directed at mobile home safety, but also dealing with RVs, that was scheduled for release in the summer of 1973. A final effort was being made in the Congress where the "National Home and Recreational Vehicle Safety Act" had been introduced in April 1973. This bill, scheduled for hearings in the summer, proposed national standards for RV construction.

Gasoline shortage

In 1973, a major threat to recreational vehicle sales was the emerging gasoline shortage associated with possible higher gas prices. Motor homes and vehicles pulling travel trailers often had gasoline mileage of only six to seven miles per gallon and tended to be concentrated in popular vacation areas, such as the Rockies, where gas shortages were ex-

---

[6] "Shifting Down: Motor-Home Firms Face Slower Growth, Many Woes," *The Wall Street Journal*, May 31, 1973, p. 23. Most of the safety activity and criticism was directed at motor homes since these were almost the only RVs that carried people while in motion. Most states had laws that prohibited travel trailer occupancy during movement.

pected to materialize first. The specter of leaving on vacation and being stranded far from home had haunted many consumers and was considered to be the primary reason for depressed industry sales during the first four months of 1973. Shipments for April 1973 were only 2.8% above those of April 1972 and manufacturers projected that shipments through July would decline by 2.7% from 1972 shipments.

Increasing competition

Another significant threat to existing RV manufacturers was General Motors, which began motor home production in February 1973. GM's initial offering was a sleekly designed, large motor home in a 23-foot model priced at $13,500 and a 26-foot model priced at $14,000. The company planned to manufacture about 5,000 units during its first year.

General Motors had taken a radically different approach to its motor home business. First of all, it was the only manufacturer that could supply its own chassis, engine, and appliances. Furthermore, it had a well-established network of over 13,000 dealers to choose from, and its motor home dealers were required to provide full service on every part in the unit. Its one-year warranty covered the entire motor home, and consumers were given a toll-free number to call for service problems. GM had committed a large amount of money to nationwide consumer advertising, and its motor home contained most of the safety features expected to become mandatory for all motor homes in the future.

Other automobile companies were expected to follow GM into the industry. In May 1973 Ford introduced a truck camper intended for use with specially equipped pickup trucks. Ford was known to have several models of motor homes and travel trailers on the drawing boards and was considering the purchase of a smaller motor home manufacturer. International Harvester produced some motor home chassis and was thought to be considering production of its own vehicle.

Foreign competition also loomed on the horizon. Volkswagen had been well entrenched in the industry for years, having sold about 11,000 units of its van-conversion camper in 1972. In early 1973 Toyota announced a September 1973 introduction of a small truck camper with a push-up top that would sell for about $4,400 and was aimed at a young-family market in need of a second car/RV combination.

Winnebago Industries Inc.

FOUNDED in 1958 to aid the depressed economy of Forest City, Iowa,[1] Winnebago Industries had become by 1973 the largest manufacturer of recreational vehicles in the world, with sales of $212 million. Operating solely from its original location, the company's growth in the period from 1967 to 1973 had been phenomenal, with sales and earnings increasing at compounded annual rates of 72% and 83%, respectively (see Exhibits 1 and 2). In a speech in early 1973, John K. Hanson, the founder of Winnebago, reflected on the company's success.

We started out some years ago with five goals: to bring a million dollar payroll to Forest City; to be listed on the New York Stock Exchange; to be among *Fortune's* 500; to have a thousand dollar investment in Winnebago in 1966 become a million dollars; and to have a billion dollar corporation.

This year our payroll is exceeding 20 million dollars; we were listed on the NYSE in September 1970, and we were the leading gainer on that exchange in 1971, the first full calendar year after listing; we should be in *Fortune's* 500 easily with this fiscal year; the thousand dollar investment became a million a year ago. We haven't reached that last goal of a billion dollar corporation yet. I'm still working on that one![2]

By May 1973, however, the situation at Winnebago had changed. Sales of the company's principal product had dropped precipitously, and earnings for the fiscal quarter ending May 26 were down 36% from the preceding year. As a result, management had canceled plans for a second plant, had cut production almost 60%, and had initiated its first factory-authorized sale.

---

[1] Forest City's population in 1973 was 4,800.

[2] This quotation is taken from a speech by John K. Hanson to the Seattle Society of Security Analysts on January 26, 1973. Other quotations in the case are taken from this speech and from quarterly and annual reports.

EXHIBIT 1

WINNEBAGO INDUSTRIES, INC.
Condensed Income Statements
(as of fiscal year end—dollars in thousands)

	February 25 1967	February 24 1968	February 22 1969	February 28 1970	February 27 1971	February 26 1972	February 24 1973
Net sales	$8,371	$17,566	$33,405	$44,961	$70,866	$133,166	$212,036
Cost of goods sold	6,382	13,546	26,288	35,360	55,388	98,394	162,145
Gross profit	$1,989	$ 4,020	$ 7,117	$ 9,601	$15,478	$ 34,772	$ 49,891
Selling expenses	604	815	1,329	2,152	4,746	5,772	9,492
General and administrative expenses	406	514	725	1,123	1,762	3,126	4,692
Total expenses	$1,010	$ 1,329	$ 2,054	$ 3,275	$ 6,508	$ 8,898	$ 14,184
Income before taxes	$ 979	$ 2,691	$ 5,063	$ 6,326	$ 8,970	$ 25,874	$ 35,707
Income taxes	468	1,306	2,633	3,120	4,355	12,277	16,335
Extraordinary item, net	...	...	...	...	...	...	2,074
Net income	$ 511	$ 1,385	$ 2,430	$ 3,206	$ 4,615	$ 13,597	$ 17,298
Net income per share*	2¢	6¢	11¢	13¢	19¢	56¢	69¢
Analysis							
(1) Items as a % of sales:							
Cost of goods sold	76.2%	77.1%	78.7%	78.6%	78.2%	73.9%	76.5%
Selling expenses	7.2	4.6	4.0	4.8	6.7	4.3	4.5
General and administrative	4.9	2.9	2.2	2.5	2.5	2.3	2.2
Income before taxes	11.7	15.3	15.2	14.1	12.7	19.4	16.8
(2) Stock price range†	...	$1–8	$5–11	$3–6	$4–27	$22–50	$5–28
(3) Return on average equity	55.2%	67.6%	26.8%	19.0%	22.3%	32.9%	29.6%

* Restated for all stock splits.
† For calendar years; 1973, through May 22. Price rounded to nearest dollar.
Source: Company records and casewriter's analysis.

EXHIBIT 2

WINNEBAGO INDUSTRIES INC.
Condensed Balance Sheets and Funds Flow
(in thousands of dollars)

Assets	2-25-67	2-24-68	2-22-69	2-28-70	2-27-71	2-26-72	2-24-73
Current assets							
Cash and securities	$ 147	$ 283	$ 7,837	$ 2,155	$ 2,093	$20,665	$ 6,038
Receivables	492	971	2,396	3,450	6,509	12,932	16,893
Inventories	1,684	3,509	4,381	18,717	12,815	26,999	42,765
Other current assets	78	78	157	427	426	734	3,575
Total current assets	$2,401	$4,841	$14,771	$24,749	$21,843	$61,330	$ 69,271
Property and equipment							
Land	$ 99	$ 107	$ 269	$ 317	$ 447	$ 577	$ 1,541
Buildings	756	914	1,787	4,455	5,416	8,219	19,655
Machinery and other	811	1,124	2,474	4,455	5,541	9,029	20,582
	$1,666	$2,145	$ 4,530	$ 9,227	$11,404	$17,825	$ 41,778
Less depreciation	247	399	556	1,001	1,660	2,728	5,036
Net plant and equipment	$1,419	$1,746	$ 3,974	$ 8,226	$ 9,744	$15,097	$ 36,742
Other assets*	$ 52	$ 59	$ 89	$ 918	$ 1,027	$ 4,512	$ 10,971
Total assets	$3,872	$6,646	$18,834	$33,893	$32,614	$80,939	$116,984
Liabilities and Equity							
Current liabilities							
Bank notes	$ 860	$ 915	$ ...	$11,000	$ 1,000	$ ...	$ 11,000
Other	1,035	2,159	3,242	4,033	7,990	20,855	27,771
Total current liabilities	$1,895	$3,074	$ 3,242	$15,033	$ 8,990	$20,855	$ 38,771
Long-term debt and deferred tax	$ 779	$ 671	$ 364	$ 426	$ 575	$ 415	$ 822
Stockholders' equity							
Common stock	$ 670	$1,388	$ 1,512	$ 3,024	$ 3,024	$12,597	$ 12,603
Paid-in-capital	29	...	9,793	8,281	8,281	21,732	22,150
Retained earnings	499	1,513	3,923	7,129	11,744	25,340	42,638
Total equity	$1,198	$2,901	$15,228	$18,434	$23,049	$59,669	$ 77,391
Total liabilities and equity	$3,872	$6,646	$18,834	$33,893	$32,614	$80,939	$116,984

PRODUCTS

Winnebago manufactured a broad line of recreational vehicles: motor homes, travel trailers, truck campers, and pickup covers (see Exhibit 3). The company's basic product philosophy was described by Hanson:

We've followed a fundamental principle that has guided us since the day we opened our doors. It is simply this: give the customer more value for his dollar than he can get anywhere else. In my opinion, this, more than any other single element, has been the basis for what success we have enjoyed to date.

EXHIBIT 2 *(continued)*

Analysis	2–25–67	2–24–68	2–22–69	2–28–70	2–27–71	2–26–72	2–24–73
Current ratio	1.3	1.6	4.5	1.6	2.4	2.9	1.8
Inventory turnover	4.8	8.2	6.7	3.0	3.5	4.7	4.7
Days receivables	22	20	26	28	33	35	29
Debt/equity	2.23	1.29	.24	.83	.42	.36	.51

Funds Flow

Sources:

Net income		76%	19%	52%	81%	36%	56%
Depreciation and other noncash expenses		8	2	9	19	4	11
Equity sales		16	79	...	...	60	1
Working capital decrease...............		...	...	39	...	...	32

Uses:

Plant and equipment additions		27%	20%	78%	42%	17%	78%
Other asset additions*.....		5	2	22	3	8	22
Working capital increase		68	78	...	55	74	...
Total funds		$1,855	$12,590	$ 6,113	$ 5,670	$38,214	$ 30,944

* Includes investments of $1,500,000 and $5,767,101 in Winnebago Acceptance Corp. for 1972 and 1973, respectively.

Source: Company records and casewriter's analysis.

EXHIBIT 3

WINNEBAGO INDUSTRIES INC.
1973 Product Line

Type	Name	Floor plans	Length in feet	Suggested retail price
Motor homes				
Class A	Brave	3	18, 21	$ 7,350–$ 8,230
	Indian	3	23, 24	10,970– 11,720
	Chieftain	5	24, 27, 28	15,815– 20,985
Class C	Minnie Winnie	2	20	$ 8,290
Travel trailers				
Conventional	Indian	2	19, 20	
	Chieftain	3	23	$ 3,000–$ 5,700
Fifth wheel........	Chieftain	2	27	
Truck campers	Indian	2	10	$ 1,200–$ 2,000
Pickup covers	Kap	13	6, 8	$ 200–$ 340

Source: Company records.

The company's products were sold under the Winnebago name and were easily identified by the famous "flying W" on the side of each unit. Even though minor annual model changes were made each August, a minimum number of variations in floor plans were offered and each model came in only one color. Options offered could mostly be "bolted on" by dealers, and consequently no custom orders were placed directly by retail purchasers.

Winnebago was the world's largest manufacturer of motor homes, holding almost a 20% share of the total U.S. market and 32% of the Type A conventional motor home market. The company's dominance in the field was exemplified by the widespread use of "Winnebago" as a generic name to describe all motor homes.

After introduction in 1966, Winnebago's motor home line changed gradually; a few new models were added each year. The evolution from three models in 1966 to 16 in 1973, however, had not been accompanied by significant exterior changes. The first Winnebago motor homes were virtually indistinguishable from the newest; the company concentrated its development efforts on engineering refinements and interior changes. Special "motor inn" models, motor homes intended for commercial purposes and sold without furnishings, were first offered in 1973.

During 1972 the company had initiated production of a Type C economy line of homes called "Minnie Winnie." John V. Hanson, Winnebago's president and the son of the company's founder, explained:

> Why buy a mini-motor home when for the same money or less you could buy a conventional motor home? Basically, it's the psychology of the driver's compartment. . . . Many first-time motor home buyers are simply more comfortable in this kind of driving situation than in a conventional motor home. That's why we're going to make them. If the first-time buyer buys a Winnebago Minnie Winnie, he's a lot more likely to buy a full-sized Winnebago the second time around.

In units, the company's 1973 sales were estimated at 60% Brave, 25% Indian, 10% Chieftain, and 5% Minnie Winnie. The success of the Brave series and the introduction of the Type C home had resulted in a lowering of the average motor home selling price by 1973 (see Exhibit 4).

In 1970 Winnebago had attempted a major diversification move by undertaking the production of low-cost modular housing on an experimental basis. The homes were designed to sell at about $10,000 exclusive of lot, and the company utilized the same production techniques for the housing that it did for the motor homes. The peak interest in this activity occurred in April 1971 when some 200 builders, real estate developers, and other interested parties attended an open house in Forest City to view the Winnebago-built homes, which had been approved by

EXHIBIT 4

WINNEBAGO INDUSTRIES INC.

Sales Analysis

	2/25/67	2/24/68	2/22/69	2/28/70	2/27/71	2/26/72	2/24/73
Percentage of dollar sales by product class							
Motor homes	27.8%	62.2%	76.9%	83.2%	88.0%	90.2%	90.6%
Travel trailers and truck campers	39.0	17.1	10.4	8.2	6.8	4.5	4.2
Pickup covers	33.2	20.7	9.0	6.1	3.4	2.4	2.4
Other*			3.7	2.5	1.8	2.9	2.8
	100.0%	100.0%	100.0%	100.0%	100.0%	100.0%	100.0%
Unit sales							
Motor homes			3,522	4,395	6,937	13,116	21,790
Travel trailers						1,309	1,667
Truck campers			1,321	2,081		943	1,050
Pickup covers						18,755	31,465
Average motor home selling price			$7,293	$8,511	$8,989	$9,157	$8,816

* Includes sales of parts and supply contracts.
Source: Company records and casewriter's analysis.

the FHA as qualifying for subsidized mortgage loans. Winnebago manufactured about three modular houses per week during 1971 and five per week during 1972. About half the total production was eventually sold to company employees. Since little interest on the part of developers could be generated, however, the modular housing activity was terminated in late 1972. John K. Hanson explained:

It comes back to just plain economics. The buildings, the facilities, the people can make a greater profit for . . . stockholders by switching from housing into our specialized fields. We gave it a try and it didn't pay off, and we're not afraid to admit that we didn't do well.

DISTRIBUTION

Winnebago products had an extensive retail market, with dealers in 49 states and in Canada and Europe.[3] The company utilized a relatively small number of mostly full-line dealers. John K. Hanson explained this policy.

---

[3] By 1973 Winnebago's foreign sales were beginning to grow. Slightly over 1% of its sales were made in Canada, and dealers were also located in England and West Germany. To facilitate growth in these markets, a subsidiary, Winnebago International Corporation, had been set up in 1972 as a channel for foreign sales.

While not all Winnebago retail dealers handle Winnebago products exclusively, the trend appears to be in that direction. A measure of the increasing strength of the dealer organization is that at Dealer Days (new model introduction) in August 1971 Winnebago honored eight dealers who had each sold more than one million dollars worth of Winnebago recreational vehicles in the previous model year. At Dealer Days in August 1972 the company honored 37 such dealers.

Beginning in 1971 Winnebago began to tighten dealer standards, which resulted in a decline in the number of dealers. All dealers were required to provide full service for the company's products, to provide indoor showrooms and other facilities similar to automobile dealerships, and to carry an estimated 90-day inventory. Each dealer had to sign a yearly agreement detailing the above requirements.

The company's 328 dealers (down from 425 in 1970) could be classified broadly according to the recreational vehicles they sold. By 1973, approximately 30% (up from 14% in 1971) handled Winnebago RVs exclusively; 32% carried products of other manufacturers to complete their line of recreational vehicles but did not carry products competitive with Winnebago; the remaining 38% carried at least one other competitive brand. Many of the company's dealers were also engaged in other areas of business, with 40% selling automobiles and/or trucks. Sales per dealer in 1973 averaged $646,500, up from $105,800 in 1970.

Dealers were supported by Winnebago's extensive home office and field sales and service organization as well as by the most extensive sales promotion and advertising efforts in the industry, including a complete assortment of product literature, point-of-sales aids, and Dealer Days. The company also engaged in considerable national consumer advertising both in magazines and on television. This program had been undertaken in 1971, and for the year ended February 1973 advertising expenditures approximated $5 million.

In 1971 the Winnebago Acceptance Corporation (WAC), a wholly owned subsidiary modeled after the financial subsidiaries of automobile companies, was formed to provide floor-plan financing for dealers and an additional source of credit for retail purchasers. Winnebago had invested $1.5 million in the financial subsidiary and had loaned it an additional $5.6 million; WAC had also obtained $11 million in short-term bank loans. By the end of fiscal 1973, WAC had outstanding credit of $17.8 million, all of it in dealer financing. Another subsidiary, the Winnebago Realty Corporation, had been formed in 1972 for the purpose of assisting in the development of dealership facilities in suitable locations by aiding in site selection, facility planning, and financing. Winnebago also pioneered another dealer aid, a standardized accounting system and business management program which it made available to all its dealers in 1972.

Some of the WAC funding had been utilized in expanding the Winnebago Rent-A-Way program in which more than half of the company's dealers participated. The rental program had been initiated in 1971 with 300 units and had grown to 1,200 by 1972 and 2,000 by 1973. Under this plan, motor homes and trailers were made available for short-term rentals. Since many potential customers preferred to rent an RV before deciding on a final purchase, this program, which was by far the largest in the industry, was considered an important means of expanding sales.

Winnebago also engaged in retail customer contact through Winnebago International Travelers, a company-sponsored club of Winnebago recreational vehicle owners set up in 1970. By 1973 the club, which was the second largest of its type in the industry after Airstream's, had 33,000 members. The club conducted caravans and rallies and, according to John K. Hanson, "generates considerable owner loyalty that tends to produce repeat sales."

Criticism of recreational vehicle warranty and service was one of the biggest problems faced by the industry in 1973. Winnebago's response to both of these issues was described by Hanson:

Warranties on Winnebago products have been broadened considerably in the 1973 model year, providing customers with the quickest and most satisfactory warranty claims service in the industry. Under the new plan, Winnebago directly warrants all components except motor homes chassis, auxiliary electric power plants, tires and batteries which are warranted directly by manufacturers of those components. Previously, a customer has had service or parts protection under as many as 14 separate warranties.

The key to long-term success in recreational vehicles is service after the sale, since satisfied customers are a company's best sales persons through word-of-mouth testimonials. Service that satisfies the customer must be provided by the retail dealers, and Winnebago currently has the most comprehensive training program for dealer service personnel in the industry. Approximately 1,000 dealer service personnel have attended Winnebago service school classes thus far.

To further improve service on its products, the company had added 11 service district managers who provided assistance to dealers. In addition, a new 90,000-square-foot parts depot was put into operation in 1973 to serve the dealer organization.

PRODUCTION AND RESEARCH

Winnebago's dynamic growth was accompanied by substantial increases in its plant. An original 90,000-square-foot building constructed after a fire in 1965 had been expanded to 250,000 square feet by 1968. Further growth is shown in the following table:

Fiscal year	Number of buildings	Square footage	Capital expenditures (in millions)
1970	10	326,000	$ 4.7
1971	15	732,000	2.4
1972	32	1,100,000	6.5
1973	39	2,403,000	24.1

By 1973 Winnebago had the largest and most advanced recreational vehicle facility in the world. The plant, situated on 860 acres of land, consisted of separate assembly buildings for pickup covers, travel trailers, and motor homes (the largest, with four 800-foot assembly lines). Travel trailers and other RVs were assembled from basically the same materials and in the same manner as motor homes. Each manufacturing operation—plastics, saw mill, aluminum extrusion, fiberglass, metal stamping, and upholstery—was located in a separate building. The remaining buildings were used for storage, maintenance, offices, and a company store.

With certain exceptions, principally chassis and engines for motor homes which were purchased from Dodge and electrical power units and appliances, the company manufactured all its parts. These included windows, doors, cabinets, seats, bathroom and kitchen fixtures, furniture, as well as curtains and drapes. The RV bodies were made principally of Thermo-Panel materials which were cut to shape to form the floor, roof, and side walls of each unit. Winnebago also produced substantially all the aluminum and plastic extrusions used in its vehicles. In total, the company manufactured an estimated 60% of its materials.

Winnebago's assembly facilities utilized extensive automated equipment and techniques similar to those commonly used by automobile manufacturers. With a limited number of floor plans and only one color offered for each model, Winnebago produced to inventory and not to dealer order. Winnebago's production practices had resulted in high productivity and enabled a pretax margin consistently in excess of the 7%–10% common in the industry. Winnebago's production strategy also resulted in a higher break-even point. It was estimated by one analyst at 10,000 motor homes yearly. In contrast to other RV manufacturers, no incentive plans were used. None of the repeated attempts of the United Auto Workers to organize the workforce had been successful.

By the spring of 1973, the Forest City facility had a capacity of 600 motor homes a week on a one-shift basis. Actual production had averaged 565 homes a week during March and 527 during April; but because of declining sales production had been cut to 450 during the first weeks in May and 350 by the end of the month. At the end of May the company announced production levels of 250 a week in June and a reduction in the workforce of 3,300 by 500 to 700 employees.

Winnebago's research and development activities were the largest in the recreational vehicle industry. Engaged primarily in product design and materials testing, the R & D staff had moved to a new building in 1972 that, according to John K. Hanson, provided "a higher level of security and the space and facilities necessary for the advanced product and engineering group to test and compare, design and improve, so that future Winnebago products and components will continue to be the best and most competitive we can make." For fiscal 1973, R & D expenditures totaled $830,000 and involved 46 full-time employees.

FINANCE

Winnebago's dramatic expansion had been financed largely with internally generated funds plus common stock offerings in 1967, 1968, and 1971 (see Exhibit 2). In 1973 the company had no long-term debt; in fact, in its entire history it had utilized only negligible amounts of such financing. Management expected that future expansion at Forest City could be financed easily from retained earnings supplemented with periodic short-term bank loans from a $45 million line of credit negotiated in late 1972. Extensive new facilities, such as a second plant, might, however, require additional external financing. Winnebago had never paid dividends.

Winnebago's margins had consistently been better than the average in the RV industry. For fiscal 1973, however, pretax profit margins had slipped to 16.8% from 19.4% for 1972. Factors contributing to this decline included government price controls, higher material costs, startup costs for the new Minnie Winnie, and shifts in the company's product mix to the Brave and Minnie Winnie, both less profitable products than the larger motor homes.

Net income for 1973 had also been severely affected by the settlement of a lawsuit first brought in 1970 by Life-Time Industries, Inc., a former dealer of Winnebago products. The suit, which had originally asked for damages of $445 million, charged that Winnebago had breached a contract to produce motor homes to be distributed by Life-Time. A federal jury awarded the plaintiff damages in the amount of $4 million in November 1972 along with $400,000 personal damage awards against John K. Hanson and another company officer. As a result an extraordinary item of $2,074,000 was charged against 1973 income.

For the first quarter of fiscal 1974 Winnebago's earnings continued to decline, although sales increased slightly.

	13 weeks ended May 27, 1972		13 weeks ended May 26, 1973	
	Millions of dollars	*Percent*	*Millions of dollars*	*Percent*
Net sales	$58.9	100%	$62.6	100%
Income before tax	12.3	21	7.8	12
Net income	6.3	11	4.0	6
Earnings per share	25 cents		16 cents	

OWNERSHIP

Control of Winnebago rested solidly with the Hanson family. Of the 25,206,808 shares outstanding by the end of fiscal 1973, the family owned an aggregate of 15,940,596 or 63.1%.

Name	*Position*	*Relation to John K. Hanson*	*Shares owned*	*% of Total*
John K. Hanson	Chairman	...	12,464,924	49.4%
G. Wallace Peterson	Vice Chairman	Brother-in-law	975,720	3.9
John V. Hanson	President	Son	838,190	3.3
Gerald E. Boman	Chief Ex. Officer	Son-in-law	819,642	3.2
Paul D. Hanson	...	Son	842,120	3.3

Despite family control the company had 21,700 shareholders of record (approximately 1,000 in Forest City) as of May 1973. An original investor who bought 100 shares for $1,250 in the initial public offering of January 1966 would have owned 32,000 shares worth over $1.5 million at the height of the stock's value in mid-1972. By May 1973, however, the decline in quarterly earnings, combined with the announcement of production cuts and the cancellation of plans for the second plant, had contributed to a significant drop in the price of Winnebago's stock from a high of $49.50 in May 1972 to $5.00 on May 22, 1973.

OUTLOOK FOR WINNEBAGO

Despite declining fortunes, Winnebago's top management remained optimistic about the company's future. John K. Hanson explained his perception of the company's difficulties and outlined his response.

In retrospect, the unexpected slackening in the growth of retail sales this spring can be attributed to a variety of factors. These include (a) buyer concern about the potential shortage of gasoline and psychological concerns of being stranded by lack of fuel while traveling to or from distant vacation locations; (b) general uncertainty of national economic conditions created by rapidly changing international monetary conditions and the negative impact of Watergate on Federal Government activities; and (*c*) increased competition from many new manufacturers of motor homes and an increase in the number of small-volume retail dealers.

We are optimistic about the long-term future of the company. We have all the essential ingredients of a healthy business: available capital, qualified people, modern production facilities, and an established product with excellent consumer brand-name recognition.

Over the long term, the recreational vehicle industry should grow at a rapid rate as more and more families experience the enjoyment and relaxation of travel and camping. And, as the established leader in the industry, we expect to fully participate in this growth through the years.

John V. Hanson continued his father's comments:

So what will we do to turn sales—and hopefully earnings—around? We are going to be more aggressive in the marketplace. Our dealers will be helped by our professional sales organization, which is the best sales organization in the country. We sell the best value products in the industry, built in the finest factory in the industry, by the best people in the industry, and in the face of increased competition and slackened demand caused by fuel shortages we hope to retain or gain market share.

A note on the mobile home industry

BECAUSE of its ability to produce a factory-manufactured home economically, the mobile home industry had rapidly moved to fill a void at the low-cost end of the U.S. housing market. With an annual growth rate of 23% after 1962, the industry had retail sales of over $4 billion by 1973 and was responsible for almost 20% of all new housing starts in the United States (see Exhibit 1).

Mobile homes were portable units designed to be towed on their own chassis (frame and wheels) and used for year-round living. They represented the most complete form of manufactured housing and were usually sold fully equipped with all major appliances, furniture, draperies, carpets, and lamps. After being towed to the buyer's site, the mobile home was stabilized and attached to utilities. It was then ready for immediate occupancy.

The success of the mobile home could be attributed in part to its exclusion from local building codes. These codes were highly fragmented regulations that made standardization of home building difficult by specifying the precise materials and methods to be used in construction. For this reason, other types of industrialized housing had not achieved cost advantages over conventional housing.

Immunity from building codes enabled the mobile home industry to innovate with new materials and building techniques. With no requirement for on-site labor, mobile homes were also not subject to restrictive work rules imposed by construction unions. To insure continued exclusion, the industry under the auspices of the Mobile Home Manufacturers

EXHIBIT 1
Growth of the mobile home industry

Year	Mobile home shipments	Retail sales (millions)	Conventional housing starts* (in thousands of units)		Mobile homes as a percentage of†	
			Single-family	Multi-family	Total housing starts	Single-family housing starts
1960	103,700	$ 518	1,008.8	390.9	6.9%	9.3%
1961	90,200	505	960.7	404.3	6.2	8.6
1962	118,000	661	972.5	519.9	7.3	10.8
1963	150,840	862	994.1	647.9	8.4	13.2
1964	191,320	1,071	946.0	615.0	10.9	16.8
1965	216,470	1,212	964.9	544.8	12.5	18.3
1966	217,300	1,239	779.5	416.3	15.4	21.8
1967	240,360	1,370	844.9	477.0	15.4	22.2
1968	317,950	1,908	900.4	645.0	17.1	26.1
1969	412,690	2,497	811.2	688.3	21.6	33.7
1970	401,190	2,451	815.1	653.9	21.5	33.0
1971	496,570	3,297	1,152.9	931.6	19.2	30.1
1972	575,940‡	4,003	1,310.7	1,067.8	19.5	30.5

* Includes manufactured housing other than mobile homes.
† Total housing starts = all conventional plus mobile homes. Single-family starts = single-family conventional houses plus mobile homes.
‡ Does not include 17,000 units sold to the Federal Government for flood victims.
Source: Mobile Home Manufacturers Association and U.S. Department of Commerce.

Association began in the 1950s to develop a nationwide construction code. The resulting code covered heating, electrical, and plumbing systems and as finally developed in 1969 was subsequently adopted by 37 states. Code enforcement, however, was often lax and was largely dependent on manufacturers themselves. The industry was facing increasing criticism and pressure from the consumerism movement in 1973; a Ralph Nader task force study was underway and three bills had been introduced in Congress to tighten mobile home construction.

THE MARKET

Families at the extremes of the age scale were the most frequent purchasers of mobile homes. Approximately half of all mobile homes were bought by young families whose head of household was under 35 years of age and about one-quarter were bought by older families whose head of household was 55 years of age or older. These two groups were expected to grow at a faster rate than the population as a whole during the 1970s. A 1967 study by the Department of Housing and Urban Development revealed that the typical mobile home family was smaller than the average, had a lower income and less education, and tended to be employed as a blue-collar worker. The study also concluded that mobile homes served only a temporary need for young families since they usually planned to obtain conventional housing when that became economically feasible.

Consumer costs

The success of mobile homes was largely attributed to the fact that a significant segment of the American home-buying public had been effectively priced out of the conventional home market during the 1960s. As a general rule, a home buyer could prudently pay two and a half times his annual income for shelter. For a typical conventional home, a minimum income of $11,000 was usually necessary to qualify for a mortgage. The 1970 census revealed that half the American households fell below this level and were thus forced either to rent housing or to buy a mobile home. Since mobile homes were the only realistic means of ownership for millions of families, 97% of all new single-family homes that sold for less than $15,000 in 1973 and 67% of those that sold for less than $25,000 were mobile homes.

Consumers generally purchased mobile homes on credit, with a 10%–20% down payment and a 5–10 year conditional sales contract, an instrument involving monthly payments and add-on interest much like an automobile loan. While the use of a vehicular financing method resulted in higher costs—effective interest range was 11%–14%—and shorter terms, it was generally a lower risk for a lending institution and thus more readily available to consumers in times of tight credit. Another benefit was that a purchaser could finance a total package of home, furniture, and appliances with one loan.

The Federal Government had assisted housing purchases by low-income families through its home ownership program inaugurated with the passage of the National Housing Act in 1968. Under Section 235 of this act, private builders constructed or renovated approved homes for purchase by eligible low-income buyers at subsidized annual interest rates of, usually, 1%. The monthly payment on a $20,000 Section 235 home was $117 as compared to $142 on a $5,600 privately financed mobile home. With such a cost advantage, subsidized housing in the United States had grown rapidly and, in 1971, 21% of all new housing (429,000 units) had been subsidized by the Federal Government. Government subsidies faced an uncertain future, however, when President Nixon declared a moratorium on almost all programs in 1973.

Other costs for the consumers came in the form of taxes. Although functionally the mobile home served as a permanent dwelling, legally it was considered a vehicle in most states and was regulated accordingly. Most states required a motor vehicle license plate for each mobile home and levied a personal property or excise tax on its value. Some authorities considered this method of taxation anachronistic and believed that mobile homes should be classified as real property and taxed as conventional housing. Only a few states had made such a move, estimated by industry spokesmen to add $200 a year in taxes to the average mobile home, but others were expected to attempt such changes in the future. While higher taxes for mobile homes could dampen demand, a change in taxation methods would have a more fundamental impact if accompanied by a legal redefinition of the mobile home as a form of permanent housing subject to conventional financing and building codes.

Geographical aspects

Roughly half of all mobile homes in the United States were located in mobile home parks near large metropolitan areas; the other half were located on private land in rural areas or small towns. While the domestic U.S. mobile home market was quite fragmented, substantial differences existed between regions. Mobile homes had gained much more acceptance in the western and southern United States than in the North. In fact, 10 states, primarily in the South, accounted for nearly 60% of the industry's growth from 1960–70 and for 70% of the growth from 1971–72.

The mobile home was an American phenomenon, having been introduced and widely used only in the United States. By the late 1960s a few manufacturers had moved into Canada and in 1972 they sold about 5,000 units there. With high demand for low-cost housing in other parts of the world, some industry experts felt that those areas represented potential markets for mobile homes.

INDUSTRY STRUCTURE

The mobile home industry was composed of four main groups: suppliers, dealers, park owners and operators, and manufacturers.

Suppliers

The typical mobile home contained most items found in a conventional home, and 255 categories of products were used in its manufacture. Supplying components to the mobile home manufacturers was estimated to be a $2 billion business, since materials accounted for two-thirds of the wholesale price of a mobile home. Most of the approximately 1,100 suppliers were small, privately held firms serving local markets. Competition among them was vigorous, and few of them held dominant positions in the industry. Because of their large number and the easy credit terms they offered (typically, 30–90 days' open credit), most manufacturers concentrated on assembly operations; few had attempted to integrate backward into the production of components.

Dealers

There were an estimated 10,000 mobile home dealers in the United States. The dealer was the only middleman between manufacturers and consumers and served as the industry's representative to the public. The dealer was especially important since almost no brand or manufacturer identification or loyalty existed among consumers. Thus dealers, who generally carried three to five brand names of an equal number of manufacturers, operated quite independently and readily switched brands if dissatisfied with a manufacturer's product, service, or delivery.

The average mobile home dealer was a small, one-lot "Mom and Pop" type of operation. An investment of $25,000 was sufficient to start a dealership, and, although some knowledge of the trade was necessary, the barriers to entry were quite low. This resulted in a large turnover in the number of dealers. By 1973, multiple lot operations had become more common, with chains ranging in size from 30 lots to as many as 250. An estimated 40% of the dealers had also moved into ownership of mobile home parks.

Retail markups on mobile homes ranged from 20%–40%, with an average of about 25%, over the manufacturer's price, although competition in local markets often led to price cutting, especially since cost was one of the main factors in a buyer's decision.

Mobile home parks

There were about 25,000 mobile home parks in the United States, of which 10,000 were small, older areas with less than 15 lots. Spaces in parks were generally rented to mobile home owners for an average of $50 a month, ranging from a low of $30 to a high of well over $100.

Traditionally, mobile home parks had been considered an esthetic and economic liability by most communities. Millions of Americans had grown up with visions of aluminum-skinned trailers densely packed in camps serving transient populations and lacking such redeeming features as lawns, curbs, or recreation facilities. In some parts of the country, however, especially in California and Florida, parks had become more luxurious in the last two decades and had therefore gained some acceptance in their communities. Quality of parks remained a major problem elsewhere, principally in the East and Midwest.

These long-standing images of mobile homes had led to highly restrictive zoning ordinances in most large metropolitan areas of the country. Communities that had attempted to exclude mobile homes from their areas had been restricted by the courts from doing so. Most had resorted to prohibiting mobile homes in certain specified areas and confining them to mobile home parks in undesirable industrial locations or on the fringes of an urban area. Restrictive zoning ordinances were especially strong in the northern states.

Primarily because of land and land development costs, mobile home parks were quite capital intensive. The United California Bank estimated that a typical mobile home park would cost $5,350 per space in 1973. Since most new parks had a minimum of 100 spaces and some had as many as 600, a substantial amount of capital was required.

Although a shortage of sites still existed, some positive trends were evident. As mentioned earlier, an estimated 40% of the dealers had become park owners, and some manufacturers as well had started park operations to provide dealers with locations for their homes.

An increasing number of new parks were being developed as subdivisions where a mobile owner could buy a lot. Other parks were set up as condominium or cooperative ownership systems. While such arrangements offered stability and added legitimacy to mobile home communities, they also increased the possibility that mobile homes would be classified as real property and regulated accordingly.

Manufacturers

At the end of 1972 there were 334 mobile home manufacturers in 811 different factory locations. According to *Automation in Housing*, the top 10 manufacturers had 45% of the mobile home market in 1972. (See Exhibits 2 and 3 for data on the major manufacturers.) Manufacturing for the most part was an assembly operation with few integrated producers. Most plants were small, averaging 64,000 square feet, with a capacity of 25–40 units per week. The industry's manufacturing strategy was greatly influenced by transportation costs (averaging $1 per mile) which made low-price homes, representing the majority of sales, only competitive within a 200–500 mile radius. The many small plants contained fairly simple equipment, and the workforce was apt to be unskilled and nonunion and was often paid on an incentive basis. Little knowledge of design, engineering, and construction was considered necessary, thus facilitating entry into the industry. Product improvements by one producer could easily be copied by others, and most manufacturers concentrated their design efforts on ways to lower material costs while retaining an overall attractive appearance for their products.

Dealers were usually serviced by local plant salesmen. A manufacturer often added new brands to his line and then offered these brands to new dealer networks in the same market area as his other outlets.

EXHIBIT 2

Operating comparison of major mobile home manufacturers

	Redman Industries Dallas, Texas		Skyline Corporation Elkhart, Ind.		Champion Builders Dryden, Mich.		Fleetwoo Enterpris Riversid Calif.	
Fiscal 1973 sales breakdown:								
Mobile homes	68%		85%		65%		56%	
Motor homes	2		3		27		14	
Travel trailers	2		12		3		28	
Modular housing	...		...		...		2	
Conventional housing	17		...		...		...	
Mobile home parks	n.a.		...		5		...	
Building products	11		...		...		...	
	100%		100%		100%		100%	
*Plants in operation:**	MH	RV	MH	RV	MH	RV	MH	
End fiscal 1970	15	1	24	6	18	6	20	
End fiscal 1972	18	2	30	7	24	9	28	
End fiscal 1973	27	5	33	11	26	14	35	
End fiscal 1974†	32	7	34	13	35	15	38	
Number of brands, 1973:								
Mobile homes	13		12		8		7	
Travel trailers	3		4		1		6	
Motor homes	4		3		3		4	
Other data:								
Mobile home dealers—1973	2,800		3,500		3,000		3,000	
Mobile home brands produced per plant	3–4		4–6		1		2	
Mobile home brands sold nationally	5		4		1		6	

* Plus 8 building products plants for Redman and 13 component plants for Champion.
† Announced plans for fiscal 1974.
n.a. = not available.
Source: Annual reports and casewriter's estimates.

Little national advertising was used, although manufacturers did some cooperative advertising with their dealers and held periodic trade shows to promote their products. Quality control in the design and assembly of the product, however, had become an important sales factor since many buyers had experienced problems with product quality and the industry had received criticism on this aspect of their operations.

There had been a proliferation of manufacturers in the late 1960s as the industry experienced large increases in demand. These included not only small firms but also large corporations such as Boise Cascade, National Gypsum, and Inland Steel which acquired established manufacturers. Several large conventional homebuilders, such as Kaufman & Broad and National Homes, had also diversified into mobile homes. The net effect of such changes was that, while in 1969 the industry produced

XHIBIT 3

inancial comparison of major mobile home manufacturers

	Redman Industries Dallas, Texas	Skyline Corporation Elkhart, Ind.	Champion Home Builders Dryden, Mich.	Fleetwood Enterprises Riverside, Calif.
les				
1969	128.8	181.2	72.4	86.5
1970	146.0	211.0	90.2	122.6
1971	148.8	252.4	113.8	154.1
1972	226.5	326.8	206.1	258.2
1973	310.3	357.4	291.0	354.1
Annual growth: 68–72	29%	32%	41%	49%
et income				
1969	5.4	8.6	2.7	3.4
1970	6.0	11.1	3.6	5.1
1971	5.2	14.4	5.1	7.0
1972	7.4	19.8	11.4	11.6
1973	9.5	17.9	16.4	12.9
Annual growth: 68–72	37%	45%	88%	62%
tal assets				
1969	32.2	37.7	23.0	22.1
1970	41.4	43.5	30.8	33.2
1971	49.9	60.2	37.4	41.5
1972	86.7	82.6	68.6	76.2
1973	126.2	96.5	92.2	111.9
73 assets:				
Cash and investments	3.8	34.0	8.0	17.8
Accounts receivable	22.4	22.9	14.6	25.8
Inventory	22.8	8.9	31.1	24.8
Plant and equipment(net)†	20.6	29.7	37.7	36.4
Other	56.6	1.0	0.8	7.1
	126.2	96.5	92.2	111.9
ong-term debt				
1969	7.9	...	1.5	...
1970	18.7	...	3.1	...
1971	20.4	...	4.2	...
1972	19.1	...	4.0	...
1973	14.5	...	2.7	...
etax margins(%)				
1969	8.4	10.1	7.8	8.5
1970	7.9	11.1	8.8	8.9
1971	6.6	11.3	9.2	8.8
1972	6.0	11.8	10.9	8.8
1973	5.7	10.1	11.0	7.7
eturn on equity (%)				
1969	41.6	50.9	30.2	41.6
1970	27.0	43.3	29.6	33.4
1971	16.7	39.6	29.9	30.5
1972	20.1	38.5	45.6	32.7
1973	20.9	26.4	42.7	21.0
ock data				
1972 average:				
Stock price	29	51	17	36
P-E ratio	19	30	35	33
ice ranges:				
1972	20–38	28–74	8–26	22–50
1973	10–23	14–33	5–15	9–27
4–30–73:				
Stock price	11	15	6	9
P-E ratio	7	8	13	7

* Dollars in millions. Data for fiscal years ending March, May, February, and April.
† Plant and equipment at cost for the four firms: $28.1, 38.6, 48.1, 44.0.
Source: Annual reports, S&P reports, casewriter's analysis.

close to capacity, in the next three years almost 10 million square feet of plant space was added, bringing the industry to an overcapacity situation by 1973 of 720,000 units annually. Most major companies had also announced significant capacity additions for 1973.

A situation of excess capacity during slowing demand could lead to tougher competition and possible price cutting. The effect of such moves was expected to be increasing concentration through attrition and merger as smaller firms were eliminated because dealers usually excluded their products first when demand slowed; large manufacturers with national purchasing power could obtain substantial cost advantages; larger firms were usually able to keep credit lines open during tight money conditions; and tighter construction standards, expected in the industry, could be complied with more effectively by larger firms.

THE FUTURE

For 1973 the Mobile Home Manufacturers Association had officially predicted a growth rate of 8% to about 625,000 units. For the first four months of the year, however, shipments had totaled 202,210—almost 15% above 1972—and some experts were predicting another banner year. Also, from January to April, mobile homes accounted for 22.6% of all housing starts and 35.9% of single-family housing starts, the highest penetration level ever.

Nevertheless, for the long run, few in the mobile home industry expected the high growth rates of the 1960s and early 1970s to continue indefinitely. Most observers agreed, however, that continual product upgrading would result in larger increases in dollar sales than in unit sales and total growth could be substantially enhanced by the industry's ability to penetrate the relatively untapped international, second-home, and commercial markets.

Fleetwood Enterprises, Inc.

ONE of the largest mobile home and recreational vehicle manufacturers in the world in 1973 was Fleetwood Enterprises, Inc., of Riverside, California, with sales of over $350 million. Fleetwood's growth from 1964 to 1973 had been spectacular, with sales and earnings increasing at annual rates of 40% and 45%, respectively (see Exhibits 1 and 2). For the year ended April 29, 1973, however, earnings had risen only 18% from 1972 as a result not only of several temporary factors such as rising material costs and price controls but also of fundamental problems experienced in the company's modular housing and mobile home park activities. As a response to the slowed earnings growth, Fleetwood's management in early May 1973 was considering a final divestiture of the modular housing business. Management also had to contend with an environment of increasing pessimism about the future of the mobile home and recreational vehicle industries, a pessimism that had driven Fleetwood's stock to its lowest price in three years.

COMPANY HISTORY

In 1950 John Crean, a Navy veteran running a small mobile home supply company, perceived a growing demand for low-cost housing and established the Fleetwood Trailer Company in Paramount, California, to produce low-price mobile homes. After some success, Crean expanded into travel trailers in 1951 and higher price mobile homes in 1952. By 1955, however, the company's rapid growth was beginning to cause problems. William Weide, president of Fleetwood in 1973, described the ensuing events:

339

EXHIBIT 1

FLEETWOOD ENTERPRISES, INC.
Income Statements*
(in thousands of dollars)

	April 30 1967	April 28 1968	April 27 1969	April 26 1970	April 25 1971	April 30 1972	April 29 1973
Sales†	$33,231	$51,877	$86,541	$122,609	$154,132	$258,189	$354,137
Cost of sales	28,396	43,139	71,873	100,063	125,224	210,243	292,969
Gross profit	$ 4,835	$ 8,738	$14,668	$ 22,546	$ 28,908	$ 47,946	$ 61,168
Selling, general and administrative	3,325	5,275	7,293	11,550	15,371	25,223	35,486
Income from operations	$ 1,510	$ 3,463	$ 7,375	$ 10,996	$ 13,537	$ 22,723	$ 25,682
Interest income	24	34	43	80	495	680	1,502
Income before tax	$ 1,534	$ 3,497	$ 7,418	$ 11,076	$ 14,032	$ 23,403	$ 27,184
Income taxes	735	1,769	4,017	5,932	7,040	11,651	13,329
Net income before extraordinary item	$ 799	$ 1,728	$ 3,401	$ 5,144	$ 6,992	$ 11,752	$ 13,855
Extraordinary item‡	...	...	...	...	...	...	(988)
Net income	$ 799	$ 1,728	$ 3,401	$ 5,144	$ 6,992	$ 11,752	$ 12,867
Income per share:§							
Before extraordinary item	$ .08	$ .18	$ .34	$ .50	$ .66	$ 1.09	$ 1.21
Extraordinary item	...	...	...	...	...	...	.09
Net income	$ .08	$ .18	$ .34	$ .50	$ .66	$ 1.09	$ 1.12

Analysis

1. Items as a % of sales							
Cost of sales	85.5%	83.2%	83.1%	81.6%	81.2%	81.4%	82.7%
Selling, G & A	10.0	10.2	8.4	9.4	10.0	9.8	10.0
Income from operations	4.5	6.7	8.5	8.9	8.8	8.8	7.3
Net income	2.4	3.3	3.9	4.2	4.5	4.6	3.6
2. Stock price range‖	1–3	3–12	8–19	7–21	15–39	22–50	9–27
P/E ratio range‖	3–16	7–35	16–37	10–31	14–36	20–46	8–24
3. Dividends per share	.03	.04	.05	.08	.08	.12	.12
4. Return on average equity	23.2%	38.1%	41.6%	33.4%	30.5%	32.7%	20.9%

* 52-week period for all fiscal years.
† All amounts restated for poolings of interest and stock splits.
‡ Extraordinary item related to Diversified Communities.
§ Based on shares outstanding as indicated in Exhibit 2.
‖ For calendar years. Stock price rounded to nearest dollar. 1973 through April 30.
Source: Company records and casewriter's analysis.

John had the right idea originally. He started with a low-cost product for the low-income market—the guy who at that time was earning $75 a week. John then lost sight of what the public wanted and ran into trouble by moving into other products. Near bankruptcy in 1955, he decided that he could not build something for everyone, and correctly cut back to just the Fleetwood line of economy-price mobile homes.

FLEETWOOD ENTERPRISES, INC.
Condensed Balance Sheets and Funds Flow
(in thousands of dollars)

Assets	4-30-67	4-28-68	4-27-69	4-26-70	4-25-71	4-30-72	4-29-73
urrent assets:							
Cash and investments ...	$2,049	$ 2,939	$ 3,118	$ 9,307	$ 7,149	$12,485	$ 17,790
Receivables	1,492	2,014	4,364	6,807	11,276	22,256	25,843
Inventories	1,636	1,994	6,211	4,155	7,636	15,418	24,808
Other current	101	151	195	510	639	928	2,337
Total current assets	$5,278	$ 7,098	$13,888	$20,779	$26,700	$51,087	$ 70,778
ixed assets (at cost):							
Land	*	*	$ 1,855	$ 2,923	$ 1,520	$ 2,816	$ 4,232
Buildings..............			5,029	7,360	12,885	19,517	31,445
Machinery.............			1,596	2,155	3,522	5,268	8,321
	2,372	3,971	8,480	12,438	17,927	27,601	43,998
Less depreciation	560	813	1,376	2,389	3,865	5,224	7,559
Total fixed assets	1,812	3,158	7,104	10,049	14,062	22,377	36,439
ther assets	151	151	151	151	...	...	...
vestment in and advances to partnership†	...	...	...	...	$ 741	$ 2,700	$ 4,650
Total assets	$7,241	$10,407	$21,143	$30,980	$41,503	$76,164	$111,867
Liabilities and equity							
urrent liabilities..........	$3,908	$ 5,625	$10,741	$12,079	$15,380	$30,305	$ 34,765
hareholders equity:							
Common stock ($1 par)	$ 565	$ 1,130	$ 2,375	$ 4,950	$ 5,310	$10,970	$ 11,470
Capital surplus	389	...	2,525	3,934	3,945	8,749	28,001
Retained earnings	2,379	3,652	5,502	10,017	16,868	26,140	37,631
	3,333	4,782	10,402	18,901	26,123	45,859	77,102
Total liabilities and equity	$7,241	$10,407	$21,143	$30,980	$41,503	$76,164	$111,867

Analysis

urrent ratio	1.35	1.26	1.29	1.72	1.74	1.69	2.04
ventory turnover	17.3	22.8	17.5	19.2	21.2	18.2	14.7
ays receivables	16.4	14.2	18.2	20.4	26.6	31.3	26.6
ook value per share	$ 5.89	$ 4.23	$ 4.38	$ 3.82	$ 4.92	$ 4.18	$ 6.72

Funds flow

ources:							
Net income		87%	50%	50%	83%	52%	35%
Depreciation and non-cash expenses		13	9	11	17	8	10
Equity sales		...	41	39	...	40	55
ses:							
Plant and equipment increase		84%	70%	40%	65%	54%	54%
Dividends		10	4	5	7	5	4
Working capital increase		6	26	55	28	41	42
otal funds (thousands)		$1,895	$6,959	$8,700	$8,446	$22,679	$36,302

* No detail available.

† Advances to Diversified Communities converted to notes receivable from Azimuth Equities, Inc., during fiscal
973.

Source: company records and casewriter's analysis.

In addition to paring his product line, Crean also developed many of the policies still operative at Fleetwood in 1973. During one of his most difficult periods, he listed the policies that were followed in successful times and those that seemed to creep in during bad times. The company was firmly committed to the former policies, such as selling only for cash, producing to order, and having no debt, and these formed the basis for a statement of corporate policies that was given to all Fleetwood managers.

In 1956 with a successful one-plant operation, Crean perceived opportunities in new markets. Mobile homes could not be moved far because of high transportation costs, so new plants were opened in Texas, Idaho, Georgia, Ohio, and Pennsylvania in 1956, 1957, 1958, 1960, and 1962. To manage these widespread units, Crean developed a unique organizational approach as described by Weide:

> John had always been an entrepreneur and felt that every individual in the company with him should also be an entrepreneur. Each plant was incorporated as a separate subsidiary, and the plant manager, set up in business for himself, was paid mainly on his plant profits. Fleetwood Management Company at the corporate level was formed with John as president, Dale Skinner as general manager, and a few functional managers, including myself. All corporate salaries were identical at that time, since John's philosophy was always "if I make a dollar, you make a dollar, too."

By 1964 with all six plants operating successfully and producing 3,800 mobile homes, Crean decided to reenter the abandoned businesses. The Broadmore line of medium-price mobile homes was introduced, and three plants were quickly put into operation near Fleetwood plants in California, Texas, and Idaho. In late 1964 the company acquired Terry Coach Industries, an established manufacturer producing about 1,500 travel trailers yearly in one California plant. Crean felt that the Terry line was too high priced, however, and went into a workshop himself in 1966 to develop the Prowler, a lower price travel trailer.

Fleetwood's acquisition policy evolved into one of buying only small, well-established companies with growth potential producing related technology products outside the company's existing product lines. In July 1969, Pace-Arrow, a small manufacturer of motor homes, was purchased. Rapid growth in the motor home industry was anticipated, and Fleetwood felt that the lead time gained by acquiring an established concern could be beneficial. Additional moves were made into modular housing in July 1970 with the purchase of DeLuxe Homes and into mobile home parks in April 1970 on a joint-venture basis with a real estate developer.

Despite these acquisitions, Fleetwood's expansion was mostly internal.

From 1967 to 1973, 12 new products were introduced and 40 new plants were added as sales grew tenfold and the sales mix shifted more to recreational vehicles. To keep pace with such growth, the company underwent several reorganizations. Although control and operating systems increased in sophistication, Fleetwood's basic policies and business philosophies remained unchanged.

FLEETWOOD PRODUCTS

In 1973 Fleetwood manufactured and sold a broad line of factory built housing and recreational vehicles under 18 different brand names. Weide described the company's basic product philosophy:

Most simply, we have always tried to build a better mousetrap. We strive to build products that give the consumer more value for the dollar than those of our competitors. We have been able to do this by not making the initial innovative efforts in the industry. Through improving the tested ideas of others we have not stubbed our toes as much, and consequently can give the consumer a higher quality product for a lower price.

Mobile homes

The largest segment of Fleetwood's business was mobile homes, which accounted for 56.3% of 1973 sales, down from 80.6% in 1967. The company's mobile home market share, as measured in units, had increased steadily from about 3% in 1967 to 5.4% for the first quarter of 1973. Fleetwood, with 31,575 units produced in fiscal 1973, was the fourth largest mobile home manufacturer; in dollar sales, however, it was third behind Skyline and Redman. This difference in position was caused by the company's higher percentage of double-wide (24 feet) mobile home sales, 22% as compared to 15% for the industry as a whole.

Fleetwood sold its mobile homes under seven brand names: Fleetwood, Glenbrook, Festival, Suncrest, and Sandpointe designed for the low-price market, and Broadmore and Barrington for the medium-price market. Several models were available in each brand in 12-foot, 14-foot, and 24-foot widths and in 44-foot to 70-foot lengths. While all seven mobile home brands were similar structurally, the price differences resulted from the use of different materials and more luxurious furnishings, appliances, and appointments.

Fleetwood was unique in the industry in that all its established brands were sold nationally with no geographical variations in design, specifications, or wholesale price. The rationale for producing a limited number of national brands was explained by Gerald G. Biddulph, financial vice president:

Ever since 1956 when we first moved into multiple plants, the design and materials content of our products have been tightly controlled by the corporate headquarters. Since we produced a standardized product, a single brand name and price nationwide made sense. In this aspect we are quite different from most of our competitors who allow their plants much more flexibility in design, brands, and pricing.

Fleetwood's growth in mobile homes had followed a definite pattern. A new brand was first introduced in one plant, usually in California not far from company headquarters. When this plant was operating profitably, plants were built in other markets and dealers in each market area agreed to carry the brand. With this first dealer network established, a supplemental mobile home brand, designed to gain additional market penetration through a second group of dealers, was then added to each plant. This strategy had been followed consistently as Glenbrook was added to Fleetwood plants, Suncrest to Festival, and Barrington to Broadmore.

Loren Schmidt, vice president of mobile home operations, described the company's mobile home business:

We have primarily aimed at the lower price end of the market since this is where we believe the greatest potential lies. More people buy Fords and Chevies than Cadillacs and the same holds true for the mobile home business. We create a high-value product that is relatively simple and service-free, with no frills or special deals.

We would rather have only one mobile home brand produced in each plant since this would result in greater production efficiencies and would avoid problems we run into with our first dealers when a second dealer network is set up. Still, using two brands per plant is one method to accomplish the objectives of filling the plant's capacity and increasing our market share in each area. I believe that using several brands in each plant might jeopardize dealer loyalty.

Fleetwood had made one excursion into the higher price mobile home market with the introduction in 1968 at a Riverside plant of the Berkshire line, a 24-foot double-wide home with a wholesale price of about $11,000. The single Riverside plant had achieved an annual sales level of almost $5 million and had been operating at a slight profit before being closed in late 1972. Schmidt explained:

We don't like to cancel any product, and so it was painful to drop the Berkshire. Nevertheless, a one-plant operation of marginal profitability draws almost as heavily on corporate staff as does a multiplant division, and the higher price segment just did not have the growth potential to justify more than one additional plant in Florida. I think we have given up on this market for now and will stay in the medium- and low-price segments that we know best.

Travel trailers

Fleetwood was the largest travel trailer manufacturer in the United States, holding over 14% of the market in 1973, with sales of 36,945 units, as compared to just 3.6% in 1967. Travel trailers had slowly increased their share of the company's sales from 14.7% in 1967 to 28.1% for fiscal 1973. They contributed the highest relative profit of any product line.

Fleetwood sold its travel trailers under the brand names of Prowler, Taurus, and Wilderness (low-price units) and Terry, Intruder, and Wild Country (medium-price units). Except for one Terry and one Prowler model, each unit was self-contained with its own lighting, heating, refrigeration, sewage holding tank, and water storage tank, thus enabling the trailer to be lived in for short periods of time without utility attachments. All brands were offered in 8-foot widths and in various lengths from 16 feet to 26 feet. As with mobile homes, all six travel trailer brands were structurally similar, and price differences resulted from better materials and appointments. Travel trailer pricing was considered very competitive, but management felt that Fleetwood's units were lower priced than comparable models of other manufacturers whose prices were constantly monitored.

Fleetwood's strategy for expanding its travel trailer business was somewhat similar to that for mobile homes. Elden Smith, vice president of recreational vehicle operations, described the basic approach:

Two years ago, with only two travel trailer brands, we decided additional brands were needed to increase our market share. Terry and Prowler had the first and second dealers in each market, so Wilderness was introduced to gain a third dealer network. Then with each dealer carrying only one Fleetwood trailer, we introduced a second, supplemental product line into each plant in a different price range. Dealers thus had two Fleetwood trailers to choose from. Wild Country, Intruder, and Taurus are secondary product lines but represent business that someone else might be getting.

The introduction of a second unit into each plant also helped fill plant capacity. Through production experience, Fleetwood had been able to reduce the number of man-hours required to produce each trailer from over 150 to approximately 90, thus creating excess capacity in several plants. Bob Graham, general manager for the travel trailer division, gave his expectations for the future:

I have a fairly short-run goal of gaining 30% of the national travel trailer market. To achieve this I want to add 10 plants in the next two years to the 15 I already have on line. In addition, we are introducing a new product, a fifth wheel trailer, into all of our plants soon. We will also be working on our dealers to carry all the models produced by a plant. This is now possible with each of our plants manufacturing trailers in two price ranges.

Motor homes

In 1973 Fleetwood produced two models of motor homes. Pace-Arrow, with fiscal 1973 sales of 3,237 units, was a Class A conventional motor home offered in six lengths from 18 feet to 26.5 feet. Tioga was an 18.5-foot Class C chopped-van motor home introduced in 1972, with 1973 sales of 2,935 units. In addition, two motor homes were planned for a spring 1973 introduction. Southwind was to be a slightly lower price Class A home and Jamboree a lower price Class C home. All of the company's motor homes were built on Dodge chassis with wooden frames and aluminum exteriors similar to mobile homes and travel trailers. The Southwind was to be an exception since it was being offered with a steel frame.

Motor homes had been the fastest growing part of Fleetwood's business, moving to 13.4% of sales in 1973. The company's market share had grown to 3.2%, and by 1973 Fleetwood was the third largest producer of Class A and Class C motor homes in the country behind Winnebago and Champion. Management expected this growth to continue, since of the 11 plants under construction on April 30, 1973, eight were motor home plants.

Unlike mobile homes and travel trailers, each motor home plant produced only one line. Additional brands in each plant had been contemplated by management, but were not considered necessary since in May 1973 all of the motor home plants were running at a high production capacity—a situation commented on by Roark Moudy, executive vice president:

> We now find a real paradox in the motor home industry as our position does not match that of other manufacturers. We are operating near capacity with high sales expectations, while Winnebago and others are curtailing their production. Some have attributed the slowdown to fears of a gasoline shortage. At this point in time, we don't think this is too serious a threat since the country can work out some solution to the problem through governmental and diplomatic channels.

Modular housing

After a year-long search, Fleetwood had entered the modular housing business in July 1970 with the purchase of DeLuxe Homes, a profitable modular builder making single-family homes from plants in Pennsylvania and Michigan. Within a year, a new plant had been opened in Ohio and plans for two more plants were under consideration. The rationale for the DeLuxe purchase and Fleetwood's plans were explained by John Crean in the 1971 annual report:

> Our major effort during the past year with DeLuxe was aimed at integrating their management into Fleetwood's, expanding their product line, adding

management personnel, and planning market strategy in preparation for expansion into new market areas. . . .

There are many similarities in manufacturing methods and materials between mobile homes and modular housing, and we anticipate no major problems in this new phase of our business. Modular housing on a national scale must be approached with a multi-plant operation. Again, we have a great deal of experience and proven management in this area . . . we are enthusiastic about the potential of this market and our ability to share in it profitably.

After the third modular plant was opened, the DeLuxe product line was expanded into multifamily dwellings. The first attempt was a 60-unit apartment/townhouse development with a Bethlehem Steel subsidiary, Multicon Properties, which proved to be quite unprofitable. Other problems with modular homes were outlined in 1972 by Hugh Scallon, a Fleetwood vice president:

> Modular housing is a different beast than mobile homes. It requires more flexibility and ability to react to local situations. Also, modular producers frequently become involved in on-site work. The industrial relations aspect is different. Construction trades have greater control at the site and this backs up into the plant.
>
> Mobile homes are pretty much a standard unit which you put on the counter. Modulars, on the other hand, are different from project to project. Each developer or builder you work with has his own ideas and problems. You literally have to design and package a new deal every couple of weeks.[1]

The various problems encountered with modulars led to substantial losses as summarized below:

Year ending	Sales	Units sold	Aftertax profits (loss)
April 30, 1971	$5.4 mm	448	$216,000
April 30, 1972	$6.6 mm	588	($1,267,000)
April 30, 1973	$8.0 mm	750	($930,000)

The Ohio and Michigan plants were closed in August and October of 1972. Each plant was operating far below its capacity of about $8 million in sales. The original Pennsylvania plant operated profitably at a higher level of capacity and had a well-established network of 78 dealers, primarily small unit developers buying single-family homes. Fleetwood, however, had not participated in Operation Breakthrough, and none of its modular homes were produced under subsidized programs.

Fleetwood's original purchase of DeLuxe in July 1970 had been for 720,000 shares of common stock which at that time was selling for about

---

[1] "Fleetwood Enterprises—Growing through Strong Management," *Automation in Housing,* February 1972.

$10 a share. DeLuxe's founder, Donald Meske, had a long-term employment contract and had stayed on as the modular division manager after the purchase. In 1973 he proposed buying back the remaining modular plant in Pennsylvania in return for 100,000 shares of Fleetwood stock. The proposed transaction did not include the two closed modular plants which Fleetwood was attempting to sell separately.

In early May 1973, Fleetwood's management was seriously contemplating Meske's offer, although acceptance would result in a large additional extraordinary charge to income of almost $1,000,000 after tax or about 9 cents a share.[2] With the outlook for the modular housing industry in 1973 rather uncertain, Roark Moudy expressed the feelings of many Fleetwood managers about the DeLuxe decision:

> The modular industry has not yet become mature enough to guarantee that multiple plants can be operated at a high enough level of capacity to warrant our involvement. A one-plant business draws heavily on financial and managerial resources at the division and corporate level. Because of our divisional structure, we cannot do profitably what a single entrepreneur can do with one plant.

Mobile home parks

Fleetwood's first and only effort at forward integration had been the formation in April 1970 of Diversified Communities on a joint-venture basis with Azimuth Equities, a real estate development firm. Diversified's primary purpose was to develop mobile home parks and to market Fleetwood's modular homes. Three parks were undertaken altogether, none of them set up as exclusive outlets for Fleetwood homes. Diversified handled modulars for only a short period of time, although it did form the highly unprofitable Multicon project.

In early 1973, Fleetwood decided to terminate its involvement in the joint venture by exchanging all of its stock for 20% of Azimuth's equity which, by the end of fiscal 1973, was written off completely for an extraordinary charge of $988,000. The balance of Fleetwood's advances to the partnership of $4.6 million was rearranged as notes payable from Azimuth over a five-year period.

FLEETWOOD'S OPERATIONS IN 1973

Organization

Prior to 1968, Fleetwood had been organized into two groups: corporate functional staff and plant operations. In 1968 the company was

---

[2] The extraordinary charge would be the aftertax difference between the book value of the modular business—$2,049,000—and the market value of the stock received.

reorganized into five divisions, and in November 1972 the company underwent another reorganization, the essence of which was to give more autonomy and responsibility to each division through the decentralization of all product development activities (see Exhibit 3 for the latest organization). Vice presidents for production, marketing, and supply remained at the corporate level in primarily an advisory capacity, although the vice president for supply negotiated with large vendors that sold to more than one division and the vice president for production headed a small engineering staff.

Division management teams were located at company headquarters in Riverside in identical separate buildings positioned around corporate headquarters. Management considered the main advantages of the new organization to be enhanced responsiveness to changing markets, decreased span of control, strengthened entrepreneurial initiative, and facilitated growth through easy addition of more divisions. Even with a divisional structure, however, major product and market decisions such as price increases, new products, plant addition or expansion, and changes in the procedure manual were made by corporate management.

Corporate headquarters was separately incorporated, and all plant subsidiaries paid management fees to headquarters based on plant profits. Out of these fees incentive bonuses were paid to both corporate and divisional management. As was also the practice at the plant level, corporate and divisional management received a low base salary and high quarterly cash bonuses. For example, during fiscal 1973, Weide was paid a $16,714 base salary plus $87,344 in incentive compensation and Moudy a $16,500 salary and $86,712 in bonuses.

Plant operations

Even though Fleetwood's 57 plants, located in 21 states and Canada, produced different types of products, there were many similarities in their operations. All of Fleetwood's plants were basically similar; they were of simple construction, contained little sophisticated equipment, and required an average capital outlay of $500,000 with additional working capital requirements of $250,000. The plants were somewhat smaller than average for the industry, but, according to Loren Schmidt, small plants were "easier to manage and control and had lower break-even points," which ranged between 25% and 30% of capacity. Plants could be switched to a different product with minor difficulty, something that the company had done several times, although none of Fleetwood's plants produced mobile homes and RVs at the same time.

Plants were generally located in small towns where land was less expensive and unskilled, nonunion workers were available. The average beginning hourly wage was $2.40, and the average wage for assembly-

EXHIBIT 3

FLEETWOOD ENTERPRISES, INC.
Condensed Organization Chart

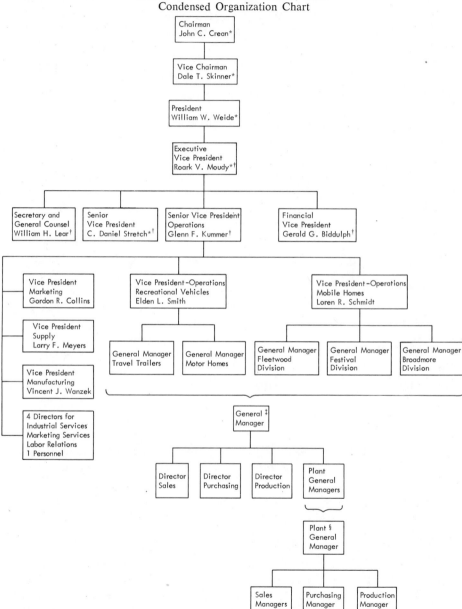

* Member of board of directors. (The board also had two outsiders.)
† Member of the executive committee.
‡ Structure of each division.
§ Structure of each plant.
Source: Company interviews.

men with over one year's experience was $3.30 before production incentives which could equal or exceed base wages. In 10 of the company's plants, production employees were represented by various unions. The union contracts were considered very weak, and there was an explicit corporate policy against union shops and dues checkoffs. Fleetwood's most recent major difficulty with unions had occurred in 1971 at its mobile home plant in Westmoreland, Tennessee, when the carpenters union had attempted to obtain a model contract to be used as a basis for eventually organizing all Fleetwood plants. Only after the plant had been closed six months did the union make major concessions, thus permitting a settlement to be reached.

Within detailed policies and procedures determined by the corporate headquarters, each plant was run autonomously by a four-man team composed of the plant general manager and the sales, purchasing, and production managers. Roark Moudy described Fleetwood's approach:

> Our system is unique in the industry since we combine decentralized plant operations with centralized services. Our competition usually stresses highly autonomous plants with little central control. Each of our plants is a separately incorporated subsidiary run by its own independent management group. I think of each plant manager as a president running his own small business. They are effective at this type of operation and they enjoy it.

Fleetwood's small procedure manual, considered the "bible" of plant operations, was described by Gerald Biddulph:

> Our procedures are designed to cover any situation a plant manager might face, and having uniform national procedures insures us of consistent handling of every situation. Through weekly meetings, the division and corporate staffs continually review the manual to stay abreast of rules guiding the plants. Over the years, while our founder's policies have remained basically unchanged, our operating procedures have been amplified and expanded. Our reporting and control systems, together with an informal internal audit system, assures adherence to the policies and procedures.

Elden Smith added to Biddulph's comments:

> One of the reasons we have been successful is because of the farsightedness of company management in requiring national uniformity of policies and procedures. My job is a lot easier when I know that all my plants are using the same methods. We have developed and refined a successful pattern that can be readily transferred to new plants.
>
> There are some violations of our policies and procedures occasionally, but we try to catch most of them. If, for example, a sales manager violates the policy of selling only for cash, he's out. We feel that our credibility is sacrificed if any manager bends the rules. The company's policies and procedures must be adhered to until changes are approved at the corporate level.

Instances when the company's procedures were compromised were attributed by Roark Moudy to "overzealous attitudes on the part of plant management in generating profits which form the basis of their compensation." The four managers in each plant comprised a plant management team. Each manager was paid a $15,000 base salary and, in addition, received incentive compensation based on a straight percentage of the plant's quarterly profits after overhead allocation.[3] These bonuses were paid quarterly in cash and raised the average plant manager's compensation to $50,000 and the three functional managers, all of whom received the same bonus, to $40,000. On a few occasions plant managers had made over $100,000 a year. While management knew that this method of compensation could encourage a short-run viewpoint, most attributed much of Fleetwood's success to the entrepreneurial zeal created by such incentive compensation.

In the late 1960s, as Fleetwood recognized the rapid increase about to take place in the number of its plants, a training program was established for plant purchasing, sales, and production managers. By 1973 about 200 people had gone through the program, which consisted of from six to nine months of basically on-the-job training in the plants. The progress of trainees was well monitored by corporate and division headquarters. The training program was important to Fleetwood since the company's top managers repeatedly stressed that the greatest resource problem facing the company was the shortage of competent plant management.

A profile of plant management is as follows:

	Ages		Longevity		Education		
	Average	Range	Average	Range	High school or less	Some college	College graduate
Plant general managers	38	28–56	4.5 years	4 months–15 years	27%	28%	45% ·
Plant functional managers	33	26–47	3.75 years	1–5 years	11%	28%	61%

Purchasing

Since the largest cost component in Fleetwood's sales dollar was purchased component parts, the purchasing function was accorded substantial importance in the company, an importance, management felt, that was much greater than its competition gave it. This enabled Fleetwood to hold its margins better in times of rising costs. Purchasing was

---

[3] Except for some direct charges, overhead from corporate and divisional headquarters was allocated equally to all plants.

performed at all three organizational levels: corporate, divisional, and plant. Corporate policy of maximizing inventory turnover allowed only 10 days' supply at the plant level.

Larry Meyers, vice president of supply, summarized the company's relations with its vendors:

We value our relationships with suppliers very dearly. We want to be the best account they have and we don't play games with them. If somebody underbids an established vendor, we will give him a chance to beat the price before we switch. In general, we are considered a "no fuss" account. We pay our bills on time, everything is done aboveboard, and there is integrity in all aspects of our relations.

Except for limited fabrication of frames, Fleetwood did almost none of its own component parts manufacturing. Some members of management felt that there was substantial profit potential in backward integration, especially in the production of plastics, windows, and lumber. Others felt that these activities in the long run were not profitable. Elden Smith expressed such a viewpoint:

I suppose that a little bit of vertical integration would be nice, but even that can hurt. Plastics, for example, are often the first choice, but there are so many innovations that by making your own components you are often stuck with an outdated design. We want to always have the best and most advanced components.

Larry Meyers, who was charged with responsibility for investigating components production, gave his opinion: "Our experience is solely in assembling and selling a quality product. We have little expertise in running a parts manufacturing plant. Our relationships with our suppliers are so strong that we get very competitive prices anyway because of our volume."

Marketing

For both mobile homes and RVs, Fleetwood's products were concentrated in low-price classes with some products in middle-price ranges. Price changes were generally made only to reflect cost increases; as explained by Gordon Collins, vice president of marketing, there had "never been a policy to price what the market would bear. We have always attempted to keep our prices as low as possible to give the customer most value for his dollar." All Fleetwood prices were set by corporate headquarters. Unlike other manufacturers, the company had a uniform national price for all products and no discounts or price reductions were granted. There were no suggested retail prices, even for recreational vehicles, as dealers were allowed to sell the company's products in line with competitive conditions in each market. Management estimated that the average dealer markup was 20% to 25%.

By 1973 Fleetwood's products were sold through almost 4,800 dealers located in 49 states and Canada. Most dealers handled several competitive product lines, and the average dealer was small, accounting for about $72,000 of Fleetwood sales (see Exhibit 4). Fleetwood avoided

EXHIBIT 4

FLEETWOOD ENTERPRISES, INC.

Dealer Data

	Mobile homes			Travel trailers			Motor homes*	
	1969	1971	1973	1969	1971	1973	1971	1973
Total number of dealers	847	1727	2944	258	566	1253	69	559
Number of plants	17	26	35	5	8	15	1	6
Dealers per plant	49.8	66.4	84.1	51.6	70.7	83.5	69.0	93.2
Fleetwood sales per dealer:								
Dollars (thousands)	$79.0	$63.7	$67.7	$57.5	$61.4	$79.2	$55.3	$84.9
Units	17.1	11.8	10.7	23.5	24.5	29.5	7.4	11.0

* Motor home data for 1969 not included since Pace-Arrow was acquired July 1969.
Source: Company records and casewriter's analysis.

selling to large chain dealers. Collins explained: "We would rather not put our eggs in one basket—we prefer the small, independent dealers. Also, I would rather have a competitor's product on the dealer's lot; I don't think that exclusive dealers are best."

Fleetwood did not enter into written dealer agreements. Selection of dealers was handled exclusively by plant sales managers;[4] the only corporate input was a credit check on all new dealers. Fleetwood had no formal requirements for dealer size, inventory level, facility, or capabilities, but sales managers were expected to consider all these matters in judging a dealer's ability to represent the company adequately. Management considered dealer turnover too high and wanted "to get it down to a more manageable level of about 15%." Unlike other manufacturers, Fleetwood's marketing philosophy would not permit use of special dealer incentives such as deals, gifts, or free trips. "Our products are of highest quality and we try to sell them in a consistent fashion," claimed one manager.

Fleetwood offered a one-year warranty on all its products. The warranty was virtually identical for mobile homes, travel trailers, and motor homes and covered primarily assembly of the units and the limited parts manufactured by Fleetwood. Warranties on purchased components such

---

[4] Unlike other manufacturers, Fleetwood in its mobile home plants employed a separate sales manager in each plant for each brand the plant produced.

as appliances were provided by original equipment manufacturers. The company had not engaged in practices employed by other mobile home and RV manufacturers, such as training dealer personnel, setting up factory service centers, or requiring dealers to give full service. However, to improve the service offered by its dealers, Fleetwood had added in 1972 a service supervisor to each of its mobile home plants.

Fleetwood first began to advertise in the early 1960s; by 1973 a small program of primarily trade advertising existed, with total expenditures equal to less than 0.5% of sales. The rationale for limited advertising was given by Elden Smith:

We feel, and we try to point this out to our dealers, that our units have better value for the price since they are not burdened with expensive advertising overhead. This goes back to a basic company philosophy. If we can succeed and not spend heavily on advertising, then both we and our customers will be better off.

Finance

Although each plant had its own accounting system and accountant, the finance function was highly concentrated in the Riverside headquarters; all cash was centralized in one bank account, and cost records and trial balances were accumulated monthly from the plants. Since several of Fleetwood's top managers had backgrounds in public accounting, quite sophisticated control and reporting systems had been developed. Boyd Plowman, the company's treasurer, outlined them:

I think Fleetwood has probably the most extensive control systems in the industry. Our cost accounting includes standard costs for all units and is updated each quarter. We also prepare very detailed budgets on a quarterly basis and a somewhat rougher forecast for an 18-month period. Each of our budgets is revised. and completely rewritten monthly. For the longer run we have a feel for sales projections, but there are no formal five- or ten-year plans.

The absence of long-range planning was explained by Elden Smith: "Things happen so fast in the company and our time frame is so short that we just don't think in five-year terms. When you are growing at 50% a year, as we have been, how can you?"

Fleetwood's financial policies were quite conservative. All plant start-up and engineering expenses were written off in the year incurred. Unlike most of its competition, the company leased but three of its 56 plants since its policy was to own facilities whenever possible. The company also had a strict policy against any long-term debt as explained by Gerald G. Biddulph: "The no-debt policy comes right from our chairman. He has vivid recollections of the depression and times when he was in financial difficulties because of debt, and vowed never to have any again." However, since much of Fleetwood's growth had been financed with equity offerings,[5] the policy against debt was being examined carefully in 1973 as the company's stock had fallen to a low of $9 per share on April 30, 1973, from a high of $49.50 in May 1972.

The decline in Fleetwood's stock price was potentially significant for company management since several held large blocks of the stock, all of which had been acquired without stock options. The 1973 proxy statement revealed that of the 11,470,000 shares outstanding, Crean owned 3,012,360 (26%), Skinner 93,800, and Weide 37,800. Nevertheless, most members of management were "philosophical" about the decline as described by Weide: "I don't understand why they are treating the industry as they are in the marketplace. My philosophy is that there is not much we can do about it anyway. The stock has been down before and it will come up again."

Gerald G. Biddulph, who directed the company's financial community relations, offered another reason:

> The mobile home and recreational vehicle industries have never been totally believed in by money managers and security analysts. They are mainly from the East and don't understand or appreciate the basics of our business since they have little day-to-day contact with our products.

Corporate management

Fleetwood's management at the corporate level was a close group that had worked together for some time. This collegiality had several roots. Most of the management team came from the western United States and their common cultural experiences were reflected in a casual "no suit and tie" atmosphere at corporate and divisional headquarters. Many members of management also had backgrounds as CPAs (see Exhibit 5) and shared the religious beliefs of the founder, beliefs that fostered the corporate policy of having an extremely cost-conscious, straightforward approach to doing business. Fleetwood had few fringe benefits and no stock options, company cars, lunch rooms, personal secretaries, or expense accounts for entertainment. Roark Moudy explained:

> Our philosophies are consistent. We pay our management people well for high performance and if they want to use their money for personal investments such as stock purchases, health plans, insurance, or pensions, that's their decision. It's their money to spend and the company does not dictate what they have to do with it. Also, if a sales or purchasing manager wants to take a supplier or dealer to lunch, the benefit should show up in increased performance for his plant and thus increased compensation for him. We feel

---

[5] The original offering had taken place in March 1965; subsequent stock offerings had been made in July 1968, January 1970, November 1971, and May 1972.

FLEETWOOD ENTERPRISES, INC.
Biographical Data on Management

Name, position and date attained	Age	Years with company	Previous positions in company	Employment prior to company	College education
John C. Crean Chairman 3–70	47	23	President	U.S. Navy Mobile Home Supply Co.	None
Dale T. Skinner Vice Chairman 12–71	50	21	Exec. V.P. President	Various construction and real estate activities	University of Nebraska, 2 years
William W. Weide President 2–73	49	15	Controller Asst. V.P. Senior V.P.	Finance and accounting in several companies	U.S.C. B.S.—Accounting
Roark V. Moudy Exec. V.P. 10–72	37	5	Asst. Controller GM–RV Div. V.P.–Operations	Arthur Andersen & Co.	California State B.S.—Accounting
Glenn F. Kummer Senior V.P.–Operations 10–72	39	7	3 Plant positions GM–RV Div. Asst. V.P. V.P.–Operations	Ernst & Ernst	University of Utah B.S.—Accounting
Gerald G. Biddulph Financial V.P. 10–72	31	5	Asst. Controller Controller Treasurer Vice President	Arthur Andersen & Co.	Utah State B.S.—Accounting
C. Daniel Stretch Senior V.P. 3–70	47	12	2 Plant positions Dir.–sales, supply V.P.–Operations	Self-employed	University of Georgia
Elden L. Smith V.P.–Operations Recreational Vehicles 10–72	32	4	Plant Manager GM–RV Division Asst. V.P.–Operations	Aerospace firm	Whittier College B.A.—Business
Loren R. Schmidt V.P.–Operations Mobile Homes 10–72	41	6	Division Manager Asst. V.P.	Various mobile home companies	Bethel University B.S.—Business
William H. Lear Secretary and General Counsel 8–71	34	2	None	Various other corporate legal positions	Yale University—B.A. Duke University—J.D.

that such policies allow us to offer products of maximum value at lowest possible prices.

Larry Meyers stated: "We really epitomize the American way of doing business in this company. We stress total free enterprise and profit motivation. All the opportunity and responsibility you might want is here in return for hard work."

The future

The vague goal of "a billion dollar" company was one expressed by many members of management. Fleetwood as a company, however, made no specific projections. Weide explained why and gave his expectations for the future:

I would rather feel that we don't have a sense for how much we want to grow. Setting specific goals forces a predetermined limit and publicly announcing a growth program might put us in a position of having to apologize. We really just want to wind up at the highest level we can, and if that means being a billion dollar company with 200 plants, then so be it.

Everyone in the company has some personal goals. Most of us would like to have the largest market shares in each of our businesses and to be No. 1 in compensation. We are far from such goals, but we constantly keep striving for them.

As regards our basic businesses, we can't be successful if we try to force the market—we must simply let it develop. We've moved away from those areas where we didn't have expertise and I think we will concentrate on maximizing our opportunities in mobile homes and recreational vehicles. Most other options are on the back burner for now.

Introductory note on Central America

Linking the two great continents of the New World is an isthmus commonly known as Central America. Although the land area is only 200,000 square miles (slightly larger than California) and the population somewhat less than 14 million, the isthmus is divided into six nations, among them Guatemala, El Salvador, Honduras, Nicaragua, and Costa Rica. Panama, the sixth country, has chosen over the years to remain apart for numerous political and economic reasons and consequently will be referred to only tangentially in this note.

Industrialization was slowly gathering force in Central America in the 1950s, sparked in part by the hope that in the future a common market would be formed to provide local manufacturers with wider opportunities. This note provides a brief description of the area and some of the factors which might influence the decision to invest in it in the mid-1950s. (See map in Exhibit 1.)

EARLY HISTORY

The Maya civilization, which had flourished in the Yucatan Peninsula in what is now Guatemala and Honduras, had substantially disintegrated in the century prior to 1502 when Columbus explored the coast in his last attempt to find the passage to the East. Balboa and Pizarro followed Columbus in search of gold and power, bringing the Catholic Church with them. Political control was eventually consolidated from 1523 to 1539 by Alvarado, one of Cortes' lieutenants, in Antigua (Guatemala).

EXHIBIT 1
Central America

When Spanish rule was peacefully cast off in 1821, a brief union with Mexico and several, often bloody, attempts at confederation ensued in the next two decades. However, each province developed separately under its own leadership, and the possibility of political union was overshadowed by a strong sense of national identity that has persisted to the present day.

DEMOGRAPHIC AND SOCIOECONOMIC CHARACTERISTICS

Some indication of population density is given in Table 1. Population statistics should be viewed with caution, however, especially those for Guatemala in which over half of the population were Indians who lived essentially outside the money economy. In El Salvador, Honduras, and Nicaragua more than 90% of the people were of mixed blood with little social discrimination. On the other hand, the population of Costa Rica was almost entirely of European stock. Central America had one of the highest population growth rates in the world (3.5%) which resulted in a "young" population (in Honduras 60% of the population was 19 years of age or younger).

TABLE 1
Central American population statistics

Country	Square miles	Population (in thousands)	Population/ square mile
Guatemala	42,642	4,420	105
El Salvador.	8,164	2,850	348
Honduras	43,277	2,135	49
Nicaragua	57,143	1,655	29
Costa Rica	19,575	1,425	74
Panama	28,576	1,160	41
	199,377	13,645	68

The capital city was by far the dominant urban center in each country in terms of population, wealth, commerce, and industry (see Table 2).[1] Each supported several newspapers and radio stations. The capitals, aside from Tegucigalpa, were connected by good roads or railroads to seaports which historically constituted for the agriculturists an outlet to world markets and for mercantile interests a means of securing manufactured goods for local consumption. In recent years the Pan American Highway had been built through Central America, linking the six countries as shown in Exhibit 1. The highway spurred the construction of subsidiary roads which had the effect of opening portions of the interior to increased traffic and commerce, though a considerable amount of it, especially on the Caribbean coast, remained isolated. Concurrent with this trend was a rapid increase in the number of automobiles and slow but steady progress in rural electrification.

Although the distribution of wealth was uneven throughout Central America, there were differences among countries. Exhibit 2 provides

TABLE 2
Population of capital cities

Country	Capital city	Approximate population
Guatemala	Guatemala City	480,000
El Salvador	San Salvador	280,000
Honduras	Tegucigalpa	125,000
Nicaragua	Managua	200,000
Costa Rica	San Jose	150,000

---

[1] With the exception of Honduras, in which San Pedro Sula in the north rivals Tegucigalpa in significance.

EXHIBIT 2
Socioeconomic characteristics of Central America

Country	Total no. of households	Urban households (percent)	Rural households (percent)	Socioeconomic class*			Literacy rate	Average income per capita (1961) (U.S. $)	Average income per household (1961) (U.S. $)
				Class A–B	Class C	Class D			
Guatemala.	764,000	35	65	10%	35%	55%	25%	$176	$ 985
El Salvador.	502,000	39	61	10	30	60	47	220	1,100
Honduras.	367,000	23	77	5	30	65	47	207	1,180
Nicaragua	258,000	41	59	5	25	70	38	213	1,300
Costa Rica	243,000	34	66	10	40	50	88	344	2,000

* Approximate incomes in each class: Class A–B: More than $300/month.
Class C: $100–$300/month.
Class D: Less than $100/month.

Source: Compiled from industry records and from information contained in *Proposed Mutual Defense and Assistance Programs FY 1964*, Agency for International Development (Washington, D.C.: U.S. Government Printing Office, 1963).

some data on this and other socioeconomic indicators for the area. Some English was spoken along the Atlantic Coast but otherwise the language was Spanish. Literàcy ranged from less than 30% in Guatemala to 88% in Costa Rica.

ECONOMIC CONDITIONS

The Central American economy depended heavily on agriculture to provide employment (two thirds of the work force were engaged in agriculture) and generate the foreign exchange necessary to finance imports and consequently was very sensitive to world commodity prices. The crop varied from country to country, although coffee tended to be the dominant one, and the top two generally accounted for 70% to 90% of the total. In all cases, the United States was the principal trading partner in the mid-1950s, followed by Germany (see Exhibit 3).

EXHIBIT 3
Foreign trade in Central America in the mid-1950s

	Principal exports	Percent	Percentage of total accounted for by U.S.*	
			Exports	Imports
Guatemala	Coffee	75	65	60
	Bananas	12		
El Salvador	Coffee	79	40	48
	Cotton	11		
Honduras	Bananas	58	52	60
	Coffee	17		
Nicaragua	Cotton, raw	36	37	55
	Coffee	17		
Costa Rica	Coffee	52	51	50
	Bananas	41		

* The second largest trading partner was generally Germany.
Source: *The South American Handbook* (New York: John T. Clark & Son, 1961).

The economies of Central American countries exhibited two characteristics which were unusual in much of Latin America. First, inflation was relatively minor, averaging from 1% to 3% a year. Second, the dollar exchange rate for local currencies, with the exception of Costa Rica, had been unchanged for many years, dating back to 1898 in the case of the Guatemalan quetzal. In Costa Rica, the colón had fluctuated in value relative to the dollar, but the net deterioration in the rate of exchange had been slight. Moreover, there had been a relative absence of currency controls; that is, funds could generally be converted into foreign currencies and removed from the country.

Tariff duties on most manufactured imports were substantial. As a means of attracting investment in industry, however, all governments employed tax incentives. For instance, it was common for investors to be granted an import duty exemption for all materials and equipment necessary to set up a factory and possibly for raw materials that could not be supplied locally. The investor might also secure an income tax exemption for a number of years. Finally, he might request, with a lower probability of success, that the tariffs on competing imports be raised to put him in a more favorable competitive position.

In the postwar years a gradual shift was occurring in Central America away from a complete dependence on agriculture and toward limited degrees of industrialization. This trend was typically manifested by the substitution of locally made goods for imports. However, there was little trade among Central American countries. Imports from other Central American countries had to surmount the same high tariffs as those from the United States and Europe.[2] Also, there was a strong consumer feeling that locally manufactured goods were inferior to U.S. and European products. As a result, markets continued to be dominated by importer-distributors who held the exclusive rights on high-quality U.S. and European merchandise.

The importer-distributor, consequently, occupied a position of considerable power in the Central American distribution system. One observer noted:

In El Salvador, for instance, less than 50 such importer-distributors handle the bulk of all Salvadoran imports, while at the same time performing the major part of the wholesaling activities in the country as well as selling at retail. Typically, these importer-distributors required an exclusive national franchise before they would agree to handle the products of any given manufacturer and tended to make a high markup (typically 10% to 20% when selling to wholesalers and retailers, but in some instances ranging up to 100%) for their services. This was true in spite of the fact that in most cases they carried overextended product lines and provided spotty coverage of retail outlets (very often not bothering at all to sell outside the capital city) and generally unaggressive marketing support. The position of power of these importer-distributors was reinforced by the fact that they tended to be the only firms within the distribution system that were strong enough financially to carry substantial inventories or to extend all-important credit to undercapitalized wholesalers and retailers.

At the retail level, prices of manufactured goods tended to be relatively high. On the theory that the uneven distribution of wealth pre-

---

[2] During the mid-1950s, there was some talk among the various Central American countries of the possible formation of a common market, which might lead to the ultimate elimination of tariffs between member countries and the establishment of common external tariffs. However, the outcome of these exploratory talks was still extremely uncertain.

vented the development of mass markets for most consumer goods, retailers preferred a "high margin–low volume" pricing policy and carried
a large, thin inventory.[3] The only exceptions to this pattern were one
or two relatively low markup food or department stores in the capital
cities. In addition, the central market, consisting of many stalls, sometimes out-of-doors, continued to be an important center of trade in towns
and cities.

POLITICS: DOMESTIC AND INTERNATIONAL

The political system in Costa Rica varied from that of the other
Central American republics in that Costa Rica supported a vocal, active
democracy. That is not to say that the others were harsh dictatorships.
Rather, they were for the most part run by strongmen, generally duly
elected and supported by the wealthy and in large measure by the
"campesinos" (rural dwellers) as well. There were no guerrillas of consequence which posed a threat to the stability of the government. For
brief periods in the postwar decade, both Costa Rica and Guatemala
were governed by coalitions including Communists but both were over-
thrown by conservative elements.

Despite the fact that the United States had intervened in Central
American politics on numerous occasions, including the presence of
marines in Nicaragua on peace-keeping duty from 1912 to 1933, relations
with the "Colossus of the North" were by and large very cordial. There
was comparatively little openly expressed hostile sentiment toward North
Americans or toward other foreigners for that matter. In business, various
kinds of working arrangements including licensing agreements and joint
ventures were common. There were no laws requiring local ownership
in industrial ventures, though it was not unusual for a well-placed private
investor to be sought as a means of securing entry to the market.

---

[3] Bank credit for working capital was available, although not always easy to
obtain. Interest rates were 12% per annum or higher.

The Central American paint market

INDUSTRY STRUCTURE

DURING the early 1950s only imported paints were sold in Central America.[1] For the most part, these imported paints came from the United States, although there were a few minor imports from Europe. As of the early 1950s, the leading brands on the paint market were those of the following companies in estimated order of importance:

1. Hathaway Paint Company[2] (U.S.).
2. Du Pont (U.S.).
3. Excello, Inc.[2] (U.S.).
4. Standard Paint Company[2] (U.S.).
5. California Paint Company[2] (U.S.).

These companies all sold their paint in Central America through what were known as "distributors." Typically in each country there were 10 to 15 of these distributors, each of whom held the rights to import and market a given brand of paint in that country. These distributors typically carried a variety of products, some of which might be related to paint (e.g., building materials and supplies, hardware, wallpaper) and some of which might be completely unrelated (e.g., whiskey, typewriters). Distributors operated one or more retail outlets of their own through which they made the bulk (80% to 90%) of their sales. At the

---

[1] Guatemala, El Salvador, Honduras, Nicaragua, Costa Rica.
[2] Some company names and financial figures have been disguised.

same time, they also functioned as wholesalers, reselling paint to a few hardware and variety stores located in or about the capital city but at substantial distances from their own retail outlets.

Sales through these "subdealers" were usually quite small and almost never accounted for more than 10% to 20% of a given distributor's total volume. Only in rare instances did distributors maintain outside salesmen to sell to subdealers, and almost never did they attempt to obtain subdealers outside the capital city. Thus, they tended to be "distributors" more in name than in fact. Rather, they might better be thought of as large retail dealers who imported paint directly from manufacturers in the United States and Europe.

Almost without exception distributors and subdealers restricted themselves to carrying the brands of only one paint manufacturer. In part this was because carrying the brands of a second manufacturer would have required tying up too much money and space in inventories; in part it was also due to the fact that most manufacturers objected to having local dealers carry competing brands.

Most of the imported paints were of high quality and were relatively expensive, retailing from $7.50 to $8.50 per gallon. Of this amount, import duties represented about $1.50 to $1.75.[3] When selling direct to the painters or the public, the distributor's margin ranged from 30% to 35% of the retail selling price. Distributors took 5% to 10% of the retail price as margin when selling to subdealers, who, in turn, received 25% of the retail selling price. The distributors were important sources of credit to both the subdealers and painters, often carrying their accounts for 60 to 180 days.

Most of the initiative for expanding the market came from local distributors rather than the U.S. paint companies. Generally speaking, the U.S. company managements considered the Central American countries to be too little and too fragmented to warrant major attention. Several of the U.S. companies, having originally been sought out by the agents in Central America, had never bothered to send a sales representative to visit the area.

PAINT MARKETING

Paint tended to be an infrequently purchased product. Moreover, its purchase was often regarded by consumers as part of a major investment which also included paying for the services of a painter. According to industry executives, "professionals" were used for most home painting jobs, while the "do-it-yourself" market was extremely limited.

---

[3] Import duties varied somewhat from country to country from year to year but tended to average out at about $.20/gross kilo plus 15% ad valorem. (A gallon of prepared paint weighs approximately five kilos.)

There was general agreement within the paint industry that in choosing a particular brand and type of paint, consumers tended to rely heavily on the advice of the painter or of a paint dealer.[4] In fact, in many cases the person whose home was being painted left the final decision up to the painter.

Typically, the first step taken by a person interested in having painting done around his house would be to engage an independent painter or a paint contracting company. The two parties would then discuss the nature of the job, the type, quality, color, and brand of paint to be used, and the price to be charged. In some cases, the price quoted by the painter or contracting company included the cost of the paint itself, while in other cases only labor was included. In the latter case, the homeowner either bought the paint from the dealer himself or else the painter bought the paint and presented the dealer's bill to the homeowner, who then made payment directly to the store.

Regardless of how the paint was obtained, the painter or contracting company usually tended to recommend strongly the brand of paint sold by his "favorite" dealer. In deciding which dealer's paint to recommend, the painter was typically motivated by several factors.

First, the paint sold by the dealer had to be of "acceptable" quality. However, since the paint handled by all dealers in Central America met this criterion, the final choice usually depended on other factors. The most important of these were, in rough order of importance:

1. The size of the discount offered by the dealer to the painter.
2. The amount of credit which the dealer was willing to offer the painter, not only on the paint itself but on other paint supplies.
3. The warmth of the personal relationship between the painter and the dealer.
4. The services offered by the dealer, including color mixing, advice on difficult paint problems, delivery, etc.
5. The breadth of the product line offered by the dealer in terms of price-quality levels, types of paint, and colors.
6. The convenience of the dealer's location for the painter.

The first of these factors, the discount to the painter, requires some explanation. In all the Central American countries it was a common practice for independent painters and paint contractors to ask for and be given a special "discount" by paint dealers. The size of the discount was typically 5% to 10% for independent painters and 10% to 20% for large paint contractors. Painters and contractors expected to be given this discount regardless of whether they purchased the paint on behalf of their clients or whether the client himself purchased the paint from the dealer. In the latter case, the payment of the discount was usually

---

[4] "Dealer" refers to either the paint outlet of the distributor or the "subdealer."

arranged after the fact between the painter and the dealer and without the knowledge of the painter's client. Once having established a satisfactory relationship with a given paint dealer, the painter usually tended to remain fairly loyal unless a major falling out occurred.

According to industry spokesmen, painters and paint contractors had a variety of ways to insure that their clients followed their advice to use the paint sold by a particular dealer. As one person in the industry put it:

If the painter's client insisted on using a brand of paint sold by a different dealer than the one recommended by the painter, then the painter might water down the unwelcome paint before applying it. Then when the client later points out that the paint job doesn't look very good, the painter will tell him it is the fault of the inferior paint which the client has insisted on using. Since the word of this sort of thing gets around pretty quickly, homeowners are usually inclined to go along with the painter's recommendations.

During the middle 1950s the size of the Central American household paint market amounted to somewhat less than one million gallons. Costa Rica, El Salvador, and Guatemala each accounted for about one quarter of the total, with one eighth going to Honduras and one eighth to Nicaragua. Most sales were made to the household market. Automotive and industrial sales were negligible.

Sales to the government, on the other hand, typically accounted for a stable 10% of the market in most Central American countries. Large consumers of paint within the governments included housing ministries, government-owned utilities, transportation ministries, local municipalities, etc.

Bids for government business were submitted by the company's distributor in each country, who, in most instances, operated a "captive" paint contracting service and hence was able to bid on the total paint job.

PAINT MANUFACTURING

From a technical point of view, the making of household paints was quite simple. Basically, it involved the following steps:

1. Mixing a white or colored pigment in powdered form with a liquid vehicle (e.g., linseed oil and turpentine or synthetic resins) to form a stiff paste.
2. Grinding the paste in a roller mill, or some other grinding machine, until it had reached a specific consistency.
3. Thinning the mixture with turpentine or some other thinner and tinting it to the proper shade with additional pigment.
4. Putting the paint in cans and attaching a label.

The technology required was readily available from many independent suppliers of paint-making equipment and raw materials. In specialty paints—such as automotive lacquers, anticorrosive paints, and industrial paints—technical know-how was more important and more difficult to obtain.

The minimum capacity for an efficient and flexible plant was 600,000 gallons per year, for which the required investment in land, building, and equipment was estimated at $300,000. It was possible to construct less efficient and flexible plants of smaller size. However, the investment required for land, building, and equipment would not decrease proportionately to size. For example, it was estimated that a 150,000-gallon-per-year facility would require an investment of $150,000. Fixed costs were estimated at $100,000 per year, covering manufacturing overhead (such as maintenance, utilities, insurance, etc.) as well as a minimum labor force to run the plant. Above a 150,000-gallon output labor costs were expected to increase by approximately 30 cents per gallon. Raw material costs were estimated between $1.50 and $2.50 per gallon depending on the quality of the paint. In addition, selling and administrative expenses as well as financing charges would have to be covered.

Note on the watch industries in Switzerland, Japan, and the United States

AN OVERVIEW OF THE WORLD WATCH INDUSTRY IN 1970

As BEST as can be estimated, worldwide watch and watch movement production in 1970 reached the level of 175 million units. At manufacturers' selling prices this production had a value of about $1.3 billion. Pin-lever watches constituted slightly more than half of the total output; jeweled-lever watches made up the rest with the exception of 1%–2% of the total which belonged to a variety of electric and electronic models.[1]

Since the early 1950s, when worldwide watch production was at an annual rate of about 45 million units, the output of the industry had increased fourfold. In the 10 years leading up to 1970, worldwide output increased at annual rates that ranged between 7% and 11%. Talk about market saturation persisted among some watchmakers, yet as of 1970 the overall growth of the industry had not shown any noticeable sign of slowing down.

Table 1 shows the origins of the 1970 output.[2]

These figures in Table 1 illustrate several important points. The first is a well-known one: Switzerland is far and away the dominant watch-making nation. In 1970 its production amounted to 42% of worldwide output.

---

[1] For a brief guide to watch technology, see Appendix A.

[2] The data presented in Tables 1 through 5 were calculated from information provided by the Federation of Swiss Watchmakers.

TABLE 1
Leading watchmaking nations—1970 (millions of watches and watch movements)

Country	Production	Exports	Exports as percent of production
Switzerland	73.7	71.4	97
Japan.	23.8	13.7	58
U.S.S.R.	21.5*	1.8	8
United States	20.0*	0.2*	1
France	11.0	4.1	37
West Germany.	8.2	4.1	50
Mainland China	5.0*	. . .	. .
East Germany	3.5	1.8	51
United Kingdom	3.2	1.0	31
Italy	2.6*	0.6	23
Others	2.0*	. . .	. .
Total.	174.5	98.7	

*Estimated.

The second point is less well known: there is considerable production in countries currently outside the mainstream of Western commerce. In 1970 output in the U.S.S.R., East Germany, and mainland China represented about 17% of the world total. For the time being, at least, the bulk of this output stays within the Eastern bloc. Accordingly, the communist countries, and in particular the Soviet Union, will be excluded from this note's analysis of the struggle for the world watch market.

With the Eastern bloc out of the picture, the Swiss domination of watchmaking becomes all the more striking. In 1970 every other watch made in the noncommunist world came from a Swiss plant.

The third point has to do with how the watchmaking industries in Switzerland, Japan, and the United States are linked to world markets. In 1970 Swiss watchmakers exported virtually all of their output, Japanese firms exported slightly more than half of their output, and American companies exported almost none of their output. In the case of the United States, the largest watch market in the world, domestic production accounted for slightly less than half of its needs. Imports, some from foreign firms and some from U.S.-controlled plants sited overseas, filled the void.

While data on the production of watches by country are readily available, figures on market size by country are hard to come by. Still, rough estimates by major geographical areas are possible. In 1970 Europe in total represented a market about equal to that of the United States: watch purchases in both markets ran at an annual rate of around 45 million units. In the same year, Japan's home market was about a third of the size of those in Europe or the United States. And as for the rest of the world (excluding the communist countries), its market roughly matched that of Europe and of the United States.

The remainder of this note examines the three watchmaking industries that, as of 1972, were the most active contenders for dominance in these markets. The Swiss, Japanese, and U.S. industries are discussed in the next three sections. The last section of this note discusses the recent technological advances and economic developments up to 1976 that have turned the contest into competitive turmoil.

THE SWISS WATCH INDUSTRY

Watchmaking, long presumed the private preserve of Swiss interests, has in the last decade or so clearly become a field that's up for grabs. The Alpine republic's one-time international hegemony in the timekeeping business is now almost as full of holes as the country's justly famed cheese.

Value Line Selection and Opinion

"Ridiculous!"

Executive Director, Watchmakers of Switzerland
Information Center

Industry highlights in 1970

Watchmaking has always occupied an especially important place in the Swiss economy, and the year 1970 was no exception. Roughly 1,000 different firms and 80,000 employees were engaged in making $630 million of watch and watch-related products.[3] Watchmaking contributed almost 3% to the total Swiss GNP; in that year it was Switzerland's fourth largest industry and it employed close to 8% of all manufacturing workers.

Of necessity, the Swiss economy depends heavily on exports, and watches have routinely been one of the country's major foreign exchange earners. In 1970 about 97% of total watch production was shipped outside the Swiss borders. Valued at $610 million, these shipments represented 12% of total Swiss exports, making watches the country's third most important export product.

In 1970 watchmaking contributed to the Swiss economy in still another important, if intangible, way. As the Swiss Bank put it:

The long-standing repute of the Swiss watch industry also provides another free benefit to the Swiss economy. Being a typical symbol of quality and

---

[3] Unless otherwise indicated all data originally stated in Swiss francs have been converted into U.S. dollars at the 1970 exchange rate of 4.3 Swiss francs to one U.S. dollar.

reliability it acts as an advertising medium for other Swiss products. Swiss industry, due to the absence of low-cost natural resources, is often at a disadvantage, in terms of cost, when competing against other countries' products. Therefore, the reputation of the Swiss watch does help to publicize the quality of the "Swiss-made" brand and acts as a powerful sales argument.

Not only was the Swiss watchmaking industry important at home, it was important to the world. Excluding production in communist countries, every other watch made in the world in 1970 came from Switzerland. And three quarters of all watches exported from any country in 1970 came from Swiss plants.

Though the Swiss hold on the world market in 1970 was impressive, it was not so impressive as it had been several decades earlier. In the late 1940s the Swiss share of worldwide production was over 80% and the Swiss share of watch exports, from all sources, was around 95%. In response to those who talked about the weakness of the Swiss industry, pointing out that its share of the world market had been cut in half during the 1950s and 1960s, the Swiss answered by referring to the threefold growth in their watch production. Back in the late 1940s the Swiss industry produced around 25 million watches and watch movements each year; by the early 1970s the industry was producing annually at close to the 75-million-unit rate. Employment in the industry had actually increased slightly since the post–World War II years. In the Swiss view the dramatic growth in their watch output represented a considerable achievement and indicated that Switzerland would remain the dominant watch-producing nation for years to come.

Swiss exports in 1970

Since, for all practical purposes, the Swiss export all the watches they make, it is necessary to look at the composition of exports in order to understand Switzerland's competitive position in foreign markets. By production category, the 1970 Swiss exports are shown in Table 2.

TABLE 2
Swiss watch exports by stage of production—1970

Category	Percent of exports in value terms
Finished watches	77.0
Watch movements	12.5
Miscellaneous watch components (including a small amount of clock exports)	10.5

The percentages in Table 2 were almost identical for jeweled-lever and pin-lever watches.

By type, Swiss exports of *finished* watches and movements are shown in Table 3.

TABLE 3
Swiss exports by type of watch—1970

	Units (millions)	Value (U.S. $ millions)	Average value per unit (U.S. $)
Jeweled-lever	38.3	440	11.50
Pin-lever	32.7	85	2.62
Electric-electronic	0.3	8	26.00

Tables 2 and 3 make one point quite clear. In 1970 the export of finished jeweled-lever watches constituted the core activity of the Swiss watchmaking industry. Anything jeopardizing this segment could jeopardize the entire industry.

Table 4 shows, by major geographical region, where the Swiss exports went in 1960 and in 1970. Several points stand out. First of all, Swiss

TABLE 4
Swiss exports by major geographical regions—1960 and 1970
(for watches and watch movements combined)

	Percent of total exports in unit terms			
	Jeweled-lever		Pin-lever	
	1960	1970	1960	1970
Europe	26.2	32.7	18.2	21.7
Africa	3.9	4.9	10.7	5.7
Middle East	7.8	14.4	1.2	2.8
Asia	13.3	11.6	9.4	26.2
USA–Canada	31.6	22.3	45.2	36.2
Latin America	14.5	12.1	15.1	7.1
Oceania	2.7	2.0	0.2	0.3

exports of jeweled-lever watches have been somewhat more dispersed than those of pin-lever watches. Second, during the 1960s, the U.S.–Canadian market declined in its relative importance to the Swiss while the European market became more important to them. And third, by 1970 Asia had become a major market for Swiss pin-lever watches. When looking at these figures, bear in mind that the value of jeweled-lever exports was almost five times that of pin-lever exports. Consequently, the shifts in market that took place with jeweled-lever watches had a far greater effect on the value of exports than did those that took place with pin-lever watches.

Table 5, which lists all the countries to which the Swiss shipped a million or more watches in 1970, rounds out the export picture.

TABLE 5
Swiss exports of watches and movements to
major markets—1970 (for all types of watches)

	Percent of total units	Percent of total value
United States	27.4	20.2
Hong Kong	14.2	10.0
United Kingdom	8.7	5.5
Arabia	4.8	3.8
West Germany.	4.1	5.7
Italy	3.7	6.5
Spain	3.6	3.8
Argentina	2.2	2.2
Brazil.	2.1	1.9
Canada	1.9	1.5
Mexico	1.6	2.0
Japan	1.4	3.7
Total.	75.7	66.8

As Table 5 indicates, 11 countries imported the bulk—three quarters in unit terms and two thirds in value terms—of Swiss watch production. As the world's largest watch market, the United States was, quite naturally, number one in importance to the Swiss. Yet, as suggested by Table 4, the Swiss share of the U.S. market has been eroding steadily. In fact, in 1950 99% of all watches imported into the United States were of Swiss origin; by 1970 this figure had dropped to around 70%. In the same period, the Swiss share of total watch consumption in the United States had declined from 50% to about 40%.

The number two export market for Switzerland in 1970, Hong Kong, was a recent arrival on the scene. One item largely accounted for the rapid emergence of Hong Kong as a Swiss customer. By 1970 almost 85% of all pin-lever movements (not finished pin-lever watches) made in Switzerland were destined for Hong Kong where they were cased and subsequently scattered over many Far Eastern markets. Determining who actually controlled what part of the Hong Kong trade in 1970 was an almost impossible task. Several Swiss pin-lever manufacturers had assembly plants in Hong Kong, yet local interests were also involved in the business. About all that could be said was that Hong Kong had become an important channel through which Swiss pin-lever watches reached many overseas markets.

One final point brought out in Table 5 needs mentioning. Note that Japan, the second largest watchmaker, was not a major market for the Swiss. This fact has certainly had a bearing on how the Swiss have viewed the competitive problems facing their industry. Whereas in any sort of contest among Swiss, Japanese, and U.S. watchmakers the Swiss could afford to give up their place in the Japanese market, they could not afford to see their hold on the U.S. market seriously jeopardized. As we shall see in a subsequent section, in 1970 the United States was also Japan's leading export market. It follows that if the 1970s were to see a struggle for leadership in the world watch industry, the battle would take place principally in the U.S. marketplace.

Fragmentation: The Swiss industry's main problem

One fact, mentioned at the beginning of the preceding section, is the key to the number one problem that faced Swiss watchmakers in 1970. The industry, which included around 1,000 different enterprises, was far more fragmented than that in any other leading watchmaking nation. To understand why this was so calls for a brief review of the development of watchmaking in Switzerland.

Early development

The Swiss did not invent the watch. Over 300 years ago the rudimentary techniques of watchmaking were brought to Switzerland by Huguenots fleeing religious persecution in France. At first they settled around Geneva; subsequently they spread throughout northwest Switzerland.

For better than a century and a half several factors combined to foster a very independent, family-oriented spirit among the early watchmakers. In part, watchmaking was a craft which depended on skills being passed on from one generation to the next. In part, where many of the watchmakers lived, in relative isolation in the mountains, prompted a very independent view. And in part, the fact that each family fabricated a few complete timepieces each year nourished a sense of a distinct family watchmaking tradition. By and large, the attitudes formed then, described by some as a stubborn individualism, persisted into recent times.

In the first half of the 1800s, in response to advances in mechanization, individual producers started to specialize: some families concentrated on making parts, others on assembling parts into finished watches. By the mid-1800s the industry had evolved into a two-tier manufacturing system with component manufacturing separate from watch assembling.

With few changes, the industry retained this characteristic up to the mid-1950s. Yet mechanization did not break down the small individual unit structure of the industry.

By 1900 watchmaking in Switzerland far outpaced that taking place anywhere else in the world. But the industry was made up of thousands of small family-owned firms. Though the Swiss dominated watchmaking on a worldwide scale and had established "Swiss made" as a symbol of quality in watches, they had done so with an industry ill equipped to cope with anything other than the most superficial economic difficulties. The crises of the 1920s and 1930s made this painfully apparent to the Swiss.

The industry's and the government's response: 1920–30

In the early 1920s Swiss watchmakers saw sales collapsing and unemployment soaring. They set out to bring order out of the chaos by organizing themselves into a number of industry associations, each made up of firms engaged in the same type of manufacturing operations. The associations that sprang up in the period 1924–27 were:

1. The Federation Suisse de Fabricants d'Horlogerie (FH): those firms assembling watches from component parts supplied by others plus those few firms with integrated manufacturing operations. All of the output of member firms was of the jeweled-lever type. These were the firms that actually sold watches in the marketplace.
2. Ebauches SA: 17 manufacturers of ebauches grouped together into a trust.
3. The Union des Branches Annexes de l'Horlogerie (UBAH): the manufacturers of components other than ebauches.

The formation of these associations laid the foundation for industry cartelization. In 1928, in a series of restrictive private agreements among the three major associations, the manufacturing, pricing, and exporting policies of member firms were brought under industry control.

No sooner had the watchmakers taken these steps when the depression of the 1930s got underway. Deteriorating conditions in the industry forced the Swiss government to come to its aid. As a first step, the government, in 1931, invested in a super holding company, the Société Générale de l'Horlogerie Suisse SA (ASUAG), which, in turn, acquired the majority of the shares of Ebauches SA and of several of the leading components manufacturers. This move eased the financial woes of a number of the watchmakers and made the government a direct partner in industry affairs. Then, in 1934, a federal statute ratified the web of the industry's private controls and imposed new ones; thereafter, watch manufacturing and exporting were permitted only with government approval. From 1934 through 1965, the structure of the Swiss watchmaking industry and the makeup of the many restrictive covenants under which it operated remained almost unchanged. A list of the principal government-sanctioned rules of the industry includes the following:

1. The members of Ebauches SA and UBAH agreed to sell components only to the members of FH.
2. In turn, the members of FH agreed, with one exception, to buy components only from member firms of Ebauches SA and UBAH. The firms in FH did reserve the right to buy foreign-made components, but they also agreed not to buy such components unless they were priced more than 20% under the Swiss level.
3. In addition, the members of FH agreed to fix their selling prices in accord with a complex interassociation pricing system and a markup formula. Ebauches SA and UBAH supplied the components at specified prices, subject to change only after interassociation negotiation. And the watch assemblers and integrated manufacturers established their prices using a standard markup above association-determined manufacturing costs.
4. Finally, FH members agreed to limit their guarantees on finished watches to one year.
5. As regards government rules, firms could only engage in watchmaking after obtaining authorization from a federal department. The federal legislation effectively froze the structure of the industry: firms could not expand, move, sell out, acquire others, or change the nature of their operations without government approval.
6. In addition, the government rules regulated the Swiss industry's links with the rest of the world. To preserve order in overseas markets, firms were required to obtain permits to export finished watches, movements, and components. More importantly, to insure that new foreign competitors would not spring up and that existing foreign competitors would not benefit from advances in Swiss technology, government approval was required for the export of tools and dies, engineering drawings, and watchmaking machinery.

This elaborate system, designed to protect the status quo in a highly fragmented industry, persisted for almost 40 years. Yet by the late 1950s events in the marketplace were making it obvious that something had to change.

The breakdown of the watch cartel

Discontent with the cartel arose first among the member firms of FH, for they were the ones who had to meet competition face to face.

Despite the Swiss attempt to pen up watchmaking technology, during the 1950s foreign rivals expanded production and began to make inroads into Swiss sales. On the continent, French and German watchmakers cut into the Swiss market share; in the United States, Timex imperiled at least a portion of Swiss exports; and in the Far East, where the threat was still in the offing, markets were ripe for an obviously impending Japanese invasion.

The malcontents in the FH claimed that the cartel rules protected the marginal assembling firms and fostered inefficiency among the component manufacturers. They also pointed out that, in the face of mounting price competition in overseas markets, the cartel promoted a type of conduct on the part of some watchmakers that jeopardized the quality image of the whole Swiss industry. Whereas the efficient producers were able to meet price competition, with sufficient residual profits to improve their manufacturing efficiency and the quality of their output still further, the marginal firms, in order to survive, had turned to producing low-quality watches which they dumped at giveaway prices in foreign markets.

After several years of negotiations within the industry, the malcontents won the first round of concessions. The industry agreements were revised to provide for greater leeway in the pricing of components to the FH members and in the application of the pricing formula for finished watches.

Then in 1961 the government bowed to the obvious necessity of bringing the industry up to date. It rescinded, effective as of January 1, 1966, the requirement for manufacturing permits. After that date firms were free to expand, contract, merge, sell out to foreign companies, or buy foreign companies. Thus the government move opened the way for industry concentration. As part of the same legislative package, the government established a watch standards commission to put an end to the debasement of the watches by the small producers. And finally, the government decreed that the requirement for export permits would expire in 1971. After that date there would be no official impediments to the transfer overseas of watchmaking technology.

The 1961 legislation sounded the death knell for the Swiss watch cartel. It finally died in 1966 when the industry associations abolished all the remnants of the fixed-price system.

The death of the watch cartel did not, however, spell the end for the important industry associations, which have continued to serve as spokesmen for the various sectors of the industry. Exhibit 1, which shows the composition of the industry as of 1970, demonstrates that its structure remained defined by the associations. Nor did the death of the watch cartel mean the end to joint actions among Swiss watchmakers. To the contrary, the associations have continued to be the backbone of a collec-

EXHIBIT 1
Structure of the Swiss watch industry—1970

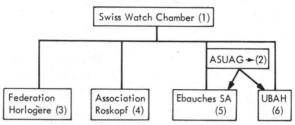

(1) The association that represents the entire industry in governmental and foreign trade matters.
(2) The holding company, 38 % controlled by the Swiss government, that owns a majority interest of Ebauches SA and of three of the largest component manufacturers.
(3) The association of jeweled-lever watch manufacturers. In 1970 it had 486 members.
(4) The association of pin-lever watch manufacturers. In 1970 it had over 50 members.
(5) A trust composed of 17 subsidiaries producing ebauches.
(6) The association of component manufacturers. It includes hundreds of small firms among its members as well as four large component producing firms or groups of firms. The four are:
  a) Fabriques d'Assortiments Réunies (escapements).
  b) Fabriques de Balanciers SA (balance wheels).
  c) Groupement des Fabricants Suisses de Spiraux (hairsprings).
  d) Pierres Holding SA (jewels).

tive approach to industry activities, especially in promotional programs and R & D projects. These collective activities will be discussed shortly, but first it is necessary to look at the steps the Swiss have taken to cope with the problem of fragmentation.

Industry concentration

In the early 1960s about 2,000 separate enterprises were engaged in one facet or another of watchmaking in Switzerland. Roughly speaking, these 2,000 firms fell into the following categories:

Finished watch manufacturers
1. About 500 firms solely assembling jeweled-lever watches.
2. About 60 integrated manufacturers of jeweled-lever watches.
3. About 70 integrated manufacturers of pin-lever watches.
Component manufacturers
4. Seventeen manufacturers of ebauches, all members of Ebauches SA.
5. About 650 manufacturers of separate parts.
6. Around 500 other firms performing miscellaneous functions.

Though these figures accurately reflect the extent of fragmentation that existed among finished watch manufacturers, they misrepresent the situation that existed among component manufacturers. Three organizations, originally trusts composed of many small companies, dominated individual parts manufacturing. They were:

Fabriques d'Assortiments Réunies SA (the major supplier of escapement mechanisms).
Fabriques de Balanciers SA (the major supplier of balance wheels).
Groupement des Fabricants Suisses de Spiraux (the major supplier of hairsprings).

Together with Ebauches SA, these three groups supplied about three quarters of the Swiss industry's requirements for ebauches and separate parts.[4] Since they accounted for such a large share of component production, it is obvious that the hundreds of other firms in the component sector either fulfilled highly specialized roles or were quite marginal firms.

As we have seen a decade later, the number of firms in the Swiss watch industry was down to around 1,000. Since 1966, when the Swiss government's restrictions on the sale or acquisition of watch companies lapsed, the industry experienced a crescendo of mergers. The Swiss were hurriedly—some observers said frantically—trying to create watchmaking firms matching the size and competitive clout of the major foreign rivals. Why the industry was caught up in the mergers' wave and where it was heading was summed up by one leading Swiss watchmaker in these terms:

For many years far-sighted representatives of the watch industry stubbornly tried to introduce new methods, to overcome outmoded structures, to eliminate the compartmentalization typical of Swiss watch production, to channel the interest of technically-minded Swiss watchmakers more into modern marketing, to overcome difficulties rooted in outmoded protectionist ideas and to surmount assorted similar problems. With few exceptions, however, they had to wait until very recently before there were any visible signs of a trend toward industry cooperation and corporate concentration.

This development is irreversible and will doubtless accelerate in the future. It is already quite conceivable that, under the growing pressure of competition from *within and without* the watch industry, there will soon be a considerable increase in the number of medium-size companies (rather than hundreds of small ones). The only product lines likely to escape this trend will be a few specialty items and exclusive products, the success of which does not depend on mass turnover.

Under these circumstances we do not think it overly bold to predict that, aside from the few exceptions mentioned, in five years there may be only about ten watch producing enterprises operating in this country.[5]

---

[4] In 1968 another holding-company-type arrangement was established within the components sector. A number of the small watch jewel manufacturers became members of Pierres Holding SA. Altogether, the members of this new group supplied about 60% of the total Swiss jewel production.

[5] Robert Brandt, "The Position of the Watch Industry," *Credit Suisse Bulletin*, December 1970. Emphasis added.

As of 1972 there was, at least on paper, ample evidence that the Swiss were succeeding at consolidating the industry. Whether the Swiss were also succeeding at converting the many newly formed companies into operationally effective organizations was still an open question. The world received a fairly steady stream of reports about mergers and plans for mergers; it did not hear much of what went on within the board rooms and corporate offices of the Swiss companies. Undoubtedly, the pains and problems of transition were taxing the managerial skills of many Swiss executives.

Still, progress looked impressive. Both horizontal and vertical mergers were changing the industry profoundly. For instance, as the result of a series of horizontal mergers, the Swiss finally had one watch company that could match the size of large foreign rivals. Founded in 1930, the Société Suisse de l'Industrie Horlogère (SSIH), the manufacturer of such famous brands as Omega and Tissot, had always been a leader in the watchmaking industry. In the early 1960s it controlled about 9% of total Swiss watch exports. But even with that share of exports, SSIH was small compared to the leading Japanese and U.S. watchmakers. Then, after 1966, SSIH broadened its activities and, in 1971, merged with Economic Swiss Time Holding (ESTH). This second group, composed of a number of pin-lever manufacturers, accounted for 20%–25% of total Swiss pin-lever output. By the end of 1971, the enlarged SSIH controlled over 20% of Swiss watch exports and had an annual turnover of close to $130 million.

ASUAG, the "supertrust" controlling a majority interest in Ebauches SA and in the three largest component manufacturers, gave birth to another large horizontal group when, in 1971, it combined the assembling firms selling seven different brands into the General Watch Holding Company. This move forged important new financial and managerial links between the component manufacturing and assembling sectors of the watch industry.

Meanwhile, Ebauches SA entered into another set of arrangements with both horizontal and vertical merger characteristics. In 1970 the Longines-Record Watch Company and the Rotary Watch Company joined to form Holdings Longines SA. Then, in 1971, Ebauches became a major partner in this new venture. As in the case with ASUAG, the Swiss joined together companies whose fundamental activities were assembling and marketing watches and simultaneously linked the amalgamation to the component manufacturing sector.

The upshot of these mergers, and dozens more, has been the creation of a partially concentrated industry. *By 1971 almost three quarters of all Swiss watch exports were accounted for by eight watchmaking groups.* But the industry structure was still lopsided. A residue of several hundred small firms contributed the other quarter of Swiss exports. Thus there was a growing gap between the big watchmaking combinations and the little independent producers. Under these circumstances, it seemed fairly certain that only one of two different futures faced most of the small companies: absorption by the big holding groups or collapse.

As for the large watch companies, the mere fact that most of them had multiplied their size through a series of mergers did not guarantee that they would enjoy the benefits of size. They still had to tackle such tasks as eliminating duplicate product lines, combining production facilities, streamlining management systems, and so on. As suggested above, in the early 1970s the evidence of progress along these lines was still sparse.

Swiss investment in the U.S. watch industry

The Swiss effort to bolster the competitive position of their industry was two-pronged. At the same time that they were concentrating it at home, they were protecting it by investing in U.S. watchmaking firms. In the second half of the 1960s they made the following moves:

1. Iseca SA, a consortium of Swiss watch manufacturers, acquired 100% of the Waltham Watch Company.
2. Sopinter SA, a Swiss holding company, acquired a 16% interest in Elgin.
3. Chronos Holding SA, a financial company set up for the express purpose of promoting amalgamation within the Swiss industry, purchased 20% of Gruen.

And in 1971 the Swiss took another step which could ultimately give them control of one of the most famous names in American watchmaking, the Hamilton Watch Company. Apart from its proud tradition in conventional watchmaking, Hamilton had been on the technological forefront on more than one occasion. In 1957 it had been the first U.S. firm to market an electric watch. In 1971, with its "Pulsar" (which used light-emitting diodes), it was the first U.S. firm to market a digital watch. Still, Hamilton came upon hard times.

The history of the Swiss move to take over Hamilton started in 1970 when Bush Universal, Inc., a diversified firm that leased piers and buildings in Brooklyn, New York, bought 50.2% of the almost bankrupt Hamilton company. Subsequently, after Hamilton's losses deepened further, Bush spun off the watch business into a new subsidiary and sold 17% of it to Aetos SA, itself a subsidiary of the leader in the Swiss industry, SSIH. Aetos, as part of the deal, also accepted a note from Hamilton which, if converted after three years, would increase the Swiss company's interest in Hamilton to 51%. Hamilton seemed destined to become a member of the Swiss camp.

The basic motivation for all these investments was fairly clear. Though the second tier of U.S. watchmakers, those that had not attained the size of Bulova and Timex, were barely able to meet the mounting competition within the industry, they all possessed one valuable asset: established trade names. To the Swiss, control of the names, in part or in whole, opened the door to increased penetration of the U.S. market. There was some evidence that the Swiss intended to fight the electronic watch battle in the United States with trade names which American consumers would assume were those of fine old U.S. watchmakers.

What else were the Swiss doing to insure the continued prosperity of their watchmaking industry?

Promotional practices

Up until the late 1960s Swiss watchmakers relied mainly on an institutional approach to promotion. They channeled a high proportion of their promotional expenditures through industrywide organizations, like the Federation of Swiss Watchmakers, into collective campaigns in overseas markets. The campaigns stressed the quality and reputation of "Swiss-made" watches rather than specific brands. Of course, a few of the larger Swiss watchmakers supplemented the industry's activities by promoting their own brands. Names like Rolex and Omega became world-renowned. Still, the sale of watches bearing established brand names constituted a small fraction of total Swiss exports. This was particularly true in the case of watches falling in the low- and medium-price categories.

As of the early 1970s this all started to change. The 1971 Annual Report of the Federation of Swiss Watchmakers (FH) described the new approach:

During 1971, the FH continued on the new course adopted after the turning point in its promotional activities in 1970, i.e., that of henceforth concentrating on designing, carrying out, and financing promotional activities with fuller cooperation from the brands involved. This change in the FH's approach to promotion consisted in a shift away from collective promotion mainly benefiting the industry as a whole in favor of programmes integrating the brands involved in every way. . . .

Even though Swiss watchmakers reallocated more and more of their promotional funds from industry to company campaigns, they still continued to support the industry's many long-standing technical programs. Since World War II, the Swiss sponsored watch-repair training schools in many countries. They established technical centers and after-sales service centers in a number of foreign markets. They frequently held seminars, in Switzerland and overseas, on a wide range of subjects related to the watch industry. And they conducted a variety of training programs covering the management, marketing, and distribution aspects of the watch business. Almost all of these efforts were collective undertakings. By and large they were regarded as essential to the success of the industry. And there were no signs that Swiss efforts along these lines would diminish in the 1970s.

Research and development

As with promotional activities, the Swiss watchmakers have tended to approach R & D from an industry rather than from an individual-firm standpoint. The two major Swiss R & D programs begun in the 1960s, both related to the development of the electronic watch, highlight this point.

In 1962 Ebauches SA, the other main component manufacturers, and a number of the watch assembling firms joined together to establish the Centre Electronique Horloger (CEH). The initial goal of the electronic watch center was to develop a new time-determining device to compete with Bulova's tuning-fork mechanism. Later, the CEH also took on the task of developing a quartz crystal watch movement. The role of the CEH was defined as extending beyond the laboratory. It was chartered to produce prototypes of new watches for the purpose of test marketing them. Once the prototypes proved themselves in the marketplace, the clients of CEH would pick them up for full-scale manufacturing and marketing.

Whether the first decade of operation of the CEH was regarded as a success or not seemed to depend on who was making the assessment. American watchmakers pointed out that the CEH failed at developing a tuning-fork device that did not violate Bulova's patents. The Swiss claimed that the CEH had come up with an acceptable alternative. Still, in 1968 Ebauches SA entered into a license agreement with Bulova to manufacture and sell watches based on Bulova's tuning-fork movement. As for research on the quartz crystal watch, the Swiss stressed that the CEH had perfected a commercial model before anyone else. Yet when the Swiss introduced their first quartz watches in 1971, American watchmakers noted that they contained integrated circuits made by U.S. firms. The Swiss had hoped to avoid this turn of events. In fact, this hope had prompted their second major R & D effort of the 1960s.

In 1966 the Federation of Watch Manufacturers (FH), two Swiss companies (Brown Boveri and Landis & Gyr), and Philips of the Netherlands formed FASEC, a laboratory for joint research in the fields of semiconductors, integrated circuits, and lasers. The purpose of the project was clear enough: to make sure that the Swiss watchmaking industry would not be dependent on U.S. electronics manufacturers.

Yet some observers interpreted the formation of FASEC as an indication of the weakness of the Swiss watchmaking industry, for it had to turn to a foreign company, Philips, for advanced electronics technology. As of 1972 there was no way for outsiders to measure what FASEC had accomplished, since Swiss electronic watches still contained American-made circuitry and the Swiss were reticent about describing FASEC's research output.

How much has the Swiss industry spent on developing the electronic watch? Unfortunately, the figures are not available to answer the question with any precision. What follows, therefore, is based on the crudest of estimates. According to some reports, the Swiss have spent around $2.5 million per year on CEH's research activities. If the Swiss industry has backed up FASEC to the same extent, the industry has been putting about $5 million a year into R & D related to the electronic watch. This figure looks respectable until it is compared to total industry turnover; it amounts to about 0.8% of industry sales. Suppose, and this is rather unlikely, that individual Swiss firms have matched the R & D expenditures of the industry-sponsored programs. Total outlays, even then, would have added up to not much more than the 1½% of industry sales.

If these figures describe, even in rough terms, the level of R & D commitment of the Swiss industry in the late 1960s and early 1970s, they raise the question of whether that commitment was high enough. It's safe to assume that the Swiss were asking themselves that same critical question.

Diversification

Throughout the last decade Swiss watchmakers have talked at length about the advantages of diversification. Yet it is fair to say that as of the early 1970s no Swiss watchmaker, big or small, was in any sense diversified. True, some produced items other than watches and clocks, but almost without exception these other goods were intimately related to the technology of timekeeping.

In the case of the many small firms, the reasons why they held fast to their narrow product lines were fairly obvious. A close family orientation, 30 years of protection under cartel rules, and a perception of their businesses in specific technical terms did not foster among the small watchmakers the inclination or the bases for diversification. And in the case of the large firms, they had been so preoccupied since the mid-1960s making and digesting mergers that it is unlikely they had either the time or the resources to pursue diversification seriously. Whatever the causes, the Swiss watchmakers faced the problems of the 1970s from a very narrowly defined business base.

THE JAPANESE WATCH INDUSTRY

A Swiss watch manufacturer was asked if the Russians posed
a threat in his business.
"The Russians!" he laughed. "They always seem to be ten
years behind."
"And the Japanese? How far behind are they?"
"About three weeks. . . ."

Jewelers' Circular-Keystone

Early development

Watchmaking started in Japan in the 1880s. For the next 50 years
Japanese watchmakers concentrated almost exclusively on supplying
their home market and on making jeweled-lever watches. They stressed
jeweled-lever production because they wanted to emulate the best in
western watchmaking. Yet, by most standards, the quality of the timepieces made in Japan in the industry's early days was inferior to that
of timepieces made in the West. And, in fact, the Swiss dominated
the premium end of the market, supplying about 90% of Japanese
imports.

By the late 1930s Japanese production of watches and watch movements had reached the level of around 5 million units per year. One
firm had emerged as the industry leader; alone it accounted for almost
one half of Japanese production. Then World War II and its aftermath
postponed further growth of the industry for almost 20 years. Japanese
watchmakers did not produce at the five-million-unit level again until
the 1958–59 period. By then, however, the industry had fully recouped
from the war, had completely retooled, and had significantly upgraded
the quality of its product. The Japanese were ready to make their presence known as a full-fledged member of the world watch industry.

The expansion of the industry in the 1960s

In 1960 Japanese production of watches and watch movements hit
the seven-million-unit level, equivalent to slightly more than 7% of worldwide watch output. Still, almost all the Japanese production was absorbed at home; the industry exported only 200,000 watches and movements that year.

Then during the 1960s Japanese watch production more than trebled
in unit terms. In 1970 the industry poured forth almost 24 million
watches and movements, about 14% of worldwide watch output. And
by 1970 over one half of this production was destined for overseas markets. Or, to put the development in perspective, the industry exported

almost twice as many watches and movements in 1970 as it had produced for total home consumption in 1960.

In part, the Japanese had pushed themselves into foreign markets; in part, they had been pulled into foreign markets. As the 1960s rolled on, the Japanese watchmakers could see that their home market was becoming increasingly saturated. Consequently, they looked overseas. They aggressively invaded the Southeast Asian market, long the private domain of the Swiss. In a somewhat more halting fashion, they started to move into Western European markets and into the United States. But in the case of the United States, the Japanese were also pulled into the market by U.S. watchmakers who imported large quantities of inexpensive Japanese movements and parts for assembly here or in 'the Virgin Islands. By the late 1960s the Japanese export push began to take on a clear pattern. Almost two thirds of all Japanese watch and watch-movement exports were destined for two markets: the United States or Hong Kong.

The growth of the industry and the success of its surge overseas was particularly remarkable because it involved so few firms.

Industry structure

In sharp contrast to the situation in. Switzerland and to the state of the U.S. industry until recent years, the Japanese watch industry has always been highly concentrated. Over the years, four firms have accounted for almost all Japanese watch production. More strikingly, two firms have accounted for almost 90% of the production. As of 1970, the industry structure was as shown in Table 6.

Obviously, K. Hattori & Co. is the General Motors of the Japanese watch industry. To understand the industry, therefore, one has to know something about this dominant leader. How did the company operate in 1970? Actually, K. Hattori was only the sales arm of a cluster of firms known as the Seiko Group. Two subsidiaries in the group, Daini

TABLE 6
Japanese watch production, 1970

Firm	Estimated share of Japanese production	Estimated production of watches and movements (millions of units)	Exports as a percent of production*
K. Hattori & Co.	60%	14	20
Citizen Watch	28	7	45
Orient Watch	9	2	60
Ricoh Watch	3	0.8	n.a.

*In terms of value.
n.a. = not available.

Seikosha and Suwa Seikosha, produced watches, movements, and components. Another subsidiary produced clocks. Still other subsidiaries manufactured products outside the timepiece field. K. Hattori managed all the sales activities for the group, marketing its products worldwide under the Seiko trade name.

By the mid-1960s the Seiko Group had become the world's largest producer of jeweled-lever watches. The reasons for Seiko's success are spelled out in the sections that follow. Bear in mind that even though the discussion focuses on the entire industry, what Seiko has done has been the key to what the industry has accomplished.

The industry's product and market strategy

Though there have been minor differences in approach among the four Japanese watchmakers, in the last two decades they all adopted more or less the same product and market strategy. As mentioned previously, the industry started out making only jeweled-lever watches. By and large, the industry has continued that practice into the 1970s. The Japanese have left pin-lever production to others.

Just because the Japanese have not made pin-lever watches does not mean that they have not competed in the low-price end of the market. To the contrary, at home and in Asian countries the Japanese have marketed a complete line of jeweled-lever watches ranging in price from the cheapest to the most expensive. Yet the main thrust of their marketing attack has been in the medium-price category. They have matched their competitors, mainly the Swiss, in terms of quality and feature of watches but have undercut them in terms of price.

In penetrating the U.S. and European markets, the Japanese have taken a somewhat different tack. They have avoided selling their own watches at either end of the market. In particular, they have let others fight it out at the bottom of the market. More so than in the Far East, they have focused their selling efforts on watches in the medium-price category. This means, for instance, that in the United States the Japanese have concentrated on marketing watches retailing in the $30–$100 range. Yet, within this segment of the market, the Japanese have relied on their usual price strategy: more watch for the same price or a comparable watch for less money.

Several reasons have kept the Japanese out of the luxury end of the watch market in the United States and in Europe. First, a few firms have dominated the luxury watch business for many years; they have created an entrenched position for themselves as prestige watchmakers. Allied to this is the fact that the luxury watch business is as much one of selling jewelry as it is one of selling watches. To penetrate the top end of the watch market, the Japanese would have had to invest heavily in building up a prestige image and in developing new marketing skills. And even if they had been successful, their sales would have been limited in unit terms. Thus, the very nature of the luxury business was contrary to a key feature of the Japanese watch strategy: mass production.

The situation at the low-price end of the market has been quite a different matter. The Japanese watchmakers have not taken on the pin-lever manufacturers, like Timex, directly. But indirectly they have been very much involved in the competitive battle, particularly the one in the United States, between the pin-lever and the jeweled-lever manufacturers.

In the late 1950s the Japanese watchmakers, especially Seiko and Citizen, became major suppliers of watch movements and components to the U.S. industry. Some American jeweled-lever manufacturers imported inexpensive movements from Japan, put the movements into their own cases, and marketed the watches at prices comparable to those for the Timex line of watches. Others imported Japanese movements and parts into the Virgin Islands, finished the watches there in company-owned assembly plants, and shipped the watches, duty-free, into the United States. Firms like Benrus and Elgin got their movements and parts from Seiko. Bulova, from 1960 on, got its movements and parts from Citizen. Generally speaking, arrangements like these have continued up through the early 1970s.

How successful have the Japanese been at penetrating overseas markets? Reliable data relating to their market share in Asia and in a number of Western European countries do not exist. Regarding the United States, official data relating to the year 1968 make it possible to arrive at a rough answer to the question. In 1968 about 5% of the watches imported directly into the United States came from Japan and about half of all the components imported into the Virgin Islands in that year also came from Japan. Adding together direct and indirect imports, the Japanese supplied about 8% of the U.S. market at that time.

Obviously, with only about 14% of worldwide sales and 8% of U.S. sales under their control in 1970, the Japanese watchmakers had a good distance to go to catch up with the Swiss. Yet the Japanese reached this point in not much more than a decade, and what worked in the past could well work in the future. Without doubt, what worked in the past most successfully for the Japanese watchmakers was related to their manufacturing capabilities.

Manufacturing

A combination of four factors has made it possible for the Japanese to be remarkably efficient low-cost watch producers. These factors have been:

1. A ready supply of disciplined, zealous workers at low wage rates;
2. Advanced mechanized and automated production techniques;
3. Vertical integration; and
4. Mass production of standardized movements and watch models.

By putting these together, the Japanese manufacturers attained economies of scale unmatched anywhere else in the world watch industry.

The labor factor is, of course, the first that immediately comes to the outsider's mind. And there is no doubt that the Japanese have had a significant edge over other producers in this respect. This has been especially true in the case of jeweled-lever watches since the labor content associated with their production is relatively high. For example, as late as 1965 the workers assembling jeweled-lever movements in Japan were earning about one fifth of what their counterparts were earning in the United States. By the late 1960s, however, rapidly rising wage rates in Japan were eroding the industry's labor-cost advantage.

The response of the industry to mounting wages highlighted its determination to preserve its competitive advantage. Japanese watchmakers were not content to stay at home seeing their costs spiraling upwards. Instead, they were prepared to shift production, or at least some of it, to new low-wage countries. By 1970 both Seiko and Citizen had established manufacturing facilities in Hong Kong. Thus, the watchmakers, like many other Japanese manufacturers, had few qualms about pursuing low-wage labor wherever it could be found. Moreover, because their overall sales were still expanding, they did not have to face the problem of protecting employment at home.

Still, Japan's labor-cost advantage should not be overemphasized. It has been only part of the total manufacturing picture. The Japanese watchmakers have also stressed the use of the most advanced production-line techniques. According to industry legend, this all came about as the result of a visit to the United States by engineers of K. Hattori & Co. After World War II they studied the production techniques used by a number of U.S. watchmakers and also visited the auto-assembly plants in Detroit. Apparently they were not especially impressed by what they saw in the watch industry but were struck by what they saw in the automobile industry. In any case, by the mid-1950s K. Hattori & Co. had adapted its watchmaking to a conveyor-belt assembly-line operation. With this type of production Hattori could use not only cheap labor but also unskilled labor. The rest of the Japanese industry soon followed Hattori's lead.

The industry took all the other steps necessary to foster low-cost production. It integrated backward into the manufacture of components, jewels, even watchmaking machinery. And it standardized production whenever and wherever it could. The result of combining all these features of manufacturing has been a total mass-production approach to watchmaking.

Comparing the Swiss industry to the Japanese industry dramatizes the difference in their approach to manufacturing. In Switzerland, as we have seen, around·1,000 firms were involved in producing, largely through a two-tier system, about 74 million watches in 1970. In the same year two Japanese firms, Seiko and Citizen, produced in-house the equivalent of 30% of the total Swiss output.

What did this difference mean in terms of actual production costs? As might be expected, the watchmakers were reluctant to give out specific figures. One has to rely on indirect measures to get at the answer. Table 7 provides at least a clue.

TABLE 7
Per-unit value of watch movements imported into the United States* (calculated from 1970 data)

Movements	From Switzerland	From Japan
0 to 1 jewel.	$ 2.08	$ 1.15
2 to 7 jewels	3.65	3.06
8 to 15 jewels†.	12.55	10.85
16 to 17 jewels	7.50	4.23
Over 17 jewels‡	28.80	6.63

*Valued at f.o.b. the exporting country.
†Imports of movements in this category were well below those in the 16 to 17 jewels category, which explains the high per-unit price.
‡Comparison of prices for watches in this category is probably invalid since the imports from Switzerland include a high proportion of luxury models.

Are these figures a valid guide to the production cost differential between Switzerland and Japan? Undoubtedly the Swiss would say no, claiming that the Japanese figures represent only marginal prices. Perhaps this is true, but even so the figures pinpoint an advantage that the Japanese have had over the Swiss. With a large home market, the Japanese have been able to absorb all fixed costs over their domestic production. They could, therefore, afford to sell at or near marginal costs in foreign markets. With practically no home market, the Swiss could pursue the same pricing strategy only with great difficulty. Whether the figures in Table 7 reflect production costs or pricing policies or a combination of the two, they show that the Japanese had the ability to undercut Swiss prices anywhere from 15% to 45% in the largest watch market in the world.

Other factors in the industry's growth

Of course Seiko and the other Japanese watchmakers did not achieve their success all on their own. They had a number of things going for them, such as a large home market fairly well protected from foreign competition. In the decades of the fifties and sixties only expensive watches were imported into the country. In unit terms these imports seldom amounted to more than 5% of Japanese production, although, because of the price factor, they did amount to as much as 20% of the market in value terms.

Government policy helped as well. To forestall the proliferation of marginal watch producers and to minimize the drain on foreign reserves caused by the importation of watchmaking machinery, the government encouraged the highly concentrated industry structure. Consequently, the leaders in the industry did not have to waste time or resources contending with new competitors.

And then there was the dramatic growth of the Japanese economy. Its expansion at a rate about two and a half times as great as that for the other advanced countries certainly prompted Japanese watch-makers to enlarge and upgrade their production facilities. The buoyant home economy undoubtedly induced Japanese watchmakers to take investment risks that competitors elsewhere shied away from.

Regarding the future, it seems likely that factors such as those listed above will play a somewhat less important role as ingredients of success. At least over the next decade or so the winners in the world watch industry will be those firms most adroit at mastering an array of new technologies and meshing the technologies with the marketplace. The Japanese watchmakers have armed themselves for the battle in their own way.

Nonwatch production: The source of new technology

Over the years the "big two" in the industry have moved into the manufacture of products outside the timepiece field. By 1970 Seiko was producing desk-top electronic calculators, high-speed printers for use with computers, miniature industrial robots, machine tools, electronic displays of various types, and information equipment. By then, Citizen Watch was producing mechanical and electronic calculators, office equipment, and machine tools. To be sure, in neither case did the sales of these items represent a major part of the firm's total revenue. But the manufacture of these nontimepiece product lines did expose the firms to technologies that were incorporated in the new types of watches under development.

And the two smaller watchmakers developed their own means for tapping new technology. Ricoh Watch, for instance, became a part of an industrial combine producing copiers, cameras, meters, clocks, and related items. Thus even these firms acquired a sort of in-house access to the skills and knowledge needed to support R & D activities for the new generation of watches.

By the early 1970s it was still too early to determine how successful the Japanese would be at transplanting the latest phases of electronic technology into watchmaking. Yet there were signs that the Japanese were not about to be outplayed. In 1970 Seiko became the first watchmaker in the world to introduce a watch employing the quartz crystal technology. Subsequently, Seiko had to withdraw the watch from the market to sort out technical problems. But within the year Seiko was back on the market with an improved quartz watch—one boasting "a special temperature compensating device designed to make the crystal's vibration as perfect as possible in order to provide extra accuracy." Clearly, Seiko was not about to give up its claim to a share of the electronic watch market.

One American, comparing the overall strategies of the Swiss and the Japanese watchmaking industries, summed up the situation in the following way:

For years the Swiss ruled the world watch market with a regiment. The Japanese are countering now with several giants. A lot of the troops in the regiment aren't going to make it in a battle with giants. Besides, the industry can't hold very many giants. How the U.S. watchmakers will come out of this, in between the Swiss and the Japanese trading punches, isn't at all clear.

THE U.S. WATCH INDUSTRY

> We've been able to beat foreign competition simply because we *are* foreign competition.
>
> Harry B. Henshel, president,
> Bulova Watch

Highlights as of 1970

In 1970 U.S. consumers spent approximately $1 billion to purchase about 45 million wristwatches, of which roughly 40%, or about 18 million, had been manufactured at home, while the remaining 60% had been imported from foreign countries or from the Virgin Islands.[6] At the same time, U.S. watch exports, as they had been for many years, were nil. Thus in 1970 the United States was both the world's largest watch market and the world's largest net importer of watches. However, as

---

[6] Since imports constituted such a high proportion of U.S. watch consumption, tariffs were obviously a factor that could not be overlooked by U.S. and foreign watchmakers. Appendix B briefly discusses the tariff issue.

we shall see shortly, these figures do not mean that foreign watchmakers supplied 60% of the U.S. market.

Although the United States was the world's largest watch market, watchmaking represented an insignificant part of U.S. manufacturing industry. Workers engaged in watchmaking constituted only one tenth of 1% of total manufacturing employment. In fact, only two U.S. watch companies, Bulova and Timex, were involved in any domestic watch production. This point is crucial. To understand anything about the U.S. watch industry as it moved into the 1970s, it is first imperative to distinguish between those watchmakers that were both U.S. manufacturing and selling enterprises and those that were merely U.S. marketing organizations. Making that distinction calls for some history.

The post–World War II shift in watch production

Since the beginning, U.S. companies have struggled to cope with the labor requirements of watchmaking. Manufacturing watches by traditional techniques has always been labor intensive; beyond that it has called for its own brand of skilled labor. Neither of these requirements has ever been easily met in the United States. Some U.S. watch sellers never tried; from the start they imported finished watches or alternatively imported movements and simply put them in watch cases here. Other firms tackled the problem by locating at least part of their production overseas. Bulova and Gruen, for example, established their own manufacturing plants in Switzerland in the early years of the 1900s. Still other companies located all their manufacturing capacity in the United States, counting on mechanization to offset foreign producers' labor advantages.

After World War II most of the big names in the U.S. watch industry had the better part of their output manufactured in the United States, though a few did obtain a significant share of their needs from their own Swiss plants. And after the war jeweled-lever watches dominated the U.S. market. Then during the 1950s and early 1960s the situation changed drastically. Timex first stormed the low-price end of the watch market and later moved up into the middle price range. At the same time marginal Swiss producers flooded the U.S. market with inexpensive pin-lever and jeweled-lever watches making price competition all the more severe. And by the early 1960s the Japanese began to carve out their piece of the U.S. market. On top of this, the mass-merchandising revolution of the 1950s threw the traditional watch distribution system, sales through jewelers and fine department stores, into chaos. To survive in a market dominated by price competition, one after another U.S. watch company gave up on domestic watch manufacturing until, as pointed out above, by 1970 there were only two survivors.

Some of those who shifted to foreign supply acquired their own overseas plants, resulting in an increase in the number of U.S.-controlled plants in Switzerland. According to one estimate, in the second half of the 1960s about 45% of the jeweled-lever watches imported into the United States from Switzerland were made in plants owned by American firms. Other U.S. companies, however, found independent Swiss or Japanese firms which supplied them with watches, which they then sold in the United States under their own familiar trade names. In addition, many of the U.S. watchmakers turned for at least part of their needs to manufacturing and assembly in the Virgin Islands. (See Appendix C.)

The upshot of all this shifting was that during the 1950–70 period a number of the well-known names in the U.S. watch industry became little more than marketing organizations. Their control of manufacturing operations, if indeed they engaged in manufacturing at all, became secondary. They survived largely by exploiting the trademarks that they had established over the years in the United States. By the early 1970s, however, it was becoming questionable whether these watch marketers could survive.

Industry structure

Even though market-share data are not publicly available, it is clear that two companies ruled the U.S. watch market in the early 1970s. Probably somewhere between two thirds and three quarters of all watches sold in the United States were made by either Bulova or Timex. Another half-dozen U.S. watch companies and a throng of foreign watchmakers scrambled for the rest of the U.S. market.

Exhibit 2 presents some of the basic facts about the firms traditionally considered to be part of the U.S. watch industry. Three points stand out in the exhibit. First, most of the companies did not manufacture in the United States. Second, most were losing money in the early 1970s. And third, several had sold out to larger U.S. companies or to Swiss interests. If Exhibit 2 included balance sheet data, it would also show that a number of the companies were heavily in debt. Apart from Bulova and Timex, the once proud U.S. watch industry was in a fairly sorry state as of the early 1970s. What had Bulova and Timex done right to separate themselves from the others?

Bulova

During the 1960s Bulova's management pursued four main goals:

1. Marketing a line of watches covering all price and user segments,
2. Creating a worldwide production base,
3. Expanding its international operations,
4. Exploiting to the fullest its tuning-fork innovation.

EXHIBIT 2
Leading names in the U.S. watch industry

Company or division	Ownership	Recent performance statistics			Watch production base
		Fiscal year	Sales	Net income (loss)	
Benrus	U.S.	1971*	$25 million	($4.5 million)	Manufacturing and assembly in Switzerland and Virgin Islands
Bulova	U.S.	1972†	$147 million	Operating at break even or loss since 1968 $3.9 million	Twenty plants around the world including several in the U.S.
Elgin National Industries	Largely U.S.; Swiss own about 5%	1971	$130 million (about 25% in watches)	($13.2 million)	Manufacturing and assembly in Switzerland and Virgin Islands
Gruen Industries	80% U.S.; 20% Swiss	1971†	$9.6 million	($100,000)	Manufacturing and assembly in Switzerland, Canada, and U.S.
Hamilton	Since 1970, a 50%-owned marketing subsidiary of Bush Universal; Swiss own 17%, with option to buy 51% in 1974	1972*	$47 million	($2.4 million)	Leases manufacturing and assembly plants in Switzerland and Virgin Islands
Longines-Wittnauer	Since 1970, a division of Westinghouse	n.a.	n.a.	n.a.	Manufacturing and assembly in Switzerland
Sheffield	U.S.	1971	$15 million	As of 1972, in bankruptcy proceedings	Manufacturing and assembly in Switzerland, New York, Virgin Islands, and Guam
Timex	Privately owned, U.S.	1971	$200 million (estimated)	n.a.	Twenty plants around the world including several in the U.S.
Waltham	Since 1968, the U.S. distribution subsidiary of a Swiss watchmaking consortium	n.a.	n.a.	n.a.	Manufacturing and assembly in Switzerland and, for its electronic watch, in the U.S.

* For fiscal year ended January 31.
† For fiscal year ended March 31.
n.a. = not available.

How Bulova tackled the U.S. marketplace is indicative of the product strategy the company implemented around the world. Throughout the 1960s and into the 1970s Bulova sold a line of watches in each of the three major market segments, low-, medium-, and high-price, and equaled or outpaced competition in each segment.

At the bottom of the market, in the price range of around $30 and under, Bulova offered its "Caravelle" line. In 1961, in response to Timex, Bulova had countered with this line which, though priced competitively with Timex's pin-lever watches, consisted solely of watches containing jeweled-lever movements. Bulova was able to challenge Timex because it had turned to a Japanese supplier, Citizen Watch, for inexpensive jeweled-lever movements. By the mid-1960s Bulova claimed that it was the leader in the jeweled-lever part of the inexpensive watch market. Parenthetically, it should be noted here that Bulova's success with the Caravelle line probably explains why Citizen, Japan's second largest watchmaker, has never moved into the U.S. market on its own.

The middle of the market, consisting principally of jeweled-lever watches selling in the $30 to $100 price range, had always been Bulova's stronghold. The company marketed literally hundreds of models under the "Bulova" name, and within this segment of the market remained price competitive by manufacturing the watch movements in its own Swiss plants. In fact, supplying the U.S. market made Bulova the largest single manufacturer in Switzerland.

At the top of the market, Bulova's tuning-fork watch, the "Accutron," was in a class of its own. Why this was so calls for a little history. Clocks based on the tuning-fork principle dated from the turn of the century. In 1952 a young Swiss engineer, working at the Bulova plant in Switzerland, got management approval to develop a miniaturized tuning-fork movement. By the mid-1950s he had partially succeeded. Bulova brought his prototypes to the United States and miniaturized them further by applying advanced electronics and metallurgical techniques. After patenting the device, Bulova put it on the market in 1960 as the Accutron watch.

Though the Accutron did not compete head-on with luxury mechanical watches, those sold more as jewelry than as timepieces, it soon grabbed the lion's share of watch purchases in the over-$100 price category. Moreover, Bulova swept the market with a watch designed solely for men; for technical reasons, "mini Accutrons" for women were not put on the market until 1971.

Whereas Accutron's uniqueness undoubtedly accounted for much of Bulova's success within the high-price segment of the watch market, uniqueness of product could not account for Bulova's success in the other two segments of the market. Instead, Bulova relied on aggressive marketing. Advertising and distribution support, for years Bulova's forte, were the two critical marketing factors.

By the second half of the sixties, Bulova was spending as much as $4 million at a crack on its seasonal advertising campaigns. By the beginning of the seventies it was spending half of all watch advertising dollars in the United States. It maintained the largest sales force within the industry and provided the distributors, particularly jewelers, with dozens of different selling and service programs. In short, Bulova, which came out of World War II somewhat larger than its rivals, increased the gap by pouring funds into marketing at a rate unparalleled in the industry.

Meanwhile, Bulova management built the manufacturing base that insured the success of its marketing strategy. It expanded the company's manufacturing operations until, by 1970, it had 20 plants scattered around the world. As suggested by the quotation at the beginning of this section, Bulova's management saw its worldwide production system as its key competitive strength. With this system Bulova could pick the time and place for producing a particular watch. For instance, it concentrated U.S. production on the Accutron, which required a low labor input but sophisticated technology.

Furthermore, as it broadened its manufacturing base, Bulova became capable of conducting R & D and market testing at more than one site. It developed its mini Accutron for women in Switzerland and first put it on the market in France.

As production spread around the world, so, too, did sales. Whereas in 1960 international business accounted for not much more than 5% of Bulova's consumer sales (these exclude defense and industrial sales), a decade later the percentage was in the 20% range. Part of this surge could be attributed to the Accutron, which Bulova introduced, with success, in a number of overseas markets. Thus, by carrying competition into its foreign rivals' own backyards, Bulova diluted somewhat the efforts they could bring to bear on the U.S. marketplace.

At the same time that Bulova was pushing out its sales base, it was also shoring up its worldwide dominance in the field of tuning-fork technology. In 1968, Swiss manufacturers, unable to develop a version of the tuning-fork movement that did not conflict with the Bulova patent, agreed to enter into a licensing agreement with Bulova. Consequently, by the early 1970s several Swiss producers, Bulova's licensees, were making and selling their own versions of the tuning-fork watch. And on the other side of the globe, the Citizen Watch Company, Japan's second largest watchmaker and a minority partner with Bulova in a joint manufacturing venture, was making and selling Accutrons under another license agreement with Bulova.

The combination of all these factors turned Bulova into the world's largest jeweled-movement watch seller, in dollar terms.

Timex[7]

Coming out of nowhere in 1950, Timex carved out a major place for itself in the U.S. watch market in the 1950s and in foreign markets in the 1960s. On almost every count Timex's product and market strategy differed from that of the traditional watchmakers. Timex did not build its reputation on the jeweled-lever watch. Instead, it took a pin-lever movement, simplified it even further so that it could be mass-produced with automated techniques, put it in simple but tasteful cases, and marketed its first watch line to retail at $6.95 to $7.95. Then Timex went outside the conventional distribution system, first selling most of its watches through drugstores and subsequently through a number of mass merchandisers. Next Timex drummed up sales through intensive advertising. Like Bulova, Timex spent far more for its advertising than was customary in the industry at the time. But unlike Bulova or any other rival, Timex promoted its line in ways that were unorthodox and, according to critics, somewhat garish. One example of Timex's off-key advertising approach, its "torture tests," became a standard of network TV in the late 1950s.

By the early 1960s Timex could claim that it was selling one out of every three watches in the United States. It then broadened its product line with electric watches and some jeweled-lever models. Consequently, by the late 1960s Timex could claim that it was selling every other watch in the United States.

While Timex was strengthening its hold on the market, it was also, like Bulova, building up a worldwide manufacturing system. By 1970, it, too, had 20 plants scattered around the world. Thus both giants in the U.S. watch industry had manufacturing bases more widely dispersed than any of their U.S. rivals or, for that matter, than any of their foreign rivals.

Lessons from Bulova and Timex

The success of Bulova and Timex calls attention to several important points, which, although they relate basically to the U.S. marketplace, may apply elsewhere as well.

1. By the end of the 1960s watchmakers could no longer base their marketing strategies almost exclusively on the push of the conventional distribution system. Both Bulova and Timex marketed their products

---

[7] For a complete description of this firm, see the case entitled "The Timex Corporation."

directly to consumers and made their brand names, not the jeweler's recommendation, the key to watch sales. In part, this switch in marketing emphasis was a natural consequence of the sweeping changes that affected the distribution and retailing of many consumer goods. In part, it was associated with the slow but steady disappearance in the United States of an important source of consumer information: the watch repairman. It was also related to consumer confusion over quality. In the 1950s and 1960s the industry baffled the consumer with literally thousands of watch models and recurrent price cutting. Unable to determine what was a good watch at a fair price, the consumer naturally turned to the one or two brands with which he or she was most familiar.

2. Unexploited niches were a thing of the past in the U.S. watch market. Bulova was very explicit about its strategy in this regard. Note this comment in its 1970 annual report:

Bulova's market researchers have sought to identify the particular needs of segmented consumer groups. That we have succeeded in this crucial phase of our operations is evidenced by the record number of more than 800 different watch models offered to the United States markets.

The report went on to note that Bulova sold watches in the price range of $10.95 to $11,000. And, of course, Timex completely blanketed the low-price field and part of the mid-price field. The rest of competition, the other U.S. watchmakers and dozens of foreign manufacturers, offered hundreds of additional models. By 1970, the chance that a watchmaker would find a niche unnoticed by competition was, for all practical purposes, nil.

3. Finally, the U.S. watch company with a strictly domestic orientation was an anachronism. During the 1960s Bulova and Timex redefined themselves as multinational firms; their outlook on markets and production became worldwide. Over time they internationalized their marketing, production, and R & D skills and competed successfully because they exploited advantages regardless of where the advantages were located. It is questionable if either firm, or any other major watchmaker, for that matter, could survive in the 1970s if it limited its operations to a single country.

What about some of the other factors that would determine the competitive ability of U.S. watchmakers in the 1970s?

Research and development

Government-supported R & D work and defense-oriented production expanded the technological base of the leading U.S. watchmakers in a way not open to the watchmakers in Switzerland and Japan. Moreover, unlike the Swiss but like the Japanese, the U.S. companies concentrated on acquiring advanced technical skills within their own organizations.

For some of the U.S. companies, the skills they accumulated, largely at government expense, added up to an impressive list. Take Bulova, for instance. During the 1950s and 1960s Bulova developed and produced a whole array of intricate electromechanical devices for missiles and was a major supplier of parts for conventional munitions. Commenting on its technical capabilities outside the watchmaking field, Bulova's 1968 annual report had stated:

> The products made in the company's four non-consumer areas have, as a common denominator, watch-making technology and miniature electronics threading through the production of artillery and mortar fuses, micro-circuit automation equipment, test instrumentation, crystals, oscillators, and servo-mechanisms, and production of millions of pin-head sized synthetic jewels.

The report went on to emphasize the advantages inherent in these activities:

> The esoteric-sounding inventory of principal products of the non-consumer units—fuses, safe and arm devices, micro-bonders, crystal filters, optical choppers, tuning-fork oscillators, laser beam choppers—seem remote from watch-design and manufacture but they represent an in-house technological base whose impact can be company-wide with consumer or non-consumer involvement.

Other watchmakers engaged in similar activities. Timex developed and manufactured gyroscopes and timing devices. Benrus supplied high-precision components for missiles, power-supply systems for naval vessels, and electronic instrumentation for satellites. Elgin made flight instruments.

To be sure, not all of the U.S. watchmakers retained the technical knowledge and expertise they acquired in the course of meeting defense needs. Those that had to sell out to other companies or that had experienced especially hard times at the end of the 1960s more than likely saw their reservoir of knowledge and skills dwindling away or becoming obsolescent. In the early 1970s the smaller U.S. watch companies showed no striking evidence that they had a technological lead over Swiss and Japanese companies. Bulova and Timex were a different matter, however. They had prospered throughout the 1960s. They, therefore, had the opportunity to build up their reservoirs of skills. In the early 1970s they were in the technological vanguard, and as the decade rolled on their accumulated technical capabilities might well turn out to be their most important competitive edge over Swiss and Japanese rivals.

Diversification

At one time or another in the fifties and sixties almost all the U.S. watchmakers experimented with diversification. Generally speaking, none of the experiments was successful. Several firms did develop lines of industrial products like precision parts or electromechanical components, but the sale of these lines never became a major part of their operations. And as for consumer goods, the watchmakers demonstrated a fairly consistent inability to market successfully a second consumer line.

Some industry observers attributed this weakness to the watchmakers' unique but specific set of marketing skills. Others claimed that the watchmakers had so many problems to deal with that they never had the chance nor the resources to pursue diversification seriously. And the cynics suggested that it was simply another case of an industry with a fixation on one technology and on one product. Whatever the cause, as the industry moved into the 1970s there was little evidence that its members could regard diversification as a readily available means for meeting adversity or for stimulating growth.

U.S. investment in the Swiss industry

The expiration, at the end of 1965, of the Swiss government's prohibition against the acquisition or sale of watchmaking companies was followed by a flurry of U.S. investments in the Swiss industry. As soon as the barriers dropped, Hamilton and Benrus each purchased Swiss watchmakers in order to obtain manufacturing sites in Switzerland. The next year, 1967, Bulova bought out Universal Geneve, a maker of quality high-priced watches. According to reports, Bulova's motive differed from that of the two other U.S. investors. Bulova had its eye on Universal Geneve's worldwide distribution system. Other U.S. watchmakers might have invested in Swiss companies as well had not the Swiss gone on the offensive and started to invest in U.S. companies.

An outsider made the next major move into the Swiss watch industry in 1971 when the American firm Zenith acquired a majority interest of the Movado-Zenith-Mondia Holding Company, Switzerland's fourth largest watchmaker.[8] The merged companies announced their intention to parlay Zenith's electronics expertise with the Swiss group's watchmaking skills to compete in the electronic watch market.

Predicting whether cross-country investment (U.S. companies in Swiss firms and vice versa) would keep up its pace throughout the rest of the 1970s was complicated by two opposing factors. On the one hand, the opportunities for this type of investment were declining. In Switzerland, the wave of horizontal and vertical mergers lessened the number of candidates for acquisition by U.S. companies. And in the United States almost all of the watch companies, with the exception of Bulova and Timex, had come under partial or complete Swiss control.

---

[8] Prior to the merger Zenith of the United States was not related in any way to the Zenith part of the Swiss watchmaking group.

On the other hand, further investment in each other's industries might be the best way for U.S. and Swiss watch companies to cope with the instability arising out of the electronic watch battle. For example, in an article entitled "Swiss Watchmakers Plan More American Mergers," the director of the Federation of Swiss Watchmakers, Mr. Retornaz, predicted more Swiss acquisitions of American watch importers. Reporters noted that he stressed one theme: "Retornaz returned again and again to a central thought with the Swiss vis-à-vis the United States: stability."[9] If U.S. and Swiss watchmakers continued to forge new links between the two industries, the quest to bring order out of potential chaos would almost assuredly be a root cause.

THE ELECTRONIC WATCH BATTLE   ·

It all shapes up as an intriguing struggle that can be safely watched by most investors from the security of the sidelines.
Value Line Selection and Opinion

Emergence of the electronic watch

As the watchmakers of Switzerland, the United States, and Japan entered the 1970s, the quartz crystal electronic watch had emerged from the prototype stage as a tempting product opportunity. Attention focused primarily on the United States, which was not only the center of the new technology but also the world's largest watch market. Since American consumers could well afford these new watches, each firm's best chance at attaining mass-production economies rode on penetrating this market.

The electronic watch differed significantly from the conventional timepiece.

1. Manufacturing the electronic watch would call for very low labor inputs. Some observers predicted that labor costs might eventually amount to no more than 10% of total manufacturing costs. In contrast, labor costs could run as high as 70% of total manufacturing costs for fine mechanical watches.
2. Unlike the situation with the tuning-fork watch, when Bulova controlled the technology through patents, no firm was likely to build up any sort of patent wall with the electronic watch. The relevant technology was widely held, in large part, by firms outside the watchmaking field.
3. Unlike the case with mechanical watches, cost reductions for the electronic watch would not come at the expense of quality. Even if the prices for it did fall to very low levels, the electronic watch, when completely perfected, would not be a junk watch. Instead, it

---
[9] *National Jeweler*, May 1972.

would have the quality associated with the most expensive mechanical watches.

4. The cost of the innards of the electronic watch would be determined by the cost-volume relationships connected with the manufacture of electronic components. Consequently, the cost advantages of volume for the electronic watch might well exceed those for the mechanical watch. Experience in the semiconductor industry indicated a 30% decline in costs with each doubling of volume.

5. And finally, the electronic watch would undergo important improvements in the next several years. As of the early 1970s, it was still far from being a completely perfected product. Neither of the two key technical components, the quartz crystal and the electronic display, was free from shortcomings. Different types of integrated circuits varied in terms of performance characteristics such as cost, reliability, size, and power consumption. Continuous efforts were being made to develop improved integrated circuits for electronic watches. Comparable efforts were being directed at improving the readability of digital displays, at adding new features to the displays, and at eliminating the need to press a button for those incorporating light-emitting diodes.

One critical question confronting the industry during the early 1970s was whether the electronic manufacturers would remain as parts suppliers or whether they would integrate forward into watch marketing. By 1976, this question had been answered: of the approximately 60 digital watch brands sold in the United States, 70% were produced by newcomers, intruders from the electronics industry. While some electronics companies limited their role to that of parts supplier, many others had introduced their own brands. Thus, the question had shifted to: What share of the watch market might the new entrants be able to conquer and what role would remain for the traditional watch companies? Would the mechanical and solid-state watch be able to coexist? If so, in what proportion? This issue obviously depended greatly on the future price and sales outlook for the electronic watch.

Outlook for the electronic watch

Prognostications on the future of the electronic watch had been a continuing phenomenon since its introduction in the early 1970s. At that time, the president of one U.S. electronics company made the prediction that received the most attention: "The solid-state watch will put 50,000 Swiss out of work."[10] Other executives in U.S. industry echoed the same

---

[10] Put in perspective for the American reader, this prediction would compare with a forecast of putting 1.3 million Americans out of work.

theme. And the president of Benrus saw the future like this: "All evidence points to the emergence of an American watch industry and to the submergence of the Swiss and non-American watch manufacturers."

These forecasts depended, of course, on assessments of the share of the market that the electronic watch would capture from the mechanical watch. The president of Benrus, for example, predicted that electronic watches would soon capture 20% of the watch market; and he added that he could foresee a time when they would control 90% of the market. Executives in the U.S. electronics industry prophesized, quite naturally, that the death of the mechanical watch was imminent.

Undoubtedly the main reason why the electronics industry held such high hopes for the new generation of watches was the long-range price prospect. Those best acquainted with the costs involved in making the electronic components predicted continuing price declines. For instance, the head of Motorola's quartz timepiece electronics division said in August 1972 that he looked for quartz watch prices to slide to $50 by 1974. Long term, he saw no reason why their retail prices could not be brought down to $10.

By 1976 many of the price prognostications appeared to be coming true. The first firms to introduce electronic watches had tried to skim the cream off the market. They had packaged the new technology in luxury cases. Bulova had launched its analog Accuquartz in 1971 in a luxury version retailing at $1,350, while Hamilton had introduced its digital Pulsar in early 1972 at a retail price of $2,100. But the cream did not last long. Within a year, electronic watch retail prices dropped to the $200–$400 range. Then the digitals began to flood into the market. By 1975, Litronix, one of the newcomers to the industry, was retailing a digital watch at $50. The Pulsar, though it was aimed at the top of the market, had become a $275 item.

In January 1976 Texas Instruments (TI) announced introduction of a $19.95 solid-state digital watch. The business press reported that Fairchild, Litronix, and National Semiconductor, by then full-fledged entrants into the watch business, were ready to follow TI's lead. This move was described by *Business Week* as a "dramatic early bid to take over the mass market from the traditional watch companies such as Timex and to block competition from the host of assemblers hoping to grab a share of this soaring market." Some observers doubted that TI, which in 1975 "had turned in disappointing sales of its initial $90-and-up watch line," could make a profit with this plastic-cased $19.95 watch requiring a factory price of between $12.95 and $13.50. TI's watch module was described as simpler than the ones produced by other watch manufacturers, and the company had shifted from batch manufacturing to a continuous assembly line. Its production goal for 1976 was rumored to be 4 million watches.

As 1976 rolled on, price reductions seemed to be moving ahead of the expected decline in the cost curves. Some of the newcomers to the industry, such as Litronix, acknowledged losses; others, such as National Semiconductor, which had encountered serious manufacturing problems necessitating curtailment of its planned output by one-half, simply announced disappointing financial results. Optel filed under Chapter IX, and American Microsystems decided to drop its line of liquid crystal display watches. A trade magazine concluded that the "long-predicted shakeout of digital watchmakers is on and will accelerate."

Clearly, the 1976 price reductions were predicated on a major and rapid rise in digital watch sales. Industry estimates placed worldwide sales of digital watches at about 200,000 in 1973, 800,000 in 1974, and 3.5 million in 1975. Worldwide, 1975 sales were estimated to be 4 million for analog electronic watches and between 200 and 225 million for all types of watches, with between 45 and 60 million watches sold in the United States.

In making forecasts, great importance was placed on the breakdown of watch sales by price categories. Industry analysts placed around 75% of unit watch sales (40% of dollar sales) in the under $25 retail price category and only 10% of unit sales (35% of dollar sales) in the over $50 retail price category. They concluded that achieving high-volume production would require industry members to offer watches retailing at $20 or under. Hence, *Jeweler's Circular-Keystone* concluded that "the watch industry moved into an entirely new era" when TI announced its $19.95 digital watch.

At this price level, what share of the watch market were digital watches expected to conquer? Various published forecasts were in relatively close agreement in estimating worldwide industry sales at 300 million units by 1980. While predictions that the new technology would almost completely take over the industry continued to be made, forecasts of electronic watch sales in 1980 generally fell in the 50 to 100 million units range. Forecasts for 1976 were between 15 to 20 million units, 80% of which would be produced by U.S. companies, mostly in Texas and California.

The emergence of the digital watch had not been without problems. The August 23, 1976, issue of *The Wall Street Journal* reported a statement from J. C. Penney Company that "about 30% of the watches it sells are returned for servicing and most of the problems are battery-related." A leading trade magazine in mid-1976 wrote about "fading digits and jammed command buttons," and predicted greater emphasis on quality and service. Accuracy, one of the chief advantages of the digital watch, was not generally accepted as a major selling argument. The senior watch buyer for Sears, Roebuck was quoted as saying: "We're getting to the point where accuracy is a little ridiculous. Most customers are more than happy with [accuracy within] two minutes a month." Industry experts continued to emphasize style as a critical element, and many of them felt that there were substantial market opportunities for the more stylish and expensive digital watches. While comparisons between calculators and watches were frequently drawn, a Benrus vice president had stated in 1975: "This is an entirely different business from calculators. The price of electronics can come down considerably. But a watch is still considered jewelry—and it is the cases that are expensive because of their gold or hand-tooling. A lot of people will go broke because they don't realize that."

The position of the mechical watch industry

"What really hurt us was that the recession and the digital watch came at the same time." This statement by the president of the Watchmakers of Switzerland Information Center summarized the predicament of the Swiss watch industry in the mid-seventies. In fact, the impact of the worldwide recession had been aggravated by the foreign exchange rate of the Swiss franc which had appreciated substantially relative to the currencies of other watch-producing countries. (See Exhibit 3.) Swiss watch exports in 1975 declined 22% from the previous year, and Swiss watch sales in the United States declined by 40%. Layoffs and plant closings shook the industry which for three decades had enjoyed full em-

EXHIBIT 3
Effective exchange rate changes (MERM-weighted index, May 1970 = 100)

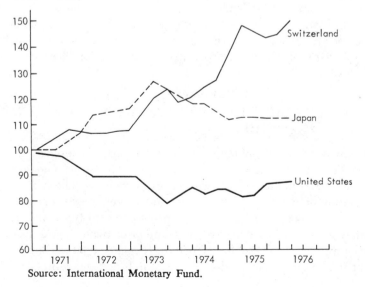

Source: International Monetary Fund.

ployment. In mid-1976 the Swiss government proposed financial assistance to the industry to support efforts toward diversification and technological innovation.

The combined impact of recession and currency appreciation was reflected in the 1975 financial results of the Swiss watch companies. Red ink was common to both small and large corporations. SSIH, the most important Swiss producer, known particularly for its Omega brand, saw its 1975 unit sales drop by 21.5% from 1974. It incurred a 6.6% operating loss on sales of about $280 million. Price pressures and technological obsolescence also impacted inventories which amounted to 55% of total assets.

Bulova, which manufactured a major portion of its watches in Switzerland, was similarly affected. In fiscal 1976 (ending March 31) its sales were down to $205 million (from $228 million in fiscal 1975) and losses amounted to $25.6 million, including a $20.5 million writedown, of which $15 million was for inventories and $5 million for sale or disposal of certain foreign subsidiaries.

In May of 1976, Stelux Manufacturing Company of Hong Kong acquired 26.8% of Bulova shares from Gulf & Western, and its managing director, 36-year-old C. P. Wong, became Bulova's chief executive officer. Stelux, founded in 1963, had become the world's largest producer of metal watchbands and employed 2,500 people. It also manufactured other watch accessories and, through a joint venture with Mostek Corporation of Texas, modules for electronic watches. Having gone public in 1972 (although remaining under family control), Stelux had acquired three Swiss manufacturers of watch parts with total sales of $6 million and had diversified into banking and real estate. This dramatic partial takeover of one of the leaders of the U.S. watch industry raised the question of why had not the Swiss made a stronger bid to gain operating control of ailing Bulova? Two reasons were given: the Swiss manufacturers' own problems and worries about antitrust implications.

APPENDIX A
A BRIEF GUIDE TO HOW WATCHES WORK AND TO THEIR PRINCIPAL TYPES

Wristwatches come in innumerable sizes, shapes, designs, and price ranges. Yet until the last decade most of the differences among watches were superficial matters of styling and extra features. The basic running mechanisms of watches were classed into a few general categories. All watches were mechanical and of the spring-powered type. And by tradition they were put into only one or the other of two categories: jeweled-lever or pin-lever. These terms will be explained later. But with the advent in the late 1950s of the electric watch and the subsequent introduction of several types of electronic watches, the problem of describing how watches work and classifying them grew in complexity.

Still, if matters are simplified considerably, it is possible to acquire without much difficulty a working familiarity with watch technology. That is the aim of this guide. It begins by describing the traditional spring-powered watch, a timepiece little changed in over 300 years, and then traces the major innovations that have so dramatically changed the nature of wristwatches in the last two decades.

THE STANDARD SPRING-POWERED WATCH

The traditional mechanical watch consists of two distinct parts: the *exterior visible elements* (the case, crystal, dial, and hands) and the *interior movement*. What happens on the outside of a watch is obvious; what goes on inside is a mystery to many. The *movement* normally consists of a hundred or more parts which form three major groups:

1. The *ebauche,* or movement blank, which accounts for more than three fifths of all parts. It comprises the framework of the watch (the plates and bridges), the gear train (the wheels and pinions), and the winding and setting mechanism. In a rough way, the ebauche can be thought of as the chassis and engine of an automobile.
2. The regulating components (the *escapement,* balance wheel, and hairspring), which make the movement work at the correct rate. Roughly, these can be thought of as the transmission of an automobile.
3. Other miscellaneous parts which cannot be classed under any generic heading.

When these hundred or so parts are assembled, how do they work? Winding a watch tightens the spiral of its mainspring. As the spring unwinds, it drives a series of gears to which the hands of the watch are attached. But the unwinding of the mainspring has to be restrained and precisely controlled to provide the right increments of time. This requirement is what makes a watch movement complex.

The task of releasing energy from the mainspring in a precise way is carried out by the regulating components, the heart of which is the *escapement mechanism.* A gear called the escapement wheel is attached to the main gear train. The escapement wheel is restrained from rotating freely, thereby blocking the unwinding of the mainspring, by two teeth in a part called the anchor fork. The anchor fork rocks back and forth releasing one tooth and immediately thereafter engaging the other tooth in the escapement wheel. This alternate release and engagement of the escapement wheel permits it to advance by tiny increments, and these increments of rotation are converted by the other gears into the second, minute, and hour movements of the watch hands.

But what makes the anchor fork move? It is connected to a balance wheel which rotates back and forth, and the balance wheel is, in turn, connected to a hairspring which coils and uncoils to keep the balance wheel in motion. As each tooth on the anchor fork disengages from the escapement wheel (the tooth actually slides away from the wheel), it transmits enough power through the anchor fork and balance wheel to the hairspring to coil it slightly. As the hairspring uncoils, it rotates the balance wheel in the opposite direction, which, in turn, rocks the anchor fork in the opposite direction starting the next cycle in the regulating mechanism. This whole complex set of movements goes on about 300 times a minute and produces the familiar ticking in the spring-powered watch.

Even though all mechanical watch movements operate according to the principle just described, not all movements are of the same quality. The quality of a movement is determined, in part, by the precision with which the many tiny parts are made and, in part, by the care that goes into adjusting the functioning of the components. For example, Swiss manufacturers of premium watches have traditionally employed master watchmakers to make all the many and time-consuming adjustments needed to produce a highly accurate movement.

Then there is the whole matter of jewels. Since watch movements consist of many tiny parts, it is obvious that friction and wear must be minimized if watches are to be accurate and long lasting. In many watches, though in far from all of them, this is accomplished by putting jewels at all the critical pivot and contact points in the movement. One standard Swiss movement, for example, contains 15 jewels. Very high-quality movements may contain as many as 30 jewels. While the purpose of jewels in watch movements is generally well understood, the contribution that they make to the cost and quality of watches is often misunderstood.

Many people assume that watches containing 15 or more jewels are expensive because the jewels are expensive. Moreover, they assume that the number of jewels in a watch movement indicates the quality of the watch. The second of these assumptions is not necessarily true; the first is just plain false. With rare exceptions all jewels used in watch-making—excluding, of course, those used on the outside of a watch for decorative purposes—are synthetic and quite inexpensive. Thus the number of jewels in a movement has little to do with the price of a watch. As regards the issue of quality, most movements containing 15 or more jewels are produced with the precision and care required to make a fine timepiece. Yet some less scrupulous watchmakers, knowing that consumers erroneously equate the number of jewels with quality, have gouged the public by putting out expensive but crude timepieces containing many jewels. It follows that establishing the true quality of the standard spring-powered watch is not an easy matter for the average consumer.

The issue is further complicated by the fact that there are two different types of spring-powered watches.

The distinction between jeweled-lever and pin-lever watches

As a rule all mechanical watches are regarded as being either of the jeweled-lever or the pin-lever variety. Although the distinction is based on specific technical differences, many watchmakers and jewelers contend that the distinction is an indication of overall watch quality. Manufacturers of jeweled-lever watches consider pin-lever watches inferior in many respects. They characterize the pin-lever watch as a crude timepiece, poorly made with low-grade materials, which will not last and which will not keep accurate time. They concede that pin-lever watches are inexpensive (they prefer to use the word cheap), but they claim that the customer is getting what he or she pays for. As the ultimate insult, they refer to pin-lever watches as "throwaways."

As might be expected, manufacturers of pin-lever watches have a different point of view. They contend that their watches do a perfectly adequate job, that their watches are durable, and that consumers do not have to pay exorbitant prices to own reliable timepieces. They also point out that there are inferior (they use words like "schlock") jeweled-lever watches.

But leaving aside all the claims and counterclaims that competing watchmakers have hurled at one another's products, what is the technical difference between the two types of watches? It relates to whether a watch movement contains jewels in its escapement mechanism. In pin-lever watches, metal pins replace the jewel-tipped teeth in the anchor fork; this accounts for the name "pin-lever." Other parts of the escapement mechanism are also simplified, further eliminating the need for jewels. Simplification, more so than elimination of the jewels, makes it possible to produce pin-lever movements at costs below those for jeweled-lever movements. Indeed, the inventor of the pin-lever movement, a man called Roskopf, had as his goal the development of a movement so simple that watches could be made for the common man. His contribution has not passed unnoticed, for even today watchmakers often refer to pin-lever movements as Roskopf movements.

Even though the distinction between jeweled-lever and pin-lever watches relates specifically to the type of escapement mechanism, the difference commonly extends to other parts of the watch. For example, pin-lever watches usually contain few or no jewels in their entire movements. And notwithstanding what many pin-lever manufacturers claim, most pin-lever watches are made to looser tolerances than those found in jeweled-lever watches. Furthermore, the materials used in pin-lever watches, and their overall styling, are often not up to the standards of the jeweled-lever watch.

The subtypes of spring-powered watches

The many ways in which mechanical watches, either jeweled-lever or pin-lever, are modified to produce a variety of subtypes can be passed over quickly. In the 1970s a number of the special features are taken for granted. By and large everybody understands what is involved when a watch is described as being shockproof, waterproof, antimagnetic, self-winding, etc. Calendar watches, those showing the day and month on the face, are common. So, too, are chronographs, watches with start-and-stop mechanisms to measure elapsed time. The important point is this: All these subtypes call for some added complexity in their manufacture, yet none represents a radical departure from the characteristics of the standard mechanical watch.

THE NEW GENERATION OF WATCHES

The electric watch

Development of miniaturized batteries and electric motors, largely the result of World War II R & D efforts, made possible the first major advance in timekeeping: the electric watch. Commercially available for the first time in the United States in 1957, the electric watch was marketed worldwide by many manufacturers in the early 1960s.

As regards its technology, the electric watch represents only a partial step away from the spring-powered watch. It does not contain a mainspring nor many of the components usually found in escapement mechanisms. Instead, current from a battery drives a tiny balance-wheel motor, which, in turn, is connected through a gear train to the hands of the watch. Yet the watch is conventional in the sense that it still depends on the oscillation of moving mechanical parts to determine time increments. For this reason the accuracy of most electric watches is not strikingly better than that of good spring-powered watches. Consequently, electric watches, though moderately successful in the marketplace throughout the 1960s, did not capture the lion's share of the medium- and high-price watch market. And the innovations that followed the electric watch severely clouded its long-run commercial future.

The tuning-fork watch

Although the electric watch represented the first break with 300 years of watchmaking tradition, its impact on the watch industry was far less than the second major innovation in watch technology, the development of the tuning-fork watch. With it, the whole principle of determining time was changed. Greatly simplified, the tuning-fork watch works in the following way. Electric current from a small battery flows through coils surrounding a tuning fork. The flow of current stimulates the tuning fork to vibrate at 360 cycles per second. A tiny strip of metal connected to the tuning fork transmits its vibrations to a set of gears, which, as in the conventional watch, convert the time increments into the sweep of the hands on the watch face. Because the time-determining element is a tuning fork which vibrates over 31 million times per day, the accuracy of the watch surpasses that of even the most finely manufactured spring-powered watches. Tuning-fork watches, if properly adjusted, should be accurate to within one minute per month.

Until 1971, all tuning-fork watches sold were men's models. Then, after further miniaturization of the tuning-fork movement was finally accomplished, models for women became available.

The quartz crystal watch

By the end of the 1960s another major innovation in watchmaking appeared in the marketplace. This newest innovation, the use of quartz crystals as the time-determining device in watch movements, could improve the accuracy of watches to unheard-of levels, and it also opened the door to the completely solid-state watch. In fact, a number of different types of watches were developed around the new technology. They all were based, however, on the same operating principle.

When electric current is passed through a quartz crystal, it can be stimulated to vibrate at a very high frequency. This oscillation can be converted into very precise time increments. Microcircuitry subdivides the crystal's frequency into electric pulses which then drive the watch in one of several different ways. In some quartz crystal watches, the pulses operate a tiny electric stepping motor which, in turn, is connected through a gear train to the hands of a watch with a conventional face. In other quartz crystal watches the pulses are used to excite a tuning-fork device. From that point on, the operation of this type of watch is identical to that of the existing tuning-fork watches. In still others, the pulses are fed into mini-computers—really integrated circuits—that convert the pulses into the usual minute and second time increments. In the case of this last type of watch, which incorporates no moving parts, the conventional face and hands of the watch are replaced by new methods of displaying time. These developments are discussed in the following section.

Changes in the face of the watch

Until 1972 the dramatic advances in watch technology remained unseen miracles to those who in the last decade or so purchased one of the newer watches. The works inside were different, but the familiar face and hands were still there. In 1972, though, innovation became visible. Watches with completely different faces, with tiny displays resembling those of a digital clock or of an electronic calculator, appeared on the market for the first time. These numerical-display watches became known as digital models, while electronic watches with conventional faces were referred to as analog models. The new faces incorporated one or the other of two different devices which were the product of quite recent technical advances: liquid crystal displays and light-emitting diodes.

The devices work on two different principles. A liquid crystal display consists of two pieces of glass with a thin coating of an electrically sensitive chemical between them. When current is passed through the chemical, it changes its crystalline structure. The altered crystals reflect ambient light, that is, they reflect light coming from an outside source. The advantage of the liquid crystal display is that it requires a very low level of current to operate since it is not actually generating light. Its disadvantage is that the quality of the image it presents, the brightness and precision of the numbers, depends on the brightness of external illumination.

As for the other device, light-emitting diodes, they are, crudely put, semiconductors that glow. In the early 1970s they found their greatest use in the displays of small electronic calculators. Whereas they give off a brighter and more precise image than liquid crystal displays, they have the disadvantage of requiring more current to operate them than liquid crystal displays. Because the diodes require so much power, no watch-size battery can keep them illuminated at all times. To read the time, the wearer had to press a button which illuminated the otherwise blank face of the watch, although for one watch the LEDs were activated by a turn of the wrist.

Digital display mechanisms were subject to continuous technological change, aimed at reducing power consumption, improving readability, and enhancing durability and stability. While initially LEDs had taken a clear lead over LCDs, many industry observers predicted that the latter might ultimately gain the upper hand. Others felt that these technologies could be used to convey the traditional analog face and hands. By the mid-1970s, announcements about improvements, combined versions, or new approaches to displays continued to be made. It was still far from certain which watch face would prevail in the future.

APPENDIX B
THE U.S. TARIFF SITUATION

The duties on watches and watch components imported into the United States were initially established by the Tariff Act of 1930.[11] Since then, Executive Orders have modified the level of duties on several occasions. In 1936, as part of a reciprocal trade agreement with Switzerland, the U.S. government reduced by one third the duties levied on movements containing 1 to 17 jewels. These concessions lasted until the post–World War II years. In 1951 U.S. watchmakers applied for relief (i.e., a hike in duties) under the escape-clause provisions of the Trade Agreement Extension Act of that year. Three years later the President, responding to the U.S. manufacturers' complaints and to the Tariff Commission's findings, raised by 50% the duties on movements in the 1-to-17-jewel category.

Throughout the 1950s the U.S. watch industry pressed unsuccessfully for additional protection by pleading the "defense essentiality" argument.

The escape-clause rates, set in 1954, were terminated in January 1967 by Presidential Proclamation: once again the duties on movements in the 1-to-17-jewel category dropped by a third. At the same time, as part of the Kennedy round GATT negotiations, the U.S. government granted the first concessions on movements containing more than 17 jewels. Beginning January 1, 1968, the duty on such movements was to be reduced, in five annual stages, by a total of 50%. The rates applicable to movements with 17 jewels or less were left untouched by the Kennedy round.

As of the early 1970s, the tariff situation was as shown in Exhibit 4.

Over the years the U.S. watch industry's increasing reliance on overseas production has prompted the industry to change its stance on the issue of tariffs. Before World War II and in the decade immediately following it, U.S. watch manufacturers, though not U.S. watch importers, lobbied hard for tariff protection. But as the industry increased its dependence on foreign sources of supply, it started to sing a different tune. The companies with overseas plants and those importing from foreign producers defected from the industry's protectionist position. By the mid-1960s the industry was divided into two camps.

The events of 1967, the termination of the escape-clause rates, and the Kennedy round concessions prodded the few firms with jeweled-lever production in the United States to transfer it abroad. By the late 1960s,

---

[11] Rates of duty are provided separately for the individual components of watches, that is, the movement and the case. Duties are assessed on each component.

EXHIBIT 4
U.S. rates of duty applicable to imports of watch movements and cases

Item	Rate as of Dec. 31, 1967	Second stage effective Jan. 1, 1969	Final stage effective Jan. 1, 1972
		Rate pursuant to concessions granted in 1964–67 trade conference	
Watch movements, unadjusted, not self-winding			
1. Having over 17 jewels	$10.75 each	$8.60 each	$5.37 each
2. Having no jewels or 1 jewel	$.75–$.90 each depending on width	No change	No change
3. Having over 1 jewel but not over 7 jewels	$.90–$1.80 each depending on width	No change	No change
4. Having over 7 but not over 17 jewels	$.90–$1.80 each depending on width	No change	No change
Additional duties on watches with 17 jewels or less			
For each jewel in excess of 7	$.09	No change	No change
For each adjustment	$.50	No change	No change
Self-winding	$.50	No change	No change
Watch cases	$.75 each plus 30% ad valorem	$.60 each plus 24% ad valorem	$.37 each plus 15% ad valorem

Source: U.S. Tariff Commission, *Summaries of Trade and Tariff Information (1970).*

when all production was either foreign-based or part of Bulova's and Timex's worldwide manufacturing systems, the industry had adopted what could be regarded as a low-key free trade position.

APPENDIX C
WATCH ASSEMBLY IN THE U.S. INSULAR POSSESSIONS[12]

Because of a loophole in the U.S. tariff law, in the late 1950s many U.S. firms turned to watch assembling in the Virgin Islands. The loophole hinged upon the stipulation that watches could be imported duty free into the United States from its insular possessions provided that no article contained foreign materials valued at more than 50% of the total value of the article. With labor costs such a high proportion of total watch manufacturing costs, it was not difficult to meet this criterion.

Watches assembled in the Virgin Islands from foreign parts first

---

[12] The U.S. insular possessions include the Virgin Islands, Guam, and American Samoa.

started to flow into the United States in 1959. Within a decade 15 different companies had assembly plants there. About half of the parts, by value, used in the Virgin Islands operations came from Japan; another quarter came from Germany. The Swiss, restricted by law until 1971 from exporting parts, never gained a foothold.

By 1968 almost 15% of total U.S. watch imports came into this country via the Virgin Islands route. By then a trickle of imports had also started to come in from Guam. In order to limit this blossoming circumvention of tariff duties, the U.S. government had, in the previous year, put a quota on imports from the insular possessions limiting them to one ninth of U.S. consumption in the prior year. Several firms, citing the quota as one reason for their decisions, shut down their Virgin Islands plants. Yet most watchmakers continued their Virgin Islands operations into the 1970s.

Timex Corporation

From industry upstart to industry leader

In 1950 the United States Time Corporation of Middlebury, Connecticut, introduced its line of inexpensive Timex watches into the U.S. marketplace. Neither American nor foreign manufacturers took much notice of the new competitor. After all, in the eyes of the traditional manufacturers, the Timex line consisted of nothing more than cheap pin-lever watches destined, at best, to meet the needs of a minor part of the U.S. market.

Twenty years later the same firm, renamed now after its world-famous Timex brand,[1] had sales in the range of $200 million, plants scattered all over the world, 17,000 employees, and rival manufacturers taking notice of its every move. In fact, Timex had become such a potent factor in the world watch industry that the Federation of Swiss Watchmakers, having studied its rival in minute detail, published a monograph entitled "The Timex Formula."

Timex had grown to be the world's largest manufacturer of pin-lever watches and a principal manufacturer of other types of watches. With its inexpensive watches it had stormed the U.S. market and so fixed the name Timex in the American consumer's mind that by 1970 every other watch bought in the United States was a Timex. And starting in the early 1960s, Timex had marched into one after another foreign

---

[1] In 1969 the firm changed its corporate name from United States Time Corporation to Timex Corporation.

market to the point where it became almost as major a factor in the watch industry overseas as in the United States.

How did Timex do it? How did Timex first reshape the watch industry in the United States and then reshape the watch industry on a worldwide basis? How have other manufacturers responded to the Timex challenge? And where does Timex go from here? These are the questions that are taken up in the pages that follow.

THE EARLY DAYS OF TIMEX

The company's founder

Since its inception, Timex has been guided by Mr. Joakim Lehmkuhl. Born in 1895 in Norway, Mr. Lehmkuhl had studied engineering in the United States, receiving degrees from Harvard and M.I.T. in 1918 and 1919, respectively, and then had returned to Norway to direct a small shipbuilding firm and eventually to publish a political newspaper. In 1940, in advance of the German invaders, he fled with his family to England. Shortly thereafter, he was sent by the Norwegian government in exile to New York to take charge of the wartime Norwegian Shipping Center. Recognizing that his assignment was temporary, Mr. Lehmkuhl soon set about looking for another opportunity to use his talents.

The birth of Timex

In 1942 Mr. Lehmkuhl found his opportunity. Seeing the need for fuse timers for bombs and artillery shells, he and a group of businessmen acquired a majority interest in the virtually bankrupt Waterbury Clock Company in order to convert the firm to fuse production. Prior to the war, the Waterbury Clock Company had manufactured the $1 Ingersoll pocket watch. Very quickly, with Mr. Lehmkuhl as its president, the firm became the largest producer of fuses in the United States.

After the war, as disappearing defense orders emptied its shop, Waterbury's total sales dropped from $70,000,000 to $300,000. Mr. Lehmkuhl reconverted his company from wartime production to watch production "because it seemed the only thing to do." But the days of the $1 Ingersoll watch were over. The U.S. market for such a watch had largely disappeared, and what market did exist was being flooded by cheap Swiss imports. On top of this, inflated costs prevented his or any firm from producing a watch to retail at $1.

Still, Mr. Lehmkuhl was convinced that a good, inexpensive watch could be produced by combining the precision tooling techniques used in making fuse timers with a high degree of mechanization. He gave Waterbury's engineers the task of designing a quality watch that could be truly mass-produced. By 1949 they had succeeded in upgrading the simple mechanism used in children's watches into the prototype of the Timex watch. It had one feature of particular importance. Picking up a development that came out of the World War II research effort, the engineers substituted new hard alloy (Armalloy) bearings for jewels in the movement. According to the company, this feature made the watch the equal of many jeweled-lever models and better than the other pin-lever models then available.

In the meantime, Mr. Lehmkuhl dropped the tarnished Ingersoll name, changed the company's name to U.S. Time, and adopted the brand "Timex" for the new product line.

TIMEX THROUGH THE FIFTIES

Product policy

The Timexes put on the market in 1950 were men's watches designed to retail at $6.95 to $7.95. Their simple, tasteful styling and modernistic lines represented an innovation in the low-price field. Gradually, the company added watches with more features and slightly higher prices. First came Timexes with sweep second hands. Then the firm introduced models that were shockproof, waterproof, and antimagnetic. In 1954 Timex brought out a line to retail at $12.95. Calendar and self-winding models soon followed. All of the Timex models, regardless of features, carried a one-year guarantee.

In 1958 Timex introduced its first line of women's watches. Promotion of the line was keyed to the idea that a woman could buy an entire wardrobe of watches—one for dress, one for sports, one for general use—for less than $50. The company claimed that by the early 1960s it had attained more than 36% of the under-$50 women's watch market.

Mr. Robert Mohr, who was vice president of sales at the time, discussed Timex's early product policy in the following terms:

> People wonder how we make a watch and sell it for as little as we do. That's all to the good. We promote the idea that the watch is not just a gift season item—something you buy for the June graduate, or at Christmas time, Father's Day or Mother's Day.
> Basically, we promote the watch as something for everyday use, that people don't have to worry about because the cost is low.
> It works out in our favor, because when you sell more watches than anyone else, you can do more.[2]

---

[2] "New TV Commercials Will Give It Even Harder to Those Hardy Timexes," *Advertising Age*, December 10, 1962.

Distribution policy

Mass distribution was the keystone to Timex's marketing strategy. At the outset, because it lacked the funds for extensive promotion of its line, the company set out to get widespread retailer support for its watches. Timex initially approached jewelers, the traditional outlet for watches. But many jewelers were reluctant to handle the Timex line. Their reluctance was based on various reasons: some downgraded the Timex line because of its price range or because of its simple pin-lever movements, others objected to the fact that they would only make a 30% margin on the retail price with the Timex line as contrasted to the 50% margin they usually made on their other lines.

Rebuffed in general by the jewelry trade, Timex tried other channels of distribution. As a result, the company started to market its watches directly through 20,000 retail accounts, the bulk of which were drugstores. In the early days almost 80% of Timex's sales were made by drugstores. Over the years, Timex constantly increased both the number and type of retail outlets through which it sold its watches. At its high point Timex had almost 250,000 retail accounts on its books.

In its approach to retailers, Timex routinely emphasized the importance of stock turnover. It also stressed retail price maintenance even though its suggested retail prices and markups were well below those traditional in the jewelry trade. Mr. Mohr described the distribution strategy:

We taught jewelers that markups don't mean a thing if you don't have the turnover. That was our story, and we preached it hard. Jewelry stores have a 1.5 average watch turnover per year. That wasn't enough for us. We put watches into drugstores, hardware and tobacco stores. Today Timex watches are sold in 80,000 of these stores. We don't sell discount, and we maintain a fair trade price, enforcing it wherever possible. We have a low price to begin with, so why cut it more?[3]

Timex management claimed that its retailers' average turnover was six times per year.

"Timex's sales approach"—according to *Tide*—"was based completely on showmanship unheard of in the conservative watch business." Timex salesmen visiting retailers slammed the watches against walls and dunked them into buckets of water to illustrate their shockproof and waterproof qualities. In 1954 the company designed a showcase for point-of-purchase display with levers which could dunk a Timex in water and smash it against an anvil. According to Mr. Lehmkuhl, these promotional tactics largely accounted for the rapid rise in sales in the early 1950s. Then in the mid-1950s Timex turned to television.

---

[3] Ibid.

Advertising policy

Prior to 1956 Timex's advertising had been on a small scale and limited mainly to magazines. In 1956 it began intensive advertising on network television. It was estimated that Timex's annual advertising budget grew from about $200,000 for the year 1952 to around $3 million for the years at the end of the decade. About 85% of the advertising budget was allocated to television.

Timex's commercials hammered home the themes of product durability and low cost. The company became renowned, first at home and then abroad, for its so-called "torture test." Its commercials featured news commentator John Cameron Swazey showing a Timex which, under varying circumstances, "took a licking and kept on ticking." In one of the early torture tests, done live, a Timex was fastened to an outboard engine propeller. In the water, the Timex inadvertently slipped off the spinning propeller. It was recovered, running, and Timex ended up with yet another highly favorable bit of publicity for its watches. One torture test followed another. The watches were shown ticking away after being fastened to the hooves of galloping horses, after surviving 135-foot dives at Acapulco, and after being attached to surfboards and amphibian airplanes.

For critics of the unorthodox advertising campaign, the company had its answer: "Timex is a watch designed for active people; then why not show it undergoing rugged tests?"[4]

Manufacturing policy

Timex could sell its watches the right way because it could make them the right way. Manufacturing in Timex was characterized by mass production with relatively unskilled labor and by constant management attention to production efficiency and to quality control. *Business Week* described the company's manufacturing operations in the following terms: "The entire operation adds up to an almost textbook example of how to run a taut ship."[5] The "simple but strict" production formula was based on: (1) rigid standardization, with full interchangeability of parts; (2) maximum mechanization to reduce human error and to minimize labor costs; and (3) centralized quality control. According to Mr. George Gelgauda, technical director, "Parts fit together whether they are made here in Middlebury, Connecticut, or in Germany." To insure standardization and the most advanced mechanization possible, the company employed 500 toolmakers who designed almost all of the

---

[4] "Rigors of Hawaii Are Setting for New Timex Tests," *Advertising Age*, October 21, 1963.

[5] "A Time Bomb for Watchmakers," *Business Week*, November 16, 1963.

firm's production equipment. Control was centralized even to the point of keeping the records on all its tools at the U.S. headquarters.

Keeping the product simple was another key element in Timex's manufacturing policy. For example, the frame of the basic Timex watch went through six manufacturing operations as contrasted with 100 for an imported watch. The Timex movement had 98 parts held between two plates, whereas foreign movements frequently had 120 parts held together by a series of five plates. The Timex had four screws; other watches had as many as 31. Of course, industry rivals tried to turn this simplicity against Timex. For instance, they pointed out that the cases of the Timex watches were riveted together, making repairs impossible. The American consumer, as will become apparent, paid little attention to these criticisms.

Another example illustrates how management achieved low-cost production. As many operations as possible were mechanized so that the end product needed little adjustment. According to Mr. William J. O'Connell, an assistant division manager:

When we put a watch together with relatively unskilled labor, it must be able to run accurately the minute the last wheel is put in place. We can't afford the petty, troublesome adjustments that are found in the handmade watch industry.[6]

More than one observer, after seeing the Timex manufacturing operations, was prone to describe Mr. Lehmkuhl as the Henry Ford of the American watchmaking industry.

Timex managed its inventories as strictly as it managed its production operations. Sales forecasting and inventory control were centralized. Sales were pinpointed through warranty cards, and estimates were constantly revised at a data processing center at Middlebury. Parts and work-in-process inventories were updated daily at headquarters. Finished-goods inventories were kept at rock bottom.

By the end of the decade Timex employed about 7,000 people in its home office and in its three U.S. and six European plants. Stateside, in addition to its main plant in Middlebury, Connecticut, it had factories in Little Rock, Arkansas, and Abilene, Texas. Overseas, it had plants in England, Scotland, West Germany, and France. Its French plant, in Besançon only 27 miles from the Swiss border, was located in a region rich in the tradition of watchmaking.

Though the company had not actively sought diversification, the firm became also an important supplier of parts for the Polaroid Land Camera. Furthermore, Timex moved into defense business. It maintained a $1 million research laboratory in Irvington-on-Hudson, New York, which featured "the cleanest room in the world" for the manufacture of gyroscopes and for the testing of timing devices.

---

[6] Ibid.

Competitive reaction: Too little or too late

Of course, competition did not stand absolutely still as Timex carved up the U.S. watch market throughout the 1950s. Yet many of Timex's rivals continued to focus most of their energies on their traditional market segments—watches in the $30 to $100 range. And when they did try to defend against Timex by adding lines of inexpensive watches, they seldom could take on Timex in head-to-head competition. Some tried, like Benrus, and eventually gave up. They lacked both Timex's manufacturing and mass distribution capabilities. Lacking these, it made no sense for them to match Timex's intensive advertising campaigns.

The other major American watchmaker, Bulova, did try to answer the Timex threat with its own Caravelle line, jeweled-lever watches retailing in the $10 to $30 range. But even though Bulova started to gear up for this counteroffensive in the late 1950s, it did not attain national distribution of the Caravelle line until 1963, 13 years after Timex hit the U.S. market.

By and large, therefore, Timex stood alone in its segment of the U.S. marketplace throughout the 1950s. Its performance statistics as it moved into the early years of the next decade reflected this fact.

Sales and financial results

The first Timex watch was put on the U.S. market in 1950. A decade later, the company was selling around 7,000,000 watches annually. In 1962 an Alfred Politz research study indicated that one watch out of every three sold in the United States carried the company's trade name of "Timex." Though Timex did not publish its financial data, its 1961 sales and after-tax income were reported by *Advertising Age* as being $71,200,000 and $2,900,000, respectively. The company, according to President Lehmkuhl, was completely free of debt, had financed all recent expansions out of earnings, and intended to continue to do so. Clearly, the Timex strategy had paid off in terms of dollars and cents.

TIMEX THROUGH THE SIXTIES

Upgrading the product line

Having established a strong foothold in the low-price segment of the U.S. market, Timex took a number of important steps in the 1960s to broaden its product line. Its first move in this program had actually taken place in 1957 when Timex introduced a line of 17-jewel watches designed to retail at $17.95. Despite predictions that Timex could not sell watches at this price level through outlets such as drugstores, the line was a success.

Then in 1962 Timex followed with a 21-jewel watch line priced at $21.95. These watches, in part because they carried a higher markup than usual for Timex, were reported to have eased the entry of the firm into distribution through the jewelry trade. Slowly Timex won over jewelers' begrudging acceptance.

Timex's next step was a response to the competitive threat posed by the electric watch. The first of these had appeared in the U.S. market in 1957, and by the early 1960s many different models were available. While the electric watch did not represent a significant technical improvement over conventional watches, it did endanger the sales growth of those firms completely committed to mechanical watches. Timex responded in typical fashion. In 1963 it introduced a line of electric watches retailing at $39.95, about half the price of its nearest competitor. *Consumer's Bulletin* had this to say about the electric Timex:

Although the Timex is very low in price for an electric watch, it was found to keep surprisingly accurate time during the first three months of operation, up to the time this issue of the *Bulletin* went to press. . . . While the case and the flexible bracelet were of lower quality than found on more expensive watches, they were judged to be satisfactory and gave a good appearance.[7]

After selling about 200,000 men's electric watches at $39.95 in 1964, Timex introduced a women's electric watch and a men's electric calendar watch, both at $45, in 1965. With the higher priced additions to the line, Timex began to run "prestige" advertising in national magazines.

Some industry observers suggested that Timex was headed for trouble by moving up out of its traditional low-price market niche. Mr. Lehmkuhl didn't see it that way. Interviewed in 1968, he had this to say about the matter:

REPORTER: Do you face any risk in moving into higher price watches?

MR. LEHMUHL: No, no. We are already the largest producers of electric watches at a higher price. That just built up the name for the lower price watches, too.[8]

Swiss watchmakers, too, didn't see Timex headed for trouble by following this policy. To the contrary, they saw it as a threat to their market position in the United States. The 1969 annual report of the Swiss Watchmakers Association, discussing mounting competition in the United States, posed the problem in these terms:

---

[7] "Timex Electric Watch," *Consumer's Bulletin*, March 1964.

[8] "Making the Most of Time," *Nation's Business*, September 1968.

As to marketing, we must take into consideration a new fact, the selling-up policy started by Timex, by adding to its range of products a certain number of more costly articles, either because they are made with higher quality movements, or because they are of a different technical construction. This new factor could possibly lead to profound changes in the market as was the case in 1950.

Going international

At the same time that Timex was upgrading its product line, it was also spreading out into foreign markets. Timex first established operations in Canada and in England. Promptly, it transplanted its marketing techniques to these new markets. Even though Timex's sales figures were not broken down for domestic and overseas markets, it was estimated that by 1965 its market share in these countries was comparable to its share in the United States. Regardless of where it was used, Timex's "torture test" advertising campaign captured the fancy of local consumers. For example, in South Africa Timex was an unknown brand in 1962. Timex launched its campaign, and in the month of December 1963 alone Timex sold 10,000 watches in that market. Timex then entered the French market, selling its line under the "Kelton" trade name, and by the mid-1960s Timex was ready to knock over the large West German market.

The West German story highlights how effective Timex had become as an international marketer. The company applied the same marketing formula, modified in several important ways, that had been successful in over 30 countries. As in many other markets, the manufacturers selling in West Germany concentrated on watches in the medium and upper price ranges, ignoring the lower price range. A Timex executive described the situation in these terms:

> They were trying to sell West German customers on the idea that expensive wristwatches added to the owner's prestige. We set out to fill the vacuum in the lower price watch market and convince buyers that good watches don't have to be expensive.[9]

But first the company had to surmount a distribution hurdle. The company knew it had to distribute through large department stores and mail-order houses to build volume. Yet over 75% of watch sales in West Germany moved through jewelers and specialty watch stores. If these outlets were antagonized, they could jeopardize all Timex's plans. Accordingly, the company set out to win their allegiance.

---

[9] "How Timex Hit German Markets with Top Quality, Durability—and the Hard Sell," *Business Abroad*, February 5, 1968.

Timex developed a three-pronged approach to convince jewelers that its business would be too good to pass up:

1. An intensive institutional campaign describing Timex and its plans for West Germany was directed at jewelers and other retailers.
2. Inducements to handle the Timex line, including margins comparable to those on other watch lines, were offered the jewelry trade. In addition, they were encouraged to send malfunctioning Timexes to its French plant for repair by granting them a 25% handling commission.
3. Sales success of the line was almost guaranteed to the trade by Timex. The company outlined its plans for its usual aggressive, imaginative advertising campaign which would fully support the trade's effort to sell the watches.

As the clincher, Timex invested almost $1 million to test-market its line and its marketing formula in one of West Germany's most populous regions. The test marketing was a success, jewelers and other retailers alike were convinced, and Timex went national in January 1967. In less than two years, Timex had captured 10% of the West German watch market with over 70% of its sales going through jewelry stores. In 1967 it sold approximately 500,000 low-price watches; estimates of its sales for 1968 ran in the range of 600,000 to 750,000 watches. By 1969 the Swiss Watchmakers Association, in its annual report, openly acknowledged that Timex was hurting Swiss export sales into Germany. The report noted that keen competition from Timex was driving down the average value of watches shipped to Germany.

Meanwhile, Timex had turned its attention to the Far East. And as in the past, Timex did not do things in the conventional way. Its venture into Japan prompted observations like the following:

> Foreign watchmakers do not always use existing sales routes. Timex of the United States, for example, has gone into a tie-up with Maruman, a leading cigarette lighter manufacturer, and is engrossed in blazing new sales routes.[10]

Elsewhere in the Far East Timex was on the move, and again the Swiss singled out Timex as a cause of some of their woes. Commenting on a downturn in exports to the Far East, the 1971 annual report of the Swiss Watchmakers Association had this to say:

> The most obvious factors which seem to have influenced our trade in this area are, broadly speaking, a major Russian commercial offensive on the Hong Kong market and aggressive Timex policies in the Far East.

---

[10] *Oriental Economist*, November 1971.

The Japanese, too, had comments about Timex's moves in the late 1960s. They didn't hesitate to point out that Timex was taking on formidable competitors. As one executive of Seiko emphasized:

. . . while Timex advertises itself as "the world's largest manufacturer," this is for pin levers. When it comes to jeweled-lever watches, Seiko occupies first place.[11]

TIMEX IN THE EARLY SEVENTIES

As the decade of the 1970s opened, quartz watches created a technological revolution in watchmaking. First introduced in early 1970 as luxury models priced above $1,000, quartz watches in early 1972 were being sold by leading Japanese, Swiss, and U.S. companies at $400 and up. In April 1972 Timex announced its entry:

"With a quartz watch priced at $125," Robert Mohr, executive vice president of the company, announced in mid-April, "we're 60% under the least expensive watch already on the market."[12] When Mohr was asked how Timex could put a quartz watch on the market at such a price, he replied:

Timex Corporation has a solid background of experience in essentials like the design and manufacture of miniaturized parts. In addition, the company has a technology geared to vast production. In making millions of watches annually, we have developed watchmaking production techniques unmatched anywhere in the world.[13]

Mr. Mohr added that Timex was so confident that its quartz watch would be a leader that the company intended to support it with a full-scale advertising and promotion campaign. The leading jeweler's news magazine noted that the Timex announcement had "stirred" the trade.

Timex's low-price leadership, however, was immediately challenged. Ebauches, the major Swiss component manufacturer, announced a line of quartz watches to retail at $30 to $300. Benrus and Gruen announced retail prices of $99 and $150, respectively, while Microma Universal, one of the watchmakers' principal suppliers of integrated circuits and liquid crystal displays, planned to sell a quartz watch under its own name for $79.50. While all the above announcements related to analog quartz watches, digital solid-state watches were also announced at price levels ranging from $149.50 to $200.

In late 1971, in spite of the impending technological and competitive changes, Mr. Lehmkuhl was optimistic about Timex's future. Sales in

---

[11] *National Jeweler*, May 1972.

[12] Ibid.

[13] Ibid.

1971 were comfortably over $200 million and up 10% from the prior year. A *New York Times* article quoted Mr. Lehmkuhl:

"We'll try to find items to fill out our line of watches," he said, "such as modern clocks, and even quartz clocks."

And Timex, which already is a major world factor in timepieces with 20 factories abroad, still doesn't think it has enough of the world market. More foreign plants are being planned.

"Volume," he adds with a faint smile, "is the oxygen of our business."[14]

---

[14] *New York Times,* December 5, 1971.

STRATEGIC ALTERNATIVES AND CORPORATE CHOICE

General Cinema Corporation

"At GENERAL CINEMA we believe that our company's growth and earning power is recession-resistant and inflation-immune," stated Richard A. Smith, president, in September 1975. "We had a record year in 1974 despite rampant inflation. This year our results will be considerably better during the most severe recession since the early thirties. General Cinema's business, although not providing necessities, does bring relatively inexpensive pleasure and satisfaction to the public. It operates from a protected base of exclusivity through unique locations in regional shopping centers or exclusive and perpetual beverage franchises. This position gives us the confidence to project continuing earnings growth in the years to come. Our objective is to increase earnings at an annual rate of 15%–20%."

General Cinema's previous growth had been impressive. Revenues had risen from $8.1 million in 1960 to $358.4 million in 1975, while earnings had increased from $870,000 to $14.9 million. Earnings growth, interrupted only once during the tremendous interest rate escalation in 1973, had been at a 23.4% compounded rate over the previous 10 years, providing a 20% return on equity. In 1976, General Cinema, with 9,600 employees, was the largest theater chain in the United States and the largest independent bottler of both Pepsi-Cola and Dr Pepper products, as well as the largest U.S. soft-drink bottling company, having passed Coke of New York in 1975. (See Exhibits 1 and 2 for income statements and balance sheets.)

432

EXHIBIT 1

GENERAL CINEMA CORPORATION
Balance Sheet—Years Ended October 31
(in thousands of dollars)

Assets	*1960*	*1970*	*1975*
Current assets			
Cash and short-term investments	$2,720	$ 12,562	$ 18,853
Notes and accounts receivable	...	4,683	9,810
Sundry deposits and receivables..............	103	1,465	6,624
Inventories.................................	65	4,788	10,067
Other current assets........................	166	1,206	1,515
Total current assets	$3,054	$ 24,704	$ 46,869
Investments and advances			
Unconsolidated affiliates.....................	$ 780	$ 942	$ 1,189
Broadcasting	...	2,153	15,138
Property, plant, and equipment.................	n.a.	$ 73,976	$137,901
Less depreciation	n.a.	(23,174)	(51,594)
	$4,743	$ 50,802	$ 86,307
Other assets*......................:........	$ 610	$ 12,669	$ 22,489
Franchises, trademarks, and goodwill	...	22,174	31,495
Total assets	$9,187	$113,444	$203,487
Liabilities			
Current liabilities			
Debt due within one year	$ 294	$ 3,629	$ 3,498
Accounts payable..........................	418	13,065	28,522
Taxes payable	568	4,679	9,478
Total current liabilities	$1,280	$ 21,373	$ 41,498
Deferred income tax	...	1,169	2,365
Long-term debt.............................	1,021	58,086	57,852
Other..	208	...	16,198†
Stockholders' equity			
Common stock	$1,186	$ 3,351	$ 5,589
Paid-in capital............................	10	4,441	11,880
Retained earnings..........................	5,493	26,252	70,607
Treasury stock	(13)	(1,228)	(2,502)
Total	$6,676	$ 32,816	$ 85,574
Total liabilities	$9,187	$113,444	$203,487

* Other assets include unamortized leasehold expense of $6,984,000 in 1970 and $13,426,000 in 1975. The remainder is largely loans and accounts receivable due after one year.
† Subordinated debt.
Source: Company records.

HISTORY

General Cinema was an outgrowth of a company organized in 1922 by Mr. Philip Smith to build and operate movie theaters. In 1935 Mr. Smith was credited with constructing and opening the first successful open-air theater. Although the company remained small, it nonetheless

EXHIBIT 2

GENERAL CINEMA CORPORATION
Financial Data for Years Ended October 31
(in thousands of dollars except per-share data)

	1966	1967	1968	1969	1970	1971	1972	1973	1974	1975
Revenues										
Theater division	$33,672	$42,386	$54,294	$ 57,926	$ 70,101	$ 80,183	$ 99,621	$117,121	$142,873	$180,006
Beverage division		....	17,552	85,964	108,757	114,792	120,385	127,756	156,641	178,441
Total	$33,672	$42,386	$71,846	$143,890	$178,858	$194,975	$220,006	$244,877	$299,514	$358,447
Costs and expenses										
Theater division	$29,711	$37,790	$46,570	$48,994	$ 59,048	$ 68,062	$ 85,964	$102,746	$127,770	$161,572
Beverage division		....	15,033	79,393	101,536	105,987	111,967	119,316	144,229	161,106
Total	$29,711	$37,790	$61,603	$128,387	$160,584	$174,049	$197,931	$222,062	$271,999	$322,678
Operating income										
Theater division	$ 3,961	$ 4,596	$ 7,724	$ 8,932	$ 11,053	$ 12,121	$ 13,657	$ 14,375	$ 15,103	$ 18,434
Beverage division		....	2,519	6,571	7,221	8,805	8,418	8,440	12,412	17,335
Total	$ 3,961	$ 4,596	$10,243	$ 15,503	$ 18,274	$ 20,926	$ 22,075	$ 22,815	$ 27,515	$ 35,769
Corporate charges										
Interest	$ 246	$ 308	$ 1,141	$ 3,940	$ 4,314	$ 4,179	$ 4,396	$ 5,893	$ 7,079	$ 5,696
Corporate expenses	352	451	428	597	537	689	627	866	845	1,755
Income before taxes	$ 3,363	$ 3,837	$ 8,673	$ 10,966	$ 13,423	$ 16,058	$ 17,052	$ 16,056	$ 19,591	$ 28,318
Income taxes	1,348	1,647	4,080	5,396	6,418	7,648	7,321	7,210	9,002	13,449
Income before extraordinary items	$ 2,015	$ 2,190	$ 4,593	$ 5,570	$ 7,005	$ 8,410	$ 9,731	$ 8,846	$ 10,589	$ 14,869
Net income	$ 1,982	$ 2,286	$ 4,988	$ 5,947	$ 7,015	$ 9,198	$ 10,349	$ 9,442	$ 11,057	$ 14,869
Depreciation	$ 1,345	$ 1,529	$ 2,669	$ 6,122	$ 7,407	$ 9,045	$ 10,764	$ 11,161	$ 11,939	$ 12,659
Capital expenditures*	n.a.	n.a.	n.a.	n.a.	n.a.	6,785	11,735	10,683	10,404	10,860
Total assets	27,151	29,876	62,472	109,790	129,144	138,782	172,385	178,999	193,208	203,487
Shareholders' equity	12,284	14,060	18,692	29,316	34,457	40,673	56,360	64,268	73,071	85,574
Per-share data										
Net income	$ .41	$ .47	$1.03	$1.14	$1.30	$1.70	$ 1.86	$ 1.69	$ 2.01	$ 2.68
Dividends paid	.12	.12	.13	.17	.23	.28	.32	.34	.41	.465
Book value	2.58	2.91	3.84	5.55	6.53	7.76	10.27	11.69	13.29	15.51
Stock price range†	4.7–3.4	10.6–3.5	33.4–8.5	31.0–18.3	26.5–11.7	40.1–25.6	55.4–31.4	37.2–7.0	14.0–5.3	24.0–7.4

* Excluding new theaters and acquisitions.
† In eighths for calendar years, adjusted for splits.
Source: Company records.

was one of the largest and most successful entrants in the open-air segment of the industry in the years prior to World War II.

Mr. Richard Smith, who became president in 1961 upon his father's death, commented on the years after World War II:

While the rest of the industry enjoyed great prosperity during the war, we just barely survived the effects of gas rationing and daylight savings time. After the war, however, the situation was reversed. Television was devastating to the indoor theater operator and the large chains were beset with legal problems. On the other hand, we found that we attracted a different kind of audience—families and young people—and benefited from laws which lowered driving ages, just as downtown theaters were penalized by inadequate parking facilities. This company was among the first to lengthen the playing season by introducing heaters to keep cars warm in the wintertime. Desirable land parcels of 25 to 35 acres were available in those days close to population centers at reasonable prices, and we expanded by building modern facilities equipped with playgrounds and amusement areas. As our position improved, we began competing for first-run movies.

The postwar period had been dismal for the theater exhibition industry. Competition from television, population shifts to the suburbs, the growth of alternate leisure activities, and a decline in the number of feature films from over 400 to between 200 and 250 had all contributed to a decline in both industry revenues and the number of theaters. The latter had dropped from 18,631 in 1948 to 16,354 in 1958, while admissions receipts had shrunk from $1.7 billion in 1946 to $1 billion in 1958. As a result, movie exhibition receipts declined from 19.8% of U.S. recreational expenditures to 6.3% during that same period.

Also of importance to the industry were the consent decrees which the Justice Department had secured from the "Big Five" (Paramount, Twentieth-Century Fox, Warner Brothers, Loew's and RKO) in 1949 and 1952 after a decade of litigation. As a result, each picture was to be rented on a picture-by-picture, theater-by-theater basis; each existing company was to be divided into a theater-exhibition and a production-distribution company; and certain theaters were to be divested. Divestitures under the consent decree amounted to about 1,200 theaters, contributing significantly to the drop in the number of theaters held by the Big Five from 2,765 in 1948 to 1,223 in 1958.

Up to that time, the Big Five had been vertically integrated, each firm possessing production, distribution, and exhibition facilities. They had dominated the motion picture industry, releasing approximately 80% of all feature films and a significantly higher percentage of box office successes. Although the Big Five controlled only 17% of the nation's theaters in 1945, they accounted for 45% of domestic film rentals. In particular, they were the dominant factor in downtown theater districts, as they operated more than 70% of the first-run movie houses in cities with populations exceeding 100,000. As much as 80% of the profits reported by integrated companies were thought to come from the exhibition activities.

In contrast to the decline in indoor theaters from 17,811 in 1948 to 14,714 in 1954, drive-ins had increased from 820 to 3,775 during the same period. In line with this favorable trend, Midwest Drive-In (the name was changed to General Cinema in 1964) had prospered; by 1959 it was one of the three largest competitors in this segment of the industry. However, as land availability declined and values increased sharply, new locations became difficult to secure and growth leveled off in the late 1950s at about $5.5 million in sales and $600,000 in aftertax profits.

In 1960, Midwest Drive-In acquired the Smith Theater Company (1959 sales of $2.1 million and profits of $136,000), owner of 14 indoor theaters in suburban and resort locations and one drive-in. Both companies were controlled by two families[1] and managed by the Smith Management Company.[2] The combined company then went public with a $2.25 million, 180,000 share offering,[3] with the proceeds from 130,000 shares accruing to certain selling shareholders and the remainder to the company. The company planned to use its proceeds for expansion of shopping center theaters and diversification into tenpins bowling.

Among the properties acquired with the Smith Theater Company was a theater in the Framingham Shopping Center. The shopping center, thought to be the first of its kind in the United States, had caught Philip Smith's imagination in 1951, and the promoter persuaded him to put a theater in it. Initially, the theater lost money and the shopping center itself, for over a decade, experienced periodic financial difficulties. By 1959, however, admission receipts were twice the initial level and the shopping center theater was contributing the largest profits in the theater group by a wide margin. A second shopping center theater had been acquired in 1955, there being at that time, according to management, about four such shopping center theaters in the entire country.

In the late 1950s, Richard Smith, who had assumed responsibility for developing new theater locations, noticed that the number of shopping centers under consideration was increasing rapidly. However, he found promoters, whom he asked to invest the $300,000 required for a 1,200 seat theater, reluctant to take the risk in a troubled industry in conjunction with a small private company. The 1960 merger and public offering were conceived to ease the financial impediments to growth.

---

[1] Prior to the public offering, the Smith family owned or controlled 45.3% and the Stoneman family 25.4% of the outstanding stock of the combined companies. These amounts were reduced to 34.9% and 20.0% following the offering. Mr. Richard Smith was not among the selling shareholders. In 1976 these percentages were approximately 25.1% and 12.4%, the reduction due largely to a secondary issue in 1968.

[2] It was common in the theater industry for individual theaters to be operated by a management company in return for a management fee.

[3] The stock was sold at $12.50 per share, a price equivalent to $2.42 in 1976 shares.

The company prospectus also indicated that the company planned to enter the tenpins bowling business through the immediate construction of three bowling centers in New England having a total of 104 lanes. It noted: "After the company has had the benefit of its experience in this area, it may expand its original goal of 300 to 400 lanes and undertake the establishment of bowling alleys . . . in metropolitan areas outside of New England." It was management's intention to proceed in bowling as it had in open-air theaters. Centers were to be "first-class," complete with restaurants and lounges and geared for use by families and young people. Tenpins bowling was enjoying a rapid rise in popularity in the United States in all parts of the country except the Northeast, which had traditionally been the province of candlepin bowling. According to the American Bowling Congress, the number of tenpins lanes increased 87% from 1955 to 1960 and individual memberships in the Congress jumped 111%.

The management group considered bowling to be a particularly appropriate opportunity for the company; it was a leisure-time business thought to appeal to the type of person who enjoyed an evening at the movies. In addition, automatic pinsetters appeared to make tenpins bowling the most attractive variety of the sport for the participant. Moreover, the company was experienced in securing sites, constructing facilities, and managing a multiple-location business. In some respects growth in bowling seemed more attainable than in theaters; locations were not so difficult to find, since they were not tied to shopping centers, and credit and marketing assistance were readily available from AMF and Brunswick Corporation, the dominant pinsetter manufacturers.

THEATER OPERATIONS

Industry trends

From a nadir in 1962, the movie exhibition business staged a comeback reflected in the statistics in Exhibits 3 and 4. Total receipts were increasing at 5% to 6% a year in the late 1960s, although attendance was growing only 2%. This growth benefited the shopping center and suburban theaters, while the traditional 2,000 to 3,000-seat downtown "movie palace" continued to lose audiences. As shopping center and new suburban theaters began to command a greater share of movie audiences and were often able to obtain higher ticket prices, they broke the dominance of downtown theaters in securing first-run movies.

Other changes occurring in the industry during the sixties were described by Mr. Smith in a 1970 speech:

The myth of the fifties that movies catered primarily to a limited, declining, nonsophisticated segment of the population has been exploded in the sixties

EXHIBIT 3

GENERAL CINEMA CORPORATION
Statistics on the Motion Picture Industry

Year	Admission receipts (millions)	Average admission price	Percent of U.S. recreational expenditures	Percent of U.S. spectator amusement expenditures	Number of feature films*
1946	$1,692	n.a.	19.8%	81.9%	n.a.
1948	1,506	$0.44	15.5	78.5	n.a.
1954	1,228	0.55	9.4	73.4	n.a.
1958	992	0.65	6.3	64.5	n.a.
1960	951	0.69	5.2	59.2	155†
1961	921	0.69	4.7	56.7	185†
1962	903	0.70	4.4	54.9	145
1963	904	0.74	4.1	53.4	150
1964	913	0.76	3.7	51.8	150
1965	927	0.85	3.5	51.2	165
1966	964	0.87	3.3	50.1	168
1967	989	1.19	3.2	47.7	215
1968	1,045	1.31	3.1	49.1	230
1969	1,099	1.42	3.0	48.6	325
1970	1,162	1.55	2.9	48.0	267
1971	1,198	1.65	2.8	47.3	281
1972	1,203	1.70	2.5	45.1	273
1973	1,292	1.76	2.5	44.6	229
1974	n.a.	1.90	n.a.	n.a.	223
1975	n.a.	2.03†	n.a.	n.a.	182

* Approved by Code Administration. In recent years, reissues of old films had become more common, averaging 39 per year from 1970 through 1975.
† Estimated.
n.a. = not available.
Source: U.S. Department of Commerce, Motion Picture Association of America, Film Daily Yearbook of Motion Pictures.

by the success of multiple-auditorium theater complexes simultaneously offering up to eight different films with the widest variety of audience appeal. Areas that only a few years ago were considered marginal for a satisfactory return on the investment required for a single theater now are capable of supporting a multiple-auditorium complex. The most fundamental change in the sixties has been in the audience profile. Today's audiences are, for the most part, younger, better educated, more affluent—many from the academic community and more of the "white-collar" rather than "blue-collar" group. They are critical, involved in the issues of the day, and shun the make-believe world that used to pass for "real life" in the movies that enchanted millions a mere 10 or 15 years ago. . . .

By the mid-seventies, Mr. Smith was even more optimistic. The 1974 annual report commented: "A marked change in movie fare away from the message, social problem, and sex films of the recent past to the pure entertainment and sometimes nostalgic films of today broadened the base of appeal beyond the youth group which had predominated in the

EXHIBIT 4

GENERAL CINEMA CORPORATION
Statistics on Motion Picture Theaters
(number of screens at end of year)

A. U.S. motion picture theaters

Year	Indoor	Drive-in	Total
1948*	17,811	820	18,631
1954*	14,716	3,775	18,491
1958*	12,291	4,063	16,354
1963*	9,150	3,502	12,652
1968†	9,500	3,690	13,190
1973†	10,850	3,800	14,650‡

B. General Cinema theater units in operation

Year	Shopping center	Resort and suburban	Drive-in	Total	Number of locations
1960	4	19	26	49	49
1963	13	18	26	57	56
1968	125	10	49	184	154
1973	387	25	46	458	289
1976	641§	22	11	674	328

* Census.
† Estimate.
‡ From 1968 through 1973 new theaters opened at an annual rate of close to 300, requiring an average investment per theater estimated at $400,000 in 1973.
§ In 1976, there were 41 shopping center theaters with one auditorium, 188 twins, 55 triples, 11 with four, and 3 with five auditoriums.
Source: *Boxoffice Magazine* and company records.

makeup of the movie audience. Now it includes virtually every age and market segment." Mr. Smith expanded in a 1975 speech:

I have been asked many times why I expect theater attendance to continue to rise in spite of its essentially flat behavior all through the sixties. The answer is that in the sixties too many of the film-makers were on the artistic perimeter of society, making films on controversial subjects or trying to make statements on behalf of political causes sometimes and social causes very often. In the last couple of years they have returned to basics. This is an entertainment medium; we do not approach it primarily as an artistic means of expression.

He stressed that these general-audience "breakout" films had attracted more 25-to-50-year-olds on a regular basis. He said: "It becomes increasingly evident that people don't stop going to the movies as they grow older, even though 52% of the population does not go to the movies at all." Mr. Smith expected attendance to increase at a rate of at least 3% over the next few years.

Theater expansion

By late 1976, General Cinema ran 674 theaters at 328 locations in 37 states. They represented approximately 4% of all theaters in the United States and around 9% of the theater industry's revenues. Over 90% of these theaters were located in or near regional shopping centers and were less than 10 years old.

Beginning in 1963, General Cinema had experimented with Cinema I and II theaters, two 500 to 1,000-seat auditoriums under one roof instead of one 1,200 to 1,400-seat auditorium. The test proved successful on several counts. First, there were some operating cost savings in personnel, advertising, and maintenance. Second, the twin auditoriums provided a means of dampening the effect of increasing construction costs while at the same time increasing revenues. The company's investment in a shopping center twin approximated $100,000 to $150,000 as compared with $75,000 to $125,000 for a single auditorium; the average revenue per location was 50% to 80% higher. Although a few auditoriums had been built with as few as 400 seats, the company had not pursued "mini" theaters (less than 300 seats). During the last several years, General Cinema had continuously converted single theaters to twins and twins to triples so that by 1976 multiple theaters dominated with only 69 single-auditorium theaters remaining, a number of which would also eventually be remodeled.

Location was considered to be crucial in determining a theater's success. In addition to the market research performed by the leading retailers in a new shopping center, management was particularly concerned about the economics of film procurement. The existence of several first-run theaters in an area could provide the distributor with leverage to drive a harder bargain and the moviegoer with competitive alternatives. Having a reliable knowledge of operating and construction costs, the company worked with the three remaining variables—ticket price, attendance, and film rental fees—to determine whether there was an opportunity for a 20% return on initial investment after taxes. Refreshment revenues were also important. For example, in 1975 they amounted to $28 million or 40 cents per capita, compared to an average admission price of $2.20. Exhibit 5 gives a breakdown of the typical cost structure of a chain theater.

General Cinema attempted, through clean, modern facilities and tasteful programming, to create an image of sophisticated entertainment that would attract family interest. It was the largest customer for Walt Disney films in the country. Mr. Wintman, executive vice president, touched on the philosophy which guided the division:

> We think we have the best theaters in the business and we don't spare the expense to keep them that way. We build functional not lavish theaters. How-

EXHIBIT 5

GENERAL CINEMA CORPORATION
Typical Cost Structure of a Chain Theater

Admissions		100.0%
Film cost		49.0
Gross profit before operating expenses		51.0%
Operating expenses (ex. rent)		
Advertising	6.0%	
Payroll	17.2	
Supervision	1.8	
Management fee and head office expense	1.5	
Repairs	0.8	
Insurance	0.5	
Utilities	3.3	
Real estate and property taxes	1.3	
Operating supplies and expenses	2.5	
Common area maintenance	1.0	
Other	1.3	
Total		37.2
Gross profit		13.8%
Concession sales	19.8%	
Concession profit		12.3
Net profit before depreciation, rent, interest		26.1%
Rent		11.5
Net profit before interest and depreciation		14.6%

Source: Company records.

ever, once a theater is built, comparatively little reinvestment is needed to maintain it at that level relative to the cash flow it generates. This provides us with a source of funds for expansion.

Two major acquisitions had been made, both departures from company policy of limiting theater additions to shopping centers. In 1970, General Cinema purchased Mann Theaters, which operated 15 theaters in Minneapolis–St. Paul, 13 of them in downtown locations, and had revenues of about $5.6 million, for $5.75 million in cash and notes. Mr. Smith explained in 1971:

We made an exception with Mann's. Minneapolis has done a nice job in resolving its urban problems; the downtown area has a lot of life in it. We had only one theater in Minnesota and had just missed a couple of shopping center deals, which had been upsetting. The Mann Theaters were in good shape and could form the nucleus of a new region. We've since added several shopping center cinemas in the area.

In 1971, the Justice Department filed a civil suit complaint requiring divestiture of the Mann circuit. Two years later the suit was settled by a consent decree whereby General Cinema agreed to sell nine of the acquired theaters, mostly located in downtown areas.

In 1972, General Cinema acquired 47 theaters from Loew's Corporation for slightly over $16 million. The acquisition provided significant initial entry into the first-run Miami, Phoenix, Albuquerque, and the greater Los Angeles markets, where General Cinema had not previously obtained desirable locations. The company expected to convert about 12 of these theaters to twin operations in order to enhance their profitability and to dispose of marginal units. One year later, 21 units, mostly neighborhood and downtown theaters, had been sold for $6 million. The 1973 annual report commented: "We felt that they could not be operated in the same manner as the shopping center theaters around which we have built our business."

Early in 1973, General Cinema announced its intention of phasing out drive-in theaters by leasing for more profitable commercial development properties it owned in fee, by selling or subleasing leased properties, and by allowing leases to expire. Attendance at drive-ins had begun to decline over the past decade due to a great shortage of family-oriented films, the traditional mainstay of drive-in operations, and to increased competition from new shopping center theaters. By 1975, the number of drive-ins had declined to 21 from a peak of 50 in 1971. They still contributed 2.5% of General Cinema's total theater revenues, but in terms of income they had recently been operating at a small loss.

A total of $48 million had been invested during the last five years in new or remodeled theaters, according to the 1975 annual report. General Cinema, given the favorable industry outlook, planned to continue expansion at a rate of about 70–80 theaters per year. Mr. Smith explained: "We have been selective, turning down each year several times the number of locations actually accepted. Our selectivity will not be compromised just to reach expected growth levels. Indeed, in order to build 75 new theaters a year we now require only 20 to 25 locations because our average new unit is a three-theater complex." General Cinema management felt that there was still major growth ahead for shopping center theaters in spite of a slowdown in shopping center construction. The greatest opportunities were felt to be in the sun belt because of its population growth and resulting need for additional retail facilities. In 1976, Mr. Smith was asked about General Cinema's rationale for building more and more theaters every year. His answer was "because we still get about a 40% pretax, pre-interest return on each new shopping center theater that we build. When you show me some better place to put my capital, I'll do it."

Competition

Mr. Wintman described General Cinema's competitive position as follows:

Although General Cinema pioneered the shopping center theater concept, it made no attempt to preempt the marketplace. As early as October 1963, the president of General Cinema publicly urged exhibitors to seek locations in suburbia. It was sincerely felt that an influx of new and viable theaters would serve as an inducement to film producers to increase their investments in films. Over the years, local exhibitors expanded into the suburbs of their own marketplaces while national circuits competed for the regional shopping center locations.

The ease of entry served to proliferate competition. Any exhibitor or entrepreneur with acceptable credit had only to furnish the theater facilities leased to him by the shopping center and built to his specifications. An exhibitor desiring further leverage could lease equipment and enter the marketplace at little or no cost.

Most marketplaces today are fairly saturated and expansion is limited to the relatively few new shopping centers being built, which in most instances will draw upon patronage already attending existing theaters. There exists virtually no market in which there is not already a competitive situation, and General Cinema faces strong competition in every one of its markets. Future expansion will of necessity be limited to marketplaces in which existing movie facilities are either old, poorly maintained and operated, or badly located with respect to population growth and highway accessibility. New shopping center theaters in these places could well prove extraordinarily successful.

Competition in the theater exhibition industry took place at the local, not the national, level. Hence, General Cinema's major competitors differed from market to market. In some places local exhibitors would aggressively compete for locations or film rentals, while in others the major pressure came from national chains. However, the dominance of the "Big Five" theater exhibition companies had long since been broken and their successor companies had evolved differently. Paramount Theaters had merged with the American Broadcasting Companies (ABC), contributing $74 million or 7% of its revenues in 1975 through 277 theaters. Stanley Warner and RKO had after a series of mergers become part of Cinerama Inc., with over 100 theaters contributing $38.5 million in 1975 revenues. Twentieth-Century Fox' theater company as National General had diversified ultimately into insurance, making it a desirable merger target for American Financial Corporation which retained only the insurance portion of the business and sold the theaters to a privately held company. Loew's, where control had shifted from Metro-Goldwyn-Mayer to the Tish brothers, had diversified into hotels and real estate and had made some major takeovers, such as Lorillard and CNA, so that by 1975 its 102 theaters contributed only 1.4% of total revenues.

In addition to competition from other exhibitors, General Cinema was confronted by alternative means of dispensing movies. Since recent box-office successes were not generally available to television and inventories of older films were being rapidly depleted, each of the television networks had begun the production of feature-length pictures for original release. Lurking in the background was the prospect of pay TV, which conceivably could offer competitive rental fees to conventional film distributors for first-run pictures. A third possibility was the video cassette or disc. The viewer would buy or rent a film on video tape or disc and replay it at his convenience on a recorder incorporated in or attached to his television set.

Back in 1971, Mr. Wintman had indicated that in his opinion these new sources of competition would not have a serious impact on theater operators:

The economics of the business work against other means of exhibition. A feature-length picture can be shown on television once or maybe twice during prime time, no matter how good it is, while we can offer guarantees of 10–15 weeks for a picture like "Love Story." As a result, television can afford perhaps $500,000 to $600,000 per picture, about the equivalent of a double-length regular hour TV program. That is a million or so less than the cost of a good low-budget film. In fact, we support the networks: the more films produced, the better. If they strike a good one, they may bring it to theaters first, or, if not, we are always interested in less expensive fillers.

Pay TV, on the other hand, could be a problem if a large enough audience could be attracted. However, the public hasn't accepted the pay-TV concept. We also suspect that the moviegoer really wants to get out of the house, especially the woman, to see a show. For this reason, I bet, except for pornography, cassettes won't generate much of a market for recreational films either, though they may be great for educational purposes.

In 1975, Mr. Smith reiterated this theme:

As happens with each new technological advance in the telecommunications field, a new round of speculation about the future of movie theaters takes place. Currently two such advances, the satellite-linked pay-TV movie service network and the video-disc players, the visual equivalent of the phonograph, are in the news. In spite of these and other remarkable technical advances, nothing major has changed or will change the basic marketing of motion pictures. According to Paul Kagan Associates, a leading authority on pay TV, there are currently ten million cable subscribers and the number should grow to 20 million by 1980. Their projection contemplates that there might be three million pay-TV subscribers by 1980. There is no way that an audience of this size can produce the income necessary to obtain first-run pictures in competition with movie theaters. We are talking about a small audience overlap in any event, without considering demographic, economic, and geographical limitations. We still feel that free home television, offering a choice from about 50 movies a week, is our principal competition, although supplemental income to film suppliers from pay TV after theatrical exhibition may eventually be a further stimulant for film production.

As to the video-disc players, it is beyond our comprehension how any but the most wealthy 1% or 2% of the population would spend the money to buy a player for more than $500 and then pay $10 to $20 to see a picture on a TV screen perhaps two or three times at the most. This device will have to find its market in something much cheaper than motion picture features or in material suitable for repeated viewing if it is to be economically viable.

Film procurement

During the early sixties, General Cinema had found it difficult at first to procure first-run movies for its new shopping center theaters. In several instances the company had to "buy its way" into markets by bidding aggressively on top pictures until its reputation had been established in the community and among film distributors. Exhibitors negotiated with film distributors, in competition with other exhibitors, for the right to show films. The terms of these arangements were influenced not only by competition among exhibitors but even more by the availability of popular films. A product shortage had gradually shifted the bargaining power to the distributors. By the seventies rentals for the popular films sometimes caused operating losses. Terms also had stiffened with respect to the number of weeks that a movie had to be shown, the guarantee of a minimum payment for which the exhibitor was obligated, payment conditions, dates when movies were to be shown (distributors tended to concentrate introductions during the Christmas and summer seasons), and the pressure on exhibitors to take several pictures from the same distributor.

In spite of this shift in bargaining position, film producers had found their business to be extremely volatile. For example, by the end of the sixties, the large old-line production-distribution companies, which continued to dominate film releases, had incurred massive write-offs of $250 million, caused by excessive inventories of high-budget films. This volatility in performance greatly affected the supply of films, which, in turn, influenced the operating results of the exhibitors.

The supply of product had become a major concern for General Cinema management. The 1975 annual report stated: "Over the past few years, the number of major new feature films produced has declined. Conversely, as we continue to expand our theater circuit, our requirements for these films are increasing." Not only the supply but also the cost of film rentals were of concern to management. General Cinema in 1975 was playing 80%–85% first-run pictures compared to 40%–50% in the sixties. As a result, film rentals had escalated from 35%–40% of box-office receipts to over 50%, and operating margins had declined somewhat to around the 10% level. Nevertheless, over the previous 15 years, General Cinema theater prices had stayed ahead of cost increases. Even though consumer resistance to ticket-price changes had not significantly affected attendance, General Cinema had not aggressively raised its ticket prices.

Since 1970, prices had increased an average of 3.7% annually, a significantly lower rate than that of the consumer price index.

To respond to these pressures, General Cinema in 1975 departed from its long-standing policy of not engaging in film production. As Mr. Smith stated:

> Our strategy to prevent further escalation of film costs and to be in a position to alleviate any future shortage of film product will be to enter the field of film financing for the benefit of established independent film suppliers and independent distributors. We will pay about $75 million in film rentals this year, and a large part is committed before the pictures open in our theaters, in line with currrent industry practice. By committing to these contracts earlier, they can become bankable collateral to help finance high-quality independent film producers without any significant change in our exposure or any major use of our capital. We are now working on a number of such arrangements and we feel confident that our film supply will be enriched in both quality and quantity as a result of these efforts.
>
> Our film financing program aims to avoid much of the volatility of production earnings and yet supply a maximum of quality popular films to a product-starved industry. In fiscal 1977 we expect to deliver a program of pictures worth over $30 million with minimal financial exposure to General Cinema. In our program we have elected to presell to the U.S. television networks the exhibition rights of our films following domestic theatrical release. In addition, we have presold foreign distribution rights. This approach cuts down the ultimate rewards on a blockbuster picture but also reduces the risk in that only 30% to 40% of the costs needs to be recovered in the U.S. market to break even. The primary objective of creating an additional supply of product is to benefit our theater division. However, if this venture's profits can meet our requirements in terms of return on capital at risk, we shall consider this as a potential area for diversification.

SOFT-DRINK BOTTLING OPERATIONS

General Cinema's entry

General Cinema's entry into soft-drink bottling operations took place in early 1968 through acquisition of the American Beverage Corporation for $18.1 million in cash. Through a sale and leaseback agreement, $12 million was raised to apply against the purchase. Exhibit 6 provides the terms and scope of this and subsequent acquisitions. This major diversification into soft-drink bottling was accomplished without substantial dilution. Financing took place largely through sale and leaseback transactions, borrowing, and internally generated funds, with only one acquisition made by issuing common stock. In 1970 General Cinema had formulated its investment policy in the beverage division as "limiting

EXHIBIT 6

GENERAL CINEMA CORPORATION
Beverage Acquisitions

Year acquired	Label	Location	Cost (millions)	No. of plants	Closed ( )
1968......	Pepsi-Cola	Dayton, Akron, Youngstown (Ohio); Miami (Florida)	$18,100	4	
	Private	Houston (Texas)		1	(1)
1968......	Seven-Up	Miami	1,500	1	(1)
1968......	Pepsi-Cola	Jacksonville, Gainesville, Ocala (Florida); Savannah (Georgia); Lynchburg (Virginia); Charleston (West Virginia); Bloomington, Seymour, Vincennes (Indiana)	8,900	8	(1)
1968......	Seven-Up	Savannah	150	...	
1969......	Seven-Up	Jacksonville	650	...	
1969......	Pepsi-Cola	Cleveland (Ohio)	4,900	2	
1969......	Dr. Pepper	Dayton, Akron, Youngstown	100	...	
1969......	Dr. Pepper	Cleveland	100	...	
1969......	Pepsi-Cola	Atlanta (Georgia)	3,300	1	
1969......	Pepsi-Cola Seven-Up Dr. Pepper	Athens (Georgia)	1,100	1	
1969......	Dr. Pepper	Vincennes Illinois (5 counties) Indiana (5 counties)	20 40		
1969......	Seven-Up	Charleston	250		
1969......	Pepsi-Cola	Gainesville (Georgia)	430	1	
1972......	Dr. Pepper	Lynchburg	440		
1972......	Seven-Up	Atlanta	888		
1973......	Pepsi-Cola	Sacramento (California); Winston-Salem, Greensboro (North Carolina); Springfield (Ohio)	15,118*	4	(1)
1973......	Pepsi-Cola	Roanoke (Virginia)	1,710	1	
1975......	Dr. Pepper	Atlanta, Gainesville (Ga.)	1,223		
1975......	Dr. Pepper Hires	Miami	800		
		Total	59,719	24	(4)

* This acquisition involved an exchange of shares; all others were made for cash.
Source: Company records.

capital outlays so that they would not exceed depreciation, leaving net profit for the retirement of debt." During the five years through 1975, capital expenditures for soft-drink bottling amounted to $45 million, slightly exceeding the total depreciation figure.

During the early years, profits were modest when compared to either the theater operations or the company's total investment in soft-drink bottling. In 1972, beverage profits even declined, explained in the annual report as "reflecting the heavy burden on gross margins resulting from the cost-price squeeze and our aggressive marketing efforts." During that

year, General Cinema restructured the divisional organization and incurred heavy marketing expenses by being among the first to initiate tests
with new resalable, returnable, 32-ounce and 16-ounce bottles which
generated a higher profit margin. The annual report stated:

> Promotional and discounting expenditures for the introduction of the new
> packages were necessarily heavy to meet competitors' responses. Although
> largely nonrecurring and in the nature of an investment from which we ex-
> pect future earnings, they were properly charged to current operating in-
> come. A second factor reduced earnings rather significantly for this division.
> Throughout most of the year we were caught in a cost-price squeeze from
> which we were unable to implement government-approved price relief until
> well into the third quarter, thus preventing us from offsetting about nine
> months of higher costs with normal price adjustments.

By 1975, Mr. Smith described the development of the beverage division as "one of the more successful diversifications of any company of
our approximate size." He continued:

> The strategy we adopted to accomplish this diversification was to seek
> leisure-time, consumer-oriented areas, where we could use our management
> skills to operate a larger pool of assets, without substantial dilution of our
> stock. The soft-drink industry, which we chose as the first major leg of our
> diversification, suited our objectives ideally. Soft drinks have enjoyed an extra-
> ordinary record of sustained long-term growth. Per-capita consumption of
> soft drinks during the past ten years (from 1964–1974) has grown 65%. Soft
> drinks, which ranked a very weak number three among beverage categories
> in 1964, should become America's favorite beverage, surpassing coffee within
> a year. Another highly favorable trend has been the growth of the national
> brands paced by the four leaders—Coca-Cola, Pepsi-Cola, 7-Up and Dr. Pep-
> per. We elected to seek a major position in the marketing of Pepsi-Cola which
> we felt offered the best opportunity in the industry for future growth.

General Cinema had pursued a multifranchise concept of adding 7-Up,
Dr. Pepper, and other nationally franchised beverages to the Pepsi line
of the acquired companies.

The organization of the beverage division had evolved from a decentralized to a centralized structure. Initially a beverage operating committee, composed of both corporate and operating managers, supervised the
acquisitions. Mr. Smith explained in 1971:

> Soft-drink bottling is essentially a local business and we bought a group
> of family-dominated companies. Other than consolidating some of the smaller
> acquisitions into the three large ones, we have left the organizations about
> as they were. I have resisted putting a single person in charge of beverages
> for a couple of reasons. First, I can't be sure whether there is anyone in the
> organization ready for the job yet. I would rather see how things go for a
> while before deciding who the person ought to be. Second, we didn't know
> much about the business when we made the acquisitions. Having someone

between us and the market might have restricted the amount of information flowing up here. I keep in contact with Pepsico, but other than putting in financial controls, evaluating capital requests, and discussing the timing of price increases, we haven't done much to interfere.

A single management team, however, was established in 1972 in Miami with Herbert G. Paige as president, to whom three geographic division managers reported. Even though local plant autonomy was partially preserved, a strong professional staff was also created by hiring several key managers from other successful consumer products companies. Mr. Smith commented in 1976:

> Following this reorganization, professional management of budgeting, purchasing, production, and marketing became more sophisticated compared to anything previously accomplished by other independent bottlers. We had waited just long enough after the initial acquisitions to understand the basics of the soft-drink business and to appraise the strengths and weaknesses of the people who had been managing the acquisitions. Thus we were able to select Herb Paige as a strong leader and to permit the creation of a strong central management. By the time we needed to restructure the organization, most of the people were prepared to support General Cinema's efforts to become "the best in the industry."

Industry trends

The soft-drink bottling industry operated on the basis of a long-standing franchising tradition. Franchised bottlers paid the franchiser for the concentrate to make the drink and were charged a fee to cover a portion of the franchiser's national advertising expenditures. In return, bottlers received exclusive rights to produce and market the product in a specified territory, an advertising allowance for a portion of their local advertising, some technical services in marketing and manufacturing, and various types of assistance in packaging, including the development of new containers. Bottlers had final responsibility for pricing, packaging, local advertising, and merchandising, although the franchisers attempted to encourage certain uniform policies.

In 1971, the Federal Trade Commission filed a suit to determine whether the exclusive sales territories franchised to bottlers represented a restraint of trade. The suit attempted to eliminate territorial restrictions in the sale of soft drinks across franchise lines, not the rights of franchised bottlers to bottle exclusively in their territories. In 1975 the administrative law judge hearing the case upheld the exclusivity of marketing areas. It was not yet clear whether the FTC would accept the decision or would initiate further proceedings. General Cinema management had repeatedly stated that its beverage business as a whole would not be adversely affected regardless of the outcome.

The three principal markets for soft drinks were food stores (44% of sales in 1975), fountains (21%), and vending machines (18%), with the remaining 17% coming from a wide variety of smaller outlets. Overall, Coca-Cola was the leader among soft-drink franchisers with a market share of over 40%, about twice that of its nearest competitor, Pepsi-Cola. Coca-Cola was particularly strong in the on-premise (fountain) and "cold drink" (vending machines) markets, while in food stores its position was less dominant (see Exhibit 7). However, competitive shares

EXHIBIT 7

GENERAL CINEMA CORPORATION
Total U.S. Soft-Drink Market Shares in Food Stores*
(8-ounce equivalent case basis)

	1965	1970	1971	1972	1973	1974	1975
Pepsi-Cola†	19.8%	19.9%	19.6%	20.2%	20.6%	20.9%	21.4%
Coca-Cola	19.5	21.4	21.1	21.0	20.9	21.0	21.3
Royal Crown	n.a.	5.1	5.3	5.2	4.7	4.7	4.8
Seven-Up	7.2	7.2	7.1	7.1	7.2	7.3	7.1
Dr. Pepper (reg.)	n.a.	3.2	3.2	3.4	3.5	3.7	3.8
All diet products	15.5	9.4	11.6	12.8	13.8	14.2	16.6
Diet Pepsi	(3.0)	(1.8)	(2.0)	(1.9)	(1.9)	(2.1)	(2.4)
Tab	(2.5)	(1.0)	(1.6)	(2.3)	(2.7)	(2.6)	(2.8)
Diet Rite	(4.3)	(2.0)	(1.9)	(1.7)	(1.3)	(1.2)	(1.3)
Diet 7-Up	n.a.	n.a.	(0.4)	(0.4)	(0.5)	(0.5)	(1.4)
S.F. Dr. Pepper	n.a.	n.a.	(0.3)	(0.4)	(0.6)	(0.7)	(0.9)
Private labels	n.a.	13.1	12.8	12.4	12.2	11.3	10.2

* Differences between 100% and totals for each year are accounted for by other brands.

† Pepsi-Cola share has always appeared relatively stronger on an 8-ounce equivalent basis since it draws very little volume from the smaller size bottles, whereas Coke, Royal Crown, and 7-Up hold significant shares in small bottles.

Source: Company records based on A. C. Nielsen data.

varied considerably among markets. In some cities, Pepsi-Cola outsold Coke by close to 3 to 1, while in others the ratio was reversed. General Cinema managers attributed such variations, in large part, to the length of time the bottler had been in the market, the quality of his route-man training and supervision, and the amount of advertising and "price-off" money he was prepared to spend. Private labels had increased their share in the take-home market during the sixties from less than 4% to over 10% (and to over 20% in chain stores), but during the seventies their position had declined.

Cola-flavored drinks continued to dominate the soft-drink market with about 60% of sales, while diet drinks by 1975 had regained the share they had held before the 1969 ban on cyclamates, which had greatly reduced their sales. Packaging changes had had a substantial impact on the industry, adversely affecting the smaller bottlers. As a result, the number of bottlers had fallen from a peak of about 8,000 in 1960 to 2,400 in

1975. It was estimated that a few hundred of them accounted for more than two-thirds of the volume.

The sixties saw a rapid acceptance of nonreturnable (NR) bottles and cans, which sharply increased packaging costs and permitted larger bottlers, who were able to effect lower production costs and lower delivery expense, to compete more aggressively on price promotions. This trend had also resulted in smaller margins for the industry as a whole. Another packaging trend favored larger size bottles, which during the fifties had accounted for only a small percentage of sales, but had captured a continuously increasing share of the take-home market (see Exhibit 8).

EXHIBIT 8

GENERAL CINEMA CORPORATION
U.S. Soft-Drink Packaging Trends in Food Stores
(in physical cases)

	1972	1973	1974	1975	1976 (6 months)
Bottles over 17 ounces					
Nonreturnable	15.4%	16.8%	17.1%	18.2%	19.3%
Returnable	5.0	7.9	10.0	12.0	14.3
16-ounce returnables	18.6	18.0	18.1	19.7	20.4
All other bottles	32.8	27.6	24.5	22.1	20.2
Cans	28.2	29.7	30.3	28.0	25.8
Total	100.0%	100.0%	100.0%	100.0%	100.0%
Returnable bottles	42.9%	41.5%	41.2%	43.0%	44.4%
Nonreturnable bottles	28.9	28.8	28.5	29.0	29.8
Cans*	28.2	29.7	30.3	28.0	25.8
Total	100.0%	100.0%	100.0%	100.0%	100.0%

* The long-term growth of cans was interrupted by the sugar-spurred pricing and discounting environment of 1975.
Source: Company records based on Nielsen data.

Growing pressure from environmentalists to limit the use of one-way containers had resulted in legislative efforts in numerous states either to ban or to tax NR bottles and cans. Oregon and Vermont had passed such legislation. These environmental pressures brought about a sizable shift in 1972 from NR to returnable bottles. General Cinema's management felt that it would be less affected by restrictive legislation as returnable bottles in 1975 accounted for 62% of its packages, a figure well above the national average. Also, the Oregon experience showed that major brands increased their market share at the expense of private labels and local bottlers.

More critical than any of the above pressures appeared to be the enormous cost increases which confronted the industry in 1974. The major escalation of the price of sugar, together with inflationary cost increases for labor, other ingredients, packaging materials, supplies, and fuel, necessitated a 50% price adjustment to offset these rising costs. After a relatively flat year in 1975, sales resumed their upward trend in 1976, leading management to conclude that the demand for soft drinks was relatively price inelastic.

In the decade preceding these drastic price increases, industry sales had grown at an annual rate of over 7%. Only 0.9% growth was attributed to a larger population and 0.1% to a changing mix in the population's age. Thus, nondemographic factors were seen as the major contributors to the growth in consumption of soft drinks. Industry observers mentioned packaging innovations, product availability, taste preferences, and marketing. They felt that soft-drink sales would continue to grow, although at a somewhat lower rate of between 4% and 5% per year. General Cinema executives were equally optimistic, as articulated by Mr. Smith in 1975:

There are a number of positive trends which augur well for the soft-drink industry. Even assuming only modest population growth, prevailing opinion is that per-capita consumption of soft drinks should continue to increase about 5% per year and we expect national brands to continue to garner a larger share of total industry volume. Demographics favor the industry in the teen to thirty age group, where the heavy consumers are. The present success of soft-drink business had been largely built on sales to less than 20% of the population who presently account for more than 70% of all consumption. Furthermore, we continue to see rapid growth in soft-drink consumption in franchise areas where per-capita levels are already double the national average.

General Cinema's position and policies

In 1976 General Cinema operated 21 beverage plants and 18 distribution centers serving 7% of the population. Products were principally distributed in trucks operated by route salesmen to retail outlets and, in some instances, to distributors. The company also owned or leased coolers and vending machines to dispense products in factories, schools, service stations, and other locations. In virtually all of the markets serviced by General Cinema, Pepsi-Cola's market share was well ahead of that of major competitors and substantially exceeded Pepsi-Cola nationally. In all these areas combined, General Cinema's corporate share in the take-home market amounted to 37.7% in 1975 versus Coke's share of 29.3%

Executives felt that General Cinema could outperform the industry. Mr. Smith explained:

The geographic location of our franchises favors us as their population growth rate is above the national average. We believe that our objective of increasing the market share of the three major brands we bottle from 35% to 50% is attainable. Also, per-capita consumption is considerably higher than the national average in many of our markets.

This optimism for the future was based on several factors which Mr. Smith described as follows:

The business is managed in a highly professional way by an experienced group, which is a blend of line managers with extensive soft-drink experience and of sophisticated specialists with other consumer packaged-goods backgrounds. We initiate our own marketing programs which, we believe, is important in our ability to outperform other soft-drink bottlers over the long run. The fact that many of our marketing programs have been imitated by the franchiser companies during the past two years suggests that we are having some success in pioneering new ideas and techniques for the soft-drink business.

Our Beverage Division management continually seeks to identify and capitalize on growth opportunities within the soft-drink market. An example of this has been our stress on the larger size growth packages. These packages represented less than 15% of food store soft-drink sales four years ago; today they represent almost 35% of sales. Computerized information systems augmented by purchased market research data is instrumental in our ability to manage our pricing policies, control costs, distribution system innovations, major marketing activities, manpower allocation, and production efficiency. Centralized management control has also permitted economies of scale in purchasing raw materials—particularly sugar, packaging, advertising, and other important items. Finally, plant modernization and automation have created increased manufacturing efficiencies.

OTHER DIVERSIFICATION

Bowling operations

The number of bowling centers operated by General Cinema grew rapidly to 15 having 494 lanes in 1963 and accounting for about 10% of corporate sales. However, difficulties were encountered from the outset, and as early as 1962 thoughts of a major expansion into bowling were put aside. The centers never quite reached the break-even point. Five of them were either sold or converted into cinemas between 1965 and 1967 and in late 1968 long-term leases with purchase options were issued to Consolidated Bowling Corporation for the remaining facilities for a fee which approximated General Cinema's annual expenses.

However disheartening the bowling interlude had been, Mr. Smith expressed the view that the experience had been a healthy one for the management group:

We made some mistakes in entering the bowling business. For one, we misjudged our market. Rather than depending on families and the casual player, the bowling alley relies on blue-collar men's leagues in the evening and daytime bowling by women's groups—frequently the blue-collar workers' wives. The work force in New England is less blue-collar heavy industry than in the Midwest and is a lot more difficult to organize this way. We started to uncover the difficulty when we opened three centers outside of New England as part of our program to learn the business.

To attract leagues you should also be able to sell beer on the lanes. We found we weren't very good at securing liquor licenses. We underestimated the competitive response from the candlepin operators in New England.

Withdrawing wasn't easy. The pinsetter manufacturers were competing with one another for good locations and putting pressure on operators to keep up. However, the operation was taking time away from theater expansion, and we began to discuss what ought to be done with it. Some of the group didn't want to accept a reverse and were in favor of trying to make it work. I thought we had given the business sufficient effort, and after a lot of discussion we finally decided to withdraw.

Communications

In 1968 General Cinema decided to enter the communications field and subsquently made investments in FM radio stations in Philadelphia, Houston, Cleveland, and Chicago; in AM and FM radio stations in Atlanta; and in a television station in Miami. By the end of 1974, however, management decided that communications could not be a major division. It was felt that profitable stations commanded extremely high prices which would not provide a satisfactory return based on the high 1974 interest rates and the requirements relating to the amortization of goodwill. In addition, management had been discouraged by continuing litigation with respect to a proposed change from classical to contemporary music for its Chicago station. "It demonstrates the special difficulties and significant potential expenses which exist in the broadcast field and its attendant increasing governmental regulation," Mr. Smith said in 1976. Accordingly, a decision was made to withdraw General Cinema's investment in radio broadcasting "as a hedge against continuing losses in Chicago and a possible adverse decision in the pending litigation." Management indicated that, assuming the pending Atlanta sale were completed, the radio investment would be recovered with

General Cinema retaining the Miami TV station and the FM stations in Philadelphia and Chicago.

Furniture retailing

In 1972 General Cinema had entered into an agreement to finance Alperts, Inc., in its development of a chain of 100,000 to 150,000 square foot retail furniture warehouse showrooms. A pilot store was opened in the fall of that year near Providence, Rhode Island, with four more openings scheduled for 1973. Although management was convinced that the warehouse-showroom concept was fundamentally sound and represented a long-overdue change in a basic $10 billion industry, it had limited its initial financial commitment to debentures convertible into 70% of the equity, with options for eventual 100% ownership. Operations were directed by the Alpert brothers, experienced and successful retail furniture merchants. General Cinema's background and expertise in the real estate field and its financial strength, coupled with the Alperts' furniture experience, were expected to provide the new company with a sound management base for significant growth.

General Cinema management felt that the warehouse furniture concept fit in with many of General Cinema's strengths and also had certain potential for growth for the following reasons: (1) General Cinema's expertise in location selection and in managing and controlling geographically separate locations was an important factor; (2) as a capital-intensive business, it permitted the use of leverage through sale and lease-back of properties and through leasing and inventory loans with General Cinema's credit; (3) as a new form of an old business, it had a similar effect to that of motels on hotels; and (4) if the initial trial proved successful, after a short period of one to two years the company could expand and open 10 to 20 locations in a two-year period, each location doing approximately $5 million. This project could then become an important segment of General Cinema's business.

In 1975, however, Mr. Smith commented:

Our investment in Alperts Furniture doesn't look too promising at this time. Like all furniture retailers in this recession, it has suffered declining volumes in its three stores (in Providence, Albany, and Buffalo). At our request, Alperts has reduced its total program to four stores, the last of which is under construction in Cleveland and will open in November. Furthermore, we have extended the time for decision about our future involvement with Alperts until 1981 and there will be no further expansion until we see some operating profits. In 1974, Alperts' operating loss was $334,000 and in 1975 it may lose over a million dollars. Although this is not a consolidated operation, we are reserving for Alperts' losses against our current earnings to prevent the buildup of any large future write-off. Our total cash investment in Alperts is about $2 million.

In 1976 the retail furniture warehouse stores were expected to lose $300,000, and management hoped that they would break even in 1977.

Diversification: A continuing challenge

After the bowling venture I didn't think seriously about diversification until our cash-flow picture started to change in 1966 and it became clear that we were going to have money to invest. We weren't afraid to think big. In 1967 we almost bought a $100 million vending machine company which in many ways complemented our theater business. However, our P/E was only 10 then and the dilution would have been substantial because a considerable amount of stock would have had to be used. Everyone here was bullish about theaters as well and didn't want to risk a conflict of interest situation with other vendor operators.

The cash-flow picture which Mr. Smith referred to was caused by the fact that movie theaters were generating more cash than could be put back into theaters alone. In the mid-sixties, management decided that it would better serve stockholders, of which about one third were financial institutions, by becoming a company with substantial long-term growth potential rather than merely a dividend payer. It was decided to develop at least one and possibly two more operating divisions, with the goal of reducing theater-related earnings to approximately 50% of the total.

This goal had been achieved by 1975 through the soft-drink bottling acquisitions and their subsequent success. Yet, as the large debt created by these acquisitions was gradually reduced and the cash flow remained strongly positive, management continued to see a need for further diversification.

In its two major businesses, General Cinema had limited its need for funds through a long-standing policy of leasing. Beverage plants were leased on a fixed rental basis and almost all the shopping center theaters on a fixed-plus-percentage rental basis. In 1975, rental expenses amounted to close to $22 million, of which $17.6 million constituted minimum annual rents. For theaters the percentage had been steadily declining, and management viewed many of the leases, which had been negotiated in periods of lower construction and interest costs, as assets rather than liabilities because it would cost substantially more to replace them at current costs.

In 1975, J. Atwood Ives, vice president and a director, commented regarding some of General Cinema's other financial policies which had recently improved the financial position:

Several years ago, we decided that improving our debt/equity ratio and increasing our liquidity should be corporate objectives. The debt/equity ratio had been increasing steadily since our first beverage acquisition and peaked at 1.77 to 1 in 1970. This year, we will attain our first objective of reducing debt to a level lower than our equity for the first time since we began buying beverage companies in 1968.

The second objective was to improve our liquidity by spreading out our debt maturities. Over the last several years, rapidly changing short-term interest rates have had a meaningful effect on our operating earnings as we have had substantial amounts of debt tied to prime. In fact, we used to point out, based on approximately $55 million of debt outstanding tied to prime, that a percentage point change in the prime rate added or subtracted five cents in annual per-share earnings. This year we greatly improved our liquidity by completing a $30 million private placement of 15-year senior notes at 11%. The proceeds will be used to fund our present bank borrowings. This financing will have the added advantage of substantially lowering the amount of debt outstanding that is tied to prime, thereby reducing the impact on future operating earnings caused by significant swings in short-term interest rates. With the completion of this financing and the retention of our bank lines, we will have sufficient funds available to us to meet all anticipated capital requirements of our present businesses. Also, we will have achieved sufficient financing flexibility to move positively and promptly on any new opportunity for expansion into a third major division.

General Cinema's improved financial posture revived discussions about what had previously been referred to as "the third leg of the stool." Mr. Smith reflected:

We are in the position again of having funds available for investment. I am interested in developing just one additional opportunity. When the company was smaller, it was O.K. to think about starting in a field from scratch, but that isn't as appropriate now as the purchase of an exisitng business. It should be big enough to have an immediate impact on earnings. It should have a capable management, good growth prospects, and a continuing need for investment. At the same time, General Cinema must be able to bring its competence to bear on the new business. I don't want to be dependent on the specialized skills of a few individuals. For that reason highly technical or stylized or even manufacturing businesses are not really of interest.

Mr. Wintman stressed certain additional concerns related to diversification:

I would like to continue in service businesses where we have some expertise. We should learn to be as proficient as those already in whatever business we enter. Rather than becoming dependent on an acquired management, I would feel more comfortable if we could do their job as well as they do if the need arose.

Mr. Lane, who had been associated with the company since 1949 and who had retired in 1976 as financial vice president, reflected on some of the reasons for General Cinema's success:

We have a tremendous pride in the accomplishments of General Cinema. Our executive group has been able to make quick decisions that have been essential in nailing down theater sites and making acquisitions. Our batting average has been pretty good so far. Dick Smith has a great deal of self-confidence and optimism that has given us the spirit to take controversial locations and make them work.

The beverage business looked like it might have been the solution to our diversification problems. We had found another noncyclical growth business that could be leveraged to the benefit of our shareholders. However, there just aren't many more good franchises around at the right price, and, if we bought one for cash, the new accounting rules for goodwill could hurt us.[4] The business is now self-sustaining and we are looking again.

As a means of internal communication and a guide for evaluating diversification opportunities, Mr. Lane in the early seventies had sum-

EXHIBIT 9

GENERAL CINEMA CORPORATION
Acquisition Objectives

We are presently engaged in two main areas: THEATRES and SOFT DRINKS. We are not interested in becoming a conglomerate; we are interested in a third major division to absorb our increasing cash flow rather than use it to pay off debt.

Describing the third division in general terms is simple; in specific terms, difficult. It should be leisure-time-oriented, consumer-oriented, perhaps service-oriented and youth-oriented. It must have good potential for expansion to keep pace with our overall corporate growth rate of 15%–20% or better, with perhaps $2–$3 million earnings. If smaller, it must be able to absorb infusions of capital for accelerated growth. In other words, it must provide a base for a third large division. Further, it should be a field in which it is possible to achieve a return on investment of at least 20% before taxes.

It is also fairly simple to rule out what we don't want: research and development, complicated manufacturing processes, involved or unique technology, cyclical or stylized characteristics; cash flow rather than earnings.

Possible fields—and these are by no means intended to be all-inclusive or exclusive—are:

BEVERAGES .... Soft drinks (major Pepsi-Cola franchises, other national brands to complement the areas in which we now operate; no private label brands)

HOUSEHOLD FURNISHINGS
COMMUNICATIONS .... (*earnings*, not just cash flow)
EDUCATION
DIRECT MAIL MARKETING
ENTERTAINMENT .... Motion pictures, musical
REAL ESTATE .... Development services (earnings, not just cash flow)

OTHER SERVICES .... Household, business, parking lots, vending
SPECIALTY RETAILING .... Gifts, novelties, greeting cards, crafts, games, sewing, hobbies

Source: Company memorandum.

---

[4] Goodwill (the excess of purchase price over net taxable assets) created by acquisitions accounted for as a purchase had to be amortized over not more than 40 years, according to a 1970 opinion of the Accounting Principles Board.

EXHIBIT 10

GENERAL CINEMA CORPORATION
Preliminary Diversification Criteria

General Cinema's business is almost equally divided in terms of revenues and earnings between its theater exhibition and soft-drink bottling businesses. Due to their nature, it is not necessary to reinvest in the business the major portion of the cash flow derived from these two operations, even though both are experiencing substantial internal growth. Over the last several years, since we have completed the major acquisition phase in the soft-drink area, this excess cash flow has been used primarily to reduce long-term debt. General Cinema's principal operating philosophy is that of a growth company. Consequently, as our debt is paid down and our existing businesses do not require available cash flow, we are looking to acquire a third major operating division.

The following criteria have been prepared to help the Company focus its search activities and to be of assistance to investment bankers and others who may be aiding us.

Financial criteria

1. The business should have pretax earnings of at least $5 million and a potential to increase to $20 million.
2. The business should have the potential for a 15% or more annual growth in earnings and a 20% or more return on additional capital employed.
3. The business could require large capital inputs in order to increase its sales and earnings growth rate.
4. The company must have reported earnings and should *develop earnings*, not only cash flow, i.e., real estate development would not be acceptable.
5. The results of the acquisition should be nondilutive to General Cinema's earnings unless it is *small* with *great* potential.
6. The purchase price should approximate book value so as to avoid the addition of an excessive amount of goodwill to General Cinema's balance sheet.

Qualitative criteria

1. The industry should not be technical or stylized, and the product or service should be immune to obsolescence.
2. The business should preferably be consumer and/or leisure oriented.
3. The business should have a relatively high barrier to entry or some other protective characteristics, i.e., brand leadership, license franchise, etc.
4. The company must have competent operating management capable of growing with the operation and of taking advantage of General Cinema's administrative and financial strengths. Basically, this new activity will be a management of assets for General Cinema with operating control in the hands of divisional management.
5. The potential market for the company's service or product should be on a large consumer base.
6. The company may be regional or decentralized, but should have a potential national scope.
7. The company's activities and primary market should be located in the United States.

July 9, 1976

marized his understanding of the criteria to be applied in a memorandum reproduced in Exhibit 9. A more recent statement is given in Exhibit 10.

Mr. Smith described the process he was employing to search for opportunities:

I am doing most of the worrying about diversification myself. The process is time-consuming; it took 15 months to work out the first soft-drink acquisition. We don't have a planning or corporate development office at General Cinema. It doesn't make much sense when we're looking for only one opportunity. Nor have I asked consultants to prepare a study for us. However, I have put the word out through our Board[5] and the bank that we want something, and we're getting a number of inquiries.

General Cinema has amply demonstrated its recession-resistant and inflation-immune characteristics during the 1974–1975 period. It continues to aspire to earnings goals of a very high standard of a 15% to 20% increase annually. The achievement of its goals requires determinations not yet made concerning (1) the proportion of future growth to be achieved by acquisition as distinct from internal growth; (2) the specific directions and operating philosophies which flow from its acquisition policy; (3) the parameters for trading off financial conservatism for leveraged earnings growth; and (4) development of its own unique professionalism required for the effective management of a company clearly moving on from its entrepreneurial stage. Of course, the solutions for these problems will be sought with the aid of the entire executive group assisted where appropriate by our board of directors.

---

[5] The General Cinema board of directors had recently been broadened and now included prominent chief executives of large companies located in the Boston area, an investment banker and the president of a major commercial bank, in addition to some of the company's top managers. Corporate headquarters had also been relocated from downtown Boston to suburban Chestnut Hill.

Philip Morris Incorporated

IN APRIL 1971 Philip Morris Incorporated was riding the crest of 17 years of uninterrupted growth in sales and net earnings. In 1970 Philip Morris' sales ($1.5 billion) and earnings ($77 million) were 296% and 369%, respectively, of the 1960 results. The company's earnings per share had grown at a compound annual rate of 13% since 1960 and 23% since 1965. In addition, Philip Morris had increased its share of the U.S. cigarette market from 9% to 16% in the decade of the sixties. In the international market (free world only), the company's market share had spurted from 1% in 1960 to 6% in 1970. Philip Morris was the third largest privately owned cigarette manufacturer in the world market, ranking behind the British-American Tobacco Company and R. J. Reynolds Industries, the leading U.S. manufacturer.

The corporation's growth had come in the face of adversities which were a continuing source of concern for the industry. Foremost among these was the decline in per-capita cigarette consumption in the United States. While total consumption had grown approximately 13% from 1960 to 1970, per-capita consumption among the over-18 population had declined 5% during the same period. Second, the debate over the relationship between cigarette smoking and health continued, with the anti-cigarette forces winning Congressional approval of a ban on TV and radio advertising of cigarettes effective January 2, 1971. Excise taxes posed a third problem. While the federal excise tax had remained constant at 8¢ per pack, state and local taxes had grown from an average of 4.8¢ in 1960 to 10.7¢ in 1970.[1] In New York City the total tax on cigarettes was 30¢ per pack and the retail price had soared to over 50¢.

THE AMERICAN CIGARETTE INDUSTRY

Structure

In 1970 American consumers spent $9.4 billion for 542 billion cigarettes and approximately $1 billion for cigars, smoking tobacco, and snuff. Per-capita consumption for the latter three products had declined slightly since 1950. Data reflecting recent trends in cigarette consumption are provided in Table 1.

TABLE 1

Year	Total unit output* (billions)	Domestic unit consumption (billions)	Nonfilter production percent of total	Filter-tip production percent of total	Over-18 years, consumption per capita (units)
Average 1955–59	447.8	428.4	63.6	37.4	3,884
1960	506.9	470.1	49.1	40.9	4,172
1965	556.8	528.7	35.6	64.4	4,258
1966	576.3	541.2	31.8	68.2	4,287
1967	576.2	549.2	27.6	72.4	4,280
1968	579.5	545.7	25.1	74.9	4,186
1969	557.6	528.9	22.5	77.5	3,993
1970	575.0	542.0	21.6	78.4	3,960

* Differences between consumption and output accounted for by exports and net inventory fluctuations.
Source: U.S. Department of Agriculture, Economic Research Service, *Tobacco Situation*, various issues.

The six major cigarette producers held 99.8% of the domestic market in 1970. Until the late 1940s, the cigarette market had been dominated by three brands: Camel, Chesterfield, and Lucky Strike. Subsequently, product innovation led to king-size, filter-tip, menthol-filter, charcoal-filter, complex-filter, and 100-millimeter cigarettes. This, in turn, led to brand proliferation. Exhibit 1 reflects market trends by brand and type of cigarette. Shown in Table 2 are 1970 sales, profits, and growth trends for the major producers.

In the sixties, after-tax profits of tobacco companies had averaged 5.5% on sales and approximately 13.5% on equity, although the perfor-

[1] U.S. Department of Agriculture, Bureau of Economic Research, *Tobacco Situation*, December 1970.

TABLE 2

| | 1970 | | | | Growth: 1966-70 | |
Company	Sales (millions)	Domestic cigarette unit sales (billions)	Sales in tobacco*	Net profits/ sales	Sales	Profit
R. J. Reynolds	$2,485	167	73%	7.7%	40.0%	38.3%
American Brands	2,674	103	77	4.1	87.3	25.6
Philip Morris.........	1,510	88	87	5.1	94.9	126.1
Brown & Williamson	890	88	99	4.5	63.1	51.2
P. Lorillard†	500	45	100	5.0	12.7	(14.7)
Liggett & Myers.......	697	34	53	4.2	20.6	29.9

* Includes other tobacco products and cigarette sales of consolidated foreign subsidiaries.

† P. Lorillard was purchased by Loew's Theatres in 1968.

Source: Annual reports of companies listed and parent companies. Domestic cigarette sales calculated from John C. Maxwell, Jr., "Historical Trends in the Tobacco Industry," Oppenheimer & Co., 1970.

mance varied substantially among six major firms. The companies also differed in their choices of financial policies (amount of debt and dividend payout) as shown in Table 3 for the four publicly held corporations.

TABLE 3

	R. J. Reynolds Industries	American Brands	Philip Morris	Liggett & Myers
Percent debt/net worth	30.6%	57.2%	81.8%	40.9%
Percent earnings/ net worth	20.6	13.8	17.2	13.2
Dividend payout percent	52.6	52.4	31.2	65.9
Price/earnings multiple (April 1971 price/1970 eps)	14.5	12.0	19.5	14.5
Other activities or companies owned ...	Mc Lean Industries (container- ized shipping) Various food products companies W. R. Grace (shipping)	Sunshine Biscuits Beam Distilling Duffy-Mott (food products)	Miller Brewing Clark gum Personna razor blades	Pet foods J & B Scotch Other liquor

Source: Arnold Bernhard & Co., Inc., *The Value Line*, Investment Survey, March 5, 1971.

EXHIBIT 1

Market share of major companies by type and brand of cigarette, 1952–70

Company and brand	Type*	1952	1961	1966	1967	1968	1969	1970
R. J. Reynolds								
†Winston	PF	···	12.0%	14.5%	15.0%	15.4%	15.3%	15.2%
Winston Menthol 100s	MF	...	···	···	0.5	0.5	0.3	0.4
†Salem	MF	...	8.4	8.7	8.4	8.5	8.3	8.5
Doral	PF	...	...	...	...	...	0.4	0.8
Doral Menthol	MF	...	...	...	...	...	0.2	0.4
Camel	PF	...	...	...	0.7	0.6	0.7	0.8
Vantage	PF	...	...	...	...	...	0.3	0.2
Tempo	CF	...	...	0.2	0.2	0.1	...	...
Camel	NFR	25.7%	13.6	8.7	7.8	6.3	6.3	5.4
Cavalier	NFK	0.5	...	...	...	...	...	...
Total market share		26.2%	34.0%	32.1%	32.6%	31.4%	31.8%	31.7%
American Brands								
†Tareyton	CF	...	2.2%	3.6%	3.6%	4.0%	4.1%	4.0%
Pall Mall 100 mm	PF	...	...	1.4	1.8	1.7	1.9	2.0
Pall Mall Menthol 100 mm	MF	...	...	0.2	0.4	0.4	0.4	0.4
Silva Thins 100 mm	PF	...	...	...	0.1	0.5	0.6	0.6
Silva Thins Menthol 100 mm	MF	...	...	...	...	0.2	0.3	0.3
Montclair	PF	...	...	0.2	0.2	0.1	0.1	0.1
Carleton	CF	...	...	0.2	0.2	0.2	0.2	0.2
†Lucky Strike	PF	...	...	0.8	0.5	0.3	0.2	0.2
Maryland Menthol 100s	MF	...	...	...	...	...	...	0.1
Other filter		...	...	...	0.2	0.2	0.1	0.1
Pall Mall	NFK	10.4%	14.6%	12.2	11.1	10.6	9.6	8.6
Lucky Strike	NFR	18.7	8.5	4.4	3.9	3.8	3.5	3.0
Tareyton	NFK	3.2	0.3	0.2	0.2	0.2	0.2	0.1
Total market share		32.3%	25.6%	23.2%	22.2%	22.2%	21.2%	19.7%
Brown and Williamson								
†Kool	MF	...	2.2%	4.5%	4.9%	5.8%	6.7%	7.7%
†Viceroy	PF	0.6%	3.7	3.9	3.7	3.8	3.8	3.7
†Raleigh	PF	...	1.4	2.7	2.7	2.8	2.8	2.7
†Belair	MF	...	0.1	1.7	1.7	1.7	1.7	1.8
Other filters		...	0.1	0.1	0.1	0	0	0
Raleigh	NFK	2.5	0.8	0.8	0.7	0.6	0.5	0.5
Kool	NFR	2.6	0.9	0.7	0.6	0.5	0.4	0.3
Wings and Avalon	NFK	0.2	0.1	...	...	...	...	...
Total market share		5.9%	9.3%	14.4%	14.4%	15.2%	15.9%	16.7%
Philip Morris								
†Marlboro	PF	...	5.0%	5.8%	6.4%	7.5%	8.6%	9.7%
Marlboro Menthol	MF	...	...	0.3	0.2	0.1	0.1	0.1
B & H 100s	PF	...	...	0.4	1.8	1.8	1.8	2.0
B & H Menthol 100s	MF	...	...	0.1	0.6	0.7	0.8	0.9
‡Parliament	PF	0.4%‡	2.0	2.0	1.7	1.7	1.6	1.6
Virginia Slims 100s	PF	...	...	...	...	0.1	0.5	0.6
Virginia Slims Menthol 100s	MF	...	...	...	...	...	0.3	0.4
Philip Morris	CF	...	...	0.7	0.6	0.5	...	...
Philip Morris Menthol	MF	...	...	0.3	0.1	0.1	...	...

XHIBIT 1 (*continued*)

Company and brand	Type*	1952	1961	1966	1967	1968	1969	1970
Multi-Filter	CF	. . .	. . .	. . .	. . .	. . .	0.1	0.4
Multi-Filter Menthol	CF	. . .	. . .	. . .	. . .	. . .	0.1	0.1
Alpine	MF	. . .	0.3	0.6	0.5	0.5	0.4	0.4
Other filter		. . .	0.1	0.1	0.1	0	0	0
Philip Morris	NFK and NFR	9.1	1.8	0.9	0.9	0.8	0.6	0.5
Dunhill.	NFK	0.1	. . .	. . .	. . .	. . .	. . .	. . .
Marlboro.	NFR	0.1	. . .	. . .	. . .	. . .	. . .	. . .
Total market share		9.7%	9.2%	11.2%	12.9%	13.8%	15.2%	16.7%
Lorillard								
†Kent	PF	0.2%	7.2%	5.8%	5.8%	5.8%	5.3%	5.0%
Kent Menthol 100s.	MF	. . .	. . .	. . .	. . .	. . .	. . .	0.1
True	PF	. . .	. . .	0.5	1.0	1.2	1.0	0.9
True Menthol	MF	. . .	. . .	. . .	0.5	0.6	0.5	0.6
†Old Gold	PF	. . .	1.0	0.8	0.8	0.9	1.0	0.9
†Newport	MF	. . .	1.5	1.6	1.4	1.4	1.0	0.8
Spring 100 mm	MF	. . .	0.1	0.3	0.2	0.2	0.1	0.1
Old Gold.	NFK and NFR	5.4%	0.7	0.4	0.3	0.2	0.1	0.1
Total market share		5.6%	10.5%	9.4%	10.0%	10.1%	9.0%	8.5%
iggett & Myers								
†L & M.	PF	. . .	5.5%	3.8%	3.4%	3.2%	3.1%	2.9%
L & M Menthol 100s	MF	. . .	. . .	. . .	0.2	0.2	0.1	0.1
Lark	CF	. . .	. . .	1.6	1.5	1.5	1.3	1.4
†Chesterfield	PF	. . .	. . .	0.3	0.3	0.2	0.2	0.3
Chesterfield	NFK and NFR	16.9%	5.3	2.8	2.3	2.1	2.0	1.8
Fatima	NFK	0.9	. . .	. . .	. . .	. . .	. . .	. . .
Total market share		17.8%	10.8%	8.5%	7.7%	7.2%	6.7%	6.5%
ll other companies		2.5%	0.6%	1.2%	0.2%	0.1%	0.2%	0.2%
Total industry		100.0%	100.0%	100.0%	100.0%	100.0%	100.0%	100.0%

*Key to abbreviations:
PF = Plain Filter   NFK = Nonfilter King
MF = Menthol Filter   NFR = Nonfilter Regular
CF = Charcoal Filter
†Includes both 85 mm and 100 mm brands.
‡Parliament owned by Benson & Hedges Company, purchased by Philip Morris in 1954.
Source: Calculated from John C. Maxwell, Jr., "Historical Trends in the Tobacco Industry,"
)ppenheimer & Co., 1970.

Operations

Table 4 gives an approximate cost breakdown of cigarettes per thousand and per pack.[2]

TABLE 4

Item	Per thousand	Per pack
Raw materials, chiefly leaf tobacco. . . . . $	2.00	$ .04
Labor and factory overhead	1.50	.03
Marketing and distribution	1.00	.02
General administrative expenses	.35	.007
Manufacturer's profit before taxes	1.00	.02
Federal excise tax.	4.00	.08
Total price to wholesaler	9.85	.197
Wholesale margin	.40	.008
State excise tax	1.00– 9.00	.02 –.18
Total price to retailer	$11.25–19.25	$.225–.385
Retail margin	1.00– 3.00	.02 –.06
State and city sales taxes.	0– 4.00	0 –.08
Total price to consumer	$12.25–26.25	$.245–.525

Source: Casewriter's discussion with various industry experts.

Even though companies could bid for government-stockpiled aged tobacco, they preferred to purchase the bulk of their requirements as cured "green" leaf at auctions and to store and age it for two or more years.

The technology of cigarette manufacturing based on cigarette rolling and packaging machines had not changed radically over the years. While machine speeds had increased and operations had become more capital intensive, economies of scale in manufacturing were not significant. Production workers in the industry had remained almost constant at 32,000 throughout the sixties. The value added per production worker increased 33% from 1960 to 1966, while wages rose 30%.[3]

Manufacturers directed their marketing toward establishing a "brand image" for their products. Once established, media advertising reinforced the image by emphasizing features of the cigarette which appealed to certain segments of the market. New variations of a successful brand such as changes in the filter, the length of the cigarette, or packaging were introduced to expand the brand's market appeal. The basic theme

---

[2] Manufacturing costs were thought to be roughly comparable in overseas operations. The end cost to the consumer usually hinged on the amount of tax added by various governments.

[3] U.S. Department of Commerce, Bureau of Defense Services Administration, Food and Tobacco Statistics, 1967.

of media advertising might also be changed in an effort to build or maintain market share. For example, Marlboro's early advertising theme emphasized "filter, flavor, flip-top box." In 1960 the famous tattooed "Marlboro man" appeared. In 1967 the tattoo disappeared from prominence as the Marlboro man appeared on horseback in a distinctive outdoor environment, "Marlboro Country."

According to industry observers, advertising as a percentage of sales averaged approximately 6%, or $.60 per thousand cigarettes. Prior to 1971 approximately 75% of all cigarette advertising had been placed on TV. Spending on individual brands varied considerably. It was common for companies to spend $5 million or more to underwrite development, test-market, and promotion costs for new brands. Conversely, advertising expenditures on a declining brand were often cut drastically, thus increasing profit on a per-unit basis. Exhibit 2 summarizes the 1969 media expenditures of the six major producers. Exhibit 3 compares TV advertising expenditures of the five leading brands with brands introduced since 1969.

The distribution of cigarettes had undergone a substantial change in the postwar years. Wholesalers at one time handled virtually all cigarette distribution, but by 1970 they had relinquished roughly half the market to chain stores and vending machine operators who purchased directly from the manufacturers, the latter accounting for about 20% of cigarette sales. Because cigarettes generated a high dollar volume per square foot of shelf space, obtaining distribution among the 1,500,000 retail outlets selling cigarettes was not inordinately difficult for a "promising" brand. Even the selection offered by vending machines, which initially had been limited to six or eight per machine, had grown to 25 or more. Manufacturers' sales were generally made on a cash basis.

Each company maintained a sales force which augmented the wholesalers' efforts by coordinating promotion of new brands with the wholesaler and checking on the placement of the company's brands in individual outlets, especially large supermarkets. Rotating stock to insure freshness was hardly ever necessary since the shelf life of cigarettes was four to six months. However, a lively competition existed in the execution of in-store promotion such as the placement of display racks and posters.

Price differentials among comparable cigarettes had been virtually nonexistent. Price cutting at the manufacturer's level was rare, because companies had discovered that price cuts were merely absorbed by wholesalers or retailers as extra profit and were not passed on to the consumer. Price increases, on the other hand, were usually initiated by R. J. Reynolds or American Brands and followed by the other companies. Manufacturers' prices had been increased three times since 1967 in this fashion in response to higher wages, storage, transportation, and marketing costs.

EXHIBIT 2
1970 media expenditures of major tobacco companies* (in thousands of dollars,

Company	Total expenditures	Magazines	Newspapers	Television	Radio	Outdoor	Total company sales*	Advertising percent to sales
R. J. Reynolds	$ 77,844	$ 9,986	...	$ 66,807	$ 805	$ 246	$2,485,000	3.14
Philip Morris.	63,598	13,746	8	48,177	834	833	1,510,000	4.22
American Brands	49,691	15,444	67	33,457	16	707	2,674,000	1.86
Brown & Williamson (British-American)	47,302	12,249	1,500	30,962	...	2,591	890,000	5.31
P. Lorillard (Loew's Theatres).	41,482	5,365	1,969	31,440	1,128	1,580	500,000	8.26
Liggett & Myers.	32,815	12,204	935	17,800	247	1,629	697,000	4.71
Industry total	$312,732	$68,994	$4,479	$228,643	$3,030	$7,586	$8,756,000	3.57

* Sales include nontobacco products and international; advertising expenditures are for domestic tobacco and nontobacco products only.
Source: *Advertising Age*, May 17, 1971, p. 32.

EXHIBIT 3
Television advertising of selected brands

Brand	Com-pany*	Date intro-duced	1970 sales dollars (millions)	1970 TV adver-tising dollars (millions)	TV adver-tising percent to sales
The top five brands					
Winston	RJR	1953	820	27.1	3.3
Pall Mall	AB	1946	580	9.4	1.6
Marlboro	PM	1954	510	18.7	3.7
Salem	RJR	1954	440	18.7	4.2
Kool	B & W	1955	400	13.9	3.5
New brands introduced since 1969 (in chronological order)					
Doral	RJR	June 1969	65	10.4	16.0
Maryland Menthol 100s	AB	Sept. 1970	4	0	0
Flair	B & W	Oct. 1970	0.5	0	0
New Leaf	PM	Oct. 1970	3	1.8	60.0
Vantage	RJR	Oct. 1970	10	6.3	63.0
Eve	L & M	Nov. 1970	4	0	0
Hallmark	B & W	Nov. 1970	0.2	0	0

* Company symbols as follows: RJR (R. J. Reynolds); AB (American Brands); PM (Philip Morris); B & W (Brown & Williamson); L & M (Liggett & Myers).
Source: *Broadcast Advertisers Reports* and casewriter's estimate of sales for individual brands based on the Maxwell report for 1970.

Taxes

Retail prices were greatly influenced by taxes. While the federal excise tax had remained constant at 8¢ per pack, aggregate state taxes had increased sevenfold since 1950.[4] In 1971 there was speculation that the federal government might increase the federal excise tax. In addition, counties and cites were beginning to follow state governments in imposing excise taxes (ranging from 1¢ to 7¢ per pack). Mayor Lindsay of New York proposed that the city's excise tax be revised to levy a heavier tax (4¢ per pack) on "high nicotine" brands and a lower tax (2¢) for "safer" brands. The attacks on smoking, added to the financial hardships encountered by all levels of government, suggested that additional "sin taxes" on cigarettes might be substantial in the seventies.

Together, these factors had caused cigarette prices to rise faster than the Consumer Price Index. Opinions among industry executives concerning the effect of higher prices varied. One experienced marketing executive commented:

---

[4] U.S. Department of Agriculture, *Tobacco Situation*, March 1970, p. 48.

We don't like to see our prices driven up by higher taxes, but, on the other hand, it hasn't affected our sales very much. People who enjoy smoking will pay the cost, just as they do for liquor. In Europe where our cigarettes retail at 75¢ to $1 per pack, our sales are going up, up, up.

On the other hand, a senior vice president of R. J. Reynolds pointed to the fact that in 14 states which increased taxes in 1970, cigarette smoking dipped 3.3%. In states which did not hike taxes, there was a 2.6% increase in sales.

Higher taxation had spawned increased bootlegging and hijacking, both of which were a concern to the cigarette manufacturers. New York City distributors maintained that approximately 20% of the cigarettes sold in the city were bootlegged from other states. Since the retail value of a truckload of cigarettes was nearly $150,000, bootlegging and hijacking had become more commonplace. One manufacturer, Liggett & Myers, had put guards on some of its trucks.

Government regulation

In January 1964 the U.S. Surgeon General's Advisory Committee on Smoking and Health issued a 350-page report in which it argued that there was no doubt about the role of cigarette smoking in lung cancer and several other diseases. It stated, "Cigarette smoking is a health hazard of sufficient importance in the United States to warrant appropriate remedial action."

Almost immediately after the Surgeon General's report was issued, the Federal Trade Commission began to hold hearings pursuant to establishing rules under which the public would be made aware of the hazards of cigarette smoking. The Tobacco Institute testified that it could police itself and that mandatory trade regulation rules were not in accord with the FTC's authority under the FTC Act. In April 1964, the leading cigarette manufacturers announced the adoption of a cigarette advertising code to be enforced by an independent administrator. The code set forth certain advertising appeals which were not to be used, for example, social prominence, sexual attraction, appeals to persons under 18, advertising on campuses and in comic books. The code did not specify separate rules for broadcasting on television or radio.

The FTC, for its part, issued the "Trade Regulation Rule for the Prevention of Unfair or Deceptive Advertising and Labeling of Cigarettes in Relation to the Health Hazards of Smoking." An Act of Congress provided that from January 1, 1966, manufacturers would be required to affix the warning: "Caution: Cigarette Smoking May Be Hazardous To Your Health" to all cigarette packages.

In 1967 the FCC ordered radio and TV stations to allow time for antismoking advertisements. Thus, stations running cigarette ads had to make available a significant amount of free time for antismoking commercials: one antismoking for every three smoking commericals. Then in April 1970 concern over public health and pressure from various anti-cigarette groups culminated in Congressional passage of legislation which revised the health warning on cigarette packages and banned all TV and radio advertising of cigarettes after January 2, 1971.[5] Moreover, beginning in November 1970, all cigarette packages were required to have the following words printed on them: "Warning: The Surgeon General Has Determined That Cigarette Smoking Is Dangerous To Your Health." This was more definitive than the previous admonition, "Caution: Cigarette Smoking May Be Hazardous To Your Health."

The FTC was empowered to enforce the ban on broadcast advertising and was armed with the prerogative of unleashing an even stronger warning label in the event that manufacturers did not comply with the spirit and letter of the law. The law also stated that the FTC could require, six months after notifying Congress, the health warning in print media after July 1, 1971, or sooner if the FTC determined that manufacturers were substantially expanding advertising in newspapers, magazines, and billboards.

The international market

The international market for cigarettes was not as concentrated as the U.S. market, although several large companies and government monopolies accounted for a sizable portion of total world production of 3 trillion units in 1968. British-American Tobacco accounted for 450 billion units, excluding its Brown and Williamson subsidiary. R. J. Reynolds and Philip Morris, the second and third largest publicly held firms in the international market, sold an estimated 110 and 90 billion units, respectively. According to industry observers, another large international firm, the Rothman Group, a consortium of privately and publicly held firms, sold nearly 300 billion units worldwide. Government-controlled monopolies in Japan, Korea, and Taiwan controlled another 250 billion units in total.

---

[5] Despite the withdrawal of cigarette advertising from television and radio, anti-cigarette commercials continued after January 2, 1971. On December 15, 1970, the FCC issued a rule that broadcasters no longer had a definite obligation to carry free antismoking messages but were expected to do so in the time they devoted to matters of public concern. At the same time, the FCC ruling indicated that broadcasters were free to decide whether the issue of smoking and health was controversial enough to warrant allowing the cigarette industry to answer attacks upon it.

TABLE 5

Region	1968 population* (millions)	1968 output† (billions)	Cigarettes per capita	Percent increase in output† 1964–68
North & Central America	285	699.2	2,450	11.8
South America	204	145.2	710	19.9
Western Europe	353	569.5	1,610	25.0
Eastern Europe & USSR	340	485.7	1,430	22.0
Africa.	336	84.2	250	22.7
Asia.	1,946	953.8	490	38.4
Oceania	19	29.4	1,540	28.4
World Total	3,483	2,967.0	855	24.5

* United Nations, *Demographic Yearbook*, 1969, p. 115.
† U.S. Department of Agriculture, Foreign Agricultural Service, "World Cigarette Output," FT 4-70, September 1970.

The problems of overseas operations were numerous and complex. First, American companies faced stiff competition in some areas such as Europe, and they anticipated increased competition in less-developed areas as the better local firms became more sophisticated. Second, nationalism was not expected to diminish in the seventies, and some industry executives believed that their companies, being highly visible, could not count on maintaining 100%-owned subsidiaries. Third, trademark laws were less stringent outside the United States; hence, American companies had to work diligently to prevent foreign firms from taking a U.S. brand and marketing it themselves.

On the other hand, factors in foreign markets such as growing affluence, craving for American brands, and less-active antismoking campaigns were responsible for the 4% annual growth rate in the overseas consumption of cigarettes. Moreover, the market share held by international companies was increasing in many areas in response to aggressive marketing techniques, new products, and the use of American brand names. Furthermore, the proportion of the free world market (excluding the United States) held by filter cigarettes had grown from about 20% in 1961 to nearly 60% in 1970, a trend thought to favor the international companies.

PHILIP MORRIS INCORPORATED

Domestic cigarette operations

The rapid acceptance of filter-tip brands introduced by competitors and the corresponding threat to the nonfilter Philip Morris brand led to the 1954 purchase for $22 million of Benson & Hedges, makers of Parliament filter cigarettes. The next year Philip Morris introduced a filter brand: Marlboro. The product was unique in that it came in a flip-top box. Marlboro was an immediate success, so much so that Philip Morris agreed to purchase the next two years' production of the patented packaging machinery from the manufacturer.

Mr. George Weissman, president of Philip Morris, outlined some of the policies that guided the company's marketing policy:

We have not often been first with a new cigarette. For example, others introduced king-sized, filters, menthols, and even 100-millimeter brands before we did. Yet, we have been successful in making our products unique. Marlboro came out in a flip-top box. We put a plastic package around Multi-Filter, our charcoal-filter brand. Virginia Slims was a "first" for us since it was the first cigarette to be directed specifically at women. We were also unique in taking a corporate name, Benson & Hedges, and putting it on a premium cigarette, Benson & Hedges 100s. We want to give the consumer a high-quality cigarette that is distinctive.

Another essential element in our success is our ability to react rapidly to changes in market or competitive conditions. We have a corporate products committee which regularly reviews the progress on individual brands. The chairman and I are personally involved with the formulation of marketing policy for our major brands. Moreover, if we have a good product idea, we can get top-management commitment in a hurry.

Mr. Ross Millhiser, president of Philip Morris U.S.A. and former Marlboro brand manager, explained certain further dimensions of the marketing task:

We want our products to have charisma, and this requires attention to packaging and advertising. When we think we have the optimal combination of product quality and consumer appeal for a certain segment of the market, we test the brand for several months. If it gets 1% of the market, we consider launching it nationwide. I don't really need market surveys to tell me how a new brand is doing. We can get some idea in a few weeks from the repurchase pattern whether it is taking hold.

Philip Morris spent roughly 80% of its $60 million 1970 advertising budget on broadcast media. The company had been highly successful in the use of creative advertising for its products. The campaigns for Marlboro and Benson & Hedges 100s had been widely acclaimed in advertising circles for their sophisticated consumer appeal.

In April 1971, company officials were assessing the impact of losing the opportunity to advertise on television. They generally agreed that television had been the most efficient means of disseminating the advertising message for cigarettes and that its prohibition was unlikely to diminish competition for consumer loyalty. On the other hand, it was not altogether clear that the long-run effects on the industry in general and Philip Morris in particular would be serious.

For one thing, company officials noted that cigarette consumption had been rising steadily long before television came into existence. Second, in the United Kingdom, where cigarette commercials had been banned in all media since 1967, consumption had risen almost 3% per year. Television advertising had never been allowed in France, yet unit sales had increased at an annual rate of 5.8% from 1964 through 1969. Philip Morris found solace in the fact that another consumer products industry, distilled spirits, had experienced sales increases of 4.5% per year without the use of broadcast advertising. Finally, the company believed that since it had well-established quality brands in the growth segments of the industry, it stood to lose least among major manufacturers.

Philip Morris International

From its founding in 1954, Philip Morris International's sales grew from 5% of the corporate total to 28% in 1970. Since 1961, sales had increased at a compound rate of 33% per year, reaching $425 million in 1970.[6] In the international market, Philip Morris was the fastest growing U.S. company, and its products were available to consumers in more than 150 nations and territories, including all the major world markets except the United Kingdom, Indonesia, and mainland China.

Philip Morris International was organized in four regions: Canada. Latin America, Asia/Pacific, and Europe, each having a regional vice president who had responsibility for profits, market share, and unit volume. Manufacturing facilities in 20 countries produced the company's U.S. brands and a wide variety of local brands tailored to the tastes of individual countries.

Philip Morris had emphasized several policies in regard to foreign operations. Mr. Hugh Cullman, president of Philip Morris International, discussed some of these policies:

We don't "wave the flag" in foreign countries. Outside the British Commonwealth where the name Philip Morris is widely known, we use indigenous names for our subsidiaries. We recognize that value systems are different in these countries, and our operations and products are designed to be consistent with these values.

We aim to develop brands which compete in the premium-priced segment of the market. Overseas, there are different price categories of cigarettes, unlike the United States. Our managers are responsible for sales and profits,

---

[6] $425 million was the total for consolidated subsidiaries, all of which were wholly owned. In addition, there was another $280 million in sales of unconsolidated subsidiaries, many of them partially owned.

but when a decision affects one of our U.S. brands such as Marlboro, the manager of a foreign subsidiary must check back with New York. Also, Joe (Cullman) and George (Weissman) like to inspect personally the progress of overseas operating units.

Diversification

Early diversification. In 1957 Philip Morris became, in management's view, the first tobacco company actively to entertain diversification. Management's reasons for seeking nontobacco enterprises at that time were threefold. First, there was a desire to move away from dependence on one product. Second, there was interest in applying the company's marketing expertise in other fields. Third, should the cigarette business, or Philip Morris' share of it, level off, a sizable cash flow would be available for investment.

In July 1957 a flexible packaging company, Milprint, Inc., was acquired for 385,000 common shares (worth approximately $16.8 million). Milprint owned Nicolet Paper Company, a producer of glassine and specialty papers. After these two acquisitions were made, the company formed the industrial division, Milprint and Nicolet accounting for 90% of the division's sales. The remaining 10% was supplied by Polymer Industries, acquired in 1958, which manufactured adhesives and textile chemicals, and Koch Convertograph, acquired in 1968, which produced bottle and other labels. While most of Philip Morris' cigarette packaging and printing was done by outside firms, management felt that having in-house packaging capability kept their outside suppliers' prices down. The industrial division's annual growth rate had averaged 3.4% since 1961.

Subsequently, three consumer products companies were acquired in the areas described below. As part of Philip Morris U.S.A. division, these companies accounted for $40 million in sales in 1970.

Shaving products. American Safety Razor Company, acquired in 1960, was the third largest manufacturer of shaving products. Its razor blade, trademarked "Personna," accounted for 12% of the domestic market in 1970 as compared with 5% in 1960.[7] Burma-Vita Company, manufacturer of Burma Shave products, was acquired in 1963.

Chewing gum. Clark Brothers Chewing Gum Company, purchased in 1963, produced a variety of chewing gums. It held 6% of the domestic chewing gum market in 1970, as compared with less than 1% when acquired.[8]

Hospital supply. The medical products' division was composed of several hospital supply companies acquired in 1967. Products included

---

[7] Gillette, the dominant producer of razors and blades, was estimated to have 60% of the market.

[8] Wrigley's, the leading gum producer, held roughly 45% of the market.

surgical blades, sutures, and sterile disposable hospital kits. The division was sold in 1971.

Miller Brewing Company. In June 1969 Philip Morris purchased 53% of the stock of Miller Brewing Company from W. R. Grace and Company for $130 million in cash. One year later, the remaining 47% was acquired for $97 million in cash from the De Rance Foundation, a charitable organization controlled by a descendant of the Miller family. The total purchase price of $227 million was approximately 25 times Miller's earnings in 1967 and 1968. Approximately $150 million of the purchase price was cost in excess of book value.

Miller produced Miller High Life beer, one of three nationally distributed premium-priced beers in the United States (the other two were Budweiser and Schlitz). Since 1960, beer consumption in the United States had been growing at a rate of 3.2% per year, but the premium-priced segment had grown at 8.5%. By 1980 total beer consumption was estimated to reach 150 million barrels, of which premium beer was expected to be 40%.

The company had three breweries, located in Milwaukee (4 million barrels), Azusa, California, and Fort Worth, Texas (1 million barrels each). Miller's output of 5 million barrels in 1969 represented 4.4% of the industry total and 16% of the premium-priced segment, as shown in Exhibit 4. Philip Morris officials viewed Miller as a stable company with a "Cadillac" reputation which marketed its products in a growth segment of a consumer-oriented industry. Philip Morris tobacco and Miller beer were sold in many of the same retail outlets.

One of the most important factors influencing Miller's 1970 results had been the continuing adverse effect of a 1969 strike in Milwaukee which affected 80% of the company's capacity. This resulted in a considerable loss of distribution, shelf space, and on-premises availability for Miller which was only partially regained in 1970. Nonetheless, the company took steps to enlarge the capacity of its Fort Worth plant by 300,000 barrels and to plan an eastern brewery (capacity, 2,000,000 barrels) in Newark, Delaware. The estimated cost of these improvements was expected to be approximately $90 million.

Mission Viejo Company. In January 1970 Philip Morris purchased convertible debentures and options in Mission Viejo Company, a land development and home construction company in Orange County, California, for $20 million. Under terms of the agreement, Philip Morris maintained temporary control of Mission Viejo until 1973. Between 1973 and 1975, for an additional $13 million Philip Morris could exercise an option enabling the company to control 52% of Mission Viejo on a permanent basis. If Philip Morris did not exercise this option and convert its debentures by December 31, 1975, it would retain straight debentures and own a fractional amount of equity in Mission Viejo.

EXHIBIT 4

PHILIP MORRIS INCORPORATED
Miller Brewing Company

I. Financial reports

Year to 12/21	Sales (incl. excise taxes) (millions)	Operating income (millions)	Operating margin	Net income (thousands)
1965	$137.6	$14.6	10.5%	$7,215
1966	154.8	15.9	10.5	8,346
1967	173.0	18.6	10.5	9,586
1968	184.4	18.1	9.8	9,035
1969	196.3	15.3	7.8	8,202
1970	198.5	11.4	5.8	7,400*

* Estimated.
Source: Company records.

II. Miller's sales compared with industry sales

Year	Thousands of barrels			Miller percent of industry	Miller percent of premium segment
	Industry	Premium segment	Miller		
1965	100,411	22,200	3,667	3.7	16.4
1966	104,262	24,200	4,146	4.0	17.0
1967	106,974	26,300	4,584	4.3	17.4
1968	111,415	28,500	4,847	4.4	16.9
1969	116,270	31,000	5,080	4.4	16.3
1970	120,100	33,700	5,113	4.4	15.8
Increase, 1965–69	15.8%	39.6%	38.5%		

Source: U.S. Treasury Department, Bureau of Internal Revenue; company data.

Founded in 1966, Mission Viejo was a new town located on 11,000 acres of land midway between Los Angeles and San Diego. By 1970, 3,000 acres had been developed and the city's population was 14,000. It was estimated that the population of Mission Viejo would reach 100,000 by 1990.

Mr. John Cookman, senior vice president, finance, believed that the Mission Viejo venture complemented the corporation's operations, since the high cash flow generated by its cigarette sales could be applied to the heavy initial cost of community development. In addition, he noted that the growth potential in real estate and the demand for competent management were considerations which beckoned to Philip Morris.

Nationally, the home-building industry was severely affected by the 1970 economic downturn. The rate of housing starts (approximately 2 million per year) dropped to 1 million in January 1970 as mortgage interest rates, housing costs, and unemployment increased. The southern California economy was particularly hard hit as layoffs in aerospace and defense industries raised unemployment in that area well above the national level. Mission Viejo, however, recorded the highest total home sales of any home builder in Orange County. A total of 765 homes were sold in 1970 for $20 million. The president of Mission Viejo Company estimated that 1971 sales would be 800–1,000 homes for a total of $30 million. In January 1971 housing starts had increased to a seasonally adjusted annual rate of 1.7 million units.

Future plans

From 1960 to 1970, long-term debt rose from $67.4 million to $370 million due largely to the acquisition of Miller. The dividend payout ratio had declined during the same period from 66% to 31%. On the other hand, cash flow relative to capital expenditures had increased steadily in the latter part of the decade.

TABLE 6
Cash flow and capital expenditures, 1963–70 (millions of dollars)

	Years ended December 31							
	1963	1964	1965	1966	1967	1968	1969	1970
Retained earnings	$ 8.2	$ 8.8	$12.7	$18.2	$27.5	$29.2	$35.7	$52.2
Depreciation	6.8	8.3	8.9	9.5	10.9	12.1	13.5	17.7
Total	$15.0	$17.1	$21.7	$27.7	$38.4	$41.3	$49.2	$69.9
Capital expenditures	26.2	19.4	12.1	17.1	25.7	26.4	23.6	39.6
Excess of funds over expenditures	($11.2)	$(2.3)	$ 9.6	$10.6	$12.7	$14.9	$25.6	$30.3

Mr. Cookman discussed Philip Morris' capital expansion plans for 1971–75:

We're going to invest $400 million in our existing businesses. First, we're building what we believe is the world's largest cigarette factory in Richmond. This will cost $80 million. We are planning a new 2 million barrel brewery in Newark, Delaware. The total investment there will be $90 million. In Europe, our plans call for $80 million for expansion of our operations there. Finally, we've planned $150 million for updating our existing facilities. Our program calls for a fairly even stream of investment each year . . . around

$80 million. Our new cigarette factory will be in operation by the end of 1973.

The company's stock, traded on the New York Stock Exchange, had been a favorite of financial institutions. Nearly one third of Philip Morris' common stock was owned by institutional accounts, compared to less than 10% for such other institutional favorites as IBM, Xerox, and Eastman Kodak. Financial data on the company are contained in Exhibits 5–7.

EXHIBIT 5

PHILIP MORRIS INCORPORATED
Consolidated Income Statements, 1966–70
(in millions of dollars)

	Year ended December 31				
	1966	*1967*	*1968*	*1969*	*1970*
Sales	$772	$905	$1,020	$1,142	$1,510
Cost of sales					
Cost of products sold. . , ...	$303	$354	$ 400	$ 455	$ 577
U.S. and foreign excise tax	265	311	338	373	519
Total cost of sales	$568	$665	$ 738	$ 828	$1,096
Gross profit	$204	$240	$ 282	$ 314	$ 414
Nonoperating expenses					
Selling, research and development	$122	$139	$ 159	$ 166	$ 220
Corporate expense	10	11	12	13	15
Interest.	8	10	16	29	35
Total nonoperating expenses	$140	$160	$ 187	$ 208	$ 270
Consolidated earnings before taxes	$ 64	$ 80	$ 95	$ 106	$ 144
Earnings from unconsolidated					
subsidiaries					
Domestic	0	0	0	3	3
Foreign	3	3	3	2	7
Other income (expense)	(1)	(2)	1	4	(3)
Earnings before income taxes	$ 66	$ 81	$ 99	$ 115	$ 151
Income taxes	32	38	50	57	73
Net earnings	$ 34	$ 43	$ 49	$ 58	$ 78
Earnings per share					
Primary	$1.54	$1.97	$2.18	$2.58	$3.36
Fully diluted	1.54	1.94	2.14	2.40	2.85

Source: Company records.

Philip Morris in the seventies

Mr. Joseph F. Cullman 3rd, chairman of the board, commented on his view of where the corporation was headed:

. . . I don't want this company to become overstimulated, to go wild. All managements are under pressure to do this . . . to pump up their earnings. We have been a disciplined company, and it has paid off. My task is to keep

EXHIBIT 6

PHILIP MORRIS INCORPORATED
Consolidated Balance Sheets, 1966–70
(in millions of dollars)

	1966	1967	1968	1969	1970
Assets					
Current assets					
Cash	$ 27	$ 38	$ 37	$ 42	$ 52
Accounts receivable	46	59	70	83	102
Inventories					
Leaf tobacco	238	327	366	364	444
Other inventory	60	60	86	83	124
Total inventory	$298	$387	$452	$447	$ 568
Prepaid expenses	2	2	3	3	7
Total current assets	$373	$486	$562	$575	$ 729
Investments in unconsolidated subsidiaries					
Domestic	$ 0	$ 0	$ 0	$132	$ 22
Foreign	18	24	68	96	68
Total investments	$ 18	$ 24	$ 68	$228	$ 90
Fixed assets					
Land	$ 5	$ 5	$ 6	$ 7	$ 12
Buildings	45	47	50	57	107
Machinery, equipment	123	142	163	173	274
Fixed assets before depreciation	$173	$194	$219	$237	$ 393
Less: Accumulated depreciation	63	70	81	90	156
Total fixed assets	$110	$124	$139	$147	$ 237
Other assets	3	6	6	13	15
Brands, trademarks, goodwill	9	9	12	13	168
Total assets	$513	$649	$787	$976	$1,239
Liabilities and equity					
Current liabilities					
Notes payable	$ 32	$ 85	$155	$158	$ 187
Accounts payable	68	75	76	78	148
Taxes payable	16	16	13	17	39
Dividends payable	4	4	5	6	7
Total current liabilities	$120	$180	$249	$259	$ 381
Long-term debt					
Senior	$129	$171	$176	$168	$ 178
Subordinated	0	0	24	164	192
Total long-term debt	$129	$171	$200	$332	$ 370
Deferred income taxes	10	11	15	18	20
Reserve applicable to international operations	1	4	4	5	9
Other liabilities	3	3	3	6	7
Total liabilities	$263	$369	$472	$620	$ 787
Preferred stock	$ 27	$ 26	$ 26	$ 26	$ 25
Common stock	23	23	23	23	24
Capital surplus	46	49	54	59	95
Retained earnings	170	197	227	262	315
Less: Treasury stock	(16)	(15)	(15)	(14)	(6)
Total equity	$250	$280	$315	$356	$ 453
Total liabilities and equity	$513	$649	$787	$976	$1,239

Source: Company records.

EXHIBIT 7

PHILIP MORRIS INCORPORATED
Financial Highlights for Individual Divisions, 1961-70

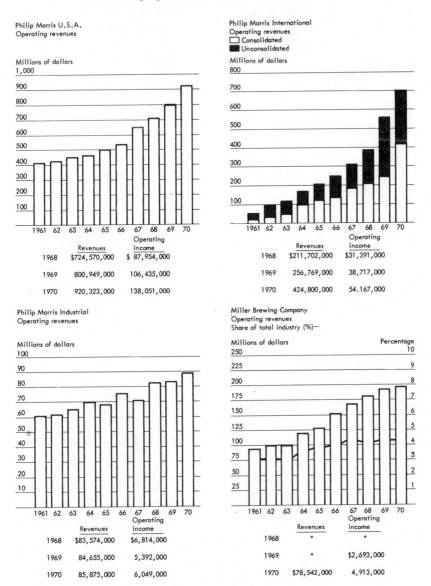

Philip Morris U.S.A.
Operating revenues

Millions of dollars
1,000

	Revenues	Operating income
1968	$724,570,000	$ 87,954,000
1969	800,949,000	106,435,000
1970	920,323,000	138,051,000

Philip Morris International
Operating revenues
☐ Consolidated
■ Unconsolidated

Millions of dollars
800

	Revenues	Operating income
1968	$211,702,000	$31,391,000
1969	256,769,000	38,717,000
1970	424,800,000	54.167,000

Philip Morris Industrial
Operating revenues

Millions of dollars
100

	Revenues	Operating income
1968	$83,574,000	$6,814,000
1969	84,655,000	5,392,000
1970	85,875,000	6,049,000

Miller Brewing Company
Operating revenues
Share of total industry (%)—

Millions of dollars   Percentage
250   10

	Revenues	Operating income
1968	*	*
1969	*	$2,693,000
1970	$78,542,000	4,913,000

* Miller operating revenues only from August 1, 1970. Philip Morris equity of 53% in Miller net income for 1969 and 100% for 1970.
Source: 1970 Annual Report.

our sales and profit momentum going. Now that we have Miller and the possibility of expanding our participation in Mission Viejo, I don't foresee a pressing need for moving off into further new directions.

We are going to devote more effort and resources to matters of corporate responsibility, especially in the areas of minority hiring and controlling pollution. Americans are becoming aware of things beyond material possessions. And American industry, which is responsible for our high economic standards, must address itself to the problems which confront our society.

The Taylor Wine Company, Inc. —Part I

THE WINE INDUSTRY IN 1961

Wine consumption

SINCE 1947, wine consumption in the United States had risen at about the rate of population growth. Thus, per-capita wine consumption, in spite of constantly rising personal incomes, had stayed constant since World War II at less than one gallon per person. This placed the United States on a par with Russia, behind Germany with 3.4 gallons per capita, and well behind Italy and France with 29.5 and 33.3 gallons, respectively.

Wine in America thus could not be characterized as a staple drink. Even when compared to its nearest beverage "competitors," beer and distilled spirits, wine came in a dismal third. Beer and spirits expenditures totaled $5 billion each in 1961, while total expenditures for wine barely exceeded $500 million. On a per-capita consumption basis, wine fell behind distilled spirits (1.4 gallons per person yearly) and far behind beer (15 gallons).

Regional consumption patterns in the United States differed considerably. Most wine was consumed on the East and West Coasts; per-capita wine consumption ranged from 2.84 gallons in Washington D.C. to 0.15 of a gallon in Iowa. The states with the largest consumption of wine were California (20.9% of U.S. consumption), New York (15.4%), Pennsylvania (5.9%), and New Jersey (5.4%).

Sources and types of wine

In 1960 nearly 80% of the wine consumed by Americans was produced in California, although that state's position had eroded somewhat since World War II. New York accounted for most of the remaining U.S. wine production, having risen in importance since the war primarily because of the popularity of its champagnes and Concord-grape wines. Imported wines, too, had steadily increased their market share since the 1940s, reaching a high of 6.6% in 1960. More significantly, since imported wines were all higher priced, they were estimated to represent about 15% of the dollar value of all wines sold in the United States. U.S. imports came from over 20 countries, with Italy, strongest in vermouths, holding 41.6% and France, strongest in table wines, holding 33.2%, followed by Germany (8.7%), Spain (5.9%), and Portugal (3.4%).

U.S. wine consumption since the war had evolved as follows:

	Percentage share in gallons		
Type of wine	*1946–1950*	*1951–1955*	*1956–1960*
Table	24.8%	28.6%	30.6%
Dessert	71.2	66.4	58.9
Vermouth and special natural	2.7	3.6	8.3
Sparkling	1.3	1.4	2.2
Average annual consumption in millions of gallons......................	126.4	138.5	155.2

Most striking was the increase in popularity of the "vermouth and special natural" category. The growing use of vermouth as an ingredient for Martinis and Manhattans was partially responsible, but most of the increase was attributed to the highly successful introduction in the late 1950s of two flavored 18% wines, Gallo's "Thunderbird" and United Vintners' "Silver Satin," which had been introduced when it was discovered that consumers were buying cheap white port and mixing it with citrus juices and herbs.

Both the dominance of dessert wines and the popularity of cheap, flavored wines tended to support the widely held belief that the typical U.S. consumer was interested only in the "most proof for the penny" and could never be influenced to drink substantial amounts of better wines. Despite this rather unpromising conclusion, there was some evidence by 1961 that the American consumer was changing. There had been a steady move away from dessert wines towards lighter, drier table wines since the late 1940s, and many observers expected this trend to continue.

Further evidence of an increasing sophistication in taste was the growth in imported wines.

Industry structure

The American wine industry consisted basically of two groups, wine producers and wine importers, both of which were highly fragmented. The 1958 *Census of Manufactures* revealed that almost 70% of domestic wine producers had less than 20 employees and only 5% had more than 100 employees. Importers had increased in number in the late 1950s as imported wines became more popular, growing from 1,309 in 1956 to 1,644 in 1961. Although there were a few notable exceptions, most importers were quite small.

Of the 495 American wineries, only one was publicly held; thus, detailed information on specific companies was almost impossible to obtain, especially given the secretive, competitive nature of the industry. The most meaningful possible difference was between wineries with "standard price" products and those with "premium price" products, a distinction created by the Wine Institute, the California industry association. There was no absolute demarcation between these categories, but the commonly accepted criterion was that standard wines were those selling at retail at approximately $.50 to $1.25 per fifth and premium wines were those selling above $1.25 per fifth.

The standard price segment was by far the largest, producing an estimated 93% of American-made wine. Two companies, E. & J. Gallo and United Vintners, dominated both this segment and the entire wine industry with 59.1% of U.S.-produced wine sales (see Exhibit 1).

The premium segment of the wine industry was much smaller than the standard segment, constituting less than 7% of U.S.-produced wine sales as measured in gallons. The four most significant premium wineries in the country were Taylor and Christian Brothers, both strongest in dessert wines, and Almaden and Paul Masson, both strongest in table wines (see Exhibit 2). Seagram's, the largest Canadian distiller, owned Paul Masson and distributed Christian Brothers, but the rest of the premium wineries were independent.

Distribution

In the United States, wine was distributed in two distinct ways. In 18 states distribution was performed by the state government. In these "control" states, wine producers and bottlers sold to a state alcoholic control board or agency which then distributed wines to state-owned retail outlets and hotels and restaurants. State markups on delivered

EXHIBIT 1
Major American wineries with standard price products*

Company	Brands	Ownership	Volume†	Market share‡	1960 Advertising expenditures	Share of wine advertising§
E. & J. Gallo Winery (California)	Gallo Thunderbird Andre	Privately held by Gallo family	46.2	30.3%	$2,086,274	24%
United Vintners, Inc. (California)	Italian Swiss Colony Silver Satin Petri	Cooperative owned by 1,500 growers	44.0	28.8	1,311,881	15
Mogen David Wine Corp. (New York)	Mogen David	Privately held	10.8	7.1	1,262,612	15
Guild Wine Co. (California)	Guild Cribari	Cooperative owned by 1,000 growers	5.2	3.4	...	...
Roma Wine Co., Inc. (California)	Roma Cresta Blanca	Subsidiary of Schenley Industries	4.8	3.1	...	...
Monarch Wine Co., Inc. (New York)	Manischewitz	Privately held	3.5	2.3	338,627	4
Franzia Brothers Winery (California)	Franzia	Privately held	3.3	2.2	...	...
			117.8	77.2		58%

* "Standard price" = less than $1.25 per fifth at retail.
† Volume in millions of gallons.
‡ Based on total U.S.-produced wine sales of 152,616,000 gallons in 1960.
§ Based on total estimated wine advertising of $8,500,000 in 1960.
Source: Casewriter's analysis and estimates. Advertising expenditures from *Newsweek* and *The Liquor Handbook* (1961).

EXHIBIT 2
Major American wineries with premium price products*

Company†	Ownership	Vol-ume‡	Market share§	1960 Adver-tising expen-ditures	Share of wine adver-tising
The Taylor Wine Co., Inc. (New York)	Privately held by Taylor family	2.99	1.96%	$356,198	4.2%
Mont La Salle Vineyards (California)	Owned by Christian Bros. Distributed by Seagram's	2.04	1.34	399,546	4.7
Almaden Vineyards (California)	Privately held	1.32	.87	95,692	1.1
Paul Masson Vineyards (California)	Subsidiary of Seagram's	1.12	.73	85,688	1.0
Pleasant Valley Wine Co. (New York)	Subsidiary of Great Western Producers, Inc.	.67	.44	43,226	.5
Gold Seal Vineyards, Inc. (New York)	Privately held	.50	.33	. . .	. . .
Widmer's Wine Cellars Inc. (New York)	Privately held	.45	.29	55,176	.6
Beaulieu Vineyard Co. (California)	Privately held	.29	.19	900	. . .
Louis M. Martini (California)	Privately held	.25	.16	. . .	. . .
		9.63	6.31%		12.1%

* "Premium price" = more than $1.25 per fifth at retail.
† Brand names same as company names except for Pleasant Valley which sold "Great Western" wines and Mont La Salle which sold "Christian Brothers" wines.
‡ In millions of gallons.
§ Based on total U.S.-produced wine sales of 152,616,000 gallons in 1960.
Source: Casewriter's analysis and estimates. Advertising expenditure from *Newsweek* and *The Liquor Handbook* (1961).

price (the producer's sales price plus federal excise tax) ranged from 17.6% to 66.3% in addition to various state sales and excise taxes.

In the 32 "open" states, wine was almost exclusively distributed through wholesalers who, in turn, sold to retailers and on-premise hotels and restaurants. Wholesalers usually carried a full line of alcoholic beverages—beer, wine, and spirits—and often carried multiple lines of wine. Retailers were generally classified as either "on-premise" hotels, restaurants, and bars or "off-premise" package stores. Relatively standard markups existed throughout the industry: 33% for wholesalers and 50% for retailers.[1] Thus, a typical bottle of premium table wine that was sold to the consumer for $1.50 would have been sold to a retailer for $1.00 and to a wholesaler for $.75.

[1] Wine was one of the retailers' most profitable items, as beer and distilled spirits carried a markup of generally less than 25%. "On-premise" outlets often marked up wines much higher than the 50% markup of package stores.

Regulation

State and federal regulation of the wine industry, like that of other alcoholic beverages, was quite stringent and complicated. The repeal of Prohibition in 1933 gave states the right to control distribution of alcoholic beverages. Each state subsequently developed its own laws, resulting in 50 highly fragmented sets of regulations that made national distribution of an alcoholic beverage difficult and created a significant barrier to entry for a small winery seeking broader distribution. The main federal influence on wine was in the area of taxation:

Type of wine	Percent alcohol	Excise tax per gallon
Table	10–14	$0.17
Dessert	14–21	0.67
	21–24	2.25
Sparkling wine	10–14	3.40

The Federal Alcohol Administration Act required that certain facts about a wine appear on the label: the brand name, the wine class or type, the geographic origin, the bottle size, the alcoholic content, and the name and address of the maker. The act also specified that (1) to carry the name of a grape variety, a wine had to contain at least 51% of that variety of grape; (2) to use a vintage year, 100% of the grapes used in making the wine had to come from one year's harvest; and (3) a wine was entitled to use a specific appellation of origin if at least 75% of its volume was derived from grapes both grown and fermented in the place or region indicated on the label.

Federal and state governments closely regulated the production of wines to insure proper tax collections and observance of labeling laws. These regulations varied in different parts of the country. New York labrusca-based wineries were allowed to add up to 53% water and sugar to their wines to tone down the excessive "grapey" flavor. California wineries, on the other hand, were not allowed by state law to ameliorate their wines with any excess water or sugar.

Economics of wine production

Due to the vast variety of wine types, qualities, and production methods, it is difficult to generalize about the economics of wine production. A few generalizations, however, are possible. For example, a fifth of premium table wine that was sold to the consumer for $1.50 would normally be sold by a winery to the channels of distribution for 75 cents, with a typical cost breakdown of:

Grapes and other raw material	$0.25
Crushing, pressing, and aging	0.02
Bottling and packaging	0.14
Warehousing and shipping	0.04
Administration, selling, federal taxes, profit	0.30
	$0.75

For standard price wines, on the other hand, grapes were a lower portion of the total cost, packages were cheaper, and selling and promotion expenses were generally higher.

The long lead time required to achieve a full grape crop (five years) and to properly process and age a wine (two years), together with the sizable investment required for land, buildings, and equipment, created significant barriers to entry into the wine business. Although estimates varied, a small winery capable of eventually producing 120,000 gallons a year commonly required an initial investment of $1 million for vineyards and plants.

THE TAYLOR WINE COMPANY, INC.

In late 1961 George A. Lawrence, secretary and treasurer of The Taylor Wine Company, Inc., was debating whether to recommend to Fred C. Taylor, the firm's president, that the company buy its next-door neighbor, The Pleasant Valley Wine Company. Since early summer Lawrence had been negotiating with Marme Obernauer, the president of Great Western Producers, Inc., for the sale of Pleasant Valley, one of the three Great Western divisions. The negotiations had reached a point where Lawrence felt that a final commitment might be imminent.

History of The Taylor Wine Company

In 1880 Walter Taylor, a 22-year-old cooper who made wooden barrels and casks, settled in Hammondsport, New York.[2] A short time after his arrival, observing the prosperity of the wine producers who had been located in the area since 1860, he bought a seven-acre vineyard and for three years grew and harvested grapes. By 1883 Taylor's wines had been so well received that he expanded his operations by buying a 70-acre farm on nearby Bully Hill and planted this land with the native grape varieties: Delaware, Catawba, Dutchess, Elvira, Niagara, Concord, and Ives. He made two basic products, red and white dinner wines, and shipped in barrels primarily to New York City markets.

Gradually Taylor's operations expanded. Dessert wines were added

---
[2] Hammondsport is located in the Finger Lakes region of western New York State. It is approximately 300 miles from New York City and in 1960 had a population of 1,112.

to the two basic table wines. The 77 acres of vineyard provided enough raw material until 1913, when Taylor for the first time purchased grapes from other growers to supplement his own crop.

As the reputation of Taylor wine spread, Walter Taylor found it necessary to concentrate on marketing. Salesmen were hired in 1915 and markets were gradually expanded. With the purchase of the Columbia Wine Company in 1919, Taylor acquired bottling facilities and began to bottle and label a few of its own products.

This expansion necessitated the addition of more managerial personnel. In 1914 when Walter Taylor was 56, two of his sons, Fred and Clarence, joined the firm. Fred, the older of the two, started in production but gradually moved into overall administration of the company. Clarence stayed with his main interest, production. In 1924 Walter's youngest son Greyton joined the firm and took over Taylor's marketing. All three sons became equal partners in the company when Walter died in 1933.

By 1961 Taylor had experienced 16 straight years of increases in case and dollar sales in almost all product classes. Average yearly growth during this period had been approximately 12%. (See Exhibits 3 and 4 for income statements and balance sheet.)

Products

In 1961 Taylor had a full line of premium price wines in all product classes (see Exhibit 5). Dessert wines were the largest selling product class with 62% of case sales, a share which had declined slightly over the last several years. Dinner wines and vermouth had remained at 21% and 3%, respectively, of case sales. Champagne, with a slowly increasing share of case sales amounting to 14% in 1961, was the most profitable of Taylor's products, contributing 26% of net dollar sales and about 22% of gross margin. Since 1948, Taylor had introduced only three new products. Speaking in 1972, George Lawrence described the firm's philosophy:

Our main concern has always been with quality of the product, and I think this is one of the primary reasons for our success. The Taylors had their name on the bottle and to them product quality and consistency was most important. Our wines are all blended and have an average age in that they come from several years' harvests. We feel that the typical American consumer, whether he buys wine or cigarettes or toothpaste, wants consistency in the product.

About the only change we could make in the production of our wines would be to give some of them a vintage year and bottle-age them for a few years before they were sold. Besides not being practical, given our volume, I don't think the consumer would get much additional quality for his money.

EXHIBIT 3

THE TAYLOR WINE COMPANY, INC.
Income Statements—1959–61
(years ended June 30)

	1959		1960		1961	
	Amount	Percent	Amount	Percent	Amount	Percent
Net sales*	$10,348,186	100.00%	$10,084,116†	100.00%	$11,437,027	100.00%
Cost of goods sold	5,561,885	53.75	5,340,288	52.96	5,845,572	51.11
Gross margin	$ 4,786,301	46.25%	$ 4,743,828	47.04%	$ 5,591,455	48.89%
Other expenses:						
Advertising	482,769	4.67	546,422	5.42	655,175	5.73
Sales promotion	116,202	1.12	136,192	1.35	207,965	1.82
Selling	1,080,839	10.44	1,053,220	10.44	1,120,713	9.80
Branch office	224,443	2.17	234,912	2.33	244,786	2.14
Officers' salaries	367,136	3.55	379,739	3.77	392,406	3.43
General and administrative	436,895	4.22	490,660	4.86	603,233	5.27
Other	103,370	1.00	133,950	1.33	125,802	1.10
Net income before taxes	$ 2,811,654	27.17%	$ 2,975,095	29.50%	$ 3,350,080	29.29%
Income taxes	1,974,647	19.08	1,768,733	17.54	2,241,375	19.60
	1,139,374	11.01	1,022,371	10.14	1,286,665	11.25
Net income	$ 835,273	8.07%	$ 746,362	7.40%	$ 954,710	8.35%
Net income per share	$9.28		$8.29		$10.61	

* After excise taxes.
† Sales decline in 1960 was due to heavy advance buying in late 1959 in anticipation of a price increase.
Source: Company records.

EXHIBIT 4

THE TAYLOR WINE COMPANY, INC.
Balance Sheet as of September 30, 1961

Assets			*Liabilities and equity*	
Cash	$ 68,597		Notes payable	$ 544,000
Marketable securities	796,615		Accounts payable	211,660
Accounts receivable	1,063,595		Accrued liabilities	1,052,149
Inventories:			Total current liabilities	$1,807,809
Raw materials	424,661		Long-term debt	2,000,000
Wine in process	3,035,305		Other liabilities	223,472
Finished goods	320,240		Total liabilities	$4,031,281
Revenue stamps	4,511		Capital stock ($20 par, authorized 100,000 shares,	
Prepaid expenses	43,674		issued 90,000)	1,800,000
Total current assets	$5,757,198		Capital surplus	99,207
Plant and equipment at cost:			Retained earnings	3,266,676
Land	51,814		Total equity	$5,165,883
Buildings	2,225,389		Total liabilities and equity	$9,197,164
Vineyards	23,292			
Machinery and equipment	1,772,808			
	$4,073,303			
Less: Accumulated depreciation	785,508			
Net plant and equipment	$3,287,795			
Other assets	152,171			
Total assets	$9,197,164			

Source: Company records.

EXHIBIT 5

THE TAYLOR WINE COMPANY, INC.
Product Line

Product	Sizes	Bottles per case	Case price to distributors and state boards	Per-bottle suggested retail price
Dessert and Aperitif Wines				
Port				
Tawny port				
Sherry				
Pale dry sherry	⁴/₅ Quart	12	$ 9.85	$1.55
Cream sherry				
White tokay				
Muscatel				
Dinner Wines				
Sauterne				
Rhine	⁴/₅ Pint	24	10.85	0.85
Burgundy	⁴/₅ Quart	12	9.85	1.55
Claret				
Rose				
Vermouth				
Sweet	⁴/₅ Quart	12	8.00	1.25
Extra dry				
Sparkling				
Dry champagne				
Brut champagne	⁴/₅ Pint	24	26.80	2.25
Pink champagne	⁴/₅ Quart	12	24.80	3.95
Sparkling Burgundy				

Source: Company records.

Marketing

In 1961 Taylor wines were sold in all 50 states. Sales to the 18 control states were made through beverage brokers to state alcoholic control boards and agencies. In the 32 open states, sales were made by 28 Taylor salesmen to approximately 200 independent wholesale distributors who resold to retail outlets. Until 1961 Taylor had sold directly to retailers in a few large domestic markets. The last of this direct selling was terminated in 1961 in the New York City market where Taylor had approximately 12.5% of its total sales. Taylor's main markets were concentrated in the East and Midwest; the top 15 states accounted for 75.7% of total case sales.

By 1961 Russell Douglas, vice president of sales, had developed definite policies for selling Taylor wines. He described Taylor's relationships with its distributors and his policies for his sales force:

A crucial aspect in this business is distributor relations. Unlike other producers, we played everything straight down the middle. We had only one price for all distributors—FOB winery—and we utilized no promotional discounts whatsoever. Every distributor had to sign a yearly written contract that detailed exactly what our relations would be, and at the end of the year we reviewed each distributor's performance.

The name of the game was control over the sales force. We didn't let our salesmen entertain lavishly and we required them to report weekly on their activities. I expected them to be working in their territories and not socializing. Their main function was to call on distributors, retailers, and restaurants.

Since the end of Prohibition, Taylor had consistently utilized national advertising and by 1961 was the most extensively advertised premium brand. Advertising was under the direction of Greyton Taylor and its budget of $655,175 was spent mainly on national magazines such as *Esquire, Time, Newsweek, The New Yorker, Holiday,* and *Sports Illustrated.*

Taylor's total marketing effort was summarized by Fred Taylor in the 1961 annual report:

The Taylor brand has become known as a mark of high quality, through the strengthening of the company's distribution and marketing program. The continuing program of advertising, sales promotion and public relations for Taylor Wine has remained the most consistent in the industry, and has, in the judgment of management, been largely responsible along with product excellence for the growth of sales and earnings. . . .

Taylor products have been advertised regularly in national magazines of high quality. . . . Feature stories in news media and corporate publicity in trade publications, tours for thousands of visitors in the winery, distribution of millions of recipe books and the utilization of a wide variety of point-of-purchase promotion material have rounded out a thorough program of product merchandising.

Production

Taylor wines were produced exclusively at the firm's winery in Hammondsport, New York. By 1961 the company's property had grown to 20 buildings containing approximately 217,000 square feet. Ten of these buildings were used for tank storage of wines that were fermenting or aging; four were devoted to champagne storage; the other six contained warehouse facilities, bottling, processing, and pressing operations, and office space. The Taylor plants had a storage capacity of 4,917,000 gallons and on June 30, 1961, when the company was operating at close to capacity, its inventory totaled 3,732,450 gallons.[3] The 1961 sales of 1,244,812 cases equaled approximately 3 million gallons of wine.

---

[3] For a New York winery with a harvest in October and November, the peak inventory occurred at the end of the harvest. June 30 marked the approximate low point, and hence this date had been chosen as the fiscal year end.

The company's 511 acres of vineyards supplied 25% of its annual grape requirements. The balance was purchased from about 300 independent growers located primarily in the Finger Lakes region. Some bulk wines used in blending and in the production of vermouth and muscatel were purchased from California suppliers.

Taylor's crushing and pressing facilities were quite old. Construction on a new pressing facility which would increase pressing capacity by 200% was underway and would be completed in time for the 1962 harvest. Taylor used redwood tanks exclusively for its fermenting and aging; the largest of these tanks held 63,000 gallons. A tank storage building for an additional 2,000,000 gallons of still wine was also under construction and was scheduled for completion in 1962. This new storage facility would alleviate the capacity problem that Taylor had been experiencing in 1961.

The remaining production facilities presented no immediate problems. Champagne was fermented in the bottle for approximately two years, and the four champagne storage buildings were considered adequate for the next several years.

Taylor employed approximately 250 regular full-time employees and added about 240 field workers during the grape harvesting season. The average plant worker made $2.69 an hour, liberal for the Hammondsport area, and received a year-end bonus equal to about one month's wages. Productivity in the plant was high; for each hour worked, 3.6 cases were produced. Management characterized its employee relations as excellent, and the senior managers in Hammondsport knew most of the plant employees on a first-name basis. There had never been a unionization attempt in the company's history, and employee turnover was extremely low.

Finance and ownership

Capital expenditures presented a significant problem. As one executive commented: "Like it or not, we are in a brick and mortar business." A better sense for capital needs for new plant and equipment could be obtained by comparing sales increases to capital additions. Such an analysis revealed that, between 1957 and 1961, for every $1 increase in sales, fixed assets were increased by about 80 cents.

The bulk of these capital needs were met through internal financing. Since internal financing also had to be used for substantial increases in working capital, the firm was forced to utilize long-term debt for the first time in 1956. Since then, Taylor had continued to use long-term debt, and on September 30, 1961, its debt totaled $2,000,000 in 5¼% 15-year notes from a life insurance company.

The demands on internally generated funds left little available for dividends. The firm paid its first dividend of 50 cents a share in 1959; in 1961 it paid 75 cents a share, for a total of $67,500.

Management

The Taylor Wine Company in 1961 could be appropriately character-ized as a family business; all its outstanding shares were owned by members of the Taylor family. In addition, the three sons of the founder, who had been with the firm all of their adult lives for an average of 44 years, constituted most of top management. Fred Taylor, described by many as the "statesman" of the company, was president and exercised overall administrative control. The younger brothers, Clarence and Greyton, were vice presidents in charge of production planning and advertising, respectively. The only other person at the vice-presidential level was Russell Douglas, who was not related to the Taylor family. He was in charge of the company's sales and had his office in New York City.

Other upper-management executives in 1961 included George Law-rence, who handled financial matters and was married to a granddaughter of Walter Taylor; Seaton Mendall, who was also married to a grand-daughter, directed Taylor's vineyard program; and Joseph Swarthout, who managed daily production operations at the winery.

The Taylor board of directors consisted of the three Taylors plus Lawrence and Mendall. The organizational setup and pertinent back-ground information on management are presented in Exhibit 6.

PLEASANT VALLEY NEGOTIATIONS

The negotiations between Taylor and Great Western had been in prog-ress since the summer of 1961. George Lawrence commented on the early discussions and on some of the difficulties that still remained to be settled late that same year:

It seemed strange at first for Taylor's to be thinking of buying Pleasant Valley. For almost 80 years these two family-controlled companies had been in intense rivalry and considered each other their greatest competition. It would have thus been virtually impossible for Taylor to buy Pleasant Valley from the Champlin family in 1956 when Obernauer took it over. Under Obernauer, however, the relations began to thaw and we realized that a purchase was possible. There were still several issues that had to be settled in future negotiations: the surviving company, the structure of the financial deal, the composition of the board, among others.

GREAT WESTERN PRODUCERS, INC.

In late 1961, Marne Obernauer, the president of Great Western Pro-ducers, Inc., was contemplating whether to recommend selling one of the company's three operating divisions, its Pleasant Valley wine and Scotch importing division. For several months he had been negotiating such a sale with The Taylor Wine Company, a major New York State

EXHIBIT 6

THE TAYLOR WINE COMPANY, INC.
Organization and Management
1961

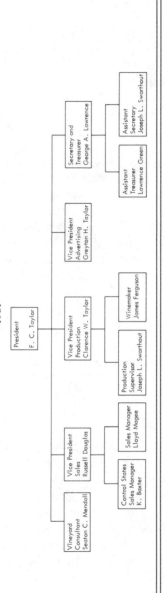

Name	Age	Years with Taylor	College education	Previous employment	Salary
Fred C. Taylor	70	47	none	none	$ 76,000
Greyton H. Taylor	58	37	2 yrs., bus. college	none	76,000
Clarence W. Taylor	68	47	none	none	76,000
George A. Lawrence	47	23	A.B., Cornell	P.R. firm, 2 yrs.	46,000
Russell Douglas	60	13	B.A., Wisconsin	American Wine Co., Exec. VP; Imperial Distributing, Pres.; Wine Institute, Mktg. Mgr.; Executive Personnel, Pres.	121,432*
Seaton Mendall	44	18	B.S., Univ. of Mass.	none	n.a.
Joseph L. Swarthout	42	15	B.S., Syracuse Univ.	none	n.a.
J. Lawrence Green	53	34	1 yr., bus. college	none	n.a.
Kenneth S. Baxter	68	2	BME, Michigan	Four Roses, VP; Copeland Refrig. Co., Pres.	n.a.
Lloyd Magee	43	7	B.A., California	Roma Wine Co., State Mgr.	n.a.

* Includes $60,000 salary plus bonus.
n.a. = not available.
Source: Casewriter's analysis from interviews and company records.

winery located next to Pleasant Valley in Hammondsport. The two parties had started negotiations with widely different perceptions of the worth of Pleasant Valley but had moved to the point where Obernauer felt that the financial terms of a sale could be readily agreed to. (See Exhibits 7 and 8 for income statements and balance sheet for Pleasant Valley.)

In 1955, Obernauer, a distributor of wines and liquors, had bought Pleasant Valley, supplementing his own capital with the backing of friends and associates. His offer of $6.60 a share for the company's stock had represented a substantial premium over the $4.00 to $4.50 market price, and Obernauer and his group were able to purchase a majority of the 250,000 outstanding shares.

The new owners, however, had not been content with merely running a winery. In 1957 Pleasant Valley was merged with Petrocarbon Chemicals, Inc., and the surviving company was called Great Western Producers, Inc. Petrocarbon's primary activity was the operation of a petroleum refinery in Irving, Texas; in addition, it owned the mineral rights to 1600 acres of California land which was leased to other producers for royalties.

Later in 1957 Great Western Producers bought the Gulf Red Cedar Pencil Slat Company, a firm that manufactured pencil slats from red cedar wood. This company, which was one of the largest of its kind in the world, had its main operations in Stockton, California. Obernauer described the reasons for the merger and purchase of these two firms:

> Petrochemical was attractive since it had a large tax-loss carry forward that we could offset against the profits of Pleasant Valley. This was the sole justification for the merger. Gulf Red Cedar represented an effort to enlarge and diversify our operations. Its purchase was supported by my partners, and I never became too involved in it.

Products

In 1961 Pleasant Valley had an extensive line of 26 varieties of premium wines resulting in 98 product sizes, even though after 1955 Marne Obernauer had reduced somewhat the complexity of the line by dropping six wines (see Exhibit 9). The main products were all sold under the Great Western name, but the firm also manufactured and marketed a secondary line of vermouth and did private-label bottling for a few large New York retailers such as Macy's. In March 1960 Pleasant Valley obtained an exclusive contract (subject to cancellation by either party) to import and market the Whyte & Mackay line of premium Scotch whiskey. Sales of this Scotch reached $349,000 in 1961.

Marne Obernauer commented on the Pleasant Valley product line and on some of his changes.

> After I took over the company, I tried to push the still [i.e., dessert and table] wines somewhat, but my emphasis was on champagne. I always viewed Great Western as a champagne name and Pleasant Valley as a champagne

EXHIBIT 7

PLEASANT VALLEY
Income Statements—1957–61
(years ended December 31)

	1957		1958		1959		1960*		1961*	
	Amount	Percent	Amount	Percent	Amount	Percent	Amount	Percent	Amount	Percent
Net sales	$2,519,754	100.0%	$2,816,158	100.0%	$3,307,867	100.0%	$3,862,680	100.0%	$4,191,226	100.0%
Cost of goods sold	1,439,536	57.1	1,526,912	54.2	1,799,139	54.4	2,096,414	54.3	2,300,228	54.9
Gross margin	$1,080,218	42.9%	$1,289,246	45.8%	$1,508,728	45.6%	$1,766,266	45.7%	$1,890,998	45.1%
Expenses:										
Selling, general, and administrative	664,905	26.4	713,180	25.3	953,514	28.8	954,106	24.7	1,168,809	27.9
Profit sharing	39,689	1.6	52,102	1.9	47,822	1.5	72,051	1.9	59,677	1.4
Interest	738	0.0	1,378	0.0	3,373	0.1	4,480	0.1	7,616	0.2
	$ 705,332	28.0%	$ 766,660	27.2%	$1,004,709	30.4%	$1,030,637	26.7%	$1,236,102	29.5%
Net income before taxes	$ 374,886	14.9%	$ 522,586	18.6%	$ 504,019	15.2%	$ 735,629	19.0%	$ 654,896	15.6%
Income taxes†	209,808	8.3	279,282	9.9	268,390	8.1	394,578	10.2	349,053	8.3
Net income	$ 165,078	6.6%	$ 243,304	8.7%	$ 235,629	7.1%	$ 341,051	8.8%	$ 305,843	7.3%
Pleasant Valley results as a percent of Great Western Producers:										
Total sales	35%		36%		31%		35%		35%	
Total income before taxes	123%		96%		62%		157%		180%	

* Includes results of Scotch whiskey imports from March 1, 1960. Net sales from this business were $279,000 in 1960 and $349,000 in 1961. Net income from this operation was approximately $9,900 in 1960 and $5,700 in 1961.

† Since Pleasant Valley was a division of Great Western Producers, it did not itself pay taxes. Income taxes have been computed at rates in effect in each year. Great Western Producers did not pay any taxes until 1961 due to loss carry forward of Petrochemical division.

Source: Company records and casewriter's analysis.

EXHIBIT 8

PLEASANT VALLEY
Balance Sheet as of September 30, 1961

Assets		
Cash*	$ 75,374	
Accounts receivable	787,656	
Inventories:		
Raw materials	224,653	
Wine in process	1,298,505	
Finished goods	239,951	
Prepaid expenses	64,502	
Total current assets		$2,690,641
Plant and equipment:		
Land	27,177	
Buildings	519,476	
Machinery and equipment	813,372	
	$1,360,025	
Less: Accumulated depreciation	511,615	
Net plant and equipment		$ 848,410
Total assets		$3,539,051†

Liabilities and Equity		
Notes payable*		$ 150,000
Accounts payable and accrued liabilities		364,929
Total current liabilities		$ 514,929
Division capital*		3,024,122
Total liabilities and equity		$3,539,051

* Since Pleasant Valley was a division of Great Western Producers, Inc., these items on the balance sheet are not meaningful.
† Total assets of Great Western Producers, Inc., at 9/30/61 equaled $8,044,842.
Source: Company records.

EXHIBIT 9

PLEASANT VALLEY
Product Line

Product	Sizes	Bottles per case	Case price to distributors and state control boards	Per-bottle suggested retail price
Dessert wines				
Port				
Tawny port				
White port				
Cocktail sherry	⁴/₅ Pint	24	$10.50	$ 0.85
Sherry	⁴/₅ Quart	12	9.50	1.55
Cream sherry	¹/₂ Gallon	6	9.41	2.95
Cooking sherry	Gallon	4	11.28	5.29
Muscatel				
Tokay				
Pink catawba				
Table wines				
Haut sauterne				
Sauterne	⁴/₅ Pint	24	10.50	0.85
Chablis	⁴/₅ Quart	12	9.50	1.55
Rhine	¹/₂ Gallon	6	9.41	2.95
Burgundy	Gallon	4	11.28	5.29
Claret				
Rose				
	⁴/₅ Pint	24	7.56	0.59
Concord	⁴/₅ Quart	12	6.56	0.99
	¹/₂ Gallon	6	7.51	2.35
	Gallon	4	8.34	3.95
Vermouth				
Sweet	⁴/₅ Pint	24	10.50	0.85
Dry	⁴/₅ Quart	12	9.50	1.55
	Quart	12	10.50	1.65
Sparkling				
Extra dry champagne				
Brut special champagne	Split (6.4 oz.)	24	17.58	1.35
Special reserve	⁴/₅ Pint	24	30.16	2.35
champagne	⁴/₅ Quart	12	28.16	4.40
Pink champagne	Magnum (51.2 oz.)	6	28.16	8.75
Sparkling Burgundy				
Extra dry champagne	Split (8 oz.)	24	30.16	2.35
	Jeroboam (102.4 oz.)	3	19.60	12.25

Source: Company price lists.

company. Our champagnes were the largest selling in the country and I think they had an elegance which was rather unique. For years Great Western was the only champagne served in the White House, and when Vice President Nixon went to Russia in 1959 he carried two cases of Great Western champagne with him.

I made several changes in products after 1955 in an effort to simplify the product line. Scotch was added purely as a diversification move. Verona vermouth was an attempt to participate in the trends towards white vermouths as it seemed to me that Great Western was just not a good vermouth name to compete with Martini & Rossi and Tribuno. The private-label business was inherited, but it served to cement relationships with large retailers and to fill our production capacity.

In 1961 champagne was the largest selling product class at Pleasant Valley. It constituted 57.5% of case sales, but more importantly it contributed over 70% of dollar sales and gross margins. The champagne labels had changed very little since the beginnings of Pleasant Valley in the 1800s, although new labels and bottles had been introduced for its dessert and table wines in 1958. These wines together accounted for about 41% of case sales in 1961.

Marketing

Although Pleasant Valley wines were sold everywhere in the United States except in the Far West, sales were heavily concentrated in the East. There were two major types of distribution: through six beverage brokers to the state alcoholic control boards and agencies in the nine control states and through 15 company salesmen to independent wholesale distributors in the 30 open states. Marne Obernauer had eliminated direct selling to retailers in upstate New York in 1958 and had increased the number of wholesalers from 65 in 1956 to approximately 125 by 1961.

The 15 salesmen were under the direction of the national sales manager, Fred Gambke, the fourth sales manager the company had had since 1956. Wholesalers were not required to take the full product line, and many of them preferred to carry only the champagnes. There were two official promotions a year, in May and in November, but one long-time employee commented that "any wholesaler who wanted a special deal could get one." Pleasant Valley's advertising budget of about $80,000 was used primarily for magazine advertising in *The New York Times Magazine* in the last three months of the year. Three different advertising agencies had been used in the period 1956 to 1961.

Production

Pleasant Valley wines were produced exclusively at the winery in Hammondsport, New York. In 1961 the company had seven buildings with a total floor space of approximately 175,000 square feet and storage capacity for 15,000 cases of whiskey and 1,665,000 gallons of champagnes and still wines. On September 30, 1961, the inventory amounted to approximately 1,450,000 gallons and the 1961 sales of 281,000 cases represented 674,000 gallons.

Pleasant Valley's winery was quite old; six buildings were of stone and brick construction and had been built prior to Prohibition. The other building, a steel warehouse, had been built in 1957. The company owned 150 acres of vineyards that supplied about 20% of its annual grape requirements and purchased the balance from independent growers in the Finger Lakes region.

Marne Obernauer commented in the 1958 annual report:

Our wines truly are among the very finest produced in this country and no effort or expense is spared in achieving this quality. This fact also presents our biggest management problem at Hammondsport; we maintain the strictest old world methods of aging, fermenting, and producing fine champagnes and we go to much out-of-ordinary expense to produce the highest quality table wines. For example, a bottle of our champagne is handled 167 times before it leaves our winery.

Some of the managerial personnel did not completely agree with this assessment. One of them commented:

The owners seemed to have one thing in mind and that was to make money. Expansion was limited and there were few resources available for maintenance. The only addition to the plant had been a strand steel warehouse, and the general condition of the winery had gone downhill in the years after 1955.

Personnel

Pleasant Valley employed approximately 125 regular full-time workers who made an average of $2.46 an hour, about standard for the Hammondsport area. Given the extensive product line, productivity was low; for each hour worked in the plant, 1.5 cases were produced.

In mid-1961 the Glassworkers Union attempted to unionize the workers. A Pleasant Valley manager described the situation:

There were just some things that the management did not understand about the wine business. In 1960 in an attempt to increase efficiency, the workers' hours were cut from the standard 45 per week to 40. This was strongly contested by the plant workers and, through the efforts of a few young ones, a union attempt was made. When it came to a vote, the older workers defeated the union, but the whole experience scared the daylights out of management.

Finance and ownership

Capital expenditures for Pleasant Valley from 1957 through 1961 had not been large. Total additions to fixed assets had been $627,167 for these five years, or an increase of about 37 cents in fixed assets for each $1 increase in sales. Great Western Producers had, however, consistently paid dividends on its preferred and common stock, and from 1957 to 1961 dividends totaled $693,766, or about 34% of net income after taxes.

Although Great Western Producers was publicly held, control rested with Marne Obernauer and his associates with 55% of the 549,296 shares outstanding.

Management

Management at Pleasant Valley consisted of a small group of men, most of whom had been with the company for only a short time (see

EXHIBIT 10

PLEASANT VALLEY
Organization and Management

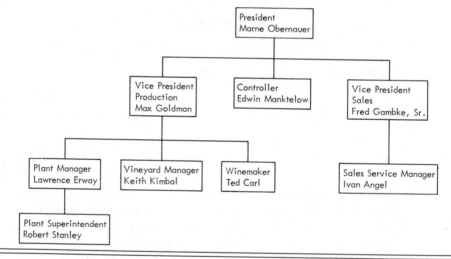

Name	Age	Years with Pleasant Valley	Previous employment	Salary and bonus
Marne Obernauer	42	5	Wine importer's agent in Pennsylvania and Ohio	$50,000
Max Goldman	51	3	General manager of a California winery	25,000
Fred Gambke, Sr.	65	1	Sales manager for wine importers	26,000
Ed Manktelow	39	6	C.P.A.	9,850
Lawrence Erway	55	28	None	10,100
Ted Carl	65	11	Production in food business	12,800
Keith Kimbal	33	3	None	10,850
Ivan Angel	40	8	Winery office manager	9,120

Source: Casewriter's analysis from interviews.

Exhibit 10). Marne Obernauer, president of Great Western Producers, described his functions:

> I had very little to do with Gulf Red Cedar or Petrochemical as these were run by my associates. I spent one week a month at the winery and the rest of the time operated out of our sales offices in New York City. While at the winery I worked with Max Goldman, but since he was in charge I left him pretty much alone.
>
> In New York City I spent my time on advertising, public relations, and wholesaler relations. I wanted to develop a personal relationship with wholesalers. Special promotions—for example, Mr. Nixon taking Great Western champagne to Russia and Mr. Richard Mellon using Great Western champagne at his daughter's wedding—took a great deal of my time also.

By late 1961 Obernauer had decided that a sale of Pleasant Valley would have to be essentially for common stock of the acquiring company. His feeling was that the amount of stock received should be in proportion to Pleasant Valley's sales and earnings contribution to the purchaser. He commented on his relations with the Taylors and the possibility of selling Pleasant Valley:

> When I first came to Hammondsport early in 1956, I found a situation that was tantamount to the Hatfields and McCoys. There existed an intense rivalry between Pleasant Valley and Taylor in both business and social aspects. In the spring of 1956 my wife and I gave a party at the winery for all the senior members of the community. When Fred Taylor came next door to Pleasant Valley, I found out that he had not stepped foot in there for over 20 years. After this a speaking relationship developed. Still, it was a reserved and guarded relationship since I knew I was considered a newcomer.
>
> As regarded a sale of Pleasant Valley, my partners had given me complete freedom to do as I saw best with the winery. My basic feeling was that I had taken Pleasant Valley as far as I could, and that future growth would be more likely as part of a larger concern.

The Taylor Wine Company, Inc.— Part II

THE WINE INDUSTRY IN 1973

Wine consumption

The U.S. wine industry in 1973 was experiencing record demands for its products. Until 1967, wine consumption had grown at an annual rate of 2.6%, resulting in a relatively stagnant per-capita figure of slightly under one gallon. The wine "boom" in the United States began in 1968 with consumption racking up consecutive yearly gains of 4.3%, 9.8%, 13.5%, 14.2%, and 10.4% and exceeding growth in both population and income. Compared to its nearest beverage competitors, however, wine per-capita consumption of 1.57 gallons in 1973 still fell behind liquor (1.89 gallons) and beer (19.3 gallons). On a national basis, the United States ranked 27th worldwide in per-capita consumption in 1971, with only 1.43 gallons compared to Italy (29.3), France (28.5), Portugal (24), Argentina (22.4), and Spain (15.8), the top five wine-consuming countries where wine was part of the everyday diet, and even behind countries such as the U.S.S.R. (3.03) and Sweden (1.8).

Reasons for the recent growth in wine demand were generally attributed to the industry's marketing efforts combined with three factors: (1) per-capita disposable income rose steadily during the 1960s and not only contributed to increased consumption of wine in general but also enabled consumers to purchase more higher price premium wines; (2) passage and adoption of the 18-year-old "right to vote" constitutional amendment in 1971 was followed by changes in many states of the "right to drink" laws, lowering the age at which wine purchases were permitted; and (3) a shift in population which was projected to continue in a direction favorable to wine consumption.

	1960	1970	1980
Under 21	39.1%	38.5%	36.2%
21–44	30.5	28.8	34.5
Over 44	30.4	32.7	29.3
Total population (millions)	181.6	203.9	227.6

General interest in wine was also enhanced through wine festivals, wine classes, wine-tasting parties, and a growing literature on wine and winemaking. Market studies presented a profile of an educated, affluent, white-collar consumer. In one market study about two thirds of the respondents rated domestic better than imported wines, wines from California better than those from New York, and higher price wines better than lower price ones.

Little change took place during the 1960s in the basic pattern of wine consumption across the United States. Regionally, wine markets were strongest on the East and West Coasts, with the Pacific area constituting 26% of the total wine market, with 21.5% of the country's sales, followed by New York (12.8%), Illinois (5.4%), and New Jersey (5.1%). On a per-capita basis, Washington D.C. was the largest single market, with a 4.74 gallon average per person in 1972, followed by Nevada (3.76), California (3.44), and New York (2.29). At the opposite extreme were states like Iowa (0.41), West Virginia (0.51), Kansas (0.59), and Tennessee (0.58).

Wine consumption was also largely an urban phenomenon, with the top five metropolitan areas accounting for 28% of total U.S. wine sales in 1972, the top 25 for 53%, and the top 50 for 66%. Concentration was even greater for imported wines, with the top 25 cities accounting for 78%. New York City alone held 23% of the imported wine market.

Sources and types of wine

By 1972, California's share had declined to slightly above 70% of U.S. consumption, while imported wines had increased their share to 14%. Industry projections expected these respective shares to amount to 63% and 20% by 1980. Imports in 1972 came primarily from five countries: France (26.5%), Italy (24%), Spain (18.1%), Portugal (14.2%), and Germany (9.9%).

While imported wines had traditionally been premium priced, a noticeable trend towards lower price imports, coming principally from Spain, appeared in the early 1970s. Despite the second devaluation of the dollar in February 1973, imports were expected to increase their share of the U.S. market. The Bank of America predicted a 1980 penetration of 20% for imports and largely dismissed effects of devaluation:

The impact of the devaluation will be different for each of the countries exporting wine to the U.S. . . . Yet, since the price of domestic wine is also increasing, the tendency of the devaluation to curtail imports is likely to be offset. With incomes continuing to rise, consumers may maintain their previous level of import purchases, despite price increases.[1]

The success of imported wines in the U.S. market was facilitated by a reasonable tariff policy, especially on table wines which were subject to customs duties of only 37.5 cents per gallon. High tariffs in most other countries kept U.S. exports low. In 1972 the United States exported only 505,000 gallons of wine, over half of which went to Canada.

Substantial shifts in the popularity of types of wine became pronounced in the 1960s:

	Percentage share in gallons			
Type of wine	1961–64	1965–68	1969–72	1980 (projected)
Table	35.9%	42.2%	50.1%	76%
Dessert	48.8	40.2	26.6	11
Vermouth	4.7	4.8	3.6	*
Special natural	7.6	7.8	12.3	*
Sparkling	3.0	5.0	7.4	13
Average annual consumption in millions of gallons	175.3	199.5	286.3	465 to 650

* Separate projections not made; included in table and dessert classes.

The special natural wine classification which in 1960 consisted of only a few flavored wines of high alcoholic content such as Thunderbird saw a proliferation of fruit-flavored, often slightly effervescent wines generally called "pop" wines.[2] Two companies, Gallo and Heublein, dominated this segment with wines such as Zapple, Boone's Farm, Ripple, Bali Hai, Key Largo, I Love You (a cola-flavored wine), and Annie Green Springs. While many observers attributed the popularity of pop wines to the rise of marijuana smoking by American youth,[3] industry spokesmen generally

---

[1] Bank of America, "California Wine Industry," September 1973.

[2] The term "pop wines" was derived from either "popular" or "soda pop" which many people felt they resembled.

[3] It was claimed that alcohol extended and intensified the feeling obtained from marijuana, and fruity, mild wine was the most palatable method of getting alcohol into the body.

felt that new consumers buying these low alcohol (9%–11%), cheaper (often less than $1 per fifth), fruity wines would eventually "trade up" to drier, higher price wines. Moreover, by 1973 there was some feeling in the industry that the pop-wine fad was slowing.

One sparkling wine that had enjoyed almost instant success was Cold Duck, a mixture of sparkling Burgundy and champagne. Cold Duck caught on in mid-1970, and the wine became so popular that it almost single-handedly contributed to a 35% increase in sparkling wine sales in 1970, despite a much higher price than other popular wines because of higher federal excise taxes. Cold Duck faded very rapidly, however, and by 1973 constituted only a small part of total sparkling wine sales.

Despite the growth of lower price pop wines, there had been a steady increase in the popularity of U.S. premium wines from an estimated 7.5% of the market in 1960 to 17% in 1972. Wine sales in 1972 by price categories and types were estimated by the *Wine Marketing Handbook* as follows:

Retail price per fifth	Table	Dessert	Sparkling	Vermouth	Total
Under $1.25	61.5%	52.7%	. . .	12.5%	53.1%
$1.25–$2.00	21.6 ´	44.3	. . .	40.0	27.4
$2.01–$3.50	8.3	2.7	63.6	47.5	11.7
$3.51–$5.00	5.2	. . .	26.0	. . .	4.9
Over $5.00	3.5	0.3	10.4	. . .	2.9
	100.0%	100.0%	100.0%	100.0%	100.0%

Wine producers

Beginning in the mid-1960s a number of large distillers and food companies entered the wine industry through the acquisition of wineries and importers (see Exhibit 1). These new firms supplied small, often family-owned wine businesses with substantial financial resources, marketing capability, and management depth. By 1972, about 75% of U.S. wines were produced by the 16 wine companies listed in Exhibit 2.

Paramount in the standard price segment was Gallo with a share of the U.S. wine market approaching 35% in 1973 and estimated 1972 sales of almost $300 million. *Time* described Gallo as follows:

. . . Just as one state dominates the industry, one company towers above the rest. . . . Family owned, the Gallo company is one of the nation's largest privately held firms. . . . The Gallos' impact on American wine making has been enormous. They were the nation's first wine makers to hire research chemists. Years ago they abandoned wooden fermenting casks for stainless-steel tanks. . . . The Gallos were the first to automate their wineries by, among other things, computerizing the blending process. They also pioneered in pop

EXHIBIT 1
Acquisitions in the wine industry

Acquisition	Year acquired	Acquiring firm	1971 Sales of acquirer (in millions)
A. *Domestic wineries*			
Paul Masson Vineyards	1945	Distillers Corporation— Seagram's, Ltd.	$1,400
Beaulieu Vineyard	1965	Heublein, Inc.	630
Almaden Vineyards	1967	National Distillers & Chemical Corporation	1,100
Widmer's Vineyards	1969	R. T. French	100
Mogen David Wine Corporation	1970	Coca-Cola of New York, Inc.	100
Beringer Brothers Winery	1970	Nestle Company, Inc. (U.S.)	300
United Vintners	1969	Heublein, Inc.	630
B. *Importer's labels*			
Browne Vintners	1940	Distillers Corporation— Seagram's, Ltd.	$1,400
Barton & Guestier (B&G)	1954	Distillers Corporation— Seagram's, Ltd.	1,400
Dreyfus Ashby	1957	Schenley Industries, Inc.	700
Alexis Lichine	1964	Bass-Charington, Ltd.	700
Leeds Imports	1966	Barton Brands, Inc.	120
Austin Nichols	1967	Liggett & Myers, Inc.	700
Frederick Wildman	1971	Hiram Walker	N/A
Julius Wile & Sons	1972	Standard Brands, Inc.	1,000
Monsieur Henri	1972	Pepsico, Inc.	600

Source: *Business Week, New York Magazine,* casewriter's analysis.

wines. . . . Last year, producing six of the dozens of entries on the market, Gallo accounted for 90% of pop wines sold in the U.S. . . .

The Gallos have a talent for sensing consumer trends and being first with new products, as they were with pop wines. Now that growth is leveling off in the pop field, the Gallos appear to be shifting their promotional efforts to more conventional wines—Chablis Blanc, Pink Chablis, Burgundy and Hearty Burgundy. . . .[4]

Gallo's allocation of promotional resources away from pop wines began in 1972. Since the firm's massive volume enabled it to produce high-quality wines at standard prices, such a shift could represent a substantial threat to the traditional premium producers. In several well-publicized tastings conducted in 1972 and 1973, Gallo's wines, especially Hearty Burgundy, were judged better than competitors' premium wines costing up to three times as much.

Behind Gallo in market share was Heublein which offered through its United Vintners subsidiary a number of standard price wines. However,

---

[4] "American Wine Comes of Age," reprinted by permission from TIME, *The Weekly Newsmagazine,* November 27, 1972, p. 81. Copyright Time Inc. 1972.

EXHIBIT 2
Major American wineries

	Ownership	Market share 1971	Market share 1972
*California "Standard"**			
E. & J. Gallo	Private	32.7%	32.4%
United Vintners	Heublein	16.7	13.6
Guild Wine	Growers' Cooperative	5.0	4.2
Franzia Brothers	Public	2.4	2.7
New York "Standard"			
Mogen David	Coca-Cola of N.Y.	3.5	3.7
Canandaigua	Public	3.0	2.9
Monarch	Private	1.5	1.6
		64.8%	61.1%
Other "Standard"		8.4	7.9
		73.2%	69.0%
California "Premium"			
Almaden	National Distillers Corp.	3.4%	4.3%
Paul Masson	Seagram's	1.9	2.0
Mont La Salle	Christian Brothers	1.8	1.7
Inglenook	Heublein	0.3	0.6
Sebastiani	Private	0.3	0.4
Charles Krug	Private	0.3	0.3
New York "Premium"			
Taylor.....................	Public	3.5	3.5
Gold Seal	Private	0.9	0.9
Widmer's	R. T. French	0.4	0.4
		12.8%	14.1%
Other "Premium"		2.2	2.9
		15.0%	17.0%
Imported		11.8	14.0
Total		100.0%	100.0%

* Refers to state location and price class of wine produced.
Source: Industry sources and casewriter's estimates.

aside from some success with its premium brands—Inglenook, Beaulieu, and Lancers—Heublein was considered by industry sources to run a poor second to Gallo in the standard price segment and to have suffered disappointing results since its 1969 acquisition of United Vintners.

While the four largest premium producers had some characteristics in common, each had certain unique aspects:

Almaden's 38 wines were sold mainly under the Almaden label, with a secondary brand of lower price "Le Domaine" sparkling wines. Eighty-five percent of the winery's sales were in table wines, some in the 14 varietals that retailed for up to $3.65 but the bulk mainly in the lower price, generic "Mountain" series of table wines. Almaden's growth had been most rapid since its acquisition by National Distillers in 1967. Markets had been opened in the East (14% of sales were in New York), and large land acquisitions for future vineyards had been undertaken.

Taylor sold 51 types of New York wines under the Taylor and Great Western brand names. The most popular products were Taylor dessert wines and Great Western champagnes. Markets were heavily concentrated in the East, and Taylor had the largest advertising budget among the premium wineries.[5]

Paul Masson sold 42 wines under the Paul Masson label. Table wines were the largest selling product class, primarily generics, but a large portion of sales came from proprietary table wines such as "Baroque." Paul Masson had been owned by Seagram's since 1945.

Mont La Salle sold 39 wines under the Christian Brothers label. The winery was unique in that it was owned by the Christian Brothers—a Catholic teaching order—who dealt only with wine production. Distribution and marketing were handled by Fromm and Sichel, a subsidiary of Seagram's. Sales were concentrated in dessert wines and, to a lesser extent, in expensive varietal table wines. Markets were predominantly western except for the Christian Brothers brandy which was the largest selling brandy in the United States.

Production

During the 1960s, largely through the efforts of state universities in California and New York, advances were made in grape growing and mechanical harvesting as well as in winery production techniques. This resulted in American wines of generally higher quality. By the early 1970s, however, grape supply and price were considered most important to the future of the wine industry. By 1973 most wineries had integrated backwards into development of their own vineyards, with the large companies usually supplying 10%–20% of their own requirements. The balance of the needed grapes came from small, independent growers under contracts of up to 20 years. Grapes were sold at open-market rates, although the dominance of a few wineries in each state, especially Gallo in California, allowed the major wineries to determine market prices.

The rising demand for wine together with damaged crops in 1970 and 1972 contributed to substantial increases in the prices of California grapes. The increases were most dramatic in the scarcer premium varieties; for example, Cabernet Sauvignon grapes that cost a winery $275 a ton in 1968 were selling for $800 a ton in 1972. Lesser increases were

---

[5] According to the *Wine Marketing Handbook*, Taylor's 1972 advertising expenditures totaled $1,589,000 as compared to $845,006 for Almaden, $1,430,391 for Paul Masson, $375,508 for Christian Brothers, and $467,657 for Inglenook.

also evident in the standard grape varieties used for making the bulk of California wines.

The surge in California grape prices had triggered a boom in grape-vine plantings. New acres planted in wine grapes totaled 6,548 in 1969, 26,844 in 1971, 48,600 in 1972, and 51,300 in 1973. Prime vineyard land prices had correspondingly soared from $1,000 to as high as $8,000 an acre. Most observers expected that this excessive planting would create a condition of oversupply in the middle and late 1970s that would drive grape prices down, drive growers out of business, and trigger a cycle of underplanting and thus undersupply by the early 1980s. Also, surplus premium grapes could be bought up cheaply and blended with standard wines, thus upgrading their quality and blurring the traditional distinction.

Marketing

Numerous changes took place during the 1960s in the marketing of wines, primarily due to the entrance of large companies. First of all, distillers could strongly influence wholesalers to take on and push the wine brands of their subsidiaries by offering discounts through package purchases of wine and liquor or by implicit threat of withdrawing their staple liquor brands.

A second change was the proliferation of nationally distributed brands. Several of the larger companies by 1973 marketed multiple brands of wine and many of the smaller premium wineries in California, traditionally content to sell their entire output within the state, were attempting to achieve national distribution. A few, such as Louis M. Martini and Wente, had been successful in selling their wines through large distillers with established channel connections.

A great expansion in wine advertising was the final marketing change in the industry. Advertising expenditures had grown from $18.5 million in 1968 to $43.2 million in 1972 (a 234% increase compared to a 60% increase in gallonage sales for the same period). The top advertisers, Heublein and Gallo, accounted for 47% of all wine advertising, and the top 12 advertisers were responsible for 89%. A breakdown of expenditures by media revealed significant differences in approach: Gallo, whose pop and less expensive wines were products aimed at a mass youth market, utilized television almost exclusively, while Seagram's, Taylor, and National Distillers, with primarily premium price products, emphasized magazines (see Exhibit 3).

By 1973 the large wineries were devoting huge promotional resources to single brands. For example, Gallo's Boone's Farm was introduced in 1970 with $785,900 in advertising, was heavily backed by $4,409,800 of advertising in 1971 and $6,236,740 in 1972, and by 1973 was the largest

EXHIBIT 3
Advertising expenditures (in thousands of dollars)

	Total advertising expenditures			1972 expenditures by category*		
	1970	1971	1972	TV	Radio	Maga-zine
E. & J. Gallo..........	$ 6,765	$ 7,352	$11,665	$11,193	$ 438	$ 31
Heublein	9,291	8,401	8,677	6,413	1,145	1,082
Seagram's............	2,433	2,194	3,556	1,510	370	1,660
Coca-Cola of N.Y.	1,726	2,365	3,191	3,012	125	50
Schenley	1,302	2,577	2,902	2,418	260	225
Renfield	1,231	1,635	1,693	1,464	19	210
Monarch	1,363	1,376	1,692	739	789	17
Taylor	1,413	1,497	1,589	572	159	843
National Distillers	718	846	1,129	...	32	1,098
Pepsico	58	224	938	478	387	73
Brown Foreman	567	953	966	230	...	735
Schieffelin	1,113	919	723	312	351	60
	$27,980	$30,339	$38,721			
Others	2,973	3,886	4,795			
Total	$30,953	$34,225	$43,516			

* Newspaper and outdoor advertising not included.
Source: Summarized from *The Wine Marketing Handbook* (1972) and (1973).

selling pop wine. Heublein in 1972 spent $2,119,205 on Lancers alone and $1,130,100 on Annie Green Springs.

The basic pattern of wine distribution had not changed much in the 1960s. In 1973, 18 states were classified as "control" states where state governments regulated distribution at the wholesale and sometimes at the retail level. The 32 "open" states, while all taxing wines to various degrees, allowed private distribution of alcoholic beverages. The various state regulations and taxes were highly fragmented across the country and as a result constituted a significant barrier to a winery seeking national distribution.

Despite this basic consistency in wine distribution, some changes were evident by 1973. Foremost was a decline in the number of open-state wholesalers, many of whom were forced out by profit squeezes, and an increase in the number of importers. A general trend towards concentration in distribution was described by the 1973 *Wine Marketing Handbook*:

There are at present approximately 350,000 retailers authorized to sell wine in the United States. Even if wine sales double in the next decade, there will be a heavy swing to chains in the ratio of total case volume. The chains have numerous advantages over independent retailers enabling them to accentuate price as an element of value.

Public offerings

By 1973 the wine industry had become one of the "darlings" of Wall Street both through a number of winery public offerings and a channeling of funds into California grape properties via tax-shelter syndications and limited partnerships. Since 1962 Taylor had been the only publicly held winery in the United States. Its stock appreciation had been substantial and undoubtedly influenced the decisions of five other wineries to offer their shares to the public in 1972 and early 1973.

Still, it soon became evident that some of the glamour of the wine business was wearing off as investors began to appraise more realistically the demanding economics of wine production. Barron's summarized the situation:

> For thousands of investors who have been beguiled by the rise in U.S. wine consumption and by TV commercials showing the rolling California hillsides with their vineyards awash in warm sunshine, the wine business may be on the point of turning sour. . . . Scanty grape harvests are beginning to pinch the profits of vintners. . . . Gallo's pervasive advertising and bulldozing merchandising tactics are making things rough for smaller publicly held competitors. Finally, a flood of Wall Street money into the wine industry, attracted more by the romance of the business than its profit potential, threatens to cause a glut in a few years which may leave today's eager investors sucking on grapes of wrath.[6]

The Bank of America speculated on the nature of the wine industry in the future:

> It is becoming clear . . . that the supply of wine from all sources seeking entry into the U.S. market eventually will exceed the market's capacity to absorb it. When that occurs, competition will assume a new character; markets will be traded rather than accumulated.
>
> As the number and capacity of wineries increase, competition for markets will become more intense. Price competition may become less important than non-price competition as greater emphasis is placed on product innovation and promotion in the years ahead. Such factors as variety, quality and bottling of the product will be stressed as well as promotional efforts. . . . Some firms may not survive in the long run because of the rigors of growth, rapid entry into the industry, and severe non-price competition. In the short run, the opportunities presented by a rapidly expanding market counterbalance the problems presented by competition.[7]

THE TAYOR WINE COMPANY, INC.

In 1973 The Taylor Wine Company was one of the largest producers of premium price wines in the United States. Its production facilities and

---

[6] "Wine and Roses? It's Time Investors Had Some Sober Second Thoughts," *Barron's,* December 4, 1972, © Dow Jones & Company, Inc. (1972).

[7] Bank of America, "California Wine Industry," September 1973.

corporate offices were located in Hammondsport, New York, and it marketed mainly New York wines under the Taylor and Great Western names. From 1962–72 its sales had grown at an annual rate of almost 13% and its profits after taxes at 15% (see Exhibit 4). The firm's operational successes were reflected in the strength of its financial position. It had no long-term debt of any significance even though total assets had tripled in the previous decade. Its current ratio stood at 6.6 to 1 (see Exhibit 5).

Taylor had benefited from the financial community's fascination with the wine business. Its common stock, traded over the counter, had reached a high of $59 a share in 1972, or 46 times earnings (see Exhibit 4). In 1973 Taylor had 4,353,748 common shares outstanding which were held by 5,825 stockholders. The Taylor family either directly or through various trusts controlled about 40% of the stock.

The Taylor company was organized along functional lines but operated the Pleasant Valley Wine Company, producer of Great Western wines, as an independent division. Almost all phases of Taylor and Pleasant Valley operations were completely separate. Each winery had its own management staff, production facilities, growers, sales forces, tour programs, and advertising agencies. Accounting and personnel for both wineries, however, were centralized at Taylor, and the two wineries jointly set prices for grape purchases and occasionally made a joint purchase of advertising media. Pleasant Valley contributed 23% of the corporation's total sales and 10% of its operating profit (gross margin less advertising, promotion, and selling expense). The 1972 Taylor annual report stated:

When Taylor acquired its long-time neighbor and rival winemaker in 1962, management decided to continue operating the two companies as competitors, each with its own staff for growing, producing and marketing wines. . . .

Time has proved that the decision to maintain separate organizations was a sound one. Since the merger, both companies have built from their strengths. Taylor, with the greater mass market and marketing organization, has added premium generic wines to its product lines. Pleasant Valley has expanded in a different way, identifying several of its wines by their varietal name to appeal to different consumers. Thanks to this marketing strategy, the two brands have found a niche side-by-side on the retail shelf, instead of growing at the expense of one another.

Looking to the future, George Lawrence, president of Taylor, explained that he had seriously considered utilizing the company's debt capacity or high P/E ratio for either expansion into Californian or European wine activities or diversification into other products.

While we have also explored joining with a large company, our current thinking is that the wisest strategy for Taylor in the foreseeable future is to

EXHIBIT 4

THE TAYLOR WINE COMPANY, INC.
Consolidated Income Statements—Years ended June 30
(in thousands of dollars)

	1962 $	1962 %	1964 $	1964 %	1967 $	1967 %	1970 $	1970 %	1971 $	1971 %	1972 $	1972 %
Net sales*	13,720	100.0	18,412	100.0	25,992	100.0	34,688	100.0	40,839	100.0	43,210	100.0
Cost of goods sold	6,962	50.7	8,905	48.4	12,189	46.9	16,274	46.9	20,462	50.1	21,789	50.4
Gross margin	6,758	49.3	9,507	51.6	13,803	53.1	18,414	53.1	20,377	49.9	21,412	49.6
Advertising and promotion	968	7.1	1,575	8.5	2,107	8.1	3,311	9.5	4,024	9.9	4,048	9.4
Selling	1,804	13.1	2,462	13.3	2,909	11.2	3,869	11.2	4,082	10.0	4,309	10.0
General and administrative	861	6.3	1,042	5.7	1,400	5.4	1,826	5.3	1,560	3.8	1,752	4.0
Other	146	1.1	175	1.0	202	0.8	295	0.9	630	1.5	305	0.7
	3,779	27.6	5,254	28.5	6,618	25.5	9,301	26.8	10,296	25.2	10,414	24.1
Income before taxes	2,979	21.7	4,253	23.1	7,185	27.6	9,113	26.3	10,081	24.7	10,998	25.5
Income taxes	1,625	11.8	2,224	12.1	3,621	13.9	4,882	14.1	5,072	12.4	5,526	12.8
Net income	1,354	9.9	2,029	11.0	3,564	13.7	4,231	12.2	5,009	12.3	5,472	12.7
Net income per share†	$0.40		$0.51		$0.89		$1.06		$1.26		$1.29	
Dividends per share	$0.03		$0.17		$0.28		$0.40		$0.43		$0.48	
Return on equity	12.6%		15.1%		18.1%		15.5%		16.4%		12.2%	
Dividend payout ratio	7.5%		33.3%		31.5%		37.7%		34.1%		37.2%	
Stock price range‡	$4–$7		$5–$8§		$7–$19‖		$13–$30#		$24–$45		$33–$59	
P/E ratio range	10x–18x		10–17		7–19		12–29		19–36		25–46	

* After federal excise taxes.
† Based on 3,990,936 shares outstanding from 1962 to 1971 and 4,353,748 shares outstanding in 1972.
‡ Adjusted for 3 for 1 stock split in 1971.
§ For 1963 and 1964.
‖ For 1965, 1966, and 1967.
For 1968, 1969, and 1970.
Source: Company records and casewriter's analysis.

EXHIBIT 5

THE TAYLOR WINE COMPANY, INC.
Condensed Balance Sheets—Years Ended June 30
(in thousands of dollars)

Assets	1962	1964	1967	1970	1971	1972
Cash	$ 640	$ 679	$ 811	$ 740	$ 1,684	$ 1,573
Accounts receivable	1,135	1,003	1,900	2,653	3,617	3,317
Inventories	6,198	8,440	10,568	16,372	18,185	24,137*
Other current assets	55	96	276	411	368	248
Total current assets	$ 8,028	$10,218	$13,555	$20,176	$23,854	$29,275
Fixed assets at cost	7,304	10,044	15,816	22,300	27,541	30,952
Less: Depreciation	1,084	2,370	4,759	7,829	9,219	10,884
Net fixed assets	$ 6,220	$ 7,674	$11,057	$14,471	$18,322	$20,068
Other assets	622	550	487	599	631	737
Total assets	$14,870	$18,442	$25,099	$35,246	$42,807	$50,080
Liabilities and Equity						
Accounts payable	$ 349	$ 354	$ 607	$ 1,059	$ 844	$ 1,104
Notes payable	165	165	867	4,200	...	1,300
Other current liabilities	1,253	2,405	2,303	1,466	1,960	2,031
Total current liabilities	$ 1,767	$ 2,924	$ 3,777	$ 6,725	$ 2,804	$ 4,435
Long-term debt	2,395	2,124	1,587	1,234	9,410	972
Equity	10,708	13,394	19,735	27,287	30,593	44,673†
Total liabilities and equity	$14,870	$18,442	$25,099	$35,246	$42,807	$50,080
Current ratio	4.5	3.5	3.6	3.0	8.5	6.6
Inventory turnover	1.35	1.24	1.18	1.29	1.18	1.03
Days receivables	24.0	15.7	20.8	22.3	26.3	23.3
Debt/equity ratio	.39	.37	.27	.28	.40	.12
Book value per share	$2.68	$3.36	$4.94	$6.84	$7.67	$10.52

* Increase in inventory due to very large 1971 harvest.
† Common stock offering in October 1971.
Source: Company records and casewriter's analysis.

continue our efforts in New York State wines. Given our people and our resources, this is what we know how to do best. I would like to see Taylor continue to grow at a relatively steady rate of 10%–12% and, if possible, to maintain our position as the number one premium-wine producer.

While Taylor's market share had grown from 1961 to 1972, its share of domestically produced premium wines had dropped from about 40% to less than 25%. According to George Lawrence:

Ten years ago, our competition consisted mainly of other New York State producers—primarily Gold Seal and Widmer's. In the last five years, however, California wineries have moved into much stronger hands, are more competitive, and have changed the rules of the game in the wine business. We are now confronted with a proliferation of new products and growing, changing markets.

The Taylor product line

The Taylor product line, except for a gradual shift away from emphasis on dessert wines (see Exhibit 6), underwent few changes during the 1960s. The major innovation was the introduction of a proprietary line of table wines under the name of Lake Country: red in 1966, white in 1968, and pink in 1970. One other new product, a premium-price Cold Duck, was introduced in 1971 with an advertising commitment of almost $300,000. George Lawrence explained:

Our marketing people thought that a Taylor Cold Duck was necessary. Our first reaction was that this was a pop wine, but they claimed that the channels were asking for a quality product. Since the production problems were not difficult—Cold Duck is merely a blend of champagne and sparkling Burgundy —we launched it in April of 1971. Ours was the first highly promoted premium-price Cold Duck, and it has been much more successful than I anticipated.

Taylor's Cold Duck in 1972 sold about 75,000 cases, or 17% of total sparkling wine sales.

The one effort at product-line diversification was the importation under the Taylor name of an Austrian brandy in 1966. Russell Douglas, vice president of marketing, commented:

The brandy idea was mine all the way, and I guess you could call it "Douglas' folly." For 20 years I had tried to convince the Taylors to get into the brandy business to compete with Christian Brothers. I was finally successful and through European contacts was able to find an Austrian producer with a special formula for a smooth brandy.

We imported the product in bulk and bottled it on Long Island. Unfortunately, bottling problems delayed our entry into the market. When we finally got in, our competitors had lowered their prices, and since I had little money in my ad budget to promote brandy, the product never went anywhere. We didn't lose anything on it, but we didn't make anything, either, so we discontinued it.

In the spring of 1973 a new Taylor wine was to be introduced: a sangria, a blend of dry red table wine and juices from lemons, limes, and oranges. Sangria was a traditional drink in Spain, Mexico, and other Latin countries and was experiencing growing popularity in the United States. The main competition for the new Taylor sangria was Yago Sant'gria, a Spanish wine imported by Monsieur Henri Wines, Ltd., a subsidiary of Pepsico, Inc. Yago was the second largest selling imported wine brand behind Mateus rose. The only other popular sangria-like wine was Gallo's standard price Spanada.

Taylor's introduction of sangria represented a marked departure for the firm. Even though the new wine was to carry a premium price, it was still an attempt by Taylor to participate in the booming flavored-

EXHIBIT 6

Percentage of Taylor and Pleasant Valley case sales by products and markets

	Taylor sales		Pleasant Valley sales		Total U.S. sales
	1961 (1,244,812 cases)	1972 (3,203,136 cases)	1961 (281,009 cases)	1972 (693,325 cases)	1971 (104 million cases)
Product class					
Dessert and aperitif	61.6%	49.0%	40.9%	13.3%	24.2%
Table	21.0	34.6		41.7	51.2
Sparkling	13.7	14.1	57.5	42.7	7.8
Vermouth	3.7	2.3	1.6	2.3	3.4
Special natural	...	...	...	...	13.4
	100.0%	100.0%	100.0%	100.0%	100.0%
Regional markets					
New England	10.9%	11.0%	12.3%	17.6%	7.3%
Middle Atlantic	41.1	32.6	46.3	43.7	22.0
East North Central	12.7	14.8	17.6	15.6	15.7
West North Central	4.7	5.6	1.6	2.9	4.0
South Atlantic	13.4	21.0	17.5	12.8	12.1
East South Central	3.4	4.2	1.4	2.3	2.0
West South Central	10.2	7.5	2.5	2.0	6.4
Mountain	1.9	2.1	0.8	1.8	4.3
Pacific	1.7	1.2	...	1.3	26.2
	100.0%	100.0%	100.0%	100.0%	100.0%

Source: Company records and casewriter's analysis.

wine segment. Management was highly enthusiastic about the new product and expected it to be quite successful.

George Lawrence explained some of the considerations that went into the choice of new products.

We can't compete in certain product segments, such as in the pop wines, due to the relatively high cost of our grapes. Where we do elect to compete— in the premium segment—we are constrained by our physical production capacity and the problems of maintaining adequate inventories for sales increases[8] and short crops; we also must plan for raw material needs five years or more in advance to insure sufficient supply for sales increases and new products.

Joe Swarthout, vice president and secretary of the corporation, continued Lawrence's theme.

At Taylor, given our volume, we do have standards for the amount of sales that would have to be expected from new products. While this depends on the complexity of the production process, I would say that 20,000 cases per year would be the minimum acceptable sales level. At Pleasant Valley, on the other hand, production is on a much smaller scale, so we can be more flexible in introducing new products.

There are still boundaries on the type of product I would want to handle. It would take an entirely different plant and group of people to compete with Gallo in the high-volume, cheaper wine segment. At the other extreme, I personally feel that there is no justification for a wine costing over $4 a bottle and would not expect to see Taylor move into such a product.

The Pleasant Valley product line

All of Pleasant Valley's wines were sold under the "Great Western" brand name. Product changes had been quite extensive in the period from 1962 to 1973; the major moves had been the switch to a Solera system[9] for dessert wines in 1966 and the gradual shift to varietal table wines beginning in 1964.

The first varietals—Vin Rouge, Vin Blanc Sec, Delaware, and Diamond—were packaged in full corked bottles and were intended to retail for $2.25 per fifth. A general consensus in the company was that this move had taken place too soon, since consumers were not willing to accept a New York State varietal wine at that time. Thus, several table wines were renamed with a varietal-generic combination, such as Delaware Moselle or Baco Noir Burgundy.

---

[8] As a rule of thumb, Taylor management tried to add two gallons of inventory for each gallon increase in sales volume.

[9] A Solera system is a unique, rather expensive method for the production of dessert wines.

By 1973 dinner wines had risen to 41.7% of case sales at Pleasant Valley, eroding somewhat the traditional dominance of Great Western champagnes (see Exhibit 6). Nevertheless, champagne and sparkling wines were still the largest selling product class, with 42.7% of case sales and over 60% of dollar sales. Fred Schroeder, managing director at Pleasant Valley, summarized the product philosophy that existed at Pleasant Valley in 1973:

> We are the specialty house of the company—the "Cadillac division"—and thus we need a broader and more unique product line. We are also not constrained by volume considerations as is Taylor and so can be more flexible in introducing low-volume new products. We now market a line of table wines with a unique combination of both a generic and varietal name. I eventually hope to be able to drop the generic name and have just the varietal designation together with a premium package. I just don't think now the consumer is completely ready.

In early 1973, Fred Schroeder, in light of the division's financial performance, was considering the elimination of some products and sizes from the Great Western line. The complexity of the line had resulted in an uneven flow of production, which in turn was thought to contribute to increased costs. Furthermore, some of the more exclusive varietal table wines such as Diamond Chablis and Delaware Moselle sold only about 2,000 cases per year, a level of production considered uneconomical for a large winery.

A more pressing product decision was the introduction of a new rose to be marketed under the proprietary name "Angel Rose." Schroeder was aware of the strong demand for premium roses. Production problems were minor, since adequate inventories existed for the blending of the wine, and the typical consumer was concerned mainly with a pinkish color and a pleasant, somewhat sweet taste. A few people in Pleasant Valley, however, felt that the proposed new rose was inconsistent with the division's existing product strategy. It could also have a negative effect on the other three roses in the product lines, two marketed by Pleasant Valley and one by Taylor. Nevertheless, all preliminary steps for national distribution of Angel Rose had been taken by the spring of 1973. An advertisement had been drawn up for the trade channels, and sales estimates of 8,000–10,000 cases a year had been planned.

Taylor organization

Management. Fred Taylor, the oldest son of the founder, had served as president and chairman of The Taylor Wine Company from its incorporation in 1955 until late 1964, when he relinquished his position as president to George Lawrence. Taylor stayed on as chairman of the board until his death in late 1968 at the age of 77. Joe Swarthout, assistant secretary in 1961, by 1973 had become a vice president, secretary and treasurer, as well as a director. Biographical information on Taylor management is presented in Exhibit 7.

Joe Swarthout summarized the general decision-making process that existed at Taylor:

How decisions are made is based on a tradition of tight Taylor control. Day-to-day operating decisions are left to the divisions, but all major capital expenditures are approved and overall policy is determined by Mr. Lawrence and myself.

George Lawrence expanded on this: "Joe acts as my alter-ego in almost everything. Outside of him most of my interactions and decisions are done on the phone. We have few meetings at Taylor."

Location. Taylor's production and corporate offices were situated in Hammondsport, New York, about 300 miles from New York City, and the village and the surrounding area had always been closely tied to the company. Estimates varied, but management felt that up to 80% of the people in Hammondsport were dependent on the wineries for their livelihood. At one time, the mayor of Hammondsport and most of the school board were Taylor employees. In the town of Urbana, of which Hammondsport was a part, Taylor and Pleasant Valley properties constituted 47% of the total assessed property valuation.

The influence of the local environment extended to all levels in the company. One top executive related it to management: "To have any understanding of this company it is necessary to realize the effects of the local culture on the values and perceptions of management. As I said before, most of our labor force comes from within a 10-mile radius of Hammondsport and the same applies to our management." In 1973 Lawrence, Swarthout, Fred Schroeder (managing director of Pleasant Valley), and Clarence Taylor (member of the board) all lived on Lake Street (Route 88), the road that extended the short distance from Hammondsport to the wineries.

The Taylor sales staff had always been housed in New York City in offices on the 29th floor of 425 Park Avenue. As Russell Douglas explained:

I was the first national sales manager that Taylor ever had and from the very beginning I have operated out of New York City. This is where the action is. New York is the headquarters for most everything that goes on in this industry. Being in New York gives us a chance to meet our distributors when they come to visit the big distillers; our salesmen can visit the national sales office easier in New York than if it was in Hammondsport; and most of the important advertising agencies are here. None of the New York wineries have

EXHIBIT 7
Biographical data on Taylor management

Name	Age	Years with company	Present position and date attained	Previous positions*
George A. Lawrence	58	34	President, 1964	Executive V.P., Secretary and Treasurer
Joseph L. Swarthout	53	26	Vice President, 1971; Secretary and Treasurer, 1965	Production Supervisor, Assistant Secretary
Russell B. Douglas, Sr.	71	24	Senior V.P.—Marketing, 1965	V.P.—Sales, National Sales Mgr.
Seaton C. Mendall	55	29	Vineyard Consultant, 1953	Vineyard Manager
Michael D. Linehan	38	12	Assistant Secretary, 1972	Personnel Manager
Edwin W. Manktelow	50	17	Comptroller, 1964	Accountant
Harland W. Tyler	51	26	Vineyard Manager, 1952	None
James W. Ferguson	57	24	Winemaker, 1950	None
Dr. Andrew C. Rice	48	10	Director of Research, 1962	Assoc. Prof., Univ. of Wisconsin; Director of Research, Seneca Foods
Lloyd Magee	55	19	Vice President—Sales, 1973	Assistant National Sales Manager, National Sales Manager
James J. Duggan	35	9 mo.	Personnel Manager, 1972	Employee Relations Manager, ITT subsidiary

* With Taylor unless otherwise indicated.
Source: Company records.

been as successful as Taylor and for years we were the only one with a New York City office.

The pressure for change comes from this office. For years we have continually bugged the people in Hammondsport for new products and new sizes. Their feeling at that time was, since we were selling all that could be made in the existing products and sizes, why create more production problems. Under present management we are now making much faster progress in this area than in the past, which augurs well for the future of our company. However, probably more from force of habit we are still inclined to keep the pressure on, and the standard reaction when I go to Hammondsport for a board meeting is, "Douglas, it's nice to see you; when did you say you were leaving?"

Douglas went to Hammondsport four times a year for board meetings. Other than that, there was little official travel between New York City and the winery by members of management.

Harland Tyler, Taylor's vineyard manager, commented on the Taylor organization:

I don't make it down to the winery too much. Each year I spend about an hour with George Lawrence and review my plans for capital expenditures and vineyard policies. I have always tried to be as conservative as they are, and I have always gotten what I needed.

Fred Taylor, George Lawrence, and Russell Douglas have always been the ones who made this thing go. The Taylors could make the wine and Douglas could sell it. They always seemed to have the right product at the right time and everything has turned out well. Now there is developing a real problem of depth of administration in the company. Joe Swarthout and George Lawrence are the whole management team up here, and if something happened to them, I'm not sure what we would do.

Pleasant Valley organization

From 1962 to 1971 Greyton Taylor had served as managing director of Pleasant Valley and his son Walter as assistant managing director. Walter left Pleasant Valley in early 1971 to start his own winery,[10] and Greyton died in July 1971 at the age of 68. Under Greyton Taylor the physical plant at Pleasant Valley was upgraded significantly[11], and considerable spirit had developed among the company's employees. This organizational climate, praised by many of the division, was described by one of the younger employees:

[10] In 1970 Walter Taylor purchased Bully Hill, the original Taylor Wine Company property. In 1973 Walter was president of the New York State Wine Association, an organization to which neither Taylor nor Pleasant Valley belonged.

[11] Almost $7 million was invested in plant and equipment from 1962 to 1971. One manager commented: "Greyton had a definite idea of what kind of a winery he wanted—a premium winery—and everything was done first class. He created a magnificent place; that was only appropriate since he spent all of his time working here."

There is a spirit in Pleasant Valley that is difficult to verbalize. People who work here mix socially with those that they work with and for. They really care about their jobs. Many of them come back on their vacations just to see how things are going.

This spirit reached its peak when Greyton was still alive. It seemed like there was a party down in the hospitality room every night. Even now with new management the spirit has been pretty much continued. I've never seen the same atmosphere over at Taylor where things are more conservative and formal.

Soon after Greyton's death, Fred Schroeder, 53, who had served as national sales manager for Pleasant Valley since 1963, was appointed managing director, a position that several Taylor managers felt should not even exist. One of them commented:

As far back as 1962 I proposed that a vice president for both the Taylor and Pleasant Valley divisions be established. But Fred Taylor was involved in the most minute details of the Taylor operation and did not want to give up anything. When Greyton Taylor died, several of us were in favor of doing away with the position of managing director of Pleasant Valley. I always felt that it had been created for Greyton and that closer cooperation between the two wineries would only be possible with single marketing and production heads for both Taylor and Pleasant Valley.

Other Taylor managers in 1973 had strong opinions on the almost total separation between Taylor and Pleasant Valley. Russell Douglas gave his viewpoint of this situation:

Fred Taylor asked me to take over Pleasant Valley's marketing in 1962. I knew that the two wineries had always been highly competitive but that Great Western could not compete directly with Taylor. Fred thought that a combination of marketing at the management level would result in considerable savings, but once Greyton was chosen as managing director I realized that this would not be possible and therefore resigned from that additional responsibility.

I now have nothing to do with Pleasant Valley marketing and Magee [vice president of sales] has nothing to do with the sales of Great Western products. We have completely separate marketing organizations at all levels and I think this is best.

Joe Swarthout, in contrast, felt that managerial relations between the two wineries were sound:

By talking to some people you can easily get the impression that there are insurmountable barriers between the two divisions and that there is no cooperation or interaction. Even though these two companies were the strongest of competitors for years, now we have the best of relations at the top levels and I expect that over time the bad feelings will disappear at the lower levels.

Note on the international bulk-shipping industry

In 1968 the international bulk-shipping business represented one of the world's few remaining examples of near perfect or classical competition. The size of the industry in dollar terms is not easily gauged, owing to the elusive and dispersed nature of the statistics and the absence of any effective central pool of intelligence, such as might have been offered by a truly industrywide trade association. A rough measure for 1968 would be about 150 million deadweight tons, tankers and bulk carriers included, valued at an average cost of $140 per DWT, or a gross asset value of $21 billion. Upon this the industry, during the boom of 1968, might be expected to generate $.35 to $.40 in revenues per dollar of assets at cost, for total revenues of some $7.4 to $8.4 billion. Of this sum, independents could be expected to earn about two thirds (about $5 billion), with the remainder going to captive fleets.

The term "international" is intended to differentiate this segment of the shipping industry from the American shipping business, and the term "bulk" is used to contrast it with the general-cargo or liner business. Somewhat simplified, a bulk ship transports a full cargo of a single commodity, such as oil, coal, or grain, and is specifically designed for that purpose. A typical bulk ship would be an oil tanker or an ore carrier; as such, it would generally be of larger size, would require fewer crew members, and could be turned around in less time than a typical general-cargo vessel, which might be required to carry anything from cases of whiskey to umbrellas. Moreover, bulk vessels are usually operated in "tramp" trades as opposed to liners, which maintain regu-

527

lar routes. In other words, bulk cargoes determine the ports of call rather than the converse.

BULK MARKETS

Shipping space was traded daily via brokers in three principal markets: New York, London, and Tokyo. The demand side was represented by anyone having a shipment to move—an oil company, a coal importer or exporter, or a shipowner having a short position. Similarly, the supply side consisted of independent shipowners or user companies with captive tonnage in excess of their requirements.

In general the U.S. bulk-shipping industry did not participate in the international market, since U.S. construction and operating costs excluded American ships from competition. In recognition of this disadvantage, U.S. law[1] excluded foreign-flag ships from American trades, that is, from any trade in which cargoes were both loaded and discharged at U.S. ports.

The market could be further broken down in terms of demand for two basic types of vessels: tankers and bulk carriers. Traditionally, a tanker could handle only petroleum products (usually crude oil) and, in some cases, a few other specialized liquid cargoes. Bulk carriers, on the other hand, could handle only dry-bulk commodities. Historically, the markets for these two basic types of bulk vessels had been isolated from each other. More recently, however, the two markets had developed strong cross-elasticities owing primarily to (1) the increasing use, through a specialized technique, of tankers in the grain trades; and (2) the emergence in 1965 of a new design of vessel known as the "OBO" (oil-bulk-ore), which was equipped to handle a full load of either liquid or dry cargoes, although only one at a time.

The tanker market

As of 1968 the tanker business had been a well-organized commodity-type market for a long time. For ease in trading, the industry employed an index of basic flat rates per ton of oil, specified for any pair of load/discharge ports desired, and variable mainly as a function of the distance between them. With the use of this rate index (called "Intascale") as a common denominator, the market price for tanker space could be determined for any pair of ports in the world, in terms of the going percentage discount from, or premium over, the flat rate. Historically, the market low had been established for one unfortunate vessel, for one voyage, during the summer of 1965 at Intascale minus 80%, at which rate even the largest, most efficient ship of the time could

---

[1] The Jones Act.

hardly be expected to cover its direct variable costs. Correspondingly, the recent historical highs had occurred at two points in time: first, during the 1956–57 Suez Canal closure when rates exceeded Intascale plus 100%, and then subsequent to the 1967 June war when rates again approached the plus 100% mark. As of February 1968 they had fallen to about Intascale flat, which was still substantially higher than the 1965–66 annual average of about Intascale minus 40%–50%.

The bulk-carrier market

For a variety of reasons, rate levels in the bulk-carrier market were not as easily ascertainable as in the tanker market. First, there was no basic index of rates to which percentages could simply be applied. Second, economies of bulk shipment had only recently been realized in a number of commodities, such as potash, phosphate rock, coal, and salt; thus, there were a number of relative newcomers (i.e., potential cargoes) to the trade. Third, owing to the increasing number of different commodities in the market, all moving to and from different ports, the market was much more heterogeneous than the tanker market. As a result, it seemed doubtful that a basic index of rates *could* be established, even if someone were to attempt it. Further, turnaround times varied with the loading and discharge capacities of the port involved, whereas in oil these were fairly standard worldwide. Finally, there was more product differentiation among the ships themselves (size, cubic capacity, draft, cargo-handling gear on board, etc.) than with tankers which, apart from size, were relatively homogeneous. Nevertheless, certain staple trades existed (such as coal from Norfolk to Japan or iron ore from Seven Islands to Baltimore) where market rates per ton were established, and these in large measure provided a base to which all other trades could be adjusted.

In both markets—tankers and bulk carriers—the key rates were "spot" rates, that is, rates for a single voyage to commence at some time in the near future (for example, anywhere from two weeks to two months from "fixing" date). Occasionally, lead times were shaved even closer, as in the case of a "spot prompt" tanker lying at anchor in the Persian Gulf awaiting cargo. Such ships were virtually at the mercy of the demand side of the market and acted in most cases as depressants upon market rates.

Long-term business

Strongly dependent on the spot-rate structure and market expectations about the future were the rates obtainable in the various types of long-term business. Term business in bulk shipping could be roughly compared to the operation of the futures market in commodities, with all the refinements such as hedging, shorts, etc. Lead times varied widely, and contracts might run for many years. (For example, a time charterer might agree today to a 10-year charter to commence one year hence.) If the spot voyage rates were high today, the period time-charter rate, translated into a single voyage equivalent, could be expected to be lower, *if* it was the general belief of the market that a decline was forthcoming.

Types of term business generally conformed to one of the following categories:

1. *Time charter:* The charterer leased the cargo-carrying capacity of the ship at a fixed dollar rate per deadweight[2] ton per month for a fixed period of time (e.g., 3 to 15 years).

2. *Bare-boat charter:* Like a time charter, except that the charterer undertook to operate the ship at his own expense (crew, maintenance, repairs, etc.), whereas under a time charter the owner absorbed these expenses, leaving the charterer only those expenses associated with the voyage itself (fuel, port charges, canal charges, etc.).

3. *Contract of affreightment:* Here the owner undertook to transport, using any ship he desired within given size limits, a certain quantity of a given commodity per annum between two or more specific points. Remuneration was set at a fixed dollar amount per ton transported. Contracts might vary in duration from 1 year to 10.

4. *Consecutive voyages:* The owner undertook to provide a specific ship (sometimes with substitution options) for consecutive voyages at a given rate per ton of cargo transported. In tankers, the rate was usually stated in terms of Intascale plus or minus a percentage. Duration of the contract might be stated in terms of a number of voyages or years, with the owner undertaking to maintain a certain average speed in transit.

SHIPYARDS, CHARTERERS, AND BROKERS

Besides the independent owners, other important factors in the bulk-shipping industry were (1) the shipyards, (2) the charterers, and (3) the brokers, whose services might be needed to bring the other principals together.

1. *Shipyards* constructed ships to owners' specifications, based on a prior order. In general, lead time between the signing of a construction contract and delivery of a vessel was two or three years. During periods of peak demand, however, such as 1957 or 1967, lead times could reach five years. Shipyards competed on the basis of price, delivery, maximum size of ship which they could physically handle, quality of workmanship,

---

[2] The "deadweight" of a ship is defined as the full cargo capacity, including water, fuel, and stores—in short, all but the hull, machinery, and fixtures.

and credit terms. One of the Japanese yards' most significant competitive advantages over European builders, aside from price, was their ability to offer the owners (through government assistance) favorable financing terms—specifically, 80% of the cost of the vessel over eight years at 5½% interest, secured by a first mortgage on the ship. These terms had been maintained without interruption for 10 years or more, despite varying credit availability elsewhere and generally rising interest rates.

2. *Charterers,* as implied earlier, were the users of bulk transportation services. They consisted mainly of the oil companies in the tanker business and the steel companies, coal exporters, and grain houses in the bulk-carrier business. Particularly in tankers, the charterers were also owners, maintaining as a rule of thumb an owned fleet equal to 35% to 40% of their requirements. Often the independent owners also acted as charterers when, for example, they found themselves short of tonnage under a contract of affreightment.

3. *Brokers* were intermediaries; as such, they performed a variety of services. Many large brokers dealt in both tanker and bulk-carrier markets, as well as in the new-building market (bringing owner and yard together) and in the secondhand tonnage markets where ships were bought and sold. The brokers' major function was to disseminate information on transactions concluded, spot or term, and on requirements overhanging the market. The majority of brokers were found in the major markets—New York, London, and Tokyo—and in other locations where a number of owners resided, such as Greece or Scandinavia. Generally, communications with owners, charterers, and other brokers proceeded via telephone, telex, or written circulars.

OWNERS

A typical owner pursued his business in the following manner: he assessed the future market and decided on the size and type of ship likely to be in demand. If lucky, he might be able to reach agreement with a charterer before committing himself to a shipyard. More often than not, however, he first contracted for the ship with the yard and then attempted, before the first significant payment on the ship was due, to obtain a long-term charter or contract with a reputable user. Then, on the strength of that charter (which was really on the strength of the charterer's credit) he obtained long-term financing, if not from the yard (which in turn was financed by someone else—for example, in Japan's case, by the Export-Import Bank), then typically from a commercial bank, life insurance company, or pension fund. With a long-term takeout in hand, he could then obtain the necessary interim, or construction financing, which might amount to 15%–25% of the total delivered cost of the ship (or approximately the usual equity left over after term financing).

Once he had obtained a vessel, the independent owner marketed its space in one or more of the ways previously described, in most cases with one or two brokers acting as intermediaries. A large majority of owners maintained their own operating staffs and had fully owned management companies. In some cases operation of a ship was subcontracted to a management specialist.

In 1968 shipowners were spread throughout the world. Leading groups, however, were centered in Scandinavia, Greece, Hong Kong, and Great Britain. Their ships generally flew the flags of the countries

EXHIBIT 1
Relative sizes of tankers presently in use

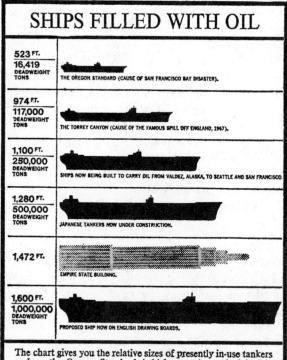

SHIPS FILLED WITH OIL

523 FT.
16,419
DEADWEIGHT
TONS
THE OREGON STANDARD (CAUSE OF SAN FRANCISCO BAY DISASTER).

974 FT.
117,000
DEADWEIGHT
TONS
THE TORREY CANYON (CAUSE OF THE FAMOUS SPILL OFF ENGLAND, 1967).

1,100 FT.
250,000
DEADWEIGHT
TONS
SHIPS NOW BEING BUILT TO CARRY OIL FROM VALDEZ, ALASKA, TO SEATTLE AND SAN FRANCISCO.

1,280 FT.
500,000
DEADWEIGHT
TONS
JAPANESE TANKERS NOW UNDER CONSTRUCTION.

1,472 FT.
EMPIRE STATE BUILDING.

1,600 FT.
1,000,000
DEADWEIGHT
TONS
PROPOSED SHIP NOW ON ENGLISH DRAWING BOARDS.

The chart gives you the relative sizes of presently in-use tankers such as the Oregon Standard (which recently crashed in San Francisco Bay) and the Torrey Canyon which crashed off England in 1967. Please note that the Oregon Standard is only one-fifteenth the size (in carrying capacity) of the ships which would bring oil down the coast from Valdez, Alaska, to San Francisco, and a sixtieth the size of a ship being proposed by the English. Most of the ships will carry oil cargoes that would nearly fill the Empire State building to overflowing. And in case you think something about their being *bigger* makes them *safer*, consider this: If the captain of one of those 250,000 tonners from Alaska sees trouble ahead while going full speed, it will take him a *half hour* to stop the thing!

Source: Friends of the Earth advertisement, *New York Times*, February 17, 1971.

mentioned, or alternatively the very popular "flags of convenience"—Panama, Liberia, or Honduras—which involved no taxation.

RECENT DEVELOPMENTS

During the decade preceding 1968, two major developments in the industry were noteworthy: a dramatic increase in the size of ships and rationalization of shipyard production methods.

The size revolution

The increase in the size of bulk ships, as best exemplified in tankers, can be demonstrated by changes over time in the average deadweight tonnage of ships under construction: whereas in 1956 projected new additions to the free-world tanker fleet (excluding that of the United States) averaged 29,000 deadweight tons, by 1966 this average had risen to 62,100 DWT and by 1967 had reached 135,000 DWT. The quantum jump in 1967 could be attributed to the second Suez closing in 10 years and to the determination of oil companies *not* to be burned a third time. They thus leaped to sizes which could economically avoid the canal, compensating by economies of scale for the extra cost of circumnavigating the cape. By 1968 the decision was even more clear. Of 52.6 million tons on order for delivery between 1969 and 1973, no less than 84% were ships of 150,000 tons or more. A graphic illustration of this trend is provided in Exhibit 1.

The average size of tankers in use remained, of course, considerably

EXHIBIT 2
Changes in total and per-tanker tonnage for the free-world tanker fleet (excluding the United States)

	1956	1959	1961	1964	1967
Fleet total (in millions of DWT)	33.7	49.2	60.0	72.5	107.0
Average size of tankers in operation (in thousands of DWT)	16.2	n.a.	21.2	25.3	35.0
Percent of fleet by size class (in thousands of DWT)					
10 to 25	75.4	59.9	48.6	34.8	21.9
25 to 35	14.5	31.6	34.0	29.4	15.0
35 to 45	10.1	5.5	9.4	11.7	11.9
45 to 75	. . .	3.0	8.0	19.7	35.8
75 and over	. . .	. . .	. . .	4.4	15.4
	100.0	100.0	100.0	100.0	100.0
Average size of tankers under construction (in thousands of DWT).	29.0	n.a.	44.7	53.3	135.0

n.a. = not available.
Source: Anglo Norness Shipping Company, Ltd., records.

lower than the average size of tankers on order (see Exhibit 2). And within the international fleet as a whole, almost 50% of the tankers in use remained below the 35,000-ton figure which was the average for 1967.

The general trend toward larger sizes was the result of economies of both *construction* and *operation*. In 1968 the shipyard price for a 25,000-ton tanker was about $150–$200 per DWT, whereas for a tanker in excess of 150,000 tons the price was $70–$80 per DWT. In addition, the variable costs of operating a tanker—exclusive of depreciation, administration, or financing charges—showed substantial economies of scale. A typical Liberian-flag 32,000-ton tanker in 1968 might be operated for about $40,000 per month, not including voyage costs such as fuel, port charges, and canal dues. By comparison, a vessel of 150,000 tons, with five times the former's capacity, might operate for $55,000–$60,000 per month, with a crew of approximately the same size. (For a sample calculation of tanker profitability on a 95,000-ton ship, see Exhibit 3.)

EXHIBIT 3
Sample calculation of tanker profitability

Vessel:	Tanker 95,000 deadweight tons
Built:	1961, Japan
Cost:	$12.4 million ($130 per DWT)
Financed:	80% over 8 years @ 5½% interest reducing
Use (1968):	15-year time charter @ $2 per DWT per month

	Thousands of dollars	*Percent*
Net revenues (95,000 × $2.00 × 11.5*)	2,200	100.0
Operating costs† (maintenance and repairs, insurance, personnel, administration)	(500)	(22.6)
Gross operating income	1,700	77.4
Fixed costs		
Depreciation (20 years straight line to 5% residual)	(590)	(26.8)
Interest (on 7th-year loan balance in 1968)	(140)	(6.4)
Net income	970	44.2
Add back: Depreciation	590	26.8
Less: Loan amortization	(1,250)	(57.0)
Net cash flow	310	14.0

* Typically, downtime for repairs, etc.. ran about two weeks a year.
† Voyage costs (fuel, port charges, etc.) excluded, since under time charter these are for charterer's account.
Source: Anglo Norness Shipping Company, Ltd., records.

Exhibit 4 reveals one oil company's estimate of the behavior of these economies of scale, including all costs, on its own fleet. The shape of the curve clearly demonstrates diminishing returns to scale, but even at 500,000 tons, which was about the limit of anyone's thinking in 1968, the curve does not appear to have flattened completely. By far the greatest cost uncertainty built into these calculations was insurance. Most

EXHIBIT 4
Economies of scale in tanker transportation

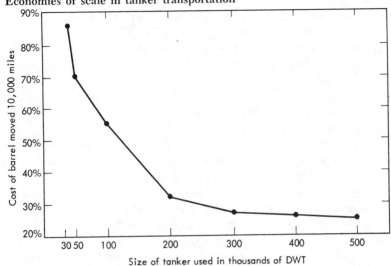

Source: Major oil company (name withheld by request).

estimates merely extrapolated past insurance-cost experience with smaller vessels. Yet a disaster like that of the Torrey Canyon, which in 1967 fouled beaches in both England and France, suggested that concentration of the world's tanker fleet into fewer and larger units would seem to increase the risk of high dollar amounts in losses. By 1968, however, the effect of this episode seemed to have dissipated. Nevertheless, repetition of a similar disaster was a possibility that the industry showed no signs of having fully appreciated.

Like tankers, bulk carriers had also undergone a size revolution, although to a lesser degree. Owing to the heterogeneous nature of the commodities moved in this market, no traffic existed in the volume necessary to justify units greater than 150,000 tons. In addition, port development, cargo handling, and storage were much greater problems with dry-bulk commodities than with liquid ones, which can be pumped through pipelines extending many miles out to offshore installations. However, as of 1968, coal and iron ore particularly were being transported in lots of 70,000 to 85,000 tons, and one example existed of salt moving in ships of 150,000 tons. By contrast, as late as 1961 bulk carriers of greater than 20,000 tons were very rare.

Rationalization of the shipyards

The second major development during the decade was the success of the world's leading shipyards in reducing production costs and increasing capacity through improved techniques in fabrication. By constructing ships in large sections and utilizing the building berths (the former bottleneck) merely for welding the completed sections together, berth time for a typical large ship was reduced from a year to about two months. The effect was a dramatic decrease in unit construction costs, over and above the effects of building larger ships, as well as a greatly increased capacity at nominal incremental investment. It was difficult to separate the effects of these two developments; suffice it to say that the combined effect was dramatic, particularly on the obsolescence of existing fleets.

In general, market rates were determined by the lowest cost unit, that is, the largest and newest tanker. Users were flexible to some extent in their size requirements and might place a bid in the spot market for a ship of anywhere from 35,000 to 60,000 tons, thus putting the two sizes in competition with each other and forcing the smaller ship to live with a rate established by the larger, probably newer, and lower cost ship. Finally, as replacement costs decreased and as market rates adjusted to the newer, larger vessels, the secondhand market followed suit, greatly depressing secondhand tonnage resale values during the decade between the Suez Canal closures.

SUPPLY AND DEMAND RELATIONSHIPS

Demand for shipping space is a function of demand for the commodity shipped or of its production, whichever is lower, adjusted for the duration of the voyage. *Supply* at any given time is a function of the size of the existing fleet plus additions through new construction and minus both vessels scrapped or lost and net layups for any purpose.

In theory, supply should adjust to demand, or at least to some expectation of demand, and rates should be a function of the balance between them. In shipping, the evidence would indicate a particularly erratic market behavior. One of the principal sources of disequilibrium lies in the tax structure of certain leading shipping nations, particularly in Scandinavia. Here, liberal accelerated depreciation allowances, coupled with high marginal tax brackets, both personal and corporate (up to 60%), are designed to encourage constant expansion of the national shipping fleets—an important source of foreign exchange. Norwegian owners, for example, are permitted to charge against current income an amount up to 25% of the cost of a new vessel during the tax year in which a new-building contract is signed. This would probably be two to four years before delivery, at which time the owner would have paid in equity only the initial installment of 5% of the contract cost.

In 1957 and again in 1968, shipyard backlogs worldwide were approaching five years under the impetus of Suez-inflated rates. Such a situation might be interpreted as indicating shortsightedness on the part of shipowners, rushing to secure new tonnage many years ahead on the assumption that current high rates would continue. In some cases, this interpretation might be valid. The main reason, however, was that in years of high profits from existing ships, taxable owners had to generate tax shields by ordering new ones. The fact that overbuilding might result in future net losses did not deter the owners, given the time value of money and their intuitive understanding of present-value theory.

Another distortion stemmed from the lack among shipowners of accurate, comprehensive statistics on developments on both sides of the marketplace. A few brokers assembled annual figures on the supply side, but little attempt was made to project demand in a rigorous fashion. Most shipowners maintained minimal staffs comprised of shipping specialists who were fully occupied with daily operations. Hence it was up to the boss himself to do the long-range strategic planning, and this he generally did by intuition. Although comprehensive statistics were very much in existence, they were all in the hands of the *users* of tonnage, who kept them to themselves.

This situation was symptomatic of a third major source of distortion—namely, the marked difference in industry structure between the supply and the demand sides of the market. On the supply side, ownership was highly fragmented and dispersed worldwide. The 10 largest independent tanker owners in 1968, for example, accounted for perhaps 15 million tons, or an estimated 15% of the world tanker fleet. The supply side was, by contrast, concentrated—dominated by a few large users. In the tanker business, demand meant the major international oil companies, of which there were nine, plus a few others—the Japanese, French, Germans, Italians, and, very recently, the Russians. Except for unusual periods such as the two Suez closings, the majors were in an ideal position to control their markets. Large operations-research staffs, using computer-aided analysis, generated and evaluated the data. As large shipowners themselves, directly owning about one third of the world's tonnage, the oil companies were intimately familiar with the independents' costs and therefore with their rates of return at any given level of freights. Through swapping tonnage among themselves across the market, they could set rates directly. Finally, there was some evidence that at least during the depressed winter of 1966–67, the oil companies were sequentially coordinating their respective entries into the spot market and thus avoiding the appearance of a marked increase in demand.

As a result of these peculiarities, plus the two major technological developments described above, the decade between the Suez crises showed a general trend toward declining rates and narrowing profit margins for shipowners. Exhibit 5 plots the bellwether indicator in the

EXHIBIT 5
Spot tanker rate composite (Intascale)

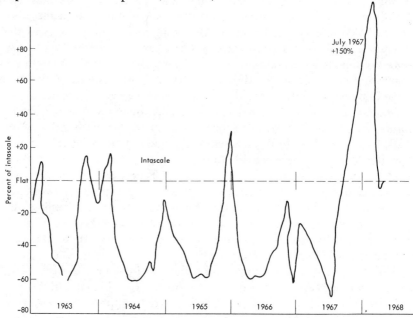

Source: Anglo Norness Shipping Company, Ltd., records.

tanker business—the spot-rate market—for the latter half of the decade. It can be noted that besides being cyclical the business is highly seasonal, with the magnitude of its swings unlikely to be matched by any other industry. Reasons for this seasonality are essentially twofold: (1) in the winter consumption of oil is higher (heating needs, etc.); and (2) winter weather slows down ships, producing in effect a curtailed supply. In an industry characterized by high fixed costs and substantial debt leverage, a year-to-year variation in the strength of the winter market could produce a much more than proportionate swing in industry profits.

A curve of the annual average rates, if superimposed on the seasonal fluctuations, would show a negative slope, bottoming in early 1967, when virtually no appreciable winter market materialized. During that period, most tankers of average size and age operating in the spot market would have shown losses, since their annual average income could well have slipped below Intascale minus 40%–50%, which might be taken as their break-even point. Without Suez, and with a continuing down trend, average rates for 1967 and 1968 would probably have reached levels where a number of owners, unable to cover the variable costs of operations, would have laid up their ships, as they did during the summer of 1963.

ENVIRONMENT SUMMARIZED

Summarizing the industry environment in which his company operated, one shipping company executive expressed himself as follows:

The bulk-shipping industry can be characterized as a Monte Carlo "crapshoot," highly volatile, where customers are highly rational and well-informed, but where suppliers are tax-motivated, unanalytic, and given to impulse—all in a world of rapid obsolescence. Most shipowners readily recognize the inequities existing in their marketplace, but when anyone refers to the bargaining advantage of the users a typical reaction is, "Don't worry—something will happen; it always has!"

Anglo Norness Shipping Company, Limited (A)

IN 1968, after a stormy five years, the Anglo Norness Shipping Company was enjoying the most dramatic bonanza in its 22-year history mainly as a result of the Arab-Israeli June war of 1967 and the increased requirements for transport which followed the closing of the Suez Canal. Profits for the year to end on June 30 were projected to exceed $15 million, or $1.58 per share, up from only $400,000, or $.05 per share for the previous year. The company's stock price had risen on the London Exchange to a recent high of about $3.15, up from its historical low of less than $1 the previous year. Even so, its market value represented a very reasonable multiple of current earnings and was well below book value, which was projected to reach about $5.50 per share by year end, including about $2.25 in cash.

As a result of this much improved position, Mr. Erling Naess and his elder son, Michael, as the controlling stockholders of Anglo Norness, were facing a critical strategic decision. Should they use their greatly increased resources to expand in any phase of the bulk-shipping business to which the company was presently committed? Should they diversify? Should they seek—or sell out to—a merger partner, inasmuch as suitors seemed bound to be attracted by the company's strong cash position and its relatively low price/earnings ratio? If so, by what criteria should possible merger offers be judged?

At the time when these choices had to be considered (February 1968), Mr. Naess, aged 65, was chairman of the company. Michael, aged 28, was vice president of one of the principal operating subsidiaries but was on leave of absence to attend the Harvard Business School, where he was halfway through his first year.

THE FLEET

In the banner year of 1968 (see Exhibit 1 for selected historical financial statistics), Anglo Norness was one of the 10 largest independent bulk shipping carriers in the world. Its fleet of 40 vessels accounted for almost 1.8 million DWT. Of this tonnage, just over half was in tankers, while the rest was divided among bulk carriers, OBOs,[1] and specialized chemical sulphur vessels (see Exhibit 2). This fleet profile represented a continuing trend toward increased diversification, for as recently as 1961 some 90% of the company's tonnage had been allocated to tankers.

As suggested by comparative figures on the average size of tankers in operation (54,000 DWT for Anglo Norness versus 35,000 worldwide), the company had been a leader in the trend toward larger and larger ships. Both the trend toward increased diversification and the trend toward larger sizes had been accelerated in 1967–68 as the company took advantage of good times to sell off some of its smaller, older tankers and to arrange for the conversion of two others to more highly specialized uses.

Of the total Anglo Norness tonnage, some 27% was not company-owned but rather leased or chartered. Leasing, like debt, was widely used as a way to finance operations in so capital-intensive an industry as shipping.

ORGANIZATIONAL STRUCTURE

A number of changes had occurred over the years in the Anglo Norness organization, but as of 1968 the company consisted of three main functional groups, each in a different location: finance and accounting and the company's official domicile were in Bermuda, chartering (sales) had its principal offices in New York, and operations were spread throughout the world depending on the nationality of the vessels and crews.

Direction of the company was in the hands of two principal individuals: Mr. Erling Naess acted as chairman; another individual, who had joined the company in 1966, was chairman of the recently created executive committee, of which the other members were Mr. Naess and two outside directors. Mr. Naess, a Norwegian citizen resident in Bermuda, maintained his principal base in New York. The chairman of the executive committee maintained a separate office in New York, one

---

[1] Oil-bulk-ore carriers.

EXHIBIT 1

ANGLO NORNESS SHIPPING COMPANY LIMITED (A)

Selected Financial Data

(dollars in millions except per-share figures)

Year to June 30	1958	1959	1960	1961	1962	1963	1964	1965	1966	1967	1968*
Total assets	$61.3	$78.7	$117.6	$156.2	$168.0	$185.1	$193.2	$172.5	$136.6	$124.2	$125.2
Vessels in operation											
—at cost	43.3	43.7	73.1	136.6	151.2	184.0	192.4	173.1	169.9	174.9	168.9
—after depreciation	41.2	40.0	66.6	124.3	131.3	152.9	151.8	130.3	102.4†	96.2†	83.6†
Investments	10.1	16.2	17.1	15.1	18.8	17.9	19.0	20.2	13.8†	12.7†	11.8†
Net fixed assets	59.1	74.2	112.3	147.6	159.9	173.6	173.9	156.5	120.3	108.9	95.6
Long-term loans	43.4	55.4	88.2	114.2	116.8	115.4	116.5	99.9	93.5	81.6	60.7
Equity	14.0	18.8	24.6	33.9	43.1	54.9	61.9	57.9	35.2†	35.2†	52.8†
Equivalent number of shares in issue	5,969,600	6,174,600	7,183,577	7,844,310	8,800,419	9,300,419‡	9,512,346	9,513,097	9,513,097	9,513,097	9,513,097
Equity value per share	$2.32	$3.04	$3.45	$4.20	$4.92	$5.94	$6.50	$6.08	$3.69	$3.70	$5.55
Gross freights	n.a.	6.4	17.6	26.3	36.4	41.4	51.5	56.3	58.1	57.2	74.1
Operating profit	6.2	2.2	9.2	15.7	18.2	21.0	23.2	18.5	20.2	16.1	33.5
Depreciation	1.4	2.2	3.1	5.9	7.6	8.4	9.5	9.5	10.7	11.7	11.1
Net interest payable	1.1	1.4	2.2	4.5	5.6	5.9	5.8	5.0	4.4	4.1	2.8
Group profit, after minority interests	3.6	3.4	4.2	5.3	4.8	6.7§	8.1	2.8	3.8	.4	16.4
Earnings per share	$.62	$.52	$.60	$.66	$.56	$.78§	$.85	$.29	$.40	$.05	$1.72
Gross freight/gross vessels	...	...	24%	19%	24%	22%	27%	33%	34%	33%	44%
Operating profit/gross freight	...	...	52%	60%	51%	51%	45%	33%	35%	28%	45%
Percent return on net fixed assets	...	4.6%	3.7%	3.6%	3.0%	3.9%	4.7%	1.8%	3.2%	0.4%	16.4%
Long-term debt/book equity	...	3.0%	3.6%	3.3%	2.7%	2.1%	1.9%	1.7%	2.6%	2.3%	1.2%
Percent return on average book equity	21.0%	21.0%	20.0%	18.2%	12.5%	14.0%	13.8%	4.7%	8.2%	1.1%	37.3%

* Estimate for the full fiscal year.
† After revaluation of assets.
‡ Including 500,000 shares issued for the acquisition of British Oil Shipping (now in voluntary liquidation).
§ Excluding the profits earned by British Oil Shipping and the shares issued for that company's acquisition.
n.a. = not available
Source: Company records.

EXHIBIT 2

ANGLO NORNESS SHIPPING COMPANY, LIMITED (A)

Composition of the Company Fleet and Relative Size of Its Tankers

(tonnage in thousands of DWT)

Year	Anglo Norness number of ships			Anglo Norness total deadweight tonnage			Anglo Norness		Average tonnage of tankers in worldwide operation†
	Tanker	Other*	Total	Tanker	Other	Total	Tanker tonnage/ total tonnage	Average tanker tonnage	
1960	15	3	18	448.5	56.6	505.1	90%	30	20.3
1961	22	4	26	820.5	84.3	904.8	91	37.4	21.2
1962	22	11	33	820.5	318.4	1,138.9	79	37.4	22.1
1963	22	16	38	909.0	786.4	1,695.4	54	41.5	23.2
1964	27	19	46	1,125.9	900.2	2,026.1	56	41.7	25.3
1965} 1966}	30	19	49	1,315.5	900.2	2,215.7	59	43.8	27.1 29.2
1967} 1968}	17	23	40	917.3	871.5	1,788.8‡	51	54.0	35.0

* As of February 1968 the nontanker components of the fleet were divided as follows:

	Bulk-carrier	Oil-bulk-ore	Chemical-sulphur	Total
Number of ships..............	17	2	4	23
Tonnage Thousands of DWT..........	655.5	113.1	102.9	871.5
Percentage of fleet total...........	37%	6%	6%	49%

† Excluding the United States.
‡ Including 27% leased tonnage, made up of 32% leased tanker tonnage and 29% leased bulk carrier tonnage.
Source: Exhibit 2 of the "Note on the International Bulk-Shipping Industry" and company annual reports.

floor above Mr. Naess, where he was assisted by a staff of three persons. In total the organization consisted of 31 different ship-owning companies and another 7 management or operating companies. Two major consulting reports submitted to the company within the previous five years had strongly recommended simplification of this structure and centralization of control in New York, Bermuda, or London. Two main factors made this difficult, however. First, the multiplicity of owning companies had originally been created to accommodate different minority interests in individual ships or groups of ships, some of which were still outstanding in 1968. Second, the company's tax-free status might be threatened if operations and management were centralized in either the United States or the United Kingdom. As it was, the subsidiaries located in those countries were officially merely "agency" companies. Centralization in Bermuda raised the question of communications and the availability of sufficient qualified staff.

COMPANY HISTORY

A Norwegian by birth and an economist by training, Mr. Erling Naess had had a brief career in British banking before turning to whaling and then permanently to shipping. In the years before World War II, he had built up a seven-vessel fleet of different types, and during the war he had emigrated to the United States to become deputy director of the agency established to manage the Norwegian fleet during the German occupation. After the war, with most of his own fleet sunk, Mr. Naess founded the Norness Shipping Company of Nassau (predecessor of Anglo Norness), in partnership with friends representing two leading Wall Street investment banking organizations.

The Norness fleet developed steadily, primarily in tankers, until 1956–57, when Norness, like most of its competitors, was inspired by the first Suez closing to embark on an unprecedented expansion. In 1958 the company had 17 ships in operation totaling 500,000 tons and another 22 ships on order totaling 1,142,000 tons, some with delivery dates six years away.

Financing such growth posed a major problem, to which three basic solutions were found: (1) obtaining prior long-term charters for as many of the ships as possible, which increased the security that could be offered to lenders; (2) ordering some ships on a lease rather than a purchase basis, which gave Norness access to assets with no equity investment at all; and (3) raising money on the capital market.

Leasing terms on the ships, which were all owned and managed from Scandinavia, were essentially as follows: Norness would use the tonnage for 15 years, during which it would pay all operating costs plus amortization on a straight-line basis, plus 5.5% to 6% interest, plus

50% of any profit. Losses, if any, would be carried forward against future profit with no interest charges, and at the end of the 15 years the ships would revert to the owners. (Some years later these terms were to come under fire from the outside investors brought into the picture when Norness sought funds on the capital market.)

To minimize the possibility that the U.S. maritime unions or the U.S. Internal Revenue Service would try to treat Norness as a U.S. company, new equity capital was raised in London, not New York. A separate corporation was formed in 1959 (Anglo American Shipping Company of Bermuda), to which Norness transferred one existing ship and four under construction, among which were two of the largest tankers then on order in the world (90,000 DWT). All five ships were tied to long-term, high-rate contracts, and when all became operational, they would earn over $2 million a year. The Norness company kept 69% of the new firm's common stock, and Norness management took over its direction.

The remaining 788,000 common shares of Anglo American were sold to the public at $2.80, along with $12.5 million in 7% "loan stock" (like preferred). The low ratio of price to projected earnings (3.5) was accounted for by the fact that several of the ships would not be "on stream" for two to three years. That the initial price was regarded as favorable was attested to by the fact that in the aftermarket the shares opened at $5.75.

As head of both a public and closely held company, Erling Naess formed a policy that "gilt-edged" long-term business would be allocated to the former and more speculative business to the latter. A question arose, however, about the allocation of a new bulk-carrier business which Mr. Naess pioneered at this time by convincing the Japanese that coal for their steel mills could be carried more economically if it were transported in larger ships. With contracts of affreightment secured, 35,000-ton carriers on order, and some "backhaul" business arranged to reduce shipping time in ballast, prospects looked so bright that the British directors of the publicly held company argued that the Naess management would lay itself open to charges of conflict of interest if the public firm were excluded from this business.

Although Mr. Naess did not feel that Anglo American should return to the capital markets so soon, he yielded to this British argument, and a merger of the two firms was arranged, the successor to be named Anglo Norness. Based on a two-year projection of the closely held company's earnings through fiscal 1964 (a projection that turned out 99% correct), each Norness Shipping share was exchanged for 820 shares of the new firm, and, on the date of its debut (December 15, 1962) the latter saw its common stock close at $6.50.[2] Shares subsequently

---

[2] After the merger, the Naess family held approximately 35% of the shares.

peaked at about $11 during fiscal 1963, but fiscal 1964 turned out to be the last good year for some time.

FINANCIAL PROBLEMS

The troubles that befell the company after 1964 show up clearly in the financial record (Exhibit 1). Problems included expiration of several of the company's high-rate time charters, delivery of the high-cost new ships that had been ordered several years earlier during boom conditions, similar deliveries to many other owners resulting in an oversupply of tonnage which weakened the spot-market rate, and Norness' obligation to amortize the cost of several new leased ships over 15 years instead of the more customary 20. The effect was a steep downturn in earnings (off 65% from fiscal 1964 to fiscal 1965) and rising stockholder discontent, the latter provoked by a relatively optimistic dividend forecast which had unfortunately been permitted to circulate via the annual report issued at the end of 1964.

The financial debacle of 1965 provoked a series of unpleasant events, among them a public meeting in London (unfavorably written up in the press), wherein management was closely questioned about such factors as the 820-to-1 exchange rate on the Norness Shipping-Anglo Norness stock, the adequacy of the financial reporting, and the propriety of having privately owned Naess family companies serve the publicly held merged company as agents on a commission basis. As a result, over the next two years the following changes occurred:

1. An executive committee of the board was created to "strengthen management and policy-making," and a new executive was imported to serve as chairman of that committee.
2. All agency companies controlled by the Naess family were acquired by Anglo Norness.
3. The entire fleet was revalued, based on an outside appraisal, resulting in an immediate charge to retained earnings of $22 million and an acceleration of depreciation with respect to certain vessels nearing expiration of their time charters.

SUEZ—1967

These changes contributed little to restoring the profit picture. Earnings were helped somewhat by a strong winter market in 1966, but then declined to an historic low with a weak winter market in 1967. Just at the end of the latter fiscal year, however, the June Arab-Israeli war broke out; Suez was closed; several Middle East pipelines were shut down; and the alternative tanker haul around the cape effectively doubled the length of the trip and halved the volume of shipping space available. Spot tanker rates responded by jumping in one month from Intascale[3] minus 70% to Intascale plus 100%, and although rates subsequently eased, they remained at Intascale flat or higher for the rest of the calendar year.

With this turn of events, Anglo Norness' controversial policy, set in 1964, of maintaining charter-free ships in the open market rather than committing them to long-term break-even business paid off royally. At the outbreak of the war Anglo Norness had no less than 15 tankers or OBOs available for spot-market oil cargoes. After the first round or two of frenzied fixtures, the company settled down to take full advantage of the situation.

Since no one knew how long the crisis would last, it became management's objective to prolong the bonanza as long as possible. Intermediate-term business was available, representing one- to three-year contracts at rates which, though certainly below spot rates, were nevertheless well above recent levels. The company took as much of this business as it could. In addition, the secondhand market had firmed up, permitting the company to dispose of a number of marginally efficient, older tankers at a book profit. Finally, a few of the owners of the troublesome leased tankers, attracted by the prospects of receiving 100% of their current operating profits, agreed to cancel the leases for nominal compensation.

On the rising tide of new-found success the troubles of 1965–66 faded. The relieved board subsided into silence. The executive committee ceased to exercise any significant function. Erling Naess reestablished his authority as the chief executive officer. The new "imported" chairman of the executive committee, his support within the board having dissipated along with the company's problems, adjusted himself and took his position as top operating man under Erling Naess.

For the first time in several years, Anglo Norness could afford the luxury of some long-term strategic thinking.

---

[3] An index of basic rates per ton of oil, specified for any pair of load/discharge ports desired, and variable mainly as a function of the distance between them.

Anglo Norness Shipping Company, Limited (B)

As the management of Anglo Norness evaluated the range of alternatives available to the company in early 1968,[1] two serious merger offers were presented to them. One came from a large oil company and the other from a small but fast-growing conglomerate with interests in various phases of what it called the "ocean industry."

THE ACQUISITION OFFERS

The oil company suitor, Occidental Petroleum, had assets of $779 million as of the end of 1967 (see Exhibits 1 and 2 for financial data). It had recently brought on stream substantial wells developed in the Libyan Desert and was accordingly seeking a way of quickly developing its own tanker fleet. What it asked for was a three-week option on the Naess family stock (35% of the Anglo Norness total), plus another major block (15.8%) held by principals of a major Wall Street firm. Should the option be exercised, Occidental would then tender for the rest. The option price would be $4.50 per share in cash.

The other suitor, Zapata Off-Shore Company, had assets of $81.1 million at the end of its fiscal year, September 30, 1967. Like Occidental, Zapata sought agreement with the two controlling blocks. Also like Occidental, it wanted Mr. Erling Naess, Anglo's chairman and founder, to continue as chief executive officer. In addition, Zapata would guarantee

---

[1] See Anglo Norness Shipping Company, Limited (A).

548

EXHIBIT 1

OCCIDENTAL PETROLEUM CORPORATION
Balance Sheet as of December 31, 1967*
(in millions of dollars)

Assets		*Liabilities*	
Current assets		Current liabilities	
Cash	$120.7	Notes and debt due	$ 17.7
Marketable securities	8.8	Accounts and accruals	109.7
Receivables (net)	136.7	Dividends payable	2.9
Inventories	35.9	Accrued taxes	3.9
Prepayments	5.1	Total current liabilities	$134.2
Total current assets	$307.1	Senior long-term debt	165.6
Long-term notes receivable	22.4	Deferred revenue on future	
Investments and advances to		production	52.2
subsidiaries, affiliates	55.6	Deferred federal income taxes	3.8
Property, plant, equipment	$503.8	Other deferred credits	1.9
Reserve for depreciation,		Minority equity	12.4
depletion, etc.	131.6	Preferred stock ($1)	$ 1.5
		Common stock ($.20)	8.8
Net property, plant,		Warrants	(under 0.1)
equipment	$372.2	Capital surplus	279.2
Other assets	21.8	Retained earnings	119.6
Total assets	$779.1	Total equity	$409.1
		Total liabilities	$779.1

*Includes companies merged in a pooling-of-interest basis through January 1968.
Note: Failure of figures to add is due to rounding.
Source: Moody's *Industrial Manual*, 1968.

a seat on its board to Mr. Naess and would change its name to incorporate "Norness" in its title.

Zapata's purchase offer was $5 per share in 4¾% debentures, convertible at $53 into Zapata common. Following a recent stock split, this common was currently priced on the American Stock Exchange at about $40. By March 1968 it would be listed on the New York Stock Exchange.

With some 9.5 million shares of Norness stock outstanding, Occidental's cash offer came to approximately $42.7 million. Owing to the conversion feature, the value of Zapata's offer would vary, depending on the company's prospects as reflected in the price of its stock.

Occidental Petroleum

Under the leadership of Dr. Armand Hammer, Occidental Petroleum had grown rapidly during the 1960s. A partial account of this growth is recorded in the following excerpt from a *Fortune* article in 1968:[2]

When Dr. Hammer (he trained as an M.D. but never practiced) took command in 1957, Oxy was an obscure and profitless little California oil and gas producer with total operating revenues (as recently as 1959) of less than $800,000. He turned it into a natural resource and fertilizer con-

---

[2] Stanley H. Brown, "Dr. Hammer's Magic Tingle," *Fortune,* July 1968. © 1968 Time Inc.

EXHIBIT 2

OCCIDENTAL PETROLEUM CORPORATION
Comparative Consolidated Income Account and Statistical Record
Years Ended December 31
(in millions)

	1963	1964	1965	1966	1967
Income account					
Oil, gas sales and revenues				$506.8	$514.9
Sulphur, agricultural chemicals					
sales				159.5	171.4
Coal sales.				135.6	139.4
Gross revenues	$514.2	$678.9	$718.5	$802.0	$825.7
Interest, dividends	1.3	0.8	1.3	2.7	5.3
Total income	$515.5	$679.7	$719.8	$804.7	$831.0
Cost of sales*	462.2	618.1	651.2	722.7	731.9
Selling, general, administrative					
expense	33.5	38.2	41.6	47.1	55.3
Interest.	2.2	3.4	4.5	8.4	10.0
Balance	$ 17.7	$ 20.0	$ 22.5	$ 26.5	$ 33.8
Federal income tax†	5.5	4.8	3.7	1.0	. . .
Minority interest	0.5	0.5	0.8	1.0	1.7
Equity in income of noncon-					
solidated subsidiaries.	1.3	3.7	6.2	0.2	0.6
Net income before extra-					
ordinary items	$ 13.0	$ 18.5	$ 24.3	$ 24.7	$ 32.7
Extraordinary items‡.	5.6	4.3	4.1	5.7	12.9§
Net income to surplus	$ 18.6	$ 22.7	$ 28 4	$ 30.4	$ 45.5

	1963	1964	1965	1966	1967
Statistical record					
Earnings per common share ‖					
Before extraordinary items . . .	$ 0.74	$1.22	$1.64	$1.63	$2.04
After extraordinary items	1.30	1.64	2.00	2.13	3.03
Dividends per common share . . .	0.50	0.50	0.55	0.70	0.80
Price range: common	34¾–	35–	35½–	57¾–	122¼–
	19⅝	23½	21	26	40⅝
Fixed charges earned					
Before income taxes	11.88	9.19	8.18	4.76	5.54
After income taxes	9.41	7.76	7.36	4.64	5.54
Number of shares outstanding. . .	. . .	. . .	. . .	11,182,274	14,688,763

*Including depreciation, amortization, and depletion of $18 million in 1966 and $22.4 million in 1967. Other years not stated.
†Represents federal income taxes of subsidiaries prior to dates of becoming subsidiaries.
‡Includes gain on sale of property, plant, and equipment; tax benefits on loss carry-overs and losses on investments; income from sale of gas, production payments, etc.
§Includes net gain of $12.8 million on sale of Kern County Land Company.
‖Includes companies merged in a pooling-of-interest basis through January 1968.
Source: Moody's *Industrial Manual*, 1968.

glomerate that earned $45,548,000 on a gross of $825,740,000 in 1967 and will crack the billion mark in sales this year. As he has assiduously sought to tell the world, he did it by finding more gas and oil in California and then by moving Oxy in several other directions: fertilizer, sulphur, petrochemicals, petroleum transportation, California real-estate development, coal mining, Libya, and petroleum refining and distribution in Western Europe. Along the way, he thought briefly about making a move to acquire Pure Oil and did make a highly profitable if unsuccessful bid to get Kern County Land

Co. And right now Occidental is involved in the acquisition of Hooker Chemical Corp. for an exchange of stock. Both Oxy's and Hooker's shareholders will vote on the deal this month, and if they approve it, Oxy will add a diversified chemical producer that last year netted $24 million after taxes on sales of $341 million. The consolidated revenues of the expanded Occidental could exceed $1.5 billion this year and net might run well over $100 million.

After 1970, what?

Occidental, which sold for 20 cents a share when Dr. Hammer first heard of it twelve years ago, lately traded around $50 after a three-for-one split. The recent performance of the stock has given rise to criticisms that the company is overzealous in promoting itself, and last year the New York Stock Exchange eliminated margin trading in Oxy stock because of its "volatility." It doesn't seem to bother investors that for all its diversity, Oxy derives much of its internal growth potential and nearly all of its recent glamour from one product in one place: oil in Libya. "It's just another oil company," one oilman says, "and should be selling for ten to fifteen times earnings."

A lot of oil companies do sell in that range, but Hammer had obviously persuaded investors that Oxy is anything but a typical oil company. Without Hooker, some analysts have been predicting 1968 earnings of $1.75 to $2 a share, putting Oxy's price-earnings ratio well above 20. But such projections are conservative in *Fortune*'s view: $2 to $2.25 a share this year seems more likely. And without any major new discoveries or acquisitions, internal growth, especially from Libyan production, can boost earnings to at least $4 a year by 1970. But that is when Libyan earnings are expected to peak. What happens then depends on Hammer's ability to solve several problems including the concentration of earning power in Libya, the absence of an apparent successor to the energetic but aging doctor, and the pressure on world oil prices as new discoveries in areas such as the Persian Gulf, Nigeria, Alaska, and the North Sea bring enormous quantities of crude oil into the market.

The essence of the doctor's success is not oil but "the deal." A man who works closely with him described appreciatively the way Armand Hammer "gets all tingly" as he begins to close one. "They call me a closer," Hammer reflected. "There's nothing worse than a deal that wasn't closed."

A further description of Dr. Hammer and the Occidental organization is provided in Exhibit 3.

Zapata Off-Shore Company

Zapata had grown, in part, as the result of a vigorous acquisition program which had carried the company into cognate industries. According to public information contained in Zapata's annual report for 1967, revenues of $36.3 million and income of about $5 million (in about the same proportions) came from the following businesses:

Offshore contract drilling of oil and gas wells for the petroleum
industry 57%
Fishing and conversion of fish into high-protein meal used mainly
for chicken feed and, to a lesser extent, conversion into fish oil
with multiple uses 17%
Service boats for servicing offshore drilling rigs 14%
Dredging 9%
Marine construction 3%
Exploring for oil and gas through a syndicate in which the company
held a 27% interest and to which its commitment was $300,000
yearly for three years . . . .
                                                                                    ——
                                                                                   100%

Financial statements and a record of Zapata common stock performance
are contained in Exhibits 4, 5, and 6.

Since Zapata had an active acquisitions program, longer run and even
immediate prospects obviously would not depend on trends in its present
businesses alone. The company's acquisition strategy had been outlined
in great detail by Mr. Robert H. Gow, executive vice president, at a
meeting of securities analysts in 1967:

I very much dislike the distinction between internal earnings growth and
acquired earnings growth. In Zapata's case, it is virtually impossible to make
such a distinction. This is because the vast majority of Zapata's growth in
earnings per share has come from what would normally be described as

---

EXHIBIT 3˙
Excerpts from "Dr. Hammer's Magic Tingle"°

**Occidental Petroleum's chairman
has a sixth sense about deals—
whether in pencils, czarist memorabilia,
or whiskey. Right now the dealing's
lifting Oxy toward the majors.**

by Stanley H. Brown

His own thing
  The doctor has never come to terms with corporate bureaucracy.
Instead, he has built a headquarters organization to serve his particular needs and style. "Unstructured," says Dorman Commons, fifty,
Oxy's uncommonly able financial vice president. A "skinny, hard-
running group," says another headquarters man. The company's home
office consists of about a dozen key men plus staff on one and a half
floors in a Los Angeles office building a few blocks from Hammer's
house.
  The front part of Armand Hammer is an accessible, often charming man, full of anecdotes, an easy smiler. But the back part is usually

* Stanley H. Brown, "Dr. Hammer's Magic Tingle," *Fortune*, July 1968. © 1968
Time Inc.

EXHIBIT 3 (*continued*)

working to conserve Hammer's time and energy. The man's schedule is wildly fluid, changing constantly, because he goes where he thinks he can serve the most productive purpose. He will think nothing of bypassing an operating executive because he can't reach the man and going direct to a subordinate. When a bypassed executive complained, Hammer apologized sincerely, and then did the same thing next day, explaining that he was only trying to help the executive. It's as though he were offering himself to the highest bidder in terms of business priority for his time and the most efficient application of his energy. That makes him extremely difficult to work with, because Hammer assumes that everyone can make as forceful and effective use of himself as he does.

Hammer describes his function at Occidental as that of "the leader of the orchestra." And like some well-known band leaders who can't read a note, Hammer has little interest in operating details. The Occidental man who said, "Dr. Hammer wouldn't know a barrel of oil if he fell into it," was not being critical at all, just a little hyperbolic. Hammer makes it a point to have able men around who know what he doesn't want to know. He gives them a free hand and pays them generously in stock options (more than 500 Oxy people are on the option list and a score are Oxy millionaires).

But the doctor guards jealously his prerogatives as chief executive officer. He surprises his staff with his decisions, sometimes based on information they didn't even know about. "He has his own sources," one high executive observes. Long before he passed his seventieth birthday last May, Hammer had already made clear that despite any indication he had given that that might have been his retirement date, he has no intention of stepping down at any time.

Hammer has put his stamp on Occidental indelibly, though he is probably no more indispensable to its future than Royal Little proved to be at Textron. There is no shortage of talented staff or operating men in the company, but neither is there an obvious successor at this point. Walter Davis, head of Permian at Midland, Texas, functions part time as head of operations at Los Angeles headquarters. "But the doctor doesn't like anyone else calling the shots," says an Oxy executive. To the question of whether there is a No. 2 man, Hammer replies with a smile, "No, but there are several contenders."

EXHIBIT 4
Price behavior of Zapata stock, 1962–67 (fiscal years ended September 30)

Year	Closing price	Percent change	Annual lows	Percent change	Annual highs	Percent change	High-low spread	Spread as a percent of close
1962	$ 2.35	. . .	$ 1.75	. . .	$ 3.85	. . .	$ 2.10	90
1963	4.63	97	2.37	35	5.37	40	3.00	65
1964	7.63	65	4.75	100	8.50	59	3.75	49
1965	8.63	13	7.63	61	11.63	38	4.00	46
1966	16.25	88	8.25	8	27.37	134	19.12	117
1967	49.12	203	15.00	82	49.12	80	34.12	70
Average. . .		93		57		71		87

Source: Zapata Off-Shore Company *Prospectus*, July 1968.

EXHIBIT 5

ZAPATA OFF-SHORE COMPANY
Consolidated Balance Sheet as of September 30, 1967
(in millions of dollars)

Assets		Liabilities and Equity	
Current assets		Current liabilities	
Cash	$ 4.20	Current maturities on long-term debt	$ 6.31
Notes and accounts receivable	10.10	Accounts payable and accrued liabilities	5.51
Inventories	2.14	Income taxes payable	2.54
Prepaid expenses	.55		
Total current assets	$16.99	Total current liabilities	$14.36
Property and equipment, net*	61.02	Long-term debt†	29.65
Deferred charges, etc.	3.11	Reserve for deferred taxes	4.81
Total assets	$81.12	Minority investment	1.27
		Stockholders' investment	
		Preferred	$ 8.77
		Common‡	.55
		Warrants§	.93
		Capital in excess of par	10.15
		Reinvested earnings‖	10.62
		Total equity	$31.02
		Total liabilities and equity	$81.12

*Property and equipment at cost by end use changed as follows from 1966 to 1967:

Use	1966	1967
Offshore drilling	$39.24	$53.57
Other vessels	7.96	20.15
Protein production	0	3.45
Oil, gas	.14	.43
Total	$47.34	$77.61
Less: Reserves for amortization and depreciation	12.14	16.59
Total	$35.20	$61.02

†Includes $19.23 million in senior long-term debt (net of current maturities of $5.30 million), mainly composed of a 6¾% mortgage note. Also includes $1.32 million long-term debt of a subsidiary, mainly a 7% note to a supplier, not guaranteed by the parent. Also includes subordinated debt:

$$
\begin{array}{ll}
6\% \ \text{debentures due } 1975 = & \$1.37 \ \text{million} \\
6\% \ \text{notes due} \quad\quad 1982 = & 1.71 \\
6\tfrac{1}{2}\% \ \text{debentures due } 1977 = & 6.02 \\
\hline
& \$9.10 \ \text{million}
\end{array}
$$

‡Par $.50 per share; authorized 5 million shares; issued 1,524,987 shares. This stock was subsequently split two for one.
§Consists of warrants to buy 232,053 shares of common at $30 per share.
‖All reinvested earnings were restricted as to payment of cash dividends on common.
Source: Zapata Off-Shore Company, 1967 Annual Report.

internal growth, that is, from the addition of new equipment to our various fleets of rigs, workboats, fishing facilities, etc. In general, what the acquisitions of the past three years have done for us is give us the asset base or the entry into the activity which made the internal growth possible. On the other hand, since this growth would not have taken place if Zapata had not made the acquisitions, it could quite correctly be viewed as "growth by acquisition." I would prefer to describe it as growth through the application of financial or corporate strategy.

EXHIBIT 6

ZAPATA OFF-SHORE COMPANY
Summary of Consolidated Earnings for Fiscal Years Ended September 30
(dollars in millions, except earnings per share)

	1963	1964	1965	1966	1967
Revenues.	$11.27	$13.23	$14.92	$16.48	$36.33
Direct costs and expenses	6.53	6.51	6.91	8.34	20.83
Depreciation.	2.10	2.18	1.92	1.52	3.35
General administrative expense	.93	1.18	1.54	1.87	2.87
Operating profit.	$ 1.72	$ 3.36	$ 4.55	$ 4.75	$ 9.29
Other income (expense)*	(.24)	(.22)	(.15)	(.59)	(2.10)
Profits before taxes and extraordinary items	$ 1.48	$ 3.14	$ 4.40	$ 4.16	$ 7.18
Provision for income taxes					
Current	.20	.42	1.08	.89	1.00
Deferred	.52	1.03	.98	.45	1.20
Profit before extraordinary items.	$ .76	$ 1.69	$ 2.34	$ 2.83	$ 4.98
Extraordinary items					
Gain on sale of marketable securities					.21
Write-off investments†				(3.21)	
Gain on sale of physical assets.		.12		1.26	
Total.		$ .12		$ (1.95)	$ .21
Net profit	$ .76	$ 1.81	$ 2.34	$ .88	$ 5.19
Preferred dividends	.07	.07	.07	.04	.17
Common dividend	0	0	0‡	0‡	0
Earnings per common share §					
Before extraordinary items.	.025	.059	.82	1.00	1.67
After extraordinary items	.025	.063	.82	.30	1.74

*Mainly interest owed ($2.17 million in 1967).
†Write-off of investments in Westec, Amata Gas, and Zapata Lining Corporations.
‡A 4% stock dividend was declared in 1965 and 1966.
§Based on average shares outstanding after giving effect to a two-for-one stock split effective January 15, 1968, and assuming conversion of the cumulative convertible preferred and 6% convertible subordinated notes.
Source: Zapata Off-Shore Company *Prospectus,* August 1968.

Mr. Gow then went on to define the five principles which he saw as having guided Zapata's behavior to date:

1. To concentrate on those areas of commercial activity where it is always possible to invest an unlimited amount of money, that is, where capital expansion can take place unhindered by a strict limit to the marketplace. Return on total investment need not be particularly high when extensive use of the second principle is made.

2. To apply, to the maximum extent possible, other people's money and credit.

3. To use listed securities primarily to acquire assets which then serve as the credit base necessary to make the down payments on some other credit-financed acquisition or investment. Here the company has adopted the phraseology "Type I–Type II" in referring to its acquisitions. Type

I is defined as the asset-type company, acquired to strengthen the balance sheet and to expand the company's credit base without contributing necessarily to earnings in the first round, but without diluting them either. Type II is an earnings acquisition. The two types are alternated sequentially, and hopefully the stock will go up and fewer shares can then be exchanged for the equivalent amount of assets acquired in the next Type I.

4. Not to hesitate to acquire so-called "cyclical" earnings if the overall trend of these earnings is upward and if the cycles have at least a minimal correlation with the company's existing business.

5. To avoid areas where management is unique, that is, areas where management can "blackmail" you through your fear of their quitting. Management, good operating management, is terribly important in the dredging business or the drilling business, for example. But you can find replacement. The situation is quite different from, for example, the conditions that would exist if we acquired a small computer company. There a team of five experts could leave you and your growth could stop altogether. A corporate strategy like Zapata's requires maximum compounding of equity cash flow. Let me repeat that because in a way it sums up all the principles: our stress is on the overall rate at which cash equity can be made to compound. This implies that the cash flows from all the divisions be invested in the one which is showing at any moment the greatest opportunity to absorb cash. The ruthlessness with which this objective of compounding return on equity cash must be followed requires that there be few if any indispensable management groups within the corporate structure.

Zapata's acquisition policy was assessed by Smith, Barney as follows:

Management's objective is to develop increased earning power through expansion of the company's present activities and by making additional acquisitions. The plan is to expand Zapata's earning power by alternately acquiring companies with strong financial positions and then purchasing companies which are less strong financially but which offer good prospects for earnings growth. Negotiations are in progress with one or more companies almost continuously. Companies of special interest are those engaged in activities related to the ocean. We are impressed particularly with the thoroughness with which potential acquisitions are studied and with the careful way in which they are integrated into the Zapata corporate structure.

As its overall view, the Smith, Barney report had added: "In our opinion the stock is an excellent long-term investment and purchase is recommended."

ANALYSIS OF THE ACQUISITION POSSIBILITIES

Michael Naess' analysis

In view of the capital appreciation opportunity contained in the Zapata offer, Michael Naess set about to analyze this proposal in detail.

A visit to the company's headquarters in Houston, Texas; annual reports; stock price records; and investment house appraisals added to his knowledge of the situation. A description of his study is contained in the Appendix at the end of this case. Assuming the Zapata shares continued to sell at 25 times earnings after the merger and assuming profits for 1968 of $8.5 million for Zapata ($1 million less than Zapata's pro-forma statements included) and $5 million for Anglo Norness, Michael Naess estimated that the debentures would sell for $126, or $6.30 per Anglo Norness share. Based on his financial analysis, he concluded that the Zapata offer was superior to that of Occidental.

A few other qualitative considerations reinforced his preference. The general area of ocean enterprise intrigued him with its promise of future growth. Zapata seemed well on its way to becoming the leading "ocean conglomerate." In addition, the offshore drilling industry had encountered two cyclical setbacks in the last 10 years, 1957 and 1967, precisely the years of shipping's greatest boom. The apparent existence, therefore, of a negative coefficient of correlation between Zapata and Anglo Norness' earnings appealed to him. Also, there appeared to be some potential synergies in the similarities between the two companies, that is, in the customers, in the use of debt to finance capital-intensive activities, and in the technologies of operating and maintaining heavy equipment at sea. Finally, the closing of the Suez Canal for the second time in a decade seemed likely to force the oil companies to seek new sources of supply in order to reduce their dependence on the Persian Gulf. This seemed to indicate strengthened demand for offshore concessions and drilling equipment.

Michael therefore decided to use whatever influence he could muster to persuade his father and the other individuals concerned to accept the Zapata offer.

The generation gap

While Michael Naess had been gradually deciding in favor of Zapata, his father, Erling Naess, had been leaning in the other direction. The latter described his reactions in a letter to his son:

You will, on your own, study the Zapata figures. It is astonishing to me that the shares of Zapata, with a net asset value of less than $7.50 per share, can sell in the market at around $50 per share. I am afraid that it illustrates the hectic nature of the market in "glamour stocks." You will note the "tight" financial situation, with current assets barely exceeding current liabilities. Also, the large number of loans, with options to purchase common stock of Zapata. I cannot help getting a feeling that the Zapata situation is one of "wheeling and dealing." Anglo Norness' position is incomparably stronger, financially.

I trust you will contact me as soon as you have studied the Zapata material.

By early February, the Wall Street principals, having studied both situations, indicated that they had a slight preference for the Occidental cash offer but would go along with whatever the Naess block decided. It was thus up to the two Naesses to decide the fate of the company.

Here Michael Naess faced a dilemma. It had become increasingly obvious that his father, age 66, opposed the Zapata offer, fearing that it was too risky. Erling Naess had been through rough times during the 1965–66 Anglo Norness troubles, and he now seemed to want security. In addition, there was the security of his four daughters, his teen-age younger son, and his grandchildren—all of whom held, either directly or in trust, large amounts of Anglo Norness stock—to think of. Michael Naess, on the other hand, found it difficult to impose his father's apparent risk aversion onto the rough probability analysis which he had done. He was too firmly rooted to his own rather neutral attitude toward risk. Hence he was concerned not only with the issue of the comparative merits of the two offers but also with the subsidiary issue of how far to push his own decision, once made. What right did he have to be contentious? His father had created the company, and although Michael had made some contribution, most of the value represented by his own Anglo Norness shares came to him by way of gifts from his father. These considerations made him extremely uneasy about his position. He resolved, nevertheless, to debate the issue up to whatever point seemed reasonable.

A series of telephone conversations followed between Erling and Michael Naess, during the course of which each became successively more entrenched in his own position. Relations became strained and then outwardly hostile. Communications had broken down. No new information or logic was being added. Erling Naess accused his son of "wheeler-dealer," unrealistic pipe dreaming. Michael thought his father afflicted with a "1929 syndrome."

At length both Zapata and Occidental applied pressure. In mid-February Occidental asked that the decision be made within 10 days. At about the same time, Zapata informed Erling Naess that its offer would be withdrawn by the end of the month.

On February 15, attempting to restore reason to the debate, Michael Naess wrote a long letter to his father, presenting the financial analysis which he had worked out and summarizing his arguments:

On balance, and in summary, our choice must rest upon an evaluation of the risk inherent in the Zapata debentures. The above analysis is conservative, in my opinion, and the near-term risk factor seems moderate. Longer term risks might be greater, and I would therefore recommend that if we were to take the Zapata route, we would sell some proportion of our Zapata stock, say, within a few months of consummating the deal, at a price between $104 and $114 per $100 face. Zapata management has offered to assist us by sponsoring a secondary offering. They have, however, made it clear that they would be disappointed if Naess family members active in the management were to dispose of a large proportion of their holding.

Nonfinancial considerations. Under this category, by necessity, analysis becomes much more subjective. Our objective, as we established it in broad terms several weeks ago, is to diversify Anglo Norness, which to me implies *both* a diversification of our investment for reasons of financial security *and* a diversification of our managerial efforts for reasons of job satisfaction. We both foresee diminishing returns in shipping during the next few years. In diversifying, we are therefore seeking to expand into areas which permit greater creativity.

Zapata's expanding position in the broad field of "oceanics" appeals to me as one of great potential creativity. Both their intentions to place you on the board and their offer to engage me as part of the "acquisitions" team satisfy me that we would both play significant roles in the creative effort.

The Occidental deal strikes me *not* as a diversification step but rather as an outright absorption. Mere size of the absorbing entity, I suppose, governs this impression. Anglo Norness' contribution to total EPS in the Zapata case is measurable in dollars, whereas in the Occidental case it amounts to cents. For me, at least, in a motivational sense, this is an important difference. In terms of our significance to the absorbing company, the difference becomes even more dramatic when you consider that within Zapata our contact had been with the two top executives, whereas, to my knowledge, you have yet to meet the chief executive of Occidental, despite two visits culminating in agreement upon the formal document of sale which, though unsigned as yet, nevertheless shows that things have gone rather far.

On the other hand, Anglo Norness fits much more readily into the Occidental picture. This might be beneficial in the sense that it offers an added guarantee for the utilization of the Anglo Norness tonnage. But it also locks us in, as managers, to the shipping business, which I thought we had agreed was not a highly creative area.

Occidental has led you to believe that, after merger, Anglo Norness would continue to operate as an autonomous entity. But the very reasons underlying the "better fit" of the Occidental deal seem to preclude autonomy. After the Signal merger, which links Signal's refining and marketing with Occidental's production, the result will be an integrated oil company *except* for one gap, transportation, which we would fill. Clearly, Anglo would have to be carefully integrated with production schedules, on the one side, and refinery runs on the other. Occidental requirements would have first preference on Anglo tonnage. Under modern management-control philosophy, Anglo would probably represent a separate profit center, and its services would be billed internally to the other divisions *at* market rates, and we have both agreed, I think, that the medium- and long-term outlook for the market, particularly tankers, is dismal. Hence, as a profit center, Anglo would probably show losses. Our investment would be safe, of course, due to the original cash exchange, and you might argue that Anglo's losses *would* be the other divisions' gain, such that if, on balance, the result was a favorable contribution to profits per share, and we owned Occidental shares, we would be helping ourselves. But the process is rather too indirect, I fear, to be of strong significance as a motivating force, or as a source of creative satisfaction. This perhaps explains why so many of the oil company executives with whom we deal, the marine VPs, have struck me as rather apathetic and not terribly enthused with their work. And I fear that the Occidental deal would place you (and later, perhaps, me if I followed you) in the same category as these gentlemen.

Conclusion. There are many other areas worthy of discussion which this memo has ignored. But it has not been my purpose to produce a definitive report. You have been astounded and perplexed at my inability immediately to perceive the vast superiority of the Occidental deal, of which you tell me you are so convinced. This memo purports to clarify some of my thinking.

A few days later, having digested Michael's letter, Erling Naess summarized *his* arguments:

The cost to Zapata of 9,500,000 Anglo Norness shares at $5 per share would be $47,500,000 in 4¾% subordinated debentures. Adding to this $47,500,000 the debentures already issued by Zapata in connection with prior acquisitions, including Paramount, the resulting capital structure would be about 85% debt and only about 10% equity (the difference of 5% being preferred stock).

Keeping carefully in mind my responsibility towards the close to 1,000 shareholders of Anglo Norness (not only the Naess family but the "grey mass" of outside shareholders, some of whom probably have an important part of their savings invested in Anglo Norness), I am unable to muster the necessary insouciance about debt to swallow this extremely top-heavy capital structure, seeing that the alternative "route," that is, Occidental, would give the shareholders CASH or the close equivalent to cash, which would completely relieve me of any further responsibility.

There hardly can be any doubt that the top-heavy capital structure of Zapata would give rise to critical comment in the financial press around the world, particularly in London. On the other hand, a cash offer of $4.50 from Occidental would go far to restore the Naess name to its glory of 1962 and 1963. At my age, and with a desire to take it more easy in the years to come, can you really blame me for not wishing to expose myself to new blasts of newspaper criticism?

In your memorandum, you yourself have conceded that "Anglo Norness fits much more readily into the Occidental picture." The fact is that Anglo Norness fits into the Occidental picture like a hand fits into a glove.

On the other hand, Anglo Norness merged into Zapata will make Zapata even more of a conglomerate than it already is. Zapata already controls subsidiaries in such different industries as

Offshore drilling
Construction (dams, etc.)
Fishing
Dredging

One or two of Anglo Norness' smaller tankers may conceivably be converted to drilling ships, but this is the only "commercial contact" between Norness and Zapata which I can discover.

You state, in your memorandum, that Zapata's expanding position in the broad field of "oceanics" appeals to you as one of great potential creativity. I agree with you. I can also understand and sympathize with your appreciation of the offer made you, personally, by Zapata, to engage you as part of the "acquisition team."

However, let us look at the offers made by Occidental in this area. Their ideas are as follows:

a) Anglo Norness will continue to function as a completely autonomous, decentralized company, only subject to their overall centralized financial control.

b) I will join the board of Occidental, apart from being the chairman and chief executive officer of Anglo Norness.

c) If you are interested, an important position in Occidental, not only in Anglo Norness, will be offered YOU. In my estimation, this is an even greater challenge and chance of "potential creativity" than the one offered you by Zapata, for the simple reason that Occidental has far greater resources to apply in "creative effort."

d) I have the feeling that Occidental is in just as great need as Zapata is of the international know-how of the Naess tribe, and that, supported by a large investment in Occidental, the Naess tribe has a tremendous future in Occidental. The opportunity is knocking on the door. You have merely to open the door.

The Zapata offer is subject to SEC registration of the $4\frac{3}{4}\%$ subordinated debentures. I am told that the granting of this registration would probably take about three months and that in the event the registration was refused, Zapata would be unable to go through with the "deal" and would be free of their commitment. In other words, we would not know for sure for three months that we have a "deal."

On the other hand, Occidental will not require SEC registration. They will pay cash in full to all the hundreds of small holders of Anglo Norness shares, thus reducing the number of persons who will receive four-year notes below the figure which compels registration to be made.[3]

Your evaluation of the attraction of Zapata's offer is based upon certain assumptions regarding Wall Street's reaction to the Zapata-Anglo Norness merger. All this assumes that the financial community in New York will believe in the future of Zapata as an "oceanic conglomerate." Only provided this belief continues STRONG will Zapata's shares be given the high market standing, that is, the P/E multiple of 25, which they are now enjoying.

One of the major reasons for my skepticism is the belief that the "conglomerate honeymoon" ended when the Litton Industries "myth" exploded and the Litton stock plunged from about $115 per share to $65. When I say that the "myth" exploded, I refer to the claim of the leading U.S. conglomerates that their use of advanced management techniques and abilities can be applied successfully to any type of business and that, therefore, a small "scientific management team" can improve the earnings of any company

---

[3] To ease the tax burden on certain of the large selling stockholders, Occidental had made available the option of four-year serial notes, which would qualify under the IRS code as an installment sale.

in any industry and, consequently, justify a much higher P/E ratio than the company had before.

When Litton Industries announced a profits drop of 30% due to "management problems," the whole house of cards collapsed.

You and I know perfectly well that to maintain Anglo Norness' earnings in the years to come will require grueling hard work and demand great skill and experience of a kind that Zapata cannot possibly supply. Managerial ability, as demonstrated in the offshore drilling business and other enterprises absorbed by Zapata, *cannot* be transferred to the business of Anglo Norness. It would still be up to you and to me to make Anglo Norness fulfill the $5 million per annum expectation upon which your evaluation of the Zapata stock is based.

The P/E multiple of 25 applied to Zapata stock is based upon the expectation of "growth." It is my belief that the headlong scramble for "growth" indulged in by the leading U.S. conglomerates has come to a sad end and that companies like Zapata will have to submit to an enforced pause in their acquisition programs. When this is realized by the financial community, it is logical to expect that the P/E multiple will drop to the more realistic one of about 15. If at the same time Anglo Norness should have a poor year and only break even, the stock of Zapata would fall to about $28—being 15 times earnings of about $1.90 per share, diluted. The 4¾% subordinated convertible debentures would probably fall to about 60, equal to about $3 per share of Anglo Norness, compared with the $4.50 cash offered by Occidental.

Except for visions of "growth," why should Zapata stock sell at a higher multiple than the shares of immensely strong companies like Standard Oil of New Jersey, Royal Dutch, etc.? It would be easy to present arguments why the Zapata shares should sell at a LOWER, not higher, multiple than these seasoned, strong companies.

Even if this letter leaves you unconvinced, I am at least hoping that you appreciate that I have studied your memorandum of February 15 carefully, weighing your arguments.

A third view

Despite the emphasis given to the merger alternatives, at least one member of the top-executive team continued to feel that Anglo Norness might have greater opportunities as an independent company. Thus, the chairman of the Anglo Norness executive committee wrote as follows to Michael Naess at the Harvard Business School:

My purpose in writing is to let you know that I believe the failure of all the current [merger] negotiations, should this occur, would not necessarily be a disaster in my opinion. There is every reason to expect that by June 1969 Anglo could have a cash availability in the order of 20 million dollars. While probably sounding exceedingly optimistic, it is more and more looking to me as if we should be the ones doing the acquiring, rather than rushing to sell out. Perhaps everyone is being overly influenced by the problems of the past, rather than looking coldly at the present as well as the near-term future.

APPENDIX
MICHAEL NAESS' STUDY OF ZAPATA OFF-SHORE COMPANY

Stock performance record. After his two-day trip to Houston, where Zapata management answered his questions and disclosed to him its forecasts, Michael Naess turned to an analysis of the past performance record of Zapata's stock. Looking at the closing annual prices from 1962 through 1967 (as adjusted for splits), he found a rise from $2.35 to $49.12, for an average yearly gain of 93%, noncompounded. Year-to-year gains, however, varied widely, and the overall average was greatly strengthened by a jump of 203% in 1967.

Michael wondered, therefore, whether the high closing price of 1967 represented a "technical climax" and whether accepting Zapata's offer would mean that Anglo would be "getting in at the top." He also noted a great volatility, as measured by the yearly high-low spreads which averaged 87%. In order to get some measure of growth besides that based on year-end changes, Michael tabulated the yearly lows and highs and figured the annual percentage change in each. From these calculations he found that the yearly growth reflected by the lows averaged 57%; as reflected by the highs it averaged 71%. Michael felt that the average of these two figures—64%—was a better yardstick of past stock price performance than the 93% computed from the year-end closes, since there seemed to be no reason to attach any special importance to the latter.

The question of whether accepting Zapata's offer meant getting in at the top could only be answered by a comparative evaluation of Zapata before and after the Norness acquisition. Accordingly, Michael Naess examined the past financial statements, especially the operating ratios, the equity structure, and the earnings per share. He appraised earnings prospects within Norness, and he went as far as he could in calculating the difference the Norness acquisition would make in this picture.

Finances. Studying Zapata's financial statements, Michael noted in particular the tight current picture with a current ratio at September 30, 1967, of slightly less than 1.2/1. He also observed the high degree of leverage in the capital structure. Adding deferred taxes and minority interest to book equity, he noted that there was about $37 million in equity against $30 million in long-term debt. He also knew, however, that since drilling rigs represented the major part of the company's assets, a high degree of leverage could be expected. Drilling rigs were normally financed in much the same way as Anglo Norness' ships. On the strength of a long-term drilling contract with an oil company, the owner could borrow heavily for the construction of a rig, in effect taking advantage of the customer's credit rating.

Turning to the equity structure, he noted that on a split basis there were 3,100,000 common shares outstanding. Potential conversion was as follows: preferred stock into 502,000; warrants, 516,000; options, 176,000; and conversion of the 6% note due in 1982, possibly 114,000. Total potential shares out were, therefore, about 4.4 million. Pro-forma earnings on this basis, assuming conversions at date of issue during 1967 and using the average number outstanding, were $1.58 per share, as opposed to the $1.76 reported. At $40, therefore, the stock was selling at about 25 times fully diluted 1967 earnings.

Outlook. Michael Naess next examined the earnings outlook for 1968. While in Houston, Zapata management had shown him their latest pro-forma income statement, which showed 1968 net income of $9.5 million, or about $3.05 per share undiluted. This projection included contribution from the purchase in January of Paramount Pacific, Inc., a heavy construction firm based in Los Angeles, for $16.7 million in convertible debentures identical in terms to those offered to Anglo Norness, plus a cash payment of $5 million to be made contingent upon future earnings.

Even apart from the Paramount or other acquisitions, Michael learned that the financial community was optimistic on Zapata's near-term earnings. Thus, one brokerage house (Smith, Barney & Co.) forecast that per-share earnings would rise, undiluted, in the neighborhood of 40% in 1968 over 1967. In support of this view, the Smith, Barney report pointed out that earnings from offshore drilling—the largest money-maker—should be improved by a full year's return on a major investment made in 1967. Earnings from the fishing fleet—the second largest source of income—should be improved by absence of the start-up costs that had accompanied acquisition of this business early in the 1967 fishing season. Earnings of the service-boat fleet, the third largest sales and income producer, would be increased by a full year's operation of four new boats, which raised the total number to 21. Earnings from dredging and marine construction should also increase, reflecting operations of a subsidiary owned for only part of the previous year.

So far as longer term prospects were concerned, the broker's report pointed out that the future of offshore drilling work looked good, based on the oil industry's prediction that crude from offshore wells would increase its share of the free-world total from 16% of all production in 1966 to 40% within the next 10 years. With demand also rising at a compound rate of 6% a year, offshore production should increase five-fold. Fishing-fleet prospects, too, appeared secure, since Zapata's break-even price for fish meal (the principal end product) was only $90 a ton, much lower than the current market price of $130, and also lower than the break-even price of the principal competition, which came from smaller, older boats owned in Peru. In addition, Zapata might prove successful in projected efforts to expand its fishing season beyond the customary six months a year.

Zapata plus Norness.   Before trying to determine how a combined Anglo Norness-Zapata would look, Michael Naess decided that to be conservative he would arbitrarily reduce Zapata's 1968 earnings forecast of $9.5 million to $8.5 million. To this he attempted to add the effects of the Anglo Norness acquisition.

At $5 per share for Anglo's 9.5 million shares, the company would cost Zapata about $47.5 million. With over $20 million in Norness cash projected by June, Michael decided to call $10 million "redundant." The net cost was thus $37.5 million. In terms of current profits of $16 million, Zapata was paying a ridiculous 2.4 times earnings. His best estimates of Anglo's earnings for 1969 and 1970, however, were about $5 million in each year, and on this basis the price was 7.5 times earnings.

Assuming the company would be purchased for 20% cash,[4] the amount of convertible debentures to be issued would be $38 million. Convertible at $53, dilution would be 720,000 shares, and contribution to Zapata's consolidated earnings would be $7 per incremental share issued, fully diluted. The deal, at this point, looked too good for Zapata. On the other hand, given Anglo's current price in London of $2.60, Zapata was already paying a premium of better than 90%.

An attempt to estimate pro-forma consolidated earnings specifically for 1968 proved to be fruitless. As a purchase, Anglo could only contribute to Zapata's earnings from the effective date of the deal, and it was impossible to predict what that date would be, given the need for proxy statements, registration, permission of the Office of Direct Foreign Investment, etc. Michael therefore assumed that it was the rate of annualized earnings, rather than the earnings reported for a particular fiscal year, that was important in predicting equity values.

Hence, he argued, at some point during 1968 Zapata would be earning at the rate of $8.5 million plus $5 million from Anglo Norness, or $13.5 million per annum, less interest on the new debentures, after tax of $900,000, or net $12.6 million. Not counting dilution, this would be $4.06 per share on 3.1 million shares. Adding conversions of 1.1 million from

---

[4] Due to Bank of England restrictions during the post-devaluation period, as well as to Department of Commerce regulations on direct foreign investment, it appeared that Zapata would not be able to offer its debentures to foreign stockholders, particularly those resident in the United Kingdom. As a result, these individuals would be offered $5 per share in cash. It was difficult to determine exactly what percentage of the company's stock was still held abroad. The stock had been traded actively since the June war, and the company's registry was known to be well behind the times. Most of the activity had been traced, however, to American buying. Accordingly, it was estimated that Zapata would end up purchasing only about 20% of the company for cash and 80% for convertibles.

the Paramount Pacific and Anglo Norness debentures to the 4.4 million previously computed, fully converted shares outstanding would be 5.5 million. Earnings in this case, however, would be unencumbered by the interest on the debentures or the preferred dividend and would presumably be bolstered by some return from the proceeds of the warrants and options. A reasonable estimate would be $14.5 million, which on 5.5 million shares would amount to fully diluted earnings of $2.65 per share.

If the combined company could maintain its former multiple of 25 times fully diluted earnings, which would in turn depend on maintenance of its growth rate, the stock would move to $67 near term. On this basis, the debentures, assuming no premium over conversion value, would sell at $126 per $100 face value. This, Michael concluded, would be equivalent to $6.30 per share of Anglo Norness. If he added back the $1 million which he had lopped off Zapata's earnings projection for 1968, earnings went to $2.80, the stock to $70, and the bonds to $132, which was $6.60 per Anglo share. Finally, slightly further out, Zapata had projected $12 million internally for 1969, based on rig contracts coming in later during 1968. On this basis, earnings would be $3.10 fully diluted, the stock $78, and the bonds $148, equal to $7.40 per Anglo share.

Finally, Michael calculated that for the Zapata offer to equate with the Occidental offer of $4.50, the bonds would have to sell at $90 per $100 face. On this basis, the stock would be at $47½, again assuming no premium. For this to happen, the multiple would have to fall to 18 times the conservative estimate, 17 times Zapata's projected EPS, and 15 times the 1969 expectation. Given the multiples applied to the rest of the offshore industry, he considered it unlikely that even with the addition of the speculative Anglo Norness to the portfolio, Zapata's multiple would fall much below 20 times fully diluted earnings.

Expressed in a different way, if the $4.50 Occidental offer was compared with $6.30 as Zapata's offer, for the latter to be equal to or worse than the former there would have to be a joint probability of only 70% that both the earnings and the multiple would turn out as expected. The earnings estimate appeared to be about 95% certain, given the 10% adjustment of Zapata's projection. The multiple was less sure. If the market valued Anglo's contribution at 10 times earnings, then the weighted average attached to the combined company should be about 19.5 times. This was still higher than the break even of 18 times derived above.

Capital International S.A.*

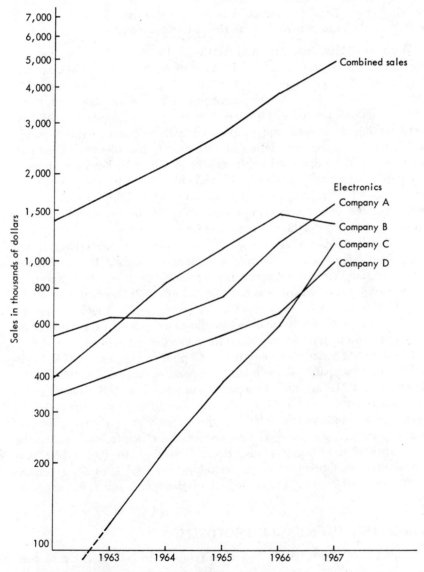

THIS CHART shows the sales performance during the last five years of four small specialized electronics companies, all from different European countries. We may have a possible opportunity of merging these four companies into one larger multinational corporation. I would like to discuss this proposition. During the next few weeks, we should reach a decision on whether or not to proceed, and, if so, how? Also, I should like to use our discussions for a consideration of mergers and the so-called merger movement in Europe. Particularly, I should like to discuss whether the concept on which the current proposition is based is viable, not just in this specific instance, but also for other European companies and industries.

With this statement, Mr. Ken Mathysen-Gerst opened a meeting of the Capital International S.A. (CI-SA) staff on August 25, 1967. Several subsequent staff meetings were devoted to this merger proposition. Mr. Mathysen-Gerst visited all four companies to discuss his plans with them. Their reactions ranged from moderate to great enthusiasm. All four were willing to explore the proposition and cooperate with a survey by CI-SA. Until the completion of this survey, the identity of no participant would be disclosed to the others. Afterwards, however, the survey would be made available to all, and this study plus reciprocal visits would permit a decision to be reached on the feasibility of the proposition. Exhibit 1, which was also presented during the initial staff meeting, provides some basic data on the four companies.

Mr. Mathysen-Gerst, age 39, a tall, lean American, formerly of Dutch citizenship, who spoke with precise sentences couched in quiet tones, was managing director of Capital International S.A., Geneva. Upon graduating from the Harvard Business School in 1959, he had joined the Capital Research and Management Company in Los Angeles. Here he had become increasingly involved in the management of European investments, and in 1962 he was asked to open a Geneva office.

CI-SA was a Swiss subsidiary of the Capital Group, Inc., a U.S. financial holding company whose principal operating subsidiary, the Capital Research and Management Company, managed four U.S. mutual funds with assets in excess of $1 billion. At one time it had managed an international fund, which, following the imposition of the U.S. interest equalization tax, was merged into one of the other funds because the tax destroyed the necessary investment flexibility. In 1967 CI-SA was providing a variety of services, including financial consulting related to mergers and acquisitions on behalf of European and U.S. corporate clients.

ORIGIN OF THE MERGER PROPOSITION

During early 1967, CI-SA had been retained by a U.S. client to conduct an acquisitions search in the European electronics industry. During this search, CI-SA had contacted 420 smaller companies, 80 of which

EXHIBIT 1
Information on the four electronics companies°

Company	A	B	C	D	Pro forma consolidated
Location	Germany	Sweden	Italy	Belgium	EEC-EFTA
Exports as a percentage of sales..............	25%	20%	15%	10%	n.a.
Market share at home.........	70%	45%	55%	90%†	n.a.
1967 forecasts (in thousands of dollars)					
Sales.................	$1,530	$1,320	$1,100	$1,000	$4,950
Net earnings.............	170	75	30	35	310
Cash earnings ....,.......	225	155	50	60	490
Financial condition (in thousands of dollars)					
Long-term debt...........	...	$ 320	$ 165	...	$ 485
Net worth..............	$1,375	453	175	$ 155	2,148
Total...............	$1,375	$ 773	$ 340	$ 155	$2,633

Product information

Company A had three product lines, with closed-circuit TV accounting for the major part of sales. The core of certain process controls, made and supplied to a leading industrial equipment manufacturer, and parts for telemetry systems rounded out its $1.5 million sales total.

Company B had achieved sales of $1.3 million on one product line, that is, motor controls mostly for industrial uses. The recent dip in sales had been due to the recent completion of a major one-time defense contract. Throughout 1966–67 commercial sales continued to increase. An upswing in the sales trend was predicted for the future. The company had a manufacturing and sales subsidiary in the Netherlands.

Company C specialized exclusively in machine tool controls with sales of $1.1 million. It had recently obtained an important contract from a major German machine tool manufacturer.

Company D produced three product lines but had most of its strength in hospital intercom systems. Closely related general intercom systems and a later addition, language labs, accounted for the remainder of its $1 million sales. It had obtained some major orders for 1968 delivery to German and French hospitals.

*Product lines have been disguised. Percentages have been rounded.
†For hospital intercom systems.
n.a. = not available
Source: CI-SA internal memorandum.

had warranted more thorough study. After this search had been completed, the U.S. client in the summer of 1967 had entered into negotiations with a Belgian company having sales of approximately $15 million. The client had decided to give priority to acquisition candidates with more than $10 million in sales.

In conducting the search, Mr. Mathysen-Gerst had been surprised by the large number of successful companies in the European electronics industry. These companies, he said, were characterized by excellent technology, specialization in a single product or product line, strong entrepreneurial owner managers (but weak second-line management and lack of control systems), rapid growth, and a predominantly national focus. On the basis of his investigations, Mr. Mathysen-Gerst became even more convinced that the much talked-about technology gap between Europe and the United States was vastly exaggerated. If any gap was revealed by the CI-SA search, it was in terms of management depth, organizational structure, and control systems.

Many of the companies investigated appeared to have excellent opportunities for growth. Most had already grown from small, garage-type operations to $1 million companies—still, however, run by their owner managers as one-man shows. Further growth was expected to take these companies into the $10 million range, at which point a larger and more formally structured organization would be required. Among these companies, some saw their future growth as going beyond their present policy of selling, in essence, a single product to their own national market. These companies were anxious to sell in other European countries as well and thus to capitalize more fully on their technological leadership. In addition, a number of firms contemplated diversifying at home, thereby reducing the risk of reliance on a single product.

Mr. Mathysen-Gerst identified the major hurdles to continued rapid expansion of these small, successful electronics companies as follows: (1) a shortage of financial resources, (2) a shortage of qualified management, and (3) the difficulty of repeating their success in different countries or product segments. One means of overcoming these hurdles was merger with a larger company. Mr. Mathysen-Gerst had argued this point in generating interest in a takeover by his U.S. corporate client. He had discovered, however, that a number of companies were not interested in takeover by a corporate giant but would consider joining forces with companies of similar size. This discovery led Mr. Mathysen-Gerst to his merger proposition.

EUROPEAN ELECTRONICS INDUSTRY

In 1967 sales of the electronics industry in Europe were estimated at about $9.5 billion, compared with $22 billion in the United States. Giants like Philips or Siemens were operating side by side with literally hundreds of small companies, some of which were successful while others were barely surviving. The large number of companies was in part a result of the marked segmentation of the industry. This, in turn, was caused by the tremendous breadth of technology employed. For example, cores for magnets were as much a part of this industry as circuits printed directly on cardboard. Each market segment, ranging from $500,000 to some $200 million, was served by from 1 to 50 companies with sales between $500,000 and $30 million. A sales breakdown by country for eight major product categories is provided in Exhibit 2; within these categories were 82 segments, 28 of which were components.

In addition to product segmentation, there was also segmentation

EXHIBIT 2
Five-country electronics markets—1967 (in millions of dollars)

	Belgium	Nether-lands	Italy	Sweden	Ger-many	Total	Europe total*
1. Consumer products . . .	46.8	46.3	257.0	55.5	462.2	867.8	1,642.8
2. Medical equipment	9.6	8.3	5.8	7.5	46.8	78.0	144.9
3. Communications, of which	67.2	72.8	108.8	63.9	453.0	765.7	1,552.8
a) Closed-circuit TV . .	0.7	0.6	2.0	0.4	4.8	8.5	19.6
b) Intercom and sound systems	3.2	5.0	6.6	3.9	24.9	43.6	123.9
4. Computer and related†	43.1	50.1	127.0	42.3	291.1	553.6	1,121.7
5. Nuclear	9.0	10.7	9.3	7.0	21.1	57.1	103.4
6. Industrial equipment, of which	79.9	76.1	86.3	67.5	296.9	606.7	1,096.6
a) Machine tool controls	8.2	9.5	11.3	10.0	33.0	72.0	133.4
b) Motor controls	8.5	8.0	5.5	5.8	25.8	53.6	88.0
c) Power supplies	11.3	11.0	10.5	10.1	22.7	65.6	119.4
d) Process controls . . .	35.0	34.0	38.0	31.0	110.0	248.0	460.5
7. Test and measuring instruments	38.4	51.4	49.8	37.5	125.2	302.3	532.0
8. Components	95.7	154.7	194.8	103.2	679.5	1,227.9	2,498.7
Total	389.7	470.4	838.8	384.4	2,375.8	4,459.1	8,692.9

*Does not include the "smaller European electronics markets" of Austria, Ireland, Greece, etc.,
which totaled about $814 million, giving a "total Europe" figure of $9,506 million.
†Not including process control systems.
Source: *Electronics*, December 26, 1966.

by countries. Most companies confined their activities to their national market. This policy was due, at least in part, to the producers' substantial dependence on sales to their governments and other public authorities. In some instances, "relationships" were essential to making these sales. Even in arm's length situations, special skills and experience were required for submitting a standard government bid. Compounded by problems of language and culture, these factors made it difficult to market in other countries, even for companies with product leadership.

During the late 1950s and the 1960s, the electronics industry had grown rapidly, doubling in size every four or five years. Growth was highly uneven, however, from one product segment to another. Annual gains ranged from 2%–4% on some consumer products, such as radios, to 35% for highly sophisticated systems and control equipment. For 1967, *Electronics*[1] magazine predicted an industry growth of 8%, or twice the rate of the GNP, with the rates for different segments ranging from −1.5% in consumer products to +27% in industrial controls. Besides

[1] By the end of 1967, the total industry growth rate had slowed from the peak of the early 1960s.

varying among product segments, growth rates also varied among countries, as suggested by the following figures for 1966–67:

Country	Electronics industry	Components sector	Nuclear equipment sector
Germany	+8%	+15%	+1%
Italy	+15%–20%	+9%	–10%

The differences in growth rates among both product segments and countries resulted primarily from different rates of technological change and different product life cycles. Government programs and policies, for example, in defense or health also helped to account for varying patterns among countries.

THE MERGER CONCEPT

Mr. Mathysen-Gerst's merger concept, which he referred to as "project synergistics," was based on five criteria. First, the participating companies were to be of equal size. This requirement ran counter to what appeared to be the trend in mergers, whereby larger companies absorbed smaller ones. The reason for this criterion was that no single partner should dominate or control the merged unit during its initial stages.

Second, all participating companies would have to be healthy. This requirement, too, appeared contrary to common merger practice. In many instances, companies in trouble seemed to be the most eager to find partners or the most likely to be regarded as a possible candidate for merger. For project synergistics, on the other hand, the members were to be leaders in their segment of the electronics industry. They had to be profitable and in good financial standing, and they had to offer the prospect of continued rapid growth. The reasons for this requirement were that the merger had to be forward-looking—oriented toward attacking new opportunities than toward correcting old mistakes. Also, rapid growth would facilitate digestion of the inevitable merger adjustments, inasmuch as a growth situation would provide opportunities for all parties concerned. Further, rapid growth would permit the newly merged unit to establish its new identity early. Growth would require major adjustments and changes by the participating companies anyway, and therefore these adjustments might as well occur within the framework of the merger. Finally, a growing company was seen as a major attraction in obtaining the manpower needed to meet future opportunities.

Third, the member companies had to be small. In these it was felt that the synergistic effects would be strongest. Also, small companies would have to change, at any rate in terms of management organization, if they were to digest further growth. If, instead of moving from domination by the owner manager to a functional setup, they moved directly to a divisional organization, the problems of adjustment would perhaps be no more grave. In fact, such problems might be less severe, since, with a divisional structure, the conduct and organization of the operating units could be geared to the personalities involved. Also, such a structure might facilitate attracting and training the manpower needed to cope with future growth opportunities, particularly those involving product diversification or establishment of operations in different countries.

Fourth, the participating companies had to be engaged in different product segments. This requirement, again, appeared contrary to the current trend, which featured mergers among companies in identical lines. Spreading of risk was one argument for this criterion, since the resulting company would be less vulnerable to technological change. Moreover, the varying growth patterns of each segment would possibly average out, thus giving the merged company a less cyclical pattern of its own. Furthermore, with participants active in different product lines, the turmoil resulting from a merger would be reduced. For example, if four companies making, say, transformers should be merged, the manufacturing, marketing, and R & D activities of each of the four would have to be integrated and coordinated in order to reduce unnecessary overlap and benefit from possible economies of scale. Such moves would have major implications, sometimes negative, for the people involved. Such action would not be required for companies in different product lines. Mr. Mathysen-Gerst was skeptical, in any case, of the alleged positive results of merging companies in the same line, especially of alleged economies of scale. Given the small size, even when combined, of the companies he was considering, he believed economies of scale would be negligible.

Fifth, the participating companies would have to be from different countries. Again, this requirement was different from the prevailing trend. Except for Agfa-Gevaert,[2] few examples of mergers across national boundaries were known. The purpose of this requirement was to achieve area as well as product diversification. Also, having partners in different countries would create a beachhead in each of them. With each participating company remaining a national unit while also belonging to the merged parent, government sales, not just of the products of the

---

[2] In 1964 Agfa and Gevaert, German and Belgian companies, respectively, merged their photographic interests, allegedly to compete more effectively with Kodak. However, both companies maintained separate corporate headquarters, and as of 1967 the operations of the two companies were far from fully integrated. Also, without a European corporation law, the merger raised complicated legal questions.

local company but of those of the other partners as well, might be facilitated.

MERGER PROCEDURE

In the area of merger procedures, Mr. Mathysen-Gerst identified five issues about which he was especially concerned. First, he wanted to determine what critical questions should be investigated in the CI-SA survey. In this connection, he had already begun work on a questionnaire to be used as a basis of the investigations he would have to conduct in each company before a decision could be reached on the operational feasibility of the merger negotiations. Among the points to be particularly investigated was how well each proposed participant measured up in terms of the criterion of health. Mr. Mathysen-Gerst had already defined health in terms of technological excellence and product leadership, profitability and financial strength, as well as rapid growth. In addition, he felt that no company should have a severely retarded functional capability in marketing, manufacturing, or R & D. He realized, however, that these conditions required further elaboration. Also, he was wondering whether this evaluation should not be made by an independent firm possessing the necessary technical expertise.

A second issue was the formula by which each partner's share in the merged venture would be determined. Should shares be based exclusively on earnings? If so, it might penalize those partners who had invested more heavily in R & D and marketing, both possibly key factors for future success. In addition to earnings, what other elements should be included in the formula? And what time span should be used? Also, to what extent should past performance determine each company's share as against projected future performance? For example, some companies might argue that they had new developments just around the corner which would greatly increase their future relative contribution. As one way to resolve their particular dilemma, Mr. Mathysen-Gerst was considering a "55% now—45% later" exchange of stock procedure. That is, 55% of the shares of the separate units would be exchanged immediately for shares of the merged company, with the formula applied on past performance. The remaining 45% would be exchanged in three to five years, with the formula applying to the results of this additional period.

A third issue related to the raising of additional funds. Mr. Mathysen-Gerst expected to find four to six additional shareholders who would be able to contribute between $1 million and $1.5 million to the merged unit. This outside money would provide additional funds to take advantage of growth opportunities. Also, the new shareholders could contribute potential contacts for obtaining new business and could permit easier debt financing. With this purpose in mind, Mr. Mathysen-Gerst had already approached a few potentially active shareholders, such as some European banks and individuals willing to invest venture capital. Their initial response had been encouraging.

A fourth issue was the compensation arrangement for CI-SA. In a number of instances, CI-SA proceeded on the basis of a fixed *per diem* compensation, while in others its compensation had been contingent upon the success of its search and related to the price of the acquisition. In the interest of project synergistics, Mr. Mathysen-Gerst was thinking of taking CI-SA's compensation in the form of stock in the merged unit. Thus, CI-SA would see a return for its extensive efforts only if the venture succeeded. However, Mr. Mathysen-Gerst hoped to develop a stock-option plan which would give CI-SA a very handsome return in case of success. In addition, he expected to request some "earnest" money from the participating firms. Even though this sum would be only a minor contribution to expenses, it would provide an early indication as to the seriousness of the participants. Given the small size of the companies involved, the payment of even a small amount of earnest money was expected to make the owner managers pause to consider whether they really wanted to proceed.

Fifth, Mr. Mathysen-Gerst wanted to proceed on the basis of a definite timetable. He was inclined to move rapidly, on the premise that speed allowed him to test the sincerity of the parties involved and would prevent tying up CI-SA's resources for an extended period. Exhibit 3

EXHIBIT 3
Capital International's timetable for project synergistics

September 22	Deliver in person detailed survey questionnaire to four participants requiring complete disclosure of all relevant data and information.
October 4	Return questionnaires to CI-SA.
October 9–14	Review and clarify each questionnaire through personal meetings.
October 18	Send to all participants copies of all completed and clarified questionnaires plus consolidation of all relevant financial and operational data.
October 23	Joint visit to Company A in Germany.
24	Joint visit to Company B in Sweden.
25	Joint visit to Company D in Belgium.
26	Joint visit to Company C in Italy.
27	Joint review.*
November 3	*Go/no go decision* regarding operational feasibility of project synergistics.
November 5	Companies pay $2,000 into joint pool to cover legal/organizational costs of project.
November 25	Capital International S.A. mails detailed financial proposal to all participants.
December 1–4	Capital International S.A. reviews financial proposal with each participant individually.
December 9	Geneva conference. Joint examination of financial proposals; reexamination of operational and management aspects.
December 15	*Final go/no go decision*, involving firm commitment to project synergistics.
February 15	Complete legal organization.
March 1	Start.

* These formally organized reviews will be followed during November by individually organized visits of each participant to the others.
Source: CI-SA internal memorandum.

provides a tentative timetable which he planned to submit to the managers of the four companies.

SYNERGISTIC EXPECTATIONS

Mr. Mathysen-Gerst did not expect that project synergistics would benefit from the traditional synergistic effects commonly attributed to mergers in textbooks: for example, economies of scale in manufacturing, R & D, and possibly marketing. Rather, he expected synergistic benefits in terms of organization, internationalization, and finance—all relatively weak areas in small electronics companies. In terms of organization, he hoped for one thing to create a base big enough to support planning and control capabilities. Bringing together four healthy companies with relatively strong functional capacities would help to achieve this objective. (Mr. Mathysen-Gerst's tentative evaluation of the functional capabilities of the merger candidates, as presented to the August 25 staff meeting, is presented in Exhibit 4.) Another organizational gain was expected to arise from the ability of the merged company, especially if successful, to attract qualified management personnel.

In terms of internationalization, the synergistic benefit would come through the assistance which each member could provide the others in his own home market. Such help would permit the partners to become international more rapidly than if each were to proceed independently.

In terms of finance, the merged units were expected to have easier access to capital markets, thus removing lack of funds as a major constraint on future growth. Another financial benefit was seen in the possibility that the merged unit might create "paper" for future acquisitions. Moreover, through the merger, marketability of the stock currently held by the owner managers in their own firms would be greatly facilitated. Finally, CI-SA's continued involvement in the merged unit was also expected to contribute to the financial synergistic benefits.

OUTLOOK

In a memo prepared for a September 5 staff meeting, Mr. Mathysen-Gerst stated the objectives, goals, and philosophy of project synergistics as follows:

Objective

To create a successful multinational enterprise. Success to be measured by:

a) Rapid growth in sales (at least 30% per year over the next three years) and increase in the share of the market.

b) Return on investment sufficient to finance internal growth and produce rapid growth in earnings per share (commensurate with sales growth).

c) Assured long-term continuity and viability (measured by management in depth, job satisfactions, new product flow, etc.).

Specific medium-term goal

Attainment of a profitable sales volume of $100 million in 1978, half through internal growth and half through acquisitions (the latter to accelerate growth in earnings per share).

EXHIBIT 4
Capabilities of the four companies and expected synergy flow

Company Location		A Germany	B Sweden	C Italy	D Belgium
Tentative ranking of *functional capabilities**					
R & D		2	1	1	4
Manufacturing.		1	3	2	2
Marketing		3	4	3	1
Control.		4	2	4	3

	To	SYNERGY FLOW			
		(7) A	(6) B	(8) C	(11) D
From A (10)	R & D		+	++	++
	Manufacturing		+	+	+
	Marketing		0	+	+
B (8)	R & D	+		+	+
	Manufacturing	+		+	+
	Marketing	0		+	+
C (9)	R & D	++	+		+
	Manufacturing	0	0		+
	Marketing	+	++		++
D (4)	R & D	+	0	0	
	Manufacturing	0	0	0	
	Marketing	+	+	+	
Controller	Cost acctg. Mgt. info. system	+++	+++	+++	+++
Board of management	Policy: strategy	+++	+++	+++	+++

+++ Extremely high synergy.
++ High synergy.
+ Some synergy.
0 Little, if any, synergy.

Other plus factors not shown: CI-SA's continuing involvement in: (*a*) acquisition/search program, (*b*) external financing, (*c*) U.S. and Japanese connections.

* Rankings went from a top figure of 1 down to 4.

EXHIBIT 4 (*continued*)

Comments:

The four companies have been selected from a group of 35 potential candidates. They have been chosen not only because of their product leadership in their home markets but also in view of the apparent high caliber of the owner managers. Aged respectively 37, 45, 47, and 50, the latter have all founded their own companies with very limited financial resources: the Belgian company about 15 years ago, although its major product line is only about five years old; the German company about 10 years ago; and the Swedish and Italian companies approximately five years ago. Three of the owner managers have advanced engineering degrees, while two of them have worked in the United States with well-known and leading electronics companies. Three of them are proficient in English, while the fourth understands that language. In addition to English and their national language, some of them speak other languages as well. One of the owner managers flies his own plane. My preliminary investigation indicates that they are self-starters and open-minded, as well as aggressive and resourceful entrepreneurs.

These companies are quite dependent on their owner managers. Such companies are usually strongest in the area where the one man has strength; and although these companies show a better than average development of supporting management, given that they are one-man shows, the loss of the owner manager would be a severe enough blow to necessitate exclusion from further negotiations. There are holes in second-line management and certainly a lack of competent successors. There is little delegation, and hence little attention has been given to formal systems in three key areas: reporting, controlling, and planning.

The German and Belgian companies have developed especially good relations and high sales to the public authorities. However, overall, the Belgian company is strongest in marketing in my tentative ranking of functional abilities. In R & D both the Swedish and the Italian companies are strong, while the German R & D effort is second only to its excellent manufacturing capabilities. The control function is rather less well developed, with only the Swedish company showing much strength. On the whole, the overall marketing function shows the inherent weaknesses expected in a technically oriented industry where manufacturing and R & D claim primary importance.

Source: CI-SA internal memorandum.

Underlying business policy

1. Products to have a satisfactory price-value relationship and to be designed to meet a definite and useful market need.
2. Business to be managed in accordance with high ethical standards relative to customers, dealers, suppliers, employees, the public (thus assume full tax burden), and shareholders.
3. Modest internal R & D to be heavily supplemented by obtaining university support, outside R & D contracts, and licensing—all to insure an adequate flow of new products, without committing a disproportionate share of total resources to R & D.
4. The companies' interests to be interwoven firmly and irrevocably to insure that owner managers will work toward common objectives.

The working paper, while setting a goal of $100 million in sales by 1978, also included a first target of $10 million by 1970. During the staff discussions, the question arose whether this was a realistic expectation. Some staff members argued that it was too ambitious, others that it was too modest. If internationalization really were achieved, companies might be able at a maximum to duplicate their national performance in the other countries covered by project synergistics. For example, since the four-nation market served by the group was 10 times as big as the home market of the Swedish member, the latter would be able to increase its size 10 times if it could repeat its past local performance elsewhere. Even though no one at CI-SA argued this optimistically, some did feel that a member firm could achieve a market share in its partners' countries of one third to one half of its market share at home. If so, the growth rate of the merged company would clearly exceed the target set in the working paper. As a result, the question was raised whether the target was not too modest, particularly in terms of the $1 to $1.5 million which Mr. Mathysen-Gerst was planning to raise.

A further question raised about the potential growth of the merged unit was that of future balance. Should equality among the units be maintained, or should it be possible for one division to dominate the others as a result of more rapid growth? This issue was viewed as particularly relevant for as long as the last 45% of the shares was still to be distributed.

The working paper stated the organizational plans as follows:

1. Engage a controller-treasurer to develop and implement an appropriate cost accounting system and a high-speed (EDP) management information system.
2. Constitute a board of management, to consist of four company managers plus a controller (the latter to act in part as a lubricant to smooth management relations and in part, if necessary, as an action expediter). This board should meet (*a*) regularly twice a month for one day on a rotating country basis; (*b*) irregularly, whenever special action was required.
3. Constitute a board of directors composed of four individual company owner managers, plus Mathysen-Gerst as *administrateur délégué*[3] until 1970, plus four outside investors.
   Note: *a*) Shareholders to have right of cumulative voting (at least for the next five years).
   b) Shareholders to elect board of directors.
   c) Directors to elect board of management.
   d) Owner managers to be assured of a seat on the board of directors through the cumulative voting, but not necessarily on the top board of management.
4. In 1970, sales should have reached $10 million, the management information system should be operative, and the evolution from confederate to federate management structure should be about two-thirds completed. Action: Take over the remaining 45% of the shares, and the board of directors elect the president of the board of managers.

Several issues concerning the organization of the merged unit were raised during the staff meetings. Organizational plans had been based on the following premises: (1) that rapid growth would result in upward mobility to jobs created as they become needed, (2) that management would thus have to develop replacements, and (3) that the company would as a result find it easier to attract capable manpower. However, would it be possible for successful entrepreneurs to grow into skillful general managers? Would previously independent owners be able to work with and take advantage of a controller? And would the collegial

---

[3] Member of the board of directors and president of board of management.

management setup work? Also, was the assumption on the development of a chief executive a sound one, namely, that he would emerge through the process of natural selection? The fear was expressed that healthy motivation might degenerate into destructive competition. Also, would it be possible for the four one-man shows to make the transition to a divisional structure? Particularly, would it be possible for the units to organize for cooperation and coordination?

In reviewing the outlook of the merger proposal with his staff, Mr. Mathysen-Gerst stressed his enthusiasm for the merger concept but also indicated that many obstacles would have to be surmounted in its implementation. Hence he assigned a high risk of failure to the project. However, he hoped that his time input could be limited to 20 days prior to the "go/no go" decision on the project. On this basis, he felt that even if a no-go decision should result, the experience gained in working with small companies and with the various elements involved in merging European firms across their national boundaries would prove beneficial. More importantly, Mr. Mathysen-Gerst believed that meaningful economic integration in Europe would inevitably require the creation of multinational European companies. For some time he had seen a major opportunity for CI-SA in contributing to this development. During the last few years he had been deeply involved in several attempts to merge major and well-known European companies from different countries. On the basis of this experience, Mr. Mathysen-Gerst was very much aware of the numerous obstacles. One seemingly insurmountable hurdle had been the difficulty of changing the national scope and outlook of large, well-established, tradition-bound organizations. In view of these difficulties, he was anxious to explore the potential of merging small, dynamic companies across national boundaries—companies whose organizational structure and physical facilities were still evolving. If this merger concept were to prove promising, Mr. Mathysen-Gerst envisaged that CI-SA's activities could be broadened to include merger assistance to smaller companies in capitalizing on the business opportunities provided by European economic integration.

CASES FOR PART II

The general manager
as organization builder

GENERAL MANAGEMENT IN THE FUNCTIONAL ORGANIZATION

Mystic Electronics Co., Inc. (A)

TOD ARMSTRONG, president of Mystic Electronics Co., Inc., viewed with mixed feelings the weekly staff meeting scheduled that afternoon, February 15, 1974. Although the company had met or exceeded his highest expectations in its first 23 months of operation, Armstrong had become increasingly aware of the impediments to continued growth as sales approached the $3 million mark. The problems seemed to him to lie in materials control and manufacturing. On the basis of the daily production report placed on his desk that morning, he feared that output would fall well below the planned amount for the third consecutive month. The staff meeting represented another opportunity to thrash out the difficulties contributing to these results. Previous meetings, however, had been marked by heated and often confused debate, which left Armstrong ill at ease. Yet he had immediate plans for expansion and was anxious to resolve the existing problems quickly and conclusively.

A personal note

Owning and managing a business had been Tod Armstrong's goal for a long time. He first became enamored with the idea during a four-year stint as a mechanical engineer for a small ($400,000 in sales) but extremely profitable ferrite core manufacturer. He left the company to enter business school in 1963 and two years later went to work for an entrepreneur who was involved in a number of small enterprises. The job proved frustrating, however, and Armstrong decided to try the big company route as one of the three men in the new product development department of USM, a large manufacturing company. Some months later, he scraped together a few thousand dollars and, with a business school classmate, acquired a small distressed furniture company in Mystic, Connecticut. For two years they struggled to breathe new life into the business with only meager results, at which point Armstrong sold his interest.

Armstrong commented on his subsequent activities:

I liked the Mystic area and had just settled in. For a while I dabbled in real estate in partnership with a radio station owner and even had a radio show on his station. Then my brother-in-law, an investment banker, told me to look up one of his clients, Elonics, an electronic components manufacturer in Mystic. The company was doing poorly and the bankers had just put in a new president. By the time I got there all the important positions had been filled. But the president said he'd find a place for me, and for the next two years I knocked around the company in middle management jobs. I helped with materials control and for a time was purchasing director for the Mystic plant. The vice president of manufacturing and I didn't get along very well, so when the vice president of sales asked me if I'd like to manage the sales service function in late 1971 I agreed.

Opportunity presents itself

Elonics was one of three full-line capacitor manufacturers in the United States and had at one time been the largest. Under a succession of managements, however, the company's facilities and market position had deteriorated steadily until by 1971 many of the lines produced in Mystic seemed to be in trouble. From his vantage point in sales service, Armstrong sensed that a decision had been made to concentrate on the strongest product line, AC oil capacitors, which accounted for most of the production in the Mystic facility.

Every afternoon at 5:00 we had a meeting to discuss quotes on potential new business. It became clear that when film, mica, and electrolytic capacitors were discussed, the sales people didn't want the business. They were careful not to hurt their regular customers, but otherwise would either not bid or submit a bid at three times the expected price.

Then in late February I read in a major financial journal that the company had set up an $800,000 reserve and was going to write off all the assets for the three lines. It also said that Elonics was losing $500,000 a year on them. The business had really gone downhill; before the bottom fell out in 1970, Elonics had sales as high as $4 million in these lines. I knew nothing about capacitors, but I went to see the sales vice president the next morning and said, "I'll buy the film and mica lines." (I wish now I'd included the electrolytic line as well.) He sent me over to the vice president of finance, and I told him, "I'll give you $50,000 for the assets." He said that was ridiculous, that he needed at least a quarter of a million, and wouldn't talk to me.

As I mulled the deal over during the next couple of days, it occurred to me that what he wanted was 50 cents on the dollar, so I went back and offered it to him with the provision that I would pay for the inventory only as I used it. He said O.K. but that the equipment was on the books for $160,000— "Where are you going to get $80,000?" Anyway, he indicated they would make an equipment inventory by the next Wednesday.

Late that Wednesday, I called and was told the inventory had been "messed up." I checked around and found that the books showed only $100,000. For another week they worked on it and finally came up with $146,000. I asked a lot of questions and we finally settled on $130,000. It was not so amicable.

On March 12, Armstrong signed a letter of intent which gave him three weeks to raise the necessary funds. In addition to the $65,000 required to purchase the equipment, he estimated that he needed $20,000 immediately for work-in-process inventory and another $5,000 for miscellaneous expenses.

As part of the deal he agreed to lease 25,000 square feet in the rear portion of the old 446,000-square-foot Elonics plant, a former textile mill, at a modest figure with an option for another 25,000 square feet. The space was easily sufficient for the existing operation which then employed 100 hourly and supervisory personnel. Armstrong also knew that, because it required large-scale expensive equipment, he would have to rely on Elonics for the critical impregnating step[1] required on about 20% of the output (a service Elonics agreed to provide at cost).

Time was of the essence. When Armstrong first began to negotiate for the two product lines, the backlog stood at $180,000; he attempted, without sucess, to obtain a guarantee that it would be at least $100,000 at the closing date. However, production was increased as Elonics ate into the more profitable orders, in some cases preshipping up to six months of standard items to major customers.

By the time Armstrong closed the deal, the backlog was $60,000. Normal monthly shipments in 1971 had been about $100,000 for film and $30,000 for mica capacitors. Moreover, for over a month, sales and service to the trade had been virtually nonexistent, customers were actively considering other suppliers, and Elonics sales reps and distributors were openly despondent.

Financing the venture

Once the letter of intent had been signed, Armstrong had two major challenges: raising capital and building an organization to manage the

---

[1] Certain capacitors, typically those made of paper, were impregnated with wax, oil, or resin to reduce the moisture in the device which would otherwise destroy its electrical properties.

newly christened Mystic Electronics Company. His first approach to the financing area was to prepare a cash-flow estimate for the next 12 months. The figures indicated a break-even profit posture with sales of about $1 million and a small positive cash flow from operations. The dramatic reduction in the losses suffered by Elonics was accounted for in large part by more realistic overhead rates,[2] the inventory purchased at half cost, and closer control over expenses.

With the pro forma cash flow in hand, Armstrong approached Walter Heller, Talcott, and others who might provide funds to be secured by accounts receivable, but the finance companies wanted more information. Next he considered a commerical loan, only to be told by the loan officer at the local bank that the proposition was too risky and by the Boston bankers that it was too small for them to consider.

With the three-week option fast expiring, Armstrong happened upon a new means of financing:

The loan officer at the First National Bank of Mystic showed me a flyer on THE Insurance Company. They offered to guarantee commercial bank loans based on an appraisal of the assets to be pledged as collateral, for an appraisal fee of 1% of the assessed value and 2% annually of the outstanding loan guarantee. I called the company, and two men came down to do an appraisal. It took us two days to find all of the equipment—it was all over the building—and I got to know them pretty well. When it was completed, they agreed to recommend a guarantee for a $75,000 three-year loan. I borrowed another $10,000 personally on a property mortgage and went to a second bank to ask for the last $5,000. They went along.

With the purchase and startup funds secured, Armstrong was then able to enter into an agreement with a local factor to finance up to 80% of verified accounts receivable for a 2% fee.

Assembling the management team

Armstrong summarized his initial thinking on management needs by stating: "I had the idea that there were two important positions—sales and production. I would handle either one and hire somebody to do the other.",However, a friend at Elonics warned him that he would not have time to manage a function as well as the overall company, and Armstrong, impressed by this reasoning, set out to locate managers for both positions.

For the sales job, Armstrong telephoned Ned Troy, then 47, an acquaintance who for 22 years had been a popular and successful salesman for Elonics. He had been transferred to a marketing job shortly after the new management took over, and in late 1971 was terminated. In March

---

[2] Elonics applied overhead as a percentage of direct labor dollars. Since the paper, film, and mica capacitors were more labor intensive than the larger AC oil line, they tended to absorb a disproportionately higher share of the overhead.

1972, he was working for another electronic components company in Philadelphia and commuting to his home in Mystic every other weekend. Troy commented on his status at the time:

I was unable to agree with the new marketing manager at Elonics. He worked quite late every night and expected others to do the same regardless of productivity. He criticized me once for not having company people to a party. But the company was not my whole life. I had two children about to go to college and a great many friends in town.

When Tod called, I had to be careful because I badly wanted to work back in Mystic. But I also had major reservations about the idea because of the history of Elonics and because I was determined to give my new employer his money's worth. I had mixed emotions but was impressed by Tod's thorough planning, the cash flows, and so forth.

After a second discussion during which Armstrong offered Troy $425 a week (Armstrong had decided to draw $350 a week himself), Troy indicated that he would decide before the IEEE convention on March 15 so that, were he to accept, an announcement to the trade could be made at that time.

Concurrently Armstrong took steps to locate a manufacturing manager. His adviser at Elonics suggested Abe Steiner, then 59, a man who for nearly 40 years had worked in various capacities at Elonics, most recently as production manager in the film and paper capacitor area. For a brief time some years before, he had been in charge of manufacturing for the entire Mystic plant. Steiner had been released just prior to Armstrong's employment and, after a brief stint as production manager for a small braided rug manufacturer and another as a maintenance foreman, was unemployed. He was described to Armstrong as "a driver, maybe not long on diplomacy, but maybe the sort of guy you need." Armstrong recalled the ensuing events in these terms:

I called Abe in Brooklyn where he was visiting relatives and waiting for the IEEE convention to begin in New York, and we met at the airport over a cup of coffee. I offered him the job at $200 a week. He said, "Yep, I'm ready." Then he drove me to the Essex House where I was going to meet with the sales representatives. Five minutes before the meeting, I called Ned, who said that his boss was off sailing somewhere but that he had talked to his boss' wife, and it was O.K. for me to tell the reps that he was joining Mystic. When I had my 30-minute session with the reps, they were ecstatic. The purpose of the meeting was to sell them our line—only one didn't sign up.

The remaining jobs were then quickly filled. Paul McCosh, the "mica king" (for the previous 15 years, he had been responsible for the mica capacitor line), agreed to stay on. Bob Merritt, formerly in production control for Elonics, accepted a position as materials control manager. Dick Curtis from the Elonics purchasing department became purchasing manager, though he had not bought production items heretofore. The quality control manager for the acquired lines agreed to join Mystic in a similar capacity. As for engineering, Armstrong concluded that little investment should or could be made in new or dramatically redesigned products. Consequently, he hired only one engineer, Ed Norris, to concentrate on spec issuance and minor adaptations of existing items. In addition, McCosh, who appeared to have some natural engineering talent, was encouraged to extend his efforts in this direction.

Only finance and accounting then remained. Armstrong decided that he could perform these functions himself for a time, assisted by his secretary who was to double as a bookkeeper. He also secured the advice of a local accountant on the type of ledgers and records to maintain.

Startup

Steiner returned to Mystic immediately and began to line up foremen and supervisory personnel from the soon-to-be-disbanded Elonics film and mica capacitor organization. He had been a well-known figure in the plant, and Armstrong felt his presence lent an air of stability and familiarity to the take-over. He then conducted an equipment inventory and organized the consolidation of Mystic's equipment into the company's designated floor space, a task which was not completed for several months. The disentanglement was not always peaceful; there were frequent vociferous disputes with Elonics manufacturing personnel over the ownership of raw material and machinery that harried Steiner and infuriated Armstrong. Steiner also retained a retired maintenance supervisor to help with the plant layout and to attend to other matters, such as overseeing the construction of office space and the rearrangement of pipes and fixtures.

Mystic was incorporated on March 20, and by April 7 Steiner had the manufacturing area in good enough shape to commence operations. Armstrong met with the employees and told them that the company was to start with 45 hourly workers—with no diminution in pay and fringe benefits—and that others would be recalled as soon as possible. In view of the high unemployment in the Mystic area, the employees were receptive to this proposition. Consequently, production was initiated in the midst of moving machines and even prior to the final closing with Elonics on April 12.

Meanwhile Troy was on the road spreading the word that Mystic was in business to service the film, paper, and mica capacitor business. His personal relationship with the three national distributors was instrumental in retaining their support for such a small volume producer. Although the distributors accounted for only 15% of the company's sales, they were vital to its overall marketing effort. Fortunately Elonics had been holding a finished goods inventory, and Elonics was able to supply them immediately at half cost to Mystic. Troy also visited sales reps and major customers. Those who were concerned about quality and service were encouraged to visit the Mystic facility; almost invariably their fears were allayed by the sight of familiar faces in manufacturing and quality assurance.

With Troy bringing in orders at a rapid rate and Steiner working the supervisory personnel well into the evening, $71,000 in sales were posted the first four weeks and a semblance of order was created in the plant. Armstrong personally borrowed an additional $4,000 to finance the initial shipments, and the factoring agreement provided sufficient funds to support continued production. Mystic was in business.

Products and competition

A capacitor is a device which is capable of storing electrical energy. It consists of two conductive plates (electrodes) separated by an insulating material called the dielectric. The capacitance of a capacitor is determined by the surface area of the electrodes, the distance separating them and the electrical properties of the dielectric. A wide range of dielectrics is employed, ranging from air to ceramics, depending on the dielectric constant of the material. For instance, impregnated paper has a constant of 4.0 to 6.0, mylar 3.0, and polystyrene 2.6, compared to an arbitrary figure of 1.0 assigned to a vacuum.

In addition to its theoretical capacitance, the circuit designer is also interested in the devices' stability over a range of temperatures, voltages, and test frequencies. Performance once again varies with the characteristics of the dielectric. For instance, paper is extremely hydroscopic, a property which tends to increase the capacitance with time (water having a dielectric constant of 81.0) and to degrade the power factor, strength, and life of the capacitor. Consequently, paper capacitors were usually impregnated with oil or, if a metalized paper was used, with a resin which provided some protection against moisture absorption. Plastic films, on the other hand, have very low moisture absorption rates and were gradually replacing paper, especially for the fast-growing, low-voltage DC applications required for many consumer electronic products. No impregnation was required in this instance, and because both the film and the casing were thin gauge, the device was smaller than comparable paper units. Plastic dielectrics included mylar, polystyrene, polypropylene, and polysulfone.

The overall noncaptive market for discrete capacitors had peaked at $492 million in 1966, according to Electronic Industries Association statistics, and by 1972 had drifted off to $438 million, as reflected in Exhibit 1. Market stagnation had been caused in part by advances in integrated circuits which contained within the same package the capability of numer-

EXHIBIT 1

MYSTIC ELECTRONICS CO., INC. (A)
Industry Sales and Market Share

Integrated Circuit and Capacitor Sales
(in millions of dollars)

	1967	1968	1969	1970	1971	1972
Integrated Circuits	$273	$367	$498	$524	$534	$718
Capacitors	441	441	490	483	435	438

Share of capacitor market
(percentage of dollar sales by type)

	1967	1968	1969	1970	1971	1972	1971 to 1972 percentage changes in		
							Price	Volume	$ Sales
Paper and film dielectric	30.4%	31.5%	32.0%	38.3%	35.1%	23.6%	(22.0%)	(13.0%)	(32.1%)
Tantalum electrolytic	22.2	19.3	21.2	20.9	18.9	20.8	(16.0)	33.6	12.2
Aluminum electrolytic......	18.8	20.0	19.6	17.0	17.7	20.0	0.6	12.4	13.0
Mica dielectric	5.4	5.2	4.9	4.1	5.1	5.0	(17.5)	20.1	(0.9)
Ceramic dielectric, fixed	14.7	16.1	16.1	15.3	18.9	24.2	3.8	23.7	28.5
All other, fixed	3.2	3.4	2.9	1.9	1.6	2.0	(9.0)	29.5	17.8
Variable	5.3	4.5	3.3	2.5	2.7	4.4	26.4	29.5	63.6
Total industry change:							(13.9)	17.0	0.7

Source: Adapted from Electronic Industries Association.

ous discrete electronic comoponents. Armstrong noted that only two companies, Sprague Electric and Cornell-Dubilier, produced the full range of capacitor products after the partial withdrawal of Elonics. In 1972, paper and film capacitors accounted for 23.6% of industry sales or $103 million and mica capacitors for another 5.0% or $22 million.

Noncaptive sales of paper and film capacitors were led by the two companies noted above plus TRW and General Electric. In addition, there were another 50 to 70 firms with more specialized product lines and sales of generally less than $2 million. Armstrong indicated that, because of the breadth of its inherited product line and customer base and its access to impregnation facilities, Mystic was unique among the small firms in having a shot at competing on even terms with the large companies.

Principal users of paper and film capacitors included the telephone, computer, instrumentation, and automotive industries. About a third of Mystic's total sales were obtained from telephone equipment manufacturers such as Western Electric, Stromberg Carlson, GT&E, Northern Electric, and ITT. This business was especially welcomed because demand was relatively stable, there was less pressure on prices, and the average price per unit was typically somewhat higher than elsewhere. Another 15% of sales came from the big computer companies in the form of orders for large quantities of low-price, small-size units. The company had some direct government business, although it was thought that perhaps only 10% of sales wound up in defense-aerospace products.

The mica capacitor market was divided between high-voltage units typically used in transmitting applications such as telephone relays and low-voltage devices found in many consumer products. Selling prices ranged from pennies in the latter case to hundreds of dollars in the former. Mystic manufactured only the high-voltage devices and, according to Armstrong, was one of the three leading firms in that segment. For some specific applications, such as in welding equipment, he estimated that Mystic had as much as half the business.

Troy summarized the company's marketing perspective in these terms:

We've attempted to sell to markets which have less price erosion and foreign competition and more stability. We've chosen to avoid the consumer products market as much as we can for these reasons. The TV industry will own you. But we have not gone after the other extreme, either—the NASA-type work—which demands very close tolerances, extra testing and record keeping. Looking to the future, maybe we'll have to enter these markets.

Distribution and sales

The network of sales representatives was viewed as a distinct asset to the company. Since the major competing firms sold through their own sales forces, Mystic was among the few independent sources of a broad line of paper/film and mica capacitors, a situation which permitted Armstrong and Troy to cultivate the most aggressive reps. Each of the 18 rep organizations had five or more salesmen and received an exclusive territory and a 5% commission on all sales in their areas, including those to the distributors. While Mystic's active accounts (ones submitting at least one order per month) numbered about 200, most of the sales originated at individual customer locations, which reinforced the need for sales force coverage.

The three distributors in some instances competed with the reps on small volume, short lead-time orders. As a matter of practice, the distributors purchased goods at the maximum quantity discount and sold them at list prices for lower quantity orders. Depending on the customer order size, the discount scheme typically provided them with a 15% margin.

Troy handled virtually all of the customer contacts himself, and much of his time was spent working directly with the reps and major OEM accounts. Although not technically trained, Troy felt that he had learned enough about capacitors to solve many of the simpler product problems in the field and to know what questions to ask should the difficulty appear more complex. He commented:

We've got no sophisticated design engineers here. McCosh, our chief engineer, is a technical school graduate, for instance. He was at Elonics for 15 years and can do things effectively and economically, but he's not polished—he wouldn't survive in a sophisticated organization. I'm reluctant to take him on the road and introduce him as our chief engineer. Also, he won't travel—recently he went to Pittsburgh by train because he's afraid of airplanes. This has forced me to solve problems beyond my engineering background.

Troy was supported by four sales service people, three responsible for order taking much of which came by telephone or through the mail, and one in charge of developing quotes and specifications for bids or inquiries. Mystic did no advertising. Instead, Troy developed a simple newsletter containing notice of product and company developments that was distributed to the reps and customers. The sales effort was highlighted by a 92-page catalog covering many of the standard items; other products were also available on request or could be made to customer specifications. Troy attempted to build into his pricing decisions a 20% profit for the company.

Manufacturing

Production was conducted on three lines. Lines No. 1 and No. 2, devoted to paper and film capacitors, shared the north end of the plant space; the foremen responsible for each reported directly to Steiner. Paper and film capacitors requiring a metal casing were produced on line No. 2, while those on line No. 1 were wrapped in flexible or tubular coverings.

Mica capacitors were produced on line No. 3, which was located at the other end of the Mystic plant. The process involved essentially the same steps. In this instance, machines built up layers of metal and mica which were then heat-treated and mounted in casings. The foreman reported to McCosh who exercised complete responsibility for the line, though in theory when the company was formed it fell under Steiner's aegis.

The first 18 months

Labor was plentiful in the Mystic area. However, as volume grew, Mystic experienced difficulty in recruiting sufficient numbers of qualified applicants. Abe Steiner commented on employee relations:

The people know me very well. There's no threat of a union. I meet with the workers' representatives from each department and we talk about their problems. I've told them the company has a future if they work hard. A couple of months ago they wanted another paid holiday. I told them why we couldn't right now, and they felt they had an honest answer. Morale seems to be high.

On the company's first anniversary, the employees staged a surprise "birthday" party for Tod Armstrong, complete with cake and champagne. Net profit for the year was $23,800 on sales of nearly $1.3 million after an intentional inventory writedown of over $100,000 in order to reduce the tax burden. The backlog was climbing as the economy picked up and Troy continued to pull one-time Elonics customers back into the fold. Of course, not all of the signs were positive. For instance, a wide discrepancy in profitability had developed between the paper/film and the mica lines; the former provided 73% of the sales but only 40% of the gross profit. Nevertheless, with employment then over 100, there was ample reason for celebration.

In the spring of 1973, Armstrong refinanced Mystic's debt by arranging a five-year, $75,000 term loan with a major Boston bank to repay the guaranteed note and to replace the factor with a $30,000 line of credit. By July, the company had no need of the bank line of credit and even had surplus funds to invest in commercial paper. Volume was running at almost $200,000 per month, and, with fall approaching and no noticeable letup in demand, further increases appeared likely. Financial statements are provided in Exhibits 2, 3, and 4.

EXHIBIT 2

MYSTIC ELECTRONICS CO., INC. (A)
Balance Sheet

Assets	March 3, 1973	February 2, 1974
Current assets		
Cash and marketable securities	$ 1,178	$ 72,893
Tax overpayment	1,700	
Accounts receivable—less allowances	191,697	377,504
Due from stockholder	5,760	(549)
Inventories:*		
Raw materials	65,235	48,450
Work in process	31,076	41,800
Finished goods	8,297	4,750
Total current assets	$304,943	$544,848
Equipment	66,550	78,177
Deposits	3,483	3,483
Organization expense, net	323	323
Total assets	$375,299	$626,831

Liabilities and Equity	March 3, 1973	February 2, 1974
Current liabilities		
Accounts payable, trade	$172,037†	$153,435
Current portion of long-term loan		
Equipment loan	25,000	15,000
Secured demand loan	50,978	…
Employee withholdings:		
Taxes	2,817	4,158
Other	2,132	1,248
Accrued liabilities		
Federal income taxes	3,500	118,185
Payroll	28,827	23,818
Payroll taxes	5,476	5,180
Vacation and holiday pay	17,093	20,926
Commissions	8,063	12,638
State income taxes	…	23,282
Interest	115	
Note payable—other	…	14,066
Total current liabilities	$316,038	$391,936
Equipment loan		
Less current portion above	$ 25,433	$ 52,131
Stockholders' equity		
Common stock, no par value:		
authorized 7,000 shares		
issued and outstanding 1,000 shares	10,000	10,000
Paid-in capital‡		6,100
Retained earnings	23,828	166,664
Total liabilities and equity	$375,299	$626,831

* Inventory is included at 50% of gross cost. An additional $17,700 was arbitrarily written off in January 1973.
† Includes a $52,000 note to Elonics, settled in fiscal 1974 for $18,000.
‡ Gain on sale of fixed assets, net of tax effect.
Source: Company records.

EXHIBIT 3

MYSTIC ELECTRONICS CO., INC. (A)
Income Statement for 1973–74
(dollars in thousands)

| | Year ending March 3, 1973 | | | | | 11 months ending February 2, 1974 | | | | |
| | Paper/Film | | Mica | | | Paper/Film | | Mica | | |
	Amount	% of sales	Amount	% of sales	Total	Amount	% of sales	Amount	% of sales	Total
Sales	$967.9		$360.5		$1,328.4	$1,879.9		$522.2		$2,402.1
Less returns & allowances	21.7		7.2		28.9	57.0		22.2		79.2
Net sales	$946.2	100.0%	$353.3	100.0%	$1,299.5	$1,822.9	100.0%	$500.0	100.0%	$2,322.9
Cost of goods sold										
Material purchases	382.1	40.4	87.7	24.8	469.8	526.5	28.9	131.3	26.3	657.8
Inventory change	(68.3)	(7.2)	(15.3)	(4.3)	(83.6)	8.6	0.5	1.0	0.1	9.6
Net material	$313.8	33.2%	$72.4	20.5%	$386.2	$535.1	29.4%	$132.3	26.4%	$667.4
Direct labor	299.4	31.6	61.2	17.3	360.6	506.8	27.8	78.8	15.8	585.6
Factory overhead	234.3	24.8	73.2	20.7	307.5	383.6	21.0	117.8	23.5	501.4
Cost of goods sold	$847.6	89.6%	$206.8	58.5%	$1,054.3	$1,425.5	78.2%	$328.9	65.7%	$1,754.4
Gross profit	$ 98.6	10.4%	$146.6	41.5%	$ 245.2	$ 397.4	21.8%	$171.2	34.2%	$ 568.6
Selling & administrative	157.7	16.7	58.3	16.5	216.0	244.6	13.4	69.0	13.8	313.6
Income from operations	$(59.1)	(6.2)%	$ 88.3	25.0%	$ 29.2	$ 152.8	8.4%	$102.2	20.4%	$ 255.0
Other income, less federal and state taxes										15.5
Short-term investment income										.2
Provision for state tax					(1.8)					(23.1)
Provision for F.I.T.					(3.5)					(104.8)
Net income for period					$ 23.8					$ 142.8

Source: Company records.

EXHIBIT 4

MYSTIC ELECTRONICS CO., INC. (A)
Monthly and Quarterly Income Statements
March 1973–January 1974
(dollars in thousands)

Total company	March 1973	April* 1973	May 1973	June 1973	July† 1973	August 1973	September 1973	October* 1973	November 1973	December 1973	January* 1974
Sales	$163.0	$207.2	$192.0	$206.9	$190.9	$207.8	$204.7	$260.4	$242.0	$234.9	$292.4
Less returns and allowances	2.7	6.6	3.1	5.8	0.1	2.8	16.1	4.7	7.0	15.9	14.3
Net sales	$160.3	$200.6	$188.9	$201.1	$190.8	$205.0	$188.6	$255.7	$234.9	$219.0	$278.1
Cost of goods sold:											
Material purchases	38.2	53.2	54.6	38.1	68.4	56.3	57.5	67.9	56.4	51.9	115.2
Inventory change						(8.1)					17.7‡
Net material						48.2					132.8
Direct labor	38.9	52.5	44.5	53.2	50.0	53.8	47.5	67.4	52.7	52.5	72.7
Factory overhead	35.6	47.5	40.5	42.7	50.8	41.1	42.2	54.6	48.1	42.9	55.3
Cost of goods sold	$112.7	$153.2	$139.6	$134.0	$169.2	$143.1	$147.3	$189.8	$157.2	$147.3	$260.9
Gross profit	47.6	47.4	49.3	67.0	21.6	61.9	41.3	65.9	77.7	71.7	17.2
Selling and administrative	19.8	27.9	25.1	21.0	29.9	26.7	28.0	31.4	28.2	35.4	40.1
Income from operations	$ 27.8	$ 19.5	$ 24.2	$ 46.1	$ (8.3)	$ 35.1	$ 13.3	$ 34.5	$ 49.5	$ 36.3	$(22.9)
Other income, less federal and state taxes thereon								0.4	(0.4)		
Provision for state tax	2.5	1.8	1.8	4.4	(0.6)	3.1	1.2	3.1	4.3	3.2	(1.8)
Provision for F.I.T.	5.6	8.5	10.8	20.0	(3.8)	15.4	5.8	15.1	21.7	15.9	(10.1)
Net income for period	$ 19.7	$ 9.2	$ 11.6	$ 21.6	$ (3.9)	$ 16.5	$ 6.2	$ 16.7	$ 23.1	$ 17.2	$(11.0)

Product line	3 months ending June 2, 1973		3 months ending Sept. 1, 1973		3 months ending Dec. 1, 1973	
	Paper/film	Mica	Paper/film	Mica	Paper/film	Mica
Sales	$426.6	$123.2	$457.8	$139.1	$539.2	$140.1
Cost of sales	331.8	73.7	367.4	79.0	396.2	98.2
Gross profit	$ 94.8	$ 49.5	$ 90.4	$ 60.1	$143.0	$ 41.9
Selling & administrative	56.5	16.3	59.3	18.3	69.8	17.8
Income from operations	$ 38.2	$ 33.2	$ 31.1	$ 41.8	$ 73.1	$ 24.1

* 5-week month.
† 3½-week month due to plant shutdown.
‡ Arbitrary inventory writedown.
Note: Numbers may not add due to rounding.
Source: Company records.

Organizational developments

The organization remained as originally constituted for about the first 18 months with the addition of a full-time accountant, Douglas Macauley, 61, who had recently been laid off from the Elonics EDP department. Although Macauley had no direct experience in accounting, he seemed to have a natural bent for the job. Earlier, Armstrong had briefly employed a retired accountant but found his system too complicated for the company's needs.

Then in the fall of 1973 Armstrong became aware of increasing problems in purchasing and materials control. The large number of products in the line required a great variety of raw materials. The stockroom was under the control of manufacturing and the inventory records were far from accurate. As material shortages began to develop and Mystic encountered increasing delays in delivery, the absence of controls and purchasing procedures began to cause unexpected production problems. Armstrong felt that Merritt, who had done a fine job in the beginning, was having difficulty grappling with his more complicated assignment. For a time, Steiner took a direct hand in supervising Merritt, but the problems, if anything, became more acute.

Armstrong then decided to look outside for a materials control manager, confiding as he did in such matters only with Troy. This plan was an outgrowth of a broader feeling on Armstrong's part that "it was time to get organized."

A short while later at a party, Armstrong met John Lysenko and learned that he was available. Lysenko, 48, was then assistant to the president of a curtain manufacturing firm in Bridgeport where he had worked for the previous seven years. Prior to that he had been employed by Cornell-Dubilier and as a result was familiar with the capacitor business. His experience had been largely in industrial engineering.

In mid-October, after several discussions, Armstrong offered him a job as materials control manager at $18,000 a year, a position to which Merritt (production control) and Curtis (purchasing) were to report. (Concurrently, Steiner's salary, which had been raised to $15,000 earlier in the year, was to be increased to $18,000 as well.) Thinking back on his decision to hire Lysenko, Armstrong commented:

I really had confidence in him. He was interested in becoming general manager. I told him when I hired him that the best way to help was to get the materials control problems fixed up. Then in a year or so, being general manager might be the next step. With the responsibility of six children, he couldn't be lazy. And his experience in the business added up to his being a good man.

Armstrong recalled the events surrounding the installation of the new manager:

John was to start work on a Monday, and I decided to tell the organization about the change at the staff meeting the Friday before. The morning of the staff meeting Bob Merritt came in and asked if he could take the afternoon off. I said "O.K." He left without knowing about the change. I was scheduled to take a two and a half weeks' sales trip starting on Monday, but I expected Ned would be there to introduce John around the office. Then on Monday morning when I called in, I found that Ned was out with a customer for a couple of days—he doesn't like personality problems. I think my secretary ended up showing John around.

When I got back Bob wouldn't speak to me. I told John that Bob was to be in charge of production control, but John kept referring to him as a "scheduler." Finally, Bob came in and said, "If I'm no better than a scheduler, I'm leaving." In a couple of days he was gone.

For the first few weeks, Abe would come fuming into my office saying "that stupid Lysenko this and that stupid Lysenko that." He would rant and rave about running up the overhead when we couldn't afford it. Actually Abe has no idea of how well we're doing—I've always told him, "we might be breaking even." One of the most appropriate ways to get along with Abe is to be a good listener. The fact that I would seldom take his advice on a subject frustrates Abe, but he always leaves saying, "If that's what you want, that's what I'll do."

During November and December Lysenko tried to get a handle on the materials control problem. Daily production reports indicated numerous stoppages due to material unavailability, and missed delivery dates were a growing concern. Lysenko's first inclination was to schedule only those jobs for which there was stock on hand. He found, however, that the orders were not documented well enough to do it systematically and that the sales department had no ready way of determining material availability prior to committing to a delivery date. In fact, the three production lines were being loaded on the basis of dollar volume and promised delivery dates, with the foreman picking through the orders to find ones that could be matched with material in inventory. He also found that his attempts to establish purchase quantities were confounded by poor yield data; that is, the yield might be only 60%, whereas standard material allotments to production were only 110% of the order total. Consequently, purchases made on the basis of sales orders fell short of requirements, creating shortages that were exacerbated by steadily lengthening vendor lead times.

Some weeks after Lysenko arrived, Armstrong asked each of his senior managers for an organization chart supported by job descriptions for the supervisors and clerks in his department. Steiner was the only one to respond despite prodding, and the matter was eventually dropped. Armstrong also became annoyed by what he considered to be a new laxness in the office. In particular, his concern centered on the materials control department. Whereas until that time all the managers and many of their people had been accustomed to working on Saturday morning and staying

EXHIBIT 5

MYSTIC ELECTRONICS CO., INC. (A)

Interoffice Memorandum

TO: People on My Staff   FROM: Tod B. Armstrong
SUBJECT: Coffee Breaks   DATE: 11/12/73

It has come to my attention that certain abuses are being made of the traditional coffee break. This is causing difficulties in contacting various people at certain times.

The reason an office coffee machine has been provided was to allow salaried people to take their coffee breaks at random times, at or near their own locations, and eliminating the need for going to the cafeteria. This lower cost coffee is not available to hourly employees and should not be drunk in the cafeteria.

I am hereby making the *strong suggestion* that the traditional coffee break for salaried people between 9:30 and 9:40 (now it is closer to 9:30–10:00) be substituted by more frequent breaks within our office areas.

Please see that your people are advised.

Tod B. Armstrong

TBA/EJ

P.S.   Please instill in your people that no one here has an 8:00 to 5:00, 40 hr/wk job. In view of our workloads and the many important accomplishments we all must make to ensure our continued successful growth, an attitude of putting off 'til tomorrow that which can be done today is not satisfactory.

I have not, I am not, nor will I ever require anyone to work beyond 5:00 PM, or on Saturday morning. BUT, on the other hand, lethargic attitudes cannot be condoned.

P.P.S.   The telephone in shipping is for use by the Shipping Department and the Q. C. department ONLY. If it is determined that an intercom phone is needed in that area of our plant, one will be installed.

Copies to: A. Steiner
            P. McCosh
            J. Lysenko
            N. Troy
            D. Macauley

into the evening if necessary, Lysenko arrived and left precisely on time, Monday through Friday. His subordinates had adopted his hours. Armstrong responded by admonishing his department heads with the memorandum contained in Exhibit 5.

Ownership compensation

Armstrong owned all the equity in Mystic. He was, however, considering the possibility of making 5% of the stock available to Ned Troy. As he put it:

Ned is key to this company. He's got a strong New England personality; his pride would never permit him to ask for a piece of the business. But I have the feeling that it's on his mind. He plays golf with many of the important people in town and he likes to think of himself as a partner. The company is a personal affair right now, and opening it up to others would probably create some problems. On the other hand, having started with absolutely nothing it's hard to determine what 5% really means to me. At this point, Ned is more important to me than 5% of the company. I take no more out of it than I need to live on, and that hasn't changed since we started.

At year end, Armstrong decided on raises for the following year. Ned Troy received $2,500, down from $4,000 the year before. Abe Steiner and John Lysenko received $500 each, and figures ranged from $10 to $20 per week for the remaining managers. Armstrong commented on this event:

I feel I've been generous with bonuses and raises. The increases for Abe and John were admittedly token amounts because of recent raises. Yet they were the only ones to complain. For Abe, making $20,000 is a life goal, and he sees the time growing short. John wanted another $10 a week; he came into my office and wouldn't leave.

Finally I said, "I'll think about it—give me two weeks." Exactly two weeks later he came back and again wouldn't leave. Then I told my secretary to give him the $10 but to charge it to miscellaneous expense—I just refused to raise his salary. ·

The problems intensify

In early January 1974, an incident occurred which highlighted certain ambiguities in the organization and differences in viewpoint among Mystic managers. Armstrong described it in these terms:

Paul McCosh had designed some racks to be used in testing an important film capacitor order. Abe came up with his own idea and had his maintenance men build the racks his way. When McCosh objected, Abe started to tell him how to manage his line—that he's too meticulous, etc. Paul has always run his own show and even handles his own purchasing. He's very quiet—not the type that would aspire to be president. But when he says it will be $49,000 in shipments next month, you can count on it. They got mad at each other— there was shouting and so forth. Then Paul came into my office with his coat on and said, "I'm going home—I'll be back in a couple days." I said, "Wait!" but he was out the door.

I waited 15 minutes and called his home. No answer. I tried again, got him, and asked if I could come over. We talked for a long while, and during the conversation I agreed that maybe Abe comes on a little strong sometimes. I also asked Paul if he thought he might like to assume the responsibility of paper/film production when Abe retires. He said, "I'm not sure I can do it, but I will accept more responsibility." He wanted to come back that afternoon, but I told him to "cool it" until the next morning. Now he makes more suggestions than before to me personally, especially about the metal-cased products on line No. 2.

Meanwhile, the backlog for both Mystic and the industry continued to grow. Troy felt that sales of existing products could be $4 million for the fiscal year beginning in March. (For the 11 months through January they were $2.4 million.) Armstrong estimated that delivery dates were missed about as often as they were met, a condition not uncommon in the industry at the time but one which invited new competition. As a result, he wrote a memorandum to Steiner and Lysenko requesting a program for increasing production on line No. 1 by about a third (Exhibit 6). Several weeks later Steiner submitted the plan shown in Exhibit 7.

EXHIBIT 6

MYSTIC ELECTRONICS CO., INC. (A)
Production increase for line No. 1

TO: A. Steiner   FROM: Tod B. Armstrong
           J. Lysenko
SUBJECT: Program to increase production   DATE: 1/3/74
           on Paper/Film line No. 1

Please get together and formulate a plan to increase production on Paper/Film line #1 from the present level of 27,000 to 31,000 per day to 40,000 per day.

Include 1—A time table (as short as possible)
        2—Increased manpower requirements w/cost
        3—Increased inventory requirements w/cost

I would like to have this plan available for review by January 15, 1974.

_____

                                    Tod B. Armstrong

TBA/EJ
cc: N. Troy   .
     D. Macauley
     P. McCosh

Historical monthly production figures for the three lines are contained in Exhibit 8.

Paper and film capacitor shipments fell about $20,000 short of the January five-week plan of $255,000. Armstrong set the February (four-week month) target at $235,000 and strongly suggested to Steiner and Lysenko that every effort be made to achieve it (Exhibit 9).

Another source of concern also emerged during January; accounts payable to raw material suppliers increased dramatically although production delays due to lack of material had not abated. On the basis of a cursory examination of the inventory, Armstrong concluded that imbalances were prevalent and he suspected that Lysenko might have been "panicked" into buying whatever material was available without regard to projected usage.

At the same time (February 7) Steiner reflected on the difficulties he was encountering:

Scheduling is a big problem. I'm unable to tell the scheduler what the machine load should be because of the variety of products, so I have to guess

EXHIBIT 7

MYSTIC ELECTRONICS CO., INC. (A)
Reply from Steiner

To: Mr. Tod Armstrong　　　　　　　　From: A. Steiner

Re: Mr. Armstrong's memo of 1/3/74
Paper/Film on Line No. 1

Production line estimate for producing 35 M to 40 M units per day are as follows:

6 weeks for winding to 35 M daily
12 weeks for winding to 40 M daily
10 weeks for Assy. & Final Test to 35 M daily
16 weeks for Assy. & Final Test to 40 M daily

Direct labor costs as follows:

Average Hr./Assy. 18 Hr./M × 2.15 = 38.70 labor/M × 16 Hr. = $619 per day
Average Hr./Wind 16 Hr./M × 2.15 = 12.90 " " × 16 Hr. = 206 "
Average Hr./Spray 2 Hr./M × 2.15 = 4.30 " " × 16 Hr. = 69 " "

Present average quantity level at Final Test is 24 M per day. My estimate on material increase in dollars would be between $30,000 to $45,000. Above estimate is based on material and labor being available to meet time table.

on how much we're able to produce and I've been high. Materials are also a big problem. Three hundred pounds of some foils will make 100,000 units, but we produce only 2,500 a day. Then another part will be missing and the inventory will pile up. Six months ago I told Tod we needed a materials control manager. It's still not working; one big order can screw you up if the supplies aren't there. As much as I don't want to, I'm still involved in it.

I deviate from the schedule because of my knowledge of the business. The

EXHIBIT 8

MYSTIC ELECTRONICS CO., INC. (A)
Capacitor Production in Units

	Line No. 1 (plastic and tubular cased paper/film)	Line No. 2 (metal cased paper/ film)	Line No. 3 (mica)
1972			
April	118,306	8,814	n.a.
May	182,607	9,886	n.a.
June	220,980	15,912	n.a.
July	222,202	9,197	n.a.
August	247,044	19,480	n.a.
September	272,067	12,842	n.a.
October	327,568	22,511	n.a.
November	299,407	21,450	n.a.
December	310,438	13,530	n.a.
Total	2,200,619	133,622	n.a.
1973			
January	414,095	19,426	4,007
February	346,983	23,659	5,462
March	402,644	27,736	4,527
April	491,791	33,684	11,171
May	420,797	17,857	9,433
June	487,425	25,868	9,174
July	410,323	18,259	7,520
August	493,446	25,441	8,202
September	512,520	26,675	9,826
October	707,799	46,197	11,881
November	546,095	29,681	7,496
December	496,197	26,413	2,649
Total	5,730,115	320,896	91,348
1974			
January	611,787	36,413	4,156

delivery schedule extends out nine weeks, and my people can work on anything in that period. We also control the stockroom. We're so small that we can keep posted on materials that are being reserved for a particular customer.

Lysenko reflected on the situation from his perspective in the following terms:

We're trying—better days are coming, but I'm the first to admit we haven't done the job so far. Scheduling is part of it. Nothing in the order form tells whether the material is available, but in six weeks to two months we should have new forms for order logging and scheduling installed which will get this under control. Right now, I can't cut Abe off from the stockroom because I can't load the department as well as the supervisors can—they're doing the scheduling. There isn't much interface between engineering and production, so I don't get very good data on yields, either.

A lot of our foil comes from Europe. Prices were lower there, now they're

EXHIBIT 9

MYSTIC ELECTRONICS CO., INC. (A)

Proposed February Program

TO: A. Steiner   FROM: Tod B. Armstrong
      J. Lysenko

JANUARY PROGRAM & PROPOSED FEBRUARY PROGRAM

Your January program for the Paper/Film departments was $255,000.00 with over $400,000.00 in the backlog to support it. Actual shipments were $235,600.00, some of which actually came from 2/4/74 production. Obviously, this cannot be considered a satisfactory performance.

Your February program will be as follows:

Paper/Film line 1	$150,000.00
Paper/Film line 2	85,000.00
Total	$235,000.00

This program again is supported by a backlog far in excess of that which is needed, and there will be no excuse for not meeting these figures.

It will take an exerted effort on your part to plan for this production and to control your department performances so that the program will be achieved without exceeding our labor cost estimates and without increasing inventory.

Please get together and list the orders to be shipped this month with their dollar values that will add up to the desired total. This list should be compiled by mid-month, and all those responsible should aim for the completion of the listed items.

I do not want you to fall short of your program a 3rd month in succession!

Tod B. Armstrong

TBA/EJ

cc: N. Troy
  .   D. Macauley
      P. McCosh

higher and we're really getting clobbered on deliveries. And with mylar, as of last Friday, the lead time went from four weeks to eight weeks—overnight. Apparently the large users are crowding the vendors and buying up the supplies. Vendors are putting minimum order sizes into effect as well.

Tod is climbing the walls because our accounts payable have gone from $100,000 to $150,000. It's true I've built some stock. I've sometimes been buying by guess and by golly—purchasing based on what orders are coming across my desk. For instance, we had a big order recently and I may have purchased too much material. But it gives me some scheduling flexibility because if another material is short, I can keep the plant busy on orders using the one in stock. I may also have more lead and copper than we need, but it was bought in anticipation of shortages. In another case, I took a big shipment to get the discount. Also, in that $150,000, I think, is $10,000 worth of 1⅝" mylar. The matching foil which was ordered at the same time hasn't been delivered yet, so the mylar just sits there. If the information was available, maybe the payables could be lower.

Armstrong's perspective

Armstrong felt that Mystic had some very significant profit opportunities and he was anxious to proceed on some of them while industry conditions favored expansion. For instance, he had discussed with Troy the possibility of supplying the electrical products industry. They were confident that entree could be secured by attracting a few major original equipment manufacturers and providing them with good service and dependable quality.

A joint venture to partially assemble low-price dipped mica capacitors in India was also under consideration to take advantage of that country's ample mica supplies, low-cost labor, and generous export subsidies. The semifinished products would be sold to an offshore trading company and then resold to Mystic, which would perform the final dipping and packaging operations and market them to high-volume users in the United States. The Indian partner would be responsible for all operations in India. Under one alternative, Mystic would have a minority interest in the Indian company and share equally in the trading company with an import-export firm that had brought the parties together and was familiar with the intricacies of such arrangements. It was possible that capacitors produced at a healthy profit in India for $.022 apiece could be sold in the United States for $.07 to $.10, with $.02 for transportation, dipping, and marketing. Mystic's investment would include $50,000 for the dipping equipment and possibly another $40,000 contributed to the Indian company. Armstrong and Troy estimated that 10% of the market could be obtained, yielding $2.5 million in sales, if quality and deliveries were on target. Three of the four firms then competing in the market were manufacturing their products in Taiwan, where labor rates were four times those in India; the fourth was producing them in the United States.

While Armstrong was enthusiastic about the opportunities open to his company, he was also disturbed by the more immediate difficulties in meeting day-to-day operating commitments. The daily production chart on February 15, reproduced in Exhibit 10, indicated that only 26% of the targeted shipments for the month had been made. The situation was frustrating, as Armstrong commented:

I know these sorts of problems are common for a growing company, but it seems to be getting out of hand here. We're a job shop; for every sale there ought to be material on order or in stock. But at the moment nothing is matched to anything. John can't relate purchasing to production. He puts out blanket orders with no regard for price. The complexity and detail has overwhelmed him. Although I make my concern quite apparent, I don't think he knows he's doing a lousy job.

No one could have done half the job that Abe did in the beginning. He drove his people and handled the relationship with Elonics. He's excellent at

EXHIBIT 10

MYSTIC ELECTRONICS CO., INC. (A)
Daily Production Chart

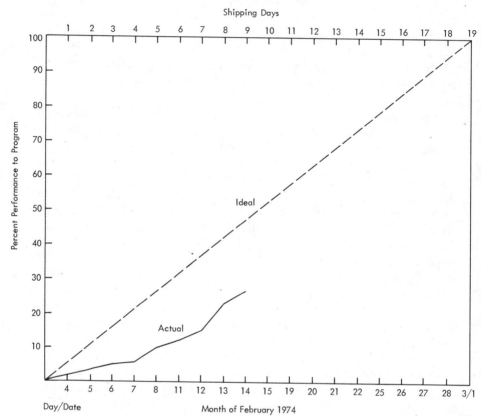

covering the bases and anticipating needs—making sure the doors are locked when the plant closes for vacation. He's been here 40 years and no one is close to taking his place. But the startup is over now and he still spends time telling the maintenance men how to put the shelves up rather than directing production.

Armstrong reflected on the upcoming staff meeting in personal terms.

These problems are getting to me. At home my mind is on them. I've rehearsed what I'll say this afternoon about the importance of making shipments, but I'm afraid I won't come across as well as I should in the meeting. I seem to be much more effective writing a memorandum. It's hard for me to be tough on people in person—most managers would be in this situation.

Vlasic Foods Inc.

VLASIC FOODS INC. processed and marketed a broad line of pickles supplemented by relishes, peppers, sauerkraut, and related items. Sales had grown rapidly from $1.7 million in 1962 to over $20 million in 1969, and profits had increased accordingly. Despite the fact that Vlasic products in 1970 were available to only about 50% of U.S. consumers, management maintained that the company had at least as large a market share in the industry as its giant competition, the H. J. Heinz Co.

The success of Vlasic Foods had increased considerably the value of the 49% interest in the company owned by Vlasic & Co., a family partnership through which Robert Vlasic, 44, kept track of a number of enterprises from his three-room suite in the Fisher Building in Detroit. Mr. Vlasic, also chairman of the board of Vlasic Foods, was instrumental in the formation of corporate policy for the company, particularly in the areas of financing, capital investment, management controls, and executive compensation. While maintaining an intensive awareness of operating results, he had encouraged his senior managers to assume the tasks of market planning and day-to-day administration. His charge to Russell Post, president of Vlasic Foods, was simply, "to grow as fast as you want, as long as you keep that 5% [net income to net sales] on the bottom line."

In August 1970 Mr. Vlasic was attempting to anticipate the consequences of continued growth. The latest plan, based on the assumption that manufacturing capacity and financing would not be limiting factors, indicated sales of over $55 million in existing product lines by 1974–75, as shown in the following table:

	1970–71	1971–72	1972–73	1973–74	1974–75
Case production (thousands)	6,700	8,040	9,648	11,580	13,900
Dollar sales (net) (thousands)	$26,700	$32,000	$38,400	$46,100	$55,500

Mr. Vlasic commented on the implications of the plan:

The numbers may seem unrealistic except that each time we draw up a plan, Russ Post and Al Dubin[1] come in with what seems like an unattainable forecast and then exceed it. I have just put together a report comparing our actual sales with those forecast in earlier five-year plans. In each case the volume estimated for a particular year increased as the year approached and still proved conservative. Assuming we are able to produce revenues of $55 million and finance it somehow, I am sure that managing a company of that size will be considerably different than it is for the one we have today. We are running very hard—I don't want us to stumble.

THE PICKLE INDUSTRY

Pickles were among the most popular vegetables in the United States. According to Pickle Packers International (PPI), the industry's trade association, pickles had passed corn, peas, snap beans, whole tomatoes, and vegetable juices in per-capita consumption from 1954 to 1967 and enjoyed a growth rate considerably higher than canned fruits and vegetables as a whole (see Exhibit 1). Some feeling for the magnitude of this growth is provided in the following table:

Year	Consumption (tons)	Per-capita consumption (pounds)
1930	107.7	2.35
1940	141.7	2.88
1950	261.2	4.62
1960	347.6	5.19
1968	542.5	7.16

Source: U.S. Department of Agriculture, Statistical Reporting Source.

Placing a value on this consumption was difficult because aggregate

[1] Treasurer and former president of Vlasic Foods.

statistics were not available on manufacturers' or retailers' sales. However, PPI published the following estimate for chain stores:

	Tons	Retail sales (millions)	Average margin	Wholesale sales* (millions)
Pickles	114.5	$168.2	24.7%	$126.2
Pickle specialties†	81.0	67.4	26.7	49.4
Total	195.5	$235.6	25.3%	$175.6

* Derived.
† Includes relish, peppers, pimentos.

EXHIBIT 1
Growth trends of pickles, vegetables, and fruit

	1952–54 average	1969	Percent change
Pickles, U.S. consumption	590	1,108	87.8
Canned vegetables	6,660	9,259	39.0
Canned fruit	3,300	5,023	52.2

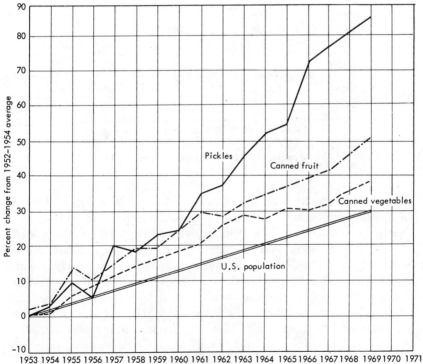

Benchmark data: Consumption, millions of pounds.
Source: U.S. Department of Agriculture.

Vlasic management estimated that total wholesale sales approximated $250 million.

Pickle products were divided into two broad categories, processed and fresh-packed. Processed pickles were manufactured by first fermenting the fresh cucumber in large open vats of brine for up to six months until they were completely cured. This brine-cured pickle was then further processed by desalting and adding sweet or dill liquors and spices to obtain the desired varieties. Additional products were obtained by cutting the cured pickles into various shapes, chopping them up to make relish, or adding other processed vegetables such as cauliflower, onions, and peppers.

Fresh-packed pickles were processed by bottling the fresh, green cucumber with sweet or dill liquor and pasteurizing. The result was a milder pickle, the most common being "bread and butter" sweet pickles and kosher-style dills. The market share accounted for by fresh-packed pickles had grown substantially during the 1960s. Vlasic had been one of the leaders in popularizing this product segment and continued to rely on it for over 50% of sales.

Percentage of sales (1969–70)

Pickle	Vlasic*	Industry
Sweet-processed pickles	10%	21%
Fresh-packed pickles†	49	35
Dill-processed pickles	11	24
Relish	16	15
Peppers (fresh-packed)	12	4
Other	2	1
	100%	100%

* Vlasic sales base of 100% does not include 9% of total sales which was divided as follows: 4% sauerkraut, 4% institutional, 1% miscellaneous.

† According to PPI, the fresh-packed share of the total market had been 19% in 1966.

The pickle industry was characterized by a large number of small family enterprises in which the art of pickle packing was passed from father to son. One Vlasic official indicated that H. J. Heinz, the Borden Company (Aunt Jane's Pickles), and Vlasic, each with about 10% of the market, were the largest producers, although most markets were dominated by a locally produced brand. Private-brand sales were estimated by Mr. Vlasic to account for somewhat less than 20% of the total market; sales were inhibited, in his view, by the contractor's inability or unwillingness to support a full line. Heinz and, to a somewhat lesser degree, Aunt Jane's were national brands while Vlasic was sold primarily in the north-central and northeastern states.

Several larger food-processing companies, including Libby, McNeill & Libby, Stokely, and Consolidated Foods, had been attracted to the industry but had later withdrawn. Mr. Vernon Filek of PPI provided one view of what had happened:

Some large companies tried to let people with experience in other areas manage their pickle operations. These people did not understand the problems of pickle manufacturing and often got a bad product. In some instances when a pickle company was acquired, the experienced pickle packers would clash with "corporate" management procedures and resign.

VLASIC FOODS

History

In 1922 Joseph Vlasic, Robert Vlasic's father, started a milk distribution business in Detroit. As the business grew, eventually becoming the largest in Michigan, the elder Vlasic found that his rapport with store owners afforded an opportunity to form a new business, Vlasic Foods, to distribute other food products. Then, in 1937, he was approached by a man who wanted the company to distribute his new "home style" fresh-packed pickles. Joseph Vlasic agreed to buy and market the pickles but only if he could control the brand name. The first Vlasic pickles were directed at the Polish community in Detroit and, in fact, the first label was written entirely in Polish.

For many years, Vlasic bought all its pickles from independent packers. However, as the business grew, it became difficult to find larger quality packers willing to pack for a private label. Moreover, it was felt a "showplace" plant was needed to convince customers that Vlasic was indeed a pickle company. For these reasons, Robert Vlasic acquired a small pickle company in Imlay City near Detroit in 1958. Unfortunately, it turned out that most of the facilities were designed for making sauerkraut instead of pickles and in large part had to be rebuilt. In 1962 Albert Dubin, one of Joseph Vlasic's first employees and later a 25% owner in each of the Vlasic enterprises, was put in charge of the pickle venture. Mr. Dubin recalled, "We learned the pickle-packing business the hard way. Those first few years were very costly."

In 1960 Russell Post was transferred from the distribution company to become sales manager. Robert Vlasic attributed most of the subsequent success of the company to the Dubin-Post team: "Russ Post is a good salesman. He and Al Dubin have worked very well together. Russ would use almost any amount of promotion to get a sale, while Al watches expenses and costs like a hawk."

Acquisitions

In 1965 Vlasic acquired the Crown Foods Company, a Detroit pickle company somewhat smaller than Vlasic, having a branded product, two plants, and three managers who had grown up in the pickle industry. The acquisition was made for stock, and the Raznick brothers, Fred, Herman, and Maurice, joined Vlasic as vice presidents.[2]

In 1968 Vlasic acquired the Shupak Pickle Company in Philadelphia, also for stock, to secure a marketing foothold in the East. In the next two years, the Shupak label was discontinued and a substantial portion of the manufacturing facilities were abandoned because of their inherent inefficiency. In 1970 Vlasic invested $700,000 in a new manufacturing facility to process deli-style kosher dills in Philadelphia and the old plant was sold. Two managers were added with the Shupak acquisition: Jerry Shupak, 33, became a vice president with the title of eastern sales manager, and his father, Morris Shupak, who was to retire in October 1970, was made vice president in charge of the Philadelphia operation.

Marketing

Russell Post commented on the role of marketing at Vlasic:

We are a marketing company. We are selling pickles while most of the other family-held businesses concentrate on making them. In fact, our major problem is getting enough products to sell. Vlasic isn't moving into any new markets in 1970 because existing accounts are absorbing all of our increased production.

The distribution of Vlasic pickle products had expanded gradually from Michigan primarily to the Midwest and East. Exhibit 2 shows sales by market. The company sought to be number one in the markets that it served rather than attempt to secure volume through nonintensive national distribution. Thus, company officials estimated that Vlasic had over 50% of the Michigan market, nearly 30% in Cleveland and northern Ohio, and approaching 20% in Chicago and Boston. The Vlasic product line of 73 items, almost equally divided between fresh-packed and processed varieties, was thought by management to be the broadest in the business. Mr. Post indicated how he approached new markets:

When we go into a new market, we know we'll be number one within two years. We get the best broker in town and convince him we can do it. When we first approach a customer, he usually says he needs another pickle item like a hole in the head. He can't believe that anyone would try to sell him 45 new items, let alone refuse to sell him any unless he agreed to take at least 15. But we start our marketing program and our

---

[2] Mr. Herman Raznick was killed in an automobile accident in 1969.

EXHIBIT 2
Vlasic's retail sales by markets

Market	Percentage of total market for year ended June 30	
	1969	*1970*
Michigan	30.9	28.1
Ohio and West Virginia	21.2	18.6
East Coast	12.4	14.3
New England	7.3	10.0
Illinois and St. Louis	7.8	9.6
Pennsylvania less Philadelphia	5.6	4.9
New York less New York City.	3.8	4.8
Indiana and Louisville	4.6	3.9
South.	2.8	3.3
West	1.7	1.7
Other.	1.9	0.8
Total retail sales	100.0	100.0

Source: Vlasic sales report.

salesman keeps calling. Eventually the customer realizes it's only a matter of time before he lets us in. If he takes 15 items, we come back the next week and try to sell him 30 more. Sooner or later we will.

Vlasic was alone among pickle manufacturers in using extensive advertising promotion. Mr. Post estimated that the company spent over half a million dollars in selected markets for animated cartoon television commercials in 1970. Mr. Post maintained that pickles were essentially purchased on impulse, and consequently volume was influenced strongly by exposure both in-store and in the media. Thus, Mr. Vlasic in 1966 commissioned a prominent designer for a substantial fee to rework the company's labeling and packaging designs. On the other hand, Vlasic rarely engaged in competition through price reductions.

Distribution

After retail accounts had purchased Vlasic products, considerable effort was devoted to enlarging the shelf space devoted to them. Mr. Post commented on the nature of the competition at this level:

A chain store typically carries only two lines of pickles and relishes. Since six key items may account for 30% of sales, the chain account may carry a narrow private-brand line. In any event, we are normally in the position of replacing a smaller line with ours, which is much broader and therefore requires more shelf space. Obtaining the additional shelf space is most difficult. Sometimes our people have to rearrange an entire grocery aisle to pick up a few more feet for pickles. But we are absolutely convinced that attractive shelf displays supplemented by special floor displays will generate additional sales without retail price reductions.

In addition to their regional sales managers, Vlasic had a staff of detail men who worked with retailers arranging for displays, checking on product rotation, and training the food broker's salesmen. The broker's men actually serviced the customer by taking the weekly order and following up on shipments, etc., but the Vlasic man was held responsible for getting the items authorized by the retail account and supervising the market's development.

Entry into New England

Vlasic's success in entering the New England market in 1968 provided an illustration of this marketing philosophy in action. Mr. Jerry Souza of Food Enterprises, the brokerage company selected by Vlasic, commented:

The pickle market in New England in 1968 was asleep. One reason was that pickles had been price imaged. When one chain in an area price images an item, the others are forced to follow. As a result of this heavy price competition, very little profit was being made on pickles in New England. The market was dominated by one local company with 45%; Heinz had 14%; and two others had about 20% between them, with the rest scattered.

The dominant company didn't advertise or offer promotions to the retailers. Heinz had spotty distribution in the area. There was general dissatisfaction with pickle marketing among retailers. Prices were low; lines were small; there were no promotion or advertising campaigns. Pickles were drab, unexciting products.

We and Vlasic offered the retailers a whole new concept, a completely new approach to their pickle departments. We gave them the opportunity to get away from image pricing. Vlasic offered the same cost per case but a higher suggested retail price. Vlasic had a good product and a wider line with well-designed packaging. It was also willing to promote and advertise. We weren't selling pickle items, we were selling an entirely new pickle department.

By August 1970 Vlasic's market share had grown to 18% and Mr. Souza was confident he would be representing the number one pickle company by the end of the year. He emphasized that the support he got from the company would keep market share.

The people at Vlasic really keep the pressure on. Russ Post accepts nothing but exceptional performance. He is also prepared to move a lot more quickly than his competition. We get a very fast response to changes in local conditions.

Farm and field

Each year the farm and field department, supervised by Mr. Leo Jokel, a veteran of 22 years with the Vlasic enterprises, contracted for the cucumbers grown on thousands of acres from Florida to Michigan.[3] Cucumbers in one location tended to mature at the same time. By purchasing over a large geographical area, Mr. Jokel was able to even out the flow of produce to the processing plants. The shortage of processing capacity and the emphasis on fresh-packed pickles increased the importance of cucumber procurement policies considerably. The matter was further complicated by uncertainties surrounding the total acres planted in the nation, the yield per acre under contract to Vlasic, and, of course, the price. To encourage loyalty during years when cucumbers were in short supply, Vlasic at times bought produce above the quantities agreed upon when yields were higher than anticipated. For 1971, Mr. Jokel intended to extend his purchases into Alabama to fill in the gap between the harvests in Florida and North Carolina.

In the South, Vlasic contracted with individual farmers for a specified acreage of cucumbers which was typically related to the amount of picking labor (e.g., the size of his family) that the farmer had available. Virtually all produce from the South was handpicked, and Vlasic supplied the seed. Farmers brought the cucumbers daily to receiving stations (Vlasic had 42 in North Carolina) and received payment; in fact, two checks were often made out because many farmers were sharecroppers who divided the proceeds with the landowner.

In Michigan and Ohio, Vlasic traditionally contracted with large growers to plant and harvest the crop. Until recently the company had supplied migrant laborers to pick the harvest and maintained extensive housing facilities for them and their families. In 1969 the company decided to discontinue furnishing the labor. Instead, subcontractors were hired who, in turn, contracted for acreage and supplied their own migrant workers. These subcontractors sold their entire output to Vlasic.

The farm and field activities were on the verge of significant change because of several external forces. In the first place, the law permitting the importation of Mexican labor was allowed to expire in 1965, and by 1970 the supply of domestic migrant labor was threatened. Cesar Chavez had successfully organized the grape pickers in California and was actively engaged in organizing workers in other agricultural sectors. Also, the increasing national concern over the plight of migrant workers was beginning to find expression in the courts. In July 1970, for instance, a Michigan apple farmer was taken to court because he did not provide adequate housing.

---

[3] Roughly 50% of Vlasic's cucumbers came from Florida, North Carolina, and Virginia, and the other 50% from Michigan and Ohio.

Secondly, the pickle industry was beginning to use mechanical harvesters to pick the cucumber crop. Vlasic owned five harvesters which were used successfully to pick about 10% of the 1970 harvest. These machines, costing over $20,000 apiece, were more effective than any developed in past years, and Mr. Jokel planned to purchase five more for 1971. Eventually he hoped that growers would buy their own machines. Currently, other large pickle companies were thought to employ mechanical harvesters more extensively than Vlasic. Mr. Jokel estimated that 12% of the total 1970 harvest was picked by machine.

Manufacturing

Cucumbers were trucked to the three Vlasic processing plants within hours after they were picked. Those to be fresh packed were sorted by size, washed, cut to the desired shape, and packed in glass jars with a sweet or dill liquor. In the harvest seasons, which extended from May through August, Vlasic processed all the fresh-packed pickles for the ensuing year; consequently, the plants operated two nine-hour shifts six days a week during this period. Cucumbers received in excess of packing capacity were placed in large open vats of brine to be packaged as processed pickles during the winter months when the plants operated on one shift five days per week.

The plants in Imlay City and Bridgeport, Michigan, were automated although hand labor was required to "top out" the jars by adding the last two or three pickles to each jar. The Memphis, Michigan, plant was a hand-packing operation for peppers and spear-shaped pickles which could not be packed by machine. According to Mr. Blum, vice president of manufacturing, all Vlasic plants were operating above capacity in 1970. While the Memphis plant was being expanded by about 30% for the 1971 season, he stated that it would be very difficult to expand the other plants because all available land on the existing sites had been used and the acquisition of contiguous space was doubtful. Exhibit 3 provides production figures for each location.

Vlasic hired women and high school students during the fresh-pack season to complement a cadre of permanent employees. Since working in a pickle plant required very little skill, wage rates were much lower than for jobs in other Detroit industries. As a result, the company experienced difficulty finding labor when employment levels in the area were high. In addition, working conditions were at times arduous.

The plants were located in three small towns near Detroit. It was possible for Mr. Blum to visit each of them in a day if he devoted about half the time to driving. Some feeling for the pace and style of the plant managers is provided in the description of a visit with one of them recounted in the Appendix.

EXHIBIT 3

VLASIC FOODS INC.
Summary Financial and Production Statistics

					Twelve months ended				
	6/30/62	6/30/63	6/30/64	6/30/65	3/30/66*	3/30/67	3/30/68	3/30/69	3/30/70
Net sales (thousands)	$1,739	$2,657	$3,802	$5,170	$5,602	$9,801	$12,724	$17,186	$20,992
Net income (thousands)	63	104	155	266	332	471	627	838	1,018†
Net income/net sales	3.6%	3.9%	4.1%	5.1%	5.9%	4.8%	4.9%	4.9%	4.9%
Earnings per share	$.15	$.25	$.31	$.40	$.50	$.69	$.91	$1.12	$1.24
Production (in thousands of cases)									
Imlay City	700	950	1,270	1,721	1,213	1,666	1,851	2,311	2,627
Bridgeport					575	895	859	1,739	2,157
Memphis					341	522	594	633	974
Philadelphia								296	115
Total	700	950	1,270	1,721	2,129	3,083	3,304	4,979	5,873

* Nine months only.
† After extraordinary charge of $14,000.
Source: Casewriter's summary of Vlasic Foods reports.

Pollution control was a continuing matter of concern to the industry because pickle plants generated a large amount of liquid waste from the washing and brine operations. Private sewer lines had been constructed at two of the plants to feed the waste into holding ponds, where it was treated and held until the state allowed it to be pumped into local rivers. In the past, Vlasic had received complaints from farmers near the holding ponds and had responded by placing aerators in the ponds, which successfully eliminated most of the odors.

Robert Vlasic

Mr. Vlasic spent approximately 50% of his time on Vlasic Foods, the remainder being consumed by a number of other businesses, including a food brokerage firm, an auto leasing company, a nursing home, and real estate developments. He explained his role in these terms:

Most of the time I spend on the pickle company is devoted to personnel planning and financial matters. For instance, I have handled our relationships with the banks and have negotiated the acquisitions we've made in the past. At the moment I've assumed responsibility for building a new plant on the East Coast, and when we go public I will assume the investor relations function as well. My theory is that the operating people have a full-time job running the business. My job should be to insulate them from outside influences so that their efforts will not be diluted. I'm also probably better qualified to handle most of these functions, too. On the other hand, I don't meddle in operations and may visit the plants only two or three times a year.

Mr. Vlasic did not receive a salary nor did he maintain an office at Vlasic Foods. Instead, he collected a management fee based on a small percentage of gross operating income from this and other ventures which he used to defray the operating expenses of Vlasic & Co. However, he maintained a very close awareness of the activities of his enterprises through a control system which he had designed.

I have a rule that one—and only one—piece of paper is to be submitted weekly to me from each business [see Exhibit 4 for an example from Vlasic Foods]. I am very concerned with the reporting forms which are used; in fact, so much so that I design them all myself. I do so partially because this type of communication is critical and partially because I enjoy it. A good deal of my time is devoted to studying the information and preparing special reports which we discuss at our board meetings.[4] [Note: Mr. Vlasic had large file cabinets behind his desk from which he could immediately produce neatly typed detailed information on any aspect of the business.]

---

[4] In addition to the weekly activity reports, Mr. Vlasic received (*a*) monthly printouts of sales in cases by product, broker, and customer; (*b*) monthly summaries of sales promotions and major sales expense items; and (*c*) quarterly financial closings by subaccount.

EXHIBIT 4

VLASIC FOODS INC.
Weekly Activity Report for Week Ending 7-24-70

SALES	$ Total	%GP
F.P. Pickles	203,334	*
Proc Pickles	125,732	*
Relishes	34,004	*
Peppers	56,213	*
Kraut	13,641	*
Institutional	32,028	*
Shupak	17,313	*
Government		
Miscellaneous (Olives)	627	*
TOTALS	482,892	*

QTR/DATE

$ Sales	1,903,109
Bal Proj	3,7.96,891
Bal Weeks	9

CASES SHIPPED	This Week	Quarter To Date
Imlay	49,767	204,184
Bridgeport	50,572	191,195
Philadelphia	3,790	11,800
Storage	2,997	14,191
TOTALS	107,126	421,370

PRODUCTION — QUARTER TO DATE

PLANTS		Bridgeport	Imlay	Memphis	Phil.	Total
THIS WEEK	$ Value	354,480	393,036	366,098	16,278	1,129,892
	Cases	73,202	91,019	74,832	2,332	241,385
QUARTER TO DATE	$ Value	1,824,775	1,966,777	1,388,033	59,565	5,239,150
	Bal Proj	3,225,225	3,283,223	2,206,967	115,435	8,830,850
	Cases	390,627	435,618	268,950	8,302	1,103,497
	Bal Proj	709,373	764,382	561,050	21,698	2,056,503

PACKING LABOR

		Bridgeport	Imlay	Memphis	Phil.	Total
THIS WEEK	$ Actual	9,572	12,308	39,424	2,432	63,736
	Standard	14,006	13,482	40,266	1,153	68,907
	FAV (UN)	4,434	1,174	842	(1,279)	5,171
QTR/DATE	$ Actual	58,820	58,738	123,430	6,757	247,745
	Standard	67,363	67,489	146,659	4,146	285,657
	FAV (UN)	8,543	8,751	23,229	(2,611)	37,912

EMPLOYEES	Admin	Sales	F & F	Bridg	Imlay	Memp	Shupak	Total
Number	53	18	21	295	314	634	34	1,369
Reg. Hrs			742	9,732	10,462	23,659	1,676	46,271
O.T. Hrs			3	368	488	653	145	1,657

* Data withheld by company.
Source: Robert Vlasic.

Major policy decisions were made by the executive committee, composed of Messrs. Vlasic, Post, and Dubin, which met twice a month in Mr. Vlasic's offices. The agenda for one meeting in July, designed and distributed by Mr. Vlasic, is shown below:

Agenda	Comment*
1. Acquisition possibility	Mr. Vlasic indicated reasons for deciding against buying a particular pickle company on the East Coast
2. Pollution control	Discussion of a consultant's proposal to study pollution problems for the company
3. Capital expenditures	Discussion of requests for 1970–71
4. Accounting format changes	Mr. Vlasic presented plans for increasing the clarity of financial data presentation
5. New corporate image	Presentation by Mr. Vlasic of the design for a new corporate logo
6. Case sales by market	Review of sales for June

* Provided by Mr. Vlasic and corroborated by Messrs. Post and Dubin.

Mr. Vlasic had also devised a formal planning system for the company. Each manager made detailed one- and five-year projections which were summarized to provide a financial forecast for Vlasic Foods. The projections were submitted to Mr. Vlasic, who approved or returned them after careful study. The first-year figures were revised quarterly, and those for subsequent years annually. Historically, sales estimates had always been low, although Mr. Vlasic commented: "In the beginning I was always adjusting their sights upwards, trying to get them to reach. Now I find myself on the other side of the table talking about restraints and getting overextended." Financial data are provided in Exhibits 3 and 5.

Ownership and compensation

On August 1, 1970, Vlasic & Co. owned 49% of Vlasic Foods, assuming conversion of certain debentures and exercise of stock options. The remainder of the ownership interests were spread among 23 individuals, 17 of whom were employees. Mr. Vlasic explained a policy he felt had contributed to the company's success over the years:

My father felt very strongly that a man works harder if he owns a piece of the business. Al Dubin was given the opportunity to become a very sizable stockholder for that reason. We have continued that policy in several ways.

First, our acquisitions have been for stock—the seller is encouraged to integrate his operation with ours and see his career tied to the success of Vlasic.

Second, we have given stock options to key men in management and recently have extended options to some men at supervisory levels.[5] I have developed a formula to set the option price: book value plus the earnings per share for the previous three years.[6] This is considered quite a bargain.

Although there was no ready market for Vlasic shares, Mr. Vlasic had always repurchased any shares offered at the current option price.

Compensation policy for top management was also based on a strong belief in incentives. Mr. Vlasic summed it up by saying, "We have a philosophy that it's best to pay a man a modest salary and give him the rest in bonus if he and the company both perform well." Although bonus determination was theoretically one of the tasks of the compensation committee,[7] Mr. Vlasic indicated that he made the final decision based on the internal reports and his subjective evaluation of the man's performance. While bonuses were paid each May for the prior year,

---

[5] Options had been granted to all men at the vice-presidential level, four men at the next level, and four more among the supervisors.

[6] Vlasic had a "qualified stock option plan" and as a result, provided certain conditions were met, the recipients did not realize income for tax purposes upon receipt or exercise of the option. Under one of these conditions, a qualified stock option could not be granted to an employee who held over 5% of the shares (which for Vlasic included Messrs. Dubin, Post, Blum, and the Raznick brothers).

[7] Composed of Robert Vlasic, Joseph Vlasic, and Al Dubin.

EXHIBIT 5

VLASIC FOODS INC.
Balance Sheets—March 30, 1969, and March 29, 1970

	1969	1970
Assets		
Current assets		
Cash	$ 546,591	$ 814,055
Accounts receivable (less allowance for doubtful accounts of $12,764 in 1969 and $23,000 in 1970)	1,178,243	1,146,997
Inventories, at the lower of cost (first-in, first-out) or market		
Produce	$ 953,578	$ 1,137,268
Containers and supplies	358,247	336,881
Finished goods	5,588,501	6,875,928
Total inventories	$ 6,900,326	$ 8,350,077
Prepaid expenses	38,088	62,664
Total current assets	$ 8,663,248	$10,373,793
Property, plant, and equipment at cost		
Land and buildings	$ 366,904	$ 604,126
Machinery, equipment, and fixtures	2,544,125	2,908,279
Leasehold improvements	1,277,489	1,357,249
Total property, plant, and equipment	$ 4,188,518	$ 4,869,654
Less: Reserves for depreciation and amortization	2,309,592	2,715,754
Net property	$ 1,878,926	$ 2,153,900
Other assets	80,300	47,800
Total assets	$10,622,474	$12,575,493
Liabilities		
Current liabilities		
Unsecured notes payable to bank	$ 975,000	$ 2,000,000
Current portion of long-term debt	304,867	315,752
Accounts payable	1,266,255	1,243,514
Accrued liabilities	478,262	438,200
Accrued income taxes	390,892	306,874
Total current liabilities	$ 3,415,276	$ 4,304,340
Long-term debt, less current portion included above	2,948,500	3,171,508
Shareholders' equity		
Common stock, $1 par value; authorized 800,000 shares in 1969 and 1,000,000 in 1970; outstanding, 735,000 shares in 1969 and 719,000 shares in 1970*	735,000	719,000
Paid-in surplus	271,550	110,450
Retained earnings*	3,252,148	4,270,195
Total shareholders' equity	$ 4,258,698	$ 5,099,645
Total liabilities	$10,622,474	$12,575,493

* Difference accounted for by the redemption of 30,000 shares for $254,700 and the exercise of options for 14,000 shares at various prices aggregating $77,600.

the managers were given some feeling for what they would be if the profit projections for the year were attained. Mr. Vlasic had concluded in 1968 that the percentage of total compensation for top management paid in cash bonuses ought to be cut back, salaries increased, and a formal profit-sharing plan introduced for all nonunion employees. In 1969, 6% of employee earnings were contributed to the profit-sharing fund, and it was hoped that eventually this percentage could be increased to 10%. Nonetheless, for the seven top-paid managers (Post, Dubin, Blum, Jerry Shupak, Maurice and Fred Raznick, and Jokel), the bonuses were substantial in relation to salary and, in Mr. Vlasic's judgment, were likely to remain an important part of the compensation package for senior management.

Year	Compensation index	Percentage of compensation			
		Salary	Bonus	PSF	Total
Top seven managers					
1968	100	53	47	. .	100
1969	112	52	45	3	100
1970	115	59	35	6	100
Three middle managers*					
1968	100	83	17	. .	100
1969	110	80	16	4	100
1970	123	82	13	5	100

* A regional sales manager, the institutional sales manager, and a farm and field supervisor. In 1968 the average compensation of these men was 40% that of the top seven managers.

Organization

The formal organization structure and assignment of responsibilities was a subject of continuing discussion at Vlasic. Each time a modification was made or a new man added, the organization chart was carefully redesigned by Mr. Vlasic to incorporate the change. The most recent chart of May 1970, reproduced in Exhibit 6, was drawn up when Russell Post assumed the presidency. Mr. Vlasic commented on this event:

Al Dubin has worked terrifically hard over the past 40-odd years and is now a wealthy man. He has talked about retiring several times to enjoy the fruits of his labor and I wouldn't be surprised if he does in a couple of years. Russell has agreed to become president and assume responsibility for manufacturing, which had previously reported to Dubin. Al is continuing to look after the control function and farm and field, though in time he may relinquish the latter as well.

When Mr. Post moved up to president, Ed VerLee was made national sales manager with the entire field sales force reporting to him, including

EXHIBIT 6

VLASIC FOODS INC.
Organization Chart
May 1970

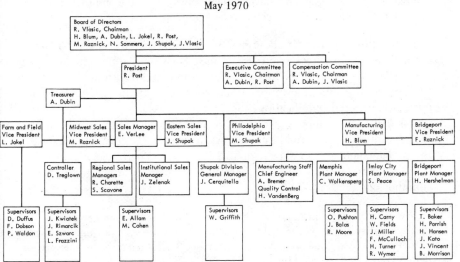

Maurice Raznick and Jerry Shupak, both vice presidents. Mr. Post retained control over marketing policy and the allocation of advertising and promotion funds. He was currently considering the addition of a high-level staff man to assist him with the merchandising function.

The three processing plants in Michigan reported to Herman Blum.[8] He described his job as follows:

> Pickle packing is a tough business, especially when you are continually pushed by sales for more production than the plants are supposed to be able to deliver. We pack over half of our annual production in four months, which means a lot of 18-hour days during the summer for our supervisors and plant managers. We have a pretty tired lot by August. A good deal of my time is devoted to touring plants, listening to problems, and helping the plant managers break bottlenecks. Meeting the production quotas is of utmost importance in the fresh-pack season because volume lost can't be regained.
>
> Developing managers is an important part of what I do. Vlasic has a more conscientious crew than any of its competitors. We've been able to hire people who are willing to get their hands dirty and work long hours. I tell them that's what it is going to be like and that we expect it. Our top management sets a good example and everyone else follows.

Mr. Blum, however, was soon to assume a new position in the company. He continued:

---

[8] At present the small deli-pickle operation in Philadelphia was directed by a general manager responsible directly to Russell Post.

Bob Vlasic has suggested that I relinquish responsibility for production and plant operations. I would keep manufacturing processes and layout, quality assurance, and research and development. No one in the industry is doing much R & D, and someday it's going to be really important.

A search directed by Mr. Post had been underway for several months for a manager to direct plant operations. He would report to Mr. Post and be at the same level in the organization as Mr. Blum. Mr. Vlasic formulated the job description and discussed with his executive committee the desired qualifications for the job.

Virtually every manager at Vlasic had had long experience in the pickle industry or in food brokerage businesses. A personal profile of the management group is provided in Exhibit 7. There was a noticeable esprit de corps in the company that Maurice Raznick attributed to being "number one":

We [the Raznick brothers] had always wanted to be number one in the pickle industry. With Vlasic, we have done it. Now we give our new salesmen the challenge that they should be number one with their accounts. Everyone here is committed to being the best.

Expansion

To fulfill the sales forecasts for the next several years, Vlasic was confronted with a need for considerable additional capacity. For a variety of reasons, particularly proximity to markets and growing areas, it was best to locate plants in different parts of the country. The Vlasic plan called for a plant in the East immediately and another in the West within five years. Mr. Vlasic described the situation as follows:

We have been looking for a company to buy on the East Coast for a year now; the ideal candidate would have a good physical plant with poor brand identification and low profits. I don't suppose we would be willing to pay for a really profitable company unless it had surplus production capacity, because that is what we are looking for. An acquisition hasn't worked out, so I'm now searching for a plant site.

The cost of this first plant was estimated at $3.5 to $4 million, and two years were thought to be necessary to have it on line at full capacity (3 million cases), during which time it would probably sustain losses.

Financing the coming expansion created certain difficulties. All the existing facilities were owned by Vlasic & Co. and Mr. Dubin and leased to Vlasic Foods. The money for this purpose had been raised through the sale of other Vlasic companies, notably the milk and food distribution businesses. Now, as Mr. Vlasic put it, "There is no more money in the barrel." His tentative plan called for a bond issue to finance the

EXHIBIT 7

VLASIC FOODS INC.
Management Profile

Executive	Position	Years with Vlasic*	Age	Previous experience	Education
R. Vlasic	Chairman		44	. . .	B.S. industrial engineering
R. Post	President	13	46	Family-owned distribution business bought by Vlasic	B.A. economics
A. Dubin	Treasurer	42	57	. . .	B.A. accounting
H. Blum	V.P. manufacturing	11	51	Manager pickle plants since 1946	M.S. biochemistry
L. Jokel	V.P. farm and field	22	53	30 years in food business in various capacities	High school
M. Raznick	V.P. midwest sales	5	60	Family-owned pickle co. acquired by Vlasic	High school
E. VerLee	Sales manager	6	41	Food brokerage co.; wholesale grocery co.	2 years college
J. Shupak	V.P. eastern sales	2	35	Family-owned pickle co. acquired by Vlasic	BBA
M. Shupak	V.P. Philadelphia	2	58	Family-owned pickle co. acquired by Vlasic	n.a.
F. Raznick	V.P. Bridgeport	5	48	Family-owned pickle co. acquired by Vlasic	n.a.
D. Treglown	Controller	7	34	CPA firm	BBA
R. Charette	Regional sales manager	5	42	Came to Vlasic with acquired Crown Co.	1 year college
S. Scavone	Regional sales manager	2	34	Food brokerage co.	1 year college
J. Zelenak	Inst. sales manager	16	44	Retail and institutional distribution co.	1 year college
J. Cerquitella	Shupak division general manager	1	40	13 years, food distribution companies	BBA
A. Bremer	Chief engineer	2	58	Plant engineer for large pickle co. 20 years	High school
H. VandenBerg	Quality control	2	56	20 years in pickle bus.	B.S. education
K. Wolkensperg	Plant manager	1	30	Experience with another pickle company	3 years college in chemistry
S. Peace	Plant manager	8	44	15 years in pickle plants	High school
H. Hershelman	Plant manager	3	43	20 years in pickle plants	High school

* Years with Vlasic includes time with any Vlasic business.
n.a. = not available.
Source: Casewriter's notes.

new plant, with the possibility at some point in the future of a public offering of Vlasic stock.

The organizational consequences of expansion were also of concern to the management group. Combined with the new roles in prospect for Russ Post and Herman Blum, they posed the need for additional operating managers and possibly a new organization structure. Already Mr. Post was devoting a portion of his time to traveling to and from Philadelphia in an effort to improve the performance of the new deli plant there (see Exhibit 4).

Mr. Vlasic had also begun to consider major changes in the function and composition of the board of directors, which currently was composed of:

Robert Vlasic	Chairman
Russell Post	President
Albert Dubin	Treasurer
Herman Blum	Vice president, manufacturing
Leo Jokel	Vice president, farm and field
Maurice Raznick	Vice president, midwest sales
Jerry Shupak	Vice president, eastern sales
Norman Sommers	Attorney
Joseph Vlasic	Director

Meetings, held quarterly, had served as occasions to discuss operating results and had been viewed by the line managers as an indication of their success in business. Though he recognized it would not be received favorably, Mr. Vlasic was disposed to replace the four vice presidents with outside directors who would be in a position to offer advice and counsel on the problems likely to confront the company in the future.

APPENDIX
VISIT WITH A PLANT MANAGER

In July 1970 the researcher visited the hand-packing plant in Memphis, Michigan, with Herman Blum, vice president of manufacturing, on one of his frequent field trips.[9] The two men passed through the front office, occupied by five girls who were busy with payroll and other clerical tasks, to another office opening out into the packing area. There they were greeted by the plant manager, Mr. K. A. Wolkensperg, dressed in a sports shirt, who had just walked in from the plant.

After the researcher had been introduced, Mr. Blum and Mr. Wolkensperg discussed production quotas and operating problems for several minutes. Mr. Wolkensperg indicated that one of his problems

---

[9] Mr. Blum visited the plants about three times a week during the fresh-pack season.

had been a shortage of labor. The conversation was concluded when Mr. Blum said that he would pay a visit that afternoon to the employment agency in [the largest neighboring town about 20 miles away] to see what could be done. Mr. Wolkensperg then offered to show the researcher the plant, commenting as they left the office:

Packing pickles is a hard business. Our people work long hours, and the jobs aren't too pleasant. But we are here to get pickles packed—not to be sociologists. We aren't like a big operation, such as General Foods which has to have a nurse in every plant. Things happen very fast during the harvest season, and we have to be able to make quick decisions. We couldn't function with a big corporate bureaucracy which had to approve every decision. I don't get to the main offices much. Most of my time is spent out here on the floor.

The work force, largely women, were returning from a coffee break, and the floor supervisors were shouting for them to come along. Mr. Wolkensperg picked up a pickle that the researcher almost stepped on and took it over to one of the cleanup crew, cautioning him to be more careful. Passing by a cucumber cutter, he told the operators to keep the chatter to a minimum. A few seconds later, a supervisor hurried up to say that one of the processing machines had broken down. Evidently Mr. Wolkensperg had pieced it together earlier with "scotch tape and bailing wire." With the assistance of a maintenance man, he proceeded to get it started again. No sooner had this been finished than several yards away one of the labeling machines jammed and bottles began to pile up in front of the machine. Mr. Wolkensperg turned his attention to this new situation, offering advice to the lead operator which resulted in a solution to the problem.

As the three men returned to the office, Mr. Wolkensperg observed:

We don't have time to overhaul our machines now. That will have to wait until fall. My job is to keep this place moving without sacrificing quality. What you've just seen is pretty typical. It would sure help if we had some more good people in the plant, though.

Walking back through the parking lot, Mr. Blum expressed his satisfaction with the way the Memphis plant was being managed. Although Mr. Wolkensperg had been with Vlasic for only a year, Mr. Blum indicated that he was viewed as "a comer" in the organization.

Vappi & Company Inc.

I SUPPOSE a consultant would consider our organization[1] a little weird in that each project has essentially two bosses—the project manager and the superintendent. In practice, I think that this arrangement may result in better decisions; there are two inputs instead of one. It is hard for just one person to consider all the factors; with two, there are more ideas and more possibilities. In this business, there are many ways of getting something done, and having two heads thinking about it seems better than one.

On the other hand, I suppose having one man in charge would give more control on project costs and schedules. There are occasional conflicts, but I think, in general, that the man in whose area of competence the crux of the decisions lies tends to take the dominant role in the decision-making process. For example, if it's a problem concerning the architect, the project manager's opinion is likely to prevail. If the problem concerns the work force, the superintendent's opinion is most important. The nature of the problem determines who is most influential. My vice presidents work well together. Each defers to the other's special area of competence. They complement each other. I think their personalities are the key to this structure.

Vincent Vappi, president of the Vappi construction company, was explaining his firm's organization in 1970. Each project was managed by both a superintendent and a project manager. These men reported to different superiors who, in turn, reported to Vappi. Under this arrangement the firm had grown from $10 million in sales in 1962 to $40 million in 1969. (See Exhibits 2 and 3 for financial data.) Yet

---

[1] See Exhibit 1 for an organization chart.

EXHIBIT 1

VAPPI & COMPANY INC.
Organization Chart—June 1970

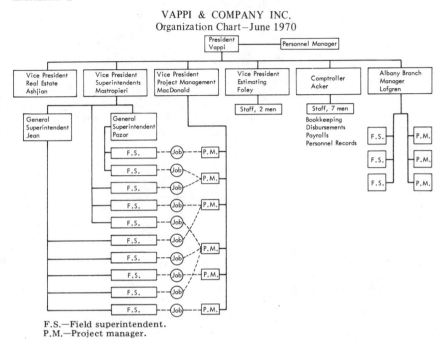

F.S.—Field superintendent.
P.M.—Project manager.

operating losses in 1969, the firm's planned entry into the real estate business, and the recent loss of three out of eight project managers[2] raised some questions as to the structure's future viability.

VINCENT VAPPI

The article was titled "How to make a million: three American success stories," the magazine was *U.S. News & World Report* for December 15, 1969. One of the three millionaires was Vincent Vappi.

For C. Vincent Vappi, an urbane 42-year-old builder from Boston, the road to a million dollars took longer to travel. The construction firm he controls—Vappi & Company—has grown steadily, and his personal fortune, now more than 2 million dollars, has risen accordingly.

Mr. Vappi's father, a brickmason, from Italy, started the business in 1927. For many years, it was a small operation—a few warehouses, small additions to plants, subcontracting work.

By 1948, when Mr. Vappi graduated from Massachusetts Institute of Technology, the company was worth $250,000. He joined it as a field supervisor

---

[2] One project manager left for health reasons. The two others went to work in firms where they felt the opportunities were greater.

EXHIBIT 2
Vappi performance versus industry median

		1962	1963	1964	1965	1966	1967	1968	1969
Profit/billings	Vappi	0.6%	0.2%	0.6%	1.4%	0.4%	0.5%	0.05%	(0.7%)
	Industry	n.a.	1.5	1.3	1.4	1.4	1.4	n.a.	n.a.
Profit/net worth	Vappi	8.9	11.5	8.3	23.6	8.0	9.0	1.2	(14.0)
	Industry	n.a.	3.0	8.5	9.7	12.4	9.9	n.a.	n.a.
Profit/working capital	Vappi	8.8	2.5	5.2	14.7	6.1	5.9	0.9	(7.2)
	Industry	n.a.	18.8	14.7	16.7	19.1	16.3	n.a.	n.a.
Billing/working capital	Vappi	14.9	14.0	8.8	10.0	14.9	12.2	17.4	10.7
	Industry	n.a.	12.6	11.1	11.1	11.5	12.2	n.a.	n.a.
Billing/net worth	Vappi	14.8	15.0	13.8	16.8	20.0	22.5	16.5	24.1
	Industry	n.a.	7.8	6.7	6.7	9.0	7.3	n.a.	n.a.

n.a. = not available.

EXHIBIT 3
Vappi contract activity, 1962–70

Year	Value of new contracts (millions)	New contracts negotiated (%)	Value of completed contracts (millions)	Value of work done during year (millions)	Net profit (loss) (after tax) (thousands)
			Total company contract activity		
1962	n.a.	n.a.	$ 8.5	$10.3	$ 61
1963	n.a.	n.a.	5.4	13.0	24
1964	$ 19.5	n.a.	17.2	12.2	72
1965	26.8	n.a.	16.3	19.9	286
1966·	26.0	n.a.	23.4	29.3	121
1967	51.0	21	26.7	31.7	153
1968	25.2	40·	31.4	43.4	22
1969	110.6	12	44.2	37.5	(253)
1970*	27.7	0	36.5†	n.a.	n.a.
			Contract activity for Albany alone		
1965	n.a.	0	$ 1.02		
1966	n.a.	0	4.68		
1967	$ 6.6	0	3.15		
1968	2.0	0	5.4		
1969	23.8‡	0	3.6		
1970	11.0‡	0	n.a.		

*To September 15, 1970.
†Projected.
‡The Albany office had four contracts in September 1970. The two largest were with IBM, one for a $10-million building and the other for a $20-million building.
n.a. = not available.

at $90 a week. Shares in the firm his father had given him were then worth less than $20,000.

In 1952, he became a vice president at $12,000 a year, then managing vice president in 1955 at $28,000. It was then that his father first became ill, and the younger Vappi began to change the nature of the business. He explains:

"It seemed to me that universities would mushroom. So we began bidding for campus jobs. A 2.5 million dollar dormitory for Boston University came first. One project led to another.

"The key events were getting the next big job—to show we could handle bigger or more complex buildings, or do big jobs in a hurry. There was a 6-million-dollar law-education building for Boston University, then a 9-million-dollar apartment house for married students at Harvard."

Business grew in volume from 6 million dollars in 1955 to 10 million in 1962. This year, Vappi & Company will put up 40 million dollars in new construction, including hospitals, libraries, government buildings.

A clash in viewpoints. Along the way, Mr. Vappi's ideas conflicted with those of his father.

"His idea was to make all the decisions, and seek higher profits on fewer jobs. I wanted more volume, even if it meant less profit at first. I wanted to adopt modern-management concepts and parcel out more responsibility to others.

"When my father said, 'Give me back more management responsibility or buy me out,' I bought him out. I paid $150,000 for his interest in 1962—$5,000 down, the rest to be paid off at $12,000 a year, interest free."

That gave Mr. Vappi 55 percent of the voting stock, then worth $337,500. He also owned part of a realty trust, valued at $100,000, that he had set up with four brothers and sisters.

Late in 1965, his holdings in the building firm and realty trust passed the million-dollar mark. At last accounting, his net worth was 2.36 millions.

His present 70 percent interest in the construction company, valued at 2 million dollars, accounts for most of his assets. The realty trust, which developed an industrial park in a Boston suburb, is being liquidated this year. Mr. Vappi expects to wind up with a gain on that deal of $600,000 after taxes.

The whopping gain will make a bulge in income this year. In recent years, Mr. Vappi's earnings had run around $100,000—$81,000 in salary as president of Vappi & Company, $12,000 salary as head of the realty trust, the rest in capital gains.

But Mr. Vappi decided to cash in the realty trust this year, rather than wait, to avoid higher rates on capital gains that he expects Congress to vote.

The $600,000 of profits—"the first significant free money I have had"—are being invested in Treasury Notes, temporarily, and in stocks. "With credit tight," he says, "this is a tough time to invest in real estate. The tax-reform bill may also make real estate less attractive an investment."

If he doesn't invest in real estate, Mr. Vappi will put money in tax-free bonds as "an anchor to windward." Still, over the long run, "you have to invest in growth stocks or real estate to keep ahead of inflation and taxes.

"I don't feel like a millionaire," Mr. Vappi comments. "I feel more like a well-off member of the middle class. We live comfortably, but not like the jet set. We have a little more of everything, but our living style hasn't changed, basically, over the years."

In 1948, Mr. Vappi and his wife lived in a fourth-floor walk-up in Cambridge. Now they own two $100,000 homes—one in Milton, Mass., and a summer place along the Massachusetts shore at Marion—three cars, and a 34-foot sloop. College for a daughter and private school for another daughter and son cost up to $12,000 a year.

Mr. Vappi spends more and more of his time on community activities, as a trustee of a hospital, private school, college and an aquarium. These outside activities "keep me up with the problems of our time, and they are also a low-key way of keeping our company's name before the community."

Though day-to-day operations of the company have been turned over to others, Mr. Vappi still visits each job site. One day, while Mr. Vappi was walking through a mental-health center his firm is building, a friend said:

"Money isn't the big thing with Vince. He gets a sense of accomplishment, going around Boston and seeing the buildings he has put up, buildings that will be around long after he has gone."[3]

Vappi's goals for the construction company were to double sales by 1980. These objectives were motivated by a desire to create more positions in the management structure for bright young men—to challenge these men so that they would stay with the firm. On the other hand, he felt a balance was needed. Vappi expressed the feeling that the extraordinary rate of growth experienced by the firm in the 1960s might have overchallenged many of his personnel. Bob MacDonald, vice president of project management, commented on this point.

The field force and the project managers are very young. The company has grown so fast that many of them have questions about their ability in their present positions. The expansion was so dramatic we've been running to catch up. We've also had problems with the blacks, unions, and even the architectural firms which have been growing so fast that their plans have suffered. Recently I lost three of my eight project managers, and as a result I am heavily engaged in projects trying to pick up the slack until our new managers learn their jobs.

Having concentrated solely on growth in the past, Vappi wanted to "fine tune" his operation so that sales growth would be accompanied by a gross income of 5% of sales and a general overhead of less than 2½% of sales. (See Exhibits 2 and 3 for financial performance from 1962 to 1969.)

Vappi was also concerned about planning for orderly management succession. "I have an emotional investment in the firm, and I naturally don't want to see it disintegrate. I might leave active management of the firm fairly soon, to pursue extracurricular activities—or fairly late, to retire. The time range, therefore, is very broad." The two principal candidates for Vappi's position as president were Bob MacDonald, the vice president of project management, and Frank Mastropieri, vice president of superintendents. Both men had been with the company since the mid-1950s and had always been treated as equals. Each man was under 45 and had an excellent reputation in the industry. (See Exhibit 4 for personal data on key managers.)

VAPPI & COMPANY INC.

Vappi & Company was considered by architects, owners, and subcontractors to be an excellent building contractor. The firm specialized in

---

[3] Copyright © 1969, U.S. News & World Report, Inc.

EXHIBIT 4
Vappi top management

Name	Age	Year joined Vappi	Positions at Vappi	Formal education
Vappi	43	1948	President	B.S., MIT 1948
MacDonald	38	1957	V.P. of project management, 1962; project manager, 1957	B.S., MIT 1953; M.B.A., HBS 1957
Mastropieri	44	1952	V.P. of superintendents, 1964; superintendent, 1954; engineer, 1952	B.S., Northeastern 1946
Foley	50	1954	V.P. of estimating, 1958; estimator, 1954	B.S., MIT 1948
Ashjian	38	1958	V.P. of real estate, 1969; project manager, 1958	B.S., Northeastern 1954; M.S., MIT 1958
Acker	55	1955	Comptroller, 1955	None
Lofgren	35	1960	Albany branch manager, 1965; assistant superintendent, 1963; engineer, 1960	n.a.
Jean	39	1954	General superintendent, 1968; superintendent, 1960; engineer, 1955	Associate, Wentworth College 1952
Pazar	41	1953	General superintendent, 1969; superintendent, 1955; engineer, 1953	B.S., MIT 1954

n.a. = not available.

nonresidential buildings and was a leader in poured concrete technology. In 1969 Vappi had $111 million in new contracts, which placed it 55th among the 400 largest contractors in the United States. During the same year, Vappi *completed* work on projects worth $40 million (see Exhibit 3).

Construction jobs were acquired in two basic ways. Using the traditional method, an owner had an architect complete all plans and specifications and then invited contractors to bid on the project. Architects thus frequently influenced the selection of the contractors. An increasingly used method of acquiring jobs in the industry involved the owner's selection of a reputable contractor in the early planning stages and inviting him to negotiate an overall cost and fee. This procedure allowed the contractor to influence significantly the design and specifications.

Upon securing a job, the general contractor immediately let subcontracts varying from 60% to 90% of the total dollar volume of construction to subcontractors in as many as 23 different trade functions. For example, Vappi was directly responsible for all concrete work (forming and pouring) and some masonry and carpentry. All other work was subcontracted.

"Subs," as they were called in the trade, were completely independent. They dealt separately with their own unions, had scheduling problems of their own, and, in general, belonged to organizations over which the general contractor had little influence or control. "Reputation" occasionally exceeded "bid price" as a determinant in selection of the "sub." Subcontracts were all fixed price, with the general contractor protected by a performance bond against subcontractor default on contract terms.

All Vappi's bids and some contract negotiations[4] were handled by John Foley and his two-man staff. Foley based his estimates on subcontractor bids as well as on an analysis of the architect's plans and an assessment of future material and labor costs. Since Vappi's average project had high architectural content, required several years to complete, involved year-round work in all weather, and was often delayed by strikes, the most difficult part of the estimating task was predicting labor productivity on the aspects of the job for which Vappi was directly responsible.

The history of the Employment Security Building contract illustrates many of the problems associated with construction projects:

August 1966:	Bids solicited, plans distributed.
September 1966:	Vappi's bid, $11,000,000; low bid, $9,900,000.
November 1966:	All bids rejected, bidders invited to resubmit.
December 1966:	Foley estimates a cost of $11,600,000. Final Vappi bid, $10,745,000.
January 1967:	Vappi awarded contract. Next lowest bid, $11,100,000. LaPlante assigned as project manager, Pazar as superintendent.
April 1967:	Vappi's attempt to change foundation design for purpose of saving money denied. Officials felt a possibility of suits from other bidders.
May 1967:	Inadequate rock formation increases foundation costs and delays concrete operations.
August 1967:	Labor shortage in Boston area becomes acute. The most skilled craftsmen drift towards jobs paying the most overtime. Vappi hampered by inexperienced laborers.
June 1968:	Ironworkers strike (they place reinforcing bar inside concrete forms). Concrete work and many other trades delayed until September 15.
May 1969:	Carpenter workers strike. Most construction delayed three months. Pazar promoted to general superintendent.
January 1970:	Partial occupancy.
March 1970:	Full occupancy.
June 1970:	All work completed. (Exhibit 5 contains a photograph of the building.)

---

[4] Foley usually made the technical estimates for negotiated contracts and either Vappi or MacDonald handled the actual negotiations with the owners and architects.

EXHIBIT 5
Employment Security building

The number of different projects managed by Vappi at any one time varied considerably. The average number during 1968–69 was 17. In July 1970 the company was managing 11 projects with values ranging from $1.6 million to $23 million. (See Exhibit 6 for a typical portfolio of projects.)

A branch office

In 1964, perceiving that construction for colleges and universities in the Albany-Schenectady-Troy area might allow him to commence operations there in a manner similar to the Boston area, Vappi opened a branch office in Albany. In 1970 the office was staffed with a branch manager, three project managers, three superintendents, and an office manager. These men managed projects ranging in value from $1 million to $20 million. Except for periodic financial reports, New York operations were completely separated from those in Boston.

Of the top-management staff, only Vappi himself made regular trips to Albany. Vappi viewed branch offices as primarily an "overflow outlet" for his young, aggressive engineers who might otherwise leave the firm in search of higher positions. Vappi was not anxious to open another branch office soon. He explained: "I'd like to see this one ripen and mature; I'd like to get some confidence in them so I don't have to put out brush fires; I'd like to see them show profits before I consider another one."

EXHIBIT 6

VAPPI & COMPANY INC.
Jobs under Construction: October 1968

	Original contract amount	Revised contract amount	Original estimate of profit	Current estimate of profit	Percent completed
B.U. instructional	$ 5,225,000	$ 6,986,777	$ 96,300	$ 275,000	88
Maine Medical	6,647,580	7,644,920	429,774	365,358	90
Rouse Co.	3,740,000	4,015,000	150,000	215,000	100
Quincy Market, Gloucester	2,300,000	1,815,000	100,000	100,000	100
Employment Security	10,745,000	11,073,397	400,000	−557,032	48
Burlington site.	1,341,000	1,339,000	30,200	− 7,000	100
Filene's, Burlington. . . .	1,922,009	1,685,103	65,000	− 14,728	100
Mental Health	10,935,400	10,936,484	1,000,000	12,997	44
Sears, Burlington	2,046,422	3,693,020	47,492	47,000	100
Paul Revere	4,777,000	5,356,766	145,000	− 53,000	85
Technical Operations . . .	834,000	832,000	47,000	47,000	100
WNAC	3,594,000	3,658,062	150,000	150,000	84
University Hospital	348,800	348,600	19,000	25,500	99
Gillette, Andover	6,695,000	6,806,557	175,000	245,022	70
Quincy Market, South Bay	3,500,000	3,500,000	140,000	140,000	22
Radcliffe, new house . . .	6,227,400	6,227,400	225,000	255,000	1
Gillette office	1,931,913	1,227,400	100,000	100,000	1
Harvard Law.	3,547,000	3,547,000	82,500	100,500	23
	$76,357,624	$81,396,999	$3,402,266	$1,457,873	

Real estate

In 1969 Vappi decided to reenter the real estate development business. (Between 1955 and 1962, the firm had been involved with real estate development on a small scale.) Peter Ashjian, previously a project manager, was given the position of vice president of real estate. In July 1970 Ashjian was studying real estate literature while phasing out the projects he was managing.

Vappi planned to enter joint ventures with real estate management firms to develop industrial parks and sell or lease buildings. He wanted to complete one project before starting another until his staff became more experienced. While profit margins in real estate were greater than in construction, Vappi felt that his reputation and skills as a professional, respectable community builder would be maintained best by keeping real estate to less than one third of the firm's sales.

Organization structure

Two key individuals, having equal status and authority, supervised each project: the project manager and superintendent. The project manager officially represented Vappi to the owner and architect and was responsible for all coordination among the three of them; he purchased all materials and negotiated the subcontracts. A project manager could have from one to three projects, depending on their complexity. The superintendent supervised, directed, and coordinated all "on-site" activities, which included determination and scheduling of manpower requirements. The remainder of the company was organized to support and control these two critical jobs. (See Exhibit 1.)

As Vappi's comments at the beginning of this case indicate, one of the questions facing Vappi and his firm in 1970 was the long-term viability of this way of organizing the company's activities. Frank Mastropieri, vice president of superintendents, commented:

> I've been plugging a long time for having one man in overall charge of each project. On big projects which require a full-time project manager, the project manager should be based on the job—he should have his office on site instead of at headquarters; this would allow us to appoint a "head man" who could then give the project tighter control, keep costs down, and insure schedules were met.

Manny Pazar, one of the two general superintendents, illustrated the problem:

> You've got to realize that the easy decisions each will try to solve—everybody takes shots at the easy ones; the hard ones everyone shuns. I think we drop some of the important decisions because no one has been assigned to take care of them. For example, a project manager ordered the reinforcing bar for a tightly confined project, not realizing that the superintendent didn't have enough room to store it. He would have had to move it five times if it had arrived when ordered. I think these functions (project manager and superintendent) should be combined into one position. We are getting further and further apart.
>
> It seems there is an overlap of effort due to this nondelineation of duties. It bothers me not to know what my job is—I think I'm more valuable if I know what is expected of me, where I'm going. I don't know where my authority starts and where it ends. There should be more coordination, more meeting of the minds. The project manager, the superintendent, and the general superintendent all have their place—but the overlap confuses the superintendent. The general superintendent might tell a superintendent something in the morning only to have it reversed in the afternoon by the project manager.

A project manager, however, was more optimistic than Pazar. He agreed with Vappi that the present structure provided a good system of checks and balances.

> As it is now, there is a system of checks and balances. I ask the super if he has been doing this and that, and he asks me if I let this subcontract

and what I included in it. Other contractors have a project manager right on the job, and that is nothing more than a glorified super.

Now I have to purchase the job and give the owner the contract. If we were under a single system, the project manager would spend a lot more time coordinating and scheduling and the super would spend more time actually supervising the job. Anyway, I am sure that working out a good personal relationship can overcome this "ball dropping" that some think can happen.

Generally the supers are the guys pushing for single responsibility. They like to run the job and are used to giving orders and having things done their own way. Supers don't have any feeling for the administrative and coordination problems, however. They don't display an awareness of the administrative aspects and they don't think in terms of protecting themselves or the owner. Supers have come up through the ranks, having worked on jobs as engineers for 10 years before being made the super of their own job.

Compensation system

The potential coordination problems caused by the dual responsibility structure were being compounded in some people's eyes by the company's evaluation and reward system. Pazar commented:

How can they really evaluate me when they won't tell me exactly what I'm supposed to do? I was so frustrated by my lack of job description as a superintendent and not knowing who was supposed to do what, that I asked to be made a project manager. When they told me I was going to be a general superintendent instead, I agreed only on the condition that they spell out exactly what I was responsible for. It's been four months now, and they still haven't told me.

MacDonald indicated that he had no specific criteria for evaluating a project manager. He based his evaluation on how well he thought the project manager handled architect relations and the subcontractors working for him and how well he coordinated with the superintendents. Mastropieri said he gave some weight to the labor-cost variance figures but that he generally evaluated his subordinates on "how well they controlled the job," their initiative, and their ability to plan ahead and see problems coming. Although Vappi had no explicit criteria for evaluating his subordinates, he felt that his daily contact with them sufficiently enabled him to determine their compensation.

Compensation was the source of much dissatisfaction among project managers and superintendents, however. Bonuses were paid to supers at the completion of a profitable project. The size of these bonuses was determined by Vappi, Mastropieri, and MacDonald and varied according to an assessment of the quality of the work and the amount of profit realized. Bonuses were paid to project managers at the end of the calendar year if the company had made a profit. Vappi devised a rough plan under which 10% of the profit before taxes and contribution to pension and profit sharing was distributed, two thirds to the vice presidents and one third to the project managers. One project manager summarized his objection to the system: "After three years, my project showed a $100,000 profit where we planned for only $50,000. Yet the superintendent who had an unfavorable labor variance of $40,000 got a $1,500 bonus, while I got nothing because the company didn't make a profit that year." (See Exhibit 7.)

EXHIBIT 7
Compensation of Vappi management

	1965	1966	1967	1968	1969	1970
Vice presidents						
Median salary	$20,000	$22,000	$23,000	$25,000	$28,000	$33,000
Bonuses	3,000	7,000	0	4,000	0	*
Project managers						
Median salary	12,700	13,500	14,400	15,100	16,600	20,100
Bonuses—High	1,500	3,000	0	2,000	0	*
Median	700	2,500	0	1,300	0	*
Low	0	2,000	0	800	0	*
Superintendents†						
Median salary	10,519	11,799	12,925	15,127	17,579	19,630
Bonuses—High	720	2,500	1,500	2,000	667	2,000‡
Median	720	2,500	715	1,300	450	1,750‡
Low	200	2,500	500	750	333	1,500‡

*Awarded at year-end.
†The two general superintendents were paid at the high end of the superintendents' salary range.
‡To date, September 15, 1970.

Career progression was also a cause of concern to some employees. One project manager claimed the position of project manager was a dead-end job. Having once attained that role, there was nowhere else to go. Inasmuch as the firm had young men at all levels, vacancies were likely to occur only when someone left the firm or if a branch office were to open. Some superintendents, perceiving the project manager position as a prestige job, had become project managers. One who had made the move said, however: "As project manager, I like the variety of work, the hours, and the contacts with the other project managers. But if I'd stayed as a superintendent, I could have been further along in the company and made more money."

Most members of the firm felt that Vappi's salaries were comparable to the industry averages, but many felt that because Vappi had such good people the salaries should be significantly above average. For example, MacDonald said that many project managers were capable of running their own companies and periodically received tempting offers.

Dansk Designs Ltd.

FOUNDED IN 1955 to market a line of stainless steel flatware, Dansk Designs' sales grew from $100,000 in its first year of operation to over $10,000,000 in 1970. The firm's 1970 product catalog listed 600 items for the "top of the table" in product categories such as china, glass, table linens, wooden accessories, flatware, and cookware that could be used for serving.

Dansk was not content, moreover, to rest on past accomplishments. Ted Nierenberg, founder, president, and sole owner of Dansk, wanted the firm to maintain a 20% growth rate per year in profits. In order to do this, he planned to enter a new market area: housewares. Whereas Dansk's existing product line consisted of eight product categories, Nierenberg expected the new housewares line eventually to have three times that number.[1]

In response to Dansk's past growth and in anticipation of its future expansion, the company's organization was changing. In the 1950s and early 1960s, Dansk had consisted of Ted Nierenberg, Jens Quistgaard, and Ed Lubell.[2] Nierenberg provided marketing insights and located manufacturing sources, Quistgaard designed all the products, and Lubell was in charge of general administration and finance and administered manufacturing. As the size of Dansk's business grew, however, these men required help. Therefore additional designers were added, a number

---

[1] See Exhibit 1 for information on the housewares line.

[2] See Exhibit 2 for information on Dansk's personnel.

EXHIBIT 1

DANSK GOURMET DESIGNS LTD.

I. *Maria Wazeter's description of the housewares line*

There has always been a tremendous gap between Dansk's products—with heavy inputs of museum-caliber design, expensive raw materials, and skilled craftsmanship (hand finishing) in the manufacturing process—and mass-produced housewares, which have usually been designed to be manufactured as cheaply as possible.

In the Gourmet collection, Dansk will be bringing the same design standards to mass production, modifying manufacturing techniques to retain the handcrafted look which has been its hallmark. The Gourmet collection has been a corporate umbrella where Dansk is developing such concepts as:

New materials: acrylic, pyroceram, ceramic crucible material, and coquille aluminum, where present design is weak and the creative potential large.

Basic, "classic" materials: for example, cast iron, copper, and automatic glass, where both functionality and style can be improved.

New processes: for example, "coquille" aluminum, where a very prosaic and utilitarian metal is given a sheen resembling hammered pewter.

These innovations alone give Dansk enough raw material to develop a marketing strategy for at least 15 years out.

Gourmet is actually something of a misnomer, for while the lines might be designed to meet a gourmet's specifications, they are intended for a much wider group, larger than the circle of Dansk's present customers. A great many people identify with the gourmet concept, even if they only heat up frozen "spinach souffle" or "green beans with almonds" instead of the traditional TV dinners. Brides, career girls, mothers of school-age children with increasing leisure time—these are some of the consumer groups whose new-found interest in cooking and corollary need for information and reassurance have spawned cooking schools, cookbook guilds, and specialty retail outlets (like The Pot Shop in Harvard Square).

From the marketing angle, the potential is enormous. First, while Dansk has always sold at a premium, Gourmet will market Dansk style at a competitive price. Dansk products have always had a "fragile-handle-with-care" stamp about them; the new Gourmet lines, on the other hand, fairly exude durability—engineered for everyday use and a more mobile population. Also, Dansk's appeal will be wider, including not only the "classic to contemporary" group of customers who buy traditional materials like wood and crystal but the younger, more avant-garde group who are willing to buy good design and acrylic.

The major issue which Dansk must resolve is the rate at which the Gourmet collections will reach the market to maximize the impact of each collection. Introducing the maximum feasible number at one time would underline the style coordination and systems advantages and, in addition, make possible the creation of a Dansk "shop" within each store (with all items or lines assembled rather than spread out in several departments).

The second alternative, which might create equal impact over the long run, would be successive waves of product introductions on a quarterly basis. Some balance must be struck between maximum impact and minimum risk. What criteria should be used to assign priorities to the various lines?

Along with the potential, of course, the pitfalls are greater. Just a few examples:

1. In the past, size and production efficiency of some of the Dansk-contracted European factories has set *maximum* sales limits on such products as Flamestone and Orecast. Many of the newer products, such as automatic glass, will have minimum sales levels to be economically feasible, which may be 3, 5, 10 or more times average volume for Dansk's regular lines.

2. As a corollary, Dansk has based its merchandising on selective distribution, usually one to three department stores in each city. While with Gourmet Dansk will be moving out of isolated departments like china and crystal into new, higher traffic areas, will this, in itself, generate enough volume?

3. The distribution problem is more acute, given that absolute dollar margins will be smaller even if percentage-wise the contribution stays the same. Or *should* it stay the same?

4. Advertising: Traditionally Dansk has spent roughly 5% of sales on advertising, in

EXHIBIT 1 (*continued*)

print media oriented toward a reasonably narrow band of customers—high income, well-educated readers of general publications and shelter magazines. With a larger budget, (e.g., based on doubled sales volume), TV, educational films, and/or pamphlets, newspaper advertising—all the more expensive media become feasible. How can we best reach that mass market?

5. Mistakes: If a current piece doesn't sell, or if Dansk occasionally has to indulge a designer by manufacturing and selling one of his favorite "museum pieces," the item can be "specialed" out of inventory. But how do you bury 25,000 white elephants? Or, more accurately, how can you abort them while ensuring that your designers feel appreciated and satisfied professionally?

II. *"For Dansk, New Line and New Image"**

By RITA REIF

Dansk Designs Ltd., a tablewares producer that has been synonymous with prestigious, high-priced modern wares for cooking and serving, is working on a new, second image.

"We think there is a terrific market for mass-produced silverplate in this country, silverplated flatware in traditional styling," said Ted Nierenberg, founder of the 15-year-old concern based in Mount Kisco, N.Y.

The statement had a startling ring coming from the president of the concern that made Scandinavian modern a style to dine by in the nineteen fifties and sixties. Retail sales in this period rose to more than $10-million annually.

The proposed plan is to produce silverplated flatware, ovenproof china, glassware, plastic-handled cutlery and three collections of cookware in cast aluminum, cast iron and enameled aluminum—all at moderate prices. The designs, to make their debut in the spring of 1972, will be marketed under a new label, Dansk Gourmet Designs Ltd.

Bruised but Shiny

"This is exactly the kind of mottled, glittering finish we're going to put on our silverplated flatware," the 47-year-old executive said during a luncheon at Sardi's earlier this week. He was holding up a bruised but shiny fork that he had picked up from the table. "We'll make it, dents and all, and in Louis XV styling."

Mr. Nierenberg said he has spent more than a year developing the collections. He worked with Gunnar Cyrén, formerly chief designer at Orrefors, the Swedish glassworks, in developing the shapes for all of the designs. Ritva Puotila of Finland, who designs Dansk's linens, is the colorist for the collections.

"Gunnar and I spent almost a month last summer touring French restaurants and hotels," Mr. Nierenberg continued. They were checking not only the materials that chefs claim are best in cookwares and the type of tablewares that stand up under continued use in commercial establishments, but they were doing design research. And, from the look of the advance sketches, Mr. Nierenberg and his cohorts also became aware of the popularity of the wares in Bonniers and in Georg Jensen's basement as well as those in the Carrier Cook Shops.

The pair decided on a return to traditional shapes for most of the wares. Molds will be fashioned to resemble fruits or baskets and the knobs and handles on pots and casseroles will be shaped like fish, bound asparagus, mushrooms, pineapples, fruits and a horse's head.

* *New York Times*, December 24, 1970. © 1970 by The New York Times Company. Reprinted by permission.

EXHIBIT 1 (*continued*)

"I think we can make six well-designed glasses to sell for the price of one glass—about $8," Mr. Nierenberg said. And with the glasses purchasers will get a rack that is part of the plastic packaging but which has been designed so that it can be used to store the wares.

"The collection may make the pegboard obsolete," he continued, producing a sketch of knives that have notched blades so that they can be hung on hooks on a rack that comes packaged with the knives.

The knife blades will be handmade in Japan, Mr. Nierenberg said, but he still hasn't decided where the plastic handles for these designs and the bistro-styled flatware (knives, forks and spoons) in the same collection will be made. He is currently checking on factories in France, Italy, Scandinavia and this country.

of MBAs were hired to assist Lubell, and Nierenberg delegated much of the marketing activity.

Nierenberg viewed these organizational changes as part of Dansk's transition from entrepreneurial to professional management. He felt that the successful accomplishment of this transition was critical if he were to realize his personal goal of withdrawing as chief executive officer by 1973.

DANSK'S BUSINESS

Products

Nierenberg described his product-market policy as anything for the "top of the table." Dansk designed and marketed flatware, china, linen, glass, decorator cookware, and wooden bowls and trays. Its products were of high quality and were priced accordingly. The firm was described by a competitor as follows:

Dansk's greatest strength is marketing and product development. They set their goals and they follow them: the "top of the table," good design, good taste, and good advertising. They are in a very good secure spot and a remarkable position today.

Because Dansk defined its market as products for the top of the dining room table, the firm competed with a broad range of companies: Lenox China, International Silver, Georg Jensen Silver and Steel, Baccarat Crystal, etc. Dansk's 1970 sales exceeded $10,000,000, and its profit after taxes was in the neighborhood of $750,000. Exhibits 3 and 4 itemize Dansk's products: their designers, manufacturers, and contribution to Dansk's overall sales.

EXHIBIT 2
Biographical summary of key Dansk people

Name	Age	Year*	Affiliation in 1970	Location	Background
Ted Nierenberg	47	1955	President	Mt. Kisco	B.S., mechanical engineering, Carnegie Tech; engineering officer, Army Air Force; Epco (5 years); Small Business Administration, 1968.
Ed Lubell	47	1956	Executive V.P.	Mt. Kisco	B.S., business administration, Hofstra University; M.S., industrial engineering, Columbia University; AMP, Harvard Business School; bombardier navigator, Army Air Force; plant manager, Epco (9 years).
Burt Klapper	44	1960	V.P. marketing	Mt. Kisco	B.B.A., marketing, University of Miami; PMD, Harvard Business School; manager, store operation, AMC.
Keld Rosager-Hansen	31	1970	V.P. overseas operations	Denmark	B.S. and M.S., chemical engineering, Denmark; MBA, Harvard University; industrial engineer, corporate secretary, Colgate-Palmolive (Europe).
Sy Baxter	40	1958	Sales manager	Mt. Kisco	B.A., journalism, New York University; graduate studies, sales management, New York University; sales, Bulova Watch Co.
Barry Ginsburg	33	1966	Asst. V.P.	Mt. Kisco	B.A., history, Colby College; MBA, Cornell University; personnel officer, Air Force; systems analyst, Bell Telephone Labs.
Jerry Lieberg	26	1969	Controller	Mt. Kisco	B.A., political science, Yale University; MBA, University of Wisconsin; government representative, ALCOA.
Maria Wazeter	29	1970	Product strategy manager	Mt. Kisco	B.A., Wellesley College; MBA, Harvard University.
Jens Quistgaard	51	1955	Designer	Denmark	Silversmith apprenticeship; chief designer, Just Anderson; ceramic designer.
Gunnar Cyren	39	1970	Designer	Sweden	Graduate, Konstfack Art School, Sweden; goldsmith-silversmith; chief designer, Orrefors Glass, Sweden.
Niels Refsgaard	36	1965	Designer	Denmark	Graduate, Copenhagen School of Decorative Arts; potter.

EXHIBIT 2 (*continued*)

Name	Age	Year*	Affiliation in 1970	Location	Background
Ritva Puotila	35	1960	Designer	Finland	Decorative Arts, Athenaeum, Helsinki, Finland; textile designer and colorist.
Richard Nissen	41	1957	Supplier, wood products	Denmark	Wood production and machine design (23 years); owner-manager, Richard Nissen
Alf Rimer	35	1959	Independent model maker	Denmark	n.a.

* Indicates the year in which the individual became affiliated with Dansk.
n.a. = not available.

Marketing

The starting point for all Dansk products was response to a perceived market opportunity. Keld Rosager-Hansen, vice president of overseas operations, commented:

Ted and others in the company have a certain ability to perceive a market need and match it with a winning design. They can see when a good design is also a marketable design. You can contrast this to selling detergent. There you can walk down the street and ring doorbells to see if people like your product. You can't do that here because the market segment is so small. How do you get at such a diffuse group? You have to rely a lot on personal judgment.

Dansk had a strong following of consumers. Nierenberg referred to them as "Dansk club members." For example, in 1970 almost 50,000 people wrote to Dansk requesting brochures or information about products, or making suggestions, etc. On the other hand, Dansk did not know very much about these customers. No market polling, panels, or research had ever been attempted.

In 1970 Dansk marketing activities were directed by Burt Klapper, 44, who had joined Dansk in 1960 as a salesman. In 1965 he was promoted to general sales manager and in 1968, upon returning from the four-month PMD program at the Harvard Business School, was named to the newly created position of vice president of marketing. Sy Baxter replaced Klapper as sales manager.

The third member of the marketing team was Maria Wazeter who had joined Dansk in June 1970 after graduating from the Harvard MBA Program. Her title was product strategy manager. Both Klapper and Nierenberg hoped that she would be able to generate some useful information about Dansk's market.

EXHIBIT 3
Product line summary of Dansk designs

Product line	Patterns	Pieces*	1st pattern intro- duced	Designers†	Country of manufacture
I					
Stainless steel flatware	8	12–15	1955	Q	Germany, Finland, France
Salt and pepper shakers	1	2	1960	Q	Denmark
II					
Enameled steel cookware (Kobenstyle)	1	18	1957	Q	Denmark, Finland, Sweden, France, Holland
Copperware (discontinued)	1	12	1962	Q	Denmark
III					
Woodenware.	1	50	1957	Q	Denmark
IV					
China dinnerware (Flamestone)	2	18	1957	Q	Denmark
Stoneware dinnerware (Generation)	10	20	1966	R	Denmark
Fine china (Epoch)	5	16	1969	R	Norway
V					
Cast-iron candlesticks	1	12	1963	Q	Denmark
Silver-plated candlesticks . . .	1	3	1968	Q	Finland
VI					
Textiles	1˙	50	1964	P	Finland, Belgium
VII					
Bar and stemware	22	4–5	1967	Q	Finland, Belgium, France
VIII					
Cast-iron cookware (orecast)	1	14	1969	Q	Finland, Belgium

*Indicates number of pieces per pattern.
†Q = Quistgaard, R = Refsgaard, P = Puotila.

Two distinctive features of Dansk's marketing strategy were the use of advertising (5% of sales) to create a strong brand image and a captive sales force (consisting of 22 men organized on a territorial basis) to offer the retailer, in Klapper's words, "far greater than normal service, greater inventory turns, and fewer markdowns."[3] Klapper touched on both these areas in the following comments:

To me Dansk advertising is one of the cornerstones upon which the company was built. There is a very special "feel" and consistency of distinctive creative elegance to it. To the retailer, it is known as the "hallmark of quality"

---

[3] On the other hand, Dansk had withdrawn from trade shows in 1965 and did not maintain showrooms, as was the custom in the industry.

EXHIBIT 4
Dansk product line statement

Product line	Percentage of gross profit		Sales by product line as a percentage of total sales						
	1969	1970	1964	1965	1966	1967	1968	1969	1970
Kobenstyle	18.4	18.3	12.6	9.9	12.4	13.9	20.8	17.5	16.0
Stainless steel flatware	19.4	18.1	22.8	18.4	17.7	15.7	18.0	18.6	16.7
Wood	19.2	17.0	24.2	32.8	20.6	17.9	17.1	20.2	21.0
Generation/Epoch	11.5	14.1	. . .	. . .	2.9	7.5	9.1	12.0	13.0
Designs with light	11.2	8.5	17.4	28.1	22.9	19.3	15.1	11.3	8.0
Orecast	2.0	5.1	. . .	. . .	. . .	. . .	. . .	2.1	4.0
Flamestone	5.2	6.8	7.3	7.0	8.0	7.4	6.0	5.4	6.0
Barware	4.9	4.2	. . .	. . .	0.7	2.0	3.7	5.1	5.0
Silver plate	3.6	3.6	4.1	3.5	4.0	4.8	3.7	3.7	4.6
Stemware	2.1	3.0	. . .	. . .	. . .	1.8	2.4	2.2	3.0
Textiles	1.8	1.6	11.6	6.3	5.6	4.5	2.7	1.7	2.0
Miscellaneous	. . .	. . .	. . .	. . .	1.1	4.4	0.9	0.2	. . .

of our industry. To consumers, it connotes the very best in taste and presentation. Nobody counts, but the number of award-winning ads are many.

We've always sold the concept—the Dansk brand. We're always selling Dansk—not an ice bucket or a salad bowl. It's undignified to discuss how much a store buyer wants of each line. I say "buy it all." That's a two-way street, though. In return for their buying the full line, they get a *real* brand name which is backed by a tightly controlled, limited distributorship (less than 500 retail outlets).

We've been leaders. We're not worried about being liked—leaders lead, they don't win popularity contests. Hence, many retailers wait for us to stumble. We are that firm in our attitudes and sales policies. The retailer has a real responsibility when he represents Dansk. I'm most comfortable with these policies.

Design

Design activity at Dansk was dominated by Jens Quistgaard. Quistgaard-designed products accounted for 75% of Dansk's dollar sales in 1970. It was generally agreed by those who knew him that Quistgaard was a most talented and temperamental artist, and he looked and played that role to its fullest. Wearing a full beard and knickers, Quistgaard, who was 51 years old, lived on an island four miles off the coast of Denmark. His comments illustrated his philosophy of design and life:

As long as there are people living here, there will always be a certain classic way of life that will not change. A certain group of intellect, a certain wish to own something that is beautiful. As a philosophy of life, it will always be so that a home will not be a garage or clinic. You will have a lot of *impractical* things around. Therefore, we will always have people that will want things that are beautiful, that are forged, that are made the classic way. People will appreciate woodenware and things that have a similarity to the human body and to movement. You will never go around with empty hands. You will want to enjoy yourself by using these beautiful things. Silk, wool, all the classic materials will never be replaced by paper or plastic.

We are having rockets, speed, hospitals, and all this kind of modern thing. When we come back to our private home, we will have fewer things, but much, much more beautiful, more artistic, and longer lasting. For the security of your inside feelings you need poetry now more than ever to combat the harsh, cold, vinegar look of the offices and factories. You will not live for your work. You will live for your private home and the classic appeal of that. All intellectual people will have it that way. You will still have paintings and a lot of things which will have changing fashions and style, but which will have the same major Gestalt. I think that's so important.

Dansk's second major designer was Niels Refsgaard. Refsgaard had joined Dansk in 1965; his china patterns accounted for 15% of Dansk's 1970 dollar sales. Like Quistgaard, Refsgaard was a Dane, although he thought of himself more as a potter than a designer:

I have been a potter for many years. When I have an idea, I only dream of a shape. Then I make many samples, and I pick the one that comes closest to that dream. You see, I come from 10 generations of blacksmiths, and, as forging is to a blacksmith, potting is a simple feeling of good proportion. It takes much hard work, but finally you have something that you can look at and feel and say, "that is right—that is what I want."

The third major designer was Gunnar Cyren, a Swede, who joined Dansk early in 1970. His primary responsibility was the new housewares line to be known as Dansk Gourmet Designs Ltd. Prior to coming to Dansk, Cyren had been chief designer at the Orrefors Glass Company in Sweden. The following comments reflect his approach to design:

It is my habit to work from 8 till 4:30 every day. In school you do it always, and then when you have been working for 10 years as an apprentice—that's ordinary work. The creativeness is only part of it. I'm not creative all the time. Even if it's not routine work, it's handicraft work. Many things have to be designed to accurate drawings. Many things are just a matter of keeping order. It is essential to have order on the table, order in your mind. From order comes good design, or design is order—a form of order.

Nierenberg compared Cyren and Quistgaard as follows:

I think Gunnar is a versatile designer and may develop to be as good or better than Jens. The temperament of these two men is very different. We are making industrially oriented (in a production sense) products. It's a combination of handcraftsmanship and mechanization. The mechanization is naturally gaining and this imposes constraints. Jens bristles with the constraints—he constantly wants the factories to design new and special machinery. Gunnar is challenged by the constraints. He wants to maximize the originality within these constraints.

As of the end of 1970, these three men, along with Ritva Puotila, a Finn, who designed Dansk's easy-care table linens and was responsible for all the firm's color decisions, and Alf Rimer, Dansk's model maker, made up Dansk's design activity. Quistgaard had the greatest experience and broadest range of talents. He had designed in wood, glass, china, cast iron, stainless steel, and silver. Refsgaard had only designed in china, and while he professed a desire to work in other materials, he had yet to do so. Cyren was considered to be an artist of considerable talent, even though his experience had been exclusively in glass and silver. It was Lubell's opinion that for the next two or three years Dansk would have to rely on Quistgaard for most of its new designs in wood, stainless steel, flatware, enamel on steel, and cast iron.

Dansk designers were paid on a royalty basis and were reputed to be paid very well. For example, Quistgaard, who had a guaranteed minimum royalty income of $50,000 a year until he was 65, had royalty income in 1969 and 1970 considerably in excess of the minimum. Dansk designers were prohibited from designing products which competed with Dansk's line. If this were to happen, Dansk could stop paying all royalties.

Manufacturing

Dansk had no manufacturing operations of its own; all its products were produced by contract manufacturers, with Dansk providing the designs and tooling. The need to provide profitability to contract manufacturers and sufficient contribution to cover Dansk's high cost of doing business[4] placed a premium on finding and developing special low-cost production techniques or competences to keep the cost of Dansk products competitive. For example, Dansk marketed glass products that looked like cut glass but actually were produced by a new injection process developed in France.

Dansk had about 30 different suppliers who were located in Denmark, Norway, Sweden, Finland, France, and Germany. Production in the Far East was being contemplated. Most suppliers were small or medium-sized and were generally under individual or family ownership. The degree of Dansk involvement ranged from situations where Dansk bought

---

[4] Maintaining a modeling shop in Copenhagen of four very skilled men; high tooling costs; high marketing expenses, including advertising and a sales force that not only sold and serviced but performed detail work as well.

only a small percentage of a supplier's volume to those where it bought 100%. In 1970 Dansk found sales of many of its products constrained by the capacity of the contract manufacturer. These suppliers were either unwilling or unable to expand production for Dansk.

The relationship between Dansk and its suppliers was an informal one: the suppliers agreed to produce a particular product for Dansk at an agreed-upon price and Dansk agreed to purchase a certain amount. The arrangements were closed by handshakes and could be terminated by either side. Dansk protected its designs by patents and copyrights and had a reputation for defending its position, having taken some imitators to litigation. As a result, in the last two or three years it had experienced little difficulty of this nature.

Richard Nissen, principal supplier of Dansk's wood products, was a good example of a Dansk contract manufacturer. He too was a Dane and prided himself on the extent to which he and Dansk had been able to preserve the handcrafted nature of the products while manufacturing on semiautomatic machinery. He commented:

By being inventive, we think we can make machinery that will do better than the craftsman himself. It might take a slight transforming of the artist's idea. It might have a curve which we cannot produce. Then we have to compromise. It can be done.

As his business expanded, Nissen had gotten more and more into management and further away from tooling and production. As a result, there had been considerable difficulty with a line of rosewood trays that Quistgaard had designed. Nissen explained:

I forgot there were very few people in the factory left that could do the work. As a matter of fact, there was only me who had the experience. Last year, the last very good craftsman died of a heart attack. So, you know: new people, a new design concept—they were not used to it. Well, I knew afterwards that they felt scared to death. They would promise you anything. The more the Dansk Copenhagen office[5] called, the more scared they were. Especially when they were threatened with competition! You know, Dansk could always send the job to another supplier.

With regard to the future, Nissen commented:

My goals are not to expand for any price. I don't want to be big in volume. I would like to be large in quality. It's not the volume that counts. In the woodworking business there will be room for quality in the future. Quantity products will be made in plastic. It's a goal that I am setting to go along with the products I know. I also know these products are of such a special nature that they will be too expensive for the consumer's need unless one

---

[5] The Copenhagen office handled Dansk's day-to-day operating relationships with contract manufacturers. In addition, office personnel participated in product-feasibility studies directed from Dansk's headquarters.

can make the feelings and emotions go along with them. That's what the
artist does—what Jens understands. Volume, no; quality and some expansion,
yes. If I have a good thing to produce, that's my job in society. If I can
fulfill this job in society, in the needs of today or tomorrow, it is my motivation.
If I can do this for Dansk, I will, but I want the name "Nissen" brought
in a little, too.

Dansk's manufacturing and other internal operations were the responsibility of Ed Lubell, executive vice president. Up until 1966 Lubell
had handled the firm's administration, inventory management, ordering,
distribution, finance, and supervision of the people Dansk employed
in the Copenhagen office. In 1966 Dansk opened a Paris production-
supervision office as its manufacturing facilities widened beyond Scandinavia. In the same year, Barry Ginsburg was hired as controller, with
particular emphasis on inventory management and factory ordering procedures. In 1969 Jerry Lieberg was hired to assume Ginsburg's activities;
Nierenberg wanted Ginsburg to take on more new product-feasibility
studies[6] and be the only person communicating with the production
offices on all but broad policy matters.

Another important organizational change involved the overseas operations. In May 1970, Keld Rosager-Hansen joined Dansk as vice president
of overseas operations. Rosager-Hansen was a Dane with an MBA degree
from Harvard. He had worked for six years with Colgate-Palmolive in
Europe, where he had established Colgate's first industrial engineering
department and had then gone through the general-management rotation
program. Rosager-Hansen was hired by Dansk with the idea of his taking
over the Paris production-supervision office as well as the Copenhagen
office. In the past, both offices had reported to Lubell (on new product
feasibility) and to Ginsburg (ongoing production). It was felt that much
work was being duplicated, whereas a single strong European manager
could exercise judgment in selecting the best supplier with whom to make
product-feasibility studies. After two months on the job, Rosager-Hansen
assessed the situation in Europe as follows:

Although there are not very many people in Dansk, they are very much
apart geographically. The communication problems that are caused by that
kind of distance are much larger than you expect till you've been in them.
So one of the problems we've got to get solved is how the proper communications with Mt. Kisco ought to be established.

At present there is a flurry of small little slips going back and forth.
The telex bills are astronomical. I believe we send a couple of yards of
telexes every day. We can't go on like that forever. The people here spend

---

[6] Two feasibility gates had to be passed before Dansk would commit to a new
product, one technical and one economic. Could the product be manufactured
as designed? If so, did the economics (investment in tooling and product costs)
make sense given Dansk's assessment of the market?

most of their time writing letters to Mt. Kisco or answering letters from them. People's time is taken up by the wrong things. Because of the communications problem, everybody's attention is really turned in the direction of Mt. Kisco. Instead, we should be looking out for the problems which are really between us here and the suppliers.

Rosager-Hansen met with Ed Lubell in Copenhagen to discuss these problems. The general conclusion of the meeting was that some standard operating procedures were needed in Dansk. Excerpts from Rosager-Hansen's minutes of the meeting are included as Exhibit 5.

Ownership

Nierenberg owned all the equity in Dansk. He was planning, however, to give part of that equity to other managers. As of the end of 1970, Lubell and Klapper were the first to receive stock in Dansk. Nierenberg explained the reasoning behind this action:

I've now completed the plan to give away stock. I don't want options or conditions. When I see some of the people here doing exactly what I would have done when it meant real personal hardship to me or my family in order to make the goal, they're not acting like owners, they are owners. So this year Burt and Ed own some of the company. And I hope it will be more and more. My responsibility is greater, but their contribution is proportionately much larger. I now see things with numbers, and yet each number represents a lot of people. And I hope it will be more people.

A public offering was also being contemplated by Nierenberg:[7]

No company that's growing 15% or 20% a year can stay private. People who do are just building a kingdom—a little fairyland where you have a king, a crown prince, and many people-in-waiting. These companies tend to be dominated by a single strong individual, and other people in the company just execute his orders. Ed Lubell has been this particular kind of executive. That's why I sent Burt off to PMD and Ed to AMP at Harvard. I wanted them to see what a manager's responsibilities were all about.

Before they went, they may have felt the gap between my contribution to the company and theirs was narrowing, and now they feel it's widening. They're beginning to become managers. They just never realized the alternatives I considered. I want to spread the responsibility, the motivation, and the ownership.

We'll either get acquired or go public. But the longer we can grow internally and keep better internal controls before we need outside financing, the greater is the equity to all of us. I don't want to go public as anything but a first-class company. I've watched a lot of people try to bail themselves out by going public—that's not for me.

---

[7] As a result, there are no detailed financial data in the case study. For the purpose of analysis, however, it can be reasonably assumed that finances were not a problem.

EXHIBIT 5

DANSK DESIGNS LTD

PRODUCTION: NYE KONGENSGADE 15, DK-1472 COPENHAGEN K TELEPHONE: *14 42 44 TELEX: 9018 CABLE: DANSIGN COPENHAGEN
HOME OFFICE: MOUNT KISCO, NEW YORK 10549 U.S.A. TELEPHONE: (914) 666-2121 TELEX: 13 74 98 CABLE: DANSKIMP MTCO

Minutes of Meeting in Copenhagen
Thursday, September 10, 1970   Copenhagen,   c.c. TN, BK
                                                            BG, JL
                                                            CA*, SP*
Present: E. S. Lubell, K. Rosager-Hansen

1) Initiation of projects to be carried out by the Copenhagen group.
   At present projects are started in Copenhagen mostly through one-way
   communication by a letter being received from somebody in Mount
   Kisco. The lack of dialogue or a feedback to the U.S. had sometimes
   caused misunderstandings in relation to unfilled expectations. In view
   of this it was decided that any major project to be initiated in
   Copenhagen as a general rule shall be agreed upon with KRH at a
   face-to-face meeting in Copenhagen, Mount Kisco, or elsewhere. In
   special cases a request for work can be submitted to KRH, who will
   evaluate the feasibility and the amount of time involved. The request
   will then be returned with a likely day of completion or with comments
   indicating why a project cannot be undertaken as is. In the latter case
   the project can be reconsidered at the first following face-to-face meeting.

   The above procedure does not concern routine operations, e.g., discussions
   of product quality and delivery times as well as price requests from established
   suppliers on basically traditional product types. However, any project
   involving new suppliers or new types of products is covered by the above
   procedure.

2) Modus Operandi.
   Basically it is the responsibility of Mount Kisco to define the problems and
   the Copenhagen group is to identify and carry out the solutions. As the
   objective is to obtain the results that are most favourable for the company as
   a whole, the origin of the right solution to a given problem is of little importance. Therefore the Copenhagen group will always welcome any suggestion
   as to how to solve a problem presented by MK. On the other hand,
   Copenhagen has no obligation to follow such proposals, and feedback on the
   proposals will not necessarily take place except when clarification is
   desired by the Development Manager.* In view of this it will be most adequate
   that said proposals are presented as straightforward statements rather than as
   questions that suggest the necessity of an answer (e.g., "Perhaps it is an idea
   also to get quotes from X " RATHER THAN "Please also get quotes from X; when
   can we expect?").

* Development managers reporting to Rosager-Hansen. Organized by materials (i.e., wood and china), these men expedited Dansk's orders.

Management

Two important aspects of Dansk management must be emphasized: delegation and style. While the firm began as a one-man show, Nierenberg consciously tried to develop managers that could assume an increasing amount of the day-to-day operation of the firm. The following comment by Barry Ginsburg reflected Nierenberg's move toward delegation:

In the last few years there has been real delegation of authority from the top down. Ted used to do everything: labels, names, new products. I'm sure he even did the doorknobs in the building. Now I do the doorknobs. Maybe they aren't as good, but that's not his job. He has become more of a chairman than president now. He piles it on Burt and Ed. As a result, they can't do what they used to, so they pile some of it on me. I think it's great—the way it should be. Maybe it should have happened earlier. This is all new since I've been here. He used to look at the new orders every morning. You know—what do you mean so and so only ordered six ice buckets? We can no longer trot in to him. We have to figure it out ourselves. This is the only way to have ongoing entity which will transcend individuals.

The second characteristic of Dansk management was its style. The high-quality, highly designed image of the firm's products carried over into the firm's operations. The headquarters building in Mt. Kisco, New York, was a striking structure placed on six acres of garden and woods. The interior decor was a blend of modern and antique.

This corporate character, moreover, went beyond the physical surroundings. Guests were taken to lunch in the finest restaurants, and there was a conscious attempt to run the firm in a first-class manner.

Another aspect of Dansk's style was its informality. Everyone at Dansk was on a first-name basis. There was no organizational chart. The atmosphere was an open one where people felt free to say what was on their minds.

THE REVENUE GAP

Nierenberg's growth goals for Dansk were ambitious ones:

The exciting thing for me is, can we keep Dansk growing at 15% to 20% a year? What other things can we do without cutting back on our Dansk line? Can we generate the same kind of growth in other areas? If we can go to $40 million on an internal basis, rather than by acquisition, we can begin to say we've got something that would be damned exciting for the people in it. You just don't see it that often. That's the kernel of the challenge.

Based on their assessment of the market, Dansk management did not feel that their existing product line would provide sufficient growth to meet Nierenberg's objectives. To fill this gap, Dansk was planning to introduce a line of houseware products to be called Dansk Gourmet Designs Ltd. (see Exhibit 1). Maria Wazeter described Gourmet:

Dansk Gourmet has developed 35–40 new product categories or product concepts, pinpointing virtually every cooking and serving function. Some may be technologically impossible at present; some may be infeasible at present; some may be infeasible for the next five years. For a few categories, the market may not be large enough to justify the design, tooling, and administrative expense.

Yet, even after these products are winnowed out, the number of categories reaching the marketplace still should at least triple what Dansk has at present. If Dansk now has close to 600 items in eight categories, the numbers involved in 24 or more new collections are staggering. In short, I can see the present Dansk line still growing yet becoming the "minor" portion of Dansk's overall sales volume within the next 5 or 10 years.

These growth goals and new product plans had significant implications for all aspects of Dansk's operations. The remainder of the case study will examine one of the most critical: new product development. The need for a steady stream of new products was apparent. Sales of some existing products were already constrained by supplier capacity; growth in these areas would mean new products and new suppliers. Gourmet represented a corporate commitment to increase the number of products that Dansk was selling by 300% in the course of 5 to 10 years.

THE DEVELOPMENT PROCESS

In Dansk's early years, the development activities were performed by Nierenberg and Quistgaard. Nierenberg's description of staved teak is a good illustration:

I had been intrigued by Danish teakwood furniture. It was beginning to be very fashionable. Teak had a magical quality. To Americans it connoted fancy yachts and boats. There were some lovely teak salad bowls in a few stores in Denmark that were expensive and made from a single solid piece of wood. I told Jens [Quistgaard] that I thought there might be a market for teak accessories such as trays and ice buckets and salad bowls because food could be placed directly on the teak and it was easy to wash off and reoil to replenish the finish if it dulled.

Jens designed some bowls and trays, but when I priced out these items with some wood turners, it meant that a bowl would have to retail for $100 and a simple tray for $30 or $40. When I analyzed the cost, it was obvious that if this product line was to come to fruition, we would have to economize drastically on the material.

I then asked Jens about the possibilities of manufacturing from staves, as in barrel production, which led to visiting barrel factories, which led to

Richard (Nissen) and the creation of staved teak. There were a few days never to be forgotten.

Jens wanted the staves bent and thought they could be bent with steam. The steam would bend them all right, but they didn't stay bent. Richard came up with the idea of cutting the staves in compound curves to form a bowl. We tried gluing together the first bowl made from staves. We were upstairs in a cruddy attic of an equipment garage. Richard, Jens, myself, and a foreman—there were 16 staves and four pairs of hands, and every time one pair of hands reached for the clamps, the bowl fell apart. Suddenly, there was another pair of hands with the clamps at the right time and the right place. It was Hans (Richard's father) who had come back late at night to see what we were doing. Jens made some designs, Richard made some calculations, and when he gave me the first prices, I knew we were on the right track.

By 1970, however, the number of participants in the development process had grown. Lubell commented:

Until recently, Ted [Nierenberg] had been the sole contact with the designers. He could not continue to be and still develop Gourmet. The logical step was to pair up Burt [Klapper] with the most important and most difficult designer, Jens [Quistgaard]. We decided to start Burt in wood, where Jens was most secure and the production parameters most clearly defined.

Furthermore, Ted was getting into the Dansk product development cycle at every step. Now Burt is conceiving the product strategy, reviewing sketches and designs, and editing. Burt's and Jens' record together on wood the last 18 months is excellent. Now they are working together on designs with light, flatware, and cookware. Maria [Wazeter] is developing product strategy for glass and china and linens.

The transition was not without its problems, particularly in the design area. After a fast and successful beginning, Dansk experienced a period of stagnation in the early 1960s. Sales growth slowed. Problems with contract manufacturers appeared. Salesmen were lost. Profits declined. The situation came to a head in 1965. Klapper commented:

It became clear that the J.H.Q.[8] china design dream was just that—a dream. Jens did not complete the job. Ted's belief in Jens' ability to "make a market" for Dansk in china was being eroded. By this time we were in a "survival strategy"—selling tremendous amounts of unproven items—clogging retail pipelines—forcing markdowns, etc. We were choking ourselves and the retailers with often undesirable inventory—trying to make our figures.

Nierenberg also commented on this situation:

Ed [Lubell] and Burt [Klapper] and I believed in our ability to execute the total top-of-the-table strategy. We were committed to a new location and warehouse in Mt. Kisco, and it was no small commitment. If I went off to Denmark, worked with Jens and saw it (the china design) through, I would have been

---

[8] Quistgaard's signature.

repeating the same annual crisis experience for the 11th time since 1955. I did not want to spend half of my life in Denmark. I also realized our survival depended on Jens—we had no depth of design resources.

Nierenberg traveled to Denmark to tell Quistgaard that Dansk would hire other designers for the first time. Quistgaard threatened to quit. Nierenberg offered him a guaranteed $50,000 a year minimum income until his 65th birthday. (Quistgaard was making about $35,000 a year at the time.) Quistgaard finally accepted the arrangement but refused to design in china ever again.

Niels Refsgaard was hired to design for Dansk and came up with the very successful "Generation" pattern. Klapper saw significance in the decision to hire Refsgaard:

"Generation" was the beginning of the real implementation of a strategy that was "top of the table": rejecting the "survival strategy" and going for a concept. As if axiomatically came the next major change: the restructuring of the Dansk-factory relationship. No more "loans and advances" to Nissen, etc. No "captive" factories—no paternalistic relationships with factories. Factories were to become sources, professionally shopped and compared. We would stand on our own two feet—so would those factories with whom we could contract and build a healthy relationship, hopefully long-term. But, realistically, profitable for both parties.

Nierenberg was not satisfied with just two designers, however. He continued to search for new design talent and in 1968 met Gunnar Cyren. The courtship of Cyren lasted two years, during which time (in 1969) Cyren was promoted to chief designer at Orrefors. Even though the promotion placed Cyren in charge of five designers, many of whom were older and more established than himself, Cyren decided to join Dansk in the spring of 1970:

The big hook for me in Ted's [Nierenberg] program was that I was responsible for the whole new collection called Gourmet. I'm not taking part of another collection. I have a whole area for myself. That's a very nice point. I don't know how much it is politics for Ted, so that he can get beside the problem with Jens. I don't think Jens wants any competitors. One way to get around that might be a new collection, and then call it Gourmet. In any case, I will be working directly with Ted. There will be no one between us, and I trust him to the utmost extent. . . . I am satisfied with that.

Quistgaard's reaction to these new designers was decidedly negative:

It is like a man who has been an opera star for many years. Then all of a sudden the owner, because of a crisis, decides to bring in a little competition to push the singer into another success. This is absolutely wrong. You cannot tell a person how he must sing and act in a role. If he could do that, he would be a superman. You can't press a man into a mold. If you

do, you are trying the wrong way. If you try to press artists into a team
when their styles do not go together, it will be a disaster.

From Quistgaard's point of view, Nierenberg's delegation of design
selection to Burt Klapper compounded the problem. Nierenberg commented on the situation:

> For the good of the company, I cannot work with Jens [Quistgaard] any-
> more. If we are to be a dynamic company, we must plan ahead—maximize al-
> ternatives—conduct feasibility studies—unfortunately, discard good designs that
> can't meet profitability criteria or duplicate a market need. We must work on
> a two-year development cycle. Jens always knew that when he was late
> with a design, I'd show up and bail him and the company out. He knew
> that I knew shortcuts nobody else knew. That's an expertise I don't want
> anybody else in the company to acquire.

Quistgaard expressed his opinion of the new approach as follows:

> I want to be in on choosing the designs myself. I want to have my voice
> there. Too much of my valuable work is going into the wastebasket. That
> I cannot stand, either as an artist businessman or as a human being. It's
> so humiliating. All the decisions are made over my head. They are not skilled
> enough to criticize this sort of thing. They don't have the talent to choose
> all that well. If they don't have me in on the design, then they are doing
> themselves more bad than good.
>
> Burt's [Klapper] letters are as sweet as can be, but he has so much to learn
> about design, style, coordination, and such. I also know from experience that he
> is a very clever guy. He won't make the same mistake twice, but he is
> too scientific in his approach.
>
> Ted [Nierenberg] and I are so close that if you change the pattern too much
> and give it to other people, no matter how nice they are, if they don't have
> the tact and respect for me, they will take out their power too much. I
> am very afraid of the future because of too much other designing, too much
> delegating to people who don't have the skill. They can perhaps gain that,
> little by little. I hope they will take me in and ask my opinion and not
> just make a calculation about the price, or something like that.

Refsgaard was also dissatisfied with the extent to which his work
was criticized:

> They should believe more in each other as people and in us as designers.
> It is not funny to have people interpret your design for you. Like Burt
> [Klapper], who is suddenly acting as new designer for Dansk. He is telling me
> that something would be a good design if I took 3 millimeters off here and
> smoothed this curve. Jens has had the same problems. Sometimes I feel they
> are trying to wring me like a sponge—get the last drop out. For example, last
> Christmas I did some patterns for decorating the white porcelain, Epoch. They
> were good designs. I sent them to Mt. Kisco, and for three months they made
> me change and develop new patterns. Now they have finally gone back and

chosen my first design. Why do I waste my time so? I should just tell them that this is my design and do something else.

At the end of 1970, Nierenberg made the following comments:

The year 1970 was very gratifying. The country has been in a slump—some of our competition was hit very hard. We have had a very good year. Gunnar Cyren looks like somebody with whom we can build. Jens is a loner! He's jealous and resentful. It's showing. Some of his resentment is carrying over to Niels—it's a little like "my enemy's enemy is my friend." I feel Keld's skills are helping us.

I've been very demanding of everybody. I guess a lot more than I used to be and more than everybody has come to expect. Sometimes I have the feeling when I'm bearing down hard on somebody in their office that they welcome a phone or intercom ringing—it takes the pressure off for a moment. Everybody is comfortable in the safe zones. Burt in sales and existing product marketing. Ed in feasibility criteria and execution of my policies. Barry where Jerry now is. Jens in wood. Niels with Generation. I have the feeling that everybody wants to hide under the table when they know I'm about to ask about alternatives for selling Gourmet—or should we continue a production-supervision office in Paris—or the source alternatives for products we've never made before—or what will be our sales compensation plan in three years? I don't want anybody to drown, but if you don't swallow a little water, you never learn how cruel that ocean can really be!

Vail Associates, Inc.

Described by *Time* magazine as "the most successful winter resort built in the United States in the past decade" and by *The New York Times* as "perhaps the most dramatic ski resort in North America," Vail, Colorado, had experienced 11 years of continuous growth since its founding in 1961. Vail Associates, Inc. (VAI), the company that had developed the area and owned the skiing facilities and much of the real estate in Vail, had shared in this success. By 1972 the company's revenues had reached nearly $7 million and total assets had grown to almost $18 million (see Exhibits 1 and 2).

In August 1972 Vail Associates' management was faced with an imminent decision on the purchase for $4,600,000 of 2,200 acres of land located nine miles west of Vail Village at Beaver Creek. An option on the land had been obtained in 1971, and VAI had immediately begun to study the area. The original option, costing $61,000, ran from September 1, 1971, through the end of February 1972. VAI had extended the option through August 31, 1972, for $123,000. The rancher owning the property had agreed to sell to VAI for the equivalent of $415,000 down, with $1,020,000 payable over five years at 7% and $3,165,000 payable over a 10-year period at 5%.

At the beginning of August 1972 VAI had attempted to extend the option for another year, but the parties selling the land had refused to accept the offer. Thus, in late August management had only a few days to decide the Beaver Creek issue—a decision complicated by the uncontrollable, unpredictable factor of the 1976 Winter Olympics for which Beaver Creek had been selected earlier that year as the site of the Alpine events. (Denver was to be the host city for the games, with various

661

EXHIBIT 1

VAIL ASSOCIATES, INC.
Income Statements
(in thousands of dollars)

	Years ending October 31						*Years ending April 30*			
	1963	*1964*	*1965*	*1966*	*1967*	*1968*	*1969*	*1970*	*1971*	*1972*
Revenues	$ 504	543	1,215	1,557	1,702	2,426	3,491	3,808	5,733	6,715
Cost of services	281	340	634	780	781	1,289	1,877	1,851	3,130	3,182
Contribution	$ 223	203	581	777	921	1,137	1,614	1,957	2,603	3,533
Corporate expenses*	567	682	793	906	752	849	961	1,727	1,908	1,952
Income before taxes	$(344)	(479)	(212)	(129)	169	288	653	230	695	1,581
Income taxes	...	...	...	...	...	134	336	103	324	769
Income from operations	$(344)	(479)	(212)	(129)	169	154	317	127	371	812
Extraordinary items†	...	...	...	...	...	277	(285)	...	311	...
Net income	$(344)	(479)	(212)	(129)	169	431	32	127	682	812
Net income per share—primary				(.15)	.19	.48	.03	.13	.72	.84
—fully diluted									.65	.71
Stock price range‡					3–3⅝	3–10¼	8¼–16½	4–13⅝	5⅞–10⅝	9⅝–16¾

Analysis

	1963	*1964*	*1965*	*1966*	*1967*	*1968*	*1969*	*1970*	*1971*	*1972*
Revenues:										
Mountain	44.8%	70.5%	54.4%	60.2%	66.2%	58.8%	56.5%	65.3%	55.0%	54.7%
Real estate	49.2	17.9	34.6	26.7	20.8	31.0	32.3	22.1	31.4	29.1
Ski school	6.0	11.6	9.9	10.7	10.3	9.0	9.9	11.7	12.4	14.6
Food concession§	...	...	1.1	2.4	2.7	1.2	1.3	.9	1.2	1.6
	100.0%	100.0%	100.0%	100.0%	100.0%	100.0%	100.0%	100.0%	100.0%	100.0%
Contribution:										
Mountain	21.1%	79.8%	45.1%	57.0%	64.7%	64.1%	72.7%	70.5%	65.4%	59.7%
Real estate	80.2	16.3	48.9	34.7	28.3	31.6	20.3	24.2	24.6	28.9
Ski school	(1.3)	3.9	3.8	3.5	2.0	1.7	4.3	3.6	7.3	8.4
Food concession§	...	...	2.2	4.8	5.0	2.6	2.7	1.7	2.7	3.0
	100.0%	100.0%	100.0%	100.0%	100.0%	100.0%	100.0%	100.0%	100.0%	100.0%
Items as a percent of total revenue:										
Contribution	44.2	37.4	47.8	49.9	54.1	46.9	46.2	51.4	45.4	52.6
Corporate expenses	112.5	125.6	65.3	58.2	44.2	35.0	27.5	45.4	33.3	29.1
Income from operations	(68.3)	(88.2)	(17.5)	(8.3)	9.9	6.4	9.1	3.3	6.5	12.0

* Includes losses of the Lodge from 1963–1967 and $350,000 provision for condominium losses in 1970. Also includes depreciation.
† Extraordinary items were gains on highway condemnation in 1968 and 1971 and loss on the sale of the Lodge in 1969 (all net of taxes).
‡ Partnership for 1963–1965. Common stock first traded OTC in 1967. 1972 price through 8-15-72 when it equaled 16¾ for a P/E of 24x.
§ Includes only lease income from restaurants owned by subsidiaries.
Source: Company records and casewriter's analysis.

EXHIBIT 2

Y/ASSETS = 4.5%

VAIL ASSOCIATES, INC.
Condensed Balance Sheets
(in thousands of dollars)

| | *Years ending October 31* | | | | | | | *Years ending April 30* | | |
Assets	1963	1964	1965	1966	1967	1968	1969	1970	1971	1972
Current Assets										
Cash	$ 101	$ 664	$ 211	$ 18	$ 76	$ 53	$ 210	$ 259	$ 1,103	$ 1,185
A/R, other	83	72	143	96	102	309	315	655	593	1,070
Land for resale	...	10	154	145	113	111	88	387	535	506
Condominium units	...	...	...	...	...	865	691	1,051	338	34
Total current assets	$ 184	$ 746	$ 508	$ 259	$ 291	$1,338	$1,304	$ 2,352	$ 2,569	$ 2,795
Plant and equipment (at cost)										
Land and improvements†	226	527	391	372	406	355	375	3,393	3,962	4,752
Ski lifts, terminals, buildings	1,310	1,310	1,995	2,020	2,028	2,338	2,297	8,436	9,016	9,160
Ski trails and slopes	110	118	165	167	193	282	282	734	786	874
Other	419	1,038	524	660	1,059	849	869	1,746	1,583	1,779
	$2,065	$2,993	$3,075	$3,219	$3,686	$3,824	$3,923	$14,309	$15,347	$16,565
Less accumulated depreciation	221	345	572	779	971	1,190	1,141	1,461	2,026	2,580
Total plant and equipment	$1,844	$2,648	$2,503	$2,440	$2,715	$2,634	$2,782	$12,848	$13,321	$13,985
Other assets	$ 366	$ 703	$ 592	$ 475	$ 430	$ 378	$ 281	$ 935	$ 1,271	$ 1,124
Total assets	$2,394	$4,097	$3,603	$3,174	$3,436	$4,350	$4,367	$16,135	$17,161	$17,904
Liabilities and Equity										
Current liabilities	$ 947	$ 500	$ 464	$ 604	$ 603	$1,618	$1,311	$ 1,859	$ 1,908	$ 2,010
Long-term debt and other	595	2,351	2,152	1,736	1,828	1,296	1,422	12,509	12,722	12,480*
Total liabilities	$1,542	$2,851	$2,616	$2,340	$2,431	$2,914	$2,733	$14,368	$14,630	$14,490
Stockholders' equity‡										
Common stock (50¢ par)				436	436	436	436	436	442	445
Capital surplus				684	684	684	684	688	765	832
Retained earnings				(286)	(115)	316	514	643	1,324	2,137
Total equity	852	1,246	987	834	1,005	1,436	1,634	1,767	2,531	3,414
Total liabilities and equity	$2,394	$4,097	$3,603	$3,174	$3,436	$4,350	$4,367	$16,135	$17,161	$17,904
Current ratio	0.2	1.5	1.1	0.4	0.5	0.8	1.0	1.3	1.3	1.4
Income from operations/equity					4.9%	3.5%	7.3%	7.2%	14.7%	23.8%
Total debt/equity	1.8	2.3	2.7	2.8	2.4	2.0	1.7	8.1	5.8	4.2

1972 detail

Secured loans	2,304
Lease obligations	156
Unsecured notes	791
Subordinated debentures§	8,033
Deferred taxes	1,196
	12,480

† Includes land to be sold after one year.
‡ Partnership capital for 1963–65.
§ The 7¼% debentures were convertible at $13.75 per share, callable at 105% in 1972, this percentage declining to 100% in 1977 when annual sinking fund payments of $800,000 would commence. VAI's vice president of finance felt that to force conversion of the debentures by calling them would require a stock price of $18 to $20 per share.
Source: Company records and casewriter's analysis.

EXHIBIT 3

VAIL ASSOCIATES, INC
Vail Properties*

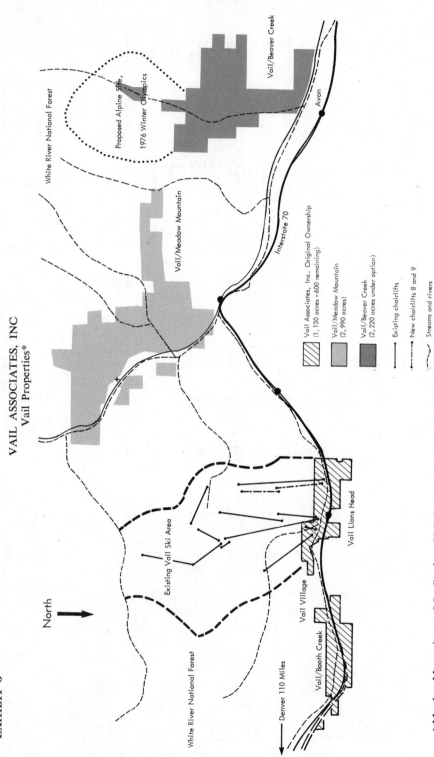

* Meadow Mountain was 5.5 miles from Vail, Beaver Creek was 9 miles from Vail.
† Location of Minturn.
Source: Company records

events scattered throughout Colorado.) By August of that year, however, significant opposition to the Olympics had arisen from a group called Citizens for Colorado's Future. This group, opposing the games on economic and environmental grounds, was responsible for putting a referendum on the November ballot that would, if passed, prevent the games from being held in Colorado. A pro-Olympic group, consisting of wealthy businessmen and prominent citizens, was heavily promoting the games. Predictions were for a very close vote in November.

On August 25, 1972, in a speech to shareholders, Dick Peterson, president of VAI, commented on the relation of the games to VAI's decision on the Beaver Creek land:

Last year about this time we were able to successfully negotiate an option on the base land of what we believed to be—and our studies this past year bear this out—one of the finest remaining undeveloped ski and summer resort locations in the world. The Mountain has similar snow conditions to Vail—the best, over 3,000 ft. of vertical, potential skiing paralleling the world's best and

EXHIBIT 4

VAIL ASSOCIATES, INC.
Projected Cash Flows*
(in thousands of dollars)

Fiscal years ending April 30

	1973	1974	1975	1976	1977
Beaver Creek contributions:†					
Mountain	$ ...	$ ...	$ 150	$ 240	$ 704
Real estate	...	250	250	375	1,000
Other	...	...	26	37	73
	$ ...	$ 250	$ 426	$ 652	$ 1,777
Vail contributions:					
Mountain	$ 2,445	$ 2,900	$ 3,440	$ 4,060	$ 4,796
Real estate	1,200	1,050	1,150	1,125	600
Other	440	530	643	771	908
	$ 4,085	$ 4,480	$ 5,233	$ 5,956	$ 6,304
Total contribution	$ 4,085	$ 4,730	$ 5,659	$ 6,608	$ 8,081
Deductions and adjustments‡	$ 3,391	$ 2,831	$ 3,546	$ 4,290	$ 5,942
Cash available for capital expenditures	$ 694	$ 1,899	$ 2,113	$ 2,318	$ 2,139
Planned capital expenditures:					
Vail	$ 1,135	$ 1,368	$ 985	$ 997	$ 660
Beaver Creek	1,078	2,190	3,545	2,620	1,455
	$ 2,213	$ 3,558	$ 4,530	$ 3,617	$ 2,115
Cash surplus (deficit)	$(1,519)	$(1,659)	$(2,417)	$(1,299)	$ 24
Cumulative	$(1,519)	$(3,178)	$(5,595)	$(6,894)	$(6,870)

* Assumes purchase of Beaver Creek by additional debt.
† Contribution = revenues minus cost of services.
‡ Includes corporate expense, taxes, depreciation, and debt services.
Source: Vail Associates, 1972 Five-Year Plan.

interconnecting easily into our Meadow Mountain property. An important verification of our assessment of the skiing potential was the designation of the site for the Alpine events for the 1976 Winter Olympics.

Management envisioned a possible development at Beaver Creek that could feasibly make it one of the most exclusive resorts in the world. Long-term plans called for a tie-in between Beaver Creek and Meadow Mountain (see Exhibit 3). Management considered Meadow Mountain, which it purchased in 1970, to be of lower skiing quality because of its gentler slopes and eastern exposure. Should Beaver Creek be developed, however, the Meadow Mountain properties would become very desirable, benefiting from the proximity of Vail on one side and Beaver Creek on the other.

It was estimated that by 1977 about $11 million in capital expenditures would be required at Beaver Creek, for which VAI estimated it would need almost $7 million in additional financing by 1976 (see Exhibit 4). The total value of the salable land was estimated to be $31 million and real estate sales could begin in 1974. The initial mountain facility would have four lifts with eventually 10 lifts possible; the projected cost of the entire Beaver Creek operation was close to $25 million, $4.6 million for the land and $10 million each for real estate development and mountain construction.

THE SKI INDUSTRY

Industry structure

The ski industry in 1972 consisted of a highly fragmented group of 1,200 ski areas in the United States and about an equal number in the rest of the world. Half of the U.S. areas were small, rope-tow arrangements open only on weekends; the other half were areas with ski lifts that varied in size and quality from day-ski operations to huge resort complexes catering to the "destination" vacation skier who traveled to the area for a stay of two or more days.

A survey of member areas of the National Association of Ski Areas (NSAA) revealed the following regional characteristics:

	East	Midwest	Rockies	West
Number of NSAA members	219	66	63	79
Average area revenues (thousands)	$ 922	$503	$1,459	$1,100
Average total assets (thousands)	$1,714	$625	$3,388	$1,789

Destination ski areas were generally the largest and received the most publicity in the industry. In Colorado, for example, resort areas accounted for 55% of skier-days, and an investor report predicted that this share would increase to 83% by 1980. The major American destination resorts—Vail, Aspen, Sun Valley, Taos, and others—were located in the western states, although large areas such as Killington, Waterville Valley, and Stowe in the East had substantial vacation business. Major European resorts such as Davos, St. Moritz, and Zermatt in Switzerland, Chamonix in France, and Kitzbühel in Austria also drew large numbers of American skiers, particularly from eastern states.

Trends in the ski industry

In the 1960s skiing literally "took off" in the United States. Increases in income and leisure time as well as improvements in ski equipment enabled the industry to grow at a solid 15% during the 1960s and early 1970s. By 1972 six million skiing Americans spent over $1.5 billion on ski-related products and services. Most observers of the industry expected the growth of skiing to continue unabated during the 1970s for the following reasons:

1. *Population growth* would continue, especially in the most active skiing ages of 20 to 34.
2. *Discretionary income* was forecast to reach $350 billion by 1979, or 30% of all income, compared with only $50 billion (10%) in 1959. Also, the number of families with incomes above $15,000—an amount considered adequate for skiing— would increase.
3. *Leisure time* would increase with shorter working hours and the four-day work week becoming more prevalent. In addition, skiing would benefit from the move to outdoor athletic use of leisure time.
4. *Improved ski equipment* would continue to make skiing simpler and safer and would help to broaden the sport's appeal.
5. *Instructional methods* such as the Graduated Length Method (GLM), which was adopted in the late 1960s by almost all ski schools, made learning to ski relatively quick and easy and opened the sport to all members of a family.
6. *Aggressive marketing* by the increasingly professional management of ski areas and by related segments of the travel industry—travel agents, wholesalers such as American Express, and airlines—would stimulate primary demand and draw newcomers to skiing.

All of these factors were expected to keep the demand for skiing growing at a 15% rate. By 1982 there would thus be 20 million skiers in the United States, a figure that even the most optimistic in the industry felt could not be accommodated comfortably unless ski area growth continued.

Threats to the industry

The threat of demand outstripping supply was very real in 1972 as the American ski industry was faced with the greatest challenge in its history from conservationists and environmentalists who demanded a stop to the construction and expansion of ski areas.

The battle was most visibly represented by the Mineral King case which began when Walt Disney, Inc., developed a plan for a $35 million resort complex at Mineral King in the Sierra Nevada Mountains of California. The plan was approved by the U.S. Forest Service[1] in 1969 but was challenged in court by the Sierra Club. By 1972 Mineral King had still not been built and the controversy promised to drag on indefinitely when in a subsequent suit the Sierra Club questioned the government's right to allow any ski area development on public lands.[2]

Caught in the middle of the controversy was the U.S. Forest Service. On one side, the Forest Service, which because of environmental criticism had significantly lengthened the time involved in gaining a permit, was criticized by the Sierra Club for its "narrow vision of bureaucracy." The ski industry's not dissimilar feeling was stated in a speech by Frank Snyder, president of the NSAA, to a U.S. Forest Service seminar in Denver:

> I'm not at all sure of the Forest Service position on [environmental] matters. What I see is a continued retrenchment—a retreat into bureaucratic anonymity. A year ago, I went into your Washington office and asked one of your officials if the Forest Service would endorse and promote skiing. The answer—delivered carefully and politely—was "No." The evidence of this neutral nonpolicy is all about us.

Environmental threats to the skiing industry had surfaced in other instances. Perhaps the most significant was the challenge to the 1976 Winter Olympics by organized groups in Colorado. Another battle in the continuing war was fought in Vermont where the state legislature adopted stringent rules pertaining to ski areas, one of its largest industries. These measures were considered so strong that they effectively cut off further ski area development and expansion.[3]

---

[1] Eighty-four U.S. ski areas in the western part of the country operated on national forest land owned by the U.S. Government. This land was under the control of the U.S. Forest Service which gave 30-year permits to private ski area operators for small yearly fees. Ski areas in the East and Midwest generally owned their own mountains.

[2] This suit, which would limit special-use grants to no more than 80 acres, could significantly affect the operation of all western ski areas. By August 1972 no decision on the suit had been reached.

[3] By 1972 several eastern ski areas were limiting ticket sales on certain days due to excessive demand. This practice was uncommon in western areas and had never occurred at Vail.

While environmental issues were far from settled in 1972, there were some obvious effects of the above-described battles. The most important was that some participants in the ski industry expected future growth to occur primarily through the expansion of existing ski areas rather than through the development of many new areas. Such a growth pattern together with the large investment required to start a destination facility attractive enough to entice skiers and well-enough planned to receive a Forest Service permit presented significant barriers to entry. A new area built at Snowbird, Utah, in 1971, for example, had an initial cost of $17 million and was not expected to break even for 10 years.

Vail's position in the skiing industry

Vail competed with a large number of ski areas both in the United States and in Europe. Its most relevant competition, however, came from other resorts in the Rocky Mountains for the vacation skier and from several areas nearer Denver such as Loveland, Winter Park, and Copper Mountain for the day skier.

By 1972, 80% of the people skiing at Vail were vacation skiers, many of whom bought tour packages consisting of transportation, lodging, and lifts. These tour packages were often sold through the Vail Resort Association (VRA), an organization of the 33 hotels and all other commercial enterprises in Vail, set up by VAI in 1964. The other 20% of Vail's skiers were mainly from Denver and stayed for only one day. Despite the tour packages, Vail's business still peaked on weekends when as many as 8,000 skiers would use the facilities compared with as few as 1,500 in mid-week.

A 1970 survey revealed that Vail drew its skiers from a variety of areas: Colorado, 23%; other western states, 13.2%; Midwest, 16.2%; Great Lakes, 16.6%; Middle Atlantic, 16.8%; South, 4.3%; Northeast, 5.3%; and Canada, 4.2%.

Most members of VAI's management considered Aspen to be Vail's strongest resort competitor even though the two areas had distinctively different characters. Aspen had more expert skiing and offered a "swinging," youthful image with superior après-ski activities. Vail was more luxurious, had a higher quality reputation, and was located 100 miles closer to Denver than Aspen, thus attracting a reasonable number of day skiers.

The basic business of the two companies operating the areas also differed. Since Aspen had been an established mining town before becoming a ski area, the Aspen Ski Corporation's[4] revenues of $6,930,300

---

[4] The Aspen Skiing Corporation (ASC) owned three of the four ski areas at Aspen and in addition owned the Breckenridge area. ASC was planning to offer its common stock to the public in late 1972 and would thus become only the second publicly held ski area operator after VAI.

in 1972 came almost totally from skiing-related activities, whereas Vail Associates derived almost 30% of its revenue from real estate. The growth of both areas had, however, been similar:

Area	Skier visits 1967–68 season	Skier visits 1971–72 season	Increase
Aspen	524,000 (29%)	1,007,000 (31%)	92%
Vail..............	280,000 (15%)	546,000 (17%)	95%
All Colorado.......	1,813,000 (100%)	3,261,000 (100%)	80%

Source: Colorado Ski Country, U.S.A.

HISTORY OF VAIL

The earliest days of Vail were chronicled by an article on skiing in *Time* magazine:

. . . Vail rises in a valley below the jagged Gore Range, and 15 years ago the area was nearly as empty as when the Utes roamed it in the days before the white man. It was developed by Peter Seibert, 48, a well-muscled, jovial man, who has dreamed of building a ski town ever since he was a boy in Bartlett, N.H.

In World War II, Seibert joined the 10th Mountain Division, which trained at Camp Hale, 20 miles away from what is now Vail. Fighting in the Italian Apennines, Sergeant Seibert was wounded three times in three days. He lost a kneecap, and doctors said that he would never ski again. But in two years, after extensive surgery, he was on the slopes at Aspen as a member of the ski patrol. Later he taught skiing, raced, worked as a logger and studied three years on the G.I. Bill at Lausanne's Ecole Hôtelière. All the time he yearned to find the "perfect" mountain for his resort.

He looked for likely peaks on Colorado maps, then inspected them on foot or horseback. In 1957 a former uranium prospector led him to Vail Mountain, and he knew that he had found his spot—the proper moisture and altitude (an 11,250 ft. peak rising from an 8,200 ft. valley), with a wide variety of slopes for beginners, intermediates and experts. With three friends, he quickly bought 500 acres at the bottom of the mountain for $55,000.

To raise more capital, the partners approached 20 wealthy people, asking for investments of $5,000 each.[5] With this money as a base, Seibert then sold limited partnerships for $10,000 each to another 100 people. Each of the initial investors got limited partnership shares in the enterprise that became Vail Associates, as well as four lifetime lift passes and a half-acre lot. The lot had to be built on immediately. "That was an ingenious idea," recalls Texas financier, Dick Bass, one of the early investors. "The obligation of shareholders to build on their property gave Vail a lot more houses much sooner than other ski developments." By late 1961, Seibert and friends had $1,500,000

---

[5] These original investments had an estimated worth of $80,000 in 1972.

including $500,000 in loans from the First National Bank of Denver and the Small Business Administration. . . .[6]

In 1961 an additional 630 acres of land was purchased for $75,000 bringing the total holding to 1,130 acres. A 30-year Forest Service permit, allowing Vail Associates to operate a ski area on 6,700 acres of the White River National Forest, was obtained on January 25, 1962. The company was all set to build.

The first years

Building commenced in the spring of 1962. By December of that year, Vail opened with the first gondola lift in a U.S. ski resort, two double-chair lifts, and 10 miles of slopes and trails—an u. precedented feat of construction. In the village itself, the company built the $950,000 Lodge at Vail (required by the SBA) and developers added another hotel and a few eating places. Vail grew steadily during the early 1960s. By 1967, the fifth season of operation, the company was making its first profit and the total value of Vail had grown to more than $40 million.

The people who contributed to Vail were a mixed lot but all played a crucial role. Some were investors, like Texas millionaire John Murchison who built a $500,000 house in Vail. Others were that nebulous group, the "jet set," who discovered Vail and added class to and generated publicity for the resort. Still others were those who committed their lives to Vail by building hotels, shops, and restaurants. This last group included a large number of Europeans such as Pepi Gramshammer, the great Austrian skier. "The Europeans were responsible for much of Vail's charm," claimed Seibert; "in the early days we had to sell our land rather than lease it because of financial considerations, but this was an advantage in that ownership of the land was important to the individual entrepreneur and helped create a permanent population, proud of their involvement in Vail."

Expansion and trouble

By 1968 VAI was operating a complete ski area facility with nine lifts and 41 trails. The totality of Vail's value was best reflected in its real estate values. An average acre of land that was bought for about $100 in the late 1950s sold for almost $100,000 in 1968. Against this background, a more ambitious strategy was outlined by Peter Seibert in the 1968 annual report:

The Company goals are to generate profits for the long-range benefit of its shareholders by pursuing those activities in which the corporation has developed, or may develop, natural competitive advantages. These activities are:

---

[6] "The Anatomy of a Ski Town," Reprinted by Permission from TIME, *The Weekly News Magazine*, December 25, 1972, p. 61. Copyright Time Inc. 1972.

(a) winter and summer sports area development and operation; (b) real estate development and operation; (c) the acquisition, development, and operation of businesses offering unusual profit potential relating to leisure time.

The specifics of these plans took several forms:

1. The Lodge at Vail, which had never made money for the company, was sold for a loss of about $285,000. "We could have probably made the Lodge profitable," claimed Seibert, "but we would have had to invest heavily in its expansion—something we were not willing to do."

2. A program was initiated in November 1968 to develop Vail/Lions-Head as an addition to Vail Village. Crash construction resulted in the completion of a gondola, terminal building, and a chairlift in just 13 months at a cost of almost $5 million—$2 million over the original estimates.

3. Twenty-eight condominium units were developed in Vail Village and were sold at a small profit by the company in 1969. A larger complex was then initiated in LionsHead in late 1969, resulting in an eventual loss of $350,000.

4. In February 1970 the company purchased 3,070 acres of land at Meadow Mountain, about five miles from Vail Village, for $3,070,000 (see Exhibit 3).

The financial ramifications of the above decisions were severe. Earnings plunged from $.48 a share in 1968 to $.03 in 1969 and $.13 in 1970. VAI's total assets rose from $4.3 million at April 30, 1969, to $16.1 million at the same date in 1970. An $8 million convertible debenture offering was made to finance the various ventures. The company's stock dropped to $4 a share in early 1970 from a 1969 high of 16½ and rumors of take-over bids were rampant as VAI teetered near bankruptcy.

New management

New management was sought as a solution to the company's problems. In March of 1970 a new vice president assumed the real estate responsibilities that had been largely Seibert's. The most significant move, however, was the addition of a new president in November 1970. Seibert commented:

I had run the company as president since its inception, but by 1970 we did not have sufficient management personnel to continue as we had in the past. So the board and I got together and decided to hire Dick Peterson to come in as president of the company.

It was a little tough at first, but in the last few years our relationship has worked out well. We have what I guess you could call a marriage of skills. Dick is a hell of a smart guy and I'm smart enough to realize that.

Peterson, who left a secure job as a consulting partner in a national CPA firm to join Vail Associates, explained his choice:

I approached my decision very much like a case study by carefully analyzing the strengths and weaknesses. What impressed me most were the fundamentals—the industry's growth, Vail's competitive position, and the people who were in the firm at the time. The big weakness, of course, was the company's financial bind. I really questioned if they could survive. When I decided to take the job, I structured an employment contract that protected my first year. If everything had gone wrong, I would have come out okay.

Peterson went on to describe his first year as president of Vail Associates:

The first move I made was to bring in Jim Bartlett in December. I needed a number two man that I knew I could rely on and since Jim had worked with me at Touche Ross he was an obvious choice. During the first year, we concentrated on day-to-day operational matters—strengthening the departments below the department head, cutting costs, and establishing new control systems.

I was confronted with obvious frictions from some of the other managers in the company. Things had been pretty loose for quite some time and they naturally resented that a new person had to be hired from the outside to tighten things up. A key element in winning their confidence was the stock option and incentive plans I instituted. During the first year, I distributed options for almost 60,000 shares to the key managers. My incentive compensation scheme allowed a department manager to earn a bonus of up to 40% of his base salary for superior performance. Finally, I raised those salaries that were obviously low.

Jim Bartlett, vice president of finance and secretary-treasurer of VAI, described his financial operation and its evolution:

When I came to the company, the financial situation was pretty serious. The personnel were weak or inexperienced, the control system was in very rough form, and the capital structure had seen the addition of $12 million in debt in one year. Within a few months Dick and I had designed new control and incentive systems, had introduced a five-year plan, and began to tighten up on expenses.

The next priority was the finance department organization. I made Gary Kehl controller and brought in Bob Momsen, an MBA from Stanford, as my assistant. Over the last year I've made an attempt to bring these guys in on everything and we now operate as a team on most matters. Dick and I now operate under a basic doctrine of "no surprises." In the middle of each month Gary and Bob visit with the department heads to elicit their estimates of how they will perform that month against their budget. This mid-month meeting has served to make results more predictable and to increase our understanding of operations on a more current basis.

Another financial effort that Peterson and Bartlett had made was in the area of the company's stock. In 1970 VAI's common stock was traded over-the-counter by four market makers with an average weekly volume of 2,500 shares. By 1972, there were 10 market makers, weekly volume was 15,000 shares, and VAI's key investment banking relationship for future offerings had been switched to Lehman Brothers.

Officers and directors of VAI owned about 17% of the 890,000 shares of common stock outstanding in 1972; another 15%–20% was closely held. The largest single individual shareholder was Peter Seibert with 41,000 shares; Dick Peterson owned 18,000 shares and outside directors about 100,000 shares. VAI had never paid any dividends. Seibert, Parker,[7] Peterson, and 12 outsiders made up the 15-member board. Almost all of the outsiders had been on the board before Peterson's arrival and several of them were among the original Vail partners. Peterson was chairman of the board's seven-member executive committee.

VAIL ASSOCIATES, INC., IN 1972

Source of revenue

VAI's primary source of revenue was lift-ticket sales. Management expected growth on Vail Mountain to continue unabated until about 1977 when the mountain's capacity of 17,200 skiers per day would be reached. (See Exhibit 5 for total mountain statistics.) Since all of Vail's expansion plans were subject to U.S. Forest Service approval, the planned growth after 1977 was questionable. Don Almond, head of the mountain department, described the company's relationships with the Forest Service:

The Forest Service is actually our "landlord," and any improvements or changes we make in their property must have their approval. This includes everything from new lifts and trails to eating facilities and lift-ticket prices. Our main contact is with the local district ranger. Because of the way the U.S. Forest Service is organized, the local ranger is in a very powerful position.

I experience a great deal of difficulty in dealing with the U.S. Forest Service. The ranger has two or three years experience compared to over 50 years for my staff. We thus operate on different levels of expertise and sophistication. Also, the Service is under extreme pressure from environmentalists and is becoming more hesitant about approving expansion plans. Their response time to our proposals is up to six months.

VAI also obtained revenues from four owned restaurants and from its ski school, the largest and most profitable in the world, in which 16% of all Vail skiers took lessons during the 1971–1972 season. Furthermore, in 1971 a program was initiated to build Vail's reputation as a year-

---

[7] Vice president of marketing.

EXHIBIT 5

VAIL ASSOCIATES, INC.
Mountain Operating Statistics

	Years ending October 31							Years ending April 30			
	1963	1964	1965	1966	1967	1968	1969	1970	1971	1972	1973*
1. Ski trails	20	23	29	30	34	41	42	58	59	61	64
2. Acres of skiable terrain:											
Most difficult	713	713	717	717	730	730	751	751	751	751	751
More difficult	75	85	103	103	128	159	159	255	255	284	324
Easiest	88	89	134	137	143	209	209	329	331	333	344
Total	876	887	954	957	1,001	1,098	1,119	1,335	1,337	1,368	1,419
3. Skier visits (in thousands)†	61	89	153	205	238	280	360	433	488	546	
4. Maximum day	N/A	N/A	N/A	N/A	N/A	4,766	5,495	6,737	6,470	7,766	
5. Single day lift-ticket price	$4.50	$5.00	$5.50	$6.00	$6.50	$7.00	$7.50	$8.00	$9.00	$9.00	$9.00
6. Annual snowfall (in inches) ...	201	190	320	185	256	325	213	324	274	364	
7. Season length (days)	122	121	152	145	152	152	157	157	157	157	
8. Lift capacity‡ (skiers per hour)	3,020	3,020	6,170	6,170	6,170	7,900	7,900	10,200	10,200	10,200	13,200
9. Number of lifts:											
Chair	2	2	5	5	5	6	6	7	7	7	9
Gondola	1	1	1	1	1	1	1	2	2	2	2
Poma	1	1	1	1	1	2	2	2	2	2	3

* Planned.
† A skier visit is one person skiing at a ski area for any part of one day.
‡ Rated capacity. The area's actual or "comfortable" capacity was about 65% of rated capacity.
Source: Company records.

round resort complex. Substantial increases had been experienced in summer business as conventions and group meetings were attracted to Vail for golf, tennis, riding, camping, and fishing. VAI's off-season revenues came from gondola ticket sales and restaurant contributions, which together totaled about $165,000 during the summer of 1971.

VAI's real estate sales were its second largest source of revenue. Vail Associates' traditional approach to real estate had been to plan and develop[8] its properties for sale to builders who in turn constructed homes, condominiums, lodges, or commercial buildings for sale or lease to others. Even though VAI sold its land, the company regulated development in Vail; builders had to submit architectural designs and construction plans before being considered as a buyer. By its approval, VAI controlled not only the type of development but also the size of the builder. No real estate project had ever failed in Vail.

The demand for land in Vail had been quite strong. During the year ending April 30, 1972, VAI sold a total of 15 acres for $1,952,700, or $130,180 per acre. This demand allowed management to control land sales and thus manage its revenues and profits from real estate. VAI sold its property on a cash or installment basis, with typical terms of 25% down payment, 25% at construction initiation, and the balance at completion of the project.

In 1972 VAI owned about 3,600 acres of land—600 in Vail and 2,990 at Meadow Mountain. Of the 600 acres of land left in Vail, about 200, with a total value of over $10 million, were to be sold.[9] The balance was committed to open space or was not suitable for development.

The town of Vail

By 1972 the town of Vail had become an entity separate from Vail Associates, electing its own officials and collecting taxes to finance basic municipal services. The town was governed by a part-time nine-member Board of Trustees, a part-time mayor, and a full-time town manager. The town's total budget was almost $1.3 million, and the town's permanent population of 750 swelled to 10,000 on some winter weekends. The town also had its own fire and police departments as well as water and sewer facilities.

In the early years of Vail, VAI had served as the local government for the area. But the constant addition of restaurants, shops, and hotels, together with expanded weekend populations, had increased the demand

---

[8] Development included subdivision and construction of roads, water, sewers, and utilities by contractors.

[9] Of the 200 acres to be sold, 25 were zoned for high-density commercial use, while the balance consisted of low-density properties zoned for townhouses or single-family homes.

for services beyond the company's capacity to provide. In 1966 therefore VAI had ceded control, and Vail Village had been incorporated with borders roughly approximating the original Vail Associates' land (see Exhibit 3).

One issue that was vigorously debated in the town was growth. Some residents, including members of the Board of Trustees, felt that the quality of life in Vail could only be preserved by stopping further development. Their attitudes were summarized by John Donovan, a supervisor in VAI's ski school, a local bar owner, and a member of the Board of Trustees:

> When I first came here it was a Brigadoon. This was the most prolific deer country. Now development and people have pushed all the game off. It's the same with fishing—just too many people. The older people lean toward slow growth but fresh money keeps showing up. I think we've been overwhelmed. The growth was faster than our thinking.[10]

The issue of growth had arisen several times during 1972 as Vail's Board of Trustees debated specific taxing and zoning proposals that could effectively clamp a moratorium on further construction. Such a move could present a severe hardship to VAI since the company planned relatively consistent annual real estate sales and almost all of its near-term land inventory was located within the town of Vail. Dick Peterson commented on the town-company relationship:

> Since we no longer can exercise direct control, my strategy for dealing with the town is to make sure the key people understand our position. I believe that they have the same long-range goal that we do: maximization of the aesthetic and economic quality of Vail. There is no doubt in my mind that at some point we have to cut off growth.
>
> In a sense, however, we do still have some leverage. The town manager, with whom I communicate a great deal, realizes that his plans will require substantial capital, and the financial community would be reluctant to lend to him if the town's economic climate deteriorated significantly.

Some people felt that the greatest danger to VAI came not from the town of Vail but rather from uncontrolled areas in Eagle County outside the town limits where developers had built many lower quality dwellings, often with inadequate attention to sewers and air pollution. Since all of VAI's property was in Eagle County, management was naturally concerned about the county government's planning process, as rapid uncontrolled expansion could dilute Vail's painfully built and maintained quality. These fears had led to the setting up in 1971 of an Advisory Planning Commission for the county, a body that management hoped would act decisively in controlling expansion.

---

[10] Christopher S. Wren, "Environmentalism, Colorado-style: I've got mine, Jack," *The New York Times Magazine,* March 11, 1973, p. 34.

Management

Vail Associates' management was generally considered by industry experts to be one of the best in the ski business (see Exhibits 6 and 7). Bob Parker, vice president of marketing, who together with Pete Seibert had been instrumental in obtaining the Winter Olympics, provided an analysis of the managerial situation in VAI:

I guess I have the best perspective of anyone on the relations of the old and new managers. I am confident that at an operating level we have blended very well and have no differences. There is still a "generation gap," however, with regard to corporate goals, image, and involvement with the community. This is a philosophical difference that boils down to the question of what is Vail? The newer people take more of a mechanistic, economic, industrial attitude towards Vail, as if Vail were a manufactured product. We take a more emotional, historical, sports-oriented attitude. Vail is not just a business, it is more—it's a place, it's people, sometimes it's a state of mind.

Pete Seibert expounded his feelings:

The biggest problem we face is how to maintain quality. Some people in the company tend to forget that we're not canning spinach but that we're in a sensitive service industry. We are in the business of taking people up on a mountain; feeding, caring, and rewarding them for their physical prowess. They come to Vail for a pleasant, enjoyable vacation, and we have the responsibility of satisfying their wishes. When directors and shareholders and their wives use the facilities as much as ours do, quality becomes especially important. If the johns are dirty or if there's mud by the ticket windows, we hear about it.

I can see our quality problems like no one else can. I guess it takes a certain dedication to go to a business school, but that kind of background doesn't guarantee you operational sensitivity. People who have grown up in the business have learned by doing and have succeeded by satisfying the basic needs of the customer.

I like to experiment with new ideas but not at the expense of quality. We are pushing our service divisions too far down, and the incentive system has encouraged people to sacrifice quality for profits. I think the only way to settle the quality issue is to go to a damn checklist and hire someone to spend all his time checking on quality, like the fellow who checks the Sunoco gas stations and Howard Johnson restaurants, for example.

I am slowly phasing out of daily operations except for monitoring our quality and attempting to develop people who believe they are in the people business. The bulk of my time in the future might be devoted to Beaver Creek and to investigating and assessing new potential recreation areas like Vail. My role at Beaver Creek would be to work myself out of a job by handling the initial development and then turning the operating details over to others. After that I might work with one or two more areas and retire to a little golf. Still, the business is too challenging to get out.

EXHIBIT 6

VAIL ASSOCIATES, INC.
Organization Chart

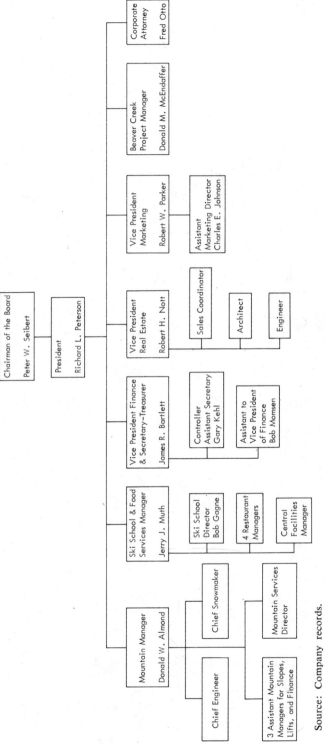

Chairman of the Board — Peter W. Seibert

President — Richard L. Peterson

Mountain Manager — Donald W. Almond
- Chief Engineer
- Chief Snowmaker
- 3 Assistant Mountain Managers for Slopes, Lifts, and Finance
- Mountain Services Director

Ski School & Food Services Manager — Jerry J. Muth
- Ski School Director — Bob Gagne
- 4 Restaurant Managers
- Central Facilities Manager

Vice President Finance & Secretary–Treasurer — James R. Bartlett
- Controller Assistant Secretary — Gary Kehl
- Assistant to Vice President of Finance — Bob Momsen

Vice President Real Estate — Robert H. Nott
- Sales Coordinator
- Architect
- Engineer

Vice President Marketing — Robert W. Parker
- Assistant Marketing Director — Charles E. Johnson

Beaver Creek Project Manager — Donald M. McEndaffer

Corporate Attorney — Fred Otto

Source: Company records.

EXHIBIT 7

VAIL ASSOCIATES, INC.
Biographical Data on Management

	Age	Joined company	Education	Previous experience	1972* salary
Peter W. Seibert	48	1961 (at founding)	Ecole Hoteliere Lausanne, Switzerland	10th Mt. Div. U.S. Army Aspen Ski Corp. Instructor Asst. Mgr. Loveland Basin Gen. Mgr.	$40,000
Richard L. Peterson	37	Nov. 1970	B.M.E.—Cornell MBA—Harvard	Touche, Ross & Co. Partner in Mgmt. Services	$40,000
Robert W. Parker	50	1961 (at founding)	B.S.—Washington Grad. Study—U. of Grenoble	10th Mt. Div. U.S. Army *Skiing* magazine Editor	$35,000
James R. Bartlett	28	Dec. 1970	B.S. (Math)—De Pauw MBA—Stanford	Touche, Ross & Co. Senior Consultant	$30,000
Robert H. Nott	40	March 1970	B.S. (Eng.)—Clemson	Coldwell, Banker & Co. DiGiorgio Corp. Real Estate Sales and Mgmt.	$35,000
Frederick Otto	33	Aug. 1972	B.S. (Acct.)—Colorado J.D.—U. of Denver	Touche, Ross & Co. Tax Staff Holme, Roberts & Owen Attorney	$24,000
Donald W. Almond	42	1961 (at founding)	B.A. (Bus.)—Idaho State	A.T.&T. lineman Vail Associates Ski Patrol Director	$24,000
Jerry J. Muth	36	1967	B.A. (Psych.)—Colorado	Arapahoe Basin Ski School Instructor Director	$27,000
Donald M. McEndaffer	30	Dec. 1971	B.S. (Math, Chem.)—Colorado	Touche, Ross & Co. Sr. Consultant	$23,100

* Salary only—bonus not included.

Peterson described his thinking about VAI's organization and management:

Peter and I haven't had the easiest relationship, but the key ingredient is that we respect each other and in the final analysis we both want the same goal of long-range maximization of the company's value. [VAI's stated objective was a 20% increase in E.P.S. annually.] I know Peter can play a valuable role in the development of this company in the future.

I interact relatively equally with everyone. I do, however, utilize Jim Bartlett for advice of a much broader nature than just financial matters. In reality he serves as the number two man in the company, a fact that I'm sure causes some obvious resentment and problems.

I will have to decide how to organize our planning, engineering, and construction skills. These now exist in the real estate and mountain departments and in the Beaver Creek group. I foresee the eventual emergence of a strong additional department for these activities. However, I have a span of control problem now, and before a new department is created I want to establish a position of vice president for operations to handle the operating departments.

The one question that I have devoted most thought to lately is our organization for Beaver Creek if we decide to exercise the option. Perhaps it should continue with its own general manager, but my thinking now is that functional centralization is necessary. After all, organization is a function of what is theoretically best and what is practically possible given personalities in a company.

As project manager for Beaver Creek, Dick Peterson had hired Don McEndaffer in December 1971. "Don has the advantage of being able to coordinate the efforts of many diverse individuals as well as having the skills necessary to control development costs. If the Olympics are approved, we will face a fixed development timetable much like that of 1968 when LionsHead was built," explained Peterson.

As to VAI's future, Peterson commented that Beaver Creek and Meadow Mountain would enable the company to continue its earnings growth for another 10 to 15 years. He continued:

Still, a publicly held company needs more than a 10–15 year time horizon, and so we are actively considering diversification into other businesses. We are one business in one location, and everything we have is dependent on the weather. This is just too risky a position. We feel that a potential acquisition should be in a leisure, recreation, or tourist type business that we understand, should offer competitive advantages, and must be basically healthy since we don't have the managerial resources to rescue a sick operation while at the same time concentrating on Vail and possibly developing a new resort at Beaver Creek.

GENERAL MANAGEMENT IN THE
DIVISIONALIZED ORGANIZATION

*United Latex Ltd.**

"OUR TASKS are not easy. We have to change attitudes of mind, find and train the right executives, and, most important, completely reorganize our accounting methods to give you measuring sticks," stated Mr. Peter Dudley, deputy managing director of United Latex Ltd. (ULL)[1] in announcing major changes in corporate organization at an executive conference in June of 1968. Mr. Dudley, 44, had joined ULL in late 1966 after holding important technical and executive positions in the chemical industry and was the principal architect of the new structure. He continued:

The ULL organization has grown as a result of the acquisition of a number of companies, many undertaking similar activities. With 9 companies and 11 factories, integration has to come but has lagged. A year or two ago the managing director had, in theory, 36 people reporting to him and received 120 reports each month. Obviously, such a state of affairs was unworkable, particularly because of the interrelation of problems, as business became tougher.

As well as providing a heavy load on top management, the centralized functional organization is defective in the lack of general business training permitted by the system. Even senior executives grow up with just a specialized training in sales or factory matters, without knowledge of each other's problems, and often in a perpetual state of war with each other.

---

[1] Names, locations, and certain financial information have been disguised.

Our plans provide for a division of company activities into cells of business activity in which those composing the cell will be responsible for the operation, development, and profitability of the company's business allotted to the cell profit centers. The decision to date is to create four operating divisions supported by the usual staff departments. These divisions follow obvious product groupings. The sales turnover of each division is substantial, and the intention is to have divisions operated by a general manager as and when appropriate personnel become available from within and without the organization. For the time being, we may have to improvise and have one executive undertaking more than one job.

For many years we have sold our goods through regional sales offices operated by ULL with certain subsidiaries playing minor sales roles because of traditional goodwill. Today we have created divisions with their own marketing responsibilities which will have to rely on these general offices. Many of the customers of divisions may be important general customers of the company within a region, so knowledge of the customer must be built up for the mutual advantage of the division and the regional sales office. Rivalry must not exist between division and regional sales, and it is hoped that effective teamwork will be forthcoming.

Divisional marketing managers can seek help from our corporate development and market research department, but that department cannot be expected to perform the day-to-day duties of a division; its prime task is to study our long-term problems and interest and pay particular attention to development projects until they are securely placed on a commercial and economic basis.

Ideally, a division—or any other cell of business activity—would operate most efficiently if the prime functions were all at one center, with the factory, the sales office, and the development laboratory under one control. However, we are faced with some large factories which may always have to be subdivided on a divisional basis. What we have to ensure is concentration of like manufacturing activities, and this must be one of the prime tasks of the divisions. But our present location problems and the inevitable consequences of development programs over the next 5 to 10 years render improbable a tidy divisional factory pattern in the sense that the divisions can have control of all our factories.

Our immediate problem is to develop an organizational structure which permits the division to exercise its full responsibility for ensuring that the products required by the division are manufactured at an economic cost and are of adequate quality. Further, the division must be able to exercise its responsibility to improve and develop the line of products allocated to it. These responsibilities can be exercised through a production manager who controls a plant within the jurisdiction of a corporate factory manager. The extent to which the responsibility for operations passes directly from division to production, or from division indirectly to production through factory management, is a matter for determination between divisional heads and factory management. The problem is analogous to that presented by divisional representation and regional sales offices.

So you will note that we have a lot to unravel, but the tasks are not insuperable. To solve them will need the closest cooperation between divisional production control and factory management. Many of you have been brought up just to mind your own business, which is a useful characteristic when interpreted as doing an effective task on your own. Unfortunately, the effect has been to discourage a sense of participation in company, factory, or divisional affairs. This attitude of mind has just got to disappear.

It has been traditional in the rubber industry that the mysteries of rubber processing and compounding are locked in the mind of the works chemist. He has become the technical dictator of control and development activity, and the rest of the organization—unable to understand what he was brewing—tended to keep him divorced from other considerations and perhaps narrowed his outlook. He has been the victim of excessive functionalism.

To be able to exercise our judgment in the techno-commercial field, we have created a corporate development department to stand aloof from day-to-day problems and guide us on how and where to concentrate our future activities. This does not mean that the divisions cannot draw upon the corporate development department. They can, but the case must be justified to corporate development and then corporate development must justify an addition or substitution in their budget.

Divisionalization, with its delegation of authority to perform in a specified area of business activity, cannot work unless those concerned have measuring sticks to control their operations and judge their performance. The essence of the reorganization is to set up profit earning centers. The company as a whole is not accustomed to be judged in monetary terms, but henceforth every senior executive will be responsible for an expense budget, a production cost, or a profit position. To achieve this has required a complete overhaul, rationalization, and modification of our accounting departments and their procedures. Divisional profitability will be judged, therefore, not on profits on sales but upon return on investment based on the fixed and working capital used by the division.

Our accounting team knows the relative importance of time and accuracy in the processing of figures, but they can get nowhere without the data on which to give you figures, and you are the people responsible for supplying the data. If you don't think you are, you had better get moving quickly to find out why you have not recognized this responsibility.

With measuring sticks available to you and to management, you are on the spot, and you will be judged by your performance against a budget you yourselves have compiled. One of our members once suggested we were bottom heavy, and this is generally true by the very fact that we have had a complex organization with considerable duplication of effort. All this is being eliminated.

To succeed we must develop people who have got a little more than other companies have got. Good men are hard to get, and it is true that there are many good men around whom we fail to recognize because we don't put opportunity in their way. Divisionalization will fail if we do not find the right leaders in the first place, and we cannot tolerate the wrong man in the wrong place. This might be management's mistake by placing a man beyond his ability to perform. Recognize your limitations or else you may well be heading for a very unhappy career. Increased responsibility is tough but fun, and we want people who are prepared to have a go at it.

CORPORATE HISTORY

ULL was a leading manufacturer in the British rubber industry. Its product line included tires, conveyor and power transmission belting, rubber hose, footwear, and a wide variety of industrial rubber products. In recent years ULL had added plastics and synthetic-fiber products to its rubber product line; these materials were replacing rubber in many applications, and their development permitted the company to diversify in associated markets.

During the 1950s and 1960s, ULL had been confronted with increasing competitive pressures resulting from (1) changed and tightened purchasing policies by its major customer, the National Coal Board; (2) the abandonment of price agreements prohibited by the Restrictive Trade Practices Act; and (3) increases in raw material prices and the entry of synthetic substitutes. ULL had entered this period with antiquated and inefficient plants as a result of policies of the then managing director who had limited plant expenditures during the years of high margins and demand. He reasoned that large cash balances were needed to take advantage of all cash discounts and to place the company in a strong bargaining position vis-à-vis its suppliers. (See Exhibit 1 for profit and loss figures from 1959 to 1970 and Exhibit 2 for the balance sheet as of December 31, 1970.)

As these competitive pressures mounted, retirement required a shift in management. The new managing director, Mr. Bradley, had previously been marketing manager. To meet increased competition, he took several steps. Time and motion study projects were introduced in the factories in an effort to increase worker efficiency and reduce costs. Second, increased efforts were made in the export market. Third, a corporate development department was created, which was responsible for handling all major products of the corporation from laboratory and market research to design. And fourth, diversification and expansion projects were undertaken by acquiring manufacturing facilities for the production of plastics and subsequently synthetic fibers. While a large proportion of its sales of these products were to the government, there was an increasing volume of business in the commercial field.

In commenting on the company's internal situation, one executive said:

After Mr. Bradley came in, I think the company tried to change, but it just did not know how. For one thing, we were extremely short of qualified staff as a result of a policy of not replacing retiring executives. Almost all

EXHIBIT 1

UNITED LATEX LTD.
Profit and Loss Statements, 1959–70
(thousands of pounds)

	1959	1960	1961	1962	1963	1964	1965	1966	1967	1968	1969	1970
Sales												
Belting and hose	14,719	15,694	15,899	15,193	14,617	13,934	14,306	14,881	13,224	13,198	13,727	13,994
Tire	3,120	2,334	2,689	4,189	3,157	3,558	3,528	3,177	4,764	3,702	4,164	4,212
Industrial products	4,295	4,211	5,357	5,553	5,474	6,052	6,181	6,101	6,920	7,603	8,325	8,987
Specialty plastics	....	....	....	....	2,132	4,404	5,407	6,263	6,315	6,690	7,257	8,113
Total	22,134	22,239	23,945	24,935	25,380	27,948	29,422	30,422	31,223	31,193	33,473	35,306
Cost of sales	19,454	19,470	20,099	21,373	22,310	24,241	25,540	26,968	28,275	28,918	31,149	32,520
Gross profit	2,680	2,769	3,846	3,562	3,070	3,707	3,882	3,454	2,948	2,275	2,324	2,786
Sales, general and administrative	1,397	1,454	1,471	1,480	1,482	1,485	1,520	1,552	1,581	1,647	1,796	1,858
Profit before taxes	1,283	1,315	2,375	2,082	1,588	2,222	2,362	1,902	1,367	628	528	928
Taxes	592	603	1,345	1,264	886	1,193	1,117	957	756	215	135	394
Net profit	691	712	1,030	818	702	1,029	1,245	945	611	413	393	534

Source: Company records.

EXHIBIT 2

UNITED LATEX LTD.
Balance Sheet as of December 31, 1970
(in thousands of pounds)

Assets

Current assets
Cash		306
Investments		729
Accounts receivable		3,613
Inventories		7,096
Total current assets		11,744

Fixed assets
Plant and equipment	10,112	
Less: Depreciation	4,363	5,749
Total assets		17,493

Liabilities and Stockholders' Equity

Current liabilities
Bank overdrafts		1,612
Accounts payable		2,870
Tax liability		512
Other accrued expenses		415
Total current liabilities		5,409

Stockholders' equity
Cumulative preference shares	470	
Common stock	4,200	4,670
Retained earnings		7,414
Total liabilities and stockholders' equity		17,493

Source: Company records.

the executives in the company were advanced in years and were quite overworked.

A second characteristic of the company's management that continued during this time was the centralization of power in the managing director, with little delegation of authority. Thus, it usually took a long time to get any decisions. Furthermore, there was little encouragement for executives to use their own initiative. And finally, I think that one of our most serious problems was that people did not talk about the future. All attention was centered on our day-to-day operating problems.

SUBSEQUENT ORGANIZATIONAL DEVELOPMENTS

In January 1970 Mr. Dudley assumed the position of managing director and Mr. Bradley became chairman of the board of directors. By March 1971 the organizational changes conceived by Mr. Dudley had been largely implemented, although in a somewhat modified manner. First, the divisions assumed complete marketing responsibility, and the position of regional sales manager was eliminated. Second, the factories were assigned to specific divisions, even though factories producing for more than one division were still operating. And third, a cor-

EXHIBIT 3

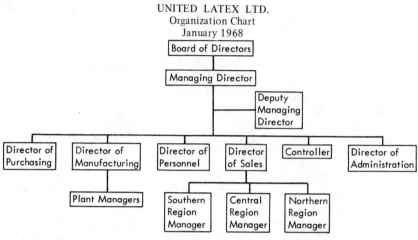

UNITED LATEX LTD.
Organization Chart
January 1968

Source: Company records.

EXHIBIT 4

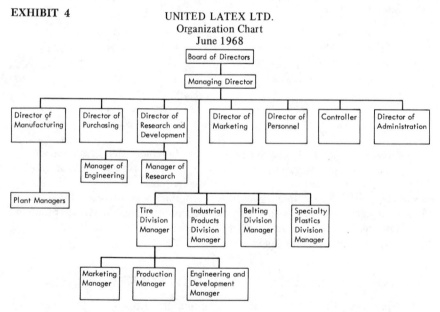

UNITED LATEX LTD.
Organization Chart
June 1968

Source: Company records.

porate director of technical operations was appointed, and the functions of the corporate development department were assumed by this more comprehensive technical organization.

As Mr. Dudley pressed ahead with his organizational plan, he noted in particular the change in manufacturing:

It became evident that without direct control of production our divisional managers were not going to understand the important production-marketing relationship. Thus, at the beginning of 1971 we assigned each factory to the division receiving the largest amount of its output. Any conflicts which the division managers cannot resolve on an informal basis can be brought to the monthly meeting of the policy committee, which is composed of the division managers and top corporate executives.

EXHIBIT 5

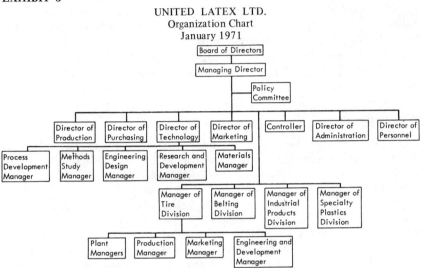

UNITED LATEX LTD.
Organization Chart
January 1971

Source: Company records.

(See Exhibits 3, 4, and 5 for organizational charts from January 1968 to January 1971.)

CORPORATE-DIVISION RELATIONSHIPS

Mr. Dudley, however, stressed that many problems remained to be worked out. He particularly emphasized the issue of corporate-division relationships: "One of my biggest problems is that I don't believe any of our division managers have really resolved this problem." The re- mainder of this case gives the views on this issue of six ULL executives representing three divisions[2] and two staff departments.

Mr. Arthur Henry and Mr. Paul Edwards, industrial products division

The industrial products division of ULL produced a broad range of products, including antivibration mountings, industrial belts, rubber

---

[2] The manager of the tire division was on vacation during this period.

and plastic mouldings, extrusions, and rubber hose. The division manager, Mr. Arthur Henry, and the assistant general manager, Mr. Paul Edwards, were interviewed together. Mr. Henry had been in his position since May 1968 and was 39 years old in 1971. Until 1968, he had been the owner manager of a small rubber products company. Mr. Edwards, 35 years old in 1971, had also worked for a small company before joining ULL in 1967.

Speaking of these two men, a corporate executive remarked: "Mr. Henry is an outstanding salesman with a volatile personality, while Mr. Edwards is the 'businessman' of the division. Due to his business abilities, Mr. Edwards is a necessary part of Mr. Henry's organization, although he tends to want to run things on his own, entirely separate from the corporation. Thus, Edwards has frequent run-ins with the corporate organization."

When asked about the new organization, Mr. Henry made the following comments:

We are new men here. We only know our division, and we don't want any unnecessary interference from the corporation. In general, we do not accept corporate staff assistance. We believe it leads to frustration and a slowing down of our operations.

Of course, we are prejudiced in this matter. We have had so little help and so much trouble from the corporation that we are sour on the whole concept. I think there are some people within this company who want to go back to the tight, centralized control we had here at one time. Personally, I'm afraid that the wise efforts to move toward divisionalization have stopped in some cases and we are now going backwards. The staff needs something to do. But Lord, they don't know a thing about industrial belts, or even our new industrial hoses. They try to make us spend more on research as if we were a Du Pont or someone. We think our marketing skill, our ability to move quickly to satisfy customer need, is our greatest asset. But Matthews (the new vice president of technology) wants us to spend as much on research as the specialty plastics division. On the other hand, we can't get any new materials out of specialty plastics because they want to exploit their own developments in some silly esoteric way.

We don't play according to the book in this division. The two of us run the show and pay attention mainly to profits. In some of the other divisions I know that the division manager is not really the boss and that they are run by the division's executive committee.[3]

In response to a question about corporate functions, Mr. Edwards commented in particular on accounting.

---

[3] Each division had an executive committee composed of top divisional managers. However, since Mr. Dudley felt that "a man should not sit in judgment on his own acts," the chairmanship of this committee was given to someone in the division other than the division general manager. In addition, the managing director of the corporation was a member of each committee.

Divisional rather than corporate accounting is absolutely necessary. We get data from the corporate accountants, and we need an interpreter in order to understand what it means. Here we are with a large number of different products and we need to know where the profit is. Yet the corporation insists upon allocating all the corporate overhead against product sales. Sometimes we tell the corporation that we don't believe their accounting data. Then they go to our plants for the information and it is passed back to the division by the corporation. All this is wasted effort and could be handled much more quickly if the divisions did their own accounting. Here's what I mean by some of the worthless information we receive from the corporation.

At this point Mr. Edwards left his office and returned a few minutes later with a 20–30 foot length of computer tabulating paper. After throwing it into the air, collecting it in a large pile on the floor, and placing it in a wastebasket, he continued:

As you can see, there are no words on that paper. There are only numbers because the machine has to work entirely with codes; and it would take me hours to translate the data. Now this is an extreme example, and I don't know why they even sent us that paper, but my point is that when you take the accounting function away from a division, you remove the intimacy with an activity which is essential to business. Unless you have this function within your organization, you are never able to see things realistically.

Mr. Henry continued Mr. Edwards' discussion of corporate functions with a brief comment on research.

Although research and development should primarily be a divisional function, I suppose the corporation can do some long-term development. As for the new function of the director of technology, it should not have any line authority. We are willing to accept technical advice if it is offered in the form of a suggestion such as we would get from an outside consultant, but we do not want to take any orders from these people.

Mr. Charles Whitney, belting division

The belting division possessed a particularly complex manufacturing organization, receiving its production from five plants. Only one of these produced exclusively for the division, and the division was responsible for operating the Sheffield factory, which produced some products for the tire and industrial products divisions.

The manager of the belting division, Mr. Charles Whitney, was a man in his early fifties. He was an engineer by training and had spent most of his career in the rubber industry. He came to ULL in 1958, and before assuming his present position in 1962 was plant manager at the Sheffield factory. Mr. Whitney was described by a corporate executive as follows:

Of all the division general managers, he has the type of background which would lead one to think that he should be the best equipped to run a division. He is a charming person, and although he does not have the dynamic qualities of Mr. Henry, I am sure that he really knows how to implement the divisionalization. On the other hand, he still hesitates to run the division as independently as he should. This is probably because he is a product of the rubber industry, which is an old-fashioned industry. For example, the industry has never paid much attention to developing people in modern management methods, and we face this problem acutely in the belting division.

For example, there is not yet an obvious number-two man in the division; this spot is probably shared by the division's marketing and production managers, neither of whom has yet developed enough drive and knowledge of business management. This is unfortunate, because the future of the division will depend to a large extent on how hard the men under Mr. Whitney set the pace.

The following statements were made by Mr. Whitney as he explained his attitudes toward the relationship he felt should exist between the divisions and the corporate organization.

During my career I have become convinced that it is of the greatest importance for people in any organization to know to whom they are responsible at the top. This is sometimes difficult to ensure in larger companies—as was the case when I first joined United. Thus, I fully supported Mr. Dudley's idea of divisionalization, which would give the divisional managers their individual organizations (rather like little companies) to look after. It seemed to me to be the right and logical thing to do.

Production

One of our biggest problems arising from divisionalization continues to be the question of how to operate the Sheffield factory. The trouble with our operations there is that the divisions are sometimes inclined to forget that there are other divisions around. We get other divisional people coming down to the plant and talking too much about what they are going to do and how much money they are going to make on their products. The result is that people at the plant sometimes become concerned about the effect of the acts of other divisions on them personally. For example, one divisional manager said that his division was going to do its own production planning. I told Mr. Dudley about this, for I considered this as the kind of case involving a change in policy which should first be discussed at a policy committee meeting. Any change in scheduling practices at the factory level should be made only after an agreement is reached at the policy level.

Policy committee

I believe the formation of the corporate policy committee was a very wise step because it provides the opportunity for the divisional managers to work together as part of a company team. We discuss each other's projects in the policy committee and we have to defend our projects on economic grounds.[4] Therefore, each divisional manager knows exactly why he does not get something he wants. He also knows that the whole matter was discussed and agreed upon among the divisional managers at this committee.

In the discussion of corporate versus divisional functions, Mr. Whitney made the following remarks:

Accounting

In the area of finance and accounting, I have no doubt it should be corporate rather than divisional responsibility. Of course, the divisions here never tried to run their own accounting, but I do not think it would be in the interest of the company if they did.

We receive a great deal of accounting information from the corporation, but we have not yet reached the stage where we know the real value of these data. Perhaps we are getting a little too much detail. The main things I want to know as a divisional manager are whether I am meeting my budgets, how much profit I am making, and if I am not making as much as I should, where I am falling down.

Research and development

The day-to-day technical problems are the responsibility of the divisions, as is divisional long-term development. At the same time, however, we have to get help from the corporation. One thing that supports the need for a corporate technology department is that there are so many technical problems within the divisions that the future seldom receives much attention. Another reason is that the divisions are short of process and design engineers.

I do not mean to say that the divisions are not responsible for performance. For instance, in my division we have just hired our own process engineer. However, as a division we have got so much work to do that we are going to need all the help we can get.

Mr. George Evans, specialty plastics division

The manager of the specialty plastics division, Mr. George Evans, had assumed this position in late 1970. Before 1968, he had been a plant chemist at one of the United factories and had started his career in one of the company's laboratories as a rubber technologist. From 1968 to 1970, Mr. Evans had held the position of director of corporate research and development. In 1971 he was in his middle forties.

---

[4] A division could invest "all its depreciation funds plus about 25% of its net profits before taxes." If additional funds were needed, a formal request was made to the policy committee.

Mr. Evans was described by Mr. Dudley as an excellent scientist with little general experience in business. "He has had no sales experience, and his only line experience was years ago when he was in charge of a small workshop. Nevertheless, I am taking the risk that he has what it takes to become a manager. He has had no opportunity to understand accounting data, but I have hired an accounting assistant for him, who can become the business manager of the division."

In commenting on corporate-division relationships, Mr. Evans made the following remarks:

Accounting

While I agree that accounting should be primarily a corporate function, I am not completely happy with some of the methods used. For instance, I suspect they are allocating factory overhead costs to products on the basis of their sales revenue. However, this does not give an accurate picture of where the overhead costs were created.

I also have some misgivings about the collection of accounting data for use in our budgetary control system. I see a variance in the red, but since the man who produced the budget is not in my division, he is not close enough to the production problems to really explain why it is in the red. Nor can he always ensure that the figures on which he bases the budget are close enough to reality. I think that the actual collection of data should be a divisional responsibility up to a certain point in order to get better reliability in the data.

Purchasing

In purchasing, the corporate people are able to get bulk contracts and therefore the divisions should utilize corporate purchasing to take advantage of the reduced prices. Plant supplies and other local purchases must be decentralized, and we have done this in the last six months.

It is also important to have someone in the corporate technical organization to help the corporate purchasing people select the proper materials. This was not so important a few years ago when we were just using natural rubber. But today, when there are three or four hundred types of synthetic materials to choose from, it is very important to have someone with technical competence coordinating these purchases.

Personnel

As far as personnel and training are concerned, in some locations we are experiencing some slowness in getting information. I also wonder to what extent we should divisionalize our personnel administration. For example, when we have two plants in two different divisions just a mile apart, are we justified in having separate maintenance departments just because the plants are being operated by different divisions? On the other hand, my division has a high number of scientific and technical people, and I find corporate personnel can't recruit the kinds of individuals we need.

Research and development

In the technical area, I think the corporation should carry out most of the long-term research, although we will also need long-term research associated with the divisions. The development of products is really a joint responsibility of both the divisional and the corporate technical people. We should put products in the corporate laboratory until they reach the stage when they can be placed in the divisions.

Production

In general, my only complaint about our divisionalization program is that sometimes we get so excited about it that we forget that the plants even exist. One man in the corporate organization made the remark that he thought that in United the tail was wagging the dog, and by tail he meant the production facilities. In my opinion, the factories are the dog and the corporation is the tail.

Mr. Adams Lowry, corporate controller

Mr. Lowry had joined United in 1953 as an accountant. In 1968 he was made corporate controller. He stated:

I would classify the divisions as being subautonomous. They are reasonably self-contained and have a responsibility for profits. The division managers are free to operate within specified target limits.

I look upon the accountants in the division as people who are under the line authority of the divisional managers. I can say that these people are my accountants, but they are not my men. I see the corporate accounting function as something that can serve as a guide, but improvements should be made by working through the line organizations. In my opinion, the relationship between the accounting people in the divisions and the corporate organization should not be a simple line relationship where a man has no route of appeal except through the line organization. In the area of accounting, a man has a functional responsibility, and he has the right of appeal to the managing director through the corporate accounting function.

You have to realize that this is not a holding company and that the managing director has operating responsibility. If I were going to decide whether to give the accounting function to the divisions, I would consider the economics of this move, and I would look at their accounting methods to see if they were the ones required by the managing director. If all of these points were satisfied, I would be happy to let the divisions handle their own accounting.

When people in the divisions complain about corporate accounting, I ask them what they would do without this central service. It is our function to draw information from the divisions, process it, and then send it back to the line organization, both downward to the divisions and upward to the managing director.

In deciding what information to send to the divisional managers, we use a process of give and take and try to find the best answer. After satisfying the requirements of the corporation, we are perfectly willing to let a man have his own type of information. We send a total of 15 reports to the divisions. Once in a while we will also give them an IBM run with some detailed figures on it, but we never give this information in this much detail unless it is requested.

A few years ago, the divisional managers were given almost no information at all. Mr. Dudley told me that we should give them every piece of information we had until they were overflowing with it. Then, he thought, they would not be able to say that they did not have enough information.

Introduction of the new system

You should also realize that there are wide differences between the divisions in the extent to which they are able to use information we give them and in the extent to which they accept the central accounting data. The important thing is to get the recipients of the information to the point where they can appreciate what it means. I think the system is working fairly well now, but this is something that takes a very long time.

Mr. Harold Matthews, director of technology

In November 1970 Mr. Harold Matthews was appointed director of technology for United Latex Ltd. Prior to 1970 Mr. Matthews had worked for a large chemical company. In his new position he had the responsibility for major engineering projects, process and machine experimentation, and the development of new technology relative to plant operations, factory layouts, work methods, and instrumentation in the field of production engineering.

I have joined a company that is still weak in the area of engineering technology. First of all, in the past the company did not employ many graduate engineers. As technical people grew up in the plants, they were trained much like chefs are trained in a London restaurant. Furthermore, the technical side of the rubber business is dominated by the compounders, who are really witch doctors and not engineers. Therefore, one of the first things I want to do is to debunk the theory that the rubber compounder is the key man in the technology of the company when, in fact, he represents only one third of the required technological team. The other two are the process engineer and the machinery engineer.

Though a much younger industry, the plastics industry was until recently just like the rubber industry today, in that it was dominated by one group of specialists—the chemists. The subsequent division of technical responsibility between chemists and engineers, who have much more to contribute to process engineering and machinery engineering, is what has made the plastics industry what it is today—an area of sophisticated processes constantly modified to achieve low cost on high volume.

The fact is, thinking in the corporation is still shaped by experience in the days when proprietary technology and scarce rubber assured it of markets. In those days synthetics were something black that cracked under severe wear. Today the materials industry is a synthetic industry and advanced processes to achieve new low-cost products are key.

Forward thinking about product development also leaves something to be desired. There are not enough people in the company with business judgment. In the past, I think that the top management tended to confuse short-term profitability with technical efficiency. Because the company was profitable, management seemed to assume that it was technically efficient.

One of the things that we must now do is to take a hard look at our present processes to determine their technical efficiency. At every level in the production process this company may need more process control. For instance, when rubber is processed one can expect to get certain variations in the thickness of the rubber, and some of these variations will result in a thickness greater than that required. It will be part of our job to point such things out to divisional management and show them that, if they can further minimize this amount of extra rubber, they will maximize the process efficiency.

I am with Mr. Dudley 100% in his plan to divisionalize the organization of the company. However, I do not think United can go far toward establishing autonomous divisions such as those in large companies. First, the company cannot afford to do this because the divisions are not very large. Second, there are not enough capable people in the divisions to permit them to be completely autonomous.

Another thing that makes divisionalization difficult from a technical point of view is that the company presently operates such an amorphous group of factories. Because the factories are so spread out, there is a serious question of whether the company can afford to put the required high-grade technical people in each unit. Therefore, I expect to take a hard look at factory rationalization.

The relationship between the divisions and the corporation should be one of plural loyalty. The people in the divisions should have their primary loyalty to their division manager. At the same time, however, they should have a loyalty to the functional heads at the corporate level where policy will be set.

In working with the divisions, my job will be primarily an educational one. In the beginning I will try to ensure that the technological structure at the plant level is right. I want to have considerable influence over these divisional technical organizations and who goes into them. For at present there are not enough people in the divisions who are really in a position to judge a person's technological ability. Once I have established satisfactory technical organizations in the divisions, I will delegate control to the divisions, continuing to support them, of course, with professional advice.

I plan to get the cooperation of the division managers by showing them that I shall recruit people with technical competence and that we can help them increase their profits. Some of the division managers have little or no technical knowledge, and these will be the easiest to work with. The hardest will be those who consider themselves to be technologists. Of course, I will also have the opportunity to argue my case with top management and get their support for the implementation of my recommendations.

The managing director's view

Mr. Dudley summarized his thinking on the status of his organization in the following terms:

As I said some years ago, we were going to try to break the organization up into cells of business activity. We have never shifted from this basic policy, and I am convinced that by so doing we are going in the right direction. I want the responsibility and full authority for operations in the hands of the divisional managers. They are responsible for the profitability and the development of the company's business in those areas allotted to them.

At the same time, however, we have not been able to delegate all functions to the divisions because some are not large enough economically to conduct their own advertising or research and development programs. Therefore, we have centralized certain functions at the corporate level and the divisional managers are expected to look to these corporate functions for help. They, of course, pay for these activities by an allocation of corporate overhead expenses.

The difficulty is that as soon as you make a man a division manager, he fights like hell for everything to be under his control and doesn't like to come to the corporation for help. For example, one of our divisions was headed by an extremely self-sufficient person who had so much a sense of independence that he insisted that his organization perform all its secretarial, accounting, and even research activities. His research activities, however, amounted to over three times his annual net profit.

We finally told him that we would approve the research but that he would have to come to the corporation for support and that the work would be financed out of the central research budget. Even under this arrangement, he wanted to have complete control over everything that was developed as a result of the research, in spite of the fact that some of the products might be more appropriately controlled by other divisions. In time, we had to withdraw the research work from his organization. He just had a tendency to overdo the development function and forget that he had to make a profit in a competitive market. Eventually we were forced to release him.

Mr. Dudley was now particularly concerned about the status of the organization because at the most recent board meeting Mr. Bradley had indicated the need for a review in this area. Mr. Dudley was aware that the chairman talked informally from time to time with members of the executive group but he had no feeling for what bearing, if any, at all, these conversations had on Mr. Bradley's desire for an organization review.

National Franchise
Management, Inc.

NATIONAL FRANCHISE MANAGEMENT, INC. (NFM) was originally formed in Houston, Texas, to provide professional management services for restaurant owners who wished to franchise their restaurants. During the company's first year of operation, food franchising fell strongly out of public favor. In March 1970 Mr. Jim Fisher, the president and founder of NFM, arranged for NFM to buy Flowers-By-Phone, Inc.*, of Tiptonville, Tennessee, an international flowers-by-wire company which served almost 9,000 subscribing florists. The retail value of the flower orders which were cleared through the Flowers-By-Phone system in fiscal 1970 was $10,805,000. The company's gross revenues were $1,861,000.

In June 1970 Mr. Fisher was faced with the problem of making changes in the Flowers-By-Phone organization so that it would fit into his plans for NFM. He planned to acquire other companies with NFM stock in order to achieve a size large enough for a public stock offering. At that time he was actively involved in bargaining for another company even larger than Flowers-By-Phone and had approached a third whose stock was already publicly traded.

JIM FISHER

Mr. Fisher had been in the acquisition business since 1959. In that year he and two other Harvard Business School graduates had formed Equidyne Industries, Inc., to buy and develop smaller industrial companies. By offering their management training, these three men were

---

* This is a fictitious name. In the 1973 First Edition the company was Phone-A-Flower, Inc., also fictitious. The names were changed to avoid confusion with the registered servicemark of Florists' Nationwide Telephone Delivery Network, Known as PHONAFLOWER.

able to buy a manufacturing concern which made satellite tracking antennas. This venture, however, met with near disaster when the company was underbid on 85 consecutive government contracts. After a change of product line, Equidyne Industries was able to sell the company without incurring heavy losses.

Jim Fisher then decided to buy the Houston Bottling Co., which bottled and distributed Coca Cola. He was able to acquire this company with only a minor investment. The company prospered; sales grew from $1.8 million in 1960 to $10.0 million in 1968. During this period the bottling company also acquired several other related companies in the Houston region. In 1968 Mr. Fisher sold his bottling company stock for a substantial financial gain. Although he retained his position as chairman of the board, he withdrew from active management of the company and began looking for another type of business venture.

Mr. Fisher's personal goals had changed with the success of the bottling company. He explained: "I enjoyed building small companies, and I learned what can be done with them. But now I want to run a large, publicly held corporation. I've made my money. I want to see what can be done with the public vehicle."

During this period Mr. Fisher became involved in political and civic affairs in Houston; one of his long-range goals was to hold an elective or appointive government office. He also served on the boards of several corporations. His extensive travel, for both business and pleasure, led one of his associates to comment: "Jim Fisher is a very hard man to catch."

In the spring of 1969, Mr. Fisher formed National Franchise Management, Inc. The company's only asset at the time was its right to franchise, in Texas and Oklahoma, Tasty Burger Restaurants, a recently formed restaurant chain based in Florida. Mr. Fisher hired Bob Trumbull, who had previously worked for the Houston Bottling Co., to be general manager. Mr. Fisher and Mr. Trumbull were shortly joined by Jim Barrett, a successful Houston restauranteur. In exchange for 30% of NFM, Mr. Barrett turned over his Big Jim's Restaurant and the franchise rights to the name. Big Jim's Restaurant was located in Houston and served higher priced lunches and dinners. NFM also bought three small Top Dog restaurants in Houston and the franchise rights to this name. These restaurants served frankfurters from drive-in windows and had only small seating capacities.

By September 1969 Mr. Fisher believed that the growth potential for the food franchising industry had become severely limited. Several food franchising companies had gone bankrupt, and many others had been accused of accounting manipulation. For these reasons, franchising stocks were out of favor with the investing public and with potential franchise buyers. (See Exhibit 1 for NFM's balance sheet at the end of 1969.)

EXHIBIT 1

NATIONAL FRANCHISE MANAGEMENT, INC.
Balance Sheet as of December 31, 1969

Assets

Current assets		
Cash		$ 3,293
Prepaid rent		90
Total current assets		$ 3,383
Investments and other assets		
Investment in and advances to subsidiaries	$98,536	
Other investment, at cost	60,000	
Deferred expense–note	30,574	
Deposits	60	189,170
Furniture and fixtures		1,576
Total assets		$194,129

Liabilities and Stockholders' Equity

Current liabilities		
Accounts payable		$ 3,617
Accrued liabilities		370
Rental–purchase contracts payable		1,202
Total current liabilities		$ 5,189
Other liabilities		
Loans from stockholder	$11,296	
Subordinated debentures, 9½%, due January 1, 1975	30,000	
Debentures and capital stock subscribed		
Less: Uncollected subscriptions ($72,464)	9,572	50,868
Stockholders' equity		
Common stock, $.12 par value; 1,500,000 shares		
authorized; 725,000 shares issued and outstanding	87,000	
Capital in excess of par value	51,072	138,072
Total liabilities and stockholders' equity		$194,129

Note: The company considered itself a nonoperating company as of December 31, 1969, and all expenses incurred to that date have been deferred. During the period from December 31, 1969, to March 31, 1970, the company sold $202,800 in stock and debentures to investors.
Source: Company records.

During this period, while Mr. Fisher was looking for another direction in which to take the company, he was contacted by Mr. Don Carty, a Houston businessman who found potential acquisitions for a fee. Mr. Carty suggested Flowers-By-Phone as an attractive possibility for NFM. Shortly thereafter, Mr. Fisher made his initial contact with the president of Flowers-By-Phone, Richard Zalisk.[1]

ACQUISITION OF FLOWERS-BY-PHONE

On March 31, 1970, National Franchise Management purchased Flowers-By-Phone, Inc., for 350,000 shares of convertible preferred voting

---

[1] In December 1969 Mr. Zalisk decided to hire Don Carty as marketing manager of Flowers-By-Phone.

stock. Included in the agreement were provisions for two smaller companies, Northwest Data Processing Company and Tiptonville Printing Company. NFM received all the outstanding stock of the former, an in-house computer facility which served Flowers-By-Phone and two very small outside customers, and it paid $60,000 in cash for an option to purchase the Tiptonville Printing Company for an additional cash payment of $240,000. The printing company was located in the same building as Flowers-By-Phone and was owned by the same three stockholders. It derived 85% of its business from Flowers-By-Phone.

The 350,000 shares of preferred voting stock of NFM that went to the former Flowers-By-Phone owners had a par value of $6 and a $.60 noncumulative dividend preference. Six percent of this preferred stock could be converted into common stock each year on a share-for-share basis. At the option of Mr. Zalisk, 20,000 shares of the preferred stock were to be redeemed at par value by NFM each year starting May 1, 1971. The $.60 dividend preference, Jim Fisher explained, was not really part of the selling price of the company but was a way of assuring Mr. Zalisk that NFM would not drain cash from Flowers-By-Phone. According to Mr. Fisher, both parties realized that the dividend would never be paid.

Each of the three stockholders in Flowers-By-Phone also received 10-year management contracts with NFM. Richard Zalisk, the president of Flowers-By-Phone, was to receive $35,000 per year; his wife, Mrs. Jackie Zalisk, $25,000 as executive vice president; and Joe Deichman, $25,000 as senior vice president of administration. There was an unwritten agreement between NFM and Mr. and Mrs. Zalisk that the business would remain in Tiptonville.

Following NFM's purchase of Flowers-By-Phone in April 1970, Jim Fisher owned 30% of NFM, Jim Barrett owned 20%, and Mr. Trumbull, Mr. and Mrs. Zalisk, and about 20 other investors owned the remaining 50%. As part of the sale agreement, NFM transferred $120,000 in working capital to Flowers-By-Phone, and Jim Fisher was elected chairman of the board.

Flowers-By-Phone, Inc., one of three wire-service organizations in the United States sharing the market for flowers wired to out-of-town recipients, had subscribers in the United States, Canada, Mexico, as well as overseas affiliates. A subscribing florist was able to transfer a flower order to a distant location to be prepared and delivered by another Flowers-By-Phone subscriber. The company guaranteed payment to the florist who prepared and delivered the flowers (the receiver); it also served as a clearing house to collect from the florist who had placed the order (the sender).

Flowers-By-Phone furnished each subscribing florist with the basic supplies and forms needed to transact an order. In addition, the subscriber received a monthly publication, *Florist News,* which contained both editorial and news articles of current interest to florists and a list of subscribers in good standing. Flowers-By-Phone's initial subscription fee was $120, which included $50 for a refundable deposit, $50 for the salesman's commission, and $20 for the cost of a credit check. The monthly charge was $2.50.

A floral order was usually communicated from one florist to another via telephone. Flowers-By-Phone furnished members with a communications system by which a florist could call the communications center in Tiptonville and send orders to several places for less than the cost of phone calls to the individual florists. However, it was estimated that the communications center, consisting of eight toll-free telephone lines, had only 50 regular users.

The florist who originated an order collected from the customer and was billed for these outgoing transactions by Flowers-By-Phone at the rate of 85% of the retail value of the order. The florist who delivered an order could immediately draw a draft on Flowers-By-Phone for 75% of the retail value as compensation for delivery of the order. In this way the delivering florist immediately received payment for the inventory and delivery costs plus profit. The drafts were drawn on the Flowers-By-Phone bank accounts in Dyersburg, Tennessee, at either the Farmers Bank and Trust Company or the First National Bank.

When the drafts had cleared the Flowers-By-Phone bank accounts in Dyersburg, they were processed by Flowers-By-Phone's computer system. Twice each month the orders so processed were billed to the florists who had originated them. The difference between the income or billing at 85% of the retail value and the cost of the draft at 75% of the retail value represented the company's proceeds for handling the transaction. Approximately 60% of Flowers-By-Phone's gross income was derived from this source. The monthly charge of $2.50 for subscription renewal dues provided 15% of Flowers-By-Phone's gross revenue. The advertising space purchased by florists in the monthly *Florist News* publication contributed another 15%; service charges to customers accounted for 6%; and other miscellaneous items contributed the remaining 4%.

THE RETAIL FLORIST TRADE

The U.S. retail florist trade included approximately 22,000 independent florists whose sales had been growing at an annual rate of about 5% since 1950 and equaled $1.2 billion in 1969. The florists' share of the total floral market, however, was being increasingly threatened by a number of nonflorist retail outlets, such as supermarkets, whose sales had reached $600 million in 1969.

The typical retail florist shop was a small proprietorship managed by the owner, 75% of whose sales were taken over the telephone on a credit basis. Consequently, the majority of the customers never saw their purchases, and the florist had to decide quickly whether to extend credit and accept the order. In spite of this method of order taking, however, only minor bad-debt losses were reported.

One characteristic of the independent dealers seemed to be a chronic need for increased operating capital. Since most of their inventory was perishable, there was little collateral to offer in obtaining loans. In addition, retail florists for the most part tended to consider themselves artists rather than businessmen and often failed to handle their business matters with the same skill with which they designed their floral arrangements.

Wire services

The annual value of the telegraphed flower orders of the three wire-service organizations in the United States approximated $160 million. According to a 1965 U.S. Department of Agriculture survey, 85% of the retail florists belonged to a wire service and one fourth of those with wire-service membership belonged to two or even three services. All three services published monthly magazines listing names, addresses, and phone numbers of all members in good standing. A recent edition of Flowers-By-Phone's *Florist News* magazine, containing 400 pages, resembled a large telephone directory.

People in the florist industry, according to Mr. Zalisk, president of Flowers-By-Phone, tended to be clannish, fostering many strong friendship ties. Most florists, for example, had developed standard correspondents in other cities. For most florists, as well, reciprocity was an important factor in determining which wire service to use and which florist shop to call when wiring an order. When one florist received an order from another whom he did not know, he often tried to return the favor. He tended, also, to use the same wire service through which the first order had been sent. The economics of the situation did not appear to dictate his choice.. One florist commented: "I really don't know which wire service is cheaper. They all have different ways of figuring the cost. I've never really given much thought to it."

Most U.S. florists charged their customers $.50 extra for a wired order, sometimes adding as well the cost of the telephone call to the wire-service communications center or to a member florist in another city. These extra charges were not included in the gross retail value which was used to determine wire service margins.

By far the largest of the wire-service organizations was Florist Transworld Delivery (FTD), a cooperative organization of florists founded in 1892. It was located in Detroit and had, among florists, a reputation for high quality. The total number of orders sent through its system had increased steadily at an annual rate of about 6% during the period 1950 to 1969. In 1969 its almost 12,000 members sent $125 million worth of orders through the system. FTD members paid an initial fee of $386.50 and approximately $4.50 monthly. Membership was limited to retail florists, and only the most successful shops in a city could meet FTD's high standards. Under the FTD system the charge to a sending florist approximated 83% of the retail value of the order. Although an FTD customer could take advantage of FTD agreements with Diners Club and other credit card companies and charge his flower order by signing the standard credit card form, this system was not extensively used.

From 1961 to 1969 FTD had experienced strong competition from the other two organizations, Flowers-By-Phone and Teleflora Delivery Service, Inc. According to an FTD official, one reason for this competition was the FTD system of variable discounts which made it cheaper for florists to send orders of under $7.50 in value through one of FTD's competitors. In 1970, however, FTD changed this discount rate, thereby becoming competitive in the lower price range. The average wire order for all three organizations in the industry was approximately $10.

Teleflora Delivery Service, Inc., was headquartered in El Segundo, California. It had over 8,000 members and had handled $20 million worth of orders in 1969. Its initial subscription fee was $139 and its monthly charge was $4. Although Teleflora did not compute its charge to a sending florist on the same basis as its two competitors, the cost to the sending florist averaged about the same as under the FTD system. The company charged 81% of the retail value of the order plus $.25 per order; the receiving florist was paid 79% less $.25 per order.

FLOWERS-BY-PHONE

Flowers-By-Phone had been started in 1961 by Mr. Richard Zalisk, who got the idea for the company while selling subscriptions to his *Florist Yearbook*. This directory, which had been published since 1955 and was recognized as the authority in the industry, contained 20,000 listings of florists along with their addresses and phone numbers. Mr. Zalisk, age 62, retained ownership of the directory when he sold Flowers-By-Phone to NFM in 1970.

Mr. Zalisk came from a small town in Arkansas. After receiving a diploma from Tech High School in Chicago, he became a tool and die apprentice and finally a quality control supervisor in a Westinghouse plant. At that point, according to Mr. Zalisk, "I decided that I wanted to get out of the city and never live in one again."

After leaving Chicago, Mr. Zalisk became a traveling salesman for

an embalming supply company. One of the towns in his territory was
Tiptonville, Tennessee, where he got to know many of the local businessmen. According to one merchant:

· Those were hard times for everybody—Richard Zalisk included. People
in town did him a lot of favors. There were always checks down at the
bank being held for payment until Richard came back through town. Why,
once I sold him a set of tires for his old Nash on credit. He would pay
me a dollar on them every time he came through. That old Nash would
always stall at the red light in the center of town, and I would give him
a push in my truck.

Mr. Zalisk decided to settle in Tiptonville and open a florist shop.
But, as he explained it:

Tiptonville is a small town. It was very hard for me to make a living
for my wife and six kids. I tried opening another shop in a nearby town
but just couldn't make a go of it. I decided to try to put together a florist
directory.
I didn't want to make a lot of money—just a good living for my family.
I wanted the kids to have a good education. I also wanted to build a service
that everyone had faith in. You know, today I have a friend in almost every
florist shop in the country.

While he was traveling for the *Florist Yearbook*, Mr. Zalisk heard
many complaints about the existing wire services. Several of his florist
friends suggested that he might start a wire service himself. Mr. Zalisk
began asking florists what they wanted in a wire service:

They told me that they resented a wire service telling them how to run
their shops, setting prices, etc. What they wanted was a way to get payment
from a wired order quickly and safely. After thinking about this problem,
I came up with the draft system. I went to the Federal Reserve Bank and
had this draft specially designed so that it would go through as a cash item.
This draft has been the cornerstone of our company, the thing which makes
us different from the others.

According to Mr. Haig Mardikian, who worked closely with Mr. Zalisk
in managing Flowers-By-Phone, "Mr. Zalisk based his new business on
a basic trust in people and especially on the honesty of members of
the floral industry. Each subscriber was furnished with a checkbook
with which he could write checks to himself on the Flowers-By-Phone
bank account as payment for wired orders which he had received."
Mr. Mardikian proudly told the casewriter: "Flowers-By-Phone has not
had a single fraudulent draft in its entire nine-year history."
This same basic trust in people was evident in the company's credit
policy. According to one manager:

The emphasis during the growth of the company was on getting new subscriptions and generally building the name of the company. Almost no credit checks were made on new subscribers, and little time was devoted to collection of accounts receivable. Often no attempt was made to collect past-due accounts. Some of these accounts were held by Mr. Zalisk's old friends who had experienced financial difficulties. During some years, as much as 10% of the accounts receivable were written off as bad debts.

A summary of accounts receivable data is shown in Exhibit 2.

EXHIBIT 2
Flowers-By-Phone's extended aged accounts receivable (in thousands of dollars)

Date	Total	Current (less than 15 days)	15–30 days	30–45 days	45–60 days	Over 60 days
12/05/69	$ 917	$338	$228	$119	$ 64	$168
12/20/69	915	428	173	106	62	176
1/05/70	822	251	260	91	66	154
1/20/70	1,115	731	113	97	32	142
2/05/70	1,207	562	390	54	55	146
2/20/70	1,098	419	318	183	36	142
3/05/70	1,148	451	268	156	101	172
3/20/70	1,064	448	242	122	70	182
4/05/70	1,042	453	236	113	61	179
4/20/70	1,140	559	235	112	46	188
5/05/70	1,235	486	356	126	68	199
5/20/70	1,151	484	258	151	52	206
6/05/70	1,517	780	304	125	79	229
6/20/70	1,351	486	452	131	64	218

Growth of the company

Since its incorporation in 1961 with 180 subscribers, Flowers-By-Phone had experienced dramatic growth:

Year	Total subscribers
1961	180
1962	450
1963	1,832
1964	3,575
1965	5,214
1966	5,423
1967	6,367
1968	7,528
1969	8,444
1970	8,984

From the beginning, Mr. and Mrs. Zalisk had been assisted by Mr. Joe Deichman who became a 31% owner of the business. Deichman, a native of Tiptonville, had been the local undertaker before joining the company. In 1970 he was 45 years old.

In 1966 Mr. Haig Mardikian, then age 61, was hired as general manager. Mr. Mardikian had been a San Francisco florist with a national reputation in the industry. He continued to be very active in industry associations and remained in constant demand for speaking engagements. His articles in *Florist News* and his speeches were usually directed toward urging florists to upgrade their business techniques and to adopt innovative marketing ideas.

In the same year, the Flowers-By-Phone family expanded further to include Denis and Leslie Bovin, highly respected designers and commentators who spent approximately 70% of their time at industry conventions and design schools. Flowers-By-Phone management considered this creative husband-and-wife team a significant asset to the business. Because of their importance to the company, the Bovins were always on equal footing with the other members of the informal management group. Both held the title of vice president of public relations.

Flowers-By-Phone stimulated the growth of two other companies financed by the same three stockholders. The Flowers-By-Phone billing department evolved into the Northwest Tennessee Data Processing Company, while the printing shop for the monthly *Florist News* magazine and the yearly *Florists Yearbook* became Tiptonville Printing Company. Joe Deichman owned a 20% share in the printing company and 33% of the data processing firm; Mr. and Mrs. Zalisk owned the remaining shares. According to one manager:

> There are really no clear lines drawn between these companies. Employees are swapped from one to the other during rush periods. After all, they are all owned by the same three people and are all still in the same building. We don't have a transfer pricing system. It all seems to even out. For example, during the Mother's Day period Mrs. Stone, the head bookkeeper, works on Flowers-By-Phone business. During slack periods, however, she also keeps books for Tiptonville Printing and does some work for *Florist Yearbook*.

The same informality existed in purchasing supplies. Any employee could make purchases in the company's name. According to one manager, "People just went out and bought what they needed."

In 1970 Flowers-By-Phone had almost 9,000 subscribers and 90 full-time employees. In fiscal 1970, the company's billings to sending florists had reached $9.1 million. Financial statements for Flowers-By-Phone are presented in Exhibits 3 and 4. Tiptonville Printing Company, with modern equipment in good condition, had total assets of $144,000. Northwest Tennessee Data Processing, the computer facility located in one

EXHIBIT 3

FLOWERS-BY-PHONE, INC.
Statement of Earnings
(in thousands of dollars)

	Year ended March 31		
	1968	*1969*	*1970*
Gross orders transmitted.	$8,053.3	$10,241.5	$10,805.0
Amount due to Flowers-By-Phone on orders	6,845.4	8,705.6	9,184.3
Less: Amount paid Flowers-By-Phone florists . . .	6,040.0	7,681.4	8,103.8
Commissions	$ 805.4	$ 1,024.2	$ 1,080.5
Other revenue.	464.2	513.7	780.5
Gross revenues	$1,269.6	$ 1,537.9	$ 1,861.0
Expenses			
Publication cost.	$ 167.5	$ 201.1	$ 210.5
Salaries and commissions	320.8	337.6	440.2
Officers' salaries	69.5	151.0	160.2
Bad debts	103.8	170.2	114.2
Taxes.	16.7	20.8	27.8
Interest	. . .	17.9	101.2
Depreciation and amortization*.	12.1	19.3	36.7
Advertising	53.2	71.5	65.3
Office supplies	37.0	22.3	61.4
Postage and mailing	39.8	57.4	62.5
Telephone and telegraph.	19.4	30.1	109.0
Credit and collection.	12.5	48.8	34.7
Convention expense	27.2	32.6	40.8
Bank charges and exchange	8.0	14.8	10.6
Travel	87.5	50.2	56.9
Equipment lease	44.8	70.0	45.6
Building lease*	13.6	15.5	. . .
Art work.	12.7	8.9	5.9
Miscellaneous	63.5	97.8	139.0
Total expenses	$1,109.6	$ 1,437.8	$ 1,722.5
Net earnings before income taxes.	$ 160.0	$ 100.1	$ 138.5
Income taxes	72.1	34.0	61.6
Net income	$ 87.9	$ 66.1	$ 76.9

*The building lease was capitalized in 1970 and was being depreciated.
Source: Company records.

room of the Flowers-By-Phone building, operated on a break-even basis
with net assets of $130,800 as of March 31, 1970.

Community relations

Flowers-By-Phone and its related companies occupied an attractive
modern building in Tiptonville, Tennessee (population 1,600). The
Flowers-By-Phone building had been built for the company in 1963 by
the city of Tiptonville and was occupied on a long-term lease, of which
16 years remained in 1970. Flowers-By-Phone and its employees purchased most of the municipal bonds which the city issued for the building

EXHIBIT 4

FLOWERS-BY-PHONE, INC.
Consolidated Balance Sheet
(in thousands of dollars)

	Year ended March 31		
	1968	1969	1970
Assets			
Current assets			
Cash	$ 64.3	$ 126.6	$ 28.2
Certificates of deposit	63.4	87.0	101.5
Net accounts and notes receivable	508.4	1,055.6	1,399.1
Prepaid expenses	1.8	3.4	. . .
Total current assets	$637.9	$1,272.6	$1,528.8
Property and equipment			
Office furniture, fixtures, and computer equipment*	$ 63.6	$ 79.1	$ 249.8
Leasehold improvements and equity†	14.6	27.2	267.2
Automobiles‡	53.4	. . .	. . .
Total property and equipment	$131.6	$ 106.3	$ 517.0
Less: Accumulated depreciation	36.2	42.7	103.7
	$ 95.4	$ 63.6	$ 413.3
Investments and other assets			
Tax credit	. . .	. . .	$ 46.6
Investments	$ 99.6	$ 77.5	11.5
Total investments and other assets	$ 99.6	$ 77.5	$ 58.1
Total assets	$832.9	$1,413.7	$2,000.2
Liabilities and Stockholders' Equity			
Current liabilities			
Accounts payable	$ 54.5	$ 40.4	$ 82.2
Accrued expenses	12.2	18.4	32.6
Federal and state taxes	71.6	8.9	52.9
Notes payable, banks	14.4	604.1	635.5
Advances from NFM	. . .	. . .	24.0
Bonds payable, City of Tiptonville	. . .	. . .	7.9
Total current liabilities	$152.7	$ 671.8	$ 835.1
Deferred liabilities			
Subscription deposits	$411.6	$ 443.3	$ 480.7
Notes payable, banks	12.0	. . .	39.6
Advances from NFM	. . .	. . .	96.0
Bonds payable, City of Tiptonville	. . .	. . .	140.4
Total deferred liabilities	$423.6	$ 443.3	$ 756.7
Stockholders' equity			
Common stock§	$ 1.2	$ 1.2	$ 180.0
Retained earnings	255.4	297.4	228.4
Total stockholders' equity	$256.6	$ 298.6	$ 408.4
Total liabilities and stockholders' equity	$832.9	$1,413.7	$2,000.2

* Includes Northwest Tennessee Data Processing in 1970 only. No computer facilities were owned by Flowers-By-Phone, Inc., in 1968 or 1969.

† The lease agreement with the City of Tiptonville was capitalized in 1970. The municipal bonds owned by the company were netted against those bonds which the company was obligated to buy. The liability shown on the books was the net amount of the outstanding bonds, the company-owned bonds, and funds in the hands of the trustees.

‡ Automobiles were leased after the year ended March 31, 1968, rather than being owned by the company.

§ During the current year the capitalization of the company was changed from 1,000 shares of no-par value stock authorized (and issued at a stated value of $1.20 per share) to 150,000 shares of $1.20 par value authorized. At the time of this change a stock dividend was declared to the effect that the outstanding shares were increased to 135,000 shares with a transfer from retained earnings of $160,800. On January 20, 1970, the company acquired all the outstanding stock of NWT Data Processing Co., Inc., in exchange for 15,000 shares of its common stock.

Source: The financial statements of the period ended March 31, 1970, were prepared by NFM's accounting firm. The statements for the years ended March 31, 1968, and March 31, 1969, were prepared by the casewriter from the records of Flowers-By-Phone's Jackson, Tennessee, accounting firm. In all three years, the casewriter has simplified the statements for the purpose of case analysis.

construction. The lease payments of $1,800 per month were used by the city to pay principal and interest on the bonds.

The physical prominence of the Flowers-By-Phone building within the town of Tiptonville was representative of the financial influence and prestige of the company within the farming community. Not only did Flowers-By-Phone merge with the community on a personal level—Mr. Haig Mardikian, for example, was president of the Tiptonville Chamber of Commerce—but it provided a new means of support to the area at a time when the profitability of farming was declining.

The Flowers-By-Phone business influenced considerably the character of the town. The modern Tiptonville Post Office was, in fact, the product of the large volume of mail which Flowers-By-Phone sent out each month. In 1961, the year in which the company was incorporated, a 12-room motel had been built next door to the present Flowers-By-Phone building. The only one in town, the motel thrived on the comings and goings of people on Flowers-By-Phone related business trips. Although the motel owner's recent business had been good as a result of the additional traffic from Houston, he was alarmed by the sale of Flowers-By-Phone and feared that the company might be moved out of Tiptonville.

While perhaps the most tangible, economic benefits were only one aspect of Flowers-By-Phone's contribution to the community. Several Tiptonville businessmen with whom the casewriter conversed conveyed a strong sense of pride in the fact that a local business had achieved national prominence. "The Flowers-By-Phone people are all local boys, and they are every bit as good as anything in Boston," commented a Tiptonville dry cleaner.

Richard Zalisk did his share to foster this close relationship between the company and the community. Page one of the 1970 edition of the *Florist Yearbook* displayed pictures of the Tiptonville High School, the Post Office, and the town's several churches.

Marketing

"Flowers-By-Phone's marketing approach in 1970 is basically the same as it was in 1961," explained Joe Rogers, manager of the 12 salesmen. "Our salesmen try to sell florists on the idea that they can have their money immediately after they receive a wire order from another florist." According to Rogers, this marketing approach was especially appealing to small florists who were short of operating cash:

The florist gets his money immediately and may not have to pay for almost a month. Flowers-By-Phone is helping him to finance his business. The small florist becomes a member to finance his business—to receive orders rather than to send them. Flowers-By-Phone's 85% billing rate to the sending florist is the highest in the industry. The other two competitors have rates of approximately 83%.

Flowers-By-Phone salesmen were paid a $100-per-week base salary plus $50 for every subscription sale and $6 for making a customer relations call on an existing member. Each salesman was asked to make 20 customer relations calls and 10 new subscription sales calls per week. A new car was furnished by the company each year, but the salesman had to bear all other expenses himself. In 1969 Flowers-By-Phone salesmen made from $6,000 to $25,000 before deducting expenses and taxes.

Mr. Rogers commented: "One of the main problems is that salesmen have such large territories that they are lucky if they visit each florist in their territory once each year." He pointed out that one salesman, for example, "has all of the New England states plus West Virginia, while his home is in Tiptonville."

Each year Flowers-By-Phone held a national convention for subscribing florists, as did its two competitors. In 1970 the company's budget allocated $50,000 for the convention, which was to be held at the Royal Orleans Hotel in New Orleans during August. It was estimated that approximately 300 subscribing florists plus all Flowers-By-Phone salesmen and officers would attend. Florists looked upon a national convention as a vacation and a time for old friends to get together; the mood was always highly festive.

Billing procedures

The distinguishing feature of Flowers-By-Phone's wire service was its draft system. The processing of the bank drafts into accounts receivable and eventually into bills mailed to sending florists was handled by an automated data processing center which employed a Univac 9300 computer. Jim Babcock, director of data processing, commented: "Our computer capacity is enough to handle twice as much business. We might possibly have to buy some extra auxiliary equipment, but it wouldn't be too expensive. Right now, we are running at about 66% capacity working one shift per day."

The computer was legally a separate company, although it occupied a room in the same building and had its bookkeeping done by Mrs. Stone of Flowers-By-Phone. Mr. Babcock noted that Northwest Tennessee Data Processing could not really compete with the special computer service companies for outside jobs, such as handling the bookkeeping for small local banks and insurance companies.

In November 1968, a billing change was made. Previously, each florist had filled out a weekly report of the orders he had sent through the system. This report, along with a check for 85% of the retail value of the orders, was forwarded to Flowers-By-Phone. In November 1968, these weekly reports were eliminated. Accounts receivable information was obtained from the bank drafts which the banks returned to the company. The receiving florist wrote the name and address of the sending florist on the draft; from this information the sending florist was billed twice monthly for 85% of the orders which he had sent. According to Mr. Deichman, Flowers-By-Phone management wanted to simplify the book-keeping job of the sending florist who used the Flowers-By-Phone system.

Financial requirements

The new system, however, caused serious problems. Previously the company had often received the 85% payment from the sending florist before the draft of the receiving florist had been deducted from the company bank account. Flowers-By-Phone had actually been making interest income on this float. Under the new system, the draft had to be received before Flowers-By-Phone even knew which florist to bill, and it was a week later before the average bill was mailed. With this development, a large amount of capital was needed to finance accounts receivable.

Due to the above circumstances, Flowers-By-Phone in December 1968 obtained a line of credit from the Merchants National Bank of St. Louis, Missouri. This loan was secured by accounts receivable and carried an interest rate of 10%. A record of the loan balances is shown in Exhibit 5.

During 1969 the bank became increasingly concerned about the line of credit. One reason for this concern was that the State of Tennessee prohibited charging interest rates higher than 10%. This 10% included fees, service charges, and other expenses associated with the loan. The only way to get around this law was with some sort of compensating balance arrangement. However, under the bank's accounts receivable formula, Flowers-By-Phone did not have the debt capacity to borrow to pay its debts and to keep a compensating balance as well. Joe Deichman stated that in his opinion the bank had been losing money on the loan because of the increased interest rates on the bank's own borrowings. "When the loan was made, no one thought that interest rates might rise as high as they did," was Mr. Deichman's explanation.[2]

Due to the above situation and the increasing size of Flowers-By-Phone's capital needs, the bank requested that additional cash of $240,000 be invested in the business in November 1969. It also requested that an additional $480,000 in collateral be pledged to offset the $50 deposit of each Flowers-By-Phone subscribing florist. These deposits had to be refunded if the individual florists canceled their subscriptions and returned their supplies.

---

[2] Yields on short-term U.S. government bonds rose from 5.23% in November of 1968 to 7.85% in 1969.

EXHIBIT 5

FLOWERS-BY-PHONE, INC.
Merchants National Bank of St. Louis
Loan Account Analysis
(in thousands of dollars)

	High daily loan balance	Low daily loan balance	Average daily loan balance	Total bankable A/R billing		Total interest expense
				High	Low	
1969						
January	$692	$371	$575	$1,048	$ 755	$4.7
February	692	521	590	1,067	893	4.6
March	620	509	571	990	841	4.8
April	731	497	608	934	836	5.0
May	906	641	749	1,057	856	6.4
June	961	787	877	1,360	888	7.2
July	832	485	584	1,178	864	6.1
August	554	478	509	943	842	5.0
September	532	444	493	924	792	4.8
October	576	444	530	925	794	5.3
November	642	541	602	955	864	5.5
December	683	565	624	1,019	912	6.1
1970						
January	953	664	860	1,262	824	8.4
February	941	738	862	1,186	1,085	7.7
March	828	691	754	1,094	1,045	7.6
April	802	610	716	1,123	1,038	7.1

At this time, Mr. Zalisk began to seek a source of capital for the company. First, he considered a public offering of stock. The stock market was in a downturn, however, so this alternative was rejected. During this period Mr. Don Carty, acquisition "finder," approached Jim Fisher about the situation.

DEVELOPMENTS AT NATIONAL FRANCHISE

Throughout the fall of 1969 and the early spring of 1970, Jim Fisher was involved in bargaining with Mr. Zalisk on the Flowers-By-Phone acquisition. In April 1970 Mr. John Gartley, a previous investor in NFM, was persuaded to join NFM as financial vice president. Gartley, age 32, was a Certified Public Accountant with seven years' experience with an international public accounting firm. After leaving the accounting firm in 1966, Gartley as an executive vice president had financially guided a medium-size industrial firm through a period of very rapid growth. Simultaneously, he had started and managed two other small manufacturing companies.

In June 1970 Jim Barrett decided to withdraw from NFM. In exchange for his 20% ownership he was given the existing Big Jim's Restaurant and the rights to franchise the name. His stock was put into the treasury.

Things had also changed in Tiptonville. Steve Hyde of Dallas had been hired from U.S. Steel and installed as Flowers-By-Phone's financial vice president in April. As of June 1970, he was the only new manager who had been brought to Tiptonville as a result of the acquisition. Mr. Hyde, who was 37 years old in 1970, had worked in the credit departments of both Texaco and U.S. Steel. His authority at Tiptonville was more extensive than his title indicated; most employees, in fact, considered him the spokesman for the new owners. Although Mr. Hyde had always lived in cities, he got along well with the people in Tiptonville. An invitation to join the Chamber of Commerce and his family's invitation to join a local church exemplified their acceptance by the community. Jim Fisher had also asked Steve Hyde to take flying lessons so that he could pilot a proposed company airplane between Tiptonville and Houston.

In another management change, Don Carty tendered his resignation because of a personality clash with Richard Zalisk. According to one manager at Flowers-By-Phone, Carty had expected to be given considerable authority because of his role in arranging the acquisition. When it was decided that Zalisk would remain as president of Flowers-By-Phone, Carty resigned in frustration. Bob Trumbull, general manager of NFM, was named marketing manager to replace Carty.

Although Mr. Zalisk remained as president and continued to occupy the very large and well-appointed office which he had built for himself in the Flowers-By-Phone building, a newly formed executive committee had final authority over all important management decisions. Joe Deichman had been made chairman of the executive committee, which was composed of Richard Zalisk, John Gartley, Bob Trumbull, and Steve Hyde. The Bovins and Haig Mardikian, who had previously reported to Zalisk, now reported to Trumbull and Deichman, respectively.

An extension of the line of credit with the Merchants National Bank of St. Louis had been secured until July 31, 1970, and Mr. Hyde had already started to overhaul the credit department. Nevertheless, the accounts receivable were still growing. Mr. Fisher approached the Citizens National Bank of Houston and made arrangements for a $900,000 line of credit beginning August 1, 1970. He felt that this would be sufficient since business at Flowers-By-Phone had been historically low during the last half of the year. (See Exhibit 5.)

FUTURE GOALS

Flowers-By-Phone was the principal asset of NFM. Mr. Fisher wanted the retail value of flowers sent through Flowers-By-Phone to reach $40 million by 1975. He stated that he wanted at least one third of the $18 million estimated annual growth in the flowers-by-wire market. He considered Flowers-By-Phone a good base for a publicly held corporation and hoped that the company's almost 9,000 subscribing florists would be a market for NFM stock.

A primary concern of Mr. Fisher was what changes to make in marketing. If Flowers-By-Phone were to grow as he projected, the company would have to get the wire business of the larger shops which handled the majority of the flowers-by-wire orders. Nearly all of these shops were heavy users of FTD. By and large, Flowers-By-Phone subscribers were smaller florists, many located in small towns. The southeastern states represented the company's area of strength.

On the afternoon of June 12, 1970, Joe Deichman presented his own proposal for changes at Flowers-By-Phone to Fisher and John Gartley. He had not informed Mr. Zalisk of his proposal. (See Exhibit 6 for a summary of the plan.)

EXHIBIT 6
Summary of proposed changes in Flowers-By-Phone procedure

> Joe Deichman
> June 12, 1970
>
> 1. The draft system will be eliminated. Receiving florists will send a list each week listing orders received. Their accounts will be credited for 75% of order value.
> 2. From the list received from receiving florists, the accounts of sending florists are debited at 82% of the order instead of the present 85%.
> 3. Monthly renewal fee will be raised from $2.50 to $3.50.
> 4. On the third or fourth day of the month statements of accounts will be sent both to florists with debit balances and those with credit balances. Payment of debit balances should be received at Flowers-By-Phone before the 25th. Checks for credit balances will be mailed on the 20th of the month.
> 5. Salesmen's compensation will no longer be based on the number of new subscriptions sold. Instead, it will be based on the dollar amount of billings coming from each account in the salesman's territory.
> 6. Flowers-By-Phone will stop accepting any florist who applies for a subscription. A strict credit-rating policy will be enforced. We will concentrate on dollar billings rather than number of members.
> 7. The listing of all Flowers-By-Phone members will not be included in the monthly *Florist News* publication. Instead we will print a yearly *Handy-Book* with this listing. Each monthly *Florist News* magazine will contain a supplemental list of changes in the *Handy-Book*. This change will eliminate 30% of the pages in the monthly *Florist News* magazine.

Mr. Deichman explained his ideas:

These proposed changes will eliminate the need for cash to finance the accounts receivable. Our checks to florists with credit balances should reach our bank at about the same time as the checks from florists with debit balances. Therefore, financing will only be needed for overdue accounts.

Changing the billing to sending florists from 85% to 82% will make us cheaper than our competition. This will give our salesmen something with which to approach the large florists. I worked this idea out with Joe Rogers [the sales manager]. He and the salesmen are very enthusiastic. This along with the change in salesmen's compensation will change our entire marketing program. We will no longer be going after large numbers of small florists but a more select group of larger florists. Flowers-By-Phone now has all the geographical coverage that it needs.

Mr. Deichman went on to explain that less than $1,200,000 in additional yearly clearings would be needed to finance his proposed changes. (See Exhibit 7 for his supporting statement.) Mr. Deichman stated that Mr. Rogers and the salesmen believed that the needed additional

EXHIBIT 7

FLOWERS-BY-PHONE, INC.
Deichman Proposal
Cost Comparison Based on 7,500 Subscribers,
$10 Million Annual Gross Clearing
(only items which would be affected, income or expense)

	Present	Proposed	Difference	
Income				
Commissions earned	$1,000,000	$ 700,000	−$300,000	
Renewal fees	225,000	315,000	90,000	
Total income	$1,225,000	$1,015,000	−$210,000	
Net decrease in income to overcome.				−$210,000

① (Need increase gross clearing of $3,000,000 to offset $210,000 loss of income.)

	Present	Proposed	Difference	
Expenses				
Flowers-By-Phone drafts*. . . .	$ 24,000	0	$ 24,000	
Bank service charges	12,000	0	12,000	
Interest.	65,000	$12,000	53,000	
Bad debt−net	75,000	45,000	30,000	
Credit and collection	45,000	25,000	20,000	
Statements†	20,000	10,000	10,000	
Clerks−2 @ $4,000 each.	8,000	0	8,000	
Total.	$249,000	$92,000	$157,000	
Decrease service charge income . .			− 40,000	
			$117,000	117,000

Net difference in income and expense to overcome . . . . −$ 93,000
② (Need increase gross clearing of $1,330,000 to offset $93,000 loss.)

Flowers-By-Phone publication
Print annual *Reference Book*. Update *Reference Book* quarterly by insert in *Florist News*. Figures reflect only printing cost. Would have additional savings on preparation each month.

$43,558 net savings 43,558

−$ 49,442

③ (Need increase gross clearing of $710,000 to offset $49,442 loss.)

* Supplies given to each florist: drafts, receipts, etc.
† 8,144 subscribers × 25¢ cost per statement × 24 billing periods.
Source: This exhibit was prepared by Mr. Deichman to support his proposal.

orders to be sent through the Flowers-By-Phone system could be achieved within six months after the marketing change.

Deichman also explained that his proposal avoided the earlier Flowers-By-Phone orders. Now larger florists will use our system to send orders. The

We want to make the Flowers-By-Phone system as easy as possible for the sending florist. My proposal puts the incentive where it should be—with the sending florist. In the past, small florists have subscribed to receive Flowers-By-Phone orders. Now larger florists will use our system to send orders. The sending florist is the one who makes the decision of which wire service to use.

Jim Fisher was also concerned about the location of Flowers-By-Phone's operations. The clearing of drafts and checks was to be moved to the Citizens National Bank of Houston. After this move occurred, the information would have to be mailed daily to Tiptonville to be run through the bookkeeping system, which would cause an unnecessary delay. Bob Trumbull also wanted to transfer the marketing function of the company to Houston, as his family did not want to move to Tiptonville. Jim Rogers wanted to resign as sales manager in order to go back to his original job as Flowers-By-Phone salesman. In addition, neither Fisher nor Gartley had any intention of moving to Tiptonville.

Hedblom (A)*

ON OCTOBER 31, 1967, Mr. Arthur Keller,[1] managing director of Hedblom, a ladies' dress company located in Boxholm, Sweden, welcomed members of the press to the company premises to show them the plant, the new offices, and the 1968 spring collection. More importantly, as he privately explained, he wanted to convey the image of the "new Hedblom":

During my first few months on this job,[2] I had to develop a strategy to ensure survival and subsequent profitability and growth. By the middle of the summer the strategy had been pretty well formulated and we are now busy implementing it. These are the crucial months during which all our decisions will be put to the test: our new collections are out, additional activities are starting, and internal changes have been made. Now we must produce the anticipated results. At the same time, we are ready to present our new image to the outside world, hence our press visit today.

Mr. Keller described the process of formulating a strategy for Hedblom as follows:

The basic strategy which I decided on during my first weeks at Hedblom had to be viable for at least two or three years. It might, of course, have

[1] Names and figures have been disguised.

[2] Mr. Keller became managing director on March 13, 1967. Events leading up to this appointment and Mr. Keller's early weeks on the job are described in the Arthur Keller case.

to be modified owing to unforeseen changes, especially with respect to competition. Nevertheless, I wanted to settle on a long-term plan which basically would avoid a zigzag course of action. However, at the same time, given the company's desperate position, I had to produce immediate results. My most critical decision was the fundamental choice between expansion or reduction of company activities. Under my predecessor the company had overexpanded: plant capacity was about four times our actual sales volume of less than Skr 10 million, while fixed expenses amounted to over Skr 6 million. With a contribution of about 35 cents on the sales dollar, to break even we almost needed to double sales or to halve our overhead expenses. While we could expect to improve our contribution by improving production, we feared that five percentage points would probably be the maximum, given our high inputs of raw materials and labor. As a result, modest measures would not restore profitability: we needed either an enormous sales effort to expand volume, or major surgery to cut fixed expenses. I decided for the first alternative.

This inevitably led us to an analysis of possible product-market relationships. Our first investigation was whether sales of Hedblom-brand dresses could be increased, and if so whether changes were required in our marketing strategy. Our second investigation related to possible sale of dresses not under the Hedblom brand. We were particularly anxious to explore ways of reaching the important and rapidly growing distribution channels, such as department store chains, which our selective policy had hitherto ignored. The third step in exploring avenues for increased sales was to look beyond ladies' dresses, considering other ladies' clothes, men's clothes, articles for the teen-age group, coats, sportswear, or fabrics. Finally, the fourth opportunity for larger sales was in markets outside Sweden or even Scandinavia. We decided to move in all four directions.

Our expanded activities on the marketplace resulted in several internal changes. The main tasks here were to improve manufacturing efficiency, and particularly to overcome our late delivery problem, as well as to make sure that our new activities would receive sufficient systematic attention. As a result, I changed the organization structure, moved all offices into the plant building, and worked on streamlining the manufacturing and control activities.

Two other aspects received my constant attention. First, I made a concerted effort to rebuild morale both inside and outside the company. Second, the relationship between the managing director and his top managers needed to be changed, and I tried to be aware of my leadership style: what signals it would convey to my men and what responses it would bring about.

A more detailed description of these changes follows.

PRODUCT LINES

The Hedblom line

After long discussions during April and May of 1967, it was decided not to change the Hedblom line in terms of distribution channels, price, styling, and image. Selective distribution accompanied by the necessary retail sales push appeared the best approach, given the price of Hedblom dresses. Price reductions of a modest scale were ruled out because (1) price elasticity at above Skr 100 was felt to be low, and (2) the company could not afford to risk a reduction in gross margin. Major price cuts would have meant a complete change in marketing strategy and would have resulted in abandoning the company's distinctive competence. Styling and image had permitted Hedblom to charge a 10% to 15% price premium, and this capability was to be reinforced, not weakened. Thus, changes in the Hedblom line would be in the direction of more collections and better services.

The first collection for which Mr. Keller would be solely responsible was that for spring 1968, and it was to receive his major attention. During April and May 1967, fabrics were to be selected and models designed for showing on September 1; thereafter the sales organization would solicit orders and production would begin manufacture so that deliveries could begin in February–March 1968. In April–May, the consumer would finally give her market verdict on efforts started 12 months earlier. The collection would include 65 to 70 dresses to be sold at an average factory price of Skr 80. A sales target of 40,000 pieces was set, and initial orders were deemed encouraging.

In addition to this "head collection," as it was called, two intermediate spring collections were also planned. A sportswear collection, with showings in early November and deliveries in April, was to include 25 to 30 dresses and suits at an average factory price of Skr 125 (with a range of Skr 83 to Skr 204). On these the sales target was set at 15,000–20,000 pieces. A "high-summer collection" was to be shown in February for delivery in May. It would include 20 dresses of which about 15,000 were to be sold at an average factory price of Skr 80.

The same approach was to be followed for the autumn of 1968. The head collection would be shown in March 1968, with August and September deliveries; a more elegant cocktail dress collection would come in May and a Christmas collection in August. Deliveries for the two interim collections were planned for October and early December. Number of models and price ranges for the three autumn collections paralleled those for the spring, except that autumn dresses were typically priced Skr 10 higher.

Mr. Keller was convinced that the increased number of collections would expand sales rather than simply shift orders. Also, he felt that adding collections was the best response to the retailers' increasing reluctance to make large and firm commitments twice a year several months ahead of sales. Finally, he expected that the extra collections would reduce the retailers' need to reorder. Mr. Keller also commented:

As long as we had only two collections, it was almost impossible to avoid large fluctuations in sales between the first and second as well as the third and fourth quarter of each year. With the above plan we not only expect to spread sales more evenly but also to assure more even utilization of the design, sales, production, and shipping departments.

As for better services, the main emphasis was on deliveries. On-time delivery was target Number One, and Mr. Keller decided to risk advance manufacturing commitments of both fabrics and dresses to ensure that goods would leave the factory on the promised date. Furthermore, for the spring 1968 head collection a catalog would be printed of the seven best selling dresses (of which only the best selling sizes and colors would be included) on which immediate delivery from stock would be provided. Special merchandising, such as labels attached to the dresses, was to emphasize Hedblom's new delivery policy.

Mr. Keller viewed advertising as another aspect of service in that it would support the sales efforts of Hedblom retailers. Special arrangements with synthetic fiber companies were investigated, and for the second 1968 spring collection Mr. Keller was able to obtain support of Skr 250,000 from one of the large synthetic fiber producers because this collection pioneered the use of its synthetic fiber for sportswear. Also, Mr. Keller shifted the emphasis from newspapers to magazines. He stated:

> I insisted that all our advertising plans be completely ready when we introduced a collection. In this way we could give the salesman all information about advertising when he started selling and this should help him in getting orders. It also forces us to plan our advertising thoroughly and thoughtfully, instead of buying space in daily newspapers at the last minute, as we did before.

Two changes were effected in the Hedblom organization. First, in-house design efforts were strengthened by hiring a new directress and the expensive Paris designer was dropped. Second, the sales organization was analyzed, with Mr. Keller going over all the accounts. As a result, the number of outside salesmen was reduced from five to four by shifting one man to an inside sales job, the aim of which was to strengthen customer services. Also, sales quotas were established.

Dress sales without the Hedblom brand

For September 1967, the introduction of a second dress collection was planned. This line was to be sold, either under the "Karin" name or unbranded, with initial efforts in Scandinavia but ultimately all over EFTA.[3] It was different from the Hedblom line in that it was (1) priced lower, to retail at Skr 90; (2) included fewer models and used less

---

[3] European Free Trade Association comprised the United Kingdom, the Scandinavian countries, Austria, Switzerland, and Portugal.

fancy fabrics and patterns, while remaining of high quality; (3) aimed at different customers, such as big chains and mail-order houses; (4) sold through a separate sales organization, composed initially of two new salesmen; (5) promoted by distinctive sales inducements, such as immediate delivery from stock or special styles for customers placing large orders; and (6) supported by little or no advertising and no public relations activities.

To get this line ready for September the decision had been made in April, and a new directress, exclusively responsible for this line, had been hired to report to work on May 17.

Fabric sales

Mr. Keller decided to expand the product line beyond dresses. One possibility considered was adding other outerwear, such as ladies' clothes other than dresses, men's clothes, articles for the teen-age group, coats, or sportswear. However, (1) it would have required a new marketing setup; (2) it would have posed entirely new problems for manufacturing; and (3) it would have taken a long time to establish a market position. Fabric sales, in contrast, appeared a more logical approach in that (1) this required only minimal marketing efforts; (2) Hedblom had both the manufacturing skills and excess knitting capacity; (3) sales would materialize immediately, particularly through aggressive pricing; and (4) Hedblom had an outstanding fabric designer, giving the company a strong competitive advantage.

Fabric sales began in the fall of 1967. A cover-up organization in Denmark was used to protect the parent company, whose Scandinavian sales manager feared losing yarn sales were Hedblom to compete openly with his customers. This company, primarily a dyer and finisher, dyed the Hedblom fabrics and sold them in Denmark through its own organization and in the rest of EFTA and the EEC[4] through its foreign agents. For this purpose a special fabric collection had been created containing seven different types of cloth, each of which came in different colors. Selling prices averaged Skr 17 per meter or Skr 51 per kilo.

FOREIGN MARKETS

Mr. Keller commented on his policies for penetrating foreign markets as follows:

One of my early decisions was to close the German sales office. The reason was that I did not believe that I could bank on anything like De Gaulle's accepting Great Britain or the other EFTA countries into the European Com-

---

[4] European Economic Community, commonly referred to as European Common Market, comprised France, West Germany, Italy, and the three Benelux countries.

mon Market. So I just forgot about the potential of markets such as Germany or France, where the duty on dresses of 30% simply makes it impossible for us to compete effectively. On the other hand, I placed major emphasis on the other EFTA markets, establishing sales offices in Austria, Switzerland, and Great Britain; hiring an agent in Finland; and placing increased pressure on our agents in Denmark and Norway. Also, this fall, I appointed an agent in the United States where the dress duty is about 25%. Dresses are sold to our overseas sales offices or agents at regular factory prices with freight paid by us.

CHANGES INTRODUCED BY MR. KELLER

Organizational changes

Besides reviewing and revising policies, Mr. Keller revised company structure:

My policy from the outset was to use everybody at Hedblom, but also to realign some of the tasks. In May of 1967, I announced a revised organization structure. The changes, compared to the previous organization, were as follows:

—Purchasing and shipping were added to production planning, and all were assigned under Carlsson.
—Merchandising would focus on the design, sales, and advertising of Hedblom dresses, with a much freer hand than before in style decisions. This area was put under Mr. Filipsson, to whom shipping had previously reported.
—Design and sales for the second dress line as well as sales of fabrics were placed under Mr. Nilsson, who previously managed purchasing.
—Production would remain under Mr. Lanner, who would be responsible for manufacturing fabrics and Hedblom dresses, as well as the second dress line.
—Fabric design for all three activities (hence on a vastly enlarged basis) would remain under Mr. Sundman.
—Bookkeeping would be enlarged to include management control and planning under Mr. Jansson.

Mr. Keller explained some of the thinking back of his decision:

The main issue which was difficult to resolve in creating the new organization was whether to place the second line of dresses under Hedblom merchandising as a separate section, or to make it an independent activity. I decided for the latter, in that one man could give his full attention to the new line without being distracted or worried by the Hedblom line. Thus, I wanted to give one man full control and responsibility for a line. At the same time, I hoped to motivate both men by having them compete with each other both outside and inside the company.

Move of offices

Late in April 1967, it was decided to convert half the top floor of the factory building into offices and the remainder into storage rooms. Costing Skr 400,000, this move occurred in August 1967. Mr. Keller decided on this change in order to permit better coordination among his top managers, closer supervision by himself, and also for symbolic reasons.

New fabric developments

As a result of the extra collections for the Hedblom line, plus the addition of the second line as well as fabric sales, fabric-design activities were increased significantly. Also, greater emphasis was placed on innovation. Hedblom pioneered a fabric made of a new 110-denier yarn produced by Wientex. It also experimented successfully with cross-dyed Dacron fabrics. There were three types of Dacron which looked alike when white but which yielded different colors if placed in the same dye. By knitting these yarns together, it was possible to obtain patterns which previously had required colored yarns. Even though some start-up problems occurred and the color flexibility was limited, use of Dacron cross-dyed fabrics promised to facilitate manufacturing and to reduce inventory. Also, Hedblom expected major advertising support from the fiber manufacturer in introducing its Dacron cross-dyed dresses.

Changes in manufacturing

General policies. As already indicated, Mr. Keller decided against contracting Hedblom's operations. This would have involved leasing some of the manufacturing space and selling several of the machines. He felt that such a move would have had a disastrous impact on employee morale and company image. Instead, a policy of filling up the plant was pursued, thereby spreading the high overhead. At the same time Mr. Keller attempted to cut costs and to speed deliveries. In attempting to achieve these goals, he relied entirely on his own people and refrained from bringing in outside help.

Additions. Mr. Keller installed three quality-control posts: one inspecting knitted goods, one inspecting goods returned from dyeing, and one inspecting completed dresses. The purpose was to make the organization more quality conscious and to discover errors early, thus reducing waste of fabrics. Constant attention to machine operations was particularly critical in knitting since an early discovery of errors could mean significant savings of otherwise wasted yarn.

By October 1967 the 10 new Jacquard knitting machines, which had been ordered prior to Mr. Keller's arrival, had been delivered and were operating. Even though total knitting capacity was far in excess of Hedblom's needs, Jacquard capacity, permitting finer and more varied fabrics and patterns, had been in short supply. Use of Jacquard machines allowed the company to specialize in so-called "knitter's dress models" which were difficult for dressmakers using merchant fabrics to copy.

Also new was an emphasis on long-term production planning, with a focus on obtaining the best prices, the best utilization of productive capacity, and improved shipping, rather than, as previously, planning only day-to-day operations.

Eliminations. Mr. Keller relieved the consulting engineer of his duties. While costing a yearly Skr 400,000, results had been meager. New piece-rate standards had not been established. The punch-card system for production control had not provided the necessary data and had to be replaced by a manual system. Finally, the materials handling system was totally unnecessary, given the size and simplicity of Hedblom's operations.

Production changes. Changes in production operations included (1) a willingness to make advance commitments on fabrics and dress manufacturing; (2) a resulting ability to spread production volume evenly over the year, thus avoiding the previous peaks and valleys; (3) a policy of maximizing long runs in sewing and minimizing subcontracting, which would be confined to short runs (during his early days at Hedblom, Mr. Keller established a policy of doing at least 90% of the sewing in-house and of personally approving any outside contracting); (4) changes in plant layout to facilitate product flow and reduce costs; (5) a focus on cutting operations to reduce the high fabric losses; (6) use of transparent thread in sewing, which permitted the use of only two threads (light and dark), thereby facilitating sewing operations and minimizing thread inventories; and (7) achievement of bulk shipments by accumulating dresses ordered by a single customer. Mr. Keller emphasized constant attention to costs in all aspects of manufacturing.

Changes in the control function

On the changes in the Hedblom control and planning functions, Mr. Keller commented as follows:

First of all, I told my people to forget about the traditional one-year time span for reports and to focus rather on three months' performance. Second, we immediately but slowly began to work with budgets. While admittedly crude (for example, for lack of standard costs we had to guess historical costs), these were total operating budgets, focusing on profits and not just on costs. We prepared the first one for May through July, which we immediately compared with actual results during the first 10 days of August. On this basis we were able to improve the next budget. Third, we began to develop a new standard cost system with a cost book consisting of new cost sheets. For this work we used a first-year student from HBS during the summer. Fourth, in terms of operations, I receive (1) a weekly sales report broken down by the various lines, by salesmen, and by area; (2) a weekly quality-control report; (3) a weekly cutting and sewing schedule; and (4) a weekly report on indirect labor. Fifth, we started to establish controls and planning for investments and major expenses and to develop source-and-use-of-funds projections for the next six months and for shorter periods whenever necessary.

Currently, we have just introduced a very comprehensive budget-control report, prepared by Carlsson and analyzed by Jansson. This report compares to the budget the quantities bought, produced, shipped, etc. We hope to simplify it in the future, making it my basic weekly report. This report, together with a three-month budget and variance analysis, should be sufficient for me to control Hedblom's activities.

As far as the controls used by my managers are concerned, I refrained on purpose from meddling with these. I gave each man freedom, leaving it up to him to design his own controls, while stressing the need for improved reports. My managers are in a better position to judge what is critical and how best to control it. Of course, they must be able to answer my questions. In this way, I check whether or not my managers have their own effective control system. Also, some of the reports I receive I do not read regularly. I just have them sent to me to make sure that people plan ahead in some of the crucial areas—for example, cutting and sewing schedules. The danger is to develop too many figures. As a result, I do not want data on the total number of workers, feeling that direct labor can best be controlled by my subordinates and that results will clearly show in the output-per-man figures. However, the indirect labor I like to watch as an overhead item.

Working on the control and planning system was no easy job. Also, I feel we still have a long way to go.

Other steps

In addition to the above steps, the obsolete inventory was liquidated. Entered on the books at Skr 4 to Skr 4.5 million, it was sold for Skr 1.5 million. The Sandvik plant was not sold, however. Mr. Keller had initially planned to do this until his managers pointed out that a sale to another textile firm would probably mean the loss of the Hedblom skilled workers who still lived in Sandvik. Potential purchasers among nontextile firms could not be found. The company Rolls-Royce, on the other hand, was sold immediately, much to the chagrin of the commercial department which considered it an excellent public relations tool.

As a source of extra, although marginal, revenue Mr. Keller entered into a licensing arrangement with a South African firm. With seasons there occurring six months later, this arrangement created little extra expense for Hedblom and resulted in a minimum annual royalty of Skr 20,000, expected to increase to Skr 100,000.

Morale building

Mr. Keller gave his constant and systematic attention to morale both inside and outside the company. He was planning an "open house" for employees and their families, during which plant tours would be organized and the entire dress collection would be modeled. Other steps to improve internal morale were (1) the creation of more work; (2) Mr. Keller's willingness to listen to employee complaints and follow up on them; (3) close cooperation with the workers' council (which told Mr. Keller after three months that he was ineffective because he had not brought more work to the plant); (4) regular plant visits by Mr. Keller, who took a detailed interest in all operations. With his managers Mr. Keller was able to move away from the previous stringent working conditions, encouraging initiative and permitting much more operating freedom.

In terms of building outside morale, Mr. Keller made the customer king, guaranteeing on-time deliveries, taking back unwanted goods, and stressing Hedblom quality. He improved bank relations, getting the prime rate with assistance of the parent company. As mentioned above, a plant visit and a showing of the collection was arranged for the press, and another one was planned for town and county officials. It was hoped that both visits would generate a great deal of publicity and goodwill. A similar purpose justified a trip by the company's public relations adviser to South America. Mr. Keller felt that Hedblom's outside image had suffered prior to the takeover and that restoration of a good image was critical for both selling and recruiting of scarce skilled knitting and sewing personnel.

MANAGEMENT STYLE

Mr. Keller commented on his management style as follows:

My main task at the beginning was to gather information and to get cooperation. Basically, I knew nothing about the dress business and little about Hedblom. I therefore conducted a detailed and systematic investigation of all aspects of company operations. Given the uneven attention paid by my predecessor to the different segments of the company, I was particularly anxious to focus on all areas. Every time I visit Boxholm, I walk around the building, meet the people, talk to them as best I can in my broken Swedish, and particularly ask questions, questions, questions. In a way, knowing very little when you start is an advantage because it allows you to ask even the most stupid questions, and by asking about so many things you are bound to discover problems and focus on critical issues. You simply take nothing for granted. By having people explain and justify what they have been doing for years as a matter of unquestioned routine you often discover what needs to be investigated and appraised. Also, in this way you learn a lot about your own people. In my questioning I usually try to get into details; only in this way do you really find out what is going on and build a platform for future action. Of course, policy and long-term planning are part of my job as general manager, but details are just as important.

With my managers I practice an open-door policy and, as a result, I see each man practically every day. Usually, our meetings last between 30 minutes and one hour, and they almost always relate to a specific operating problem. About twice a month I meet with all six managers together, but these meetings are largely to convey information: on policies, on results, etc. I do not believe in committees for decision making and coordination. Particularly at Hedblom we are still small enough so that these things can take place on a daily and informal basis. At the beginning I was more meeting-oriented. To get to know the managers better and to facilitate coordination, I scheduled regular luncheon meetings. After several weeks, however, I learned that lunch was a sacred time for one of my managers who used to go home during this time for a nap. Incidentally, this man rarely leaves before 8:00 P.M. in the evening and his siesta is more than justified. After I learned about this, we stopped our luncheon meetings and nothing formal or regular took their place. Also, I often have dinner with the managers since I am usually alone in Boxholm, but this is mostly on an individual basis.

My policy is to delegate. Because of my language handicap, I am in fact forced to do so, and this is a good thing. I have also tried to encourage initiative by the managers and even arguments. This is not easy, given the leadership style under which they had worked previously. Also, I am trying to make everybody cost-conscious. Watching costs is critical in our business, and cost reduction is imperative to restore Hedblom to profitability. Yet there is really nothing dramatic that you can do to cut costs: no shortcuts, no labor-saving machinery, and no great economies of scale. Thus, it is very necessary to watch every step and every penny. In a recent meeting the production manager mentioned that his direct-labor-per-kilo-of-fabric-knitted ratio would go up because he had hired extra people in view of a large fabric order which was subsequently canceled. This concern about costs and awareness about his department's efficiency is quite a change from a few months ago.

My job naturally is to think ahead. Hence I try to focus the attention of my managers not only on today's problems but also on what we might be facing in six months or one year. This is especially important given the lead times in our business. Another job I have is that of arbiter. Fortunately, there is not too much conflict around here, and so this role is not a very active one. Sometimes I try to avoid conflicts by making the decisions myself. For example, I anticipated conflicts in allocating fabrics among our three basic activities. Every line (Hedblom, Karin, and fabrics) of course would want the best cloth, so I allocated fabrics to each of them.

Hedblom (B)*

On Wednesday, March 13, 1968, Mr. Arthur Keller,[1] age 32, managing director of Hedblom, a ladies' dress company located in Boxholm, Sweden, entered his office to find a big bouquet of flowers with a card from his six top managers expressing their gratitude and conveying their best wishes. "Yes," Mr. Keller remarked, "today is my anniversary here.[2] It has been an exciting and rewarding year, and we look forward to the future with confidence. Our goal is to make Hedblom into one of the leading dress companies, not just in Sweden, but in all of EFTA."

In looking back at the results of the past year, Mr. Keller stressed the full cooperation and complete devotion of his associates. "If, during the remainder of my career, I get the same support from my associates as I have received here during the past year, I will be very fortunate," he said.

The feeling was mutual. One of the managers said, "Since Mr. Keller has been here I feel several years younger." Another manager commented that he now was able to work more freely, to make his own decisions, and to use initiative. A third manager liked the open-door policy and the attention he received. He also appreciated being informed

* Copyright 1968 by l'Institut pour l'Etude des Méthodes de Direction de l'Enterprise (IMEDE), Lausanne, Switzerland. Reproduced by permission.

[1] Names and figures have been disguised.

[2] Mr. Keller became managing director of Hedblom on March 13, 1967. Events leading up to this appointment and Mr. Keller's early weeks on the job are described in the Arthur Keller case. The strategy which Mr. Keller decided upon during his first months on the job is described in the Hedblom (A) case.

about what went on in the entire company, and he liked the high degree of delegation. Finally, he was delighted that Mr. Keller took a keen interest in the company, and especially that he took walks through the plant.

In appraising the results of his actions during the past year and in assessing the future outlook for Hedblom, Mr. Keller commented as follows:

Our three 1968 spring collections of Hedblom dresses sold well, and results exceeded our targets. The initial results of our 1968 autumn collection are most encouraging, especially since autumn was typically Hedblom's weak collection. Our style reputation has increased during the past year and our on-time deliveries have enhanced trade goodwill. Our advertising has become more effective and should support even larger sales. We expect to sell between Skr 12 and Skr 14 million of Hedblom dresses. Also I feel that we now have a basis for profitable long-term growth with Hedblom dresses in Sweden, averaging about 10%–15% per year.

Initial results with our second [Karin] line and with our fabric sales have been encouraging, but some major issues have to be resolved before we can achieve our true potential. In 1968 we expect to get Skr 2 to Skr 4 million in sales revenues from our second line and Skr 2 to Skr 4 million from fabric sales, but with more and better efforts we should be able to reach, respectively, Skr 10 to Skr 12 million and Skr 4 to Skr 6 million. We expect yearly growth rates of 10% to 15% for our second line of dresses and of 15% to 20% for fabrics.

Foreign markets are also still mostly potential, although we have made good progress during the past year. Our potential could be fantastic. Sweden's GNP is 13.5% of the EFTA total (excluding Portugal), and if we were to do equally well elsewhere in EFTA as in Sweden, we could expect 7½ times as much sales as now, or up to Skr 100 million. Of course, it is unlikely that we will achieve the same market penetration as in Sweden, at least in the near future, but nevertheless this is our target. Before we get that far, some issues here, too, have to be settled.

Our organization seems to have digested the change and growth very well. The office move worked out perfectly, as did the changes in organization structure. There is only one issue which comes back all the time: whether the second dress line should be independent, or organizationally part of merchandising.

Fabric design has been doing a tremendous job, but I begin to get complaints that with our three lines too many demands are placed on our designer. Manufacturing has also made great improvements, but here, too, some of the strains of our broader product line are being felt. In the management control area we still have to make most of our progress, but, after all, this is the area where we really started from scratch.

All in all, I am most happy about the past year and confident about the future. In 1967 we closed with a loss, but very much reduced from previous years. During 1968 we expect to make a decent profit, and all indications point to a profitable first quarter. [See Exhibit 1 for recent financial

EXHIBIT 1

HEDBLOM
Abbreviated Operating Statement
(in millions of Swedish kronor)*

	7/1/66 to 6/30/67	7/1/67 to 12/31/67	1/1/68 to 6/30/68 (budget)
Net sales†	10.3	4.8	9.3
Gross margin	1.1	1.5	2.5
Selling and administrative expense	3.6	1.7	1.6
Income from operations	(2.5)	(0.2)	0.9

*Skr = 19.3 U.S. cents; $1 = Skr 5.17.
†Net sales = gross sales minus sales taxes, rebates, and shipping.

Tentative Breakdown of Manufacturing Expenses
Developed during the Summer and Fall of 1967
(in percentages)

Yarn		45.1
Accessories		3.9
Knitting		
Labor	2.5 }	8.5
Overhead	6.0 }	
Cutting		
Labor	2.8 }	4.3
Overhead	1.5 }	
Sewing		
Labor	16.0 }	20.8
Overhead	4.8 }	
Dyeing		5.8
Development and samples		5.8
Other costs		
Variable	4.0 }	
Overhead	1.8 }	5.8
		100.0

Source: Company records.

data.] For the future there are two more issues that occupy me: Hedblom's relations with its parent company, which is also its major supplier; and our distinctive competence, especially whether it will ensure sufficient long-term profitability.

In his appraisal of past results and future outlook for Hedblom, Mr. Keller mentioned nine issues which he had to face in March of 1968. These are described in more detail below.

THE RETAIL REVOLUTION

The crux of this issue, as Mr. Keller described it, was that (1) Hedblom's selective distribution ruled out certain large and growing dress distribution channels, and (2) these channels wanted to retail dresses at below Skr 100—in other words, at much lower prices than Hedblom's. Could Hedblom cater to this market segment without damage to its bread-and-butter line? Particularly, how would its traditional channels, the small dress shops, respond if Hedblom dresses were sold in the mass merchandising outlets? Also, could Hedblom continue to command high prices if under the same brand dresses at half that price were sold? The company had looked at four basic alternatives: (1) continue to ignore these growing channels; (2) make sales to these channels at lower prices but use unbranded merchandise or else the store's own brand; (3) sell through these outlets, but use a second, different company brand; or (4) try to make sales to these outlets under a different parallel brand, but at the same prices as Hedblom dresses.

With the Karin brand the company had opted for the third alternative, but the issue was far from settled. Initially, the plan was to sell Karin dresses to every potential client, but when the time came the company proceeded very carefully and slowly for fear that an aggressive approach might jeopardize sales of Hedblom dresses. The commercial manager estimated potential losses in Hedblom dress sales at 50% of current volume. As a result, Karin dresses were sold in Sweden to only six large department stores and three mail-order houses. The commercial manager kept pushing for the alternative of supplying the mass retail outlets with unbranded, low-price dresses. He argued that unbranded sales, rather than use of a second brand, offered protection to the Hedblom line, thus permitting aggressive sales. Also, he felt there was no future in department stores for dresses over Skr 100, and therefore he did not believe in a parallel high-price brand.

ORGANIZING PARALLEL ACTIVITIES IN DRESSES

Early in 1968 Mr. Keller was faced with increasing pressure from the commercial manager, Mr. Filipsson, to make Karin sales his responsibility. His reasoning was that Karin styling and sales greatly influenced the market position of Hedblom dresses. Hence it was essential to assure close and continuous coordination of the merchandising of both lines. This could be done better, Mr. Filipsson argued, if the Karin directress and the two salesmen were to report directly to him.

Mr. Nilsson, to whom the Karin line was currently assigned, did not have strong feelings about the issue. He regretted that he had not been able to pursue a more aggressive sales policy, and, lacking this, he wondered whether all his troubles had been worthwhile. He had encountered difficulties in getting the fabrics he wanted, with the Hedblom dress manager using a preemptive strategy in asking for his fabrics. There had also been some conflicts on dress models, with the Hedblom dress people arguing that the Karin models too closely resembled the Hedblom ones. All in all, Mr. Nilsson indicated, Karin was treated pretty much like a stepchild. Operating problems, on the other hand, had been few.

Most important, he had been able to deliver his Karin dresses on time, with the manufacturing department always meeting its promises.

FABRIC SALES

We started fabric sales with great enthusiasm to fill up the plant, but now some people are beginning to have second thoughts. By selling fabrics to makers-up you help your own competitors in a way. But the biggest resistance to our fabric sales has come from our parent company, Wientex.

With these words Mr. Keller described his main issue in regard to selling fabrics. The parent company's argument was that this activity put Hedblom into competition with companies that were Wientex's yarn customers. These customers, Wientex's Scandinavian sales manager feared, might retaliate by not buying from him. He was particularly afraid of this retaliation if Hedblom were to force its way into the fabric business through a low-price strategy. He cited Wientex's strong position in Scandinavia, where it had a 60% market share in texturized yarns.

On Hedblom's side the argument was that Wientex would lose customers anyway because two yarn producers in Finland and Norway had established texturizing facilities and would definitely take market share away from Wientex. At any rate, intense price competition in texturized yarns was predicted for Scandinavia, and this would make fabric sales preferable to yarn sales. The latter were entirely price sensitive, and since yarn was a commodity, customer loyalty was nil. With fabrics, on the other hand, it was possible to achieve some product differentiation, especially through excellence in designs. Furthermore, Hedblom management cited the U.S. integration of yarn and fabric facilities and predicted such a trend for Europe. Finally, Hedblom's managers cited the example of a British yarn producer which had a subsidiary selling fabrics. This subsidiary had sold Crimplene-based fabrics in Scandinavia without provoking retaliation from the British company's customers. On balance, Hedblom management felt that the gains on fabric sales far outweighed possible losses on yarns.

The above issue, however, had prevented Mr. Nilsson from pushing fabric sales aggressively. He had to rely exclusively on the Danish cover-up organization, which he considered to be (1) too costly, (2) too complicated, (3) poor in terms of its sales organization, (4) wholly dependent on small customers, and (5) unable to reach large accounts. Mr. Nilsson felt that if fabric sales could be made under the Hedblom name, the company's reputation plus aggressive selling would enable him to move up to 100 tons of fabrics per year in EFTA instead of the currently expected annual sales of between 40 and 80 tons. He did not see much long-term potential in the European Common Market, given its high import duties of about 14%. Some temporary sales could, however, be made in Germany, where yarn prices higher than in Sweden allowed absorption of the import duty. He expected yarn prices to drop in Germany, at which point Swedish fabric sales would be priced out of the market.

FOREIGN MARKETS

Mr. Keller identified his chief issue in this area as follows:

The only way to make real headway in foreign markets is to have your own sales organization which is well qualified and dedicated. We have made a great deal of progress, but the road ahead appears both long and strenuous. However, we feel that the sales potential in EFTA is worth the trouble and money. At this point, however, foreign sales amount to 20% to 30% of the total, but this includes fabric sales through Denmark.

The foreign markets are giving us more problems than we anticipated. Each country has different demands, and the timing of introductions of dress collections also varies. Furthermore, we did not give our distribution setup enough thought. Should we rely on agents who get a 10% commission and who carry other lines? Or should we hire our own exclusive salesmen? In this case, should their compensation be through straight salary or through commissions, or, if both, in what proportions? Motivation, compensation, and control of our foreign sales activities is still an unresolved issue. In Norway and Austria results have been fine, while in Switzerland and Denmark they have been below expectations.

PARENT COMPANY SUPPLIER REGULATIONS

In contrast to the hitherto prevailing product shortages, Hedblom management predicted excess capacity for texturized yarns and therefore expected severe price competition. Price pressures on yarns, of course, would be beneficial to Hedblom as a purchaser. However, relations with the parent company had to be considered. One of the reasons for the Hedblom purchase by Wientex had been the desire to secure a stable outlet. By March 1968 Hedblom absorbed about 15% to 20% of the output of Wientex's Austrian texturized yarn plant and thus was an important factor in this plant's profitability. Within this setting, would Hedblom be able to shop around freely for yarn bargains? Would it be able to demand lower prices from its parent?

Related to the above issues was the question whether Hedblom should continue to purchase, and emphasize in its merchandising, the Crimplene branded texturized polyesters. Wientex sold Crimplene branded yarn, passing on a Skr 1.50 advertising allowance per kilo received from its raw materials supplier. Other texturizers also sold mostly branded polyesters. With the possibility of excess capacity, yarn producers might attempt selective price cutting by reducing prices on unbranded polyesters while maintaining them on branded sales. It was rumored that some companies were already doing this, allowing price cuts up to 15% (or about twice the usual advertising allowance which, of course, would not be granted for unbranded sales). The possibility of a dual market raised implications for Hedblom, which had always emphasized Crimplene in its dress sales. Should Hedblom continue this emphasis, particularly in view of the increasing brand proliferation of synthetics and the resulting consumer confusion? Also, the aggressive sale of cheap U.K. Crimplene dresses in Scandinavia might weaken the prestige of Crimplene for Hedblom. The question was raised among Hedblom managers whether there would not be, particularly in the long term, greater security in the Hedblom brand than in the Crimplene brand.

STYLING DEMANDS

In March 1968 Mr. Sundman, fabric design manager, commented on styling issues as follows:

With our new activities, the demand on my department has increased greatly. Last year we developed more fabrics than in the previous four to five years together. In fact, for 1968's high-summer and autumn dress collections, along with fabric sales, 63 qualities in all have been developed. [See Exhibit 2.] And that only covers half a year. At this rate we have to develop

EXHIBIT 2
Fabric qualities for 1968

Brand	Purpose	Qualities developed	Qualities on Jacquards
Hedblom	High-summer collection	6	3
Hedblom	Autumn head collection	17	11
Hedblom	Autumn cocktail collection	12	11
Karin	Autumn collection	21	11
Fabric.	Sales	7	2

about 125 qualities yearly, which amounts to one design every second working day. Up to now, we have been able to produce this many designs because we had some ideas in reserve from previous years, but these will soon be exhausted. Also, we can reintroduce some fabrics of earlier years, but that will not get us far either. Thus, I frankly cannot see how we can continue to satisfy the enormous demands of our product line. My department consists of only myself and an assistant. Furthermore, fabric designs have to be tried on the machines, and this too imposes some restrictions and costs.

MANUFACTURING DEMANDS

Mr. Lanner, production manager, discussed manufacturing problems as follows:

I think we have too many collections. Also, manufacturing does not have enough influence on dress choices. As a result, our efficiency is reduced.

Mr. Carlsson, manager for production scheduling, purchasing, and shipping, added the following points:

Changing style trends make it necessary to purchase more and more colored yarn. Earlier, close to 80% of our purchases were of white yarn, but if the present trend continues it may soon be only 50%. This change makes our purchases more costly and increases wastage as well as risk of obsolescence. We are doing our best in purchasing to reduce the percentage of dyed yarns, but there is only so much you can do.

MEASUREMENT CONTROL

Mr. Keller discussed what he saw as a key issue here as follows:

I am supposed to make long-run decisions, and yet I am measured on the basis of Hedblom's quarterly results. Also, I am measured on the basis of the bottom line: profit and loss. But I cannot measure any of my subordinates on this same basis. I cannot measure fabric design on profit or loss, or manufacturing or merchandising. If I were to try to do so, they would blame one another: merchandising would say that manufacturing made the wrong dresses, made them poorly, or delivered late. Manufacturing would accuse merchandising of placing all sorts of special orders, of not selling enough, etc. Yet, my boss doesn't care about any of these excuses; he simply points at me. Under these conditions how can I design a control system which focuses on the criterion by which I am measured, and yet is meaningful to my subordinates, particularly in guiding them to make profit-oriented decisions? This is currently my biggest problem in the area of internal management and organization.

LONG-TERM OUTLOOK FOR HEDBLOM

Mr. Keller continued:

Is this business attractive long term, and how can we profitably beat competition? In purchasing we have no advantages: everybody can buy yarn at the same price and we face no shortages. In knitting we have a certain advantage with our Jacquard machines; these permit us to use our design skills and to achieve great pattern flexibility which gives us an edge over the makers-up. In cutting we have no advantage; all still hinges on the pattern girl. I have been talking to one of the computer companies to see whether something can be done to minimize fabric losses, but this does not look immediately feasible. In sewing we do not have an advantage, just more sewing machines. I see no way to gain an advantage here except through radically different techniques such as using adhesives, possibly with other materials—for example, paper. In shipping we do not have an advantage either, except that, given our size, we can possibly ship more in bulk. Thus, in manufacturing we do not have much of an edge.

Merchandising is different. Through our advertising and public relations we have achieved quite an image, and I think we are on the way to achieving a customer franchise. Still we are not sure how far advertising will carry us, how much we will have to spend continuously, and how durable the impact will be for ladies' dresses. Also, we have two types of competition: the small makers-up of which there are many, given the ease of entry into the dress business, and the large sophisticated retail outlets like the department store chains. What long-term threats do these two types of competition pose for a company like Hedblom? Furthermore, the economics of our business should be considered, especially in terms of variable costs and working capital requirements. Given these conditions, what are the implications both in terms of size and in terms of growth?

I think that we have rescued Hedblom, and all our attention up to this point was focused on this task. Now, as we used to say at the B-School, we can start thinking about whether this is the business we should be in.

Hedblom (C)*

On June 19, 1968, while reviewing the Hedblom (B) case for release, Mr. Keller commented: "The nine issues which I faced back in March are accurately portrayed. However, some major new developments have occurred in the meantime, particularly in terms of the Hedblom product line and fabric sales." Mr. Keller continued as follows:[1]

As part of our Hedblom intermediate spring sportsclothes collection, which we started selling in early November 1967 for delivery in April 1968, we included ladies' slacks to retail at Skr 59. Initial orders through the sales force totaled 3,000 pieces, while orders written for the whole collection amounted to 16,000. Since April, reorders by telephone have been for 8,000 pieces. This success and some market studies indicate that there must be a market for high-priced wash-and-wear slacks and other types of sportswear, for both women and men. We do not think, however, that European men will buy polyester wash-and-wear suits, even though only the expert eye can tell the difference between our knitted and the traditional woven fabrics. Slacks of knitted polyester, on the other hand, appear to have a great potential. Clothes care for them is different, and the European housewife, who has been putting her dresses in the washing machine for some years, may like to do this for her husband's slacks as well. Also keep in mind that permapress is less useful in Europe because most households do not have tumble dryers.

We are now considering hiring another directress to concentrate entirely on

[1] Names and figures have been disguised.

739

the trouser business and possibly even a special salesman to sell trousers on a year-round basis.

In fabric sales we face a much greater opportunity. When put in charge of Hedblom, I also retained my earlier duties as assistant to the president of Wientex, our Austrian parent company; here my work primarily involved planning and implementing Wientex's forward integration from spinning and texturizing into knitting, weaving, possibly dyeing and finishing, and, eventually, dressmaking. In this part of my job I looked at several companies as possible acquisitions and also investigated some projects which we could start from scratch. I rejected all these except two. One was the potential acquisition of a $10 million fabric company in the European Common Market, on which negotiations are proceeding slowly. The other project, to be started by us, involved making circular double-knits at a company to be located in Germany but set up to supply the entire European Common Market with fabrics. I finished preparations for this project by September of 1967, and it was approved by the Wientex board of directors. Permission was granted to purchase knitting machines, to hire people, to open sales offices, and to build a new plant. The only restriction was that the company would not be involved in dyeing and finishing. Deliveries were to start during the early part of 1969. On this basis I proceeded with preparations. Support within the company was strong, since the texturizing division saw the German project as a large captive account and outlet.

Less than a month ago the board reversed its decision, and the German project was canceled. The same pressures against forward integration as described in the "B" case led to this decision: our yard-goods people were afraid of losing some of their customers if we competed with them in fabrics. By last month, however, we had 23 circular knitting machines on order for a total purchase price of $544,000. We had hired two sales managers (for France and Germany, respectively), two fabric designers, two knitting technicians, and two secretaries. Up to now I have not succeeded in convincing top management to revive the German project. Hence I face the decision of what to do with the people I have hired and the machines on order.

At the same time, we are reaching the conclusion that the Danish cover-up organization which sells our Hedblom fabrics under another name is not performing satisfactorily. They do not sell enough, have no important customers, and simply are not in touch with the market. Yet we see a tremendous demand for knitted fabrics, and we believe that with our reputation and skills we should succeed.

The cancellation of the German project now provides us with the following opportunities at Hedblom. Our expected rise in dress sales necessitates, in any event, an additional seven Jacquard circular knitting machines. Instead of taking seven of the 23 machines on order for Germany, why not gamble and take all of them? If so, the time appears ripe to negotiate, as a *quid pro quo*, for permission from the parent company to sell fabrics under our own name, thus doing away with the cover-up restrictions. With the pressure of the 23 machines on order, I feel that I have a good chance to persuade top management. Incidentally, these machines are scheduled for delivery at a rate of four per month, starting in about four weeks. Thus, a decision to take delivery or to cancel has to be made immediately. Also, if at Hedblom we move into fabrics in a major way, we can employ most of the people I have hired for the German project.

The additional 16 machines, costing about Skr 2 million, would add an incremental fabric capacity of between 240 and 250 tons a year and could produce about Skr 12 million in fabric sales. For 1968, in contrast, we expect fabric sales of between 40 and 80 tons, or Skr 2 to 4 million. Also, our total current knitting output, serving dresses and other finished clothes as well as fabric sales, now amounts to about 250 tons yearly. A ton of fabric sales is expected to yield profits before taxes of between Skr 5,000 and Skr 6,000, or $1,000–$1,200 per ton, or about 10% on sales.

Of course, in the short run, this move would create excess capacity again, but this time of the most modern types, involving high-production 36 "systems" machines with fine gauge and excellent styling capabilities which could provide us with further competitive advantages.

BCI Ltd.*

"In today's world, we do not think that our subsidiary companies can expand to their full potential without some help from central advisory services provided by our headquarters staffs," stated Mr. Henry Lampton, one of BCI's executives and a leading contender to succeed the BCI managing director, who would retire within one year. British Commercial Investments Ltd. (BCI), a London-based industrial holding company, comprised 16 subsidiary companies, with operations ranging from the manufacture of oil drilling equipment to electrical components and from special steel fabrication to the construction of agricultural buildings. Originally, the company had been involved solely with Malayan rubber plantations, but in the fifties it was decided to diversify entirely out of these politically risky activities through acquisition of small- to medium-size private companies, mainly in the United Kingdom. During the preceding seven years, partly through acquisition and partly through internal growth, gross tangible assets had risen from £9 million to £31 million and pretax profits from £900,000 to £3.4 million. A recent shift in emphasis had occurred, however. According to one executive:

Our present investment effort is directed mainly towards internal expansion by existing subsidiaries and the acquisition of no new subsidiaries unless they complement technologically those we already have. These two efforts, growth from within and acquisition of *related* companies, is what will produce the

---

* This case was written by Professor C. E. Summer. Copyright 1972 by l'Institut pour l'Étude des Méthodes de Direction de l'Enterprise (IMEDE), Lausanne, Switzerland. Reproduced by permission.

kind of profit we are interested in. Also, we have instituted what we call the BCI Three-Year Forecast, which involves much forward thinking-in-detail. This kind of planning is accepted as essential in modern company planning, but, even if it wasn't, something very similar would be needed to ensure the continued strength of BCI.

PARENT-SUBSIDIARY RELATIONSHIPS

The shift in emphasis in corporate objectives as well as the increased attention to formal planning had also led to changes in the relationships between BCI and its subsidiaries. According to Mr. Lampton, who had been instrumental in bringing about these changes:

We have been trying recently to provide additional help to our subsidiary companies. Until very recently, however, we were rather diffident about providing these services to give specialized advice in particular fields; it would be fatal to try and force them on unwilling subsidiary managements. But recently the success of our operations research group, the welcome accorded to the monthly economic bulletins of our chief economist, and the demand for the services of our BCI marketing adviser all attest to the need felt by subsidiary managers. Only in the last three weeks a computer adviser has joined our staff and has begun to familiarize himself with existing EDP installations and projects. We have been too slow in recognizing the part which EDP techniques will play in the future. We hope to provide companies individually too small to justify their own EDP units with access to facilities, and to reduce costs for all by organizing a coordinated network available on a BCI-wide basis.

It is, however, a part of our philosophy that our underlying principal subsidiaries (or, if you like, divisions) should be of a size that they can support their own local functional staff of a high caliber. We are not suffering under the delusion that we can operate a large central services team capable of resolving the local problems of such a diverse organization. Our advisory staff are used as catalysts.

Finally, I would like to say something about the services rendered to subsidiary operating companies by our BCI nominee director. We like to think that the personalities, experience, and sometimes wider contacts which our directors have are an important source of help to managements of BCI subsidiary companies.

Another executive elaborated:

BCI maintains a (nonexecutive) director on the board of each of its subsidiaries, usually as chairman. Although nonexecutive, the BCI nominee normally visits each of his two or three companies about once a week, or twice every three weeks. The BCI nominee typically has had considerable industrial experience before joining our organization, either with a firm of accountants or management consultants, or with some other industrial corporation in an executive capacity. Many of them have university education and have also attended advanced management programs such as the Administrative Staff College at Henley, Harvard Business School, Stanford Business School, or IMEDE in Lausanne.

Mr. Lampton continued:

The position of a BCI nominee director involves a rather heavy responsibility. We are not bankers, interested only in the financial aspects of the business. We are not there to take a normal dividend and let it go at that. In some financial holding companies, the local managements have the idea that they are entirely self-sufficient, except for dividends. At the same time, the directors nominated by the parent company to the boards of those subsidiaries create the impression that they are banker types—somewhat superior to getting into real operating problems. I personally believe that in some such holding companies the subsidiary managers are being supine; they sit there with talent which could add to operations, but which they abdicate. Specifically, I am certain that in this day of complex technology and society, the director has a moral responsibility to help his managers—to encourage them to do planning for the future, to aid them in selecting and staffing their operations, and to give advice where the director has talent or knowledge.

I can give you one example. Most recently, BCI acquired the L. M. Trowbridge Company from the Trowbridge family. This company specializes in construction projects using asphalt products—parking lots, tennis courts, large industrial asphalt areas. It is to the benefit of everyone—BCI, Harrogate [another subsidiary which produces asphalt materials] and Trowbridge managers, and employees of both companies—to merge the operations of the two companies. In this way, both will be more profitable, enjoy more growth, and stand a much better chance of survival in the British economy. Next year we plan to form a company to hold both Harrogate and Trowbridge in the interest of better all-round operations. The move was, inevitably, initiated by the BCI nominee chairman; the managers of Harrogate and Trowbridge don't have the same chance of standing back and taking an overall view of their operations. Without our BCI man, the merger would never have been initiated.

This shows how far we have moved from our position when BCI was still mainly involved in Malayan plantations and when our United Kingdom subsidiaries were regarded merely as diversified investments to be bought and sold, managerial responsibilities resting wholly with the underlying unit. Gradually we have come to acknowledge that this is an untenable position and have taken on full responsibility for the underlying units while allowing them a very wide degree of local autonomy in the main areas of their businesses.

THE ACQUISITION OF HARROGATE

Seven years ago, Mr. Jack Stanley, a man of 82 and the owner of a number of family companies including Harrogate Asphalt, wanted to put his estate in order so that it could be passed on to his heirs.

His brother approached a member of BCI management in London with the idea that BCI might be interested in acquiring Harrogate Asphalt. Mr. Lampton, then 31 years old and living in Birmingham as the BCI Midlands representative, was assigned the job of doing a management evaluation of the Harrogate company, which was located in Frampton, a small town in Yorkshire near Harrogate.

Lampton's general conclusion was that Harrogate represented an excellent investment. He based this on a thorough analysis of finances, management, marketing, production, and raw material procurement. He also found that the Harrogate management had sold a less profitable coal business some years earlier, had concentrated on the more profitable asphalt operations, had introduced a revolutionary technological process in the late fifties, and had expanded production and sales. He found that the company was in sound financial condition and that profits had increased at a fast pace.

Mr. Lampton's management evaluation report described Mr. Paul Denham, Harrogate's managing director and secretary, as follows:

Mr. Denham is 48 years old. He has spent the last 25 years with Mr. Stanley and has grown up with the business. He has been the prime mover in the expansion of Harrogate over the past several years. Despite Harrogate's rapid growth, the company is still relatively easy to administer and Denham has a tight personal control over it. He has a very pleasant personality. He is a strict disciplinarian and is respected for it. As the company is in a rural area and there is a very low labor turnover, Denham regards the employees with Edwardian paternalism. He has three sons at public school; the eldest (at 16) works in the company during vacations. Denham hopes one of the three will join him in the business later.

The works, transport, and sales managers were seen by Lampton as capable but "only one is likely to grow to sufficient stature."

Lampton pointed out that the workers in the plant earned very good wages compared to general conditions in British industry. The wages were exceptionally high in relation to the surrounding agricultural area. Wages of between £30 and £40 per week were due to the fact that when the new revolutionary production machinery was purchased, neither the manufacturer of the machinery nor the Harrogate management knew that it would be so productive. Piece rates were established based on what the machines were estimated to produce, but these were "grossly wrong."

Lampton continued:

The company (in the event, wisely) did not change these rates but reserved the undisputed right to trim all production units to a bare minimum of labor. As the company has constantly expanded, no surplus labor has been laid off but merely transferred to new units.

Needless to say, at these rates competition for jobs at Harrogate is very high. There was an intensely "brisk" air about the whole place. It is nonunion labor. There is no pension scheme. Hours worked are long (normally 07:30 to 18:30) and annual holidays are split, a week in the summer and another in the winter. The work is arduous and in the winter conditions are not good by the very nature of the business. As the rates are all fixed by team output, there is no room for individual slacking. Relations with management appear to be good. Total labor force has risen rapidly in the past year to around 100.

Lampton concluded his report:

The reason for the company's success is probably due to its geographical position (both for raw materials and markets), the fact that it invested early in a revolutionary production machinery (outside engineers reckon that Harrogate has more of these than anyone else, but Denham has no proof of this), very efficient management (mainly by Denham), and because it is supplying a material in increasing demand over the past decade.

As a result of this report, BCI made an offer to Mr. Jack Stanley for his company. This was accepted, and Harrogate became a subsidiary of the London holding company. At the time of acquisition, Jack Stanley, with his wife, daughters, and grandchildren, owned 90% of Harrogate, and Paul Denham and his wife owned 10%. This latter represented an interest which Stanley had permitted Denham to buy. During the first three years of BCI ownership, Denham retained his minority ownership, but this was subsequently sold to BCI on recommendation of his own financial adviser.

Because the future of the company's sales and profits looked so good, Stanley had proposed that Denham receive £4,000 net salary per year, and 2½% of net profits over £100,000. Previously, he had received a lower salary (£2,000) plus 5% of total net profits. Lampton stated that Denham agreed with this, and that at the time it meant a total take-home of £5,000. His total earnings had risen consistently over the years, culminating in £17,000. This was considered by the casewriter to be a relatively high remuneration in British industry.

The first five years of operation

During the first year, the board of directors of Harrogate consisted of Jack Stanley, Paul Denham, and Gerald Kemp, a full-time executive of BCI who was assigned as the parent-company representative.

During those years, Mr. Henry Lampton was serving as BCI representative in the Midlands and as nominee director of two BCI subsidiaries located near Birmingham. Nevertheless, Mr. Lampton recalled certain things which he knew went on during the first five years.

In that period, the new equipment installed from Mason & Grant gave Harrogate an overwhelming competitive advantage in a business mainly served by fairly small companies, with the result that profits, sales, and return on new capital increased dramatically. Here is a company whose return on net worth was among the highest of any BCI company. Nevertheless, in my judgment, there were definite signs of trouble. Stanley died at the end of the second year. This left the BCI director and Paul Denham. About a year later, these two directors recommended as the third director Roger Sample, a young man who was hired by Denham in the second year of our ownership. I'll have more to say about him later, but I acknowledged Roger from the first time I met him to be a capable chap, though his experience in Harrogate was limited.

The board meetings of those days consisted of a rather formal, cut-and-dried reporting of figures, once a month.

At this point, the casewriter asked: "Was Paul Denham making the policy decisions?" Mr. Lampton responded: "If there were any policy decisions being made—though I doubt there were."

Lampton continued:

Also, in about the second year, Harrogate suddenly found itself with a strike on its hands. Denham was at loggerheads with the union and he was at a loss as to what to do. The BCI director had to go up there and deal with the union, and a settlement was reached. As I recall, Denham simply gave up and said that he could not deal with them.

Also, Denham operated by turning up at 8 A.M., opening the mail, then sitting in the sales (internal) office for two hours, returning to his own office where he would incarcerate himself and merely look at figures of past performance. He rarely went to see customers off site or saw customers when they came in.

Recent events

About two years ago, while some other changes were being made in the BCI organization, Mr. Lampton, at age 36, returned from Birmingham to the BCI London head office as a director of BCI; at the same time he was also assigned to the board of the Harrogate subsidiary. Mr. Lampton commented on his new Harrogate assignment as follows:

I arrived on the scene of this highly successful company (60% on net worth is remarkable by any criteria) full of youthful bounce and asking why they don't look at the situation in the building products industries for growth. I knew that the company was doing no real forward planning, and that with the addition of a lot of hard work along this line the company could do much better. I also had a certain amount of good will and ambition—and the knowledge that I would have a delicate time with Paul Denham.

But I soon found that it was an unusual company. I saw a managing director making £15,000 a year but no other men of responsibility. His four top men, including Roger Sample, were making £3,000 or under. This came as a surprise. Here was an outstandingly successful company, profit-wise, with no staff in depth. In fact, in addition to Roger Sample, the only talent I could see was a good production assistant who had just given notice of his termination.

First let me say that I am not adverse to local autonomy—I believe it is best—but not for one local autocrat. Let me also say that my relationship with Denham was a good relationship, personally speaking, but when I tried to bring some things up for improvement around the board table (I had instituted more frequent board meetings and insisted that we discuss company policy problems rather than just review figures of past performance) he did not want to discuss them. Instead, he would say, "This is not a matter for formal board—why don't you come around to my office and let's talk about them informally." Nevertheless, I thought that all three board members (including Sample) should be in on important matters, and that there should be formal board meetings, with the board having the responsibility for making decisions.

Let me give you an example. Our operators in the plant were getting very high piece rates, but it was physically very hard work, 58 hours a week, and two one-and-a-half-week holidays that had to be split, one-and-a-half weeks in summer and one-and-a-half in winter; anyone absent without a doctor's note got instant dismissal. When Denham asked me not to bring this up in the board but to come to his office, I said, "No, this is a board matter." I could see that these conditions would mean trouble, and Roger Sample was telling me—not as a moral issue at all, but as a practical issue—we couldn't keep things this way. For my own part, I regarded it as a practical issue *and* a moral issue. In a way, we were blackmailing the workers with high pay and not providing opportunity for recreation. They were spending money in considerable amounts in gambling and drinking (this seemed to be a problem in the town). So I proposed that we allow them to take their two one-and-a-half weeks together, thus affording more of a real holiday and rest away from the job.

As I persisted in placing this matter before the board, Denham finally said: "I don't want any part of this discussion. If you want to make board policy, do it." Notice that he wasn't saying, "I am the managing director, I will think and be responsible about this." Instead, he was abdicating the managing directorship to us.

I mentioned Roger Sample. Denham had hired him some years ago from a local construction firm, and he subsequently became production manager. While he had rather narrow experience working locally up there in Yorkshire, he is a man of talent. He knew I thought highly of him, but he was reticent with me at first because he didn't know what kind of game I was playing. He did not have much confidence in pushing his ideas, because when Denham resisted he did not know if I would back him. Gradually, however, we established a relationship of trust. It came about through situations like the following. On my side, I could see great need for looking beyond the narrow confines of present products and processes. The company needed market research and research on new technology. On Roger's side, he had been reading magazines of the industry and had become aware of some new processes which were being developed in Sweden. He wanted to go there to investigate but had been forbidden by the managing director. Later, I raised this at the board table, but Denham's reaction was, "Don't let's meddle outside the company now. We have a system which is producing high profit." Why he took this attitude I don't know. I suspect that the real trouble lay in the fact that Denham had been outgrown by the company he managed, and he was afraid that anything new might put him still further out of his depth. Harrogate's very success was against him.

Some time later, the accountant for the plant quit. I think it was because he was mistreated by Denham. At this point, I tried to get Denham to go out and find a really top-flight managerial accountant, one who could think and plan rather than simply be an audit clerk. As things proceeded, I could see that Denham just wasn't capable of doing this, so I persuaded him that we should go out and hire an outside firm of consultants to do the recruiting. The consultants presented four candidates for our approval. I was party to interviewing them. We rejected two immediately, and there were two left, in my opinion, who were suitable. About this time I left to attend the 13-week Advanced Management Program of Harvard University in the United States. When I returned, I found to my amazement that he had rejected both of them and instead had hired a local accountant at £1,800 a year rather than the £4,000 man I had envisaged.

About this time I recognized that Paul Denham was a man who was going to reject any sort of idea, and any sort of talent, that he was not familiar with. I was utterly disenchanted with what he was doing. When I got back from Harvard, Paul Denham also recognized that I was a chap who was going to stick to his guns. I could see trouble ahead and was determined to do something about it, even though the company's profit record continued to be outstanding.

Mr. Lampton continued:

At the second board meeting after I returned, Roger Sample brought up a subject which I had encouraged him to study. (I had encouraged him to look at all facets of the business.) Our office staff had very high turnover. The staff was working on Saturday mornings, but there was no need, no work, for this. When Roger proposed it, Paul again said he wanted no part of it. He wasn't even fighting it. I suspect it was because he knew it was going to be put into effect anyway.

At any rate, I was intent on pursuing this to some sort of conclusion. The meeting became heated and intense. Denham said: "Hell, why do we waste our time on these matters; go out and find out what the order position is and let's get down to work." At this point, and in front of Roger, I blew my top. "This is real business," I said, "and if we don't pursue it, we have a real crisis."

One BCI executive commented that during this time,

Lampton was very conscious that the company's success was in some measure due to the tremendous pace which Denham had set for the company in earlier years. Indeed, the competitive edge which Harrogate had gained came largely from the fact that the company utilized its machines so intensively—the credit for which, at any rate initially, was Denham's.

(See Exhibit 1 for Harrogate's sales and profit performance.)

EXHIBIT 1
HARROGATE ASPHALT PRODUCTS LTD.
Selected Financial and Operating Results

Year	Sales	Profits before taxes
−14 . . . . £	31,000	n.a.
−13	55,000	£ 22,000
−12	83,000	28,000
−11	110,000	39,000
−10	178,000	62,000
− 9	224,000	87,000
− 8	361,000	136,000
− 7	520,000	150,000
− 6	867,000	260,000
− 5	1,053,000	310,000
− 4	1,096,000	300,000
− 3	1,638,000	450,000
− 2	1,922,000	595,000
− 1	2,050,000	600,000
Current year	2,500,000	750,000 (estimated)

Figures are rounded to nearest £1,000.
n.a. = not available.
Source: Company records.

After the above incident, Mr. Lampton upon returning to London wrote Denham a letter stating:

I have given myself some cooling time since our last meeting to consider its implications. I believe that it is most important that you and I meet away from Harrogate to discuss both the future of the business and the way in which you and I can operate together constructively for its good.

The letter then requested Denham to come to London for a meeting. According to Lampton:

I felt that it was stupid to keep this up and that we must resolve it somehow. Anyway, Denham had not once been to London in all the years we owned the company. I always invited him to the annual dinner we hold for subsidiary managing directors, but he always accepted and then sent a last-minute excuse.

The night before the meeting was to take place here at the head office, Paul Denham telephoned to say that he was not feeling well. He had shut himself off and did not realize that someone else owns the company and that he was not, as he thought, master of his own domain. I drove all the way to Yorkshire the next day. He was surprised to see me. I said that it is intolerable to go on this way and that we must cooperate if the company is going to progress. I told him also that we must educate Roger Sample in a wider sphere, that we must move him out of the production manager position and give him experience on the commercial side. He agreed to this, and to promote Roger's assistant to production manager.

On his return from Yorkshire, Mr. Lampton also sent to Denham the letter which appears as Exhibit 2. He continued:

During this entire period I had been getting close to Roger Sample, but at this point I got very close. He said, "I don't want to be disloyal to the managing director. You are moving me from an area where I know the work and feel secure to an area where I do not. But I am going to be of no use to anybody if I go on not being allowed to be in contact with customers. I wonder if Paul, who is 54, knows that, at 38, I am cornered?"

EXHIBIT 2

BCI LTD.

Mr. Paul Denham, Managing Director
Harrogate Asphalt Products Company
Frampton, Yorkshire

Dear Paul:

Although I was disappointed that you did not feel fit enough to come down here yesterday, I am glad that we had our discussion about the future, and I hope that you now understand and sympathize with our determination to strengthen the management at Harrogate so that it can be in a position to maintain its leadership in its own field and to exploit other opportunities in allied fields. I am sure that our decision to put Roger in full charge of sales is sound.

At the same time I hope that you understood that the BCI management is insisting that the individual subsidiaries institute, this year, a formal approach towards three-year planning and forecasting (the majority of the companies did this last year, of course). This is not an academic exercise but, in our opinion, an essential step both for the operating companies and for BCI. The preparation of such a report must essentially be a team effort that has your full backing, and as it is sometimes difficult to start viewing the future in this way I have, as I told you, arranged for James Kemp, our management accountant and planning specialist, to be free for a week (or more, if necessary) at the end of this month or in September to give you any help you may need. I sincerely hope that I have managed to persuade you that one is not just looking for a "figure pledge" that you would consider you had broken were it not achieved. When you look at the framework around which such a report is constructed, you will see that it requires the participation of the whole management team.

Naturally, I am anxious about your health and I do hope that you can soon discover what is wrong with your arm. What you said about overworking and the need for a really worthwhile break of two months or more seems to me not only desirable but necessary if you are going to be able to maintain your energies in the future. You have our complete backing for this, and I hope you can manage this as soon as possible.

Yours,

H. Lampton

Source: Company records.

Mr. Lampton said that he then offered Sample a service agreement (contract) to insure that he would not be summarily fired. Sample responded, according to Lampton, "No, that is not what I want. I will give you a pledge to stay three years, but I will leave if there aren't some changes in the way the company is running."

Mr. Lampton continued:

Naturally, I did not put it to Denham that way. I told him it would be a good thing to send Roger to a three-week marketing course I knew about at the University of Glasgow. He said that this is not productive for the company, but that if Roger wants it and I approve, he would go along.

On the very day that Roger left, Paul Denham took sick. Roger phoned from Glasgow (Paul had phoned him) and wanted to know if he should go back to Frampton.

Omar Industries, Inc.

OMAR INDUSTRIES was a diversified manufacturing company with sales in 1971 of about $1.0 billion. It was composed of eight operating divisions, half of them producing chemicals and packaging products for industry and the other half consumer durables. In all, the company had over 40 manufacturing locations in the United States and several more overseas under the direction of the International Division. Assisted by one acquisition, corporate sales had grown at a rate of about 10% over the previous decade. Although net profit to sales had slipped from 5.3% to 4.0% during this period, return on equity had held constant at roughly 10% as the company increased its debt to equity ratio from .30 to .67. During 1972 renewed emphasis was placed on improving margins and increasing earnings per share. Moreover, in view of the increased debt levels, the president had made it clear to his division managers that the corporation was going to "live within its means" by not spending more on capital investment than its cash flow after dividends (about $62 million in 1971) justified.

ENVIRONMENTAL CONTROL DEPARTMENT

In 1970, the Environmental Control Department (ECD) was formed to consolidate a number of corporate staff activities related to Omar's concern with the environment. The company was recognized as a leader in the control of air and water pollution in its manufacturing operations, at times pioneering in the adoption of new control technologies. During his years as president, the current chairman of the board had stressed the importance of providing "the best pollution control equipment to meet or exceed community criteria."

ECD performed a variety of functions including (*a*) assisting the operating divisions in achieving compliance with government regulations, (*b*) keeping the corporation current on changes in regulation or control technology, (*c*) reviewing capital requests from an environmental viewpoint, and (*d*) encouraging the divisions to incorporate environmental concerns and potential expenditures in their planning. The department did not, however, have the authority to force action on the operating divisions, though in some respects it shared the responsibility for the implementation of the corporate policy on pollution.

ECD was directed by John Carpenter who reported to Fred Phillips, an administrative vice president for special services, a position that included responsibility for several corporate-level technical service groups and various external programs related to environmental affairs. ECD was divided into sections responsible for air, water, testing, and environmental hygiene. This latter section was acquired from the corporate personnel group when ECD was formed on the premise that much of the effort required in the occupational health and safety area was related to engineering rather than personnel.

Occupational health and safety

In the summer of 1972, Phillips and Carpenter were becoming increasingly concerned about a growing public interest in the work environment in general and the requirements posed by the 1971 Occupational Health and Safety Act (OSHA) in particular. They were especially worried about the 90-decibel standard for noise included in the Act as the maximum allowable for sustained exposure. Carpenter commented:

OSHA inspectors have been hammering some of our divisions for noise. We know there are some places where the levels get as high as 130 decibels— that's way above the new national standard of 90 decibels. I've been going to the technical directors in the divisions to try to get them to write down their existing situation. They're annoyed with me at the moment. They say they don't have the time or the money to spend on worrying about noise at the moment. My argument is that if they get it written down, they can at least (1) ask for some money to work on the problem and (2) show to OSHA that they're acting in good faith.

The divisions are different. The Chemical Division is doing an excellent job. The Packaging Division is giving us no response. We had a meeting with them a little while ago to discuss it and they took the position, "We hear you but until we have a specific problem, in other words a citation, we're not going to do anything. There are other pollution problems right now that are of more importance to us."

In the first week of July, Carpenter called Fred Bellows, manager of plant construction and engineering in the Automotive Parts Division, to arrange a meeting to assess the division's status in the areas covered by the Occupational Health and Safety Act—chiefly noise abatement. While he had been working with several of the other divisions on formulating action programs to bring their operations into compliance with the new regulations, Carpenter had had little contact with this division on this particular issue.

The Automotive Parts Division had been acquired by Omar in the late 1960s. Its sales had remained more or less constant at $90 million since that time and as a result had not been keeping pace with the corporation's overall growth. Profit margins, always tight, had been under increasing pressure in recent years as the division worked to develop new products in a highly competitive field. It operated four general line and two specialty plants in addition to several technical centers.

On July 13, Carpenter, Bellows, and Walter Gardner, an engineer who worked for the director of environmental hygiene, met in Carpenter's office. The following discussion ensued:

CARPENTER: I wrote to all of the technical directors in the divisions recently outlining goals and objectives for engineering noise out of our operations. We see OSHA inspectors telling us to engineer the noise levels down to the point that employees don't have to wear earplugs within maybe a two-year time frame. We also have the feeling that, if we have programs prior to the time they demand them, they will be willing to accept a more reasonable compliance schedule.

BELLOWS: We have already had one citation on noise.

CARPENTER (to Gardner): Did you know that?

GARDNER: No.

CARPENTER: Was the citation given by the state or OSHA?

BELLOWS: OSHA. They gave us a citation and were going to give us until July 1 to correct it. That was ridiculous—only four weeks away. I talked with the enforcement officer and told him so. I told him we were spending 5,000 hours of engineering time working on the problem. That's stretching the truth a bit, though we can justify it if they ask us by stretching the description of what our engineers are doing. But we do have mandatory ear-protection rules in areas of 100 decibels and down to 85 decibels it's encouraged but optional. On this basis, the inspectors closed the file.

On the basis of our efforts—a continuing long-range program—they said O.K. I gave them no numbers, no details, and no schedules, but if they have another complaint, they said, "we'll open it up again."

CARPENTER: Let's say they did.

BELLOWS: We would use the same argument—a long-run argument.

CARPENTER: Do you have a schedule with definite programs and goals?

BELLOWS: No, it's a long-term project but one that falls short of redesigning the machines. We have 250 stamping machines, and there just isn't enough money to do it. One of these machines, even running by itself, generates 90 decibels. I don't know how we can do it.

CARPENTER: That's what the Chemical Division people told us about the forming machines, but now they have redesigned them so that noise levels have dropped from 114 decibels to 90. You need a schedule and some objectives.

BELLOWS: But as soon as you have a schedule, you need a budget and people assigned to it.

CARPENTER: That's just what I am trying to get you to do.

BELLOWS: The noise problem is really a problem, no denying it.

CARPENTER: Then why don't you want to take out the noise?

BELLOWS: The noise on a machine is important. That's the way the operator tells if something is wrong. That's the reason I'm not happy with the ear-protection devices. The operator with earplugs in can't listen to the equipment as well.

GARDNER: I'd like to see ear-protection devices eliminated, too, but you can only do that by eliminating the noise.

BELLOWS: We've got noise control on all new equipment.

CARPENTER: You've put it on the purchase order?

BELLOWS: Yes.

CARPENTER: That's great.

BELLOWS: No, it's not great. We often need special machines, and with these new requirements some suppliers just won't bid on them.

CARPENTER: Not even for money?

BELLOWS: We didn't say we would pay a million dollars. They weren't sure they could come up with a new technology for what we pay. Somewhere along the line, John, it's got to be economical. You can't put the machine in a room by itself.

CARPENTER: That's a point, though. Have you thought about shielding?

BELLOWS: Have you ever run a machine? At some point it's going to be uneconomical to do this. We've got a problem here that won't be solved in your lifetime.

CARPENTER: The Chemical Division is going to do it on all their forming machines.

BELLOWS: What's it going to cost them and how long will it take?

CARPENTER: $8 million. They've got a program for doing it that may take six or seven years, but it looks like OSHA may buy that. However, we had another situation at the Wilton plant. The OSHA inspector didn't like what we are doing. She told us to put together a program for meeting the national standards but said that an eight- to ten-year time frame would be unacceptable.

BELLOWS: That's unrealistic.

CARPENTER: But at least they are going to have a program which can be used as a basis for moving ahead toward controlling the problem.

BELLOWS: It's unrealistic for us. We can't replace all those machines. Maybe we'll change the product. We are moving from some lines to others which aren't as noisy on the machinery. But there are no stamping machines like ours in the United States which can meet the OSHA standards. You aren't going to get that to change.

CARPENTER: I can't buy the comment that there never will be a machine that can't do it.

BELLOWS: Sure, you can have what they call administrative controls—putting the machines off by themselves or having them run automatically by a guy at the end of the plant—but we are a low-profit operation. You're going to have to accept some of these unpleasantries in our case to stay in business.

GARDNER: Who says this will cost too much?

BELLOWS: We [engineering] never say that. Division management does.

CARPENTER: Somewhere along the line this decision gets made. Maybe by the division manager.

BELLOWS: It's the division manager, all right.

CARPENTER: The division manager has got to weigh these things and put them all together.

GARDNER: Has he been given a program?

BELLOWS: No, he only knows the problem in general terms.

CARPENTER: In fact, you have a new division manager.

BELLOWS: We haven't talked with the new one about it yet. Look, we know that noise reduction means machine redesign. I could go to him and tell him that. But I don't know the cost. We have never built machines with a design other than the one we have now, so we would need a study project—maybe $200,000 with a two-year timetable. Then a replacement project at $100,000 a machine. That's a lot of money. I don't have to present him with that. I know what he'll say—no.

Maybe if OSHA says shut the plant down, that will be something else. But for a business grossing $90 million, it's ridiculous to invest $25 million on a replacement basis.

GARDNER: I have just been here for a short time, and I don't know much about costs or about the operation. But I have been in government and I know OSHA is tough.

BELLOWS: They have been good to us so far.

CARPENTER: We can't say what your program ought to be . . .

BELLOWS: John, I don't object to writing a program. It's necessarily going to be a little nebulous and long term. The amount of money involved is going to be nebulous, too. We can say we know it's about $25 million in the long run.

CARPENTER: Unless you change the product . . .

BELLOWS: But as far as what happens then . . .

We could put an engineer on design . . . I don't mean to say we aren't trying to control the noise. Maybe we ought to just bumble along as we are. We don't have the capability to redesign.

CARPENTER: You have no incentive to do it now. In fact, you have an incentive to do nothing.

BELLOWS: OSHA told me that Northern Can has the same problem. OSHA made them make a schedule for compliance and so forth. We will probably have to do this next time. But the inspector said, "If no complaint, then you have seen the last of us for four years."

GARDNER: But he said that because OSHA has no inspectors. They will have them very soon, however.

BELLOWS: Actually, we have had another complaint at Middleton by the state control people. I have been away and I don't know any more about it than that. In a way, I am more worried about that one. But we will argue on the basis of our activities as we have with OSHA already.

CARPENTER: It sounds like you're just reacting. What you need is a program. Even your current program might do if it were just written down.

BELLOWS: Actually we have safety committees at each plant now. They're usually chaired by the plant manager. It's new—just started a month ago. I've seen some preliminary reports. They are pretty grim. If OSHA saw them, they would be unhappy.

(For several minutes the three men discussed the makeup of the safety committees. Because of union considerations, all were salaried personnel. They then discussed the sources of noise department by department.)

BELLOWS: Everything you say is possible, but it costs money and we aren't prepared to spend much.

GARDNER: Unfortunately, OSHA doesn't think much about costs. I have been there and I know how they feel.

CARPENTER: On the other hand, the OSHA people have got to see that $25 million is a lot of money for that operation.

BELLOWS: I am in favor of much of this ecology kick, but I also like TVs and automobiles and so forth. Someone has got to make a decision on where money is to be spent. I really don't think OSHA will be too tough if they're dealing with people who are making an honest attempt to make the plants clean and safe within their ability to do it.

GARDNER: I don't think this attitude will continue. The magic number for OSHA is now 90 decibels, and there is some talk in Washington about reducing it to 85.[1] OSHA will become tougher. They will come into the plant and test for specific noise levels, for instance, and not pay any attention to how clean the place is if that's their mission.

CARPENTER: We would really like to know what your general hearing conservation program is.

BELLOWS: I will send you a copy of our procedures for employee hearing tests. It depends on the size of the plants. In general, the large ones do the testing themselves and the smaller ones send employees to local doctors. All employees are tested when they are hired and periodically thereafter.

CARPENTER: O.K. That's part of it. Where from there?

BELLOWS: We issue earplugs, we test employees again after a period of time. We are looking for deteriorating conditions. It is a very disquieting thing to me. At the Durby plant, I can look at the tests and tell how long the employee has worked there by how his hearing has deteriorated.

CARPENTER: Do the employees have to wear them?

BELLOWS: Yes.

CARPENTER: How often can they leave them at home before they are fired?

---

[1] Decibel levels are calculated on a logarithmic scale. A reduction in the maximum allowed for sustained exposure from 90 to 85 would have a substantially greater impact on the noise level than the percentage reduction in decibels would indicate.

BELLOWS: The warning system varies, but in most cases it specifies "repetitive violations."

CARPENTER: Tell you what the Chemical Division does. The first time it's a warning, the second time the employee is docked one day, the third time it's three days, and after that he is out.

BELLOWS: My plant managers would have problems with something like that. You think I'm tough to work with, you ought to talk with some of them.

CARPENTER: You should see what we have to deal with in other divisions.

BELLOWS: I really don't think the next five years will be too bad. In the long run I agree with you, but those stamping machines may not be around that long. I don't see spending money on them. The problem may just go away.

CARPENTER: You can always change your plan or even put a probability of a change in the plans when you write them, but at least have the goal—85 decibels—and some goals for getting there. Put what it would cost to redesign the machine, but also take a look at alternatives. I don't have the answers, but that sort of program should be salable to your management and by itself it might be enough. . . . In addition to what you're doing with your plant committees, which would also be included, this program should be in the hands of the plant manager so when OSHA people come, he can tell them, "here's what we are doing."

BELLOWS: These inspectors are like other inspectors. It depends a lot on how they are handled. If you keep them waiting in a waiting room for two hours, then they won't take kindly to you. But we have got some pretty good people as plant managers. I really don't think we will have a problem. I see where we could have a tough time if we got a series of complaints and we don't show progress in between. . . . Tell you what I can do. I can sit down and dream up something which I can take to management as long as I don't spend anything on it.

CARPENTER: That would be very helpful. Who do you work for?

BELLOWS: Nelson. He is manager of engineering service, I think, though I am not sure of his title. He reports to the division manager.

CARPENTER: Well, we have a lot better feel for what's going on in the Automotive Division. People ask me how things are going in various divisions, and when I come to yours I have never had very much to say.

(After five minutes of informal discussion the meeting ended with the following comment by Bellows, speaking softly and looking at the floor.)

BELLOWS: Do you think I can last for five more years? I will be 60 in October.

After Bellows and Gardner left, Carpenter turned to the afternoon mail. In the pile was a capital request form from the Automotive Division for a $1.2 million stamping line. Carpenter indicated that he wished he had known about this project before the meeting with Bellows. A quick review of the document revealed that the new line was to be used for an important product and involved a change in technology from the existing machinery in the division. No explicit attention had been given to possible noise problems, and it would, as a result, have provided a useful vehicle for discussing the issue in concrete terms. This being a large investment for the division, Carpenter wondered why Bellows had not mentioned it.

The next morning Carpenter called in Ted Hawkins (director of environmental hygiene) and gave him the capital request with the following comment:

Ted, get on this one fast. Find out the noise levels and what, if anything they're going to do about it. If we wait until the thing is built, they'll say, "The line is already in. We can't afford to do anything about it now."

Later that day, Carpenter discussed the OSHA situation with Phillips in the context of a general review of the department's activities.

PHILLIPS: We know what the major engineering questions are with OSHA. There is stamping noise, radiant heat, vapors, and noise in areas other than stamping.

CARPENTER: We got a capital request from the Automotive Division yesterday that gets into this. It's for $1.2 million—a new stamping line.

PHILLIPS: I had heard about that. How many lines are there?

CARPENTER: I don't have the details exactly. I'm not sure whether it's new or a rebuild. Bellows didn't mention it when we talked last week.

PHILLIPS: He may not have known about it. Not very many people do— maybe only four people at corporate. It would have to be a new line.

CARPENTER: It's a good example. How do we tackle that one?

PHILLIPS: O.K. You've got to give this to someone and get it straightened out now.

CARPENTER: Another thing. Hawkins has been talking about going into a plant in the Chemical Division with some mufflers and physically shutting off all compressed air sources that are not absolutely necessary—actually taking the feeder lines out so the operator can't turn the air back on when he leaves. If it is really necessary, he'll put a muffler on it. He says he can cut the noise by 20% or more.

PHILLIPS: He's said that to me, too. I don't believe it—but let's give him a try.

CARPENTER: That would worry me . . .

PHILLIPS: No, let's do it someplace where we know the plant manager— like Richards.[2] He'll let us know if Hawkins gets in trouble so we can yank him before it gets out of hand. Let's call Richards while we're both here. [On phone] Say Pete, we have a young man—Ted Hawkins—here on our staff who's been talking about cutting noise out of plants by eliminating or muffling compressed air sources. If we send him up to you for a while, would you be willing to have him around to see what he can do?

[Richards responds in the affirmative.]

---

[2] Richards was Phillips' replacement as plant manager in the Chemical Division in Akron when the latter became vice president of operations services.

PHILLIPS [continuing]: His position demonstrates that he is a bit naive but it also reflects that he's interested in doing something. This is a good time to say "Put up or shut up." He may have something and, if so, we should take advantage of it. If it's O.K. with you, I'll let him get together with Williams [manufacturing manager at the Akron plant] and John [Carpenter] and work out a program. Then if he gets in trouble, send him home.

About three weeks later, Hawkins, accompanied by a man from the engineering staff, spent three days at Akron. He then returned and wrote a report to the plant manager, including recommendations for reducing noise. Carpenter was upset, however, when he learned that Hawkins had taken no direct action during his visit, such as disconnecting the compressed air sources, to reduce noise levels.

EXHIBIT 1
OMAR INDUSTRIES, INC.
Partial Organization Chart

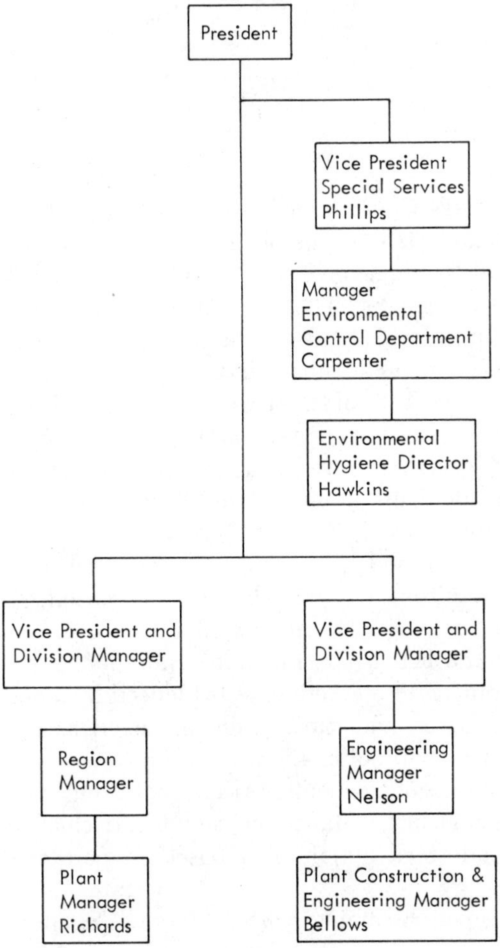

American Industries Corporation (A)

AMERICAN INDUSTRIES Corporation (AIC) was the outgrowth of a small but profitable real estate development company which had been established in 1950 by three investors, all of whom had been successful in their respective careers. The company purchased, developed, and sold properties in Florida and southern California, and by 1965 the investors had accumulated substantial retained earnings. They were, however, all over 60 years old and were anxious both to diversify their interests and to establish valuation and liquidity for estate purposes. Therefore they decided to hire an aggressive younger person as president to take the company public and use it as a base for diversification.

After a lengthy search, the trio located Justin J. Marwick, 42, a partner in a Boston-based consulting firm. Marwick had had 15 years' experience in consulting and was desirous of becoming president of a growth-oriented company. He impressed the investors on two counts: first, he had established a considerable reputation in the development of a systems approach to marketing, as evidenced by a number of articles and books; second, he had successfully managed a sizable division in the consulting firm with ultimate responsibility for a wide variety of large and complex engagements. After conferring with Marwick at length, the investors hired him as president and chief executive officer with a salary and stock option plan based in part on the company's earnings growth.

Immediately upon assuming office, Marwick changed the corpora-

tion's name to American Industries, and the real estate firm became the
Real Estate Group. Between 1965 and 1970, American Industries acquired companies in diversified fields: modular housing, mobile homes,
electronic components, and packaging. Following the acquisition of the
modular homes company in 1965, the company went public, and in 1967
its stock was listed on the New York Stock Exchange. Sales increased
from $22 million in 1965 to $216 million in 1969, and net income rose
in the same period from $1.8 million to $13.8 million, as shown in the
financial statements in Exhibits 1 and 2.

EXHIBIT 1

AMERICAN INDUSTRIES CORPORATION (A)
Sales and Income by Group, 1965–70
(in millions of dollars)

American Group	1965	1966	1967	1968	1969	Six months 1970
Real estate sales	$10.2	$10.8	$11.3	$ 12.7	$ 13.3	$ 5.8
Net income	1.0	1.6	2.2	3.0	3.5	1.4
Housing sales	12.2	36.1	61.2	79.4	101.3	56.6
Net income	0.8	2.0	2.5	6.0	8.1	3.9
Electronic sales			20.8	23.4	28.2	12.8
Net income			1.2	1.4	1.2	0.6
Packaging sales				68.4	73.3	34.0
Net income				0.9	1.0	0.2
Corporation sales	22.4	46.9	93.3	183.9	216.1	109.2
Net income	1.8	3.6	5.9	11.3	13.8	6.1
Common shares outstanding (millions)	2.1	2.5	3.1	4.0	4.0	4.0
Earnings per share	$ 0.86	$ 1.44	$ 1.90	$ 2.83	$ 3.44	$ 1.53
Stock price*						
High	$17.50	$32.25	$55.75	$ 64.50	$ 68.75	$ 41.25
Low	8.75	21.00	39.00	48.25	38.50	24.00

* AIC was first traded publicly in 1965 (over the counter) when an offering was made of 1.5 million
shares at $12. The company was listed on the New York Stock Exchange in 1967. Price on July 28, 1970,
was $25.50.
Source: Company records.

Seated behind a large desk in his walnut-paneled office in the company's New York headquarters, Marwick commented on AIC's multi-
market orientation:

We started out buying companies which complemented our real estate operations (modular housing and mobile homes) but then saw some opportunities
to breathe new life into staid old companies by rethinking the opportunities
in their markets. That's how we got into packaging. By infusing new technology in manufacturing, better management controls, and a systems-oriented
marketing concept, we will be able to improve our earnings and provide a

EXHIBIT 2

AMERICAN INDUSTRIES CORPORATION (A)
Consolidated Balance Sheets, 1969–70
(restated to include all acquisitions—in thousands of dollars)

Assets	December 31 1969	June 30 1970
Current assets		
Cash	$ 3,141	$ 2,113
Accounts receivable	12,703	13,481
Inventory	14,083	15,584
Notes and mortgages receivable	3,567	3,499
Prepaid expenses	2,308	2,100
Total current assets	$ 35,802	$ 36,777
Property, plant, and equipment	$120,932	$126,536
Less: Accumulated depreciation	(31,631)	(36,172)
Net property, plant, and equipment	$ 89,301	$ 90,364
Real estate held for investment		
Land at cost	$ 4,223	$ 5,516
Buildings and equipment	10,013	12,381
Total real estate	$ 14,236	$ 17,897
Goodwill	$ 17,254	$ 16,016
Other assets	1,713	2,016
Total assets	$158,306	$163,070

Liabilities and Equity	December 31 1969	June 30 1970
Current liabilities		
Accounts payable and accruals	$ 22,767	$ 21,989
Long-term debt current portion	5,339	3,716
Taxes payable	2,305	2,418
Total current liabilities	$ 30,411	$ 28,123
Long-term debt less current	$ 45,525	$ 47,724
Deferred income taxes	2,333	1,749
Total noncurrent items	$ 47,858	$ 49,473
Equity		
Preferred stock, $100 par	$ 4,000	$ 4,000
Common stock, $1 par	4,003	4,003
Capital surplus	30,167	30,167
Retained earnings	41,867	47,304
Total equity	$ 80,037	$ 85,474
Total liabilities and equity	$158,306	$163,070

Source: Company records.

stable base for future growth. I have a "think tank" of staff consultants who are searching for companies or industries offering these kinds of opportunities.

. . . older companies are typically overstaffed and unsystematic in their approach to problems. To correct this, we're putting emphasis on two things: (1) decentralization of responsibilities and (2) the application, wherever possible, of advanced techniques for decision making and communication. We are already developing a system new to land development, integrating the efforts of our Real Estate and Housing Groups.

In February 1970 Marwick realigned the corporate-level organization. Brian Flint, 46, a former group vice president of a large container company, was hired as chief operating officer and given overall responsibility for existing businesses, thus permitting Marwick to devote more time to the search for additional growth opportunities and the management of AIC's external affairs. The 18-member corporate staff was divided between the two men: planning and finance remained with the president and systems development and personnel were assigned to Flint. An organization chart is shown in Exhibit 3.

EXHIBIT 3

AMERICAN INDUSTRIES CORPORATION (A)
Organization Chart—July 1970

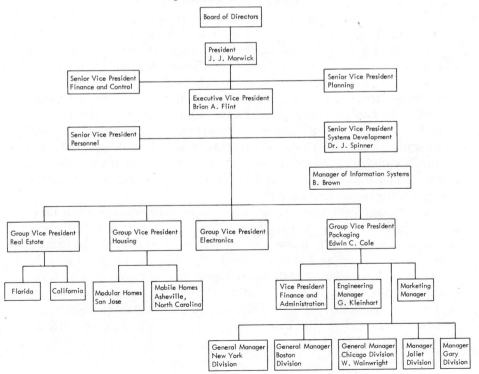

THE PACKAGING GROUP

One acquisition opportunity that had come to Marwick's attention in the fall of 1968 was Eastern Packaging, a leading independent producer of corrugated and folding (cardboard) cartons. Eastern Packaging had been incorporated in 1927 by a Chicago entrepreneur who had later acquired companies with similar facilities in New York and Boston. The home office, however, had remained in the original Chicago plant.

The founder's sales abilities were complemented by the skills of William Wainwright, an engineer and 1942 business school graduate who had joined the Chicago operation immediately after completing his education and had become vice president of manufacturing in 1950. Under Wainwright's leadership, the Chicago plant had become a technological innovator. Wainwright had adapted web-offset printing techniques to paperboard manufacturing and had invented a rotary die cutter which greatly speeded up the manufacturing time for die-cut corrugated boxes and innerpacking. In addition, he had designed custom machinery for forming, filling, and closing folding cartons, an innovation that had gained wide acceptance among food processing companies which required packaging equipment to complement their food processing lines. Eastern Packaging's success as an independent packager was in no small measure due to the technology introduced by Wainwright.

In 1965 the founder had turned the reins over to his son. Between 1965 and 1968 the company's sales had increased from $51 million to $64 million but profits had steadily declined from $1.8 million to $600,000 during that same period. Then, in the fall of 1968, a Chicago investment banker who was familiar with the Eastern Packaging situation contacted Marwick. After investigating the packaging firm and concluding that it fit his concept for AIC and had substantial untapped earnings potential, Marwick negotiated a merger for $26.5 million in AIC common stock. The founder's son agreed to withdraw from the company following the acquisition.

In October 1968, two months before the acquisition of Eastern Packaging had been formally completed, Marwick began looking for a general manager to head up the organization, which was to be the foundation for the American Industries Packaging Group. Through a friend, he located Edwin Cole, 44, then marketing vice president for a major packaging company where he had been employed for 20 years, having started as a salesman in 1948. The plaque on the wall of Cole's office at AIC reflected, in the casewriter's view, Cole's attitude toward his job and his employers.

Loyalty

If you work for a man, in heaven's name work for him, speak well of him, and stand by the institution he represents. Remember, an ounce of loyalty is worth a pound of cleverness. As long as you are part of an institution, do not condemn it.

Soon after joining AIC, Cole discovered that the Eastern Packaging plants had been subjected to strong, centralized management in Chicago. The founder had personally controlled the company's sales force and had established cost centers in his manufacturing plants. Hence, plant managers were primarily responsible for cost-effective production and had little to do with pricing decisions. In December 1968, Cole decided to unify responsibility for sales and production at the plant level, thus creating three divisions. He commented that this change had been made to increase profit consciousness at lower levels in the organization and to promote greater adaptability to customer needs, which he considered an essential part of his plans for a thrust into specialty packaging. Other than a small national accounts sales force,[1] a staff engineer, and a three-member finance/planning department, all functions and personnel were reassigned to the divisions. Two of the new division managers, one of whom was Wainwright, were long-service managers with Eastern Packaging; the third had been hired in January 1969 from another packaging company.

While Marwick was completing the deal with Eastern Packaging, he and Cole began searching for further acquisition prospects to round out what Marwick was coming to see as a major opportunity for AIC. He commented:

Although packaging isn't considered one of the great growth industries, it's a classic opportunity to apply new technology and service-oriented marketing to a business that has become obsessed with high-volume, low-cost commodity products. Take the case of Marcor (Montgomery Ward and Container Corporation), for example. Packaging and retailing go hand in hand, and the more that a packager can assist the customer in marketing his product, the better his margins will be. For years, the industry has sold on the basis of price, and there are few firms with the ingenuity to innovate in marketing.

. . . In addition, to be effective in this industry we have to understand the marketing problem of our customers, and that, in turn, leads to a whole host of opportunities. Beyond integrating across packaging mediums—plastics, paper, aerosols—we can develop graphics and other related fields. We will have to be innovators, able to turn on a dime, and able to take advantage of specialty markets effectively.

---

[1] National accounts represented about 30% of group sales. In many instances, however, the accounts were themselves geographically dispersed and contracted directly with the plants.

A short time later, Cole located two small but profitable packagers, E-Z Pack, a manufacturer of corrugated specialty products and styrofoam innerpacking, and Illini Bag, a producer of plastic and foil-lined paper bags. After conferring with the owners of the two small companies, Cole introduced them to Marwick, who was immediately interested in having the firms join American's Packaging Group. Marwick subsequently offered the two owners AIC common stock in exchange for their companies. Both accepted and agreed in the process to continue as division managers with AIC.

The packaging group strategy

Cole outlined the long-range goals he and Marwick had established for the Packaging Group when Cole had joined AIC in 1968:

First, we wanted to identify profitable market segments in paper packaging which would grow at a 12% compound rate in the 1970s in line with Justin's goals for AIC as a corporation. Second, we wanted to generate profit before taxes of 11% of sales. Finally, we wanted to find some way of becoming an integrated producer of paperboard without getting into the economies of scale problems that plague the big companies. We could see that the independent producers were getting squeezed by companies which produced their own paperboard, especially the board for folding cardboard cartons.

In October 1968, the first thing I did was to have some of Justin's former consulting associates do a marketing study on growth rates and trends in the folding carton segment of the industry, since we were pretty sure we'd be acquiring some companies in paper packaging. They told us that the most promising product areas were in composite packaging, utilizing plastics. The profitable market segments in folding cartons would be cosmetics, hardware, medical products, and users of multicolored specialty cartons with eye appeal.

We were already doing some selling in those niches of the folding carton market, so we knew we had the right markets if only we could concentrate our efforts.

We were already strong in corrugated markets, so we focused our efforts on folding cartons. In order to capture a larger share of those markets, we felt we needed two things: better technology and marketing techniques. We took a look at the industry environment and then bet our chips.

In January 1969, Marwick met with Cole and the Packaging Group's division managers to discuss plans for penetrating the folding carton market. Cole referred to the consultant's report and recommended that his group initiate a search for a new machinery design that would enable the Packaging Group to increase its folding carton sales by combining lower costs, increased flexibility, and high quality.

Wainwright, general manager of the Chicago division, was assigned to head a task force to undertake this search. Utilizing two senior managers within his division, Wainwright contacted several domestic and foreign machinery manufacturers to design a new machinery configuration which would give the Packaging Group a competitive advantage. In May 1969, after four months of intensive effort, Wainwright presented his recommendations for "the ultimate in folding carton machinery" to Cole, who then conferred with Marwick. The proposed machines would permit AIC to apply low-cost yet versatile processing techniques to the manufacture of specialty packaging products. The result would hopefully enable the company to make substantial inroads in markets that offered relatively higher margins.

The new machines, called "PFP" because of their capability of producing composite paper, foil, and plastic folding cartons, combined the papermaking process with conversion and finishing operations, all in a long series of interconnected operations which speeded up the manufacturing process and reduced labor and handling costs. In addition, despite their size (100 feet long) the machines could be set up rapidly, allowing flexibility for shorter runs of 160,000 cartons. The entire operation could be run by 16 workers per shift. Commenting on the economic aspects of the PFPs, Cole said he believed that the two units could average a total of $16 million in sales and $3.2 million in earnings before interest and taxes annually over a 10-year investment horizon (see Exhibit 4 for the pro forma figures on the PFPs).

Shortly after the recommendation had been submitted, Marwick and Cole signed a contract with the Lugen Corporation of Philadelphia to develop two machines, costing $8 million apiece, which were originally slated for installation at the New York and Chicago divisions. An additional $2 million for plant expansion at the two locations brought the total investment to $18 million.

The PFP decision: A view from Chicago

Wainwright recounted the developments preceding the decision to purchase the machines:

In December 1968, when Justin Marwick decided to purchase Eastern Packaging, he came to me and said, "Will, we're new teammates now. How do you feel about the Packaging Group's growth prospects?" I replied, "Justin, tell us how far and how fast to go."

Justin wanted us to become fully integrated and double our sales in five years. At our historical growth rate, we would have taken a hell of a lot longer than that. To meet Justin's objective, we had to make a major push forward. We couldn't be a "me-too" company. We had to innovate.

After Ed Cole got a consultant's study on prospects in paper packaging, he came to me and said, "Will, here's where the market growth is: now what kind of machinery can we build to compete in these segments?"

I worked with my managers of engineering development and manufacturing

EXHIBIT 4

AMERICAN INDUSTRIES CORPORATION (A)
Pro Forma Estimates on the PFP Program
March 11, 1969

Assumptions
1. *Machines running at* 90% of capacity around the clock
   (90% capacity = 100% efficiency)
2. Average yearly sales per machine: $8 million over a 10-year period
   (includes inflation adjustment of 3% per year in sales)
3. Straight-line depreciation: 10-year life
4. Interest rate: 8.5% on average debt of $9 million

Income statement (total for 10 years, in thousands)

Sales		$160,000
Cost of sales		112,000
Gross margin		$ 48,000
General and administrative	$ 9,600	
Selling	6,400	16,000
Earnings before interest and taxes (E.B.I.T.)		$ 32,000
Interest @ 8.5% × $9,000 (average debt)		7,650
Earnings before taxes		$ 24,350
Taxes @ 50%	$12,175	
Add: Investment tax credit 7% × $18,000	(1,260)	
Net taxes		10,915
Earnings after taxes		$ 13,435
Average earnings after taxes (E.A.T.)		$ 1,344

Return on investment

$$\text{Average investment:} \quad \frac{\$18,000}{2} = \$ 9,000$$

Average working capital	2,400
Average total investment	$11,400

$$\frac{\text{Average E.B.I.T.}}{\text{Average total investment}} = \frac{\$ 3,200}{\$11,400} = 28.2\%$$

$$\frac{\text{Average E.A.T.}}{\text{Average total investment}} = \frac{\$ 1,344}{\$11,400} = 11.8\%$$

Source: Company records.

in looking at various machinery designs. We needed faster machinery which could give us a cost advantage and allow us flexibility in scheduling.

The manager of engineering development explained why Chicago had acquired two machines:

Ed Cole was so enthused about the PFPs that he wanted to order three—one for each of our divisions. His marketing staff had been working on determining how much volume we could land if we had the machines.

When the contract for two machines was signed in May 1969, it was intended that New York and Chicago would each get one. The ink on the contract had barely dried when the people at the New York plant discovered that they didn't have as much business as they thought they'd have. So Will Wainwright offered to take the second PFP, since the market here in Chicago has more growth potential than either Boston or New York.

Another senior manager added a further dimension to the rationale behind the PFP decision:

Actually, none of the processes we've incorporated into the PFP are entirely new, but the combination of capabilities is unique. Will Wainwright was aware of the problems that manufacturers had with paper machinery, and he took his manufacturing manager around with him to talk with domestic and foreign manufacturers. None of the existing equipment on the market had all the features we wanted. So we worked with the Lugen people to develop a special generation of PFP machines.

Getting the PFPs underway

A new addition to the plant specifically designed for the PFPs had been constructed. Crews, made up mostly of senior employees, were carefully selected from the best employees in the division. Extensive training was then conducted. The manager of engineering development wrote training manuals for the machines, and the crews were flown to Lugen's plant in Philadelphia for training on the machines. At the end of the training session in November, each participant received a diploma. To assist Wainwright in getting the new equipment running properly, Cole transferred his staff engineer, Charles Mack, to Chicago in January 1970.[2] Cole anticipated that Mack would remain in Chicago after the machines were fully on line to devise process-control systems that would better integrate production capabilities with market needs.

Wainwright had estimated that six months would be required to get the machines running at 100% efficiency. Since paper machines were never run before they were installed in a customer's plant, time always had to be allocated to "de-bugging" mechanical problems and getting the crews accustomed to the peculiarities of a new machine. Management felt that the superior design of the equipment, coupled with the crew training program, would shorten the traditional 12 months' start-up time.

The first PFP was installed by mid-December 1969. Morale was high as the crew, outfitted in special uniforms, began cranking up the giant machine. Hopes for an easy start-up period soon had to be abandoned, however. Wainwright related some of the problems which occurred during the early months:

It was a mechanical can of worms. Normally, you figure on spending 80% of your start-up time on operating problems and 20% on de-bugging design faults of the manufacturer. The design was a can of worms, however, and we spent 80% to 90% of our time on Lugen's problems. The ink fountains on our

---

[2] Mack's position on the group staff was filled the following month by George Kleinhart, 37, a former manufacturing executive with an automotive company. An engineer by training, Kleinhart had interpreted his role, with the encouragement of Cole and Flint, to include troubleshooting in the operations area.

eight-color rotogravure unit didn't work properly. Bearings in our foil unit burned out every five weeks right on schedule. All the water fountains were made of carbon steel which rusted, and we had to have all new stainless steel fountains installed. Gauges didn't register properly. There were problems in every major assembly of these machines. You've heard of Murphy's Law: "If something can go wrong, it will go wrong"? That has been our experience.

The manager of manufacturing at the Chicago plant summed up the problem this way:

There's still some magic in running a paper machine. By that I mean that the crews have to get a "feel" for the thing. We've solved many of the mechanical problems with parts, but the crews haven't learned to cope with all the technical aspects of the PFPs. They set up a machine the same way to run a particular job. One time it works, and the next time around the paperboard breaks.

Wainwright outlined his own plan of attack on the problem of the PFPs:

My personal target for getting the machines operating at standard is April 1971. It's a nagging problem, but here's what I've done. First, I got an inventory of problems from everyone connected with the PFPs. I classified the inventory according to the type of problem and assigned a priority to various classes of problems. Second, I've assigned a task force of high-level people to work on each problem. I don't want our lower level line people interrupted because they have enough problems with manning and morale. Finally, I've assigned a time frame for solving each problem.

. . . We've had so much trouble getting either one of these monsters running right . . . I've decided to shut down one of them completely while we concentrate on solving the basic problems.

The Chicago manufacturing manager was optimistic about the progress made on the machines by his team:

We've solved many design problems, and we're working on the mechanical problems. Our raw materials suppliers are working on special chemicals, foil, plastic compounds, and inks, and we've made some headway in getting a combination of stuff which will run through the machines. When you're living with these machines day and night, as I am, you can see progress, even though as yet we cannot know whether the equipment will produce according to design specifications. Hopefully, within the next six months or so we will be able to make this determination and begin to work like a team.

Meanwhile, both machines remained well below scheduled output and Chicago was incurring heavy losses ($300,000 before taxes in June alone). As a result of the Chicago division's problems, estimated profits for the entire group were down 64% for the six months ending June 30, 1970, as compared with the same period in 1969. (See Exhibit 5 for the income statements of the Packaging Group and the Chicago division.)

EXHIBIT 5

AMERICAN INDUSTRIES CORPORATION (A)
Statement of Income, 1967–70
Packaging Group and Chicago Division
(in thousands of dollars)

	Packaging Group Six months		*Year ending December 31*		
	1969	*1970*	*1967*	*1968*	*1969*
Sales	$36,720	$39,431	$62,305	$68,430	$73,341
Cost of sales	28,870	32,519	48,505	54,590	58,239
Gross profit	$ 7,850	$ 6,912	$13,800	$13,840	$15,102
Selling, general, and administrative	6,480	6,423	11,280	11,910	13,001
Income before taxes	$ 1,370	$ 489	$ 2,520	$ 1,930	$ 2,101
Depreciation	2,407	2,613	3,413	3,728	4,813
	Chicago Division				
Sales	$15,548	$16,234	$22,407	$25,434	$30,023
Cost of sales	12,530	14,621	18,327	20,918	24,101
Gross profit	$ 3,018	$ 1,613	$ 4,080	$ 4,516	$ 5,922
Selling, general, and administrative	2,608	2,647	3,478	4,096	5,087
Income before taxes	$ 410	($ 1,034)	$ 602	$ 420	$ 835
Depreciation	1,431	1,570	1,651	1,703	2,881

Source: Company records.

A major concern related to the PFPs was the possibility of losing customers. Cole commented:

With all the problems we've been having, it's a miracle that our customers have stayed with us. Fortunately, we've had some spectacular results on some items, and the hope that the PFPs have offered has kept our customers with us. I don't know how long we can keep them if we don't start developing consistency in our operations.

In reviewing the $18 million outlay for the PFP machines and related equipment, Cole told the casewriter:

Justin [Marwick] has been trumpeting about our new technology and systems approach. Everybody from the American Paper Institute to the guys on the Street [Wall Street] have heard our story. If our PFPs run right, we'll have our competition flat. If we fail, all the old-timers in the trade will get a good laugh.

. . . As far as the Packaging Group is concerned, the PFPs are the nucleus of our expansion efforts. AIC has spent $33 million (in stock) on acquisitions and has plunked $18 million into the PFP program. If we don't produce profits, the corporation will find other places to invest its money. Right now, the Housing Group is screaming for capital.

American Industries Corporation (B)

COMPUTERIZED INSTRUMENTATION PROJECT

In July 1969, two months after the contract for the PFPs had been signed with Lugen, Jeremy Spinner, corporate vice president for systems development, and Charles Mack, staff engineer for Cole, had discussed the idea of making technical advances on the machines which were then under construction. Dr. Spinner, 39, was a highly respected consultant on systems theory and computer technology and a former associate of Marwick's who had joined AIC in 1968. Charles Mack, 42, had had 20 years' experience in the paper industry, most recently in the area of process controls with a major paper company.

The technical advance worked out between Spinner and Mack involved a system of computerized process controls which would virtually enable the PFP machines to run themselves and would certainly reduce the possibility of human error in controlling operations. As a first step toward this instrumentation program, Spinner had recommended a computerized monitoring program. He described the rationale behind this proposal as follows:

We both agreed that it would lead to closed-loop process control but that in the short run instrumentation could help us in getting the machines running at standard efficiency. Rather than ask for money to fund research for the entire closed-loop system, we decided to ask for just enough to solve the short-run problem.

Spinner described the circumstances immediately preceding the dispatch of the $280,000 capital expenditure request (CER) for the instrumentation project:

. . . There was some provision in our contract with Lugen about instrumentation, as we began working immediately on a project which would involve both Lugen and AIC on a joint basis. Shortly after the first PFP was installed in November, we had a proposal ready to go. Lugen liked the idea. Around the first of December, we drafted a CER for our half of the project, and Ed Cole wrote a covering letter and sent the CER to Will Wainwright in Chicago. We planned on having the system installed and running by April 1970, but the CER sat on Will's desk.

Since it was American Industries' policy to have division managers take responsibility for capital expenditure requests, Wainwright's inaction on the CER could not be overruled by Cole if corporate precedent was to be preserved. It was in this context that Spinner in June 1970, again with Cole's concurrence, decided to send Bentley Brown to Chicago. Brown, who had just graduated from business school as one of the top members of his class, had been appointed corporate manager of information systems and reported to Spinner. Brown's first assignment was to visit Chicago to determine the status of the project and, if possible, persuade Wainwright to sign the CER. After his visit, Brown wrote the following memorandum:

Date: July 24, 1970

TO: J. R. Spinner
FROM: Bentley Brown
CC TO: B. A. Flint
          E. C. Cole
          C. E. Mack

SUBJECT: Trip to Chicago, July 20–21, 1970
The object of this visit was to see if the Chicago division could be persuaded to take the initiative to insure successful installation of the PFP instrumentation project.
In summary, I believe the visit was a success. All affected people had a chance to talk with each other and arrive at a set of common goals as well as an understanding of the mechanical aspects of the problem.
From this meeting came an informal understanding (to be confirmed on Friday, July 29) that John Smith would be appointed Project Director. Because John has a 10-hour-a-day job making the PFP machine work, he will have an assistant.

Present Status of Project
1. The CER has been rewritten [see Exhibit 1] based not on potential savings but on "Research and Development." The CER has not, however, been signed.

2. Chicago's operating and technical people are devoting maximum effort to getting the PFPs off the ground. They still have many problems, such as high paper waste, low productivity, many web breaks, and shipping schedules. As a result, they are not ready to proceed with instrumentation right away.
3. Many Chicago people are asking embarrassing questions about the spelling out of responsibilities between Lugen and American Industries: "Where is the written contract?"

Summary

I believe that all people involved in the successful use of the PFP equipment realize the need to take the initiative. This does not mean that there will not be frustrating delays, because everyone at Chicago feels that the project must take second place to getting the PFP equipment running. Until this happens, it will be hard to get people's attention. At least now there is an understanding of the needs of the project and a realization of the work that needs to be done, as well as a skeletal mechanism for carrying out the work.

Bentley Brown's memorandum, however, resulted in an immediate reply from Will Wainwright:

MEMORANDUM

Date: July 26, 1970

TO: Bentley Brown (New York)
FROM: William I. Wainwright
CC TO: Ed Cole (New York)
           Jeremy Spinner (New York)
           Charles Mack
           Brian Flint (New York)

SUBJECT: PFP Instrumentation

Bentley, I am sorry that your memorandum of July 24, 1970, gives a premature and erroneous picture of what we plan to do with the PFP instrumentation project.

Chicago has no plan of action and no skeletal mechanism for carrying out the work.

The fact of the matter is that no one in Chicago has sufficient knowledge of the equipment involved, the original objectives of the program, or the potential short-term payback to make an intelligent plan of action. The instrumentation project was designed primarily by Jeremy Spinner and Charlie Mack in New York in conjunction with Lugen research engineers. Their specific plans for the use of the equipment are shrouded in mystery and are not clearly set forth in the ream of correspondence which has flown to and from Chicago.

Before we can decide what approach we will take to this program, we must have a meeting with Lugen in which Spinner, Mack, and you participate. This meeting is tentatively set up for July 31 in Philadelphia. Perhaps by that time you will have located the contract which spells out our specific responsibilities in regard to instrumentation.

Again, let me emphasize that no one here in Chicago has sufficient facts to set up an intelligent program on this project, and that there is very obviously a difference in viewpoint between what we originally intended to do and what it now appears we must do from the short-term payback standpoint.

In future, it would be a help if you would clear with me before you make judgments on the status of affairs here in Chicago.

The hour of decision

The deadlock on the instrumentation project left Cole feeling uneasy. The six months' start-up period had already elapsed, but Chicago's income statement continued to deteriorate, pulling down with it the overall corporate performance. There seemed to be little agreement between the corporate staff and the Chicago division over the instrumentation issue.

Spinner and his associates had provided no assurance that instrumentation would reduce losses. However, they argued that the $280,000 needed for the first year of the project was less than Chicago's losses for one month. With instrumentation, data recorded from the sensors could be reconstructed chronologically after a breakdown had occurred. Then a "replay" of the machine's performance prior to the breakdown could be made to determine any unusual tension on a certain component of the PFP. In this way, according to Spinner, the problem areas could be isolated.

Wainwright and other members of his Chicago management team had unequivocally stated that progress was being made in eliminating difficulties; after all, he had been the principal architect of the PFP program. He claimed now that both machines would be operating at standard by April 1971 and would pass the break-even point by the end of 1970. With steady improvement expected on the machines, he maintained that profits for the Chicago division as a whole would reappear in October. Cole recalled, however, that during their last conversation the previous week Wainwright had indicated that the market prices negotiated thus far by the Chicago sales force for work done on the machines had been running "somewhat lower" than the prices included in the PFP capital request.[1]

Cole was scheduled for a monthly progress review meeting with Brian Flint on the following day. Shortly after coming to AIC, Flint had asked each group vice president to prepare a list of "key events" for the remainder of the year. In his words, these were "tracking elements of a

[1] Orders from companies in the Chicago area had been accepted but in only limited quantities until production could be assured.

group's short-range plans which are usually reflected in accounting numbers at some future time." The instrumentation project had been at the top of Cole's list. Cole had not remembered his last two monthly review sessions for their levity, and he was not relishing the one coming up. He wondered how his division managers would feel if they were in his shoes. He picked up Bentley Brown's memorandum and tried again to figure out what it meant.

EXHIBIT 1

AMERICAN INDUSTRIES CORPORATION (B)
Capital Expenditure Request
PFP Instrumentation Project

July 21, 1970*

PROPOSAL: Instrument one PFP machine at Chicago as a joint research and development study between the Packaging Group, AIC, and the Lugen Corporation. The installation will cost $200,000 and will involve a yearly expense of $80,000. Lugen to be responsible for developing programming for the study at a cost of $200,000.

OBJECTIVES: The primary objective is to improve operation of the PFP machine and to develop principles influencing computerized process control. Data will be collected from sensors installed on the machine and will be recorded on magnetic tape for short- and long-run data reduction.

ANALYSIS: No savings are predicted for this project, as we do not know what we may discover or what we will do with the information. It is safe to assume that, when we go from our present crude data gathering system to the sophisticated installation inherent in this project, there will be important information generated and, hopefully, principles uncovered which will be of immediate operating assistance as well as for long-run computerized process control.

INVESTMENT:

Transducers	$110,000
Brackets, cables, etc.	20,000
Data reduction equipment	30,000
Installation	30,000
Computer equipment room	10,000
	$200,000

Expenses (per year)

Computer rental	$ 50,000
Additional personnel	25,000
Supplies	5,000
	$ 80,000

AUTHORIZED SIGNATURE:

William I. Wainwright, General Manager
Packaging Group—Chicago Division

* Amended version, prepared by Bentley Brown, manager of information systems on the corporate staff in New York, and the management of the Chicago division.

American Industries Corporation (C)

In EARLY AUGUST 1970, Bud Sharpe, recently hired as operations manager for the Packaging Group's Chicago division, was wondering what he should do about the $280,000 PFP instrumentation capital expenditure request (CER) which his boss had just tossed on his desk (see Exhibit 1 of the "B" case). Computer monitoring, Sharpe knew, was a proposal which AIC's corporate executives believed would solve machine start-up problems in the short run while paving the way for a new system of semi-automatic process control later. Sharpe's boss, Will Wainwright, general manager of the Chicago division, was no less interested than headquarters in solving the technical problems of the machines, but he was extremely busy working on them in his own way with the same long-standing members of his management team who had assisted him in the initial PFP decision. It was partly for this reason that Wainwright had asked Sharpe to make a decision on the CER which had been prepared the previous December. Headquarters was now becoming insistent on an answer.

When he had asked Sharpe to study the issue of signing or not signing the CER, Wainwright had indicated that Chicago would go ahead if Sharpe decided the project was feasible. Sharpe knew that Wainwright was not convinced of the project's necessity and that Chicago executives believed that if accepted the project should not be at Chicago's expense since it was the "brainchild of the corporate staff."

Still another related issue for Sharpe to consider was the part which the machine manufacturer, Lugen Corporation, should play. Hoping to

779

draw on a broad market for the new generation of PFP machines, Lugen had agreed to develop software at its own expense. Sharpe believed, however, that Lugen might be willing to allow the Packaging Group to purchase the software because of the unexpectedly heavy costs Lugen had already incurred in replacing malfunctioning parts on the machines after they had been installed in Chicago. The advantage of buying the software package would be that the information related to the performance of the machines would become proprietary. The chief disadvantage would be that the Packaging Group would incur the total cost of the instrumentation package itself instead of dividing the risk. Sharpe knew that a recommendation to buy Lugen's software package could easily increase the total cost of the project by $200,000.

As he rearranged the papers on his desk, placing the CER to one side, Sharpe glanced at his watch and noted that it was already 6 P.M. Working late was not unusual for him since his arrival in Chicago the previous month. Taking out a yellow pad and pencil, he began to mull over the considerations he should weigh in making a decision on the instrumentation project.

Sharpe, 33, was one of the three persons reporting to Wainwright (see Exhibits 1 and 2). He had obtained an MBA from Seton Hall evening school while working for a large container company. After successfully managing plants in Pittsburgh and Chicago, he had been recruited by Brian Flint, corporate executive vice president of AIC, who had formerly been an executive of the same container company. Wainwright commented on Sharpe's appointment:

> Early this year [1970] when we decided to move Max Dooley from operations manager to controller, my first choice for operations manager was an older and more seasoned manager. Brian Flint asked me, "But can your first choice sprint?" Bud Sharpe was Brian Flint's first choice, so I abdicated my position on the older man. The theory was that Bud would take over here in 60 days, and I would be utilized somewhere else in the Packaging Group. Because of Bud's lack of experience, I stayed on to see that the PFPs would get into operation efficiently.

THE CHICAGO DIVISION

In 1969 the Chicago division had $30 million in sales, $16 million from corrugated shipping containers and $14 million from folding cartons. (See Exhibit 5 of the "A" case for financial data.) The division had 1,000 employees, many of whom had been with the division for several years, although a substantial number of younger men and women had been hired since 1965. The director of manufacturing was responsible for 750 hourly employees who belonged to six different unions, each with a separate contract. The division purchased wood pulp for

EXHIBIT 1

AMERICAN INDUSTRIES CORPORATION (C)
Organization of the Packaging Group Chicago Division
August 1970

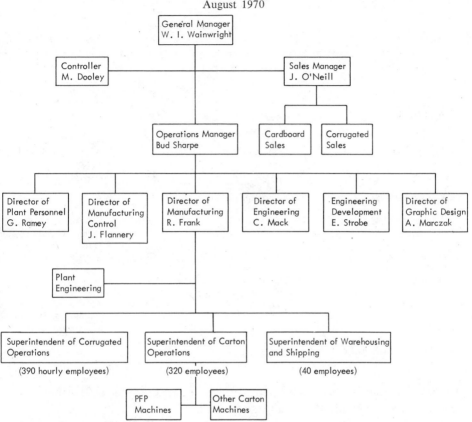

Source: Company Records.

making folding cartons from several large fully integrated paper manufacturers, some of whom were competitors of the division. The pulp was
then converted into finished products which were shipped to customers
by rail or truck. The plant operated around the clock seven days a week.

Among the division's folding carton customers were large consumer-
products manufacturing companies, including Coca Cola, Beatrice Foods,
Parke-Davis, Bristol-Myers, and Heublein. Sales efforts for these customers were coordinated through the national accounts sales force in
New York. The division's own 20-man sales force operated in the field
within a 300-mile radius of Chicago (dictated by transportation economics) and remained in contact with manufacturing control personnel
who would, in turn, consult with manufacturing concerning machine
requirements and scheduling of orders. The director of manufacturing

EXHIBIT 2

AMERICAN INDUSTRIES CORPORATION (C)
Background Information on Chicago Management

Manager	Age	Position	Years with Chicago	Experience before joining
William I. Wainwright	55	General Manager	28	M.B.A.
Bud Sharpe	33	Operations Manager	1 month	M.B.A., general manager f a large container corporation.
Max Dooley	41	Controller	19	B.A., was operations manager for one year pri to Sharpe's arrival.
Jack O'Neill	36	Sales Manager	1	B.A., sales manager for another paper company
Art Marczak	40	Director of Graphic Design	19	B.A.
Gordon Ramey	50	Director of Plant Personnel	25	B.A.
Charles Mack	45	Director of Engineering	6 months	B.S., worked on Edwin Cole's staff until January 1970
Emory Strobe	55	Development Engineering	28	B.S.
Richard Frank	45	Director of Manufacturing	21	M.B.A.
John Flannery	34	Director of Manufacturing Control	6 months	B.A., sales service for another paper company, worked for Jack O'Neill

Source: Company Records.

control explained the department's function and the interrelationship of the various elements at the Chicago division:

Because we do the scheduling, we have to coordinate with the graphic designers, then with manufacturing, and finally with our suppliers of wood pulp, ink, and printing plates. We write up the specs for the plant and also handle customers every day, so the customers call us if they have problems. We have to be on top of everything, it seems, and I can tell you that teamwork is vital to our business.

Reactions to the instrumentation project

Will Wainwright commented:

Lugen has an obligation to do something for us in the way of instrumentation. This project was initiated by Jeremy Spinner and Charlie Mack and dumped in our lap. Our corporate "space-agers" think that we'll be able to have closed-loop process control by 1973, but a whole lot has to be done before then. I'd say we're 10 years away from closed-loop process control.

. . . Somehow New York assumed that everything was all set up and ready to go on this instrumentation project. It wasn't. We don't have the staff to handle this thing. Secondly, we don't have any idea how to implement it.

Richard Frank, director of manufacturing:

A lot depends on timing. Right now is not the time. I can't afford to shut down a machine for three or four days and let them hook up computer terminals. I have to solve the problem my own way . . . today.

The manager of information processing:

The operations people have to be shown that something really works. The reactions to computers range from extremely negative to bare toleration. We're putting a computer terminal in all foremen's offices throughout the plant . . . bringing the computer to them. If we can convince them that the computer can help, it'll be a lot easier for them to accept something like the instrumentation project in the PFP area of the plant.

Morale in Chicago, July 1970

Opinions on morale varied among younger and older managers. Some younger managers commented:

. . . The crews are highly motivated. In view of all these problems, they've blamed Lugen.

. . . We're going it alone. We have no specialists to turn to. We're it.

. . . There is a little more esprit de crops in the PFP area, and we're noticing a change in attitude among the crew.

. . . Any company which gets hooked onto a conglomerate is bound to have some people problems. Eventually, the people here will adjust to a less personal atmosphere.

Some of the older managers expressed their views:

. . . Morale is inversely proportional to the introduction of business school techniques. We're no longer a group of good buddies. We don't have a feeling for the top guy, Marwick. In the old days, the workers could communicate with the president. Today, we have several layers of management between those guys and the president. We never see Marwick or Cole around here. This may be a necessity, but it doesn't help morale.

. . . My understanding is that Justin Marwick and his team are trying to pattern American Industries after Boise Cascade. They're hiring a lot of business school types. The company's becoming a machine.

. . . One of my friends, a 15-year veteran here at Chicago, was cut from the payroll because corporate headquarters wanted us to cut overhead expenses 10%. Who'll get the axe next? Will Wainwright?

Reactions to Bud Sharpe

Rich Frank (manufacturing):

We felt that a person like Bud would be brought in. We knew paper but were searching for a man with a different approach to general management. If Bud had come in here and told me how to run the manufacturing end of the plant, it would have been gangbusters. People in the paper business, and I'm sure one of them, I guess, are a close-knit lot, and they view outsiders with suspicion. Bud was smart enough to sit back and see how we ran the show from a technical point of view.

The personnel director:

He [Sharpe] gained the respect of foremen by showing interest in them and keeping them informed. Bud spends time in the shop, and he even came in some evenings.

Max Dooley (controller):

He doesn't get into manufacturing too deeply. He likes to set procedures and make organizational changes. He's rational and doesn't pound the table.

Some comments from Sharpe

In a luncheon conversation with the casewriter, Sharpe commented on his role as operations manager:

You have to realize that there's no formula which applies to every situation. When you're the quarterback, you look at both sides of your line, your back-field, and those guys across the line. I rely heavily on the strata below me and also on my peers. I spend time in the plant after work reading reports and ask, "Is it happening?" I depend on measurement systems, and I look especially at controllable changes.

. . . I'm a realist. Sometimes I think there's too much business school-type planning back there in New York. They attempt to plug figures into a set format instead of asking what is realistically possible.

. . . Motivation is based on mutual respect, trust, and a common goal. People don't have to like you personally. I'm not running a popularity contest. A general manager is like an admiral in combat. The sailors may hate your guts, but they're glad to have the "old man" up there on the bridge.

Chicago looks at New York

The following are selected comments made by seasoned managers in the Chicago division:

. . . Out there they're concerned about the stock price because they want to make more acquisitions. Justin Marwick is a tremendously motivated guy, and his track record so far is up, up, up. He's always been on a winning team, and it's a bitter pill for him to swallow when he can't achieve his goals.

. . . They've taken our feedback and have used their leverage to help the situation. For example, they've put pressure on Lugen to help us.

. . . They're extremely nervous. They're wondering how long it will take to turn these machines around profitwise. We thought this instrumentation project was long-range R & D, but since March [1970] they've acted like it's the cure-all to the immediate problem.

To sign or not to sign

Sharpe glanced again at his wristwatch and noted that it was already seven o'clock. He had scribbled two pages full of notes. It seemed to him that his problem was not just a matter of signing or not signing the CER. First of all, was he responsible for the PFP instrumentation project? Was anyone in the Chicago division? Secondly, even if he decided that Chicago was responsible for the project, should they have to pay for it?

Sharpe sketched out a decision tree with three branches. Under alternative one, he could disclaim responsibility, refuse to sign the CER, and send it back to Cole via Mack, who reviewed all CERs before they were sent to Cole. Alternative number two would be to acknowledge responsibility but refuse to pay (i.e., refuse to sign). Under alternative three, Sharpe would acknowledge responsibility and agree that Chicago should pay. Under either of the latter two alternatives, he could suggest that American buy out or not buy out the software development from Lugen.

As Sharpe looked at the three roughly drawn branches on the decision tree, two important thoughts came to mind. Corporate headquarters had said that any operating expenses associated with starting up the PFPs would be capitalized on Chicago's balance sheet up to $1 million pretax. This included any operating losses. If he or Wainwright signed the CER, the entire amount would go into Chicago's P&L because the plant had lost more than $1 million pretax since the machines had been installed. On the other hand, he had asked Rich Frank how much lead the Chicago division would have over its competition, should competitors try to install equipment similar to the PFPs. Frank had commented that if competitors could not get a lot of technical information on the machines, Chicago would have a lead of at least two years. Frank felt that Lugen didn't possess a great deal of information on how to make the machines run properly. Although the Chicago managers did not have much information, either, it seemed that Chicago might increase its competitive lead without Lugen in on the instrumentation project.

Placing the CER and his notes in the top drawer of his desk, a fatigued Sharpe prepared to leave the office. A look at his calendar reminded him that George Kleinhart, a troubleshooter on Cole's staff, would be visiting the Chicago division the next day. Since joining AIC in February 1970, Kleinhart had gained a reputation as a "hard-nosed German," a steely-eyed, incisive questioner who got down to "brass tacks" immediately. During his last visit in early July, Kleinhart had mentioned that AIC officials in New York were anxious to see the division "get on with the instrumentation project" as soon as the CER arrived at headquarters. Sharpe felt that he had to have an answer ready by the next day.

American Industries Corporation (D)

LATE IN OCTOBER 1970, Ed Cole, group vice president of the Packaging Group of American Industries, was considering restructuring the group in order to enhance the attainment of his long-range objective of "increasing earnings before taxes to $9.4 million by 1975."

In a conversation with the casewriter, Cole discussed factors favoring a change in structure:

> None of our general managers has an overall marketing approach. Basically, they want to run manufacturing operations. The result is that we aren't matching our production capabilities with markets. For example, we have different types of machines at our various plants, but managers are concerned about getting business only in their geographical area. The Boston division just sent me a CER for a third rotogravure press, but the justification had no information about the prospects for business outside the Boston area. This indicated to me that there is a lack of coordination between the New York and Boston managers. New York doesn't have rotogravure capability, but there may be some good accounts down there which could use rotogravure printing. If we had a centralized marketing function, we could get some cross-fertilization which we're not getting at present.
>
> . . . I don't go along with Justin Marwick's theory that you can go out and find "wonder-boys" who can be good general managers. It's not that easy in the packaging business. The type of functional specialists we have in paper converting suggest that we could maximize performance in a functionally oriented business.
>
> . . . A functional system has worked for one of our largest competitors and they're making 7% after taxes year in and year out. They have strong

general managers at the top of the organization but rely on separate marketing and manufacturing people. The manufacturing people work on a cost-center basis and are decentralized, while the marketing people are centralized at their home office.

Cole continued by enumerating possible drawbacks of an organizational change:

There would be conflicts between marketing and manufacturing. We now work closely, because each division manager has his own sales and marketing staff. These people work with manufacturing and manufacturing control to arrive at pricing and scheduling decisions. Our fine tuning of pricing decisions might be impaired.

. . . I don't know how Justin Marwick would react toward moving away from the general manager concept. He likes having responsibility vested in one guy on a decentralized basis.

. . . The functional approach didn't work at the company I was with before AIC, because they lacked strong general managers at the top.

. . . It's hard to gauge how a change would affect our present division managers. I know they wouldn't go along with it initially. We'd have a selling job to do.

Cole sketched out his plan of reorganization (see Exhibit 1) and commented:

EXHIBIT 1

AMERICAN INDUSTRIES CORPORATION (D)
Proposed Reorganization of the Packaging Group

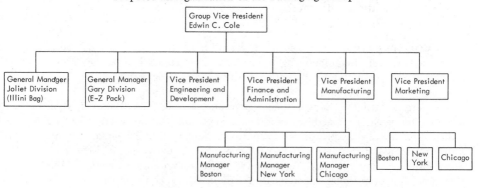

I'd leave some of our specialty operations alone, but I'd create manufacturing divisions at Boston, New York, and Chicago. We'd have a centralized marketing function which could match markets with our various production facilities. We've already moved in that direction by having each division make a product-market matrix.

Exhibit 2 contains information on the Packaging Group's various operating divisions.

EXHIBIT 2

AMERICAN INDUSTRIES CORPORATION (D)

Data on Packaging Group Divisions

	Joliet, Illinois (Illini Bag)	Gary, Indiana (E-Z Pack)	Boston, Mass.	New York, N.Y.	Chicago, Illinois
1969 Sales (thousands)	$2,328	$2,542	$18,047	$19,401	$30,023
Production capabilities (machinery)	Converting machinery only. Late-model bag manufacturing equipment.	2 injection molders, plus corrugated container converting equipment.	Corrugated board manufacturing and converting equipment. Some folding carton equipment	Same as Boston division, but more carton equipment	Corrugated board and folding carton manufacturing and converting equipment.
Types of products (percent of sales)	Paper, plastic, and composite bags lined with foil. (100%)	Corrugated boxes (80%) Styrofoam inner-packing (20%)	Corrugated boxes (70%) Folding cartons (30%)	Corrugated boxes (50%) Folding cartons (50%)	Corrugated boxes (53%) Folding cartons (47%)
Major customers (percent of division sales)	Midwest bakeries (30%) Food processors (15%) Fast food chains (35%) Industrial customers (20%)	Primarily manufacturers of consumer products in the Chicago–Gary area.	Consumer products manufacturers (50%) Electronics companies (10%) Food processing companies (30%) Other (10%)	Consumer products manufacturers (40%) Food processing and beverages (20%) Cosmetic companies (20%) Industrial products and other (20%)	Consumer products manufacturers (36%) Food processing and beverages (28%) Pharmaceutical (12%) Cosmetic (8%) Industrial products and other (16%)

Cole had arrived at 8 o'clock that morning and had found on his desk a copy of Flint's third quarter report to AIC shareholders, indicating that the $2,640,000 net income represented a decline of 24% from results last year, even though sales had increased by 2.1%. The report stated:

The reduction in earnings is primarily a result of continuing unplanned start-up problems with the $18,000,000 PFP machinery program at the Packaging Group's Chicago division. This program lowered income before taxes by approximately $1,100,000 during the third quarter. Frequent mechanical failures have interrupted and detracted from the development of an efficient machine operation. Modifications were made to the machines in September which appear to have resolved the major reason for these failures. Although this operation will continue to have serious adverse effect on fiscal 1970 profits in the fourth quarter, operating and marketing programs initiated upon completion of the modifications should result in a substantial improvement in fiscal 1971 income.

All other operations are performing on plan:

American Real Estate: As expected, sales and profits are off as the money market continues to remain tight.

American Housing: Sales are up 12% and profits up 5% as a result of the continuing strong demand for mobile homes.

American Electronics: The strength of the Trutone line of products plus improved operating efficiency have kept profits at 1969 levels despite a softening of the economy.

The group controller had also prepared financial data on the Packaging Group and its Chicago division for the same period, indicating continuing losses in excess of $1 million for the Chicago division. The initial budget-setting meeting for 1971 was scheduled for October 28, and Flint had indicated that Cole should be prepared to present a plan for profit improvement in the Packaging Group. As he sipped his morning cup of black coffee, Cole wondered if a change in structure should be the focal point of his profit improvement plan.

Bancil Corporation[*]

STRUGGLING to clear his mind, Remy Gentile, marketing manager in France for the toiletry division of Bancil, stumbled to answer the ringing telephone.

"Allo?"

"Remy, Tom Wilson here. Sorry to bother you at this hour. Can you hear me?"

"Sacre Bleu! Do you know what time it is?"

"About 5:20 in Sunnyvale. I've been looking over the past quarter's results for our Peau Doux . . ."

"Tom, it's after 2 A.M. in Paris; hold the phone for a moment."

Remy was vexed with Tom Wilson, marketing vice president for the toiletry division and acting division marketing director for Europe, since they had discussed the Peau Doux situation via telex no more than a month ago. When he returned to the phone, Remy spoke in a more controlled manner.

"You mentioned the Peau Doux line, Tom."

"Yes, Remy, the last quarter's results were very disappointing. Though we've increased advertising by 30%, sales were less than 1% higher. What is even more distressing, Remy, is that our competitors' sales have been growing at nearly 20% per year. Furthermore, our percent cost of goods sold has not decreased. Has Pierre Chevalier bought the new equipment to streamline the factory's operation?"

"No, Pierre has not yet authorized the purchase of the machines, and there is little that can be done to rationalize operations in the antiquated Peau Doux plant. Also, we have not yet succeeded in securing another distributor for the line."

"What! But that was part of the strategy with our increased advertising. I thought we agreed to . . ."

Tom Wilson hesitated for a moment. His mind was racing as he attempted to recall the specifics of the proposed toiletry division strategy for France. That strategy had guided his earlier recommendation to Gentile and Pierre Chevalier, the Bancil general manager in France, to increase advertising and to obtain a new distributor. Tom wanted to be forceful but tactful to insure Gentile's commitment to the strategy.

"Remy, let's think about what we discussed on my last trip to Paris. Do you recall we agreed to propose to Chevalier a plan to revitalize Peau Doux's growth? If my memory serves me well, it was to increase advertising by 25%, groom a new national distributor, reduce manufacturing costs with new equipment, increase prices, and purchase the 'L'aube' product line to spread our marketing overhead."

"Oui, oui. We explored some ideas and I thought they needed more study."

"Remy, as you recall Peau Doux has a low margin. Cutting costs is imperative. We expected to decrease costs by 5% by investing $45,000 in new equipment. Our test for the new strategy next year was to increase advertising this quarter and next quarter while contracting for a new distributor. The advertising was for naught. What happened?"

"I really don't know. I guess Pierre has some second thoughts."

Tom spoke faster as he grew more impatient. Gentile's asking Tom to repeat what he had said made him angrier. Tom realized that he must visit Paris to salvage what he could from the current test program on Peau Doux. He knew that the recent results would not support the proposed toiletry division strategy.

"Remy, I need to see what's going on and then decide how I can best assist you and Chevalier. I should visit Paris soon. How about early next week, say Monday and Tuesday?"

"Oui, that is fine."

"I'll fly in on Sunday morning. Do you think you can join me for dinner that evening at the Vietnamese restaurant we dined at last time?"

"Oui."

"Please make reservations only for two. I'm coming alone. Good night, Remy."

"Oui. Bon soir."

COMPANY BACKGROUND

Bancil Corporation of Sunnyvale, California, was founded in 1908 by pharmacist Dominic Bancil. During its first half century, its products consisted primarily of analgesics (branded pain relievers like aspirin), an antiseptic mouthwash, and a first-aid cream. By 1974, some of the top-management positions were still held by members of the Bancil family, who typically had backgrounds as pharmacists or physicians. This tradition notwithstanding, John Stoopes, the present chief executive officer, was committed to developing a broad-based professional management team.

Bancil sales, amounting to $61 million in 1955, had grown to $380 million in 1970 and to $600 million in 1974. This sales growth had been aided by diversification and acquisition of allied businesses as well as by international expansion. Bancil's product line by 1970 included four major groups:

	Sales (in millions of dollars)	
	1970	*1974*
Agricultural and animal health products (weedkillers, fertilizers, feed additives)	$ 52	$141
Consumer products (Bancil original line plus hand creams, shampoos, and baby accessories)	205	276
Pharmaceutical products (tranquilizers, oral contraceptives, hormonal drugs)	62	107
Professional products (diagnostic reagents, automated chemical analyzers, and surgical gloves and instruments)	60	76

In 1974, Bancil's corporate organization was structured around these four product groups which, in turn, were divided into two or three divisions. Thus, in 1973 the consumer products group had been divided into the Dominic division, which handled Bancil's original product line, and the toiletry division, which was in charge of the newer product acquisitions. The objective of this separation was to direct greater attention to the toiletry products.

INTERNATIONAL OPERATIONS

International expansion had begun in the mid-1950s when Bancil exported through agents and distributors. Subsequently, marketing subsidiaries, called National Units (NUs), were created in Europe, Africa, Latin America, and Japan. All manufacturing took place in the United

States. Virtually the entire export activity consisted of Bancil's analgesic Domicil. An innovative packaging concept, large amounts of creative advertising, and considerable sales push made Domicil a common word in most of the free world, reaching even the most remote areas of Africa, Asia, and South America. A vice president of international operations exercised control at this time through letters and occasional overseas trips. By the mid-1960s, overseas marketing of pharmaceutical and professional products began, frequently through a joint venture with a local company. Increasing sales led to the construction of production facilities for many of Bancil's products in England, Kenya, Mexico, Brazil, and Japan.

Bancil's international expansion received a strong commitment from top management. John Stoopes was not only a successful business executive but also a widely read intellectual with an avid interest in South American and African cultures. This interest generated an extraordinary sense of responsibility to the developing nations and a conviction that the mature industrial societies had an obligation to help in their development. He did not want Bancil to be viewed as a firm that drained resources and money from the developing world; rather, he desired to apply Bancil's resources to worldwide health and malnutrition problems. His personal commitment as an ardent humanist was a guideline for Bancil's international operations.

While Bancil had been successful during the 1960s in terms of both domestic diversification and international expansion, its efforts to achieve worldwide diversification had given rise to frustration. Even though the international division's specific purpose was to promote all Bancil products most advantageously throughout the world, the NUs had concentrated mainly on analgesics. As a result, the growth of the remaining products had been generally confined to the United States and thus these products were not realizing their fullest worldwide potential.

According to Bancil executives, these problems had their roots in the fact that the various product lines, though generically related, required different management strategies. For consumer products, advertising consumed 28% to 35% of sales; since production facilities did not require a large capital investment, considerable spare capacity was available to absorb impulses in demand created by advertising campaigns. For agricultural and animal health products, promotion was less than 1% of sales, but the capital-intensive production (a facility of minimum economic scale cost $18 million) required a marketing effort to stimulate demand consistently near full production capacity. Furthermore, the nature of the marketing activity for the professional and pharmaceutical products placed the burden on personal selling rather than on a mass-promotion effort.

In response to this situation, a reorganization in 1969 gave each product division worldwide responsibility for marketing its products. Regional marketing managers, reporting to the division's vice president of marketing, were given direct authority for most marketing decisions (e.g., advertising, pricing, distribution channels) of their division's products in their area. The manufacturing division, with headquarters in Sunnyvale, had worldwide responsibility for production and quality control. (See Exhibit 1 for the 1969 organization chart.)

EXHIBIT 1

BANCIL CORPORATION
1969 Organization Chart

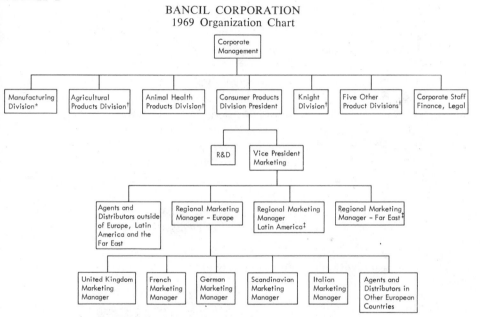

* The manufacturing division manufactured products for all the product divisions. Overseas manufacturing (not shown) reported to the manufacturing division in Sunnyvale.
† Organization similar to that of the consumer products division.
‡ Organization similar to that for Europe.
Source: Company records.

Corporate management also identified a need in key countries for a single local executive to represent Bancil Corporation's interests in local banking and political circles. There was no single criterion for selecting, from the divisions' representatives in each country, the Bancil delegate, the title given to this position. A corporate officer remarked: "We chose whom we thought was the best business executive in each country. There was no emphasis on functional specialty or on selecting an individual from the division with the greatest volume. In one country, the major candidates were opinionated and strong-willed, and we therefore chose the individual who was the least controversial. The Bancil delegate generally had a marketing background if marketing was the primary

Bancil activity in the country or a production background if Bancil had several manufacturing facilities in the country."

While international sales had grown from $99 million in 1970 to $147 million in 1972, profit performance from 1971 to 1972 had been disappointing. A consultant's report stated:

> There are excessive communications between the NUs and Sunnyvale. The marketing managers and all the agents are calling for product-line information from the divisional headquarters. Five individuals are calling three times per week on an average, and many more are calling only slightly less often.

It appeared that a great deal of management time was spent on telex, long-distance communications, and travel. In response to these concerns, the divisions' staffs increased in each country. Overhead nearly tripled, affecting the growth rate of profits from international operations.

With the exception of financial decisions which were dictated by corporate headquarters, most decisions on inventories, pricing, new product offerings, and facility development were made by corporate headquarters in conjunction with the local people. Local people, however, felt that the key decisions were being postponed. Conflicting demands also were a problem as every division drew on the local resources for manpower, inventories, receivables, and capital investment. These demands had been manageable, however, because even though profits were below target no cash shortages had developed.

Current organization of international operations

To improve the performance of its international operations, Bancil instituted a reorganization in mid-1973. The new organization was a matrix of NU general managers and area vice presidents, who were responsible for total resource allocation in their geographic area, and division presidents, who were responsible for their product lines worldwide. (See Exhibit 2 for a description of the matrix in 1975.)

The general manager was the chief executive in his country in charge of all Bancil products. He also was Bancil's representative on the board and executive committee of local joint ventures. The Bancil delegate usually had been chosen as the general manager. He was responsible for making the best use of financial, material, and personnel resources; pursuing approved strategies; searching for and identifying new business opportunities for Bancil in his NU; and developing Bancil's reputation as a responsible corporate citizen. The general manager was assisted by a financial manager, one or more plant managers, product-line marketing managers, and other functional managers as required.

The divisions were responsible for operations in the United States and Canada and for worldwide expertise on their product lines. Divi-

EXHIBIT 2

BANCIL CORPORATION
Shared Responsibility Matrix

Product Group Vice Presidents	Division Presidents	Vice President International Operations Clark B. Tucker						
		Area Vice President, Europe Andre Dufour			Area Vice President, Latin America Juan Vilas			Area Vice President, Far East
		General Manager, France P. Chevalier	General Manager, Germany D. Rogge	General Manager, Four Other National Units	General Manager, Argentina and Uruguay S. Portillo	General Manager, Brazil E. Covelli	General Manager, Two Other National Units	General Manager, Four National Units
Agricultural and Animal Health (3 divisions)	Rodgers Division							
	Division B							
	Division C							
Consumer Products (2 divisions)	Dominic Division							
	Toiletry Division (Robert Vincent)							
Pharmaceuticals (2 divisions)	Division A							
	Division B							
Professional (3 divisions)	Knight Division							
	Division B							
	Division C							

Source: Company records.

sions discharged the latter responsibility through local product-line marketing managers who reported on a line basis to the NU general manager and on a functional basis to a division area marketing director. The latter, in turn, reported to the divisional marketing vice president. Where divisions were involved in other functional activities, the organizational structure was similar to that for marketing. The flow of product-line expertise from the divisions to the NUs consisted of (1) operational inputs such as hiring/termination policies and the structure of merit programs and (2) technical/professional inputs to the NU marketing, production, and other staff functions on the conduct of the division's business within the NU.

Only the Dominic division was represented in every NU. Some divisions lacked representation in several NUs, and in some cases a division did not have a marketing director in an area. For example, the Rodgers division had area marketing directors in Europe, the Far East, and Latin America, all reporting to the divisional vice president of marketing to whom the division's U.S. marketing personnel also reported. However, the Knight division, which had a structure similar to that of the Rodgers division, could justify area marketing directors only in Europe and Latin America.

The new matrix organization established for each country a National Unit Review Committee (NURC) with its membership consisting of the general manager (chairman), a financial manager, and a representative from each division with activities in the NU. Corporate executives viewed the NURC as the major mechanism for exercising shared profit responsibility. NURC met quarterly, or more frequently at the general manager's direction, to (1) review and approve divisional profit commitments generated by the general manager's staff; (2) insure that these profit commitments, viewed as a whole, were compatible with and representative of the best use of the NU's resources; (3) monitor the NU's progress against the agreed plans; and (4) review and approve salary ranges for key NU personnel. When the division's representatives acted as members of the NURC, they were expected to view themselves as responsible executives of the NU.

Strategic planning and control

NURC was also the framework within which general managers and division representatives established the NU's annual strategic plan and profit commitment. Strategy meetings commenced in May, at which time the general manager presented a forecast of Bancil's business in his NU for the next five years and the strategies he would pursue to exploit environmental opportunities. The general manager and the divisional representatives worked together between May and September to develop a mutually acceptable strategy and profit commitment. If genuine disagreement on principle arose during these deliberations, the issue could be resolved at the next level of responsibility. The profit commitment was reviewed at higher levels both within the area and within the product divisions, with the final approval coming from the corporate executive committee (CEC) which required compatible figures from the vice president of international operations and the product group executives. CEC, the major policy-making forum at Bancil, consisting of the chief executive officer, the group vice presidents, the vice president of international operations, and the corporate secretary, met monthly to resolve policy issues and to review operating performance.

For each country, results were reported separately for the various divisions represented, which, in turn, were consolidated into a combined NU statement. The NU as well as the divisions were held accountable, though at different levels, according to their responsibilities. The division profit flow (DPF) and NU net income are shown in the following example for the Argentine National Unit in 1974:

	Rodgers division	Dominic division	Toiletry division	National unit
Division sales	$250,000	$800,000	$1,250,000	$2,300,000
Division expenses	160,000	650,000	970,000	1,780,000
Division profit flow (DPF)	$ 90,000	$150,000	$ 280,000	$ 520,000
NU other expenses				
(general administrative, interest on loans, etc.)				350,000
NU income before taxes				$ 170,000
Less: Taxes				80,000
NU net income				$ 90,000
Working capital	$100,000	$300,000	$ 700,000	

The product divisions were responsible for worldwide division profit flow (DPF) defined as net sales less all direct expenses related to divisional activity, including marketing managers' salaries, sales force, and sales office expenses. The NU was responsible for net income after charging all local divisional expenses and all NU operating expenses such as general administration, taxes, and interest on borrowed funds. Because both the general managers and the divisions shared responsibility for profit in the international operations, the new structure was called a shared responsibility matrix (SRM). The vice president of international operations and the division presidents continually monitored various performance ratios and figures (see Exhibit 3). In 1975 international operations emphasized return on resources, cash generation, and cash remittance, while the division presidents emphasized product-line

EXHIBIT 3

BANCIL CORPORATION
Control Figures and Ratios

Vice president of international operations for national unit		Division president for product line
X	Sales	X
X	Operating income: % sales	X
X	General manager expense: % sales	
X	Selling expense: % sales	X
X	Nonproduction expense: % operating income	
X	Operating income per staff employee	
X	% staff turnover	
X	Accounts receivable (days)	X
X	Inventories (days)	X
X	Fixed assets	X
X	Resources employed	X
X	Return on resources	X
X	Cash generation	
X	Cash remittances	
X	Share of market and share of advertising	X
X	Rate of new product introduction	X

X indicates figure or ratio on organization's (national unit or division) performance of interest to the vice president of international operations and the division presidents.
Source: Company records.

return on resources, competitive market share, share of advertising, and dates of new product introductions.

The impact of the 1973 organizational shift to the SRM. had been greatest for the general managers. Previously, as Bancil delegates, they had not been measured on the basis of the NU's total performance for which they were now held responsible. Also, they now determined salary adjustments, hiring, dismissals, and appointments after consultations with the divisions. In addition, general managers continued to keep abreast of important political developments in their areas, such as the appointment of a new finance minister, a general work strike, imposition of punitive taxes, and the outbreak of political strife, a not-infrequent occurrence in some countries.

Under the new organizational structure, the area marketing directors felt that their influence was waning. While they were responsible for DPF, they were not sure that they had "enough muscle" to effect appropriate allocation of resources for their products in each of the countries they served. This view was shared by Nicholas Rosati, Knight division marketing manager in Italy, who commented on his job:

The European marketing director for the Knight division keeps telling me to make more calls on hospitals and laboratories. But it is useless to make calls to solicit more orders. The general manager for Italy came from the consumer products division. He will neither allocate additional manpower to service new accounts for the Knight division nor will he purchase sufficient inventory óf our products so I can promise reasonable delivery times for new accounts.

Divisions, nevertheless, were anxious to increase their market penetration outside the United States and Canada, seeing such a strategy as their best avenue of growth. The recent increase in international sales and profits, which had by far exceeded that of domestic operations (see Exhibit 4), seemed to confirm the soundness of this view. Not all NU

EXHIBIT 4

BANCIL CORPORATION
Sales and Profits for Bancil Corporation
Domestic and International
(in millions of dollars)

Year	Domestic		International		Total	
	Sales	Profit	Sales	Profit	Sales	Profit
1955	$ 61	$ 5.5	—	—	$ 61	$ 5.5
1960	83	8.3	$ 6	$ 0.2	89	8.5
1965	121	13.5	23	1.3	144	14.8
1969	269	26.7	76	9.2	345	35.9
1970	280	27.1	99	12.3	379	39.4
1971	288	28.7	110	14.2	398	42.9
1972	313	32.5	147	15.8	460	48.3
1973	333	35.3	188	21.4	521	56.7
1974	358	36.7	242	30.9	600	67.6

Source: Company records.

general managers shared this approach, as exemplified by a statement from Edmundo Covelli, the general manager of Brazil:

The divisions are continually seeking to boost their sales and increase their DPF. They are not concerned with the working capital requirements to support the sales. With the inflation rate in Brazil, my interest rate of 40% on short-term loans has a significant effect on my profits.

The Peau Doux issue

The telephone conversation described at the beginning of the case involved a disagreement between Tom Wilson, who was both marketing vice president for the toiletry division and acting division marketing director for Europe, and Pierre Chevalier, Bancil's general manager for France. It also involved Remy Gentile, who reported on a line basis to Chevalier and on a functional basis to Wilson.

Pierre Chevalier had been a general manager of France for 18 months after having been hired from a competitor in the consumer products business. Upon assuming the position, he identified several organizational and operational problems in France:

When I took this job, I had five marketing managers, a financial manager, a production manager, and a medical specialist reporting to me. After the consumer products division split, the new toiletry division wanted its own marketing manager. Nine people reporting to me was too many. I hired Remy for his administrative talents and had him assume responsibility for the toiletry division in addition to having the other marketing managers report to him. That gave me more time to work with our production people to get the cost of goods down.

In less than two years as general manager, Chevalier had reduced the cost of goods sold by more than 3% by investing in new equipment and had improved the net income for the French NU by discontinuing products which had little profit potential.

Remy Gentile had been the marketing manager for the toiletry division in France for the past year. In addition, five other marketing managers (one for each Bancil Corporation division operating in France) reported to him. During the previous six years Gentile had progressed from salesman to sales supervisor to marketing manager within the Knight division in France. Although he had received mixed reviews from the toiletry division, particularly on his lack of mass-marketing experience, Chevalier had hired him because of his track record, his ability to learn fast, and his outstanding judgment.

The disagreement involved the Peau Doux line of hand creams which Bancil Corporation had purchased five years earlier to spread the general manager's overhead, especially in terms of marketing, over a broader product offering. Wilson's frustration resulted from Chevalier's ambivalence toward the division's strategy of increasing the marketing effort and cutting manufacturing costs on the Peau Doux line.

The total market in France for the Peau Doux product line was growing at an annual rate of 15%–20%, according to both Wilson and Gentile. However, Peau Doux, an old, highly regarded hand cream, had been traditionally distributed through pharmacies, whereas recently introduced hand creams had been successfully sold through supermarkets. The original Peau Doux sales force was not equipped to distribute the product through other outlets. To support a second sales force for supermarket distribution, the toiletry division sought to acquire the L'aube shampoo and face cream line. When Gentile had informed Chevalier of this strategy, the latter had questioned the wisdom of the move. The current volume of the Peau Doux line was $800,000. Though less than 10% of Chevalier's total volume, it comprised the entire toiletry division volume in France.

Tom Wilson viewed the Peau Doux problems primarily in terms of an inadequate marketing effort. On three occasions within the past year, he or his media experts from Sunnyvale had gone to Paris to trouble-shoot the Peau Doux problems. On the last trip, Robert Vincent, the toiletry division president, had joined them. On the return flight to Sunnyvale, Wilson remarked to Vincent:

I have the suspicion that Chevalier, in disregarding our expertise, is challenging our authority. It is apparent from his indifference to our concerns and his neglect in allocating capital for new machinery that he doesn't care about the Peau Doux line. Maybe he should be told what to do directly.

Vincent responded:

Those are very strong words, Tom. I suggest we hold tight and do a very thorough job of preparing for the budget session on our strategy in France. If Chevalier does not accept or fundamentally revises our budget, we may take appropriate measures to make corporate management aware of the existing insensitivity to the toiletry division in France. This seems to be a critical issue. If we lose now, we may never get back in the French market in the future.

After Wilson and Vincent had departed for Sunnyvale, Chevalier commented to Dufour, his area vice president:

I have the feeling that nothing we say will alter the thinking of Wilson and Vincent. They seem to be impervious to our arguments that mass advertising and merchandising in France do not fit the Peau Doux product concept.

Andre Dufour had been a practicing pharmacist for six years prior to joining Bancil Corporation as a sales supervisor in Paris in 1962. He had progressed to sales manager and marketing manager of the consumer products division in France. After the untimely death of the existing Bancil delegate for France in 1970, he had been selected to fill that position. With the advent of SRM he had become the general manager and had been promoted to vice president for Europe a year later. Dufour had a talent for identifying market needs and for thoroughly planning and deliberately executing strategies. He was also admired for his perseverance and dedication to established objectives. Clark B. Tucker, vice president of international operations and Dufour's immediate supervisor, commented:

When he was a pharmacist he developed an avocational interest in chess and desired to become proficient at the game. Within five years he successfully competed in several international tournaments and achieved the rank of International Grand Master.

In the fall of 1974, Dufour had become the acting vice president of international operations while his superior, Clark Tucker, was attending the 13-week Advanced Management Program at the Harvard Business School. Though Dufour had considerable difficulty with the English language, he favorably impressed the corporate management at Sunnyvale with his ability of getting to the heart of business problems.

The toiletry division had only limited international activities. In addition to the Peau Doux line in France, it marketed Cascada shampoos and Tempestad fragrances in Argentina. The Cascada and Tempestad lines had been acquired in 1971.

Tom Wilson and Manual Ramirez, toiletry division marketing director for Latin America, were ecstatic over the consumer acceptance and division performance of Cascada and Tempestad in Argentina. Revenue and DPF had quintupled since the acquisition. In his dealings with Gentile, Wilson frequently referred to the toiletry division's success in Argentina. Given this sales performance and the division's clearly stated responsibility for worldwide marketing of toiletry products, Wilson felt that his position in proposing the new strategy for France was strong.

On the other hand, Sergio Portillo, general manager of Argentina and Uruguay, and Juan Vilas, vice president for Latin American operations, had become alarmed by the cash drain from marketing the toiletry division products in Argentina. The high interest charges on funds for inventories and receivables seemed to negate the margins touted by the division executives. In describing the Cascada and Tempestad operation to Vilas, Portillo commented:

I have roughly calculated our inventory turnover for the toiletry division products marketed in Argentina. Though my calculations are crude, the ratio based on gross sales is about four, which is less than one-half the inventory turnover of the remainder of our products.

Neither Portillo nor Vilas shared the toiletry division's enthusiasm and they suspected that Cascada and Tempestad were only slightly above break-even profitability. Chevalier and Dufour were aware of this concern with the toiletry products in Argentina.

As Chevalier contemplated the toiletry division strategy, he became convinced that more substantive arguments rather than just economic ones would support his position. In discussing his concerns with Dufour, Chevalier asked:

Are the toiletry division product lines really part of what John Stoopes and we want to be Bancil's business? Hand creams, shampoos, and fragrances belong to firms like Colgate-Palmolive, Procter & Gamble, and Revlon. What is Bancil contributing to the local people's welfare by producing and marketing toiletries? We have several potentially lucrative alternatives for our resources. The Rodgers division's revenues have been increasing at 18%. We recently completed construction of a processing plant for Rodgers and we must get sales up to our new capacity. The Knight division is introducing an electronic blood analyzer that represents a technological breakthrough. We must expand and educate our sales force to take advantage of this opportunity.

Chevalier sensed that Gentile was becoming increasingly uneasy on this issue, and the feeling was contagious. They had never faced such a situation before. Under the previous organization, NUs had been required to comply, although sometimes reluctantly, with the decisions from Sunnyvale. However, SRM was not supposed to work this way. Chevalier and Gentile stood firmly behind their position, though they recognized the pressure on Tom Wilson and to a lesser degree on Vincent. They wondered what should be the next step and who should take it. Due to the strained relationship with Wilson, they did not rule out the possibility of Wilson and Vincent's taking the Peau Doux issue to the consumer products group vice president and having it resolved within the corporate executive committee.

Business Products Corporation— Part I

CORPORATE POLICY

In July 1972 all managers of the Business Products Corporation (BPC) in the United States received the following letter from Graham Moore, chairman of the board:

A very high priority for BPC in 1972 is to improve significantly the position of minority group employees and women in the company.

This doesn't mean we've been ineffective in years past, but it does mean we must do considerably better. The number of minority employees in the last four years has increased from 5.2% of our total U.S. employment to 10.4%, with significant increases at most job levels. And in a period of sharply rising employment this has meant almost a fourfold increase in minority employees, from 1,150 in 1967 to 4,100 at the end of 1971. By ordinary standards this is a very creditable record. By BPC standards, it is not.

I am not satisfied with our progress in the placement of minorities and women in upper level and managerial positions. I am disappointed, too, to find that, despite frequent statements of corporate policy, there are still departments within the company which are sharply deficient in the employment of both minorities and women.

I expect these situations to change this year. This is the year in which we are putting in place a system of equal opportunity planning and implementation which we intend will make meaningful progress in 1972 and will carry forward that momentum into succeeding years.

The most significant change this year—the one that is basic to all others— is to place responsibility for achieving equal opportunity objectives where it rightfully belongs: with operating management, with each of us. Achieving these objectives is as important as meeting *any other* traditional business responsibility.

It follows, of course, that a key element in each manager's overall performance appraisal will be his progress in this important area. No manager should expect a satisfactory appraisal if he meets other objectives but fails here.

The vehicle for developing and specifying budgets is what we call our Employee Resource Plans. I can assure you that these plans were not developed in a vacuum. We have input from senior line management. Additionally, our thinking has been influenced significantly by dialogues we have had with minority employees singly and in groups. The members of a minority Employee Advisory Committee were particularly helpful in reviewing the plans and suggesting important revisions.

Because our communications are not perfect, I expect that some of you may not yet be fully informed about this program and your part in it. If you are not, talk to your manager and get clear what he expects of you and what his manager expects of him.

We recognize that, like all major new programs, this one requires tangible budgetary support as well as personal commitment. We've already authorized supplemental budgets of over $600,000 in the operating groups to support these programs, and we expect to commit additional funds for other programs before the year is out.

I am often asked why this is such a high priority at BPC. There is, of course, the obvious answer that it is in our best interest to seek out and employ good people in all sectors of our society. And there is the answer that enlightened self interest tells us that more and more of the younger people, whom we must attract as future employees, choose companies by their social records as much as by their business prospects.

But the one overriding reason for this emphasis is because it is right. Because BPC has always set for itself the objective of assuming social as well as business obligations. Because that's the kind of company we have been.

And, with your participation, that's the kind of company we'll continue to be.

THE ORGANIZATIONAL SETTING

Business Products Corporation was a highly successful producer of office supplies and products and specialty equipment with sales of over $1.8 billion. It was acknowledged to be a marketing and technological leader in many of the businesses in which it participated. Overall growth in sales and profits had averaged 12% to 15% for over a decade, and top management had expressed its intention of maintaining this performance record in the future. Although acquisitions had been made from time to time, the growth had been largely accomplished internally through the addition of related product lines and more recently through expansion overseas.

BPC was divided into a number of divisions, each managed by a vice president who reported to one of two group vice presidents at the corporate level. (See Exhibit 1 for a partial organization chart.) The corporate organization, located in New York and numbering roughly 200, was not normally involved in the operating decisions of the divisions. However, an extensive financial budgeting and reporting system provided corporate executives with a means of assessing the expected and actual performance of the operating units. In addition, the corporate personnel function kept close watch on movement through the executive ranks and provided assistance in management development activities. Due in part to the company's rapid growth, the average age of the management group was young, advancement was often swift, and terminations or lateral moves were not unusual. Nevertheless, the company maintained the policy that no "exempt" employee with over seven years' service could be released without the president's approval.

Since the early 1960s, BPC had participated in programs designed to contribute to the advancement of minorities. For instance, funds were funneled through a community development corporation into minority-owned businesses in inner city areas and stress was placed on the employment and training of so-called "hard core" unemployed. Through these efforts, BPC became widely recognized as a leader in minority affairs. Such recognition on issues of social concern was not unusual in BPC. The current and former chairmen of the board had often spoken out on the importance of accepting the corporation's wider responsibilities to society and on numerous occasions had sponsored programs which provided tangible evidence of their convictions.

Of the operating divisions, the Graphic Systems Division (GSD), with sales of about $750 million, was the largest and historically the one that provided BPC with consistent growth and the resources to finance new activities. The division's offices and most of its manufacturing facilities were located in Indianapolis. Sales, distribution, and customer services activities were handled by five regional organizations, each directed by a vice president.

The midwest region, based in Chicago, was responsible for about $150 million in sales. Toward the end of the year, the regional general manager negotiated sales targets and expense budgets for the region with division management; these were ultimately included in the plan agreed upon with corporate. It was characteristic in BPC for corporate to receive "stretch" commitments from the operating units. For the first several months of 1972 the midwest region had ranked fourth in sales performance against plan. However, improvement had been steady, and by the end of July Daryl Roman, regional vice president since May 1971, reported that his organization had nudged into first place by one percentage point at 91% of plan on a year-to-date basis.

During the late sixties, GSD management had decided to phase out its centralized national distribution service and assign this function to

EXHIBIT 1: BUSINESS PRODUCTS CORPORATION
Partial Organization Chart

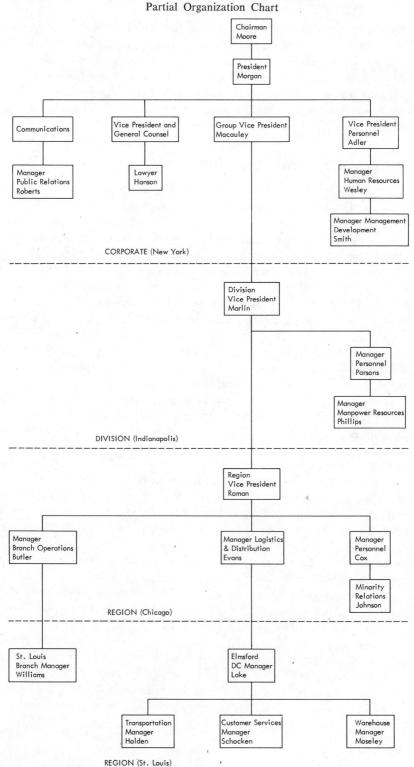

Chairman
Moore

President
Morgan

Communications

Vice President and
General Counsel

Group Vice President
Macauley

Vice President
Personnel
Adler

Manager
Public Relations
Roberts

Lawyer
Hanson

Manager
Human Resources
Wesley

Manager Management
Development
Smith

CORPORATE (New York)

Division
Vice President
Marlin

Manager
Personnel
Parsons

Manager
Manpower Resources
Phillips

DIVISION (Indianapolis)

Region
Vice President
Roman

Manager
Branch Operations
Butler

Manager Logistics
& Distribution
Evans

Manager
Personnel
Cox

Minority
Relations
Johnson

REGION (Chicago)

St. Louis
Branch Manager
Williams

Elmsford
DC Manager
Lake

Transportation
Manager
Holden

Customer Services
Manager
Schocken

Warehouse
Manager
Moseley

REGION (St. Louis)

the five regional organizations, which in turn created several geographically dispersed distribution centers. The last of these new distribution centers to be established was located at Elmsford, a suburb of St. Louis. The work force of these centers was largely clerical and female. For instance, in August 1972, of the 32 employees at the Elmsford facility, four were managers, eight were warehousemen, and the remaining 20 were women working in traffic, customer services, and inventory analysis.

THE ELMSFORD DISTRIBUTION CENTER

The Elmsford distribution center had begun operations as a separate entity in May 1969, even though it did not move physically to Elmsford until November 1970. During this 18-month period, the new distribution center's manager, Peter Lake, had operated under difficult conditions. Forced to vacate his old quarters in the modern GSD building on three days' notice to make room for a new marketing group, Lake relocated his work force, which he had inherited from the disbanded distribution service, in a rundown, rat-infested loft in the Indianapolis central city. Work-force turnover in the warehouse was over 300% per year; the better employees moved on to more skilled jobs in the GSD manufacturing facilities around Indianapolis, and the rest suffered from the varied afflictions of ghetto residents. On one visit to the warehouse, Lake recalled, 14 of the 23 employees had been absent.

When the operation was transferred to Elmsford, the entire management team composed of the managers of traffic, customer services, and the warehouse moved with it. Shortly before the move took place, however, Lake had approached his new boss, Alex Evans, regional manager of logistics and distribution, with the request that Joe Schocken, then 30, the manager of customer services, not make the move. Evans agreed. Schocken had worked with Lake for three of his six years at BPC, one and a half of them as Lake's direct subordinate. He had been put on probation by his previous superior from September 1968 to March 1969 (a long time in BPC) for marginal personnel skills and was viewed as moody and erratic though hard working and loyal. On the other hand, his technical and operational skills had been rated high.

For two months Evans looked for reassignment opportunities for Schocken in Indianapolis to no avail; in essence, Evans was told, "You've got him, his record is cloudy, he's yours." Schocken had at first been reluctant to move, citing family reasons, but when he was told that his job could not be guaranteed otherwise, he agreed to go. He was not told, however, that the region had sought his transfer. Not long after the move, tragedy struck Schocken when his wife committed suicide. At the time Schocken was reluctantly attending a company seminar at the region's request.

The first months in Elmsford brought little relief for the management team. The capital request for a new facility had languished at the division for over a year with the result that the distribution center was located 15 months in temporary quarters. These quarters were six trailers fastened together and parked in a middle-class suburb not far from where the permanent building was to be constructed. Conditions were primitive. The trailers were cramped and broken up into numerous little working areas. The septic system froze from time to time, causing the toilets to fail during the winter months, and it was not unusual for the temperature differential between floor and desk level to be 30 degrees.

In this context Lake had two major tasks. The first was managing a volume of work that was 50% larger than it had been in Indianapolis because new territories had been added without the relinquishment of old ones. For some months operations were conducted at both the new and old locations, and Lake recalled that he could not get his entire management group together for weeks at a time.

The second task was building an organization, a process complicated by several factors. First, BPC had instituted a corporate-wide hiring freeze in the latter months of 1970 due to lagging budget-actual financial comparisons. As a result, until the new year the work force was interviewed by Lake and his managers but hired through a third party as temporary help. This created a good deal of uncertainty and some resentment among the new people who did not see why they were not entitled to all the fringe benefits normally accruing to BPC employees.

Furthermore, all the applicants obtained through initial advertising in the Elmsford area were white in keeping with the profile of the surrounding communities. Lake, desirous of operating in the spirit of the corporate minority relations policy, sought minority candidates in greater St. Louis where the local sales branch was experienced in recruiting minority employees, and he worked through them to identify, interview, and test minority applicants. In Elmsford, Lake selected much more informally from among applicants coming to him directly, not having facilities or staff for testing. When the distribution center opened, five of the 13 newly hired employees, including Lake's secretary, were minority.

Despite these obstacles, the organization appeared to Evans and Lake to be developing nicely. The caliber of the new employees was considered excellent, and a pioneering spirit took hold that helped them through the uncomfortable winter of 1971. Reducing the backlog became a challenge prompting a high level of commitment and motivation. Lake described some of his activities:

In a way, the trailers had a positive influence in the sense that we tried to pay attention to the employees in lots of little ways. You know, nameplates for their desks, roses for girls out sick. One time we were without toilets for seven days. By coincidence, we had a Muzak system hooked up the first day. I went around as the office clown, asking them, "What do you people want, both toilets *and* Muzak?" There was a common enemy, and everyone pulled together to work down the tremendous backlog. The trailers may have put us in awkward positions, but they made us do some good things, too.

In the fall of 1971, Lake again approached Evans with the suggestion that a transfer be considered for Schocken. Evans discussed this with Daryl Roman in the context of moving him to the regional office in a staff capacity. The matter was given some study but nothing came of it. However, the Manpower Resources Plan at year end contained the recommendation that he be moved at the end of 1972 to a position in which his operational skills would be more central to his job. In the meantime, he continued as manager of customer services, responsible for roughly a dozen female employees.

In mid-1971 construction on the new distribution center finally commenced. As the work progressed, Lake took pictures and displayed them in the trailers as a sign that better times were ahead. Performance indicators in the distribution center reflected steady improvement from the low point of the first months when Elmsford had the worst record in the country. Evans commented on his evaluation for 1971:

Elmsford got the job done in 1971. And without much administrative support from the region. We asked from both supervisors and employees a tremendous amount of effort. I can remember writing in Lake's review, "He's great at jerry-rigging. Give him any task and he can do it and keep his people motivated and committed. But the critical question is, can he run a refined operation?"

When the distribution center moved to its new quarters in February 1972, Lake felt that the time had come to tighten discipline, especially for attendance and lateness, which he had not emphasized as strongly earlier because of the poor working conditions. He "rattled the cage" from time to time, stressing that customer services, the distribution center's primary concern, depended on employees being on the job. While he did not want time clocks, he made it clear that time cards were to reflect latenesses as well as absences. The employees responded by achieving an absentee record of 0.9% for the first half of 1972, which was considered extraordinarily low. Both Lake and those who reviewed the performance of the distribution center took this as a good indication that morale and dedication continued on a high level.

After the move to the new building had been completed, Evans reviewed the functions of the distribution center. He found that customer services and traffic were "coming on strong," the warehouse was improving, and the equipment control group was the best in the country. When the center was established, Evans and Lake agreed that the functions should be put in first-rate order sequentially, and now only inventory control posed a problem. In May, responsibility for this function was shifted from customer services to the warehouse manager, and a specialist from Evans' staff conducted a study which pointed to the need for an additional inventory clerk. Evans concurred with this recommendation and suggested to Lake that he pick the very best person in the distribution center to be lead clerk, with special emphasis on her analytical skills. At the end of May, Lake chose a woman in traffic who had been with the center since it opened. At the time, Evans asked if her transfer would create a problem for the current clerk, Shirley Gaynor, a black woman, one of the original employees. Lake responded that he felt he would be able to "console" her. The correctness of Lake's choice appeared to be confirmed in the following weeks as the inventory control function exhibited steady improvement.

By July, the region could point to the Elmsford distribution center with some satisfaction. Its performance was then among the best in the country. Evans recalled that Roman had complimented him after a visit to the facility, saying in effect, "They should all be like that one." The friendliness apparent in the work environment, it was noted, generally impressed visitors.

Minority relations—some early rumbles

Behind the commendable operating results and the pleasant atmosphere, Evans and Lake had on several occasions become aware of dissatisfactions expressed by several of the black employees. However, in the context of the myriad problems encountered and for the most part being overcome, they were viewed as either understandable or relatively insignificant.

The first involved the resignation in March 1972 of Susan Wilson, one of the original minority employees. Schocken indicated that he had placed her on probation for absenteeism in late 1971, her record at the time reflecting more than twice the number of lost hours as the next highest employee. In February she had been in an automobile accident and had lost several more days. There was some evidence to suggest that the temporary disability form which she had filed after her return and which presumably had been signed by a physician had been falsified, though this suspicion had not been discussed with Wilson at the time. Then in March her doctor advised her that, in view of other medical problems, she would probably be absent quite a bit more in the near future. At this point Lake explained to her the possibility of a leave of absence and also questioned her about the earlier medical slip, which she denied falsifying. She then resigned. As these events unfolded, Lake kept Evans informed.

The Wilson episode did not end there, however. Just before she resigned, but without Lake's knowledge at the time, she filed a suit with the Missouri Equal Employment Opportunity Commission charging BPC with forcing her to resign under duress. She was regarded as something of a martyr by the other black women. Hannah Hill, Lake's secretary, had several long discussions with Lake about the handling of the Wilson case. Hill emphasized the numerous problems Wilson had: poor housing and transportation, an illegitimate child, and so forth. Lake retorted that, in view of her record, he had been justified in his actions. Moreover, he suspected that she had resigned rather than chance an investigation into the authenticity of the disability form.

Several weeks later Shirley Gaynor, another of the original black employees, had a two-hour session with Lake in which she lodged a complaint against Schocken. She maintained that he was a racist and provided a series of incidents to support her contention. Lake had had previous discussions with other (white) employees about Schocken's insensitivity toward the needs of his people. As Lake listened to Gaynor, he had the feeling that he was picking up further evidence of Schocken's managerial weakness. After this meeting, he spoke to Schocken "briefly and honestly" about what had happened but with no more emphasis then he had used on earlier occasions.

The next straw in the wind involved Evans. In May, GSD held an open house at Elmsford to inaugurate the new building. Hannah Hill came with her husband, Nathan Hill, a black activist and community organizer in St. Louis, who was currently involved in establishing a drug rehabilitation center (the Black Community House). Nathan Hill took Evans aside and "laid it on him." In the noise and confusion it was hard for Evans to understand all that was being said; he did not entirely grasp Hill's outside affiliation, though he knew Hannah Hill was Nathan's wife. Much of the monologue related to the problems Hill was having in St. Louis, to his need for financial support for his drug program, to a fundamentally racist society, and in vague ways to the existence of racism in BPC. However, Evans heard no specific charges leveled against the distribution center. In the next few days, Evans relayed the sense of his conversation to the regional personnel manager, Mike Cox, and checked with Lake, who indicated that he knew of no serious racial problems in Elmsford.

Then in late May the lead inventory control clerk's job was filled by a white woman from traffic, as described above. When Shirley Gaynor had been hired, she had expressed an interest in inventory control, and Lake had assigned her to the one slot then available. Her performance over the next year and a half was satisfactory. However, while she was considered very intelligent, Lake felt she had a narrow view of the job. She was difficult to counsel and was viewed as disruptive in the work force; management, as Evans put it, "couldn't come to grips with her." The woman who had been transferred from traffic and who, along with Gaynor, had been a Grade 3, received a two-grade promotion. Gaynor had never received a promotion at Elmsford nor had she been interviewed for the lead job. As Evans put it, "She hadn't received much training. No one had ever given her a job she couldn't do." Gaynor was upset.

For the next two months little of significance to management transpired in minority relations. Evans commented: "We didn't see Hannah's criticism as serious. She is a very sophisticated person. From a look at her resume, it's pretty clear she is way overqualified for the job she's in. She can be criticizing but in such a pleasant way you might not catch it." As Lake's secretary she had access to the personnel files and most of the information flowing to and from the office.

A nightclub affair

On the evening of Thursday, August 10, Sam Johnson, the regional manager of minority relations, flew to St. Louis to preside over an open house for minority candidates for service representative positions at the sales branch. His visit came at the conclusion of a four-day advertising campaign on radio stations popular in the black community.

Just before Johnson left he touched base with his boss, Mike Cox. At the conclusion of their conversation, Cox mentioned in passing the discussion he had had with Evans about the latter's meeting with Nathan Hill. Cox said he thought Hill might be a minister—the Black Community Church (House)—who wanted BPC to contribute to his drug rehabilitation program. He also indicated that Hill had met with the St. Louis branch manager, Brad Williams. In any event, he asked Johnson to get in touch with Hill to learn more about the drug program and to find out whether Hill might wish to help identify minority candidates for employment in GSD.

When Johnson arrived in St. Louis, he contacted Hill and arranged to meet for lunch the next day. That evening Hannah Hill called Johnson and said she wanted to talk with him about some problems at the distribution center. Johnson asked if she had talked with her husband about his call earlier, to which she replied that she had not. Later Nathan Hill called and rescheduled his meeting for the evening.

Nathan Hill picked up Johnson after work and, as they headed for the nightclub that had been agreed upon for the meeting, Hill related some of the difficulties he was having with the city bureaucracy. After a drink at the bar they went upstairs to a private room. Inside were 27 people: 19 men from Hill's Black Community House, 4 black women from the distribution center, 2 black salesmen from the St. Louis branch, an aide from Representative Charmichael's office (a black Congressman), and a reporter from the largest St. Louis newspaper. Johnson, himself a black, described the ensuing events:

The first thing Nathan said when we got inside was, "The reason we're here is to talk about racism at BPC!" I said, "Wait a minute, why am I here? I thought it was to talk about a drug program with you." Hill went into the meeting he had had with Brad Williams. After this went on for a while, I turned to Hannah and said, "Why are you here?" She said she had some complaints at the distribution center she wanted to talk about. Then I asked one of the salesmen, "Why are you here?" He started saying, "I don't know . . . ah . . . we were told there was a meeting. . . ." and was pretty uncomfortable about the whole thing. Then I balked. I told them, "I'm only a functionary. I can only bring information back but can't make decisions on the spot." At this point Nathan put on his show . . . 300 years of slavery, how the black man was exploited, how "you are being bought off by whitey . . ." There was a lot of strong language. Some of the girls were crying. I listened for a while and then I picked up my things and started for the door. Nathan said, "Where are you going?" I told him I was not going to talk about this kind of thing. If they wanted to talk about BPC, O.K., but not with that crowd of people there. With that, everybody left but the four girls and the salesmen.

Shirley Gaynor started in on Lake. She said he was a figurehead, that Schocken was the real power in the distribution center and he [Schocken] was a racist, a bigot, and so forth. I said, "O.K., but can you give me some facts?" They gave me a lot of incidents, and I wrote them down. Then I asked the salesmen to give me some facts, too. They began to talk about being assigned to ghetto sales districts where there was less money to be made, about thinking they got lower starting salaries, and so on. But when they saw me starting to write them down, they said: "Stop. The sisters have more problems than we do. You work on them first."

It was 9:00 P.M. by this time. The others came back. I went out for a break and tried to call Cox but couldn't get him. Then I came back and we had another long discussion about the narcotics program and everything else again 'til 11:00 P.M. Finally, the meeting broke up. I said to Nathan, "You'll have an answer from BPC on the drug rehabilitation program in three weeks." Nathan said, "When are we going to hear about the sisters?" I told him next Wednesday or Thursday. He asked why that long; I said it would take some time to communicate with other people, get things typed, etc. Then one of his lieutenants said, "Where is Roman?[1] Why don't you find him and tell him *now*?" I replied that Roman was probably back home in Chicago for the weekend. It wasn't that I couldn't, it was that I didn't *choose* to. Then he said, "I'll bet you would if it was a matter of getting your breath straight." I had to admit he was right. That really got me thinking. . . .

---

[1] It had come out earlier in the discussion that Roman had been in St. Louis for a sales meeting that day.

Johnson immediately wrote up his notes on the meeting in the following form:

MEMO TO MYSELF!
SUBJECT: Notes from Meeting with Black Employees/Black Community House, St. Louis

Sometime during the period between March and June 1972, four (4) black clericals [Hannah Hill, Shirley Gaynor, Wilma Green, and Jennie Williams] in the Elmsford distribution center filed a Class Action Suit[2] claiming racial discrimination against BPC, listing among their indictments the following:

A. *Discrimination in employment practices*
   1. In the start-up of the distribution center all of the black clericals were tested; none of the whites were tested.
   2. Joe Schocken hired Elise Rawlinson (referred by Aileen Lambert) because she was blond and wore miniskirts—she was never tested.
   3. Carolyn Moody was hired as a temporary on March 19. Carolyn, a black girl, was processed initially by Pete Lake and told that she would be hired. Before her papers could be processed, Joe Schocken found out about the offer, came into Pete Lake's office, and insisted that this girl be hired as a temporary so that they would have a chance to observe her. Pete Lake agreed, Carolyn was hired as a temporary, and told that there were no allocations at the time.

B. *Segregated Facilities*
   The sole content of this area of alleged discrimination refers to the physical setting when the distribution center was located in a series of trailers. Wilma Green and Shirley Gaynor allege that they were physically segregated from the white girls and placed in a remote corner of one of the trailers.

C. *Discrimination in Performance Appraisals and Promotions*
   1. Shirley Gaynor alleges that she was discriminated against in terms of receiving a promotion to lead inventory control clerk.
   2. Aileen Lambert allegedly was promoted twice in three months while her attendance record in terms of absenteeism and tardiness was just as bad as a black girl's, Susan Wilson, who was fired.
   3. Wilma Green alleges that she was told: "You are good at your work. However, you do not help the other girls, and therefore we cannot give you a high performance appraisal." She received a "4."
   4. The comment was made by Hannah Hill that no black in the distribution center had ever received a rating higher than a "4."

---

[2] In August, no one in BPC was aware of any legal action involving the Elmsford facility other than the pending Susan Wilson case.

5. The charge was made that Elinor Stewart had a performance appraisal which reflected good attendance. When the appraisal was submitted to Hannah Hill for typing, she brought it to Pete Lake's attention, saying "This is a blatant lie, she has missed well over 80 hours." The performance appraisal was then returned to Joe Schocken. He changed the comment about her attendance being good, indicated that it was not so good, yet he did not change her performance appraisal.

D. *General Allegations*

1. Allegedly Susan Wilson was "railroaded out of the distribution center because she was black and because she was not liked by Joe Schocken."

2. Allegedly, a representative from Matson Employment Agency was visiting the distribution center when she was shown into Schocken's office by Wilma Green. Wilma and Shirley alleged hearing the following dialogue: The representative from Matson saying, "Oh, I see you hire blacks." Answer from Joe Schocken, "Yes, we have to hire them whether we want to or not."

3. Statement made by Shirley Gaynor agreed upon by the other girls: "The racist situation is so bad out at the distribution center that the white girls feel absolutely free to reprimand blacks about petty and menial stuff when they have no supervisory powers. They feel all they have to do is to tell Joe Schocken and he'll get right on the black's case."

4. A meeting was held to discuss the abuse of overtime and all employees were told that if they came in late they could not make it up through lunch. No black has been allowed to make up late time since then, yet whites have been allowed to make up that kind of time on numerous documented occasions.

Business Products Corporation— Part II

THE EVENING of Thursday, August 10, 1972, Sam Johnson, manager of minority relations for the midwest region of the Graphic Systems Division (GSD) of the Business Products Corporation (BPC), had met at a St. Louis nightclub with a local black leader, Nathan Hill, and several black BPC employees. At this meeting Hill and the BPC employees had confronted Johnson with charges of racial discrimination at Elmsford, one of the region's distribution centers. At the heart of the racial discrimination complaints was Joe Schocken, the distribution center's customer services manager, whose previous job history included high ratings for his technical and operational performance but low marks (including a lengthy probation period) for marginal personnel skills. The distribution center, prior to its move into a new building in February 1972, had operated out of temporary quarters for close to three years, requiring a great deal of adaptation and improvisation on the part of its manager, Peter Lake. Regional management had given the distribution center high praise during this difficult transition period and after the move in February had rated its performance as among the best in the country. In line with BPC's corporate minority relations policy, Lake had made special efforts to recruit minorities and, when operations started in Elmsford, five of the 13 newly hired employees were black. The Business

Products Corporation (Part I) case provides more detailed background on the Elmsford situation; Exhibit 1 of that case portrays BPC's multilevel organization structure.

On Sunday, August 13, Johnson called Mike Cox, the regional personnel manager, to tell him briefly what had happened in St. Louis. The next day Cox alerted the regional vice president, Daryl Roman, who asked Alex Evans, regional manager of logistics and distribution, and Johnson to join him and Cox to discuss the situation as it had been presented by Johnson and to determine what ought to be done. Evans was aware that Lake had been attending a meeting of the distribution center managers in Indianapolis that week and might not have known about the nightclub affair. Roman pressed for answers to two questions: First, what was the problem at the distribution center? Second, to the extent that it related to Schocken, what should be done about him?

THE REGION'S RESPONSE TO THE ELMSFORD SITUATION

The region's approach to resolving the issue raised by the four black employees was described by Johnson:

Daryl [Roman] wanted to do something quickly. We concluded that Lake and Schocken should investigate the allegations by looking into the personnel records at the distribution center. In the spirit of continuing a dialogue, Lake was to have the black girls conduct their own investigation. In other words, Lake was to meet with them and ask their help. Then the information would be pulled together and we'd move on to recommendations.

With regard to personnel, Evans argued that Schocken should be pulled out and Hannah Hill transferred to a less sensitive job where she would not have free access to personnel records and all communications to and from Lake's office. He reasoned that, whether the allegations were justified or not, the best way to turn the situation around was to remove the primary irritant before matters became worse. His position was strengthened when Schocken's job history was reviewed, and it was recalled that Lake had requested his transfer previously. In Evans' view, Schocken had the potential for being valuable elsewhere in the division. He had done an outstanding job, for instance, in implementing a computer system for processing customer supply orders—better than anyone else in the company, according to Evans. His record suggested that he might well turn in a fine performance in staff work. Moreover, his dedication to BPC was enormous; he worked long hours and followed company rules to the letter. However, his weak people skills in a supervisory role were again causing difficulties. Evans also suggested Jim Atkins as Schocken's replacement. Atkins, a black working in the other midwest distribution center, had been requested by Lake earlier. Evans said he was the best man available.   .

While Roman agreed that Schocken should be moved, he also wanted to determine if there was substance to the charges of discrimination. Consequently the investigation was to proceed while the division was sounded out on the possibility of a transfer. In the meantime, both Schocken and Hill were to remain in place.

On Wednesday, August 16, Lake flew to Chicago where he met with Cox, Evans, and Johnson; they thrashed out a more detailed course of action. Cox notified the black women that the region was investigating their concerns as Johnson had promised and would like them to meet with Lake as soon as he returned from Indianapolis. Division and corporate headquarters were alerted to the problem in conference calls on August 15, 17, and 18. Cox asked about corporate policy on meeting with outside representatives such as Nathan Hill. The corporate headquarters' response was that BPC did not as a matter of principle deal with parties who were not either duly elected union representatives or legal counsel. This position confirmed an earlier one taken by Roman and subsequently concurred in by the divisional vice president.

The following Monday, August 21, Lake met with the four black women for seven hours in his office. He had the feeling that the women viewed this meeting as an obligation to local management and a necessary step prior to taking their charges to higher levels of management. Lake said: "They felt they had received no satisfaction from me in the past. They accused me not of discrimination but of condoning it." The women made a number of allegations which Lake noted, but no formal demands were articulated and Lake recalled no mention of the possible intervention of Nathan Hill on their behalf.

On Wednesday afternoon, August 23, Cox, Evans, and Johnson flew to St. Louis. Cox called Hannah Hill and asked if she would meet with him alone. She agreed. Cox commented on their conversation:

> She said the situation was serious, adding "I doubt if we'll meet with you without Nathan." I asked her why she didn't stay inside the company. She said it was no use—distribution center management was not responsive.

That evening and for 10 hours the next day, the three regional managers met with Lake, Schocken, and Moseley (the warehouse supervisor at Elmsford) to review the results obtained thus far in their investigation and to formulate a course of action. They also went over, point by point, the charges and incidents emphasized by the black women. Lake admitted that there were a lot of inconsistencies in administrative procedures, especially with regard to testing, promotions, and absences, often affecting whites as well as blacks, and a degree of insensitivity to minority relations that he had not been aware of before. He maintained that they were not overt but in large measure a function of the distribution center's difficult history. On the other hand, the regional managers all felt that Schocken either evaded the questions or insisted that he did not see how the actions ascribed to him could have been misinterpreted.

By Thursday evening a plan was put together which included specific responses to the problems identified by the black women. Some of the corrective actions applied to the whole distribution center while others related to redressing individual grievances. The plan proposed to change performance appraisal weightings and specifications; to establish a program of cross-training employees to enhance promotional opportunities; to have supervisors/managers hold monthly meetings with their subordinates to improve on-site dialogue, especially with black employees; to take an attitude survey on human relations problems at the distribution center; to hold a minority awareness training education session; and to institute an experimental policy for effective and equitable monitoring of absence and lateness performance. Evans raised a question about what the white employees should be told. The group discouraged him from saying anything at that time. The feeling was that the problems would be settled in a few days—no use stirring up the matter any further.

Early Friday morning, a surprise meeting was called with the black women attended by Cox, Evans, Johnson, and Lake to review the results of the investigation and present the remedial program. The women then said they would not discuss substantive matters unless Nathan Hill was allowed to represent them. Their argument was more or less as follows: "We are four poor little girls without training or experience in the matters that should be discussed. You people have your experts whenever you need help. How can we possibly get a fair deal when the odds against us are so high? Therefore, we need our expert, Nathan Hill, to represent us. He can make you understand our problems." For two and a half hours the discussion revolved around the women's insistence and the managers' intransigence on outside representation. The women's argument was received with some sympathy, however, and at one point the managers caucused to discuss whether they ought to meet with Hill. In view of the specific instructions they had to the contrary, however, they decided against it.

At the airport that afternoon, Cox called Wesley, manager of human resources at corporate headquarters, to advise him that the employees had not agreed to the region's approach and in fact had even threatened to take the dispute "to the streets." Cox tested corporate again on the strength of the policy ruling out negotiations with third parties. He also raised a further point: "If there is publicity, is the corporation going to bend? If so, let's do it now." Wesley reaffirmed the policy on third parties. He further assured Cox that the corporation would do what it felt was right and would not be dissuaded by the prospect of adverse public comment.

The following week at the distribution center, Lake was informed by the black women that there was an increasing amount of animosity between blacks and whites in sharp contrast to the harmony that had prevailed before. In an effort to allay the tension, Lake decided to make himself available after work on Wednesday, August 30, to discuss with the white employees in general terms what had been happening between the black employees and management. Most of the white employees stayed for a two-hour meeting, which Lake described in these terms:

> I told the white employees about some of the problems brought up in the blacks' allegations. I tried to defend the blacks' complaints and to explain what affirmative action means and what their rights are with EEOC. The whites didn't buy it. They felt there was a bigger design here. "What are their complaints? They've gotten promotions, haven't they?" And so forth. There was a real lack of understanding on their part of what was going on. I was also under instructions not to say anything specific to them about the charges or the corrective action. I wasn't successful in getting the point across. They believed that there had been equal treatment in the past and couldn't understand what the problem was. There was a lot of tension.

PUBLIC EXPOSURE

On the afternoon of Labor Day, Monday, September 4, the public relations director of the Graphic Systems Division (GSD) received a call at his home in Indianapolis from a reporter for one of the network television stations in St. Louis, who indicated that some charges had been leveled at BPC in a story to be aired on the 6 o'clock news that evening. The GSD official, knowing nothing of the preceding events, refused to comment until he had further information. He immediately telephoned Scott Parsons, the GSD vice president of personnel, who, having just returned from vacation, had heard nothing about the problem since shortly after Johnson's meeting with Hill in August. Parsons then called Cox and alerted him to what was coming, receiving in exchange a briefing on the intervening events in St. Louis. After trying without success to reach the GSD divisional vice president, John Marlin, Parsons next talked with Philip Adler, corporate vice president of personnel. Adler had been in Europe and his only previous contact with the situation had been a brief phone conversation with Wesley in which the latter had mentioned the Johnson meeting with Hill and had indicated that the region appeared to be on top of the matter. Parsons' call now took the form of a briefing. Adler, in turn, reached Wesley, and they agreed to touch base as necessary with Brian Macauley, the group vice president, and Howard Morgan, the president of BPC, both located in New York.

Meanwhile, Marlin had returned Parsons' call. Marlin's previous exposure to the problem had been a brief discussion with Parsons on a plane trip in mid-August in which he was told of a situation involving some black employees in the Elmsford distribution center. He had not pursued it, simply telling Parsons to keep him informed. Now he became aware of a nine-year supervisor with a spotty employment record named Schocken who, from what Parsons knew at the time, seemed to be at the heart of the difficulty. Marlin recalled getting the impression in either this conversation or a subsequent one with Roman that Schocken was poorly thought of by *all* employees, not just the blacks. In any event, he told Parsons that should it appear appropriate to transfer Schocken to Indianapolis, he [Marlin] would "make it happen" and gave Parsons permission to arrange it.

Concurrently, Cox was also on the telephone to spread the news to Roman and Evans. Roman had Cox get back to the GSD public relations director to confer on an appropriate response to the press. Roman contacted Marlin himself to indicate that the region was prepared to deal with the problem. Meanwhile, Evans talked with Lake who, in turn, called Schocken and Holden, the transportation manager at Elmsford. The three managers in St. Louis each agreed to monitor one of the network television stations and record the story with dictaphones quickly procured from the office.

The story, in somewhat different versions, ran on both the 6:00 and 11:00 P.M. news programs. A transcript of the earlier broadcast follows:

ANNOUNCER: Four black BPC employees held a news conference today at the Westview Plaza Mall. They were accompanied by Nathan Hill, a local resident who has been quite active on a number of racial fronts.

A spokeswoman for the group today explained what action they'll be taking if BPC does not respond to the charges by this coming Thursday.

S. GAYNOR: #1. Obtain letter of suit from EEOC to take Federal Action against BPC in forms of individual and class action suits for punitive and civil damages.

#2. Request Congressman Charmichael's office to investigate the gross violation adhering to Federal Compliance as it relates to advertising.

Due to improper management an otherwise affable relationship of white co-workers was jeopardized and caused a near racial clash.

We have a series of nine local and six national demands which we will make public if BPC refuses to meet with and discuss the existing problems.

ANNOUNCER: A company spokesman who was reached in his home in Indianapolis today said that BPC could not possibly have a comment until the group's charges had been investigated.

The upshot of the news conference was that BPC faced a series of unspecified local and national demands and an ultimatum to respond by Thursday. A press release was issued by the black employees containing the same information that had been given in the newscast.

SUBSEQUENT EVENTS

Tuesday, September 5

At the distribution center Tuesday morning the atmosphere was described by Lake:

I don't think any of the white girls had seen the TV news program but they had heard about it from friends and relatives. One of the lead girls came in with a real disgusted manner. She couldn't believe it. They thought they had a great situation here, and I had them believing we were No. 1. They just couldn't see how things could be interpreted this way. Black and white employees weren't speaking. The atmosphere was "rock bottom."

In mid-morning, Cox, Evans, and Johnson arrived, unannounced, at the distribution center and immediately held a meeting with the black employees. In particular, the regional managers wanted to learn the nature of the demands referred to in the broadcast and whatever further evidence there might be for accusing Schocken of racism. The employees again refused to talk unless Nathan Hill were allowed to represent them. The meeting was perfunctory. Cox reported to both Parsons and Roman that their latest efforts had been unsuccessful. Evans remained in St. Louis and Cox and Johnson flew back to Chicago.

At the division, Parsons began to arrange interviews for Joe Schocken as well as to prepare a memorandum summarizing the situation for Brian Macauley at corporate. Meanwhile at corporate Chuck Smith, manager of management development and a black himself, contacted Hill ostensibly to discuss the drug rehabilitation program, as had been promised by Johnson during the August 10 nightclub meeting. A lengthy but inconclusive discussion ensued, mostly about the distribution center. According to Smith, Hill agreed that the commitment of corporate headquarters to contact him had been fulfilled with this telephone call.

Wednesday, September 6

At corporate, Philip Adler had become increasingly concerned about the apparent scope of Hill's charges and the implied threat to other BPC locations. The newspaper coverage of the incident did not allay his concerns. Adler and Wesley met for lunch with Macauley. The group vice president took the position that the problem was GSD's and that Marlin and his regional organization were responsible for resolving it. The corporate staff was to provide counsel as needed. Macauley also wanted the facts on Schocken before countenancing his transfer; he did not want GSD simply to put Schocken somewhere else rather than face up to the charges against him. "If Schocken is guilty, he should be fired or at least suspended; if powerful steps aren't taken, why will operating management take the minority relations policy seriously?" It was further agreed that Wesley, someone from public relations, and someone from the legal staff would go to St. Louis that evening.

After lunch, Macauley telephoned Marlin and, affirming GSD's responsibilities, argued that, if Schocken were guilty of the charges leveled against him, he should be fired and not transferred. Marlin retorted that, given what he knew then, a transfer was all he could justify. The upshot of the conversation, as Marlin perceived it, was that cause had to be shown to Macauley for *not* terminating Schocken.

In a subsequent call to Roman, Marlin indicated that the investigation as it related to Schocken was to document why he should or should not be terminated. Plans to pull Schocken off the job were also discussed, and it was agreed that interviews could be arranged for him in Indianapolis the next day (rather than the following Monday). It was also agreed that the employees would now be met at a higher level; Roman himself would take charge, supported by staff from the division and corporate as well as the region.

In mid-afternoon, Evans received word from Cox that Schocken was to be pulled out and sent to Indianapolis the following day for interviews. Evans again pointed out that Atkins was the most qualified candidate to replace Schocken. Cox agreed, after which Evans contacted Atkins and offered him the job as customer services manager at Elmsford. Atkins accepted.

Late that afternoon in New York, Macauley and Adler briefed Morgan on the situation in St. Louis and on a suggested press release from public relations. Morgan recalled his reaction to the proposed course of action.

I objected to the press announcement that they were going to issue in answer to Hill and put a stop to it. It was bad public relations but beyond that it was just bad business judgment. They also said that it was to be announced to everybody that Schocken was being removed. While this was being said, I began to have some doubts about the information on which we were basing our decision. I also objected to the timing of Schocken's removal; it shouldn't be on the deadline set by Hill. I don't think we were necessarily in full agreement, but we finally did agree that Schocken should not be pulled out until we had more information.

Meanwhile, at the distribution center Evans had Lake keep Schocken until about 7:00 P.M. to work after hours on assembling records pertinent to the Susan Wilson case soon to be investigated by EEOC. Evans recalled his impressions of the subsequent meeting with Schocken:

Earlier I had been for removing Schocken, but now I felt all we were doing was reacting to the press. Public exposure was going to blow the lid off, but the decision on the timing of his removal had been taken out of my hands.

I told Schocken that "for operational reasons" we were pulling him off the job. A lot of evidence pointed to his area, and in our judgment all we could do was make a change in management. Schocken objected to being pulled out but said he'd been expecting it. He was very concerned about going to Indianapolis—said he didn't want to go, couldn't arrange a babysitter in time, and so forth. We spent an hour discussing it. He said: "Maybe I'll resign, but how will that make the company look?" I told him that didn't matter. He kept on, however, saying he had to make a stand to clear his name. "Maybe I should sue the blacks," he added. I argued that the best thing for him to do was to go to Indianapolis the next day and try like hell to sell himself. Finally, he agreed to go.

After the meeting Evans went to a nearby motel where a crowd of BPC managers had assembled. The corporate jet had arrived with Wesley, Roberts (public relations), and a member of the corporate legal staff from New York and Roman and Johnson from Chicago. Also present were Cox and the regional manager of branch operations from Chicago, the St. Louis branch manager, and Parsons from Indianapolis.

In the ensuing meeting Roman was recognized as the manager in charge. He summarized the discussion:

We started mapping out a strategy for the distribution center for the next day. We asked a lot of "what if" questions. What do we do if there is a strike? If no one shows up? If there is another press conference? If the sales branch is picketed? And so forth. The multifunction group was a good idea—we were ready for just about any contingency.

I had instructions from Marlin that I should meet with the black employees. We decided that night to do it unannounced the next day so as not to alert Nathan Hill and increase the possibility of a demonstration. As far as Schocken was concerned, I was told to prepare a case if he was not to be dismissed by the end of the week. So in the worst case, fire him; in the best case, transfer him. Parsons had talked with Marlin before he had left for the meeting and had told him that Schocken was being pulled out. Everyone was 100% sure that Schocken was coming out of Elmsford; the only question was when.

We were then in a position that no matter what we did we lost. If Schocken is removed, we have caved in; if he is not, Nathan Hill may make it worse. I felt that the sooner he was pulled out the better. Who knows what the situation might be like in the event he remained until the following week?

The decision was made during the meeting that Schocken, instead of returning to the distribution center on Friday, would remain at home until he received further instructions.

Also discussed that evening was a proposal that Wesley visit with Hill. It was affirmed that Wesley should talk with him about national issues and whatever ideas for training programs might be forthcoming but that he should also reiterate BPC's position on third-party negotiations.

Thursday, September 7

At the distribution center, Roman, Parsons, Cox, and Johnson called the black women into the conference room. The initial response from the employees was the same as it had been in the past: they would not talk with management unless Hill was present to represent them. Gradually, however, a rapport was estabished, helped along by Roman's announcement that Schocken had been removed and would be replaced by Atkins. Johnson recalled, "This was the first productive meeting because they felt that now they were talking with someone who could make some decisions."

At about noon, after what seemed to the managers to be an increasingly positive discussion, the women agreed to reconsider. They left the room and tried to call Nathan Hill, but he had already left for his meeting with Wesley. The session then adjourned for lunch, Johnson leaving with the black employees and Roman, Parsons, and Cox, in a hopeful mood, joining up with Evans and Lake.

The morning had been considerably less pleasant for their associates. Evans and Lake called the white employees together for a brief "stand-up" meeting to bring them up to date on what was taking place. Aside from Lake's earlier attempts in August, this was the first occasion anyone had talked with them about it. Evans described the event:

> I announced that Joe Schocken was in Indianapolis and was to be transferred and that Jim Atkins was taking his place. There were murmurs, "Those four blacks did that . . ." and one girl whispered loudly, "Jim Atkins is a black . . ." which was followed by a number of gasps. Someone asked me, "Is this related to the newspaper article?" I said, "No. For operational reasons only." Another asked, "Is Atkins being moved here to pacify the blacks?" I said, "No. He's the most qualified for the job." The answers really got them mad.

As the meeting closed, the white employees were told that Roman would have a response for them by the end of the day. Evans called Schocken in Indianapolis and told him that his transfer had been announced at the distribution center that day and that he was to remain at home until given further instructions.

Downtown, Wesley was lunching with Hill. A three-hour discussion followed. Wesley remained firm on BPC's refusal to negotiate with Hill, who subsequently seemed to soften. Wesley commented:

> I began to feel he was looking for a way to save face in view of the representations he had made to the girls. So I said: "Let's assume we could arrange a meeting with top-management people in St. Louis without the employees. You don't talk about local issues but present the larger picture." He agreed. I said I'd run it by local management.

At about 3:00 P.M. the black employees at the distribution center reached Hill. Immediately thereafter their meeting with Roman, Parsons, Cox, and Johnson reconvened. The women announced that they had talked with Hill and were again convinced that only through his intervention would the issues be properly identified and resolved. The meeting continued unproductively for another hour and then disbanded.

Later in the afternoon, Roman met with all employees and read a prepared five-paragraph statement which stressed the importance of minority relations. He then indicated that he did not want to discuss specific issues or answer questions at that time. However, he said an investigation was underway and he would be back to review it with them no later than the following Friday. The reaction to this session was negative. One manager commented: "I'll bet this was the most hostile meeting ever conducted by a BPC vice president."

The BPC managers then met again at the motel. Wesley raised the proposition he had made to Hill about a presentation to management. The response continued to be "no," such an interchange would still be interpreted as negotiations with an employee representative. Wesley relayed this message to Hill, who commented: "If that's the decision, we'll see you on the battlefield."

Calls to Marlin and Adler brought the division and corporate officers up to date on the day's events. Marlin agreed that Roman should return to Chicago for an important conference the next morning with an unhappy client. Johnson, on his way to Detroit to meet with a group of unhappy black salesmen, rode as far as Chicago with Roman on the corporate jet. On the plane, Roman asked Johnson what he thought of the situation. Johnson proceeded to lay his frustrations on the line. He indicated that there was no operating machinery to back up minority affairs; he was out in the field with no authority to get policy implemented. Moreover, his function was buried in the personnel department and had little visibility. There was really nothing different about the Elmsford distribution center except that Nathan and Hannah Hill were involved. Johnson said that he and Cox had been trying to get the minority relations job done but that the priorities given to it in relation to salesmen's quotas, for instance, reduced their efforts mostly to talk.

Friday, September 8

Evans and Lake arrived at the distribution center before starting time on Friday. Soon the white employees, one after another, began to call in sick; within a few minutes it was clear that BPC now had a boycott on its hands. The black employees were shaken and asked for a meeting with Lake in which they indicated they had not intended such a thing to happen, that they had no quarrel with the other employees.

Hannah Hill also exhibited a piece of "hate" mail that her husband had received which included a threat to his life. She was upset. Later in the morning, Parsons, Evans, the member of the corporate legal staff, and Hannah Hill took the letter to the police, requesting at the same time greater surveillance for the distribution center. The remainder of the day in Elmsford was spent scrambling around answering the phones and trying to keep customers happy (the backlog having been accumulating all week). In Chicago, Roman spent most of the day at a large client's office trying, without success as it turned out, to resolve some major difficulties; the account was lost.

Elsewhere the day was devoted, in part at least, to report writing. At the motel in Elmsford the previous evening and most of Friday, Parsons and Cox assembled the study requested earlier in the week by Macauley, Marlin, and Roman summarizing the problem and justifying, if possible, Schocken's transfer. Johnson's initial description of his August 10 meeting continued to be the primary source of problem identification. The tentative conclusion from their work was that some of the allegations could not be attributed directly to Schocken, others were unfounded, and still others he denied. On this basis, they faulted him for poor management but could not, with confidence, accuse him of discrimination.

Contingency plans were also made for Monday. Parsons, Cox, and Wesley decided that Friday's absences should be laid to emotion and no disciplinary action taken even though it was clearly a concerted and deliberate violation of company procedures. However, if they called in sick on Monday, they would be told to bring in a doctor's slip if they expected to be paid and, if they were absent without one for four days, they would be dismissed in accordance with established policy. If the black employees picketed, they would be asked to return to work or face disciplinary action also.

Saturday, September 9

A number of the white employees met on Friday and prepared a press release. They contacted the same newspaper reporter who had covered the story earlier in the week and they held an interview with him. The next morning an article appeared in the paper, excerpts of which follow:

10 BPC aides deny bias by boss

Ten white office workers at BPC's regional distribution center in Elmsford rose to the defense yesterday of their customer services manager who had been accused by four blacks of racial discrimination.

The 10 white women denied that discrimination had existed in the office and said the black workers, rather than the manager, had created tension by taking grievances to management without discussing them with white workers.

High-level BPC executives from New York, Indianapolis, and Chicago were in St. Louis yesterday and Thursday to work out the problems and to meet with Nathan Hill, spokesman for disgruntled black BPC employees in St. Louis and elsewhere. It was learned that the customer services manager, Joseph Schocken, was abruptly transferred out of town during the talks. Both white and black employees described Schocken's removal as an attempt to placate the black workers.

Willard Roberts of New York, head of public relations for BPC, confirmed that Schocken had been reassigned during investigations into racial problems at the distribution center. Roberts said a number of other actions had also been taken but declined to discuss them. Roberts stated that the service manager had not been transferred because of the racial situation and he added that it was a coincidence that the transfer had been made on the day of Hill's deadline. Roberts did say, however, that Schocken had not asked for a transfer.

The 10 white employees declined to name a spokesman and issued their statement jointly. They all work for the customer services manager and denied any racial motive. They insisted they would not have issued their statement if they suspected racial discrimination in their office.

Also on Saturday, information was exchanged by managers in New York, Indianapolis, and Chicago. A further complication was unearthed. The white employees had approached the union which represented most of the BPC factory workers in Indianapolis and elsewhere. They reasoned that, with their greater numbers, they would be able to outvote the blacks on matters affecting employment through the democratic process of the union. In view of the union's good record in minority relations in Indianapolis, Parsons doubted if the International would permit organization under these circumstances but he could not be sure. It was generally agreed, however, that the white employees had gone further than anyone had anticipated.

The Week of September 11

Lake was sitting in his office early Monday morning watching the entrance to the parking lot. At 7:50 the white employees arrived en masse. Lake called Evans at the motel, and the latter told him to "get it straightened out." Lake described the statements made by the white women:

Girls were up tight and claimed "Roman blew it." They said Roman did not answer questions truthfully. "We found out more from the newspaper reporter than we did from our own management." They said the newspaperman "knew" that Joe was going to be fired and that the handling of Joe had been poorly done. "Joe didn't even have a chance to say goodbye. Evans lied to us by telling us it was not related to the racial thing." They mentioned going to a union for representation because "no one is representing us and, with Joe gone, no one will protect us. If it could happen to Joe, it could happen to us." The black girls never tried to talk to Joe, the women said; "he would have listened to them just as he listens to us. The removal of Joe won't satisfy Nathan Hill, and where does it stop? If four black girls can get Joe, then they could get us. Do we [BPC] have to hire a black manager? BPC will suffer a great loss with Joe gone; he knows his job, tells us when we're wrong and why we're wrong. He's tough but he's doing the job for BPC. Blacks have banded together, and with a black supervisor coming in, what chance do we have? Bringing in a black will make the situation worse. Even the blacks agree to this. How could four black girls do this to the distribution center? Black girls did not go to Joe first. Jim is black and is one of them. Therefore, a union is needed to protect the rights and jobs of the white workers. After this trouble, will whites ever be able to go to their black supervisor and discuss their problems? Why was Joe pulled out so abruptly? You're moving people based on allegations. How can you do that? Everything was equal, but not any more." Joe was not racist, they said; "he overlooked a lot of things the black girls did that we would have been reprimanded for." They said Shirley Gaynor threatened "not to take this lying down" after she wasn't promoted. Also, they said Shirley had no respect for the American flag; it "does not represent equality." Hannah Hill was "planted" by her husband two years ago to further his cause. "How could the press get all this information if our personnel clerk wasn't passing it out? We're tired of being puppets and lied to. Management doesn't care since they refuse to answer our questions; we find out more through newspapers. What do you expect us to do with treatment like that?"

At 10 o'clock Evans arrived and the meeting was moved to the conference room. The white employees then delivered an ultimatum: either Schocken is reinstated in his old job at the distribution center by Thursday or they would (*a*) join a union, (*b*) retain a lawyer, or (*c*) quit.

As if to emphasize their point, the union representative arrived. Evans "hid," telling Lake to be cordial but to say that he would have to contact Indianapolis before doing anything further. The union people talked briefly with the shop steward in the warehouse which was already organized, brought up one minor grievance, and told Lake that they would probably make an organizing attempt later. The discussion was amicable and, after a brief meeting with the white employees, they left.

At noon Evans and Lake concluded their session with the white employees and went to the motel to join Wesley and Butler, the manager of branch operations for the midwest region. After they heard the news, Wesley and Butler retired to another room to caucus; they concluded that any further action at this point would only be the subject of increased criticism. However, after a further investigation by people not already involved (neither Wesley nor Butler had been to the distribution center at the time), the employees might calm down and subsequent decisions could be related to this new study. They called New York, Indianapolis, and Chicago to find that others were reaching similar conclusions. It was quickly cleared with Adler, Roman, and Marlin that Wesley would represent corporate and Butler the region.

That afternoon Evans and Lake returned to the distribution center and called the employees together. Evans read the following statement:

All of us are concerned about the events of the past few days and we want to resolve any differences which exist here. Senior management has asked two people who are not connected with the center to examine all the questions that have been raised.

Frank Wesley from the corporate staff and Greg Butler representing GSD management will be here tomorrow to talk with many of us. Their conversations will be private and impartial. Their purpose will be to arrive at a full report and recommendations to management. Let's all cooperate with them fully.

The atmosphere continued to be tense. The husband of one of the white employees called and said he felt it was too dangerous for his wife to work there. Evans managed to convince him otherwise.

While these events were occurring, the Parsons-Cox report, which had been completed the previous Friday, was working its way up the line. The covering memorandum from Roman to Marlin indicated that "in spite of the large amount of circumstantial evidence, there remains in my mind a sincere doubt regarding intentional discrimination." The covering memorandum from Marlin to Macauley recommended, based on a similar reading of the evidence, that "Schocken be offered a position in Indianapolis with the understanding that if the current or any subsequent investigations demonstrate that he, in fact, is a racist, he will be immediately terminated." The memoranda were written more or less concurrently after the two managers had conversed by phone. Both stated that the future organizational health of the distribution center depended on a "timely resolution of the Schocken issue."

That evening Jim Atkins arrived in St. Louis and had dinner with Wesley, Cox, and Butler at the motel. They apprised Atkins of the dimensions of the backlash. Roman, Cox, and Evans were convinced that the transfer under the circumstances was not in Atkins' or anyone else's best interests. Atkins began to reach the same conclusion, and the next day he told Roman that he had reconsidered.

On Tuesday morning Wesley and Butler began their investigation. They divided the work force and interviewed each employee individually, including the warehousemen who had not previously been involved and who had little to say about the matter. They also interviewed Lake, who again acknowledged numerous inconsistencies in the treatment of employees but indicated that they were both unintentional and often more general than simply black versus white.

That evening at the motel Wesley and Butler spent more than four hours with Schocken, the first time he had been contacted since the previous Thursday. The investigators discussed with him the allegations first collected by Johnson and a few others that had surfaced later. Butler summarized Schocken's reaction.

As an operating manager Schocken concurred with his initial removal. He was told it was for operational reasons and he agreed that if he was a hindrance he had to go. But he had no understanding at all of his lack of sensitivity. He just could not see racial bias in what he had done and he categorically denied making the statements attributed to him.

On Wednesday Wesley and Butler finished their interviews and began to formulate conclusions. Before 5 o'clock when Wesley left to catch a plane to New York, they agreed in general terms on the findings, conclusions, and recommendations and on the format for the report. They collaborated in writing up the portion of the report dealing specifically with Schocken, as shown in Exhibit 1. After Wesley had gone, Butler dictated the remainder of the report to one of the secretaries from the St. Louis

EXHIBIT 1

BUSINESS PRODUCTS CORPORATION, PART II
The Wesley-Butler Report as it Pertains to Schocken

Schocken issue
1. Hard working, dedicated, bright, but inflexible manager who lacked awareness of and sensitivity to minority issues as well as the degree of BPC commitment in this area.
2. The action removing Joe Schocken was hastily taken in the heat of defensive emotion, with insufficient investigation and knowledge of the real issues, without hard factual data, and based on an inadequate assessment of the situation.
3. Although the allegations made against Schocken occurred over a one and one-half year period, they were only brought to management's attention, by the employees involved, within the last three months. In fact, many of the specific incidents were communicated only within the past several weeks.
4. Of the specific allegations made against Schocken:
    a. Some questionable practices were equally applied to blacks and whites.
    b. Some alleged Schocken statements were denied by him and may never be resolved.
    c. Some Schocken admitted to, but claimed his actions were taken without racial motivation.

Conclusions

Schocken was singled out for his ineptness in dealing with minority relations matters. Responsibility for the disparate treatment that did occur to minority employees should be shared by the distribution center manager—who, in fact, was the one to whom problems were pointed out. In most cases, he delayed or took inadequate action.

Ample consideration was not given to Joe Schocken as an individual or as an employee in this matter. He was abruptly removed without adequate explanation or investigation (under the demand of management and the pressure group's deadline).

Recommendations

Schocken should be admonished for his handling of people in general and his minority awareness in particular. He should be transferred, laterally, to a nonline position in Indianapolis, because:

1. He was untrained and poorly counseled to handle the problem.
2. The emotionalism of the minority issue has made his continued effectiveness at the distribution center questionable.

branch. Cox, Evans, and another lawyer from corporate reviewed the draft and offered a few comments but expressed no major hang-ups.

The remainder of the report, as written by Butler, proposed that payroll and appraisal changes for the black women should be made immediately and retroactively, that James Atkins should be promoted to the traffic position in the distribution center, and that Fred Holden should be moved from traffic to customer services. BPC's Equal Employment Opportunity commitment was to be reemphasized to all employees, and it should also be communicated that "Schocken is: (*a*) not hurt—he gets a lateral transfer; (*b*) happy with change and accepts it." It was also stated that Schocken should be made visible by bringing him back to spend two days with Fred Holden.

The report went on to make these additional recommendations: a communication meeting explaining problems and actions should be conducted by the regional manager as soon as possible, preferably by September 15 at the latest; Lake should be admonished and placed on probation, although his removal at this time would be disastrous; the region should prepare an action plan to implement minority awareness training promptly; BPC should not engage Hill as an employee representative, but should continue to evaluate his interest in minority training and need for assistance from BPC. By the time the report had been finished, Roman, Parsons, and Marlin had been apprised and were in basic agreement with its contents.

Regional management had two concerns as the week progressed: securing a replacement for Schocken as rapidly as possible and explaining the results of the investigation to the employees. The Wesley-Butler report was received in Chicago late Thursday morning. Roman made a few minor changes and forwarded them to Indianapolis and New York. There seemed to be general agreement among Marlin, Parsons, and Macauley on the report. Evans and Lake were anxious to get the management question settled and the distribution center back in production. Furthermore, Roman had made a personal commitment to the employees to advise them of the outcome by the end of the week and, under the circumstances, he felt it particularly important to honor it.

The necessity for proceeding expeditiously was reinforced Thursday morning when the white employees approached Lake and requested a meeting. They feared a return of Nathan Hill and again indicated that they would only be satisfied with Schocken's reinstatement. Finally, they apparently sensed that the decision was now out of Roman's hands; Roslyn O'Neil, one of the white women, asked, "When is Howie Morgan coming down?"

Evans then called Roman at about noon and asked for permission to contact Atkins under strict secrecy and give him the alternative of the traffic job in Elmsford or a probable promotion at his present location in several months time. Evans also requested authority to approach Holden in confidence about a transfer to customer services manager. Roman acceded to both requests.

The president intervenes

Early Thursday morning in New York, Adler alerted Wesley that he was attempting to arrange a meeting with Morgan and Macauley to discuss the Elmsford investigation. Wesley sent copies of the "Schocken issue" portions of the report (he had not at this point received the remainder of the report dictated by Butler the previous evening) to the three managers indicating that it could provide a basis for discussion.

At about noon, Macauley, Adler, and Wesley met with Morgan. Wesley presented the findings and recommendations contained in the report, the latter supported by both Macauley and Adler. No resolution on the Schocken issue was reached, however, other than Morgan's firm indication that he was going to make the final decision.

At 2 o'clock, as soon as the meeting was over, Wesley called Roman in Chicago to tell him that Morgan was going to make the decision on Schocken (though at the time Wesley did not know what the decision was going to be) and, in the meantime, the region was not to initiate any moves. He also advised Roman that it was not possible to say whether a decision would be available in time for him to hold the meeting with the employees before Friday as promised.

Wesley's call was a couple of minutes late. Evans had already talked with Lake about the Holden transfer and at 2 o'clock Lake had begun his interview with Holden. At 2:03 P.M., Butler burst into Lake's office, having just received the call from Roman advising him of Morgan's instructions. Butler stopped the meeting and, after apologizing to Holden, told him: "All bets are off. No commitments can be made. Turn the clock back five minutes. You are subject to dismissal if one word of this leaks out!"

By this time Roman began to sense that the Friday meeting was in jeopardy. He called Marlin, who was in Miami at a sales convention, and said that from his point of view a delay was unacceptable. Marlin discussed it with Macauley but to no avail. When no further word had been received from New York by late afternoon, Butler concluded that the meeting was off for the time being and he returned to Chicago, leaving Evans and Cox in St. Louis. Word was received during this time from Atkins, who had decided he would rather not accept any opening in St. Louis.

Meanwhile in New York, after Macauley, Adler, and Wesley had left his office, Morgan called Moore (BPC's chairman of the board) and indicated that he was contemplating offering Schocken the opportunity of returning to his old job at the Elmsford distribution center in addition to the possibility of a transfer to Indianapolis. He reasoned as follows:

I was mad when I found out that Schocken's removal had already been announced the previous week after we had decided here to wait. After the investigation, what bothered me was that there was no way to make the transfer without also making Schocken guilty. I also learned of the white backlash and the fact that we had acted too hastily. Everyone would be mad at us, both blacks and whites, and the factual basis on which Schocken was removed was questionable if not wrong.

The region's judgment had been to sacrifice the person and not the company. But Elmsford is probably just the first in a long series of problems like this. So we might as well start by doing what is right. We should not make a bad decision and then try to rationalize it afterwards.

Moore agreed.

On Friday Macauley, Adler, and Wesley met again with Morgan, this time for four hours. Wesley reported on some of the discussion:

After a time Howie [Morgan] said: "What if we put him back in Elmsford?" The rest of us said that would be an impossible situation from a management standpoint. Finally, he asked: "We've just had an inquisition, and now you're telling me we have no hard facts to justify the result. What is the right thing to do?" I said: "Put him back in Elmsford; but why take that risk when it's not in the best interest of the company?"

Macauley stated his position:

My position was that we haven't proved the blacks wrong, either. They would see putting Schocken back as a whitewash. In my judgment, such an action wouldn't be right in the larger sense of overall black-white relations. Howie felt it was morally wrong to have relieved Schocken. In the long run, he argued, doing what was right for Schocken would be in the best interests of the company. I thought in this case that was debatable.

Adler indicated the eventual resolution:

Finally, Howie made the decision on the basis of what was equitable for the employee. It was a moral decision, not a business decision. If it costs the company, that's a cost we have to bear. In addition, he made the decision that the employees should be told about the offer whether it was accepted or not. The white employees had some gripes and in the interests of full honesty we should tell them we made a mistake. Pragmatically we had the feeling they would probably find out anyway because of the close relationship between Schocken and Holden.

Morgan reflected on the group's reaction to his decision:

Everyone agreed that offering him his job back was the right thing for Schocken. But there was great argument about what was right for the company. I think they finally came to see that these eventually were the same.

No one really liked the decision, but I really believe they felt better after it had been made in the way it was.

At about 1:30 Friday afternoon, the second Morgan-Macauley-Adler-Wesley meeting broke up. Wesley called Parsons and Roman to say (*a*) Schocken was to be offered his old job or an equivalent one in Indianapolis, (*b*) those alternatives were to be announced to the employees, and (*c*) the meeting would probably be the next week but Morgan wanted to review an outline of what was to be covered beforehand.

Index of cases

Index of cases

840

This book has been set in 10 and 9 point Caledonia, leaded 2 points. Part numbers and titles are in 24 point Scotch Roman. Chapter numbers are in 36 point Scotch Roman, chapter titles are in 18 point Scotch Roman. The size of the type page is 27 by 45½ picas.